METHODOLOGY
OF ECONOMICS AND
OTHER SOCIAL SCIENCES

ECONOMIC THEORY, ECONOMETRICS, AND MATHEMATICAL ECONOMICS

Consulting Editor: Karl Shell

UNIVERSITY OF PENNSYLVANIA
PHILADELPHIA, PENNSYLVANIA

Franklin M. Fisher and Karl Shell. The Economic Theory of Price Indices: *Two Essays on the Effects of Taste, Quality, and Technological Change*

Luis Eugenio Di Marco (Ed.). International Economics and Development: *Essays in Honor of Raúl Presbisch*

Erwin Klein. Mathematical Methods in Theoretical Economics: *Topological and Vector Space Foundations of Equilibrium Analysis*

Paul Zarembka (Ed.). Frontiers in Econometrics

George Horwich and Paul A. Samuelson (Eds.). Trade, Stability, and Macroeconomics: *Essays in Honor of Lloyd A. Metzler*

W. T. Ziemba and R. G. Vickson (Eds.). Stochastic Optimization Models in Finance

Steven A. Y. Lin (Ed.). Theory and Measurement of Economic Externalities

David Cass and Karl Shell (Eds.). The Hamiltonian Approach to Dynamic Economics

R. Shone. Microeconomics: *A Modern Treatment*

C. W. J. Granger and Paul Newbold. Forecasting Economic Time Series

Michael Szenberg, John W. Lombardi, and Eric Y. Lee. Welfare Effects of Trade Restrictions: *A Case Study of the U.S. Footwear Industry*

Haim Levy and Marshall Sarnat (Eds.). Financial Decision Making under Uncertainty

Yasuo Murata. Mathematics for Stability and Optimization of Economic Systems

Alan S. Blinder and Philip Friedman (Eds.). Natural Resources, Uncertainty, and General Equilibrium Systems: *Essays in Memory of Rafael Lusky*

Jerry S. Kelly. Arrow Impossibility Theorems

Peter Diamond and Michael Rothschild (Eds.). Uncertainty in Economics: *Readings and Exercises*

Fritz Machlup. Methodology of Economics and Other Social Sciences

In preparation

Robert H. Frank and Richard T. Freeman. Distributional Consequences of Direct Foreign Investment

Elhanan Helpman and Assaf Razin. A Theory of International Trade Under Uncertainty

Marc Nerlove, David M. Grether, and José L. Carvalho. Analysis of Economic Time Series: *A Synthesis*

Thomas J. Sargent. Macroeconomic Theory

METHODOLOGY OF ECONOMICS AND OTHER SOCIAL SCIENCES

Fritz Machlup

ACADEMIC PRESS
New York   San Francisco   London   1978
A Subsidiary of Harcourt Brace Jovanovich, Publishers

ACADEMIC PRESS, INC.
111 Fifth Avenue, New York, New York 10003

United Kingdom Edition published by
ACADEMIC PRESS, INC. (LONDON) LTD.
24/28 Oval Road, London NW1 7DX

Library of Congress Cataloging in Publication Data

Machlup, Fritz, Date
    Methodology of economics and other social sciences.

    (Economic theory, econometrics, and mathematical
economics series)
    Bibliography: p.
    Includes index.
    1. Economics--Methodology.   2.   Social sciences--
Methodology.   I.   Title.
HB131.M3   330'.01'8   77–25734
ISBN 0–12–464550–X

CONTENTS

v

PREFACE

I have often been asked how I developed such a strong taste for methodological discourse. The answer is easy: In the intellectual milieu in which I lived it would have been surprising for any student at the university to remain uninterested in methodology. Vienna was the place where Carl Menger, the founder of the Austrian School of economics, had led the *Methodenstreit,* explaining the three different approaches to economic inquiry—the exact–theoretical, the empiric–realistic, and the historical. It was the place where Ernst Mach had formulated his views on procedural conventions in physics. It was the place where Max Weber had taught until just the time when I began my university years and where his methodological essays were eagerly read by all who took their studies seriously. It was the home of the "Vienna Circle" of logical positivists—Moritz Schlick, Friedrich Waismann, Rudolf Carnap, Otto Neurath, Hans Hahn, Herbert Feigl, *et al.*—who, determined to exorcize metaphysical speculation from scientific theorizing, formulated their strongly empiricist tenets. Vienna was the place where Ludwig Wittgenstein, the founder of linguistic philosophy, Karl Popper, the dissident who substituted

falsificationism for verificationism, and Kurt Gödel, the logician, lived and worked. It was the place where Ludwig von
Mises, my teacher, taught his aprioristic methodology; and it
was the place where my close friends Felix Kaufmann and
Alfred Schütz were working on the idea of merging Edmund
Husserl's phenomenology with a conventionalist or ideal–
typical methodology of the social sciences. How could I have
escaped the lure of such discussions?

Thus it came about that I read, reflected, conversed, and
wrote about methodology from the early 1920s to the present. I
often tell my students that they should not publish any methodological notes, papers, or books until after they have done years
of substantive research in their field and attained recognition
for their mastery of its technical aspects. The danger of vacuous
chatter is great if one engages in methodological discourse
without previous work on substantive problems. On the other
hand, even a lifetime of scientific research does not generate,
let alone guarantee, comprehension of methodological problems. It also takes years of studying philosophy, not limited to
just one philosophical school, but catholic in scope. No one
should attempt to be a self-made methodologist.

By the mid-1960s I had published a sufficient number of
papers on methodology to give some of my friends the idea of
arranging a volume of collected essays. This idea was revived
a couple of years ago by Mark Perlman and accepted by
Academic Press.

The present volume should perhaps be placed in perspective
with three other volumes of collected essays of mine. The first
was arranged in 1962 by my former graduate students to honor
me on my sixtieth birthday; it was edited by Merton H. Miller,
and entitled *Essays in Economic Semantics* (Englewood Cliffs, N.J.:
Prentice-Hall, 1963; second printing, New York: W. W. Norton,
1967; third printing, New York: New York University Press,
1976). The second collection was of papers in international
monetary economics, published under the title *International
Payments, Debts, and Gold* (New York: Charles Scribner's
Sons, 1964; second, enlarged edition, New York: New York
University Press, 1976), and in England under the title *Interna-*

tional Monetary Economics (London: Allen and Unwin, 1966). The third collection, arranged by the Department of Economics of New York University and edited by George Bitros, was *Selected Economic Writings of Fritz Machlup* (New York: New York University Press, 1976). The papers for that volume were chosen by the editor with the advice of committees consulted on different fields of specialization.

The present volume does not contain all my papers devoted to problems of methodology. I am most conscious of two omissions: "Marginal Analysis and Empirical Research" (1946) and "Equilibrium and Disequilibrium: Misplaced Concreteness and Disguised Politics" (1958). The former had been included in *Semantics* as well as in the *Selected Writings*; the latter in *Semantics* as well as in *International Payments*. Although these two papers were largely methodological in character, I flinched at having them included in a third collection. Twice may be excusable, thrice is not.

If twice is excusable, I admit several such duplications: 5 of the 20 papers chosen for the *Selected Writings* are also included in the present collection. These papers were clearly concerned with methodology and belong in this volume. That they had been selected for the earlier collection merely shows that they were deemed eligible also for readers not primarily interested in methodological discussion.

The 26 papers in this collection were written between 1935 and 1977. Two of the essays are entirely new, written for this volume, and a third essay has never been published in English. It happens that these three pieces account for roughly one-third of this book—much more than is usual in volumes of collected papers. Acknowledgments to the publishers and editors of the earlier publications are made on a separate page following this preface. References to these earlier publications are also included in the introductions to the seven parts of this volume, along with abstracts of each of the chapters.

Acknowledgment to the publishers and editors who have kindly permitted reproduction of my earlier publications is made on pages xiii—xiv. This preface, however, is the appropriate place to express my gratitude to Jessica Kennedy, my research assistant. Not only did she do the proofreading, but she checked the references, collaborated with me in preparing the unusually comprehensive index, and did much of the library searches that enabled me to write the survey of the methodological literature for the first chapter.

Fritz Machlup
New York University

ACKNOWLEDGMENTS

Acknowledgment is made to all publishers and editors of the books and journals in which the texts of most chapters of this volume were first published. The following list names the journals and the titles of the books and their publishers. The author is grateful to them for their permissions to reprint.

Chapter 2: Economica, New Series Vol. III (February 1936), pp. 39–45.

Chapter 3: Fritz Machlup, *The Economics of Sellers' Competition* (Baltimore: Johns Hopkins University Press, 1952), pp. 4–14, and 414–428.

Chapter 4: Fritz Machlup, *The Political Economy of Monopoly* (Baltimore: Johns Hopkins University Press, 1952), pp. 439–468.

Chapter 5: Southern Economic Journal, Vol. XXII (July 1955), pp. 1–21.

Chapter 6: Giornale degli Economisti, New Series Vol. XIX (September–October 1960), pp. 553–582.

Chapter 7: Sherman Roy Krupp, ed., *The Structure of Economic Science* (Englewood Cliffs, N.J.: Prentice-Hall, 1966), pp. 53–67.

Chapter 10: Maurice Natanson, ed., *Phenomenology and Social Reality: Essays in Memory of Alfred Schutz* (The Hague: Nijhoff, 1970), pp. 122–131, 134–137.

Chapter 11: Maurice Peston and Bernard Corry, eds., *Essays in Honour of Lord Robbins* (London: Weidenfeld & Nicolson, 1972), pp. 99–117.

Chapter 12: Sidney Morgenbesser, Patrick Suppes, and Morton White, eds., *Philosophy, Science, and Method* (New York: St. Martin's Press, 1969), pp. 286–305.

Chapter 13: Mary Sennholz, ed., *On Freedom and Free Enterprise: Essays in Honor of Ludwig von Mises* (Princeton, N.J.: Van Nostrand, 1956), pp. 161–172.

Chapter 14: Southern Economic Journal, Vol. XXVII (January 1961), pp. 173–184.

Chapter 15: Proceedings of the American Philosophical Society, Vol. 109 (February 1965), pp. 1–7.

Chapter 16: American Economic Review, Vol. LVII (March 1967), pp. 1–33.

Chapter 17: Robert L. Heilbroner, ed., *Economic Means and Social Ends: Essays in Political Economics* (Englewood Cliffs, N.J.: Prentice-Hall, 1969), pp. 99–124.

Chapter 18: The Review of Economics and Statistics, Vol. XXXIII (May 1951), pp. 145–151.

Chapter 19: American Economic Review, Vol. XLV (December 1955), pp. 948–952.

Chapter 20: American Economic Review, Vol. LIV (September 1964), pp. 733–736.

Chapter 21: American Economic Review, Vol. XLV (June 1955), pp. 394–396.

Chapter 22: Southern Economic Journal, Vol. XXIII (January 1957), pp. 330–332.

Chapter 23: Southern Economic Journal, Vol. XXII (April 1956), pp. 483–493.

Chapter 24: Robert L. Heilbroner, ed., *Economic Means and Social Ends: Essays in Political Economics* (Englewood Cliffs, N.J.: Prentice-Hall, 1969), 124–129.

Chapter 25: The Swedish Journal of Economics, Vol. 76 (December 1974), pp. 498–531.

Chapter 26: British Journal for the Philosophy of Science, Vol. 25 (September 1974), pp. 271–284.

ON THE NATURE AND SIGNIFICANCE OF METHODOLOGY

INTRODUCTION TO PART ONE

The two essays that make up Part One of this volume were written 42 years apart. Chapter 1, "What Is Meant by Methodology," is entirely new, written for this collection of essays in the summer of 1977. Chapter 2, "Why Bother with Methodology?" was published in *Economica*, New Series Vol. 3 February 1936.

The new essay engages only for the first few pages in a semantic discussion, reporting on the language pollution which in recent years has led to a vulgar use of the word *methodology* in a sense violating all philosophical traditions. The bulk of the chapter is given to a survey of methodological writings; it is designed to give the reader an idea of the variety of views on methodology and, in some instances, also on epistemology. The reader will become acquainted— only slightly, of course—with some of the relevant views, presented here in quotations or paraphrases, of the following 19 philosophers: Immanuel Kant (1724–1804), Wilhelm Windelband (1848–1915), Josiah Royce (1855–1916), Benedetto Croce (1866–1952), Max Weber (1864–1920), William Pepperell Montague (1873–1953), Percy Bridgman (1882–1961), Alfred North Whitehead (1861–1947), Morris R. Cohen (1880–1947), Hans Reichenbach (1891–1953), Felix Kaufmann (1895–1949), Alfred Schutz (1899–1959), Rudolf Carnap (1891–1970), Henry Margenau (born 1901), Karl R. Popper (born 1902), Herbert Feigl (born 1902), Richard B. Braithwaite (born 1900), Ernest Nagel (born 1901), and Carl G. Hempel (born 1905).

Why I chose just these and not others for inclusion in the survey, I will explain in the text of the chapter. The 19 vignettes of methodological discourse may not succeed in developing an unitiated reader's taste for methodological discourse, but they should leave him with a better awareness of what it is all about.

Chapter 2 undertakes to answer the question "Why Bother with Methodology?" Although this short piece was written a very long time ago—in 1935, when I taught for a term at Harvard—I have not found it necessary to make any changes of substance. I changed only a few words—fewer than 10—for purely stylistic reasons.

The main point of this short paper is that statements of an "if–then" type may have very different degrees of validity within a given conceptual scheme. To illustrate the point, I present three propositions where the "consequences" of the conditional premise (or independent variable) depend on unstated assumptions of various degrees of plausibility. One of the consequences is based on competitive mass behavior, the second on a state of technological creativity, the third on the political judgment and convictions of a handful of persons in power. In order to appraise the probability of the "predicted" consequence, one has to examine the nature of the tacit assumption and decide whether it is somehow implied or associated with the fundamental postulate or whether it had better be made explicit as a specific condition without which the consequence would not be realized. To bother with methodology is more than a pastime: It may be of substantive help.

Chapter 1

WHAT IS MEANT BY METHODOLOGY:
A SELECTIVE SURVEY OF THE LITERATURE

In the classification system of the Library of Congress, *methodology* has the code BD 240–241, where B stands for "Philosophy, Psychology, and Religion," and BD for "Speculative Philosophy." In the BD category, *methodology* is predeced by Metaphysics and Epistemology (Theory of Knowledge) and followed by Ontology and Cosmology.

No one vaguely familiar with logic and philosophy will be surprised by this arrangement. He knows that Kant had presented a Methodology of Pure Reason and a Methodology of Practical Reason; [1] and that, during the nearly 200 years since then, philosophers have argued over the relationship between methodology and epistemology on the one hand, and methodology and logic, on the other. For example, the *Encyclopaedia of the Philosophical Sciences*, vol. 1, *Logic*, contains three articles entitled "The Principles of Logic," by a German, an American, and a Frenchman. Wilhelm Windelband (of Heidelberg) divides his article into four parts: I. Phenomenology

---

[1] Immanuel Kant, *Critique of Pure Reason* [First German edition, 1781], and *Critique of Practical Reason* [First German edition, 1788]. In the Chicago edition (Encyclopaedia Britannica, 1952), the "Transcendental Doctrine of Method" appears on pp. 210–50, and the "Methodology of Pure Practical Reason" on pp. 356–61.

of Knowledge, II. Pure or Formal Logic, III. Methodology, and IV. Theory of Knowledge. Josiah Royce (of Cambridge, Massachusetts) gives to the first part of his article the title "The Relation of Logic as Methodology to Logic as the Science of Order." And Louis Couturat (of Paris) has a section on methodology follow the section "The Logic of Relations."

THE DEBASING OF THE TERM

In any living language, new words are coined and old words acquire new meanings. Words coined for scientific usage may be given new technical meanings; eventually they may enter common language with meanings drastically changed. This process sometimes deprives prior users of a term with definite intension. In some instances, the debasing of the coinage is the result of malapropism.[2]

Mrs. Malaprop Takes Over

Some time before 1940, Mrs. Malaprop discovered "methodology." Enamored of the learned word, yet too lazy to look it up in a dictionary, she began using it for what she *thought* it meant: a description of a method or even a synonym for method. The propensity of many people to substitute technical terms for ordinary, well-understood words from the vocabulary of everyday speech has long been an effective force in the development of language, often leading to its enrichment, but sometimes to its pollution. The adoption of the term *methodology* by people ignorant of its original and proper meaning is a case of language pollution, probably of the irreparable sort, because we now find the word more often misapplied than not.

---

[2] The word malapropism goes back to Mrs. Malaprop (from French *mal à propos*, out of place), a comic character in *The Rivals*, who is noted for her blunders in the use of words. Eager to show off with her knowledge of high-class words, she misapplies them in the most grotesque fashion. A few examples may be helpful to readers who have not read or seen the play: Mrs. Malaprop would have her daughter "instructed in geometry, that she might know something of the contagious countries." She finds her niece "as headstrong as an allegory on the banks of the Nile." And she is full of praise for a young man because "his physiognomy [is] so grammatical." Richard Brinsley Sheridan, *The Rivals. A Comedy* [1775] (Oxford: Clarendon Press, 1935), pp. 18, 60, and 75.

I have not searched for the first Malaprop who debased *methodology*, but I would not be surprised if he were found to be a statistician trying to explain the procedures and techniques he used in collecting, arranging, and analyzing his numerical data. Be this as it may, the term *methodology* was soon used in all sorts of statistical studies. But it became equally popular among accountants, especially those engaged in justifying their practices in writing down certain types of assets, writing off some frozen receivables, presenting consolidated financial statements, and the like. These experts in the numerical arts would have been flabbergasted if a philosopher, noticing their interest in the "methodology used" in their statistical or accounting statements, had asked them what they knew of Kant's transcendental methodology. Such danger, however, was slight, since few philosophers read either statistical tracts or financial statements and, similarly, few experts in these practical professions seek the company of philosophers.

Public Documents and Private Researchers

The habit—the ill-informed use of the philosopher's term—spread to other fields. Sadly enough, some of the officers and editors of the National Science Foundation adopted the word for use in official documents, and soon every applicant for a grant in support of research thought it wise to include in his proposal a section on "the methodology of [his] research" and later to repeat such disquisition under that title either at the beginning or at the end of his final report. The NSF published its own study, *Methodology of Statistics on Research and Development*, devoted to discussions of "problems of definition," "interpretation of R&D statistics," and "accounting systems for measuring the intersectoral flow of R&D funds in the United States." [3] Some discriminating writers of NSF documents—perhaps products of a liberal education—resisted the new fashion and, modestly and appropriately, wrote "Technical Notes" for their discussions of scope and method, definitions, weighting and estimating procedures, standard errors, the process of sample selection, and

[3] The document bears the number NSF 59-36 (Washington: National Science Foundation, 1959).

similar problems, without any incantation of "Methodology." [4] These writers seem to be exceptional, however. A survey published in the same year presented the reader with a section on the "Methodology of Survey," to describe the sample, the variances, and even the mailing of the questionnaires.[5]

With the government setting the example, no wonder that its grantees follow it. An increasing number of social scientists, especially those engaged in quantitative research projects, speak of methodology when they discuss their correlation coefficients, partial regressions, and the least-squares method of curve fitting. In an article, "Methodological Developments," in *Survey of Contemporary Economics*, the author discusses "specialized methodological techniques"—note the redundancy!—and holds that "every research project . . . may have a unique methodology." [6] The honor of the economics profession was upheld, fortunately, by the invited commentator of the article, who complained that the paper in question "is concerned not with methodology as a part of the philosophy of knowledge, but rather with a description of present-day economic research. By choosing . . . this orientation, the author missed his opportunity to say something worthwhile on an interesting, if difficult, subject." [7]

To recount these instances is not to level a general charge against our contemporary economists and other social scientists of having abandoned a serious concern with genuine methodology. Such a charge would be completely unwarranted. Economic theorists have never stopped examining and reexamining the methodological foundations of their system: the nature of their axioms, theorems, postulates, and hypotheses; the roles of historical records, fertile intuition, speculative interpretation, logical deduction, inductive generalization, heuristic fiction, observation and experimentation, introspection, intervening variables and other nonobservables. This is only a sample of the topics of methodological investigations em-

---

[4] The authors of NSF 76-323, Part 2, deserve commendation.

[5] NSF 76-322. In fairness to the authors, it should be said that the particular section is attributed to the Industry Division of the Bureau of the Census, a group that may be more strongly addicted to the habit.

[6] Richard Ruggles, "Methodological Developments," in *A Survey of Contemporary Economics,* edited by Bernard F. Haley, vol. 2 (Homewood, Ill.: Richard D. Irwin for the American Economic Association, 1952), pp. 408 and 411.

[7] Evsey D. Domar, "Comment," in Haley, ed., *Survey*, p. 453.

bodied in an unending flow of publications. None of their works confused methodology either with method or with a description of methods. Concern with methodology proper has been even more preeminent among sociologists, some of whom came to devote the bulk of their treatises and courses on "social theory" and "sociological theory" to methodological discourse in the uncorrupted sense.

Dictionary Definitions

Up to 1971, when the third edition of Webster's dictionary appeared, no one who consulted a dictionary could have been left in doubt about the meaning of *methodology*. The second edition of Webster's *New International Dictionary* [1953] offered the following definition: "The science of method or arrangement; hence a. A branch of logic dealing with the principles of procedure whether of theoretical or practical science." [8] *Webster's Collegiate Dictionary*, fifth edition [1945], reproduced these definitions without essential change.

The *Oxford Universal English Dictionary* [1937] defines *methodology* as "the science of method; a treatise or discussion on method." The unabridged *Oxford English Dictionary* [1933, new printing 1971] adds to the first definition, in parenthesis, "methodics" as an equivalent, and gives "systematic classification" as a special meaning for "*Nat. Hist.*"

In Lalande's French *Vocabulaire technique et critique de la philosophie* [5th ed., 1947], methodology is defined as "the subdivision of logic concerned with the study, *a posteriori*, of methods and, especially and ordinarily, of scientific methods."

So far so good. However, in 1971, the third edition of Webster's appeared. Dedicated to the indiscriminate listing of literary, scientific, and colloquial word meanings (as also of correct and incorrect versions in spelling and grammar), the *Third New International Dictionary* "legitimized" the corrupted meanings of methodology. Indeed, it gave precedence to the meanings intended by the ill informed, and relegated to last place the original meaning intended by those who had coined or introduced the word. The entries (with-

---

[8] It gives also a second definition: "b. *Educ.* The science which describes and evaluates arrangements of materials of instruction." This concerns only those in schools of education.

out the illustrative quotations from the literature) read as follows:

"1a. a body of methods, procedures, working concepts, rules, and postulates employed by a science, art, or discipline . . . b. the processes, techniques or approaches employed in the solution of a problem or in doing something: a particular procedure or set of procedures . . . c. the theoretical foundations of a philosophical doctrine: the basic premises, postulates, and concepts of a philosophy . . . 2. the science or the study of method; *specif.*: a branch of logic that analyzes the principles or procedures that should guide inquiry in a particular field."

Note that even the *"specif."* meaning given with the last entry—the only one that does justice to the second half of the compound word, *-logy*—commits the blunder of using a normative "should," in flagrant contradiction to the *"a posteriori"* explicitly stated in Lalande's definition and implicit in that of the *Oxford English Dictionary.*

In the recent editions of *Webster's New Collegiate Dictionary* [1963, 1973] only two definitions are furnished: "1. a body of methods, rules, and postulates employed by a discipline: a particular procedure or set of procedures . . . 2. the analysis of the principles or procedures of inquiry in a particular field." Thus, only *particular* procedures and procedures for a *particular* field are given as the meanings of methodology; for collegiates, it seems, Kant has never lived, and logic, evidently, is not relevant.[9]

WHAT METHODOLOGISTS ACTUALLY WROTE

If I call certain writers methodologists, I shall for the purposes of this discussion limit myself to those who have used the term methodology in their published work, especially those who have given it prominence, for example, by including it in the titles of their books

[9] The apparent irrelevance of logic for collegiate studies in the United States is reflected also in "the New HEGIS Taxonomy," published in 1970 by the U.S. Department of Health, Education, and Welfare under the title *A Taxonomy of Instructional Programs in Higher Education.* It enumerates 24 "discipline divisions," each subdivided into between 2 and 44 "specialties" denoted by altogether 403 code numbers. The alphabetical index, referring to 440 subject titles, includes "weaving," "metalsmithing," and "home decoration," but philosophy is merely another specialty in the subdivision "Letters"—and there is no entry at all for logic, either as a discipline or as a subdivision or a specialty!

or articles, or of parts or sections of their books or articles. I shall offer a selective survey of such writings but must warn that it is difficult, if not impossible, to choose a sample that will be truly representative of the population of methodologists. I shall try to exhibit such a variety of positions that the reader will be quickly disabused of any suspicion that this is a monolithic discipline. On the other hand, the sampling of the pronouncements on methodology will succeed in conveying to the reader that the different writers have more in common than the employment of the term in question.

Some of the most influential treatises on methodology will be left out of this survey on the (perhaps simplistic) ground that they did not employ the term. This refers to the work of David Hume, with its important discussion of causality; Hume wrote before the word methodology was coined. But it also refers to Mill's *Logic*, which was probably the most complete work on methodolgy of the mid-nineteenth century.[10] It examines a large variety of scientific methods, inductive, deductive, concrete–deductive, inverse–deductive, and all the rest; also the methods of experimental inquiry—the method of agreement, the method of difference, the method of residues, and the method of concomitant variations. It also discusses the principles of abstraction, concept formation, inductive inference; the formation of hypotheses, empirical laws, derivative laws, verification—in short, virtually everything that forms the content of the theory of scientific method. But the word *methodology* does not occur in the two volumes. Two other works of great influence will be absent from my survey: Lord Kelvin's *Treatise on Natural Philosophy* [11] and Karl Pearson's *Grammar of Science*.[12] Some of their views were discussed and criticized by later writers on methodology, but I stick to my criterion and omit the works in which I could not find the term in question.

The author with whom to start this survey is, without serious question, Immanuel Kant, chiefly because *methodology* appears in the titles of chapters or parts of three of his books. As my next wit-

[10] John Stuart Mill, *A System of Logic: Ratiocinative and Inductive, Being a Connected View of the Principles of Evidence, and the Methods of Scientific Investigation* (London: Parker, Son, and Bourn; 1st ed., 1843, 5th ed., 1862).

[11] William Thomson [later Lord Kelvin] and Peter Guthrie Tait, *Treatise on Natural Philosophy* (Cambridge: The University Press, 2d ed., 1879).

[12] Karl Pearson, *The Grammar of Science* (London: Adam and Charles Black; 1st ed., 1892, 2d ed., 1900).

nesses, I choose Wilhelm Windelband, Josiah Royce, and Benedetto Croce, because they were the three writers on methodology in the *Encyclopaedia of Philosophical Sciences*. Max Weber, the sociologist, comes next, who devoted himself exclusively to the methodology of the social sciences in articles and books published between 1903 and 1922. Three philosophers—William Pepperell Montague, Alfred North Whitehead, and Morris R. Cohen—will be presented with excerpts from books published in 1925, 1929, and 1931, respectively. Two physicists will be produced in their capacity as methodologists: Percy W. Bridgman of Harvard and Henry Margenau of Yale, the former with a book published in 1927, the latter with one in 1950. The views of nine other philosophers of different schools will be reviewed: Felix Kaufmann and Alfred Schutz, both phenomenological philosophers specializing in methodology of the social sciences in works written between 1932 and 1958; Hans Reichenbach, Rudolf Carnap, Herbert Feigl, Ernest Nagel, Richard Braithwaite, and Carl Hempel, six members, followers or descendents of logical positivism, whose writings were published between 1921 and 1970; and Sir Karl Popper, who has propounded Popperian methodology from 1935 to the present.

Just as the selection of writers, the selection of representative samples from their writings for quotation or paraphrase in this essay cannot help being arbitrary. Let me admit, there is not consistent design in choosing statements for exhibition in these vignettes. The choice has sometimes been determined by where the book happened to fall open. None of the sentences or passages chosen can possibly do justice to the total contribution made by a particular author.

Kant

In three different works, Kant treats of the "methodology of pure reason," the "methodology of practical reason," and the "methodology of teleological judgments." In an "explanation of terms" Haywood, one of the translators of Kant's *Critique of Pure Reason*, offers the reader this all too brief definition: "Methodology (*Methodenlehre*), Transcendental doctrine of method." This is, in fact, nothing but Kant's title of the second half of the volume, the first half being devoted to Elementology (*Elementarlehre*). But Haywood tries to help the reader by contrasting the two: "The elementary . . . doctrine has been called . . . the science treating of the forms of a metaphysical system."[13] Not very illuminating for anyone who has not studied Kant's work! Still, one can get a vague idea of what methodology of pure reason (or "transcendental methodology") may be about if one learns (1) that it keeps company with transcendental elementology, which includes aesthetics and transcendental logic, and (2) that Kant treats transcendental methodology in chapters on disciplines, canons, and the architectonic of pure reason.

Kant tries to illuminate the meaning of "methodology of pure *practical* reason" by contrasting it with that of "*theoretical* philosophy," where method is shown to be

> a process, according to *principles of reason,* by which alone the manifold of any branch of knowledge can become a system [and, hence, a science]. In contrast, by the methodology of pure *practical* reason . . . is understood the mode in which we can give the laws of pure practical reason *access* to the human mind, and *influence* on the maxims, that is, by which we can make the objectively practical reason *subjectively* practical also.[14]

This is probably more than enough of Kant's thought to prove to the reader that the man who gave prominence to the science of method, called *methodology,* was not concerned with mailing questionnaires or calculating least-squares estimates. On the other hand, the reader will not yet know much about what methodology is actually about. We shall turn to later methodologists to find out.

Windelband

For Windelband, there are "three fundamental philosophical sciences: Logic, Ethics, and Aesthetics, corresponding to the fundamental psychical activities of knowing, willing, and feeling and to the forms which human culture has taken: Science, Morality, and

[13] Immanual Kant, *Critick of Pure Reason,* translated by Francis Haywood (London: William Pickering, 1848), p. 600.

[14] Immanuel Kant, *Critique of Practical Reason* (Chicago: Encyclopaedia Britannica, 1952), p. 356. The "Methodology of Pure Practical Reason" is Part 2 of this work and covers pp. 356–61 of the volume.

Art." [15] It is not the object of logic to "shake the foundations" of any special sciences but, instead, "to study their philosophical significance." Logic can do this "partly as Methodology, partly as Theory of Knowledge" [p. 20]. Formal or pure logic must abstract from every relation to any particular knowledge-content and develop forms that are

> valid for all kinds of thinking which have truth [validity] as their object. [The] second part of Logic, namely Methodology . . . is to exhibit the purposive interconnexion of logical forms by which the particular sciences attain their end with regard both to the formal and the essential nature [of the relevant objects; and] to show in how many different ways the individual disciplines are able to exhibit the systematic interconnexion of all the elements of knowledge which lie within their province. In this sense Methodology is chiefly concerned with immanent truth, i.e., the agreement of ideas amongst themselves [p. 22].

Methodology, for Windelband,

> is a technical discipline, and might also be called . . . the doctrine of the *systematic* forms of thought. [In its universal aspects, it] deals with the *methods of proof and of refutation* which are equally valid for all the sciences and also for extra-scientific thought. For all these are only more or less complicated ways of inference and therefore have their principles in syllogistic. We are, however, obliged to pass beyond this schematization as soon as we reflect on the character of the *major premisses* which, themselves not demonstrable, must . . . form the starting point of all proof. [These] major premisses are either *axioms,* i.e., general presuppositions which cannot be grounded in experience, or *facts* which are given in perception" [p. 43; I corrected the misplacement of two commas].

On this difference rests the distinction between *rational* sciences (mathematics) and *empirical* sciences, though "we must not imply that" the empirical sciences "are based exclusively upon facts," since they also need "the help of axiomatic presuppositions." Philosophy holds a special place: its "method . . . is neither rational nor empirical, but *critical.*" The "general premisses" in empirical sciences need neither be facts nor "axioms in the strictest sense: they may also consist of defining determinations or of hypothetical concept-and-

[15] Wilhelm Windelband, "The Principles of Logic," in Arnold Ruge *et al., Logic, Encyclopaedia of the Philosophical Sciences,* vol. 1 (London: Macmillan, 1913), p. 9.

judgment constructions; or finally, they may be more or less certain results of inductive thought." Depending on the nature of the premisses, "the results of the deductive proof" are "apodeictic," "problematic," or "probable" [p. 44].

Windelband emphasizes the distinction "between nomothetic and idiographic inquiries," the former dealing with "laws," the latter with "events" [pp. 47–48]. The methodology of historical science is characterized by the fact that "historical investigation is *science related to values*, [though] this methodological view does not have anything whatever in common with the ethics of desire and volition" [p. 49]. In other "*human* sciences . . . generalizing and individualizing thought interpenetrate. . . . Every inquiry, however, natural or human, inevitably makes assumptions. Hence the *logic of hypothesis* is the most important part of the Methodology of inquiry" [pp. 48, 53].

Royce

Josiah Royce accepts the customary division of logic into formal and material, but prefers to call the former "the General Science of Order" and the latter "Methodology" (which incidentally he considers "the mother of Logic in the other sense"). Methodology, "in its usual sense [is] a study of the norms and methods of thoughts used in the various arts and sciences." [16]

Royce gives a brief and lucid exposition of "Socratic and Platonic Methodology" and then (skipping the "Aristotelian Logic," the "Baconian reform of scientific methods and . . . the vastly more important consequences of the experimental methods" of Galileo and his contemporaries) turns to "the doctrines of modern scientific Methodology" [pp. 69–74]. Royce enumerates and discusses various methods that are used in making an ordered system, a science, out of a heap of records of facts of experience. He includes methods of classification, methods of comparison ("comparing the corresponding stages in the various processes or products of natural Evolution"), statistical methods (to see "how two or more aspects of the phenom-

[16] Josiah Royce, "The Principles of Logic," in Arnold Ruge *et al., Logic, Encyclopaedia of the Philosophical Sciences,* vol. 1 (London: Macmillan, 1913), p. 69. Reprinted in Josiah Royce, *The Principles of Logic* (New York: Wisdom Library, 1961), p. 11. The page references in the text are to the *Encyclopaedia.*

ena in question tend to vary together"), and methods of organized combination of theory and experience ("inductions . . . which employ the principle of 'fair sampling' [to judge] with probability . . . the constitution of the whole collection) [pp. 74–88]." For the arguments in support of some of the methods, that is, for the "methodology of inductive generalization," Royce gives credit to Charles S. Peirce, especially his 1883 article on the logic of induction.[17]

What makes

> the union of Theory and Observation . . . most effective, depends upon the possibility of defining hypotheses in terms of certain conceptual order-systems whose exactness of structure far transcends, in ideal, the grade of exactness that can ever be given to our physical observations themselves. . . . One often meets with the remark that a scientific hypothesis must be such as to be more or less completely capable of verification or of refutation by experience. The remark is sound. But equally sound it is to say that a hypothesis which, just as it is made, is, without further deductive reasoning, capable of receiving direct refutation or verification, *is not nearly as valuable to any science as is a hypothesis whose verifications, so far as they occur at all, are only possible indirectly, and through the mediation of a considerable deductive theory,* whereby the consequences of the hypothesis are first worked out, and then submitted to test [pp 88–89].

Since some of these tests rely heavily on quantitative concepts, Royce emphatically warns against a widespread confusion between "exactness" and "quantitative": "Exact Deductive Theory and Quantitative Theory are by no means coextensive" [p. 92].

Croce

Benedetto Croce, in his article, "The Task of Logic," argues against the "separatists" in philosophy who have also tried to separate "Elementary Logic from Applied Logic or Methodology."[18] He presents a list of methodological problems which includes the nature of concepts, definition, syllogism, perception, the existential predicate, counting and measuring; the relation between distinct and contrary concepts; the nature of a system, the employment of empirical con-

---

[17] "A Theory of Probable Inference," *Studies in Logic: By Members of the Johns Hopkins University* (Boston: Little, Brown, and Company, 1883), pp. 126–181.

[18] Benedetto Croce, "The Task of Logic," in Arnold Ruge *et al.*, *Logic, Encyclopaedia of the Philosophical Sciences,* vol. 1 (London: Macmillan, 1913).

cepts in history, the value of natural science and of a mathematical science of nature; the philosophical theory of error, either as "a pathology of thought" or as a "phenomenology of truth" [pp. 213–14].

Max Weber

Max Weber, probably the most influential thinker in theoretical sociology, wrote several long essays on methodology of the social sciences.[19] While many of his statements on the functions of methodology would deserve inclusion in this survey, I confine myself to quoting a rather innocuous one:

> Methodology is neither able nor does it aim to prescribe to anyone what he should put into a literary work. It claims for itself only the right to state that certain problems are logically different from certain other problems and that their confusion in a discussion results in the mutual misunderstanding of the discussants. It claims furthermore that the treatment of one of these types of problems with the means afforded by empirical science or by logic is meaningful [pp. 32–33].

This statement is cryptic out of its context: It is part of a discussion of "The Meaning of 'Ethical Neutrality' in Sociology and Economics" and, specifically, of the need to distinguish causal analysis, aesthetic valuation, and other value interpretation.

Weber's major methodological contribution was to the theory of concept formation in social theory, history, and cultural sciences.[20] He held that in the social sciences, and particularly in history

[19] Max Weber, *The Methodology of the Social Sciences,* translated and edited by Edward A. Shils and Henry A. Finch (Glencoe, Ill.: Free Press, 1949). This book contains three of the numerous articles published by Weber in German between 1904 and 1917, and later collected in *Gesammelte Aufsätze zur Wissenschaftslehre* (Tübingen: J. C. B. Mohr, 1922; 2d ed., 1951).

[20] Max Weber, "Roscher und Knies und die logischen Probleme der historischen Nationalökonomie," *Schmollers Jahrbücher,* [1903 27], [1905 29], and [1906 30]. Reprinted in Max Weber, *Gessammelte Aufsätze,* 2d ed., pp. 1–145 (no English translation); *idem,* "Die Objektivität der sozialwissenschaftlichen Erkenntnis," *Archiv für Sozialwissenschaft und Sozialpolitik,* Vol. 1 (1904). Reprinted in *Gesammelte Aufsätze,* 2d ed., pp. 146–214. (English translation in *Methodology,* cited in note 19). The latest and best exposition of Weber's ideas appears in his volume *Wirtschaft und Gesellschaft,* part 3 of the *Grundriss der Sozialökonomik* (Tübingen: J. C. B. Mohr [Paul Siebeck], 1922, 2d ed. 1925). An English translation of Part 1 of that volume was made by Alexander H. Henderson and Talcott Parsons and published under the title *Max Weber: The Theory of Social and Economic Organization* (Glencoe, Ill.: The Free Press, 1947).

we are concerned with the fact that among the relevant events there are mental processes whose "understanding" through re-experiencing naturally is a task which is specifically different from the one which the models of the exact natural sciences can and try to accomplish [*Gesammelte Aufsätze*, p. 173].

The specific conceptual tool in the process of "understanding" the subjectively meant meanings of individual actors, and hence the understanding of human actions and results of actions, is the "ideal type." This mental construct is not supposed to copy reality, or to average observed cases; instead, the ideal type

is like a *utopia* which has been arrived at by the analytical accentuation of certain elements of reality. Its relationship to empirical data consists solely in the fact that where . . . concrete relationships of the type referred to by the abstract construct are discovered or suspected to exist in reality to some extent, we can make the *characteristic* features of this relationship pragmatically *clear* and *understandable* by reference to the ideal type. [It is] an analytical construct, which is "ideal" in the strictly logical [not normative] sense of the term. It is a matter here of constructing relationships which our imagination accepts as plausibly motivated and hence as "objectively possible" and which appear as *adequate* from the nomological standpoint [*Methodology*, pp. 90, 92].

Weber's methodological writings have been misunderstood by several generations of interpreters, critical or admiring, chiefly because Weber's writing style is awkward and his exposition arcane. For the few who have understood it, his contribution to the methodology of the social sciences is of supreme importance.[21]

Montague

One of the most lucid writers on methodology was William Pepperell Montague.[22] He distinguished three "grand divisions of philosophy": Methodology, Metaphysics, and Theory of Value [p. 31].

---

[21] For a closer examination of Weber's methodology, see my essays included in the present volume as Chapters 8 and 9. There are many secondary sources available. The most recent is Thomas Burger, *Max Weber's Theory of Concept Formation: History, Laws, and Ideal Types* (Durham, N.C.: Duke University Press, 1976). The definitive interpretation and elaboration can be found in the writings of Alfred Schutz, cited in notes 31 and 32. Burger, unfortunately, has failed to take full advantage of Schutz's work.

[22] William Pepperell Montague, *The Ways of Knowing, or the Methods of Philosophy* (New York: Macmillan; London: Allen & Unwin, 1925).

The last of these is subdivided into Ethics and Aesthetics. Metaphysics has three subdivisions, Ontology (analytic metaphysics), Cosmology (synthetic metaphysics),[23] and Theology or Religion (evaluative metaphysics) [p. 411]. Methodology is defined as the study of "the ways of knowing," and subdivided into two parts: Logic, defined as the study of the ways of *attaining* knowledge (either formal logic, concerned with relative validity, or material logic, concerned with absolute validity through the validation of the premises); and Epistemology, defined as the study of the ways of *interpreting* knowledge and concerned chiefly with the relations between the known and the knower [p. 33].

It is interesting to find epistemology treated, not as a part of metaphysics (as it has been from the earliest times until the present),[24] but with logic as one of two parts of methodology. The most fundamental question of epistemology is "To what extent, if any, are the things and qualities of the world dependent upon their being related as objects to a knower or subject?" [p. 32]. The reader may be helped in his orientation by looking at a sample of epistemological positions (or *isms*): the four basic ones are epistemological realism, idealism, dualism, and relativism.[25] (Each of these nouns has to be modified

[23] Cosmology has lately been promoted from a "metaphysical science" to an "observational science," together with astrophysics, astronomy, and cosmogeny. See the writings by Erwin Finlay Freundlich, Edwin Powell Hubble, Paul Oppenheimer, and others.

[24] For example, Victor F. Lenzen, "The Methodological Import of Scientific Facts," in *Studies in the Nature of Facts*, University of California Publications in Philosophy, Vol. 14 (1932), p. 151. Whether Cohen and Nagel assign epistemology to metaphysics is not entirely clear from their formulation. "The essential purpose of logic is attained if we can analyze the various forms of inference and arrive at a systematic way of discriminating the valid forms from the invalid forms. Writers on logic, however, have not generally been content to restrict themselves to this. . . . They have engaged in a good deal of speculative discussion as to the general nature of knowledge and the operations by which the human mind attains truth as to the external world. . . . Indeed, the answers to the questions of metaphysics, rational psychology, or epistemology (as they are variously called) are admittedly too uncertain or too questionable to serve as a basis for the science of all proof and demonstration." Morris R. Cohen and Ernest Nagel, *An Introduction to Logic and Scientific Method* (New York: Harcourt, Brace, 1934), pp. 20–21. The comma between "rational psychology, or epistemology" may be a clue for us to interpret the two as not being included in metaphysics.

[25] Epistemological dualism is also known as *critical realism* or as *representative theory*; epistemological relativism also goes under the name of *pragmatic theory of knowledge*.

by the adjective *epistemological*, since each is also used, with different meanings, in other fields of inquiry.) Besides these four basic positions, reviewers of the epistemological literature have distinguished extreme materialism, scientific materialism, sensationalistic empiricism, naturalism, naturalistic rationalism, scientific rationalism, fictionalism, conceptualism, irrationalism, and some more.

Bridgman

An experimental physicist, Percy W. Bridgman, published in 1927 a strong endorsement of strict empiricism. His book, *The Logic of Modern Physics,* advocated a method of concept formation that became known as "operationalism." [26]

Bridgman is suspicious of "abstract science . . . as far removed from reality as the abstract geometry of the mathematicians, built on postulates [p. 5]." He prefers concepts based on operations, indeed he means

> by any concept nothing more than a set of operations; *the concept is synonymous with the corresponding set of operations.* If the concept is physical, as of length, the operations are actual physical operations, namely, those by which length is measured [p. 5]. [He calls this] the proper definition of a concept. . . . For if experience is always described in terms of experience, there must always be correspondence between experience and our description of it. [p. 6. A patently redundant statement.] If we have more than one set of operations, we have more than one concept, and strictly there should be a separate name to correspond to each set of operations [p. 10].

Operationalism becomes for Bridgman a criterion of meaning:

> If a specific question has meaning, it must be possible to find operations by which an answer may be given to it. It will be found in many cases that the operations cannot exist, and the question therefore has no meaning [p. 28]. I believe that many of the questions asked about social and philosophical subjects will be found

[26] Percy W. Bridgman, *The Logic of Modern Physics* (New York: Macmillan, 1927). For a critical discussion of operationalism, see my essays reproduced as Chapters 6 and 7 of the present volume.

to be meaningless when examined from the point of view of operations. It would doubtless conduce greatly to clarity of thought if the operational mode of thinking were adopted in all fields of inquiry as well as in the physical [p. 30]. To adopt the operational point of view involves . . . that we shall no longer permit ourselves to use as tools in our thinking concepts of which we cannot give an adequate account in terms of operations [p. 31].

It is a general consequence of the approximate character of all measurement that no empirical science can ever make exact statements [p. 34]. The essence of the explanatory process is such that we must be prepared to accept as an ultimate for our explanations the mere statement of a correlation between phenomena or situations with which we are sufficiently familiar [p. 47]. Poincaré . . . showed that not only is it always possible to find a mechanistic explanation of any phenomenon . . . , but there are always an infinite number of such explanations. This is very unsatisfactory. We want to be able to find the *real* mechanism [p. 49].

Bridgman is aware of the fact that physics is "full" of mental constructs and mental models. Many of the constructs "are made by us to enable us to deal with physical situations which we cannot directly experience through our senses but with which we have contact indirectly and by inference. Such constructs usually involve the element of invention to a greater or less degree" [p. 53]. Bridgman gives examples of "good constructs" and constructs to which no "physical reality" can be ascribed [p. 57]. He admits that constructs are "useful and even unavoidable things [but he warns] that they may have great dangers" [p. 60]. His hope is that the future will bring "a closer analysis of our inventions . . . , a search for new physical facts which shall give to our inventions the character of physical reality [or, failing that, an explicit admission] that we are dealing with pure inventions and not realities" [pp. 225–26].

Whitehead

The philosopher Alfred North Whitehead was especially effective in elucidating the relationships between so-called facts and "mere" thoughts, and in showing the fallacies of the long-standing distinction between "immediate perception" and "hypothetical reconstruction." His essay, "The Anatomy of Some Scientific Ideas," contains the most profound statements on "sense objects" and "thought objects." [27]

> A distinction is sometimes made between facts and thoughts. So far as physical science is concerned, the facts are thoughts, and thoughts are facts. Namely, the facts of sense-presentation as they affect science are those elements in the immediate apprehensions which are thoughts. Also, actual thought-expressions, primary or secondary, are the material facts which science interprets. The distinction that facts are given, but thoughts are free, is not absolute. We can select and modify our sense-presentation, so that facts—in the narrower sense of immediate apprehension of sense-presentation—are to some degree subject to volition [p. 184].

> Now science aims at harmonising our reflective and derivative thoughts with the primary thoughts involved in the immediate apprehension of sense-presentation. It also aims at producing such derivative thoughts, logically knit together. This is scientific theory; and the harmony to be achieved is the agreement of theory with observation, which is the apprehension of sense-presentation [p. 185].

Whitehead asks himself whether "the cat"—not the family of felines or the species housecat, but his own pet—was a sense-object or a thought-object. Most readers of philosophy would not have expected his conclusion:

> The perceived object is largely the supposition of our imagination. When we recognised the cat, we also recognised that it was glad to see us. But we merely heard it mewing, saw it arch its back, and felt it rubbing itself against us. We must distinguish, therefore, between the many direct objects of sense, and the single indirect object of thought which is the cat. Thus, when we say that we perceived the cat and understood its feelings, we mean that we heard a sense-object of sound, that we saw a sense-object of sight, that we felt a sense-object of touch, and that we thought of a cat and imagined its feelings. . . . For example, we hear mewing and say there must be a cat in the room. The transition from the sense-object to the cat has then been made, by deliberate ratiocination [p. 187].

[27] Alfred North Whitehead, *The Aims of Education and Other Essays* (New York: Macmillan, 1929), pp. 180–231.

There is no directly perceived time-relation between a present event and a past event. The present event is only related to the memory of the past event. But the memory of a past event is itself a present element in consciousness. . . . By proceeding according to this principle the time-relations between elements of consciousness, not in the same present, are established. The method of procedure here explained is a first example of what we will call the Principle of Aggregation. This is one of the fundamental principles of mental construction according to which our conception of the external physical world is constructed [pp. 190, 191].

The space-relations between the parts are confused and fluctuating, and in general lack determinate precision. The master-key by which we confine our attention to such parts as possess mutual relations sufficiently simple for our intellects to consider is the principle of convergence to simplicity with diminution of extent. We call it the "principle of convergence." This principle extends throughout the whole field of sense-presentation. . . . Thus the sense-object is the result of an active process of discrimination made in virtue of the principle of convergence. It is the result of the quest for simplicity of relations within the complete stream of sense-presentation [pp. 191–92].

There are other sense-presentations occurring in association with that composite partial stream which can be determined by rules derived from analogous composite partial streams, with other space and time-relations, provided that the analogy be sufficiently close. Call these the "associated sense-presentations" [p. 193].

The thought-objects of perception which are presupposed in the common thought of civilised beings are almost wholly hypothetical. The material universe is largely a concept of the imagination which rests on a slender basis of direct sense-presentation. But none the less it is a fact; for it is a fact that actually we imagine it. Thus it is actual in our consciousness just as sense-presentation also is actual there. The effort of reflective criticism is to make these two factors in our consciousness agree where they are related, namely, to construe our sense-presentation as actual realisation of the hypothetical thought-objects of perception. The wholesale employment of purely hypothetical thought-objects of perception enables science to explain some of the stray sense-objects which cannot be construed as perceptions of a thought-object of perception: for example, sounds [pp. 199–200].

The thought-objects of science are molecules, atoms, and electrons. The peculiarity of these objects is that they have shed all the qualities which are capable of direct sense-representation in consciousness. They are known to us only by their associated phenomena, namely, series of events in which they are implicated are represented in our consciousness by sense-presentations. In this way, the thought-objects of science are conceived as the causes of sense-representation. The transition from thought-objects of perception to thought-objects of science is decently veiled by an elaborate theory concerning primary and secondary qualities of bodies. This device, by which sense-presentations are represented in thought as our perception of events in which thought-objects of science are implicated, is the fundamental means by which a bridge is formed between the fluid vagueness of sense and the exact definition of thought. In thought a proposition is either true or false, an entity is exactly what it is, and relations between entities are expressible (in idea) by definite propositions about distinctly conceived entities. Sense-perception knows none of these things, except by courtesy. Accuracy essentially collapses at some stage of inquiry [pp. 200–201].

Morris Cohen

A wise book on scientific method, *Reason and Nature* by Morris Cohen, published in 1931, is conspicuously absent from many lists of references in contemporary methodological literature.[28] The reason for this neglect, I suppose, lies in the tides of philosophic fashion: Soon after Cohen's book appeared, logical empiricism and linguistic philosophy began to dominate the theory of knowledge and the philosophy of science, and these schools had no sympathy for Cohen's rationalistic leanings. I begin by quoting some of his statements on the errors of inductivism.

"Scientific method is popularly associated with the cult of induction. But clear thinking as to what precisely induction is, and how it is related to discovery and truth, has been blocked by three traditional confusions" [p. 115]. Confusion No. 1 is the alleged contrast between deduction as reasoning from universals to particulars, and induction as the exact reverse. Confusion No. 2 is between reason as a logical and reason as a psychological term. Confusion No. 3 is the notion that induction is a method of discovering general truth, while deduction is merely a method of exposition.

[28] Morris R. Cohen, *Reason and Nature: An Essay on the Meaning of Scientific Method* (New York: Harcourt, Brace & Co., 1931).

Induction and deduction are not . . . antithetic terms in the realm of purely formal logic. The difference between them is one concerning material evidence. Instead of being absolute, this generally reduces itself to a question of the *degree* of conclusiveness of the initial evidence in favor of the homogeneity of the class concerning which we wish to establish a law [p. 119].

According to the currently fashionable view, it is of the very essence of scientific method to distrust all reason and to rely on the facts only. The motto "Don't think; find out," often embodies this attitude. Scientific method is supposed to begin by banishing all preconceptions or anticipations of nature. In the first positive stage it simply collects facts; in the second, it classifies them; then it lets the facts themselves suggest a working hypothesis to explain them. It is only in the last stage, in the testing or verifying of hypotheses (so as to transform them into established laws) that the rational deduction of consequences plays any part. Such deduction, it is maintained, brings us no new information. It only makes explicit what experience has already put into our premises. . . . Begin with collecting the facts? Ay, but what facts? Obviously only with those that have some bearing on our inquiry. Attention to irrelevant circumstances will obviously not help us at all, but will rather distract us from our problem. Now, the relevant facts of nature do not of their own accord separate themselves from all the others, nor do they come with all their significant characteristics duly labelled for us. Which of the infinite variety of nature's circumstances we should turn to as relevant to or bearing on any specific problem depends upon our general ideas as to how that which is sought for can possibly be related to what we already know. Without such guiding ideas or hypotheses as to possible connection we have nothing to look for [pp. 76–77].

Certainly, if the term *scientific method* is used in any significant sense it cannot be said to begin with a *tabula rasa* and pure sense-impressions on it, such as the newborn babe is supposed to have. Sensations, like relations, are elements in a logical analysis of what we know and not actual starting points in scientific investigations. Science properly begins rather when there is wonder or active curiosity and an effort to answer questions or problems that arise out of intellectual difficulties which reflection finds in common knowledge [pp. 78–79].

Scientific method is a systematic effort to eliminate the poison of error from our common knowledge. If common knowledge were entirely wrong in substance and method, science could not have any base from which to start or any certain direction in which to proceed. It would be impossible for science to arise out of common experience and reflection if the latter did not contain the seeds of truth as well as the noxious weeds of error and illusion. But it is precisely because common sense is such a mixture of sense and illusion, of enduring truth and superstition, and because even its truth is so vaguely and inaccurately expressed, that under certain conditions it arouses dissatisfaction in sensitive intellects and compels them to go beyond common knowledge and endure the rigours of scientific research to attain purer and wider truth. If science thus begins with the facts of common sense it is only to organize or transform them radically [p. 79].

It simply is not true that the facts themselves suggest the appropriate hypothesis. The same facts do not always suggest the same hypothesis to everyone who looks at them. The history of science indicates rather that fruitful hypotheses have generally come to certain gifted minds as musical themes or great poetic expressions have come to others. You may call them the gifts of the gods to their favourites. But it is certain that it requires a plenitude of previous knowledge to enable one gifted with fortunate insights or guesses to develop them into successful scientific hypotheses [p. 80].

When facts do not fit in with our idea or hypothesis, we re-examine the process by which the facts are obtained, and try to correct them by other observations and to discover hypothetical causes of the irreducible divergences or perturbations. It is only as a last resort that we modify (as little as possible) the old ideas. If we did not hold on to our old ideas tenaciously, if we threw them away the moment they encountered difficulties, we could never develop any strong ideas and our science would have no continuity of development. Reason thus plays a more active part in scientific method than is accorded to it by the usual positivistic, anti-rationalistic account. Our safeguard against fantastic speculations and hardened prejudice is not to try to clear the mind of all prejudgments or anticipations. That is neither possible nor desirable. We cannot by mere resolution get rid of all preconceptions, since most of them seem to us obvious or unquestionable truths, and it does not in fact occur to us to question one of them except when it conflicts with some other preconception. The hampering effect of narrow prejudice or prejudgment is reduced rather by logical analysis or reflection, which, by making our premises explicit, shows them to be a part of a *larger number of possible assumptions*. Reason thus enriches us with a greater number of possible hypotheses or anticipations of nature, and this makes possible a richer variety of observation. Certainly great contributions to science are not made by those who go to nature innocent of all preconceptions but rather by those who have acquired the most knowledge and fruitful ideas on the subject of their inquiry. . . . Though no number of single experiments and observations can prove an hypothesis to be true, they are necessary to decide as to which of two hypotheses is the preferable as showing greater agreement with the order of existence. This shift from the question of whether a general proposition is absolutely true to the question of whether it is better founded than its rival is the key to the understanding of the rôle of probable and inductive reasoning [pp. 81–82].

There are still scientists who were told by their teachers that the task of science was to describe, not to explain. Cohen deplores that the truth on this subject

is obscured by the positivistic dogma (made popular among certain men of science by Karl Pearson) that the laws of nature are mere descriptions of the routine of our perception or habitual sequence of our sensations. Whatever may be the historic or psychologic origin of scientific laws like Newton's laws of mechanics, or Maxwell's laws of the electro-magnetic field, or Planck's Quantum Law, they certainly do not describe the order of our perceptions or the sequence of our sensations. For the laws are stated in terms of abstract elements like mass, time and space intervals, electric permeability, etc., which are not as such sensations. Nor do these laws assert any temporal sequence. They assert rather a mutual implication between the parts of an equation, though the elements of the equation refer to what is in time. Indeed, even what we have called factual laws are concerned with abstract elements [p. 101].

The most powerful organon for the apprehension and controlling of nature that man has as yet discovered is description in terms of ideal entities such as perfect levers, ideal gases, perfectly continuous bodies, the velocity of light in an unattainable perfect vacuum, and the like. For explanation of this paradox we must fall back on the fact that while the so-called perceptual order of commonsense experience is the source of scientific truth it is also full of illusion and error, so that the conceptual order which science seeks to attain must depart from it to attain coherent truth [pp. 104–5].

Every abstract or universal law asserts what would happen if only certain conditions prevailed and everything else remained indifferent. Prediction is possible to the extent that nature does offer us instances where the action of bodies can be accounted for by a limited number of factors, and the effects of all other influences either balance each other or are so small as to be negligible or unnoticeable. But theoretically it is true that no actual phenomenon can exclusively embody a single universal law, since in general every actual phenomenon is the meeting place or intersection of many laws. Yet every true law is actually embodied in all instances of it, and it is that which enables us to analyze phenomena and arrange them in significant order. But while abstract laws are always necessary for the understanding of phenomena, their sufficiency varies in different fields [pp. 105–6].

No one human being develops all or most of his generalizations. Each one of us is born into a community and the general ideas of that community are imposed upon us through language and through other social molds which emphasize certain aspects of existence to the neglect of others. There is therefore no reason to suppose that the perception of particulars always precedes the perception of the universal. . . . But it would be fairer to say that universal idea and particular fact generally develop into clearness together, the particular instance helping to give body and prehensibility to the idea, and the idea making the instance clearer and more definite. Even psychologically, however, it is true that some ideas, notably of method, must precede in time the recognition of certain particular facts which would not be otherwise sought for or observed. . . . Logically, however, a proposition is a priori if it must be presupposed and cannot be proved or disproved within the system to which it is a priori [p. 138].

Science can never dispense with unproved universal propositions. Of these unproved assumptions some can be disproved by their consequences,—while others can not be. Ordinary hypotheses belong to the first class, while those of the second class may properly be called a priori. For an hypothesis in science is an anticipation of experience (in plain language, a guess) that may turn out to be false and refutable, while it is the essence of the a priori to be irrefutable [p. 140].

In a fairly uniform realm like that of physics, where we can vary one factor at a time, it is possible to have a crucial experiment, that is, it is possible to reduce an issue to a question of yes or no, so that the result refutes and eliminates one hypothesis and leaves the other in possession of the field. But where the number of possible causes is indefinitely large, and where we cannot always isolate a given factor, it is obviously difficult to eliminate an hypothesis; and the elimination of one hypothesis from a very large number does not produce the impression of progress in the establishment of a definite cause [p. 352].

Reichenbach

Hans Reichenbach wrote, in the preface to his book *Experience and Prediction*,[29] that "the key to an understanding of scientific method is contained within the probability problem" [p. vii]. And he is credited with having replaced the competing theories of cognitive meaning—pragmatic theory, verifiability theory, falsifiability theory, confirmability theory, etc.—with his "probability theory of meaning."

Reichenbach distinguishes three tasks of epistemology: descriptive (as a part of sociology and psychology), critical (as a part of the logic of cognition), and advisory (as a part of decision-making processes). For him, "any rationally reconstructed knowledge can only be given in the language form [p. 16]. A theory of knowledge must consequently begin with a theory of language. Knowledge is given by symbols [and] symbols are . . . physical bodies," such as ink spots or sound waves [p. 17]. But symbols have also another property—meaning: "Only the rules of language confer meaning on a symbol [p. 18]. Linear arrangements of symbols are divided into units, called propositions. There are three predicates of propositions: meaning, truth-value, and weight. Only very few propositions occurring in speech have a known truth-value; most of them, with their truth-value unknown, have only some weight:

> The weight is a quantity in continuous scale running from the utmost uncertainty through intermediate degrees of reliability to the highest certainty. The exact measure of the degree of reliability, or weight, is probability [p. 23]. [Thus,] in the system of propositional weights we construct a bridge from the known to the unknown [p. 24]. Whether a sentence is true depends on the sentence alone, or rather on the facts concerned. The weight, on the contrary, is conferred upon a sentence by the state of our knowledge and may therefore vary according to a change in knowledge [p. 27].

[29] Hans Reichenbach, *Experience and Prediction: An Analysis of the Foundations and the Structure of Knowledge* (Chicago: University of Chicago Press, 1938).

Regarding the application of the "truth theory of meaning" to "observation propositions" and to "indirect propositions," Reichenbach distinguishes technical possibility, physical possibility, and logical possibility of verification. The first criterion is surely unacceptable, the second may still be too restrictive, the third, however, too lenient; "the concept of physical meaning looks sounder than that of logical meaning" [p. 45]. However, if we were to apply this standard consistently, "all that physics states would be a summary of observation propositions" [p. 50]. Reichenbach concludes that we must "renounce absolute verifiability as the criterion of meaning" [p. 53]. He proposes that *a proposition has meaning if it is possible to determine a weight, i.e., a degree of probability, for the proposition* [p. 54]. But, since "logical probability meaning and logical truth meaning are identical—because logical relations are truisms—it "is always physical probability meaning" that matters [p. 55].

The reference to "indirect propositions" calls for an explanation. Reichenbach divides

> propositions into direct and indirect sentences. *Direct sentences* are sentences concerning immediately observable physical facts; such sentences . . . are absolutely verifiable, i.e., accessible to a determination of their truth-value within the frame of two-valued logic. Only for *indirect sentences* [is] the predicate of weight needed; such sentences are not controlled directly, but by means of their relation to direct sentences which confer on them a certain degree of probability [p. 83].

However, even observation sentences are not absolutely verifiable, because "the difference between the material object" observed and a mere illusion can be formulated only on the basis of a prediction of certain "future observations" [p. 86], as, for example, "if I were to put the book on the table now, it would not fall" but would be supported by the table, which thereby would prove itself as a material object. Hence,

> There is no statement concerning physical objects which is absolutely verifiable. [For,] if we admit the possibility that later observation can control [test] our statement about a present observation, we cannot exclude the case of a negative result of this con-

trol—that is, our statement cannot be maintained as certain. If in spite of that we take such statements as certain, we perform an idealization; we identify a high degree of probability with certainty. But, strictly speaking, this is not a case of truth but one of weight; even the observation sentences of daily life are not to be considered as direct sentences but as indirect sentences judged by the predicate of weight instead of the predicate of truth [p. 87].

Felix Kaufmann

Many propositions on methodology and its cognate fields in the work of Felix Kaufmann are more detailed and explicit than those found in other sources.[30] Kaufmann sees methodology, "the logical analysis of scientific procedure," as "related to deductive logic," but he wants methodology and deductive logic clearly distinguished and recognized as autonomous rational disciplines [p. vii]. He also warns that "the conflicting epistemological doctrines 'behind' the methodological controversies"—for example, rationalism–empiricism, realism–idealism, subjectivism–objectivism, monism–dualism, determinism–indeterminism—do not lead to the core of general methodological issues. These issues can be properly interpreted only "by an analysis of the fundamental rules of empirical procedure." Finally, he distinguishes the methodologies of particular (natural or social) sciences from general methodology. He holds that "the major methodological controversies in the social sciences cannot be settled if we regard them as peculiar to particular fields of social inquiry or even to the entire domain of social research. . . . Issues of general methodology play an essential part in these controversies" [p. 2].

Kaufmann sees a clear-cut difference between methodology and formal logic in the proofs by which their rules are judged:

> The adequacy of rules of deductive inference, e.g., of moods of the syllogism, can be proved by analysis of propositional meanings. However, such a proof is not possible for the rules of empirical procedure [p. 32]. Empirical procedure is concerned with a division of synthetic propositions into two disjunctive classes, accepted propositions and non-accepted propositions. A decision by which

[30] Felix Kaufmann, *Methodology of the Social Sciences* (New York: Oxford University Press, 1944). German edition, *Methodenlehre der Sozialwissenschaften* (Vienna: Julius Springer, 1936).

the status of a proposition is changed, e.g., by which its transfer from one class into the other is performed, must not be arbitrary; grounds must be offered to justify it [p. 39].

It is a "misconception" to think that there is "a single adequate approach" to all problems in a given field of inquiry. It leads to methodological conflict about

what is *the* appropriate method. . . . In certain circumstances . . . one method is plainly preferable to another because it makes possible the solution not only of all problems soluble by the other methods, but of additional problems as well. . . . Very often, however, different methods will coexist within a certain field of inquiry, each leading to certain achievements denied to the others. The idea that for a given field . . . one method is exclusively appropriate is less harmful in physics . . . than in psychology and the social sciences. It seems that we shall have to resign ourselves for some time to methodological pluralism in these sciences [p. 74].

Methodology has been plagued by the importation of epistemological questions such as

whether the laws of nature have "objective" existence . . . or merely "subjective" existence . . . ; whether they are real bonds between things or merely theoretical constructs [and whether] the laws [are] discovered or invented. The genuine methodological questions are: (a) What is the logical form of law? (b) Under what conditions are such propositions accepted? (c) Under what conditions are such propositions eliminated? (d) What functions do such propositions have in the control of other propositions? (e) How far does the system of laws established at present fulfill the conditions implied in the ideal of a rational cosmos? [p. 77].

"Methodological analysis of social laws has been largely concerned with the question why social science is not so successful as natural science in making predictions." Kaufmann's answer is chiefly in terms of determinateness: "Every physical event down to its most minute details is governed by a system of laws. But in dealing with human action, we must take into account a factor that is exempt from these laws, namely, free will" [p. 169]. However, Kaufmann immediately qualifies these statements, both with respect to "radical determinism" in physics (where it has been renounced in order to accommodate quantum physics) and with respect to the "free will," which has been found to be a highly ambiguous term. Kaufmann shows this by presenting nine different theses concerning "free will," each with a different methodological implication or application [pp. 170–72]. In these matters, as regarding several others, Kaufmann warns against "exaggeration of the disparity between natural and social science" [p. 177] and holds that so-called "rigid theoretical laws"—in contrast to "strict (empirical) laws"—are equally useful in social and natural sciences [p. 175]. He admits, however, that there are differences in the degrees to which the traditional ideals of "Unity and Simplicity, Unrestricted Universality, Precision, [and] Persuasiveness" apply to the different sciences [pp. 179–81].

Schutz

Alfred Schutz, philosopher and sociologist, confined his methodological studies to the social sciences. His *Phenomenology of the Social World*,[31] first published in German in 1932, constituted an ingenious intertwining of two very different strands of thought: the methodological concepts of Max Weber and the phenomenological philosophy of Edmund Husserl. Although this work contained the foundation of Schutz's methodology of the social sciences, several later essays offered more concise statements of the major principles.[32]

A fundamental issue had to be settled first: the meaning of empirical observation. Schutz insisted "that we do not restrict this term to sensory perceptions of objects and events in the outer world but include the experiential form by which common-sense thinking in everyday life understands human actions and their outcome in terms

[31] Alfred Schutz, *Der sinnhafte Aufbau der sozialen Welt* (Vienna: Springer Verlag, 1932); English edition, *The Phenomenology of the Social World*, translated by George Walsh and Frederick Lehnert (Evanston, Ill.: Northwestern University Press, 1967).

[32] Alfred Schutz, "The Social World and the Theory of Social Action," *Social Research*, Vol. 27 (No. 2, 1960), pp. 203–21; reprinted in *Collected Papers*, vol. 2 (The Hague: Martinus Nijhoff, 1964), pp. 3–19; *idem*, "Common-Sense and Scientific Interpretation of Human Action," *Philosophy and Phenomenological Research*, Vol. 14 (September 1953), pp. 1–37; reprinted in *Collected Papers*, vol. 1 (1962), pp. 3–47; *idem*, "Concept and Theory Formation in the Social Sciences," *Journal of Philosophy*, Vol. 51 (April 1954), pp. 257–73; reprinted in *Collected Papers*, vol. 1, pp. 48–66. All page references in the text are to the *Collected Papers*.

of their underlying motives and goals" [*Concept,* p. 65]. While this insistence was necessary vis-à-vis epistemologists of the "sensory-experience only" persuasion, it would not have been necessary to stress it vis-à-vis the many philosophers of science who include "inner experience" as a source of empirical knowledge (Alfred North Whitehead, Richard B. Braithwaite, and even Rudolf Carnap may be counted among those who have admitted "private facts" to the class of eligible empirical data).

Schutz adopted the ideal type which Weber had introduced as the basic concept of social theory and social history, and adapted it in several respects. He held that "the goal of the social sciences is the explanation of the 'social reality' as experienced by man living his everyday life within the social world." But since "the subjective meaning an action has for an actor is unique and individual," the question arises how it is "possible to grasp subjective meaning scientifically" [*Common-Sense,* p. 35]. Moreover, since scientific knowledge must be objective in the sense that it is "accessible equally" to all scientists, to be tested and potentially disconfirmed, how can "subjective meaning structures" of acting persons be grasped by a system of objective knowledge? Schutz answers the first of these questions by offering "particular methodological devices" by which "the social scientist replaces the thought objects of common-sense thought relating to unique events . . . by constructing a model of a sector of the social world within which merely those typified events occur that are relevant to the scientist's particular problem under scrutiny" [p. 36].

His answers to the second question rely on similar "methodological devices," which have to satisfy three methodological postulates. (1) *The postulate of logical consistency*: "The system of typical constructs designed by the scientist . . . must be fully compatible with the principles of formal logic," which "warrants [their] objective validity." (2) *The postulate of subjective interpretation*: "The scientist has to construct a 'model of an individual mind' endowed with such 'typical contents' [as can] explain the observed facts as the result of the activity of such a mind in an understandable relation" [p. 43.] (3) *The postulate of adequacy*: "Each term in a scientific model of human action must be constructed in such a way that a human act performed within the life-world by an individual actor in the way indicated by the typical construct would be understandable for the actor himself as well as for his fellow-men in terms of common-sense interpretation of everyday life. [This] warrants the consistency of the constructs of the social scientist with the constructs of common-sense experience of the social reality" [p. 44].[33]

Carnap

If Rudolf Carnap is characterized as one of the chief protagonists of logical positivism—evolved in the Vienna Circle that had formed around Moritz Schlick—this does not signify a fixed epistemological and methodological position. The point is that the views of several members of that school developed from a rather radical empiricism ("scientific," "logical," "logistic," "logicist" empiricism)—in the form of an extreme physicalism—to a gradually more liberal emphasis on the methodical application of logic to the philosophy of science.[34] The transformation from intransigence to philosophical tolerance is best described in "Carnap's Intellectual Autobiography."[35]

> I came to hold the view that many theses of traditional metaphysics are not only useless, but even devoid of cognitive content. They are pseudo-sentences, that is to say, they seem to make assertions because they have the grammatical form of declarative sentences, and the words occurring in them have many strong and emotionally loaded associations, while in fact they do not make any assertions, do not express any propositions, and are therefore neither true nor false. Even the apparent questions to which these sentences allegedly give either an affirmative or a negative answer . . . are not genuine questions but pseudo-questions. The view that these sentences and questions are non-cognitive was based on

[33] For more on Schutz's work see my essay included in this volume as Chapter 8.

[34] Carnap's major works include *Physikalische Begriffsbildung* (Karlsruhe: G. Braun, 1926); *Der logische Aufbau der Welt* (Berlin-Schlachtensee: Weltkreis-Verlag, 1928); *Abriss der Logistik* (Vienna: Julius Springer, 1929); *The Unity of Science* (London: Kegan Paul, Trench, Trubner & Co., 1934); *The Logical Syntax of Language* (London: Kegan Paul, Trench, Trubner & Co., 1937); *Introduction to Semantics* (Cambridge, Mass.: Harvard University Press, 1942); *Formalization of Logic* (Cambridge, Mass.: Harvard University Press, 1943); *Meaning and Necessity: A Study in Semantics and Modal Logic* (Chicago: University of Chicago Press, 1947); *Logical Foundations of Probability* (Chicago: University of Chicago Press, 1950); *The Continuum of Inductive Methods* (Chicago: University of Chicago Press, 1952); *Philosophical Foundations of Physics* (New York: Basic Books, 1966).

[35] In *The Philosophy of Rudolf Carnap*, edited by Paul Arthur Schilpp (La Salle, Ill.: Open Court, 1963), pp 3–84. All page references in the text are to this volume.

Wittgenstein's principle of verifiability. This principle says first, that the meaning of a sentence is given by the conditions of its verification and, second, that a sentence is meaningful if and only if it is in principle verifiable, that is, if there are possible, not necessarily actual, circumstances, which, if they did occur, would definitely establish the truth of the sentence. This principle of verifiability was later replaced by the more liberal principle of confirmability.

Unfortunately, following Wittgenstein, we formulated our view in the Vienna Circle in the oversimplified version of saying that certain metaphysical theses are "meaningless." This formulation caused much unnecessary opposition, even among some of those philosophers who basically agreed with us. Only later did we see that it is important to distinguish the various meaning components, and therefore said in a more precise way that such theses lack cognitive or theoretical meaning. They often have other meaning components, e.g., emotive or motivative ones, which, although not cognitive, may have strong psychological effects [pp. 45–46].

In his earliest works, in the 1920s, Carnap regarded

a phenomenalistic language as the best for a philosophical analysis of knowledge. I believed that the task of philosophy consists in reducing all knowledge to a basis of certainty. Since the most certain knowledge is that of the immediately given, whereas knowledge of material things is derivative and less certain, it seemed that the philosopher must employ a language which uses sense-data as a basis. In the Vienna discussions my attitude changed gradually toward a preference for the physicalistic language. Against the conception that this language may serve as a total language for all knowledge, sometimes the objection was raised that on a physicalistic basis it is impossible to reach the concepts of psychology [p. 50].

Carnap held that this objection could be overcome by "the construction of concepts concerning other minds on the basis of the observed behavior of other human bodies" [p. 51]. However, "our initial formulations of physicalism . . . can only be regarded as a first rough attempt. In view of the liberalization of the empiricist conception . . . the assertion of the definability of psychological terms on the basis of the terms of the thing-language must be weakened to an assertion of reducibility" [pp. 52–53].

According to the original conception, . . . we assumed that there was a certain rock bottom of knowledge, the knowledge of the immediately given, which was indubitable. Every other kind of knowledge was supposed to be firmly supported by this basis and therefore likewise decidable with certainty. . . . This view . . . was difficult to reconcile with . . . the methodology of science. . . . The important feature in our methodological position was the emphasis on the hypothetical character of the laws of nature, in particular of physical theories. . . . It was clear that the laws of physics could not possibly be completely verified. . . . we had to look for a more liberal criterion of significance [no longer: "meaning"] than verifiability [p. 57].

Later I introduced the quantitative concept of degree of confirmation or logical probability. . . . In addition . . . we must abandon the earlier view that the concepts of science are explicitly definable on the basis of observation concepts; more indirect methods of reduction must be used. . . . Our earlier thesis of phenomenalistic positivism was in need of a more liberal reformulation in an analogous way, so that translatability was replaced by confirmability [p. 59].

I have the impression that, among empiricists today, there is no longer strong opposition to abstract entities, either in semantics or in any field of mathematics or empirical science [p. 67].

As early as 1936, in an essay, "Testability and Meaning," [36] Carnap "stressed . . . the impossibility of translating the sentences of the scientific language into terms designating observables" [p. 78]. Twenty years later, in his article, "The Methodological Character of Theoretical Concepts," [37] he reached his final position on the differences between theoretical and observation languages:

The interpretation of theoretical terms is always incomplete, and the theoretical sentences are in general not translatable into the observation language. These disadvantages are more than balanced by the great advantages of the theoretical language, viz. the great

[36] Rudolf Carnap, "Testability and Meaning," *Philosophy of Science* [Baltimore] Vol. 3 (October 1936), pp. 419–71, and Vol. 4 (January 1937), pp. 1–40.

[37] Rudolf Carnap, "The Methodological Character of Theoretical Concepts," in *The Foundations of Science and the Concepts of Psychology and Psychoanalysis,* edited by Herbert Feigl and Michael Scriven (Minneapolis: University of Minnesota Press, 1956), pp. 38–76.

freedom of concept formation and theory formation, and the great explanatory and predictive power of a theory. These advantages have so far been used chiefly in the field of physics; the prodigious growth of physics since the last century depended essentially upon the possibility of referring to unobservable entities like atoms and fields. In our century, other branches of science such as biology, psychology, and economics, have begun to apply the method of theoretical concepts to some extent [p. 80].

This position, Carnap admits, is incompatible with the

empiricist criterion of meaningfulness, . . . since the connection between a theoretical term *t* and observation terms, which is the basis of the interpretation, becomes weaker as the chain from observation terms through rules of correspondence and postulates to the term *t* becomes longer, it seemed plausible to think that in this context we must speak of a degree of significance [p. 80].

Carnap proposed a different solution, for terms as well as for sentences:

A theoretical term *t* is significant if there is an assumption *A* involving *t* such that from *A* and additional assumptions involving other theoretical terms that have already been recognized as significant it is possible to derive with the help of the postulates and the rules of correspondence an observation sentence that cannot be derived without the assumption *A*. This criterion is meant as a minimum requirement. For sentences I proposed the following criterion. An expression of the language *L* containing theoretical terms is a significant sentence if it satisfies the rules of formation for *L* and if all theoretical terms occurring in it are significant [p. 80].

As to the modified requirement of confirmability, Carnap still resists accepting "logical possibility"; he insists on "physical possibility" ["Replies and Expositions," p. 877]. On the other hand, the requirement is not very restrictive, since Carnap states: "I regard as meaningful for me whatever I can, in principle, confirm subjectively"; and "everything I know, including what I know by introspection, is in principle confirmable by others on the basis of their observations" [p. 882].

Margenau

For the physicist–philosopher Henry Margenau, methodology is the part of metaphysics that studies the methods for determining what is real. Since his book is entitled *The Nature of Physical Reality*, and since concern with reality and existence is the avowed objective of ontology, one is not surprised at Margenau's admission of metaphysical discourse.[38]

> To deny the . . . necessary presence of metaphysical elements in any successful science is to be blind to the obvious, although to foster such blindness has become a highly sophisticated endeavour in our time [p. 12]. Every scientist *must* invoke assumptions or rules of procedure which are not dictated by sensory evidence as such, rules whose application endow a collection of facts with internal organization and coherence, makes them simple, makes a theory elegant and acceptable [p. 13].

Many of the scientist's rules of procedure rest on "metaphysical convictions, not perhaps of a grandly ontological sort, but certainly epistemological in character" [p. 13]. Metaphysics, since Kant,

> has tended to designate two large branches of thought, ontology and epistemology. We hold with Kant that epistemology must precede ontology and that epistemology denotes the methodology of the cognitive process. The methodology of science involves deliverances of sense as well as rules of correspondence, constructs, and principles regulating constructs. Having learned that the latter are not conveyed by sensory data and yet function in guiding experience, we should call them metaphysical principles in the modern sense of the word [p. 81].

According to Margenau,

> All sciences start upon the correlational level and evolve progressively toward the theoretic stage. At any given stage, no science is entirely correlational, and none is entirely theoretic. Nevertheless, if there is a significant methodological distinction, it is this, that a science is either predominantly correlational or predominantly

[38] Henry Margenau, *The Nature of Physical Reality: A Philosophy of Modern Physics* (New York: McGraw-Hill, 1950).

theoretic [p. 29]. [As they] have abandoned the correlational method and have embraced the use of theoretical hypotheses, from which facts can in a certain sense be *deduced,* . . . sciences have become *theoretical,* exact, or deductive [p. 30].

To each of these two methods belongs a different kind of concept: to the former, empirical or epistemic concepts that are related to perception and sensory evidence [pp. 54–65]; to the latter, invented, completely abstract and theoretical, mental constructs which are purely rational elements of a deductive system [pp. 69–73]. "It is the principal business of a methodology of science, and indeed of all epistemology, to investigate what requirements a construct must satisfy to be admitted as valid" [p. 70]. The connections among epistemic concepts are presented as correlations; the connections among theoretical constructs form a deductive system.

Margenau lists six requirements for the validity of constructs and systems of constructs: A. Logical Fertility, B. Multiple Connections, C. Permanence and Stability, D. Extensibility, E. Causality, and F. Simplicity and Elegance [pp. 81–99]. He calls these requirements, which are not much different from those enumerated by other methodologists, "metaphysical, for their function approximates closely the role which was played by metaphysics in the older systems of philosophy" [p. 100].

In contrast to the fashion of scientific methodology around 1900, but in conformance with the position of the wide majority of modern philosophers of science, Margenau emphasizes the difference between description and explanation. A

"*descriptive* theory" involves constructs that are not very distant from "the plane of perception, [whereas] an *explanation* involves a further progression into the constructional domain. We explain by going 'beyond phenomena'" [p. 169]. Apposite to the domain of data (Domain P, for perception or protocol statements) and the domain of construction (Domain C) are two kinds of definitions: "epistemic" (or operational) definitions for P-statements, and "constitutive" definitions for C-statements [pp. 220–43]. A constitutive definition represents a postulated grouping of constructs, remains wholly within the C field, and is therefore empirically not verifiable. An epistemic definition is always a rule or a set of rules of correspondence [p. 240]. Without epistemic definitions science degenerates to speculation; in the absence of constitutive definitions it becomes a sterile record of observational facts [p. 243].

Popper

The methodological writings of Sir Karl Popper, beginning with the German edition of his book, *The Logic of Scientific Discovery*,[39] have been exceptionally influential, chiefly because of his opposition to the teachings of the neopositivistic school with its (now retracted) contention that nonverifiable propositions were "meaningless." Contrary to their emphasis on reductionism to sense perceptions of the physical world and on inductive inference, Popperian methodology "rejects inductive logic" altogether [p. 35]. Popper sharply distinguishes

> between the *psychology of knowledge,* which deals with empirical facts, and the *logic of knowledge,* which is concerned only with logical relations [p. 30]. [He points to] four different lines along which the [deductive] testing of a theory could be carried out. First there is the logical comparison of the conclusions among themselves, by which the internal consistency of the system is tested. Secondly, there is the investigation of the logical form of the theory, with the object of determining whether it has the character of an empirical or scientific theory, or whether it is, for example, tautological [as a completely axiomatic system would be]. Thirdly, there is the comparison with other theories, chiefly with the aim of determining whether the theory would constitute a scientific advance should it survive our various tests. And finally, there is the testing of the theory by way of empirical applications of the conclusions which can be derived from it [pp. 32–33].

This testing of empirical applications, however, is not designed to verify the theory or the system of which it is a part. Indeed, while a theory may have "proved its mettle" [p. 33] and thus survived its test, theories are *"never* empirically verifiable" [p. 40]. Hence, "we must choose a criterion which allows us to admit to the domain of empirical science even statements which cannot be verified. [The]

[39] Karl R. Popper, *Die Logik der Forschung* (Vienna: Julius Springer, 1935). English translation, *The Logic of Scientific Discovery* (London: Hutchinson; New York: Basic Books, 1959).

problem of demarcation, [the separating line] between the empirical sciences on the one hand, and mathematics and logic as well as 'metaphysical' systems on the other" [p. 34] cannot be solved by way of induction, for "there is no such thing as induction. [Hence] not the *verifiability* but the *falsifiability* of a system is to be taken as a criterion of demarcation" [p. 40]. The "logical form" required of a scientific system "shall be such that . . . it be possible for an empirical scientific system to be refuted by experience" [p. 41]. The point is that a statement about a singular occurrence may contradict a universal statement which denied the possibility of such occurrences. Strictly speaking, even such a disproof is impossible, inasmuch as the particular statement may be the result of a faulty experiment, an error of observation, etc. [p. 50]. This explains the difference between potential falsifiability and actual falsification, which requires "a *reproducible effect* which refutes the theory"; even so, the "falsifying hypothesis" has to pass severe tests before it is accepted as conclusive disproof of the theory [pp. 86–87].

Popper defines methodology as the theory of the "rules of scientific method" and explains "why methodological decisions are indispensable" [p. 49]. He regards "methodological rules . . . as conventions. [They are] the rules of the game of science" [p. 53]. Among the methodological rules on which Popper elaborates are those concerning the "principle of causality: . . . that we are not to abandon the search for universal laws and for a coherent theoretical system, nor ever give up our attempts to explain causally any kind of event we can describe" [p. 61]. The rules concerning the "axiomatization of the system" demand that the system be (1) "free from contradiction," (2) "independent (i.e., it must not contain any axiom deducible from the remaining axioms)," (3) "sufficient," and (4) "necessary" (i.e., it should contain no superfluous assumptions [pp. 71–72]. As regards auxiliary hypotheses, Popper's rule is that we accept only those which do "not diminish the degree of falsifiability . . . of the system" [p. 83]. The rules implied in the requirement of falsifiability demand that the theory circumscribe "the class of all those basic statements with which it is inconsistent, [that is,] the class of the *potential* falsifiers" [p. 86]. The rules securing the requirement of consistency hold for "*every* theoretical system, be it empirical or nonempirical" [p. 92]. Popper rejects as mere "psychologism [the] doctrine that empirical sciences are reducible to sense-perceptions" [p. 93] or must be based on, or tested by, "protocol sentences [or] records . . . of immediate observation" [p. 96]. The customary requirement of simplicity, sometimes interpreted as conformance with preferences of practical or aesthetic character, is taken by Popper to be merely another way of requiring a high "degree of falsifiability, [just as also] the degree of universality and of precision of a theory increases with its degree of falsifiability" [p. 141].

In addition to the methodological principles of the scientific enterprise, Popper has presented rather revolutionary ideas on the epistemology of "objective knowledge," independent of a knowing subject. There will be an opportunity in a later section of this essay to report on these views.

Feigl

Giving credit to others, including the chemist Ostwald, Feigl effectively expounds, in a well-known address,[40] "the modern idea of philosophy of science as the logic, epistemology, and methodology of the scientific enterprise" [p. 1]. He takes pains to combat the frequent confusions between the genesis and the logical analysis of scientific ideas:

> We have learned to distinguish investigations of the origin and the development of scientific ideas from studies concerning their meaning, logical structure, and validation. Logical and methodological studies amount to an explication, analysis, or reconstruction of scientific knowledge claims. Historical studies concern the evolution of scientific knowledge in the context of psychological, social, cultural, political, and economic conditions [p. 3].

Feigl, like virtually all contemporary philosophers of science, has relegated the once widespread methodology of inductive generalization of observed regularities to the museum of specious antiquities. He holds that "axiomatization—that is, the reconstruction of a scientific discipline in the form of a deductive system, with precisely

[40] Herbert Feigl, "Philosophical Tangents of Science," in *Current Issues in the Philosophy of Science,* edited by Herbert Feigl and Grover Maxwell (New York: Holt, Rinehart, and Winston, 1961).

formulated sets of postulates, definitions, and derivations—has become the order of the day" [pp. 3–4]. And, in opposition to radical empiricists but in conformance with Einstein, Braithwaite, Duhem and many others, Feigl has concluded that "there can be no crucial experiments for single isolated assumptions, and that rival theories can be tested only as 'organic wholes'" [p. 4].

In an article on "Other Minds," [41] Feigl offers telling arguments concerning the supposedly "'unbridgeable chasm' between two minds (as William James chose to describe it)" and the traditional denial of "cognitive status to the 'avowals' of one's experience" [pp. 981, 982].

> We do have "criteria" for discriminating between mere pretending and genuine feeling, but these criteria are never statable in the form of necessary and sufficient conditions. They must be regarded as probabilistic indicators very much in the manner in which symptoms in general medicine are regarded as probabilistic indicators of diseases [p. 980].

> Introspective statements formulated in phenomenal terms can be verified by direct confrontation with immediate experience. . . . There is indeed no other criterion but intuitive cogency for the correct recognition of one's own private states [p. 982].

> Since introspective statements about my own direct experience can be clearly true or false (false at least in the case of lying or mis-speaking), I cannot accept this latest version of a behavioristic rejection of the subjectively given [p. 983].

> A fully explicit understanding of the rules of correspondence between "subjective" avowals and "objective" (intersubjective) statements will go a long way toward dispelling the philosophical puzzles about other minds [p. 983].

Feigl discusses the correspondence between a doctor's prediction that his operation will hurt the patient, and the patient's subsequent feeling of pain. He holds that

> A more detailed analysis of both the scientific methodology as well as of basic epistemology may provide a more satisfactory answer.

[41] Herbert Feigl, "Other Minds and the Egocentric Predicament," *Journal of Philosophy,* Vol. 55 (October 23, 1958), pp. 978–87.

It has become increasingly clear that the early ("radical") be-havioristic identification of the meaning of subjective terms with behavioral terms (designating symptoms) will not do. Embarrass-ment is not identical with blushing; pain is not identical with cring-ing or writhing [p. 984].

Once it is realized that almost all of our knowledge is capable of confirmation only (and not of direct verification), the torments of the other-minds problem should fade away [p. 985].

Braithwaite

In his book *Scientific Explanation*, Richard Braithwaite leaves no doubt that for him theoretical, deductive systems are the essence of explanation, and that observed facts include "private data" of inner experience.[42] Thus, although he is regarded as a philosopher close to logical positivism, he is definitely not a radical empiricist with physicalist inclinations.

In a prefatory pronouncement he makes this statement:

It is almost a platitude to say that every science proceeds, more or less explicity, by thinking of general hypotheses, of greater or less generality, from which particular consequences are deduced which can be tested by observation and experiment. . . . Science, as it advances, does not rest content with establishing simple generali-zations from observable facts: it tries to explain these lowest-level generalizations by deducing them from more general hypotheses at a higher level. Such an organization of a science into a hierarchical deductive system requires the use of subtle deductive techniques, which are provided by pure mathematics. As the hierarchy of hy-potheses of increasing generality rises, the concepts with which the hypotheses are concerned cease to be properties of things which are directly observable, and instead become "theoretical" concepts —atoms, electrons, fields of force, genes, unconscious mental proc-esses—which are connected to the observable facts by complicated logical relationships [p. vii].

[Braithwaite uses] experience, observation, and cognate terms . . . in the widest sense to cover observed facts about material objects or events in them as well as directly known facts about the

[42] Richard Bevan Braithwaite, *Scientific Explanation: A Study of the Function of Theory, Probability, and Law in Science* (Cambridge: The University Press, 1953; New York: Harper, 1960).

contents or objects of immediate experience. It may be said that it is unnecessary to include this second class of facts at all, if all the empirical data of science are facts about material objects or events in them. But this would be to exclude psychology from the status of a science, unless, indeed, the data of psychology be limited, as behaviourists would wish, to public observable facts about the behaviour of human bodies. Since I do not wish to limit psychology from the beginning in this way, nor so to limit sociology and economics should these also wish to use facts of immediate experience as data, such facts will be included among the observable facts which can be taken to be the empirical basis of a science. In using experience and observation in this way, I am following common usage; I speak of observing that I have toothache as well as of observing that I have a pen in my hand, and both my toothache and my pen are experienced by me, though the latter experience will not be immediate if phenomenalism or a representative theory is the correct philosophy of perception [p. 8].

The publicity of its data is therefore not used (as many writers would wish to use it) as the hall-mark of a science. The physical and the ordinary biological sciences use only public data open to observation by all, but the psychological and social sciences may also use private data of immediate experience. These private data are in certain cases deducible from general hypotheses in the same way as that in which public data are so deducible; it is this hypothetico-deductive method applied to empirical material which is the essential feature of a science; and if psychology or economics can produce empirically testable hypotheses, *ipso facto* they are sciences, whether or not the consequences of the hypotheses are private and incommunicable [pp. 8–9].

What is a scientific law? [asks Braithwaite.] The one thing upon which everyone agrees is that it always includes a generalization, i.e., a proposition asserting a universal connexion between properties. It always includes a proposition stating that every event or thing of a certain sort either has a certain property or stands in certain relations to other events, or things, having certain properties. The generalization may assert a concomitance of properties in the same thing or event [p. 9].

Scientific hypotheses, which, if true, are scientific laws, will then, for the purpose of my exposition, be taken as equivalent to generalizations of unrestricted range in space and time of greater or less degrees of complexity and generality. . . . . A scientific system consists of a set of hypotheses which form a deductive system; that is, which is arranged in such a way that from some of the hypotheses

as premisses all the other hypotheses logically follow. The propositions in a deductive system may be considered as being arranged
in an order of levels, the hypotheses at the highest level being those
which occur only as premisses in the system, those at the lowest
level being those which occur only as conclusions in the system,
and those at intermediate levels being those which occur as conclusions of deductions from higher-level hypotheses and which
serve as premisses for deductions to lower-level hypotheses. . . .
The hypotheses in this deductive system are empirical general
propositions with diminishing generality. The empirical testing of
the deductive system is effected by testing the lowest-level hypotheses in the system [pp. 12–13].

Braithwaite was quite firm about the status of theoretical terms:
They "can only be defined by means of observable properties on condition that the theory cannot be adapted properly to apply to new
situations" [p. 76]. More bluntly, a useful theory cannot have its
terms defined by means of observables; if there are such terms, the
theory cannot predict, and hence is not useful.

Ernest Nagel

Ernest Nagel presented his methodological system in his book,
The Structure of Science.[43] His chief concerns are the principles of
scientific method.

Implicit in the contrasts between modern science and common
sense . . . is the important difference that derives from the deliberate policy of science to expose its cognitive claims to the repeated
challenge of critically probative observational data, procured under
carefully controlled conditions. . . . The difference . . . can be
expressed by the dictum that the conclusions of science, unlike
common-sense beliefs, are the products of scientific method. However, this brief formula should not be misconstrued. It must not be
understood to assert, for example, that the practice of scientific
method consists in following prescribed rules for making experimental discoveries or for finding satisfactory explanations for matters of established fact. . . . Nor must the formula be construed
as maintaining that the practice of scientific method consists in the
use in all inquiries of some special set of techniques (such as the

[43] Ernest Nagel, *The Structure of Science: Problems in the Logic of Scientific Explanation* (New York: Harcourt, Brace & World, 1961).

techniques of measurement employed in physical science), irrespective of the subject matter or the problem under investigation [p. 12].

The practice of scientific method is the persistent critique of arguments, in the light of tried canons for judging the reliability of the procedures by which evidential data are obtained, and for assessing the probative force of the evidence on which conclusions are based. . . . While common-sense beliefs are usually accepted without a critical evaluation of the evidence available, the evidence for the conclusions of science conforms to standards such that a significant proportion of conclusions supported by similarly structured evidence remains in good agreement with additional factual data when fresh data are obtained [p. 13].

Nagel distinguishes four types of explanation: (1) deductive explanations; (2) probabilistic explanations; (3) functional or teleological explanations; and (4) genetic explanations.

A deductive explanation has the formal structure of a deductive argument, in which the explicandum is a logically necessary consequence of the explanatory premises. Accordingly, in explanations of this type the premises state a sufficient (and sometimes, though not invariably, a necessary) condition for the truth of the explicandum [p. 21].

[Probabilistic explanations] are *prima facie* not of deductive form, since their explanatory premises do not formally imply their explicanda. Nevertheless, though the premises are logically insufficient to secure the truth of the explicandum, they are said to make the latter "probable." Probabilistic explanations are usually encountered when the explanatory premises contain a statistical assumption about some class of elements, while the explicandum is a singular statement about a given individual member of that class. . . . The distinction between deductive and probabilistic types of explanation . . . is based on patent differences in the way the premises and the explicanda are related to one another, and not on any supposed differences in our knowledge of the premises [pp. 22–23].

Functional or teleological explanations— especially, though not exclusively, in biology and in the study of human affairs— . . . take the form of indicating one or more functions (or even dysfunctions) that a unit performs in maintaining or realizing certain traits of a system to which the unit belongs, or of stating the instrumental role an action plays in bringing about some goal. . . . A functional explanation may be sought for a particular act, state, or thing occurring at a stated time. . . . Or alternatively, [it] may be given for a feature that is present in all systems of a certain kind, at whatever time such systems may exist. . . . Some teleological explanations patently do assume the existence of deliberate plans and conscious purposes; but such an assumption is not illegitimate when, as in the case of teleological explanations of certain aspects of human behavior, the facts warrant it [pp. 23–24].

[Genetic explanations] undertake to explain why it is that a given subject of study has certain characteristics, by describing how the subject has evolved out of some earlier one. Such explanations . . . have been given for animate as well as inanimate things, for traits of an individual as well as for characteristics of a group. . . . The task of genetic explanations is to set out the sequence of major events through which some earlier system has been transformed into a later one. The explanatory premises of such explanations will therefore necessarily contain a large number of singular statements about past events in the system under inquiry. . . . Those events . . . are selected on the basis of assumptions (frequently tacit ones) as to what sorts of events are causally relevant to the development of the system. Accordingly, in addition to the singular statements the premises will also include (whether explicitly or implicitly) general assumptions about the causal dependencies of various kinds of events [p. 25].

In opposition to extreme empiricists who wanted to admit "description only" and regarded causal explanation as metaphysical humbug, Nagel states "that it is entirely appropriate to designate an answer to a 'why' question as an explanation, even when the answer does not supply reasons for regarding the explicandum as intrinsically necessary" [p. 27].

Analyzing the logical character of scientific laws, Nagel makes a distinction between "accidental and nomic universality" [p. 51], and points to a "*prima facie* difference" between the two, in that "a universal of law 'supports' a subjunctive conditional, while an accidental universal does not [p. 52]. This means that a nomic universality allows us to assert with confidence that if a certain event were to occur another specified event would follow. Even "contrary-to-fact conditionals" may be supported by a universal-law statement; for example, that if a certain event had occurred—which in fact had not occurred—another specified event would have followed. Nagel discusses the status of "laws of nature" and "causal laws" with great care: he rejects the use of "vacuously true laws"—why would scientists "seek experimental and observational evidence" for a law that expresses a logical necessity? [p. 53]—and he seems sceptical about the cognitive value of the practice of "transformation of an ostensible empirical law into a rule of inference" [p. 67].

Nagel devotes three chapters to methodological issues in the study of human affairs: "Methodological Problems of the Social Sciences" [pp. 447–502]; "Explanation and Understanding in the Social Sciences" [pp. 503–46]; and "Problems in the Logic of Historical Inquiry" [pp. 547–606]. He is out of sympathy with the approaches of Max Weber, Alfred Schutz, and others who stressed the importance of constructs involving the understanding of meanings meant by persons acting in the social world.[44]

Hempel

The distinction of Carl Gustav [Peter] Hempel is his fairness and gentleness in critical analysis, his understanding for other views, naïve or sophisticated, and his good sense in presenting a position that will appear sound even to those who have held different opinions. His major essays are brought together in his book *Aspects of Scientific Explanation*.[45] It deals with the Logic of Confirmation, Inductive Inconsistencies, Science and Human Values, Empiricist Criteria of Cognitive Significance, a Logical Appraisal of Operationism, Fundamentals of Taxonomy, Typological Methods in the Natural and Social Sciences, the Logic of Theory Construction, the Function of General Laws in History, the Logic of Explanation, the Logic of Functional Analysis, Deductive–Nomological Explanation, Statistical Explanation, the Concepts of "Covering-Law" Explanation, Pragmatic Aspects of Explanation, Models and Analogies, Genetic Explanation, Dispositional Explanation, Rationality and Explanation by Reasons—a set of problems that may well serve as a

---

[44] A discussion of these differences in methodological problems, with special reference to Nagel's position, will be found in Chapter 11 of this volume.

[45] Carl G. Hempel, *Aspects of Scientific Explanation and Other Essays in the Philosophy of Science* (New York: The Free Press, 1965).

FRITZ MACHLUP

representative sample of the major concerns of present-day methodology.

As for virtually all modern philosophers of science, for Hempel the essential distinction is between "empirical generalizations"— expressing "regular connections among directly observable phenomena"—and "scientific theory formation"— connecting theoretical terms and sentences in the form of "strictly universal statements" [pp. 173–75]. Hempel asks "Why should science resort to the assumption of hypothetical entities when it is interested in establishing predictive and explanatory connections among observables?" The answer is that generalizations about the latter "have a rather limited range of application, and even within that range, they have exceptions, so that actually they are not true general statements [pp. 179–80].

> It is a remarkable fact that the greatest advances in scientific systematization have not been accomplished by means of laws referring explicitly to *observables,* i.e., to things and events which are ascertainable by direct observation, but rather by means of laws that speak of various *hypothetical,* or *theoretical, entities,* i.e., presumptive objects, events, and attributes which cannot be perceived or otherwise directly observed by us" [p. 177].

The set of sentences asserted by a theory "falls into two subsets: *primitive sentences,* or *postulates* (also called *axioms*) and *derivative sentences,* or *theorems.*" Theories "in the form of axiomatized systems" require a listing of the terms and their definitions, as well as of the postulates, and they are subject to "the rules of deductive inference" [p. 183]. In order to "function as a theory in empirical science" it requires also a reference to its range of application, which is done through a "set of *interpretative sentences,* which connect certain terms of the theoretical vocabulary with observational terms" [p. 184]. However, assuming that "the observational vocabularly is finite, . . . it can be proved that not all scientific terms are definable in a way that provides them with finite criteria of application" [p. 199]. "In effect . . . most theoretical terms are presently used in science on the basis of only a partial experiential interpretation; and this use . . . appears to offer distinct heuristic advantages" [p. 206].

Hempel examines and rejects "the general view of explanation as a reduction to the familiar." Familiarity is "relative to a questioner," whereas explanations in empirical science are "to exhibit objective relationships" [p. 430]. He shows that "it is neither necessary nor sufficient for the scientific adequacy of an explanation that it should reduce the explanandum to ideas with which we are already familiar" [p. 433]. As to the explanatory value of models and analogies, Hempel grants that they "may provide effective heuristic guidance in the search for new explanatory principles" [p. 441], but he questions their direct contribution to explanation. He recognizes that certain theoretical models in psychology, sociology, and economics may have the character of theories "with a more or less limited scope of application. . . . The resulting explanations and predictions may be deductive–nomological or inductive–statistical depending on the form of the hypotheses included in the model" [p. 446].

A deductive–nomological explanation "effects a deductive subsumption of the explanandum under principles that have the character of general laws. . . . Given the particular circumstances and the laws in question, the occurrence of the phenomenon *was to be expected;* and it is in this sense that the explanation enables us to *understand why* the phenomenon occurred" [p. 337]. These "general laws" are sometimes regarded as "inference rules." They have long been denied the logical character of propositions because they were not directly verifiable "by particular experiential findings. [However,] the requirement of strict verifiability for sentences that are to qualify as empirically significant has long since been abandoned as too restrictive" [p. 354]. Statistical laws may be deductive—if they can be inferred, like the probability of 0.5 for each side of a flipped coin to come up if the coin is perfect—or inductive—if the probability value is the result of observation or experiment, that is, "*relative to some body of evidence*" [p. 382]. Statistical laws "play a very important role in science. Rather than deny them explanatory status on the ground that nonrealization of the explanandum is compatible with the explanans, we have to acknowledge that they constitute explanations of a distinct logical character, reflecting, we might say, a different sense of the word 'because'" [p. 393.] The chief point is "that *the concept of statistical explanation for particular events is essentially relative to a given knowledge situation as represented by*

FRITZ MACHLUP

a class of accepted statements." Hempel refers "to this characteristic as the *epistemic relativity of statistical explanation*" [p. 402].

METHODOLOGY, LOGIC, EPISTEMOLOGY, PHILOSOPHY

Writers dealing with methodology have not always been careful in distinguishing their immediate concerns from those of logic, on the one hand, and those of epistemology, on the other; and some have preferred to eschew fixing their place in the spectrum by using the all-embracing term *Philosophy* as designation of their reflections. In a superficial test, I checked the titles of volumes, parts, or chapters of books, essays, and articles cited in the references listed in a few books on the subject. The word *philosophy* appeared in seven titles, *methodology* in four, *logic* in four, *method* in one, and *metaphysics* in one.[46]

[46] The titles are listed here in order of their publication dates:

Edwin Arthur Burtt, *Metaphysical Foundations of Modern Physical Science* (New York: Harcourt, Brace, 1927);

Percy W. Bridgman, *The Logic of Modern Physics* (New York: Macmillan, 1927);

Hans Reichenbach, *Philosophie der Raum-Zeitlehre* (Berlin: Walter de Gruyter, 1928);

Albert Einstein, "On the Method of Theoretical Physics," *Essays in Science* (New York: Philosophical Library, 1930);

Henry Margenau, "Methodology of Modern Physics," *Philosophy of Science*, vol. 2 (Nos. 1 and 2, 1935). Part 1, pp. 48–72, Part 2, pp. 164–87.

A. C. Benjamin, *Introduction to the Philosophy of Science* (New York: Macmillan, 1937);

William H. Werkmeister, *A Philosophy of Science* (New York: Harper, 1940);

Alexander Tarski, *Introduction to Logic and to Methodology of the Deductive Sciences* (New York: Oxford University Press, 1941);

Felix Kaufmann, *Methodology of the Social Sciences* (New York: Oxford University Press, 1944);

Hans Reichenbach, *Philosophic Foundations of Quantum Mechanics* (Berkeley: University of California Press, 1944);

Filmer S. C. Northrup, *The Logic of the Sciences and the Humanities* (New York: Macmillan, 1947)

Hermann Weyl, *Philosophy of Mathematics and Natural Science* (Princeton: Princeton University Press, 1949);

Henry Margenau, *The Nature of Physical Reality: A Philosophy of Modern Physics* (New York: McGraw-Hill, 1950);

Philipp Frank, *Philosophy of Science* (Englewood Cliffs, N.J.: Prentice-Hall, 1957);

Epistemological problems were discussed along with methodological ones, but epistemology did not make the title of any of the works on the list. In this connection, it is interesting to see how different philosophers have placed epistemology, methodology, and logic in relation to one another. For some (for example, Lalande and Margenau) methodology is a part of epistemology; for others (for example, Montague) epistemology is a part of methodology. With respect to all three subjects, the chances for inconsistent placements are increased, and philosophers are not likely to pass up such chances. For some (for example, Montague) methodology contains both epistemology and logic; for others (for example, Windelband) logic contains both methodology and epistemology; again for others (for example, Cohen and Nagel) epistemology stands alone, whereas logic contains methodology. I shall not at this juncture go through all possible combinations; this will be easier after I furnish a set of acceptable definitions for the disciplines in question.

Definition of Methodology

In our survey of fundamental methodological positions stated by various methodologists, we encountered several definitions of methodology, some explicit, others merely implied. I shall now try my hand at formulating a definition that avoids as much as possible any metaphysical commitment and acceptance of any particular epistemological position. (In this endeavor I have been influenced chiefly by the writings of Felix Kaufmann.)

I submit that we understand by methodology the study of the principles that guide students of any field of knowledge, and especially of any branch of higher learning (science) in deciding whether to accept or reject certain propositions as a part of the body of ordered knowledge in general or of their own discipline (science).

This definition excludes from methodology several tasks that some writers have assigned to it. Before all, methodology has nothing to say on the best way, let alone the only way, by which to approach any substantive problem in any field of inquiry. Furthermore, al-

---

Karl R. Popper, *The Logic of Scientific Discovery* (London: Hutchinson, 1959) [German original, 1934];

Alfred Schutz, "On the Methodology of the Social Sciences," Part I of *Collected Papers*, vol. 1, *The Problem of Social Reality* (The Hague: Martinus Nijhoff, 1962).

though methodology is *about* methods, it is not *a* method, nor a set of methods, nor a description of methods. Instead, it provides arguments, perhaps rationalizations, which support various preferences entertained by the scientific community for certain rules of intellectual procedure, including those for forming concepts, building models, formulating hypotheses, and testing theories. Thus, investigators employing the *same method*—that is, taking the same steps in their research and analysis—may nevertheless *hold very different methodological positions*. Obversely, supporters of the *same methodological principles* may decide to *use very different methods* in their research and analysis if they differ in their judgments of the problem to be investigated, of the existing or assumed conditions, of the relevance of different factors, or of the availability or quality of recorded data. Thus, while we use a method, we never "use" methodology; and while we may describe a method, we cannot "describe" methodology. The confusion of methodology with method is, for a literate person, inexcusable.

Perhaps we should explicitly deal with the question of whether methodology is a positive or a normative discipline.[47] Does it inquire into what *is* or into what *ought* to be? Is it a set of prescriptions for research and analysis? It would be easy to develop sound or unsound prescriptions such as, for example, "You ought to use only operationally defined terms; you ought to avoid making deductions from unverified assumptions; you ought not to admit normative statements or value judgments into scientific analysis." It would be just as easy, however, to translate such normative statements into positive statements about rules of procedure actually adopted or rejected by respected scientists. However, as I have just proposed, methodology is neither a study of "good methods" nor a study of "methods used," but rather a study of the reasons behind the principles on the basis of which various types of propositions are accepted

---

[47] For Popper, methodology consists of the "rules, or . . . norms, by which the scientist is guided when he is engaged in research or in discovery." Karl R. Popper, *The Logic of Scientific Discovery* (London: Hutchinson, 1959), p. 50. This has sounded to some as if it were normative. In any case, however, "Methodology in this sense must be clearly distinguished from a *description* of actual research processes—past or ongoing—and the methods actually used in such processes." Gerard Radnitzky, "Popperian Philosophy of Science as an Antidote against Relativism," in *Essays in Memory of Imre Lakatos*, edited by Robert S. Cohen *et al.* (Dordrecht, Holland: D. Reidel Publishing Company, 1976), p. 507.

or rejected as part of the body of ordered knowledge in general or of any special discipline.

The Cognate Subjects

While I was bold enough to propose my own definition of methodology, it would be sheer impertinence if I undertook to formulate definitions of the cognate subjects, particularly after having observed how some of the most respected writers disagreed on the relative places of epistemology, logic, and methodology within the spectrum of philosophy; and on which of these subjects were or were not included in metaphysics. But, for the orientation of readers who would like a quick refresher sketch of the history of philosophy, I may offer a few paraphrases from the pertinent literature.

Metaphysics comprised in times past (but does so for some philosophers also today) a large variety of "speculative" inquiries: Ontology, Epistemology, Cosmology, Psychology, Logic, Ethics, Aesthetics, and Natural Theology. Most of these subjects have been "promoted," not unanimously but by many, to the status of empirical sciences. Regarding psychology, the promotion is now uncontested. Ethics and aesthetics, sometimes merged into Theory of Value, are for many philosophers empirical sciences,[48] while others insist that they are nonsciences, metaphysical systems, or even nonstatements, devoid of sense.[49] Cosmology became empirical in the

---

[48] "Evaluations are a form of empirical knowledge, not fundamentally different in what determines their truth or falsity, and what determines their validity or justification, from other kinds of empirical knowledge." Clarence Irving Lewis, *An Analysis of Knowledge and Valuation* (La Salle, Ill.: Open Court Publishing Co., 1946), p. 365. Many other philosophers have included ethics and aesthetics among the sciences, but they characterized them as normative, not empirical sciences. For C. I. Lewis they are empirical sciences.

[49] "But actually a value statement is nothing else than a command in a misleading grammatical form. It may have effects upon the actions of men, and these effects may either be in accordance with our wishes or not; but it is neither true nor false. It does not assert anything and can neither be proved nor disproved." Metaphysical propositions "do express something, but nevertheless they have no sense, no theoretical content." Rudolf Carnap, *Philosophy and Logical Syntax* (London: Kegan Paul, Trench, Trubner, 1935), pp. 24, 27. In a similar vein: "Sentences which simply express moral judgments do not say anything. [And] ethical statements are expressions and excitants of feeling which do not necessarily involve any assertion. [Finally,] ethical philosophy consists simply in saying that ethical concepts are pseudo-concepts

course of developments in physics, astronomy, and astrophysics. The places of logic and epistemology are controversial; that they are not empirical does not make them necessarily metaphysical, in the opinion of some. Between *empirical* sciences and *metaphysical* inquiries (or sciences) are the *formal* sciences. Thus, logic, the science of valid inferences and valid generalizations, and epistemology, the science of the nature and limits of knowledge, are neither empirical nor metaphysical branches of learning.[50] After this succession of expulsions or promotions from metaphysics, only ontology and natural theology would remain as its constituents—if all status changes were generally accepted, which they are not.

That philosophers disagree on such seemingly fundamental questions is unavoidable because the exact meanings of the disciplines in question vary among schools.[51] This uncertainty of meaning prevails also with regard to metaphysics. Its widest meaning is that of reflections that transcend observed phenomena or immediate perceptions of physical facts or events.[52] The realization that this broad

---

and therefore unanalysable." Alfred Jules Ayer, *Language, Truth and Logic* (New York: Dover Publications, 1946), pp. 108, 109–110, 112.

[50] "Logic is the autonomous science of the objective though formal conditions of valid inference [and] the science of the weight of evidence in all fields." We should, however, recognize "the metaphysical significance of logical principles," especially the fact "that they are inherently applicable because they are concerned with ontological traits of utmost generality." Morris R. Cohen and Ernest Nagel, *An Introduction to Logic and Scientific Method* (New York: Harcourt, Brace, 1934), pp. iv–v. The nonempirical nature of logic is brought out in this statement: "Logical principles in their full generality cannot be proved, since every such attempted proof must assume some or all of them. That which is required in every proof cannot itself be demonstrated" [p. 187].

[51] "The different schools [of logic], the traditional, the linguistic, the psychological, the epistemological, and the mathematical, speak different languages, and each regards the other as not really dealing with logic at all." Cohen and Nagel, *Logic*, p. iii.

[52] "From the point of view of methodology the term *'positive'* is conceived in polemical opposition to the *metaphysical* abstractions of traditional philosophy. One calls *'positive'* the facts and things of immediate perception as well as the relations and uniformities which thought may discover in them without transcending experience. On the other hand, one calls *'metaphysical'* every inquiry which claims to go beyond the sphere of the empirical and seeks either hidden essences behind phenomenal appearances, or ultimate efficient and final causes behind things, as well as any attempt to attribute reality to species, ideas, concepts or the mind's logical 'intentions' in general." Guido de Ruggiero, "Positivism," *Encyclopaedia of the Social Sciences*, vol. 12 (New York: Macmillan, 1937), p. 260. [Emphasis supplied.]

concept of metaphysics confuses objectivity with materiality, disregards psychic facts and inner experience, and would (if taken literally) exclude all nonobservable relationships among experienced phenomena, has led to successive modifications, and thus to the increasing ambiguity of the concept.

Epistemology has been called the science of the nature and limits of knowledge, but also the science of the sciences (in the sense of systematic knowledge of [interconnected] things, tangible or intangible, natural or cultural, physical or mental). Sir Karl Popper calls it "the theory of scientific knowledge." [53] Other writers, preferring a wider but more specific notion of epistemology, divide it into (1) the theory of knowledge and (2) the study of concepts, methods, principles, and hypotheses of the sciences (in accordance with Margenau's dictum that "Epistemology denotes the methodology of the cognitive process" [Margenau, *Physical Reality*, p. 81]). The theory of knowledge has also been defined as the study of the mutual relation between the subject and the object in the process of cognition, or (in Montague's words) as the study of the relation between the knower and the known. This "subjectivist" notion of epistemology is rejected by Popper, for "scientific knowledge belongs . . . to the world of objective theories, objective problems, and objective arguments" [Popper, "Epistemology," p. 228].

Equipped with all these definitions, we can now design a scheme that exhibits the surveyed subjects in a reasonable order without prejudice to their historical origins, hierarchical order, or logical interconnections.

A Map of the Territory

Seven cognate subjects will be shown on the map.

Subject	Main concern
A. Formal logic [Pure logic, Deductive logic, Analytical logic]	Concerned with "valid inferences" based on study of objective relations between propositions; deals with implications; a priori

[53] Karl R. Popper, "Epistemology without a Knowing Subject," in Jerry H. Gill, ed., *Philosophy Today No. 2* (New York: Macmillan, 1968), p. 227.

Subject	Main concern
B. Inductive logic [Applied logic, material logic, Empirical logic, "Scientific method"]	Concerned with "valid generalizations" based on study of weights of evidence to test impressions, opinions, and surmises; deals with truth and probability
C. General methodology	Concerned with relations between observation, conceptualization, and judgment; "fact" and "theory," rules of scientific procedure
D. Special methodology	Concerned with rules of procedure in special fields of inquiry; differences between various fields; special situations calling for special "methods"
E. Epistemology	Concerned with relations between subject and objects of cognition, between the knower and the known; with the nature and limits of knowledge; alternatively, the theory of "objective" scientific knowledge
F. Ontology	Concerned with the nature of reality and of "being"

Using various *broader* definitions of logic, methodology, and epistemology, we can "unite" any two, three, or four of these subjects under one heading. This may explain the different places to which the subjects have been assigned in the spectrum of philosophy. Logic as taught in most college courses and textbooks comprises subjects A and B; but in many older treatises it extends to C. Methodology, according to the majority view, comprises subjects B, C, and D, but some methodologists restrict their field to only C and D, whereas others extend it to include either B or E, or both, or even A. Hence the great variances in the meaning of *methodology* in the philosophical literature. Epistemology in a wider sense would comprise C and D in addition to E. Metaphysics in the narrowest sense would include only subject F from our list, but in a wider sense, favored by a fair number of philosophers, it would extend to E, perhaps also to C and D and, for a small minority, it would take in the entire list.

It remains to settle the meaning of Philosophy of Science. In the narrowest sense it would include C, D, and E, but most philosophers would extend it to include B, and perhaps also A, on the one side, and F on the other side. But this is not all. Various subjects beyond our list deserve treatment under the heading of Philosophy of Science; among them would be Phenomenology of Science, Psychology of Science, Linguistics of Science, Semiotics and Hermeneutics of Science, and undoubtedly also the Ethics of Science. Some additional aspects of scientific activity are no part of the Philosophy of Science but merit study in connection with it: Sociology of Science, Politics of Science, and Economics of Science.

Methodolatry and Methodophobia

Some scholars have an insatiable appetite for methodological discussion, while others cannot stand it and are quickly bored when they hear the word *methodology*. There was a time when at German universities virtually all doctoral dissertations, especially in the social sciences, began with a chapter on general methodological problems. The students' excessive concern with methodology reflected their professor's position in the *Methodenstreit*, their commitments to the tenets of the historical school, the abstract–theoretical school, or anything between these extremes. The readers' exposure to methodology was sometimes intolerable, and many became fed up with the quasi-philosophical blabber.

In American graduate departments, many professors, and consequently their students, had little or no interest in methodological discourse. Indeed, most of them were contemptuous of "impractical speculation" and considered it a waste of time. A great American philosopher, Arthur O. Lovejoy, coined the word *methodolatry* to denote "the worship of method apart from subject matter." No doubt, one can overdo a good thing, and there is little use talking about, say, the methodology of the social sciences if the talker has only a slight acquaintance with research undertaken in any of the social sciences.

On the other hand, there is ample evidence for the existence of the contrary attitude. I may coin the word *methodophobia* to denote an explicit disdain for methodological reflection by researchers who *think* they are *not* "wasting time" on "useless" methodological discussion but in fact are quite unwittingly taking strong methodological positions on all sorts of issues. They criticize fellow workers for making "unrealistic" or "unverified assumptions," for using "ideal types" in place of "operational concepts," for being "too abstract," or for failing to use "dynamic" analysis. All of these charges are based on particular methodological positions taken in ignorance of the issues involved. No one should be compelled to study methodology. But if he prefers to remain uninformed about the subject, then he should kindly abstain from making judgments for which he lacks competence.

-logy and -graphy

After all that has been said in this essay, the reader can hardly be in doubt about what is meant by methodology when methodologists talk about it. They understand by it a part of philosophy of science. They do not mean a description of a method or a set of methods. This should, of course, have been clear from the second half of the compound word *methodo-logy*. A *-logy* is not a *-graphy*. A *-graphy* means drawing or writing, that is, a description, while a *-logy* is a theoretical system.

There is a difference between geology and geography: the former is the science that studies the [crust of the] earth, the latter is the science that *describes* the [surface of the] earth. Likewise, there are biology and biography: the former is the science that studies life, the latter is a *description* of a person's life. There are physiology and physiography: the former is the science that studies the functions of the parts and organs of living things, animal and vegetable, the latter *describes* natural phenomena. There are ethnology and ethnography: the former is the science that studies races and racial characteristics, the latter *describes* human races, customs, and habits. In all such combinations with particular objects, the *-logies* are systems of theories, and the *-graphies* are descriptions. If *methodology* is the science that studies the principles of validation and rejection of scientific propositions; and if a word should be needed for the description of a method or methods employed in a particular research project, that word could possibly be methodography. But "Notes on Methods Used" would be more simple, and hence preferable.

Method and Methodology

The worst misuse of the word *methodology* is its substitution for method. To say *methodology* when what is meant is *method* or *methods* is sheer illiteracy. I am returning to this point partly in order to reinforce the lesson, partly because it gives me that chance of concluding this essay on an amusing note. Edwin Newman, the author of *Strictly Speaking* (a book about the gradual demolition of the English language), wrote an article on the language of American athletes and sportscasters under the title "Regulated to the Bench, Sportswise." It was published in *Sports Illustrated* in 1976. Newman made fun of the Malaprops in the sports world, especially those who misappropriate words that sound very learned to replace straightforward language. He quotes a baseball player who said "My studiology of baseball is better," and another, "It's all a matter of a poor field position situation." But the best sentence is one in which Newman ridicules those who substitute *methodology* for the simple word *method*, by having Hamlet upgrade his famous comment about the crazed Ophelia: "Though this be madness, yet there's methodology in't."

Chapter 2

WHY BOTHER WITH METHODOLOGY?

The antipathy to methodology among a good many economists originated in the times when such discussions consisted mainly in advertising the writers' and maligning others' methods. Everybody wanted to promote his method among his competitors and colleagues. After a while economists became disgusted by these advertising practices and wanted to work, undisturbed by methodology, on problems of immediate practical interest. A pronounced indifference toward philosophising about methods developed.

Professor Robbins' *Essay on the Nature and Significance of Economic Science* [1] was taken as a challenge. His critics expressed the reluctance of economists to accept any "regimentation" of their subject-matter and their methods. However opposed they were to the "laissez-faire system," they wanted to enjoy laissez-faire in the production and distribution of their ideas without any (logical or methodological) barriers between the various fields of research. Dr. Souter took up the case against the regimentation of economics,

---

[1] Lionel Robbins, *Essay on the Nature and Significance of Economic Science*, London, 1932.

but his plea, the *Prolegomena to Relativity Economics*,[2] was more heavily interlarded with Hegelian philosophy than a normal economist can stand. A still greater antipathy to methodology was the outcome of the discussion.

I wonder whether it is necessary to write on methodology in a form so forbidding that it is likely to drive away the reader from any attention to methodological problems. It can be shown, I believe, that esoteric philosophy is not essential to expounding methodological thought and, moreover, that certain methodological questions are directly relevant for discussions of immediate practical interest to any economist. The aim of this note is not at all to present a complete discussion of my subject, but to call attention in a simple manner to the significance of methodology for quite elementary economic propositions. If the alternatives are naïve, simplification on the one hand, and unintelligible profundity on the other, I would rather choose—for the purpose of this note—the former. (I do think, however, that "simple" and "profound" are relative to the knowledge and interest of the reader). Simple reasoning about a few simple economic propositions will show whether or not methodological reflections can do anything for the economist's work.

Statement (1): "If, because of an abundant crop, the output of wheat is much increased, the price of wheat will fall."

Statement (2): "If, because of increased wage-rates and decreased interest-rates, capital becomes relatively cheaper than labour, new labour-saving devices will be invented."

Statement (3): "If, because of heavy withdrawals of foreign deposits, the banks are in danger of insolvency, the Central Bank Authorities will extend the necessary credit."

Are these three statements imposed, so to speak, by "economic laws"? Are they of equal economic relevance? Are they equally true or false, equally certain or probable?

Professor Robbins undoubtedly would hold only the first statement to be based on the "pure theory of economics." He would consider the others merely "data" of economic relevance. Dr. Souter

---

[2] Ralph W. Souter, *Prolegomena to Relativity Economics*, New York, 1933.

would protest against such hierarchical division. He would hold that all three statements are of the same logical nature, all equally hypothetical, all based upon certain assumptions, all of equal "necessity" or dignity.

A "verification" of the hypothetical statements by "real facts" would offer the same problems in all three cases. For each of them, of course, historical or statistical illustrations might readily be produced.

All three statements are concerned with human conduct or human behaviour. Can a distinction be made between the motives underlying these various types of behaviour? (1) The wheat-growers sell their product cheaper because nearly every one of them prefers to take lower prices rather than not to sell at all. The rationale of such a decision is familiar. It is ordinarily labelled as "economic conduct." (2) The engineers rack their brains to invent labour-saving devices because they expect high compensation. Manufacturers establish new laboratories because the expected inventions may be extremely profitable now that capital has become cheap and labour dear. The rationale of such thinking is in principle not different from that of the wheat-growers. (3) The Central Bank Authorities consider it their duty to provide the member banks with liquid funds. The extended credits increase the profits of the Reserve Banks by increased income from interest payments; moreover, the member banks must fail if the credits are denied, and this is regarded as highly harmful for the whole economic system and would certainly raise powerful opposition against the directors. The latter want to keep their jobs. The rationale of such thinking is not much different from that of the wheat growers, the engineers, or the manufacturers. In principle, no essential distinction could be made between the character of the motivation of the conduct described by the three statements.

All three statements are "true" under certain assumptions and not true under others. Suppose they have proved untrue and we have to give reasons for it.

Statement (1a): "The wheat prices did not fall, because a Farm Pool bought the whole surplus."

Statement (2a): "No new device was invented, because in spite of all efforts no creative idea occurred to the would-be inventors."

Statement (3a): "The Central Bank Authorities turned down the request of the member banks, because Professor von Mises convinced them that the economic evils of credit expansion would be greater than those of the bank failures."

The reasons given for the cases in which the statements did not prove true are of course arbitrary. But we may perhaps find in the nature of the supposed (not improbable) reasons some essential differences which help us to clarify our problem.

Let us begin with the second statement, about "induced" inventions. When it is stated that under certain conditions "induced" inventions will come about, the tacit assumption is made that the disposition to expend effort in this way is practically all that is needed; hence, that there is something like a stock of unborn inventions available, quickly called into existence when a strong incentive is present. It is true that in reality creative minds regularly succeed in finding some new things if strong efforts are put forth. But there is no "a priori reason" why the wish to invent should be successful. It can easily be imagined that the inventors' efforts will not be successful.

The third statement proved untrue when the Authorities consulted a "stony-hearted" expert and followed his advice. It is true that authorities do so very rarely. It is conceivable, nevertheless, that they will do so. There is neither an "a priori reason" nor a reliable statistical probability that they would not. There may be one man, or two or three, really influential in the Central Bank management. History gives us many instances of the one kind (readiness to support the banks), but also some of the other kind (refusal to support) of bank authorities' behaviour. We can imagine that their decisions are at times of the so-called deflationist type; and statement (3) would become untrue.

The first statement, concerning the wheat price, can hardly be invalidated so easily. As compared with the third, one difference becomes obvious. The decision of the one, two, or three managers of the official Bank Monopoly is uncertain. The tendency of the decisions of thousands and thousands of wheat-growers is far from being equally uncertain. It is, of course, probable that some sellers may decide to hold back and to wait until trade is better. It is even possible that other sellers may be willing, influenced by an adviser, to sell only a portion of their crop, provided they expect the others to do the same. But it is entirely improbable that all of a great many sellers will act in this way. If only a few producers were to sell their whole increased output (and the price tendency stated in (1) then would be true!), more and more producers would follow suit and the statement would be proven to the hilt. The type of the competitive seller is not so likely to disappear from the economic stage as the type of the benevolent central bank manager. In other words, while it is conceivable that the men responsible for the money-system may or may not act in conformity with statement (3), it is not so conceivable that the men responsible for the wheat supply and therefore for the wheat price will fail to act in conformity with statement (1). As a result of this very fact politicians who are uneasy about a decline in wheat prices devise specific political measures in order to make statement (1) untrue, such as founding a farm pool which buys the wheat surplus. No one would make a *Statement* (1*b*): "If, because of an abundant crop, the supply of wheat is much increased, a farm pool will buy the surplus," and attach to this statement the same validity (within the particular conceptual scheme) as to statement (1). The foundation of the farm pool is no doubt an effect of the increased supply; but it is an effect which can be stated only with many additional assumptions about actions which are colloquially called political.

Most economists would confine the title "proposition in *economic theory*" to statement (1), and would not assign it also to statement (1*b*). This, because under (1) we think of a more general (more "anonymous") type of behaviour than under (1*b*). If this is right, it is only a matter of terminology whether one calls (1) a statement of a higher degree of generality than (1*b*) or whether one calls (1) a statement of economic theory, and (1*b*), with Professor Robbins, the statement of an economic datum.

The wish to avoid the drop in wheat prices is the economic incentive for the formation of the farm pool. This wish is by no means always fulfilled. If it is fulfilled, we state this fact as a new economic datum, the consequence of which may be explained again in terms of general economic theory. We may apply the same principle to statement (2). The conditions expressed in statement (2) present a strong economic incentive for inventing new labour-saving devices. But the actual success of the induced efforts is better stated as a new economic datum. If this datum is given, we begin, with a fresh breath, thinking about the economic effects of the newly invented devices, all the more so because the effects of "induced" inventions are not different from those of "spontaneous" inventions of the same kind. There is no disadvantage perceptible in such a procedure. One may, however, stress that the changes in data (namely the occurrence of induced inventions) have developed from the economic situation itself.

According to the previous considerations it is by no means a "crime against logic", and indeed has its definite usefulness, to hold that only statement (1) is based on pure economic theory, while statements (2) and (3) are best regarded as data for the application of further economic analysis. To say this is not to belittle their relevance nor to question their derivation from economic changes. They are effects of economic forces as well as the causes of further change. But the causal relations such as stated in (2) and (3) are derived from types of human conduct of a lesser generality or anonymity. To make a statement about the actions of the bank authorities (such as (3)) calls for reasoning in a stratum of behaviour-conceptions of much less anonymous types of actors. We have to know or to imagine the acting persons more intimately. It will make a great difference whether Mr. Keynes or Professor von Hayek is governor or expert adviser of the central bank. To deal with conduct of types of higher intimacy and, therefore, lesser anonymity means to deal with phenomena in a stratum of lesser generality.[3]

Dr. Souter will hold that the logical character of all the statements is the same. All of them are hypothetical, based on certain assumptions, and no discrimination of their logical dignity is justifiable. This is not questioned here. The point in question is whether or not the general validity in terms of a particular conceptual scheme is the same. We have found that this is not the case.[4]

An economist's reasoning may be seriously impaired if its causal

[3] This analysis is an application (somewhat crude) of the excellent and extremely subtle apparatus of methodology in the Social Sciences, given by Dr. Alfred Schütz in his *Der sinnhafte Aufbau der sozialen Welt* (Vienna, 1932). A more precise use of Dr. Schütz's terminology would have to draw certain distinctions between degrees of anonymity and generality.

[4] Whether the distinction between the characters of the different statements is to be regarded as one of kind or only as one of degree does not affect our argument. These concepts involve difficult problems, which we may leave alone.

FRITZ MACHLUP

chain contains links of minor general validity (in terms of the particular conceptual scheme) together with those of major general validity. This may be responsible for the divergence of a good many theoretical inferences of various economists. An example will illustrate what is meant.

In the theory of international exchange there are many statements of the type having high general validity. They enjoy widespread recognition among almost all students of this area of economic theory. But violent disagreement replaces unanimity as regards the problem of international transfers. One point of dissension lies in the assumptions regarding the methods of raising the money required for the purchase of the foreign exchange which is to effect the transfer from a debtor country to the creditor countries. One can find, for instance, the following statement: "The withdrawal of foreign loans was so extraordinarily heavy that the demand for foreign exchange could not be met. The balance of trade cannot be adjusted to such unnatural movements of capital." This argument assumes that the creditor's wish to be repaid and the debtors wish to repay really mean that these wishes produce a movement of capital. But, surely, the cash balances available would restrict actual payments within very narrow limits. There is no chance that all debtors have at their command, within a reasonable period of time, sufficient free cash balances to buy the exchange wherewith to repay the debts. Hence, no heavy demand for foreign exchange, no immense outflow of capital is to be expected unless an auxiliary statement holds true—namely, our old statement (3), that a central bank supports the needy debtors with new credits. Then, and only then, the demand for foreign exchange can become insatiable and the exports unadaptable to the flow of capital.[5] The statement quoted above is valid only on the tacit supposition of central bank policy stated in (3); otherwise it is false. The mingling of assumptions of different degrees of validity (validity, again, in terms of the particular conceptual scheme) is acceptable only if the assumptions are fully stated. If they are made tacitly (perhaps even unconsciously) the argument is methodologically unsound; one may condemn it as invalid.

[5] Cf. Fritz Machlup, "Die Theorie der Kapitalflucht," *Weltwirtschaftliches Archiv*, Vol. 36, 1932, p. 527.

The assumption of new givens, new "data" such as political actions and governmental measures not logically implied in the fundamental hypotheses (integral parts of the conceptual scheme) should be explicitly stated, since they are of a lower degree of general validity within the particular scheme. Statements of "pure economic theory" are statements which assume only the most general and anonymous types of behaviour. They allow us, therefore, to proceed in the economic analysis without restating and reiterating the assumptions again and again.

The failure to make distinctions between statements of different order often has serious practical consequences. For such reasons, we ought sometimes to bother with methodology.

ON FACTS, MODELS, AND THEORIES IN ECONOMICS

INTRODUCTION TO PART TWO

The pieces collected in Part Two come from my twin books on monopoly and competition, published in 1952. "A Note on Models in Microeconomics" consists of the first two subsections of Chapter 1 of *The Economics of Seller's Competition* (Baltimore: Johns Hopkins Press, 1952) with side-headings "A Note on Model Analysis" and "The Economy, the Industry, the Firm," and one subsection of Chapter 13. The other piece, "Fact and Theory in Economics," was Chapter 11 in *The Political Economy of Monopoly* (Baltimore: Johns Hopkins Press, 1952).

These selections from my books expressed my methodological views in such down-to-earth language that I felt they belonged in this volume on methodology. Only stylistic changes have been made from the original texts; in Chapter 3 I inserted a few lines as a transition from the material taken from Chapter 1 of the book to that taken from Chapter 13. In Chapter 4 of the present volume, I made slight changes only in the introductory paragraph, in footnote 13, and in a few clauses referring to other parts of the book.

Chapter 3, "A Note on Models in Microeconomics," begins with the degree of abstraction involved in the formation of mental constructs and models for different purposes. Models, mostly in verbal form, are used by everybody who thinks, talks, and acts in everyday life; models are used also by the historian, when he tells his story;

models are used by descriptive economists, lawyers, and politicians, when they talk about economic situations, events, and policies; and models are used by the pure theorist in his hypothetico-deductive system. Only the degrees of abstraction and generality of all these models are apt to differ. That theorists often substitute algebraic symbols for words makes little difference to the nature and functions of their models. What *is* important is to understand the differences in applicability of alternative models in particular instances. For example, in price theory, models of the individual firm, the whole industry, and the entire economy will be more suitable for application to some problems and less suitable to others. It takes judgment to select the most appropriate model for the problem at hand.

From this discussion, I jump to some observations on the theory of oligopoly. I first examine the meaning of indeterminacy. Then I go into the problem of the methodological differences in the analysis of a purely competitive firm, where a very anonymous model will do, and in the analysis of an oligopolistic firm, where idiosyncratic decision-making is part of the game.

The chief message of Chapter 4, "Fact and Theory in Economics," is that virtually all so-called facts in economics, even if they are stated as supposedly observed events occurring at a specified time and place, are largely the results of theories and are questionable on the ground that they are inferred with the aid of theoretical universals, from untested (and probably false) factual assumptions of an undetermined level of abstraction. I offer a detailed examination of the speculative contents of alleged facts in a case of a simple statement about a change in the price of steel by a particular corporation at a specified time. It is shown that most of the supposed facts are in effect "implied theory." Other themes discussed in the chapter relate to differences in the ways in which I have approached different economic problems; the logical relationship between explanation and prediction; the almost unavoidable intrusion of value judgments concealed in supposedly factual statements; and the implications of measurement and fictitious accuracy.

Chapter 3

A NOTE ON MODELS IN MICROECONOMICS

Discussion in economics abounds with references to "models." The chances of misunderstanding this word are so great that we should not grudge the time for a few comments on "model building" that may allay the fears of some readers who dislike new-fangled words and distrust abstractions that have proceeded so far that the feeling of familiarity is lost.

Abstractions, Constructs, Models

Every one of us thinks almost exclusively in abstractions, only the degree of abstraction varies. When we come to speak of classes or types of things or events, abstraction has already gone a considerable way. For as soon as we group several single things or events into classes or types, we have abstracted from many of their individual attributes and have to that extent deprived them of some of their individuality or uniqueness. As long as the "type" contains still enough of the attributes and features which we know in individual specimens, we retain a feeling of familiarity and regard the abstraction as relatively "realistic." But for purposes of analysis we must often go much further and abstract from still more of the familiar features of the thing or event or whatever it is we are thinking about. Eventually, what is left is merely a phantom of the real thing, a mental construction that may contain more things that we have not noticed or perceived in reality than things that we have. Now, if our abstraction or mental construction contains several parts in whose interaction and interrelationships we are interested and which we may in our imagination combine in several ways to derive different "results" we speak of an analytical model.

The economic theorist is, of course, not alone in the business of constructing analytical models. Anybody at all who thinks about

In this extract from my book first published in 1952 references are to other chapters of that—not the present—book.

causal relationships, about "how things work," builds himself a "model." And he does not even have to be a theorist by profession or avocation. The man in the street who describes for himself or for others how something has happened does this by using a mental model. And so does every historian, every lawyer, every scientist. We think with the aid of models, whether we know it or not. If we do not know it, we are like the unschooled upstart who did not know that he knew how to speak prose.[1] Of course, there is no need to use the word "model." Other words have been used in the same sense—for example, "construct" and "schema"—and most people can get along without any such term, because they feel it unnecessary to explain to others or to themselves the processes and techniques they use in their thinking.

Theoretical and Descriptive Economics

Many economists are not conscious of the use of analytical models unless these models are made out of algebraic functions or geometric curves or some other fancy building material. It is true that the econometricians or the addicts to geometric analysis talk more about models than do other economists. But there is no reason why models cannot be described entirely in plain words, and indeed most models are. We can take any book of economic history or institutional economics and find analytical models on almost every page. And I am not referring to "pure" fictions, like pure competition; I am referring to constructions that are needed for the description of business practices, government policies, legal provisions, or historical events. For example, "price leadership," "collusion," "restraint of trade," "price discrimination," "concentration," "consumer deception," "foreign exchange control," "support prices for potatoes"—every one of these matters implies the use of analytical models.

All theorizing involves model building. Does then the fact that some of our work in economics is "theoretical" while some is "descriptive" indicate that models play a greater part in the former than in the latter? The answer is "no." The difference is merely that in our theoretical work we construct new models, adapt old ones,

[1] Molière, *The Bourgeois Gentleman* (1670).

FRITZ MACHLUP

modify this or that part of a model, manipulate or "operate" models to examine and re-examine various combinations of assumptions, whereas in our descriptive work we use ready-made models and the results of previous (conscious or unconscious) model analysis without necessarily being aware of the amount of "theory" that is involved.

There are, to be sure, wide differences in degree. For example, in my book on *The Political Economy of Monopoly* the chapters on monopolistic wage determination are "more theoretical" than the chapters on monopolistic business practices. But this is chiefly because the theoretical foundation on which business practices can be discussed is much firmer than that on which a discussion of labor practices can be placed. Thus, we are able to *apply* theory to the one discussion, while we have to *make* or *examine* theory in the other. But there should be no mistake about the amount of theory, good or bad, that goes into so-called "purely descriptive" economics. Anyone reading with a critical mind the description of a law case, for example, a case involving discriminatory pricing techniques or restrictive patent licensing, must realize that the argument rests largely on economic theories developed by means of model analysis—sometimes sound, sometimes unsound, but always of a degree of abstraction much higher than may have been apparent to the lawyers who presented or examined the argument.

Models in the Theory of Price

Some of the models in economic theory are designed for a degree of generality that can be attained only by a level of abstraction which is incompatible with realistic details. It is customary to divide the theory of relative prices into three parts, or three "levels of analysis": the theory of the firm, the theory of the industry, and the theory of the whole system. The first two are "partial equilibrium" analysis, the third is "general equilibrium" analysis, where "equilibrium" stands by and large for "initial position" and for "end result" of the operation of assumed "forces" or conditions.[2]

[2] The equilibrium concept in economics is primarily a tool for the explanation of *movement:* we "explain" a movement by pointing to "causes"

The division into the three levels is a matter of methodological convenience because different kinds of assumptions are made for the basic models used. Our conception of "how the economy works" is greatly aided by the construction of these basic models which schematize some of the interrelationships that we think exist between various phenomena.

The models of the firm, the industry, and the whole system that are used in price theory are so "shockingly" unrealistic that a few comments might be added to give the reasons for it. The purpose of an analytical model is to demonstrate the operation of the factors considered most relevant for the problem under examination. In order to be most useful for such a purpose the model should omit everything held to be of small or no relevance for the particular problem. Any part of a model that merely serves to make it look more realistic becomes an unnecessary burden in the use of the model. Of course, one must distinguish two kinds of protest against lack of realism: first, that certain realistic assumptions were omitted in the construction; second, that the assumptions made were unrealistic. The answer to the first of these protests is that realism in a model constructed for purposes of analysis is undesirable if it reduces its simplicity, and may cause confusion by "cluttering up" the model with irrelevant details. People who are superficial, who prefer to "look" rather than to "think" and are more interested in the outer trappings than in the inner workings of things, are wont to complain about models that are "unrealistic" in this sense. But a complaint of unrealism in this sense should be taken seriously only if the critic can prove that the missing parts in the model essentially change the end results of its operation and

---

that are responsible for a departure from one position and an approach to another one. These two positions are idealized as positions of *rest*, an "initial" equilibrium and a "new" equilibrium. The movement is thus "understood" as an adjustment to a "disequilibrating" change. We need the assumed "balance of forces" in the *initial* position in order to isolate the disequilibrating change, that is, in order to make sure that nothing else has occurred and that the movement exhibited by the operation of the model can be attributed without any doubt to the specified disturbance. We need the assumed "balance of forces" in the *new* position in order to make sure that the adjustment is complete and all effects of the disequilibrating change have been fully recorded. But let no one make the mistake of interpreting the "equilibrium theorist" as trying to detect equilibrium positions in reality.

that a "more complete" model yields results much more closely conforming to generally observed or experienced reality.

The second kind of protest can be answered only by an invitation to provide a substitute model with more realistic assumptions which nevertheless does all that the rejected model can do. Models are not selected chiefly for their input of assumptions but for their output of results. We know what we want to have explained, and then construct models that can aid in explaining it. Of all the models that might explain the result, we choose the one that works with the assumptions that we believe conform most closely to observed reality. Models with "more realistic" assumptions but not yielding results conforming to observed reality are disqualified.[3]

The models now generally used in the theory of relative prices —generally used because the results appear to conform to our observations and the assumptions seem the most plausible—are certainly unrealistic. The model of the individual firm does not bear any close resemblance to anything that we in the real world know as a firm; the model of an industry is quite dissimilar to what is popularly understood to be an industry or what the statisticians understand by that term; and least of all does the model of the economy as a whole look like any picture that a close observer of reality may ever have drawn for himself.[4]

The Economy, the Industry, the Firm

The fact that economic theorists engaged in price analysis have constructed models of the firm, the industry, and the economy as a whole does not mean that they need all these models for every

[3] We hear sometimes suggestions to the effect that we should *begin* with realistic assumptions. This suggestion overlooks the fact that observation provides *millions* of *realistic* assumptions for each "case" or "problem," but no guide for selecting the relevant ones. One must work backward from the result that is to be explained, and construct models with constellations of assumptions which would approximate the result. These alternative models then provide several sets of possibly *relevant* "causes"; finally one selects the model whose assumptions appear most *plausible* on the basis of observed reality.

[4] No more does the model of a magnetic field which the physicist constructs for his analytical work look like anything anybody has ever "seen" in the real world; nor has any physicist ever "observed" a neutrino; nor a biologist a gene. [Published in 1952.]

problem of price theory. The selection of models in each case is a matter of relevance and convenience.

The Selection of Models

For some problems of the interdependence of economic magnitudes in the economy as a whole, we can do without the models of the firm or the industry. For example, we often feel that a "solution" based on the assumption of pure competition may serve as a reasonable "approximation." But for the theory of an economy in which all firms operate under pure competition it is unnecessary to spend much time on the theory of the individual firm, because the relationships are so simple that no separate models of the individual business unit are needed to demonstrate them. Even more frequently can we dispense with the model of the industry. On the other hand, there may be problems for which the model of the whole system would be an unnecessarily clumsy thinking aid and which can more simply be analysed with the help of the theory of the industry. Needless to say, there is more than one model of the firm, of the industry, and of the whole economy. Economists have constructed whole sets of models for each and select the ones they think are most handy for tackling the particular problem that they may wish to analyse.

Assume for example we wish to analyse the effects of a cartel agreement on the output of the commodity concerned. We shall first find it convenient to examine how an imaginary individual firm will adjust itself to the change in selling conditions. We do this by selecting two models of firms, one of a producer acting under conditions of unregulated competition, another of a producer with the same cost conditions acting under the cartel restrictions imposed upon him and with the knowledge of similar restrictions imposed on the other suppliers of the "same" commodity. We can thus compare the equilibrium output of "the" firm in the two models. Then we ask ourselves what the possibilities are of new firms taking up business in the same field. If no such possibilities exist, we are satisfied with the results indicated by the theory of the firm. If the possibility of new firms entering the field is open, we shall resort to an industry model, analyse the profit rates a newcomer might expect to obtain if he started production, compare the profit rates with those obtaining elsewhere, and examine the combined effects of the output restrictions by the insiders and the new production by newcomers. We may be satisfied with these results, or we may decide to go further if we believe that we can fruitfully analyse the indirect repercussions of the changes which have resulted from the operations of the models up to this point.

Taking another example, let us assume that we wish to analyse the effects of an import quota on the price and output of a certain commodity. If the number of domestic producers is large, we may decide that the assumption of pure competition, unrealistic as it is, will yield sufficiently close results. We shall then skip experimenting with models of the individual firm and start immediately with an industry model, making assumptions about the supply by domestic producers and about the total domestic demand for the commodity. Depending on our assumptions about the case of entry of new firms into the industry, the assumed supply will include or exclude the potential output of potential newcomers.

Let us refer, as a third example, to a problem that I have discussed elsewhere,[5] the effects of a pay raise obtained by a trade union for the workers of a particular industry. Depending on the number and size of firms in the industry, we shall either begin with individual-firm analysis or immediately proceed to industry analysis. But we shall probably not be satisfied with studying the effects upon prices and production of the commodities made by the industry directly affected. We shall need to go into the further repercussions on other industries, other commodities, other worker groups. The kind of repercussions studied will be suggested to us by a general-equilibrium model, a model of the economy as a whole.

The Comparison of Prices

In each of the models prices play a major role. But as we move "up and down" the various levels of analysis the meaning of price may often undergo slight variations. For example, one may assume

---

[5] Fritz Machlup, *The Political Economy of Monopoly: Business, Labor and Government Policies* (Baltimore: Johns Hopkins Press, 1952), Chapter 10.

that the subjective price expectations of some particular firm may be translated into a definite price "given" to all firms as we move "up" from the theory of the firm to the theory of the industry. Or the prices paid by the consumer, as assumed for the demand curve in an industry model, will call for several translations as we "move down" to the model of the individual firm and its expected average net revenue. Yet, although we might be strict and not forget to shift methodological gears as we ascend or descend between the different levels of analysis, we shall for many problems be permitted to neglect such exactitude and, for the sake of simplicity, assume that the price to the firm is the same as the price to the industry.

Simplifications of this sort presuppose another "unrealistic" kind of assumption, the assumption of homogeneous commodities and homogeneous factors of production. Let no one believe that a critic who proves that there are wide differences between labor and labor has demolished economic theory where homogeneity of labor is often assumed. Economic theory is equipped to deal with any number of different factors of production; indeed, if it were proved that no two hours of labor, or no two tons of coal, were alike, economic theory could proceed on the assumption that the relative efficiencies of all the different factors, the substitutabilities of one for another, were given. But things would certainly be more complicated and, hence, regardless of how different or alike the various units in a class of productive factors are in reality, we must first learn how to operate models in which "homogeneity" is assumed.

This assumption, that the various units of what we call one factor of production are perfectly alike, is a great help in the theory of monopoly. For example, if we say that a restriction of entry may allow the price of a productive service employed within a field to remain above the price of the *same* services elsewhere, we certainly imply that the excluded ones are just as good, in every respect, as the ones employed. That is, we affirm (or complain) that they receive different prices although they are theoretically interchangeable. Of course, before one can apply this theory to a case where monopolistic restrictions are suspected, one would have to make a judgment about the extent to which the productive factors within and outside the "industry" are really the same. This judgment involves much more than technological substitutability; it involves views about the changeability of social, political and economic institutions.

Assume two pieces of land, exactly the same size and possessing the same physical and chemical quality of soil, and in the same climate, but located in different parts of the country, or merely at different distances from a particular city, railroad station, river, or harbor. No one will doubt that location is an important quality of such resources and therefore that their productive services are different, no matter how alike they are in all other respects. No one will be surprised if the two pieces of land command different prices and no one will blame monopolistic restrictions for it.

Assume now two groups of workers, exactly alike in physical makeup, in personal characteristics, in skill, industry, ambition, willingness and capacity, but located in different parts of the country. If they receive different prices for their services, shall we also accept this as a necessary consequence of the difference in location? We are not inclined to do so, for while we accept the immobility of land as natural and inevitable, we do not so accept the immobility of labor. The difference in the location of labor is not a part of its quality as it is of land. Any lack of mobility that exists with regard to labor may possibly be due to monopolistic restrictions. For example, closed-shop contracts between industries and local unions may prevent the movement of workers. On the other hand, the workers' failure to move may be due to other circumstances. There may be, on the part of the workers, an unwillingness to move. Both groups may be equally unwilling to move, but one of them may have the good luck to be in the location with superior job opportunities. Surely we cannot in this case attribute the difference in wages to monopoly restraints. But how shall we judge the situation if it is lack of information that explains the failure of the workers to move to the better-paying jobs? And how, if they know about the better jobs and would like to move, but lack the necessary funds and cannot borrow them? Are we to regard the two worker groups as the "same" factors of production, whose movements are impeded by institutional impediments to competition, or as factors as different from each other as the two pieces of land at different locations?

The difficulty is not one of theory but of judgment and appraisal. The theorist can deal with the situation equally well as a competitive one involving different productive resources or as a monopolistic one involving the same resources. It is not the price difference that indicates the presence of monopolistic restrictions, for an examination of the nature of any impediments to mobility and substitutability is necessary before we can decide whether the resources whose prices are compared are to be regarded as the same or different resources.

The Profits of Enterprise

While it is easily said that the presence of monopoly profits indicates the presence of monopoly, it is not easily said what monopoly profits are and how they can in concrete cases be distinguished and separated from normal profits, from profits due to differential managerial ability, to differential exposure to uncertainty, or to mere windfalls.

Those who regard "enterprise" as a factor of production, and profit as the income earned by this factor, have a particularly difficult time disentangling differences in the "quality" of this factor from differences in monopolistic position when differential profits in different firms or industries are to be compared. Other models of the economic system, reserving the concept of productive factor to physically measurable things, avoid this particular difficulty, but the task of dissecting the business profit as computed by the accountant, and of sorting its various parts into different boxes, labeled "resources cost," "windfalls," "monopoly profits," etc., remains formidable.

In any case, it is helpful to understand that this important phase of the discussion of cost-price relationships is part of the theory of the transfer of enterprise and resources between different fields of activity. That is, it is part of the theory of the industry, part of the theory of open or barred access; and it plays a major role in the theory of profit and newcomers' competition. The trouble with most of the analysis of the industry is that its concepts are so highly abstract that they cannot be made practically operational. That is, we cannot find for them any counterparts in the real world that could be objects of statistical measurement.

One should think that we are much better off in this respect when we come to the theory of the firm. Unfortunately one finds that matters there are not a great deal better as far as the availability of data is concerned.

We shall not, however, at this juncture go into the business of data and empirical counterparts of mental constructs. We shall instead look into the theoretical and methodological questions concerning the construct of the oligopolistic firm.

OLIGOPOLISTIC INDETERMINACY

What is "oligopolistic indeterminacy"? Is it merely a sophisticated word for a rather simple idea? or is the idea behind it very intricate, if not mysterious? or is it perhaps a word standing in lieu of an idea, a high-sounding phrase to cover up a void of thought? Frankly, any one of these suspicions may prove true, for it is in a variety of meanings that the word is being used. We feel obliged to look behind the phrase, especially since the role which "oligopolistic indeterminacy" plays in the literature of the subject is very much greater than has been indicated thus far.

The General Meaning of Indeterminacy

In a general way, economists speak of indeterminacy if not enough information is available to give a safe and unambiguous answer to a question before them. If they wish to solve a problem —for example, how the price of a certain commodity will change under certain conditions—but find that the data which are assumed to be "given" would permit of two or more (perhaps of an indefinite number of) answers, they will state that the problem has no determinate solution.[1] Such a statement does not mean that the problem is insoluble. It means only that more must be known before it can be solved.[2]

The realization that a problem has no determinate solution will not be disturbing in the least, if we know what additional data we need and how we can get them. Often it is clear that the additional data cannot be obtained. If this is merely a "practical" impossibility, the theorist will not be much worried. As far as he is concerned, the solution of his problem is determinate as soon as he assumes as given what in practical fact may not be known. It is really bad only if he must admit that the data in question cannot even "conceivably" be known. For then his model will not be operational either practically or conceivably. But this will rarely happen. Most things which we do not know are "conceivably knowable" even if we have no hope of ever knowing them in the world in which we live. Thus, if we find that a problem has no determinate solution, all we have to do is to make additional assumptions which will remove the indeterminacy.[3]

[1] Economists usually speak of indeterminacy where mathematicians would speak of a multiplicity of solutions.

[2] Depending on the number of additional independent variables they want to be given, economists sometimes say that the solution has still one or more "degrees of freedom." It will be determinate when enough is given to remove all "degrees of freedom." See Erich Schneider, *Einführung in die Wirtschaftstheorie, II. Teil, Wirtschaftspläne und wirtschaftliches Gleichgewicht in der Verkehrswirtschaft* (Tübingen: J. C. Mohr-Paul Siebeck, 1949), pp. 295 ff.

[3] The following types of indeterminacy—chiefly with regard to oligopoly analysis—may be conveniently distinguished:

(1) Two or more solutions, perhaps an infinite number of solutions, are compatible with the data assumed as given. We need more data to determine the outcome. The needed additional information may be about

Why, then, should we so often resort to the disclaimer of determinacy instead of filling out the gaps in our sets of data? There are at least two good reasons for it. First of all, the "missing" data may be of a nature entirely different from that of all other data assumed to be given. We may be reluctant to "mix" indiscriminately assumptions of too dissimilar or diverse character. Secondly, the problem for the solution of which more data are wanted may be very much like many other problems, which however are soluble without such additional data. We may be reluctant to furnish an extra supply of data to one problem when apparently very similar problems can do with less. Let us look more closely into both these reasons.

(a) external (environmental, objective) conditions, affecting the conduct of the actors concerned;

(b) subjective (inclinational, psychological) conditions, affecting the conduct of the actors; or

(c) external forces or interventions by third parties, including government, affecting the results of the conduct of the actors.

(2) Only one solution is compatible with the data assumed as given, but upon closer inspection it can be seen that there is only apparent determinacy due to the fact that one or more variables about which no explicit assumption is made are implicitly assumed to be zero. Knowing, however, that they cannot be zero, one realizes that the problem has not a uniquely determinate solution. If the magnitudes of these neglected variables are assumed to be known, other additional data may now be required for a determination of the outcome. [Example: Uncertainty implicitly assumed to be zero. If it is not zero, several more assumptions must be made.]

(3) The given sets of data result in a succession of merely tentative (provisional) solutions, each inherently unstable because whenever one actor attains equilibrium the equilibria of others are upset. The continuing shifts of positions may lead to oscillatory (or even explosive) movements which make the maintenance of the original assumptions impossible because they prove to be inconsistent with other, possibly implicit, assumptions. The problem can become determinate only through additional data concerning

(a) changes in the external conditions, brought about by the oscillatory (or explosive) movements and affecting the conduct of the actors concerned [Examples: plant deterioration, reduction of financial strength];

(b) changes in the subjective conditions, brought about by the movements and affecting conduct [Examples: tiredness, resignation]; or

(c) new external forces or interventions by third parties, including government, affecting the conduct of the actors or its result [Examples: government price control, buyers' cooperative movement].

This list is probably incomplete and perhaps unsystematic. The distinction between (a) and (c) may not be justified by any real differences.

Pure and Applied Economics

The question how far one should go in supplying additional assumptions in the analysis of particular economic problems has long been a matter of convention, if not fashion, among economists. A large number, perhaps a majority, of economists have adhered to the rule that "pure" theory should operate with a minimum of assumptions and that they must all be of the broadest, most general type. Anything else is "applied" theory, where many more assumptions, and assumptions of a more specific nature, are introduced. Needless to say, "concrete" problems approaching the complex situations prevalent in the real world ordinarily require a great many and very specific data for their solution and can, therefore, be accommodated only by applied economics. But even in a relatively general form, certain kinds of problems may not be soluble with the scant rations and the non-specific types of assumptions furnished in "pure" economics.

Depending on the various epistemological views, the propositions of "pure" theory have been interpreted alternatively as basic postulates of economic conduct, as fundamental assumptions of evident empirical validity, as ideal types of great explanatory value, as aprioristic truths inherent in the rationality of human thought, as logical inferences from useful tools of analysis. Accordingly, any problems not completely soluble in such terms were contrasted with propositions of pure theory, and the additional raw material required for the solutions was referred to as non-economic, more specific, less generally applicable, empirical, descriptive, or factual. It is on the basis of these methodological distinctions, much disputed although largely a matter of taste, that the comments of certain economists on oligopolistic indeterminacy within "pure economics" must be understood.[4]

---

[4] For example, Pareto said that "pure economics" cannot tell us anything about the continuing shifts of position of competing oligopolists and that we must turn to "the observation of facts," which may show us a large variety of actual solutions: cartel, trust, price leadership, cut-throat competition, live-and-let-live policies, etc. Vilfredo Pareto, *Manuel d'Economie Politique* (Paris: M. Giard, 2nd ed., 1927), pp. 601–602. In the same vein, Triffin said that "the limited tools of pure economics are powerless to yield by themselves a determinate solution," and that the actual solution is "an empirical question,

There is no need for us in this context to examine the different methodological positions of different schools of economics. (It is difficult, though, to resist the temptation on this occasion to criticize the notion that there is a difference in kind, rather than degree, in the logical nature of pure and applied economics and that the latter is empirical while the former is not. But we shall restrain ourselves.) The point here for us to focus on is that the line drawn between pure and applied economics can often explain what is meant by "indeterminacy" of the solution of a problem: it is indeterminate inside the line because the data needed to make the solution determinate may lie beyond the line.

Anonymous Masses and the Conduct of Individuals

Where thousands or even only hundreds of firms sell in the same market, we are usually able to do with much less information than if only a few sellers share the market. In the analysis of mass action, where each individual actor counts only a little, we need not know them intimately in order to explain the combined result. A very "anonymous" model (or ideal type) of the relevant kind of actor will suffice for an explanation of the process in question and its outcome. Not so when only a few people are involved; where each individual actor counts heavily, a much more intimate

---

and not a matter of logical deduction." Robert Triffin, *Monopolistic Competition and General Equilibrium Theory* (Cambridge: Harvard University Press, 1940), pp. 124–25. The following excellent statement by K. W. Rothschild characterizes different methodological positions towards oligopolistic indeterminacy: "But while thus the increasing acceptance of the indeterminateness of the problem was an advance towards a more realistic treatment of the subject, it was also a retreat from the former belief that price theory could be sufficiently developed to deal with all possible market phenomena. Indeed, the majority of these writers, once they have shown the inadequacy of the determinate solutions, take up an almost nihilistic attitude towards the theory of duopoly and oligopoly. They may, like Chamberlin, just add a short list of "uncertainties" to an artificial, determinate solution; or they may deny the possibility of a general theory covering industry under oligopolistic conditions and substitute for it voluminous case-studies describing the behavior pattern of particular industries; or oligopolistic industry is just viewed as a chaotic mess where practically anything may happen, and about which economic analysis has very little to say." K. W. Rothschild, "Price Theory and Oligopoly," *Economic Journal*, Vol. LVII (1947), p. 304.

knowledge about every one of them may be needed for an explanation of the combined result.

The important difference between ideal behavior-types (conduct models) of a high degree of "anonymity" and those of a high degree of "intimacy" has been developed in formal sociology.[5] It is related to the fact that analysis may deal with phenomena in very different strata of generality (in terms of particular conceptual schemes). The legitimacy of the reliance on the applicability of highly anonymous types may or may not be related also to the "law of large numbers," explaining the greater reliability of propositions about mass phenomena.[6]

This points to a very important difference between the theories of polypoly, on the one hand, and monopoly and oligopoly, on the other hand. Assume, for example, we knew perfectly well the cost conditions of every single plant in an industry and knew also the conditions of demand for its homogeneous product sold in large central markets. If there were, let us say, two hundred plants of approximately equal size and they were owned and operated by two hundred different capitalists, we could make a reasonably good prediction of the aggregate output that would be produced in the two hundred plants and of the price at which the product would be sold. There may be very odd characters among the two hundred producers; and some of them may be smart, others dumb; some lazy, others industrious; some venturous, others timid; some imaginative and optimistic, others pessimistic and pedestrian; some

---

[5] See Alfred Schütz, *Der sinnhafte Aufbau der sozialen Welt* (Vienna: Springer, 1932); Alfred Stonier and Karl Bode, "A New Approach to the Methodology of the Social Sciences," *Economica*, New Series, Vol. IV (1937), pp. 406–24; and my own article, "Why Bother with Methodology?", *Economica*, New Series, Vol. III (1936), p. 44.

[6] "It is a well known phenomenon in many branches of the exact and physical sciences that very great numbers are often easier to handle than those of medium size. . . . This is, of course, due to the excellent possibility of applying the laws of statistics and probabilities. . . ." John von Neumann and Oskar Morgenstern, *The Theory of Games and Economic Behavior* (Princeton: Princeton University Press, 2nd ed., 1947), p. 14. The authors warn, however, against premature reliance on this principle for generalizations in economics. While they "hope" that the principle will be found to apply there, they state: ". . . only after the theory for moderate numbers of participants has been satisfactorily developed will it be possible to decide whether extremely great numbers of participants simplify the situation." *Ibid.*

FRITZ MACHLUP

short-sighted, others far-sighted; some penny-pinchers, others spendthrifts; yet, we should not have to worry about these differences. There would be no need of knowing any of the sellers individually, because no one of them would make enough of a difference in the outcome. The most anonymous behavior type, the model of the perfect polypolist trying to make as much money as he can, would suffice for our analysis of the combined outcome. The more specific behavior types—and, of course, every one of the above mentioned fourteen personal qualities would represent another ideal type—would be of no use in improving our prediction.

Let us now assume that all two hundred plants are under unified control and the product is sold by a monopolist. Now to make a prediction of price and output—not merely a prediction of the decisions of an anonymous, "typical" monopolist, but rather a prediction of the real man acting in the real world—would call for a different method of analysis. We should have to know a good many of the personal qualities of the man, and about his background and experience, his friends and associates, his political ambitions, and perhaps also his digestive troubles; and even then we might not know half enough to come very close to the actual outcome.

The difficulties are not less but even more serious if the two hundred plants are divided among a few independent owners. What kind of people are they? If two or more of them are typical leaders, what kind of battle will they fight? Which of them will give in and after what length of time? How spiteful are they, or how complaisant? How much money have they to lose? Are they emotional or cool-headed? Are they good bluffers and good mind-readers? If we knew all this about our men, and a thousand other things too, we still should not know enough to make a prediction which—even if neither cost nor demand conditions had changed—would have a fifty percent chance of hitting the actual outcome with a twenty percent margin of error.

Have we exaggerated the differences in complexity between the analyses of polypolistic, monopolistic, and oligopolistic selling? The differences are so enormous if the comparisons are made, as we have done, in terms of predictions rather than merely explanations. This is probably not quite fair, since we are often satisfied to explain and do not always aspire to predict. Surely the explanatory value of a theory may be great even if its predictive value is small.[7] While the future may hold an infinite number of possibilities, the past has eliminated all but one. The reconstruction of the data which may have led to the actual outcome need no longer be encumbered with the infinite possible "solutions" that existed before the course of events unfolded itself. Looking backward we may select those givens which would make the operations of our theoretical model yield just the result that in actual fact has emerged from the operations of the real world. Thus, a theory which has merely the task of explaining, not of predicting, may be much less formidable and perfectly manageable. But even for this much more modest task the assumptions required for a model with only a few actors will nevertheless be much more numerous and much more specific than the assumptions required for a model in which a large number of actors are involved.

Extra-Economic Factors

If, in order to achieve determinacy, more specific assumptions are needed for a model schematizing the interactions among a few than for one schematizing the interactions among many, does this requirement for more detailed specification imply a departure from purely economic factors and the indiscriminate inclusion of non-economic ones?

To some extent the answer will depend on what one chooses to call an economic factor, and what a non-economic or extra-economic one. Are we dealing with an "economic" factor if we make assumptions about how great a man's ability is to estimate the production cost of an output he has not produced before? or about his confidence in his own ability to gauge the market and

---

[7] The meteorologists are much better in explaining why it rained yesterday than in predicting that it will rain tomorrow. The physicists may have a fully satisfactory explanation of all causes of an explosion last month, without being able to predict an explosion next month. And the physician may not be able to predict the death of a patient although he may afterwards explain what led to it. The economist's capacity to explain economic phenomena must not be judged by his small success in predicting them.

the elasticity of the demand? about a man's inclination to look far ahead into the distant future? a man's willingness to take risks? Is financial strength [8] an extra-economic factor? or the pride of leadership in an industry?

In a large measure, however, the factors that have to be introduced in order to make the outcome of oligopolistic competition determinate will be considered non-economic in almost any sort of classification. For example, assumptions about how much fun a man will get out of being in a good scrap with a competitor; how quickly a man will get tired and will acquiesce in a position he first vigorously rejected; how conscientiously a man, when he is in a pinch, will adhere to a gentlemen's agreement to maintain prices; how good a man's political connections are enabling him to bring off or to stop some governmental intervention in the industry. A thousand and one of such things may be the crucial factors in an oligopolistic situation. Disregard them—and the solution may be indeterminate.[9]

Does the realization of this mean that in order to analyse oligopoly we must psychoanalyse each member of each group? Does it mean that we should give up studying the "theory" of oligopoly and engage instead in a thousand different descriptive industry studies, considering each situation as a separate and unique one which has nothing in common with any other oligopoly situation? Indeed not. We have always known that no single science is self-sufficient or could explain a concrete situation of the real world fully to the last detail without recourse to theories, constructs, and models from many other fields of learning or every-day intelligence. Such is not the aim of scientific work in general or of economic analysis in particular or, in the present case, of the theory of oligopoly. All we want to say is what *can* be validly said about a general class of phenomena. Where the phenomena become so unique that they no longer fit into any class, we may still be interested—as we may be in something without equal or parallel

[8] Triffin lists "financial backing" among extraneous factors. *Op. cit.*, p. 71.
[9] Some of such factors may also be important in a polypolistic situation. But there they may merely affect and change the actual outcome, which is determinate in any event. Disregard them—and the solution will be *different*, but not indeterminate.

—but our interest is no longer that of generalizing scientists.[10] The theory of oligopoly must stop before it becomes too specific— that is, so specific that it applies only to unique cases—and even if it has not by that time arrived at complete determinacy.[11]

On the other hand, the theory of oligopoly must not stop too early, that is, it cannot be satisfied with the general assumption made for the economic analysis of the business firm, namely, that it will maximize its profits. This clearly is not enough. More is needed even for a rather general theory of oligopolistic behavior and, of course, still more for the theories of each of the main types of oligopoly which a classification chooses to distinguish. In exercising one's judgment about how far to go in introducing more specific assumptions, one should not be influenced by narrow partisanship to the "schools" of "abstract" versus "institutional" economics.[12] In the question of admitting additional assumptions into a theoretical model their relative usefulness should be the only decisive consideration. If an assumption seems to be in reasonable conformance with observation or reliable testimony in a large number of instances and with the findings of imagined intro-

[10] The very fact that students of supposedly purely descriptive case histories do not ordinarily publish within one book the unique cases of a melancholic mass murderer, a paraphlegmic concert violinist, a universal chess, track, and wrestling champion, and a guaranteed non-collusive oligopolist proves that they do recognize that even most unique cases somehow belong into general classes and that generalizations about types abstracting from all specific details are necessary and useful.

[11] In answer to an appeal for more empirical research into the thinking, prejudices, temperaments, intuitive judgment, and shrewd knowledge of entrepreneurs as a prerequisite of a proper analysis of price policy, K. W. Rothschild commented as follows: "But, surely, the peculiarities of price behaviour under oligopolistic conditions are not due to any peculiarities in the psychology of duopolists and oligopolists, but to the different economic environment in which they work. By all means let us have more research into the psychology of the business-man in all the various market situations, but the distinguishing feature of oligopolistic price theory cannot lie in additional psychological investigations, but in the provision of a framework which will show the actions of a "normal" business-man under the specific conditions of an oligopolistic environment." Op. cit., p. 306.

[12] "The theory of oligopoly has been aptly described as a ticket of admission to institutional economics." Edward S. Mason, "Price and Production Policies of Large-Scale Enterprise," American Economic Review, Supplement, Vol. XXIX (1939), pp. 64–65.

spection, and if it modifies the operations of our models in a way as to achieve greater conformance with observed phenomena of the real world (and if this degree of conformance cannot be achieved with fewer or simpler assumptions) such assumption should be eligible for admission to our models no matter whether it is labeled "economic" or "extra-economic."

The "extra-economic" label might be hung either on the *motivation* of the oligopolistic seller's actions, or on the *nature* of their actions, or on some *outside influences* on these actions. The motivation may be one competing with the profit motive, which is commonly assumed to be the chief or sole guide of the actions of polypolistic sellers. The nature of the oligopolists' actions may be political—e.g., inducing an intervention by the government—or social—e.g., instigating other members of the trade to ostracize a rival—instead of strictly economic, that is, consisting (in our society) chiefly in selling, buying, offering, and bidding. The outside influences may, again, be governmental or corporative [13] policies.

Position, Security, and Profit

The "monistic" place given, in the theory of the firm, to the principle of profit maximization has been subject to severe criticism. Other motives are seen to be competing with the profit motive in entrepreneurial considerations. The desire for "position" and the quest for "security" are said to be on a par with the striving for maximum profits. Profit, security, and position are named as three separate objectives of the firm, one economic, the others "non-economic."

Two questions suggest themselves in connection with the proposed "inclusion of these 'non-economic' elements" [14] among the essential elements for an explanation of oligopolistic behavior and price: (1) To what extent are the two "non-economic" motives, the desires for position and security, separate from and independent of the profit motive? (2) To what extent is it true that the need for distinguishing position and security as separate motives

---

[13] "Corporative" are the policies of the trade associations.
[14] K. W. Rothschild, *op. cit.*, p. 319.

(or sub-motives) for the behavior of the firm arises in the theory of oligopoly, but not in the theories of polypoly and monopoly?

Taking the second question first, we can see immediately that attempts to improve a firm's *position* in the industry are foreign to polypolistic as well as to monopolistic behavior, because both the polypolist and the monopolist take their positions for granted. This is true regardless of whether "position" is defined by the seller's share in the total market for the products of the industry or, subjectively, by the importance he attaches to himself or by his feeling of being recognized as an important factor in his industry or line of business.[15] A seller is a polypolist if he considers himself too insignificant in the market to be recognized by any of the other sellers as an important factor in the market. A seller is a monopolist if he considers himself as the only one in the market and, thus, thinks of no one who would or would not recognize his importance. He is a perfect monopolist if he is not even afraid of any potential newcomer who might disturb the situation. In no event can he improve his position. The oligopolist, on the other hand, has, at any time, a certain share in the market and enjoys a certain recognition as an important factor in the industry. He may be bent upon improving his position, and he may fear to see it reduced. Position, thus, is a consideration that may count a good deal in the mental make-up of the oligopolist.

The same reasoning holds to a large extent for *security* as an objective of the firm. In polypoly the problem of security can hardly arise independently of the problem of maximum profit. The same policy which promises a maximum of money profits to the polypolist will also give him maximum security. The more money he makes, the more secure he will feel.[16] In perfect monopoly the seller feels absolutely safe; hence, he never needs to pass up any profit opportunities for the sake of his security. The imperfect monopolist is not in this happy situation. He does have to look out for his security and may have to forsake chances of juicier profits in order to safeguard his financial and market position,

[15] This is only one of several meanings of "position." Some writers use the term interchangeably or correlatively with "security"; to them the position which the seller desires is one of security.

[16] See Fritz Machlup, *The Economics of Sellers' Competition*, (Baltimore: Johns Hopkins Press, 1952), pp. 51–56.

chiefly against potential newcomer's competition, but also against government intervention or public opinion. This is even more so in the case of an oligopolist. The oligopolist must look out not only for potential newcomer's competition, potential government intervention, and potential public disapprobation, but in addition also for potential misunderstanding with, and retaliations from, his competitors. Indeed, we have made the concern with rival's reactions the characteristic of oligopoly and must certainly not fail to give it—and, in connection with it, the desire to avoid excessively costly conflict—a most prominent place in the explanation of oligopolistic behavior.

It remains to be seen, however, whether these security considerations can be clearly distinguished from profit considerations. This is, of course, nothing else but the first of the two questions raised above, namely, whether the security motive can be, and should be, distinguished from the profit motive.

There is a strong separatist movement agitating for the autonomy of the security motive.[17] It is admitted that, even under oligopoly, actions motivated by the desire for maximum security will in most instances be the same as actions motivated by the desire for maximum profit. But it is contended that there are instances in which "the two motives lead to conflicting patterns of behavior. Where profit maximization demands prices fluctuating with every change in revenue and cost conditions, security maximization may demand rigid prices; while profit maximization should tend to create firms of optimum size, security considerations will favor the oversized firm; again, where we should expect reserve funds to be invested in response to expected returns, we may find their practically unconditional reinvestment in their own firm."[18]

The separatist movement is opposed by those who campaign for maintaining the union of profit and security considerations under the banner of "long-run profits." If every price change may involve the risk of a price war cutting down the profits or even

[17] Rothschild declares that "the security motive must be given the same pride of place as has been occupied by the profit maximization principle for such a long time." *Op. cit.*, p. 309.
[18] *Ibid.*

turning them into losses, the avoidance of price changes can be fully explained in terms of long-run profits. If the oligopolist believes that a reserve of unused capacity, which he can threaten to utilize at any time, may help him maintain or even increase in the future his share in the market—be it in the form of agreed quotas or through silent acquiescence on the part of his competitors—his policy is perfectly explicable in terms of long-run money profits. Indeed, one may well insist that policies which fail to take account of all these factors should not properly be regarded as policies designed to maximize profits. For, after all, what sense can there be in calling "profit maximization" a course of action which *would* maximize profits only *if* half the facts of the situation were different from what they are? Is the separation of the security motive from the profit motive fundamentally anything but an arbitrary separation of some data from the rest of the data relevant in the situation?

The trouble with both the separatists and the unionists is that they fight for the universality and exclusive truthfulness of their respective points of view and fail to see that there can be many different models schematizing the same set of facts. Whether one model or another is "better" is often merely a matter of taste or habit of thought. That a separation of data is "arbitrary" is not a decisive criticism of the autonomy of the security motive. Likewise, that the merger of all pecuniary considerations under the name of long-run profit maximization may look "tautological" is not a decisive criticism of the subsumption of security considerations under the profit motive. One can deal with these considerations equally well whether they are treated under the heading of a separate security motive or as additional points under the all-inclusive profit motive. The main thing is that they are treated; under what heading they are treated is irrelevant.

There is much more justification in the demand for separating the firm's desire for "position" from the objective of maximum profits if position is merely a matter of vanity and conceit and not a means of making or safeguarding profits. In principle, of course, it is again true that it does not matter under what heading this sort of consideration is introduced in the analysis. But while the question of safe profits will hardly be overlooked when maximum

FRITZ MACHLUP

profits are being discussed, there is a possibility that prestige considerations get lost in the shuffle. In order to guard against such an oversight one may well insist on a separate listing for the oligopolist's desire for position.

Chapter 4

FACT AND THEORY IN ECONOMICS

Discussions of practical economic issues are commonly, and perhaps inevitably, mixtures of fact and fiction, logic and preconception, history and theory, political philosophy and plain common sense. What are the mixtures expediently chosen for the discussions of various topics? I may illustrate some variations in method that I deemed appropriate for different parts of my book on *The Political Economy of Monopoly* (Baltimore: Johns Hopkins Press, 1952).

VARIATIONS IN METHOD

I set out with the preparation of a "conceptual framework" appropriate for the description, analysis and appraisal of the phenomena referred to by the terms monopoly and competition. Part I was devoted to this task. Part II dealt with business policies, and attempted to describe monopolistic business practices in general terms, using a rather "taxonomic" approach. Part III, the discussion of government policies concerning monopoly and competition,

[439]

In this extract from my book first published in 1952 references are to other chapters of that—not the present—book.

was more "historical" in nature than any of the other parts of the book. Part IV treated the implications of labor policies and their probable effects on organized bargaining power, wage determination and income distribution in a more deliberately "theoretical" analysis than was employed in the rest of the book. Thus, these four parts are rather different as to the methods of discourse practised. It seems worth our while to ask whether these variations in method were appropriate in view of the problems examined.

Conceptual Framework (Part I)

It would be pretentious if I claimed that it was absolutely necessary to begin with the construction or justification of a conceptual framework for the discussion, or that this was the only intelligent thing to do. After all, there are enough books on our subject that do not follow this procedure. Can the subject perhaps be treated without any conceptual framework at all? Of course not. A writer surely "means" something when he uses such words as monopoly and competition, and what he means is usually rather involved; nevertheless he often assumes that his readers will know what he means even if he does not bother with definitions and with attempts to ascertain the place of his concepts in his universe of discourse.

Such a confidence in the possibility of achieving a meeting of minds without the benefit of "preliminary negotiations" may be based on one of three presuppositions: (1) all of the words used are part of the common vocabulary in every-day parlance and have clear unambiguous meanings; (2) the terms and concepts used have been satisfactorily discussed, explained and consistently defined in previous writings by the same or other authors with which one may assume most of the readers to be familiar; or (3) the terms and concepts used are such that the reader, even if he is not at the outset familiar with their precise meanings and connotations, can be expected to grasp the ideas as the discussion proceeds.

It is the last of these presuppositions on which many writers in economics count when they choose not to bother with a discussion of their conceptual framework. Many a writer proceeds on the assumption: "You will get what I mean as I go on." This is a very sensible procedure in many instances. But I felt it was not reasonable to follow it for that book. In the very first pages we found that most of the popular notions of monopoly and competition were vague, ambiguous, confusing; and that we had to clear the ground and start with some simple idealized "models" if we wanted to obtain manageable tools of reasoning. Moreover, we found that there was little point in talking about competition and monopoly if we had not a pretty clear idea of their effects on the performance of the economy. These effects are obviously connected with the price mechanism. It follows that competition and monopoly have to be understood in the light of the insight gained from working with a model of an economic system in which productive resources are steered to their uses by a price mechanism whose functioning is affected by the more or less "monopolistic" market positions of sellers and buyers. Thus, the concepts of competition and monopoly are firmly "bound up" with the concepts of price mechanism, resource allocation, consumer preferences, productive efficiency, total output—in short, they are part and parcel of a conceptual framework which had to be introduced and exhibited if the whole discussion was to make good sense.

There are of course many central and side issues that had to be dealt with in this connection. If one were to appraise monopolistic "deflections" and "deviations" of the performance of the economic system only in the light of standards developed from mental experimentations with an abstract "model economy" with the very "simplest" set of assumptions, serious errors of judgment would be inevitable. For example, the simplest assumptions would postulate a much greater degree of divisibility of resources than exists in reality. But one can understand the problem of "natural monopolies" only by using models providing also for indivisible resources; and thus the conceptual framework appropriate for the tasks for which we were preparing had to include certain special assumptions. This enabled us to discuss in Part I the inevitability and desirability of monopoly in certain fields or under certain conditions before embarking in Parts II and III on descriptions of the policies of businessmen and of governments with regard to the creation, reinforcement, maintenance, and exploitation of monopoly positions. Descriptions of these policies would have been largely meaningless without the benefit of findings about their probable effects and at least some presumptive appraisals of these effects. Why should we ever care to describe a "policy" or "practice" if we did not suspect that it had some significant effects or implications? Descriptive accounts, therefore, are more illuminating if they are preceded by an exposition of the conceptual framework that enables us to sense or check the suspected or asserted effects or implications of the phenomena described.

Taxonomic Approach (Part II)

It is impossible to describe anything without the use of general categories. Even so, it would be possible to take these categories for granted and to give a description of monopolistic business practices by telling what certain companies have done at certain times at certain places. Indeed, such "case histories" are very important, if not indispensable, to our understanding of the issues involved. Fortunately numerous good case studies of monopolistic business policies are available, and students of industrial organization and control are always adding to our knowledge of "cases."

An alternative approach to the description of business policies is to omit names, dates, and places, and to classify the reported actions according to some significant aspects. This is the classificatory or taxonomic approach; it is the one that I chose for Part II of the book. Just as the case approach presupposes some prior classificatory attempt, however tentative, the taxonomic approach presupposes some prior case studies, however incomplete. In other words, the two approaches are interdependent, each being based on some previous steps along the other. But where the number of cases is very large and the main purpose is to arrive at generalizations, the taxonomic approach will be more manageable.

Classifications must be on the basis of some principles, and one may well argue about their selection. But any such argument can be meaningful only in view of the explicit or implicit purposes the classification is to serve. Speaking of monopolistic business practices a lawyer will most probably group them according to the major provisions of the laws actually or potentially violated, while economists may choose among several possible distinguishing criteria. In the discussions of Part II we favored some of the classificatory principles that had suggested themselves in the course of the discussions of the conceptual framework in Part I. But we felt it necessary to engage also in cross-classifications according to other characteristics more commonly selected for emphasis.[1]

It probably goes without saying that classifications not only serve analysis but also presuppose analysis. For example, it would surely not be possible to group certain actions according to their effects if we did not have a theory to help us. The theories prerequisite to various classificatory principles are of different degrees of complexity. Thus it takes less analysis to sort types of conduct according to technique employed than according to purposes served.

Historical Approach (Part III)

When I say that I followed a historical approach in discussing government policies regarding monopoly and competition, I am exaggerating, perhaps more than is legitimate, in order to bring out a contrast. The contrast that I wish to point up is this: while we spoke in Part II of the actions of unidentified business firms, without regard to time or place, we discussed in Part III the actions of particular governments—chiefly the United States, but also some individual states—as particular events in time.

The exaggeration involved in my suggestion does not consist in the fact that the discussion in the three chapters of Part III was systematically subdivided according to different kinds (classes) of governmental measures; such systematic subdivisions are perfectly compatible with historical accounts. The exaggeration lies in the fact that the emphasized features of the treatment—the

[1] At one point I enumerated more than twenty different types of price discrimination. (Chapter 5, pp. 135–63.) This may look as if I had allowed my taxonomic zeal to go to some extremes. But the stringing together of this large number of "types" was not excessive taxonomy—but too little. Separate classifications according to different principles, such as according to techniques employed, purposes served, effects achieved, or special conditions required, would each distinguish only a handful of categories. But a cross-classification could yield many more "types" than I had the space to present.

selection and presentation of individual, unique events and the placing of these events in time—are, though necessary, not sufficient characteristics of historical work. Although it is often done, one should not regard dates as the essence of history, or a writer of chronology as a historian. Some of the main tasks of the historian— the search for and evaluation of documents, the interpretation of evidence, the linking of events in time by detailed analysis of causes, conditions, motives, and effects, and the presentation of the findings in the whole "historical setting"—were not brought into play in our account of government restraints of and aids to monopoly. There was no need, in the chapters of Part III, for first-hand historical research or for new critical historical analysis. For our purposes we were able to rely on accepted accounts of governmental actions in our field of interest and we could be satisfied with a recapitulation of the highlights or, in certain areas, of some representative instances.

But why did we choose to make the treatment of this phase of our theme as historical as it was? Would it not have been neater to continue with the taxonomic approach used in the preceding part? It certainly would have been possible to do so. We could have described in general terms the economically significant features of the different kinds of measures which government in general may take to foster competition and restrain monopoly, and to aid monopoly and restrict competition,—any government, at any time, anywhere. Instead, we reported on particular acts passed by the United States Congress or on particular decisions pronounced by the Supreme Court of the United States in certain years and under specific circumstances. The reason, of course, is that the historical approach is preferable where it does not unduly lengthen the account.[2] The chief advantage of the taxonomic approach is that it eliminates masses of details and boils down enormous num-

---

[2] This should not be misunderstood as an endorsement of the so-called "historical method," or of the doctrine of the "historical school" in economics, according to which history was prior to theory—if theory was to be recognized at all. This methodological view was untenable and all attempts to support it have failed. "There is no reason to regard this failure as less than definitive." Thorstein Veblen, "Gustav Schmoller's Economics," *Quarterly Journal of Economics*, Vol. XVI (1901), p. 7.

bers of individual cases to a small number of types or classes. Where we were dealing with millions of business firms and billions of business actions, we availed ourselves of the space-saving distillation accomplished by the taxonomic process. Most of the color and of the flavor of the individual stories are lost in such distillation, and the reader was advised to sample some of the case histories in order to make up for the loss. But even if only one representative case for each type of monopolistic business practice mentioned in Part II had been selected for illustration, the reports on these cases would have filled several volumes.

Dealing with government actions to *restrain competition* we were also faced with too large a number of instances to make it practical to use historical reporting. This is the field where local and state governments have been so terribly active, and where laws, decrees and ordinances have poured forth in such profusion, that the taxonomic method is the only feasible one. The same is true of the actions of national governments to restraint competition in international trade and in other respects. It is in the fight *against monopoly* that the actions of individual governments become sufficiently unique, and the number of significant measures or decisions sufficiently small to enable us to use the historical approach. Thus it was chiefly in the chapter on the antitrust policy of the United States that we could present an account more historical in nature than the treatment of other topics.

The historical approach, where it can be used without undue demands on space, has many advantages over taxonomic distillation. We have only to imagine how an entirely unhistorical, taxonomic treatment of the American antitrust policy would look, and we can readily sense what it would lack. Indeed, the present state of the antitrust law and the possibilities of its further development could not be understood without the benefit of the insight gained by a historical review.

On the other hand, there is no lack of "implicit analysis" in a historical account of economic policies. When reasons, motives, purposes, and effects are discussed in connection with specific measures, economic theory must be used. Frequently, however, the writer of a historical account has so much confidence in the theoretical analysis which he or others have employed, that he announces the results of the analysis as if they were findings of fact.

Theoretical Approach (Part IV)

When it came to the discussion of labor policies, there was no widely accepted body of theory that could be taken for granted and relied on with confidence. The examination of the conceptual framework in Part I may have prepared us sufficiently for the discussions of business policies in Part II and of government policies in Part III, but not for the discussion of labor policies. One should think that the analytical models employed as aids in visualizing the effects of cartel price determination for industrial products or of increased concentration of industry control by corporate mergers would be equally helpful in visualizing the effects of union wage determination for industrial labor or of increased union control over the labor market through industry-wide collective bargaining. Yet, whether because of differences in the kinds of analysis employed, or because of differences in the effects inferred from the same kind of analysis, or because of differences in the evaluation of the same effects, at the present state of professional thinking the problems of competition and monopoly in the labor market cannot be meaningfully discussed without first laying a more solid foundation of economic analysis suitable to these problems.

Awareness of this situation led me to use in Part IV of the book an explicitly theoretical approach, abstracting from all descriptive and historical material. After all that I have said about the advantages of the historical approach wherever it is practicable, I need hardly emphasize that by not following it we sacrificed valuable familiarity with trade union development and a great deal of information about things worth knowing. But a history that cannot say anything about the most significant relationships among the events which it reports is not very meaningful. Before one has an idea, for example, how changes in union membership, in money wages rates, product prices, real wage rates, and employment can be connected with one another, a historical, or rather chronological, approach to these matters cannot enlarge our understanding.[3] Likewise, a taxonomic treatise of trade union practices would not be very revealing before we have more confidence in our ability to judge the various types of practices according to their economic effects.

Can abstract theorizing help us here, can it do for us what we need? The reader who happens to know the book and particularly its Part IV may have some idea about this. I hope he has come to share my appreciation of the fact that "reality" is much too complex to be understood unless we abstract from most of it and break the rest down into a few crucial elements the relationships among which we can examine in isolation. In reality too many things happen at once, so that we can never "observe" what causes what. If by some magic we could arrange that absolutely everything in the world remained unchanged while we experimented with a single change, say, an increase in the wage rates paid in a particular industry, and watched what happened—then reality could become a laboratory for experimental research in economics. In want of such magic we must resort to mental experiments with abstract models where we can move one thing at a time. This is what the "theoretical approach" tries to do, and I believe it is the only approach that can lead to answers, however tentative, where we still lack understanding of fundamental relationships.

Nevertheless, I know that many have found the analysis presented in Part IV "too abstract" and "too unrealistic." Quite possibly it can be shown to be deficient; its validity or applicability may well be questioned. But I hope those who did will point to the flaws and make the corrections instead of confining themselves to the complaint that there was "too much theory and not enough facts." About this complaint and the relationship between economic fact and theory some further comments are in order at this point.[4]

[3] This is not to deny that the inspection of different time series may give the investigator an idea for the development of a theory, although of course he must have some hunch about relevant connections before he selects his series.

[4] For an excellent exposition of the relationship between fact and theory in the natural and social sciences see Morris R. Cohen, *Reason and Nature*

ABSTRACTION, THEORY, AND FACT

Theorizing means abstracting from many things and isolating a few things with a view to grasping an otherwise hidden connection between the latter. Few people are given to this kind of mental exercise, chiefly because of a lack of training in abstract thinking. Some dislike high degrees of abstraction because, not used to it and unable to participate, they find it tedious, others, because they distrust it when they see how the theorist comes out with conclusions they cannot check. More often than not, he who distrusts and disparages theory will regard as "theory" anything that calls for his mental effort or disagrees with his prejudices, while he will uncritically accept as an axiom, if not as "fact," many an old theory which others have long abandoned as invalid or inapplicable.

"It's a Fact"

When a trusted theory is considered as a "fact," this is merely a naive misunderstanding by an unschooled mind. All of us have heard people say "it's a fact" when they merely meant "it's true" and were referring, not to observation, but to hypothetical propositions and presumed "rules" of experience, or even to exploded theories and plain superstitions. This indiscrimination in the popular use of language is mentioned here only because we shall find that it is part of a much broader and yet more subtle problem of confusing facts and theories. Any number of intelligent people, well trained in some branch of knowledge, are wont to accept as "fact" what on inspection turns out to be merely the result of inferences resting on rather special if not specious theories.

In the strictest sense of the word, a fact is an event in time that has been *observed,* that is, for which we have evidence, based on sensory perception, which is accepted as conclusive. But there is a large category of *"inferred* facts" and, depending on the methodological point of view, some kinds of inferred facts are given the full status of facts.[5] There are, for example, events in

(New York: Harcourt, Brace & Co., 1931), especially the chapters on "Reason and Scientific Method" (pp. 76–146) and on "The Social and the Natural Sciences" (pp. 333–68).

[5] To many, however, a fact is strictly "a datum of experience as dis-

time, certain particular occurrences, which—although occurrences of the type are observable—have not been directly observed but merely inferred from other observations, yet where (because of an established one-to-one relationship, or perfect correlation, between the class of the facts observed and the class of the facts inferred) the occurrence is regarded as just as certain as if it had been directly observed. There is another kind of inferred "facts" —which may be denied the status of fact—where the certified observations plus inferences do not guarantee that the inferred event has actually taken place. This is the kind of conclusion which in law cases is referred to as "circumstantial evidence": the observed facts are taken as strong indication, but not as absolutely incontrovertible evidence, of the suspected occurrence. If other interpretations of the observed facts are possible, the "fact" that is inferred from the observed ones is surely not as good a fact as one directly observed.

A third kind of "inferred fact" relates to occurrences that are never directly observable. They are facts by construction only, but a one-to-one relationship may have been postulated between a certain kind of observation and a certain "construct." The impossibility of direct observation may be inherent in the construct, yet scientists may be satisfied that the construct is no less part of "reality" than the results of direct observation based on sense perception.[6]

It has been denied that there are in the world of human actions —and, hence, in the social sciences—any facts in the strict sense of the word. Whatever may be called a fact in the social sciences is certainly of a nature rather different from that of the fact of the natural sciences. The latter is concerned mostly with physical properties and, indeed, the bulk of the facts of physics are "data"

---

tinguished from conclusions." *Oxford Universal English Dictionary* (Oxford University Press, 1937), Vol. III, p. 667.

[6] For example, the atom "is evidently a construct, because no one ever experienced an atom, and its existence is entirely inferential." But, although first "a pure invention, without physical reality," we have accumulated so much "information all pointing to the atom, until now we are as convinced of its physical reality as of our hands and feet." This and similar "constructs" are regarded as "good" because "there is a unique correspondence between it and the physical data in terms of which it is defined." P. W. Bridgman, *The Logic of Modern Physics* (New York: Macmillan, 1927), pp. 59 and 55.

read from the indicators of scientific instruments. The social sciences are concerned with human actions, or with certain aspects of the results of human actions, which may have real existence (as "social" phenomena) only in the minds of the actors and of other parties concerned.[7] Thus, there is a serious difficulty in establishing what it really is that economists (or historians or sociologists) can "observe."

But we need not here go into these profound questions of methodology.[8] Perhaps we can be satisfied for our purposes with the simple device of regarding as facts those data of direct observation or of "record" which are so firmly established that they cannot reasonably be questioned. Anything that looks substantially different to different observers or from different points of view, or that lends itself to different "interpretations" should not be called a fact.

"It's Just a Theory"

The question how two or more separately observed facts hang together, whether some may be causes or effects of others, is tentatively answered by a mental scheme of interrelationships which we call theory. Often the validity of a theory is distinguished from its applicability. For it may happen that a theory "explains" the relationships between certain "hypothetical facts" which are so different from and incomparable with any actually observed facts that it can never be applied to anything. Most controversies among economists concern the applicability of theories, and especially their applicability to particular ("concrete") situations. The chief disagreements are matters of judgment: whether the facts are such that the theory applies.

---

[7] "Action" is defined as "human behavior when and insofar as the acting individual attaches a subjective meaning to it." An action is a "social action" when and "insofar as, by virtue of the subjective meaning attached to it by the acting individual (or individuals), it takes account of the behavior of others and is thereby oriented in its course." Max Weber, *The Theory of Social and Economic Organization*, ed. by Talcott Parsons (London: Hodge, 1947), p. 80.

[8] For an excellent and brief exposition of the essential problem involved see Friedrich A. Hayek, "The Facts of the Social Sciences," *Ethics*, Vol. LIV (1943), pp. 1–13. Reprinted in Friedrich A. Hayek, *Individualism and Economic Order* (Chicago: University of Chicago Press, 1948), pp. 57–76.

According to the degree of abstraction we may distinguish general theories, special theories, applied theories, and implied theories. In the latter two forms, theory is sometimes not identified as theory and may pass as description, historical narrative, purely factual account, statistical data. This is particularly so in the case of implied theory, where concrete cases, events or situations are discussed as if they were nothing but objective facts, while upon close inspection these so-called facts turn out to be inferences based on theories and would look quite different from the point of view of other theories. Let us illustrate this by an example.

Facts or Implied Theories?

The following statement looks to most people like a straight-forward account of historical facts: "From January 1946 to December 1952 the steel workers union, in a strong bargaining position, aided by government policies, was able to obtain for its members wage increases of x percent; and the steel companies, using their monopolistic position in the market, boosted steel prices by y percent."

This statement is chockful of theories, some of rather questionable validity. Let us examine the assertions made in the statement and see to what extent they are facts or implied theories. (a) That the union was or is in a "strong bargaining position" cannot be established by direct observation, but only inferred from certain impressions on the basis of some very special theories, most of which have not even succeeded in defining the main concepts employed. Vague concepts and poor data are sufficient grounds to question the assertion. (b) That the union was "aided by government policies" is an assertion that can be supported only by theories concerning the effect of certain kinds of government measures upon trade union strength. The assertion implies that in the absence of certain government policies the union would have been weaker. It is not impossible to assert the contrary and make a plausible case for such an assertion. (c) That steel workers' wages increased by x percent can be said only on the basis of a considerable number of conceptual and statistical conventions which in turn are based upon certain propositions of wage theory, index number theory, etc.[9] (d) That the union "obtained" these wage increases for its members is an assertion which rests on the hypothesis that there would have been no wage increase had it not been for union pressure. The statement gives no justification for this hypothesis. (e) That the steel companies were in a "monopolistic position" is an assertion the very meaning of which depends on the theory held. The particular theories used to support the assertion are rejected by many, including the steel companies. (f) That the companies "used" their monopolistic position is equally questionable, especially if it is argued that they used it for boosting steel prices. The opposite may be argued. (g) That steel prices rose by y percent can be said only on the basis of certain conceptual and statistical conventions which in turn are based upon certain propositions of price theory, index number theory, etc.[10] (h) That

[9] "Wages" may refer to contractual wage rates, average hourly earnings, average weekly earnings, total weekly payroll, average hourly labor cost (including the cost of fringe benefits), and perhaps other things. Which of these figures is considered relevant depends on several questions (including the theory of collective bargaining). It should be clear that these different wage data may change not only by different percentages but also in different directions. For example, when contractual wage rates increase average hourly earnings may decline if the percentage of unskilled labor employed becomes much larger; or average weekly earnings may fall as contractual wage rates rise if the number of hours worked is reduced. For want of an index of contractual wage rates, we must usually consult the published statistics of average hourly earnings, although this is affected by the amount of overtime worked as well as by the composition of the work force. Since the fringe benefits granted the workers during the period in question would figure among the obtained improvements of the wage contract, the cost of these concessions to the companies must be added to the wages paid. From all this it will be clear that there may be an indefinite number of findings for the "wage increase."

[10] For each steel product and each steel producer there are differences between base prices, mill net prices, and delivered prices, and the choice between these depends on certain theoretical considerations. There is also the difficulty in computing an average price increase. If an average price were calculated by dividing total sales proceeds for all steel products by total tonnage sold, one might find the average price reduced if the composition had changed from more expensive to less expensive products—even while every single steel product were sold at an increased price. This explains the need of using "appropriate" index number methods which make "adequate" allowance for changes in the composition of the product mix, for differences in specifications and qualities, for differences in transport costs and distances of deliveries, etc.

the companies "boosted" the steel prices is an assertion which, to be meaningful in the context, implies the hypothesis that steel prices would not have increased in a perfectly competitive market. One may argue differently and, indeed, we shall presently do so.

While it may now be patent that not one of the eight assertions is a simple fact directly ascertainable by observation,—that, instead, every one involves inferences linking, through implied theories, the asserted facts to other facts presumably established by observation or casual impression,—the most essential points of the statement can be found to rest on the weakest hypotheses, not even conceivably amenable to empirical tests or observation of any sort. I refer to the assertions (d) and (h) that increases in steel wages and steel prices are attributable to the particular policies and actions of steel workers unions and steel companies, respectively, in the sense that the increases would not have occurred if unions and companies had had no control over wages and prices, respectively. These assertions are open to question; a very strong case can be made against the theories on which they rest.

I am willing to argue that the existence of unions and of union contracts running for periods such as a whole year was, during 1946–1952, a stabilizing factor and that wage rates in these years would have risen more often and more sharply if the labor market had been more competitive.[11] I should argue with even more conviction that unrestricted competition in steel products would have driven steel prices higher than they were "set" by the companies. These were times of distinct "excess demand" with deferred deliveries, customer rationing and allocations; unrestricted competition would have driven prices to levels at which enough would-be buyers were squeezed out of the market to reduce total demand to the scarce supply. The steel companies used their control over prices to hold them below the competitive levels.[12] If my reasoning and my judgment of the actual facts are correct, any monopoly

[11] Cf. Albert Rees, "Postwar Wage Determination in the Basic Steel Industry," *American Economic Review*, Vol. XLI (1951), pp. 389–404.

[12] Whether this was "good" or "bad" for society can be decided only on the basis of a whole system of theory and valuation. I regard it as "bad," on the basis of my scheme of social values. But there is no agreement on this.

power possessed by unions and companies was used to keep steel wages and prices from rising as much as they would have in free competitive markets.

Surely, I am not presenting these counter-assertions as facts. They are conclusions based on hypotheses which happen to be different from those on which the original assertions rested. But, I submit, that this theorizing is better than the implied theorizing of the pseudo-factual statement under examination, first, in that it admits the hypothetical character of the findings and discloses the underlying hypotheses and, second, in that it is more consistent with the concepts used in the rest of the statement. For the references to "bargaining position" and "monopolistic position" are meaningful only in (implied) comparison with a situation where the parties concerned are not enjoying such positions, that is, in comparison with a more competitive situation, if not with a state of pure and perfect competition. Such a comparison is carried through in the counter-assertions, but is disregarded in the original assertions.

We shall not take more space to illustrate the contention that most of the so-called facts in economics are really "implied theory." [13] But we should demand that theory be made explicit whenever it can be done without undue effort. If this were done, people would become more critical of "facts" and less averse to "theory"; at least they would know that the so-called facts cannot be better than the theories implied.

EXPLANATION, PREDICTION, EVALUATION

Theory, the schematic linking of hypothetical facts in our minds, is used for purposes of fact finding, explanation, prediction, and evaluation. In fact finding, theory is a means of establishing "inferred facts" from observed facts. In explanations, theory leads us from certain given facts to others that are regarded as their "causes" and are selected out of the vast array of facts observed or inferred. In predictions, theory goes from given facts to their

[13] I recommend as a healthy exercise for students of economics to collect (or invent) additional examples of historical statements of (supposed) facts inferred with the aid of implied theory.

future "effects." In evaluation, theory links facts with systems of values or "ends."

Prediction versus Explanation

If it is as easy as all that, one might wonder why scientists and philosophers have been puzzling throughout the ages about the logical and methodological relationships in question. Let us admit then that we are indulging in great simplifications. But it is better to have vaguely correct ideas about these matters than downright false ones or none at all.

In predictions of future events we believe that we know the conditions and factors at work and can tell what the outcome will be; in explanations of past events what we know is the outcome and we are called upon to tell what were the responsible conditions and the significant factors at work. Thus, logically there is little difference: in the one case, we go forward from causes to effects, in the other, backward from effects to causes. Practically, the difference may be great: it is easy to show that a prediction was wrong —at least, if the timing of the effect was included in the prediction and we can wait long enough—while it may be difficult, if not impossible, to disprove an explanation.

For example, if I make a diagnosis of the situation in the tin industry and then, on the basis of my judgment about all observed, inferred, and anticipated facts and on the basis of my theoretical insight, make the prediction that the price of tin will be at least 20 percent higher within six months, all it takes to prove me wrong is—six months and reliable reports on tin prices. On the other hand, if I observe that tin prices have increased by 20 percent in the last six months and now give an explanation for it, pointing to increased demand and increased production costs, it would not be easy to prove me wrong. It might be possible to prove that production costs have not increased,—which would throw out half of my explanation—but it would be difficult to disprove the asserted increase in demand. If someone should find evidence of a price fixing agreement among the largest tin producers, he could point to it as another explanation of the price increase. But it would be hard to present conclusive proof that the agreement, rather than the demand or cost increase, was the "real" cause and would have caused the price increase in the absence of any increase in demand or cost.[14]

The word "prediction" is often used for merely hypothetical statements. In a real prediction the forecaster assumes the responsibility for all the conditions on which his prediction depends; he says not merely what will happen *if* . . . , but what will happen, *period*. Not so in hypothetical predictions. The practical value of such "iffy" predictions depends on how many ifs are included and how hard it is to find out whether they are actually realized.

Hypothetical Predictions

To say, for example, that sugar prices will fall by at least fifteen percent within a year if the quota restrictions on imports are abolished, may be very helpful advice because it states only one condition, and an easily ascertainable one at that. Less helpful, on the other hand, would be a "prediction" that enumerates many of the conditions on which it depends and leaves it to the "clients" —legislature, administration, business management, general public—to judge for themselves how likely it is that all the listed conditions will be fulfilled. Something like this: "If the quota restrictions on sugar imports are abolished, if the import tariff and the sugar tax are left unchanged, if no great changes occur in the conditions of foreign cane production and of domestic sugar beet production, if transport costs remain the same, if the domestic fruit crops are not substantially increased, if national income does not rise by more than ten percent, and if the income-tax structure is not markedly altered, then we may expect sugar prices to fall by at least fifteen percent within a year." Yet this is still a modest

[14] If in the natural sciences more stress is laid upon prediction than upon explanation, the reason is that they are so much concerned with controlled experiments. Explanations of past events where no checks are possible as to the actual circumstances and operative factors are equally difficult and controversial in the natural and social sciences. To establish beyond doubt or controversy the causes responsible for the explosion of a boiler or a tank or for the collapse of a structure is sometimes as impossible as it is to establish the causes responsible for explosion or collapse in the economy. Several different explanations may fit the data and there is no way of knowing for sure what may have caused things to come out as they did.

example of a conditional prediction; we could easily expand the list of ifs to several times its present length. Moreover, all of the stated conditions are of the ascertainable, or approximately ascertainable, sort, while we could easily add a few where no one could possibly know how to go about finding out whether they were fulfilled or not.

There is a good reason for denying that hypothetical predictions are predictions at all. For we may go on adding necessary conditions until no doubt remains and the outcome is absolutely assured. The last condition to be added, making the "forecast" 100 percent certain, might read: ". . . and if nothing else happens that could interfere with the predicted outcome." This, of course, transforms the statement into a pure tautology, that is, it becomes equivalent to saying that a certain event will occur if and when it occurs. Between a real forecast, or unconditional prediction, on one end and, on the other end, a tautological statement enumerating all the conditions that would make the predicted outcome an absolute certainty, there is a long range of hypothetical statements and it is a matter of methodological taste where one wishes to draw the line between propositions one agrees to call predictions and propositions one refuses to call predictions.[15]

But if the difference between real and hypothetical predictions, or unconditional and conditional forecasts, consists in whether the forecaster bears the responsibility for the fulfillment of all conditions on which the prediction rests or whether he leaves some of them to his "clients" to judge for themselves, one will quickly appreciate that, from the "clients'" point of view, the difference is more or less a formality. For in the end it does not help the "clients" if the forecaster has the self-confidence or the gambling spirit that it takes to assume responsibility for an uncondi-

[15] Some reasonable points for drawing the line:
(a) immediately after the unconditional prediction and before the stipulation of any conditions at all;
(b) between conditional predictions providing only for such conditions as are under our control and propositions providing also for conditions we cannot control;
(c) between conditional predictions providing only for conditions whose realizations we can clearly ascertain before the event and propositions providing also for conditions whose realization we cannot ascertain at all or only after the event.

tional forecast. If it is uncertain whether all the conditions will be satisfied, the cocksureness of the forecaster making an unconditional prediction will not reduce the risk of anybody acting on the basis of this prediction. The really important question is whether we can rely on the forecaster's judgment or our own that all the conditions implied in the unconditional prediction or spelled out in the conditional prediction, respectively, are going to be fulfilled. And this depends on the degree of control we have over the conditions and on the degree of certainty or measure of probability that the conditions we cannot control will nevertheless be realized. Neither of the two is very great in economic affairs. And it is for this reason that economists are better in explaining than in predicting. Nevertheless, any policy recommendations that are made by economists presuppose some degree of confidence in their ability to predict.[16]

Evaluation

Policy recommendations presuppose more than some ability to predict that certain "effects" will follow from certain measures; they presuppose also some ability to compare alternative effects and to know which are preferable. In other words, political economists must also seek to formulate guiding principles for the comparative evaluation of alternative states of affairs.

This statement will be protested by many who have fought hard to keep economics pure, free from "value judgments," cleanly segregated from politics. Their idea is that the economist should merely present his list of probable effects to be expected from alternative policies and let the politician choose from the list. Working under such directives an economist must refrain from saying that free trade or low tariffs are better than high protective tariffs and import prohibitions; that free access to trades and occupations

[16] Perhaps it should be mentioned that prediction in economics is rarely concerned with the actions of *particular* consumers or firms. There is much confusion on this point because we speak of theories of the "individual" consumer and the "individual" firm. But these theories presuppose merely that there are *enough* people who will act in such a way that the results will correspond to the results of the "model action" of the idealized individual.

is preferable to a system of franchises and licences; that a scheme of subsidized production of potatoes with fixed price supports and destruction of the surplus output is undesirable; that price-fixing combinations and industrial monopolies are against the public interest. Of course, the purists who oppose the admission of value judgments into economics will not deny that the economist has the right as a citizen to have and express his ideas about what he likes and what he dislikes—provided that he makes it clear that he speaks as a citizen, not as an economist.

I have much sympathy with this view and with the demand that the economist in his professional work should maintain objectivity and not "take sides." Yet I am not convinced that it can be done with full consistency. Perhaps complete freedom from value judgments in economics can be achieved if a great many things remain unsaid which ought to be said and which only an economist is qualified to say. Many economists, incidentally, believe they have avoided value judgments when they have skirted the words "good" and "bad," "desirable" and "undesirable," or "superior" and "inferior," and instead have spoken only about optimum allocation and misallocation of resources, efficient and wasteful use of resources, or economic and uneconomic organization of production.[17] The implications are that everybody agrees society ought to work economically, efficiently, optimally; that economists need not evaluate this objective but can impartially analyse and report on the ways of approaching it; and that there are standards, not subject to diverse interpretation, by which the optimum and the deviations therefrom can be ascertained. All this, however, is controversial.

Implied Value Judgments

The controversy extends even to such seemingly simple things as an "increase in aggregate real income." According to most economists, the idea of an increase in real income can be distinguished from the idea of an increase in welfare. For any change in income

---

[17] "Misallocation," "inefficient" and "uneconomic" use of resources are understood here to be synonymous. A few writers have developed narrower meanings of "efficiency."

there will probably be *some* members of society who are worse off
while others are better off and, hence, a judgment about *total welfare* implies either that we can measure, compare and add up the
utilities or satisfactions of different persons, or that we have some
objective standards by which to weigh the importance of changes
in income distribution for the total welfare of the community. If
we can do neither and if we thus cannot "objectively" say that an
increase in total real income is equivalent to an increase in total
welfare, we might omit statements about welfare and be satisfied
with the "objectivity" of statements about total real income. But
even this is denied by some economists. For there will probably
be *some* products in the total real income of society of which less
is produced while more is available of others and, hence, a judgment that *total output* on balance has increased implies that we
accept some weights, such as market prices, by which to measure,
compare and add up the values of different goods and services.
But the acceptance of market prices for this purpose involves,
according to these dissenters, certain conventions or hypotheses
that rest on value judgments.[18]

[18] The majority of economists is quite willing to accept market prices for
the purpose of real income measurements without admitting that this implies any value judgments. However, since market prices change over time,
they would employ a double test for the comparison of the incomes of two
periods: the bundle of goods and services of the second period, in order to
deserve a plus sign in the comparison with the first period, must be bigger
in value both on the basis of the prices prevailing in the first period and on
the basis of the prices prevailing in the second period.

Yet, even this test cannot satisfy everybody for it fails to take account of
the effects of income distribution upon prices. The following argument will
explain one of the difficulties. Assume that the value of total output (goods
and services) of Situation II is greater than the value of total output of
Situation I, no matter whether it is calculated in terms of prices of Situation
II or in terms of prices of Situation I. But the change in the composition of
total output may have been associated with a change in the distribution of
income such that some groups of people receive, not only a smaller relative
share of the total, but actually less than before. One might be satisfied with
the "imaginary-compensation test," that is, with estimating whether compensation payments from those who have gained to those who have lost (in
comparison with Situation I) would leave the former still better off after
the latter were fully compensated for their losses. But assume now that
such compensation payments are actually enforced through a system of taxes
and bonuses; that this redistribution of income leads to shifts in demand and,
consequently, changes in prices; and that calculated in terms of these prices

The bearing of all this on the economic theory of monopoly is probably clear.[19] Are we entitled to say in scientific objectivity that the abolition or reduction of monopoly will lead to a more efficient use of resources and thus to an increase in real income? Or does such a statement depend on value judgments? A verdict confirming the suspicion that value judgments are involved would not, however, weaken the case against monopolies, provided the implied value judgments can be ferreted out, made explicit, and shown to be generally accepted; at least the case would hold for all those who are willing to subscribe to the postulated value judgments—as well as to the theories on which the particular argument is based.

An Illustration

Perhaps we should offer an illustration showing how closely pure "causal" analysis and "welfare" analysis are connected in the comparative evaluation of two situations. Assume that a locally produced building material has been generally used by all contractors in a city; that a less expensive out-of-state product becomes available and threatens to replace the local product; that, in order to protect the business of the local producer and the employment of his workers, the use of the substitute material in local building construction is prevented through appropriate "safety regulations"

---

the bundle of goods and services produced in Situation II would be worth less than the output in Situation I. In other words, the comparison between the two bundles of output would depend on whether the changes in income distribution that were associated with the change in output were or were not "undone" through income transfers; output would appear to have decreased in the one case, but increased in the other. To measure real income in terms of prices prevailing without compensation payments to losers is to accept an implicit value judgment to the effect that the subjective valuations by the beneficiaries of a change should win out over the subjective valuations by the losers.

Quite apart from such sophisticated arguments, the use of market prices as weights in the aggregation of heterogeneous goods and services is rejected by most Marxist economists as based on a "bourgeois-capitalist prejudice."

[19] For a thorough and refined treatment of the subject from the point of view of modern welfare analysis see Tibor Scitovsky, *Welfare and Competition* (Chicago: Richard D. Irwin, 1951).

in the building code of the city or by the refusal of local building unions to handle the imported material. If these "monopolistic" interventions by the local government or local trade unions are dropped, benefits will accrue to certain groups of people while others will be harmed. On balance, what will be the effects? How can the economist justify his recommendation that the monopolistic restraints be abolished?

His argument will have to be divided according to several points of view: (1) taking account of all people concerned, those in the state where the new material is produced as well as those in the city; (2) taking account of the city people only; (A) taking account of the long-run effects; (B) taking account of the near future only. Moreover, he will have to consider the possibilities (a) that the displaced city workers will easily find other jobs, almost as good as the ones they lost; (b) that they will find employment only on much less favorable terms; or (c) that they are unfit for any other employment. (All this, incidentally, will be relevant only upon the assumption that the new building material is so much cheaper or better than the city product that the latter, if the new material may be used, could not be sold even at a price barely above direct costs.[20])

Most economists would have no difficulties in recommending against the monopolistic interventions from any points of view if assumption (a) can be made concerning reemployment opportunities. Difficulties begin with assumptions (b) and (c), where serious losses of income to the displaced workers (in addition to the long-run income losses of landlords owing to rent reductions resulting from an increased supply of housing) must be set against the gains of builders, contractors, building laborers, tenants and new home owners in the city, and of workers employed in the production of the new building material outside the city. Theorizing on the basis of (2A)—the long-run interests of the city people alone—will be complicated by the fact that, deducing from balance-of-payments principles, one may anticipate eventually the development and production of some "export item" in the

[20] This assumption is necessary because the city plant ordinarily would not be shut down as long as by continuing operations more than all variable costs (inclusive of the "user cost" of fixed resources) could be earned.

city, which may help to outweigh the losses involved in the displacement of workers. Arguing on the basis of (2Bb) or (2Bc)—only the city, only the short run, with reemployment trouble—the economist may have to concede much to the advocates of restriction, though of course the argument would be explicitly narrow and short-sighted, that is, confined to the effects upon local interests in the near future.

It must be left to the reader to figure out for himself the possibilities and probabilities of the case from the different points of view and upon different assumptions. But it is probably sufficiently clear that all relevant arguments will involve comparisons of alternative situations for different groups of people over different periods of time, comparative evaluations which can be made comprehensive only with the help of economic theories linking changes in prices, production and incomes with changes in the welfare of different people, communities, and generations.

Conflicting Values

Welfare analysis solely in terms of consumable goods and services is not enough. There are also other considerations for the evaluation of the performance of the economic system, and for the comparison of alternative states of affairs. But society is not unanimous with regard to the objectives of its economic organization. It is hard to choose among social goals and it is not possible for society to strive at the same time for the attainment of a maximum of consumable income, of progress, of stability, of employment, of equality, of security, and of freedom. To the extent to which these social goals conflict with one another, compromises will be necessary. But different people attach different degrees of importance to these social goals, and compromises on these matters cannot be reached solely in the market place. These compromises are made through political machinery, though in a very rough and inefficient way.[21] Political scientists and economists have to collaborate on

[21] To illustrate this point: Theoretically it is possible to let the conflict between current consumable income and rate of progress be solved by the savings decisions of individual households and business firms, guided by relative prices and interest rates in conjunction with income anticipations and personal time preferences. But society is not satisfied with such an ar-

the task of evaluating the machinery by which conflicts in the hierarchy of social objectives are ironed out or compromised. The tools of economic theory can to good advantage be applied in the analysis of issues of this sort.

Measurement

The difference between scientific knowledge and knowledge acquired and used in the ordinary business of every-day life is that the former always strives to be clearer, more systematic, more definite and more exact where the latter is vague, unsystematic, indefinite and approximate. From the emphasis on the ideal of greater accuracy has developed a boastful slogan: "Science is Measurement."

"Science is Measurement"

This slogan has had some good and some bad consequences. The good ones are too obvious to call for discussion. The bad ones

rangement and interferes in a variety of ways on behalf of faster progress, that is, on behalf of higher future incomes relative to current consumption. These interventions are through the patent system, by which resources are lured into research and development work; through conservation measures, by which natural resources are kept from current use under the pretense that more should be left for future generations; through inflationary monetary policies, by which credit is created to finance additional investment; through fiscal policies designed (not as counter-cyclical measures, but) to finance government investment in generous amounts and in areas in which competitive enterprise could adequately function (and, paradoxically, at the same time to reduce private saving through sharply progressive tax rates); through direct controls allocating strategic materials for selected investments; etc., etc. The merits and demerits of such policies must be analysed by economists and explained to the public, which in its "selection" of political leaders may exert a modicum of influence on governments.

Perhaps the present author should be allowed to express a value judgment in opposition to most government interventions in the operation of competitive markets. He is an old-fashioned liberal who prefers to leave as much as possible to the anonymous decisions in competitive markets, and as little as possible to decisions by men in power, partly because he is convinced that the interventions are necessarily clumsy and wasteful (and, as a rule, exploited for the benefit of private interests at the expense of the public and almost without regard to social costs), partly because he fears that they seriously encroach upon individual freedom—which in his scale of values holds top place in the hierarchy of objectives.

are that, in an attempt to be "more scientific," people have tried to measure where there was nothing to measure, have slighted important studies where numerical relationships were not of the essence, and have promoted an excessive allocation of intellectual resources to "measurement at all cost" at the expense of other kinds of research and analysis.[22]

To be sure, where a description involves discrete units of any kind of object, it is desirable that they be counted; where a description or a theory involves comparisons of extensive or intensive magnitudes,[23] they should be made in numerical terms; and where a theory involves quantitative relationships, numerical ratios ought to be developed if possible. Yet there are descriptions or theories where none of these operations is relevant or meaningful and attempted measurements are useless or inappropriate.[24]

Some Implications of Measurement

In certain fields of inquiry measurement affects the measured objects or even annihilates them.[25] To what extent, if any, does

[22] "We cannot refuse the name *science* to logic or to the non-quantitative branches of mathematics such as analysis situs, projective geometry, etc. Nor is there good reason for refusing the adjective *scientific* to such works as Aristotle's *Politics* or Spinoza's *Ethics* and applying it to statistical 'investigations' or 'researches' that do not advance the understanding of anything." Morris R. Cohen, *op. cit.*, p. 89.

[23] Extensive magnitudes can be meaningfully added, subtracted, multiplied, and divided; intensive magnitudes cannot. The usual examples of the former are length or weight, and of the latter temperature or hardness. The term "measurement" is used for both, though in somewhat different senses.

[24] "There has been a lot of foolishness connected with this attempt to measure everything. There is, for example, this statement of Lord Kelvin's . . . : 'If you cannot measure, your knowledge is meagre and unsatisfactory.' Its practical meaning tends to be: 'If you cannot measure, measure anyhow.'" Frank H. Knight, on "Quantification: The Quest for Precision" in *Eleven Twenty-Six: A Decade of Social Science Research*, ed. by Louis Wirth (Chicago: University of Chicago Press, 1940), p. 169.

[25] The "Heisenberg principle of uncertainty," concerned with the effects of observation upon the observed, relates to quantum mechanics in physics and the impossibility of determining "position" as well as "momentum" simultaneously. Analogous principles may apply in other fields. Examples of victims of destruction by measurement are photons, mesons, neutrinos. Cf. Henry Margenau, *The Nature of Physical Reality: A Philosophy of Modern Physics* (New York: McGraw-Hill, 1950), p. 373.—Margenau believes that

this apply to economics? One thing seems unavoidable: measurement in economics presupposes that many individuals and organizations make disclosures about their private affairs; hence, their privacy is interfered with and the freedom of the individual may thereby be encroached upon. Often, however, the disclosures are obtained in connection with government interventions that are undertaken for other purposes, so that data for measurement are "by-products" available without any *additional* encroachment upon individual freedom.

Most of the phenomena that are significant for problems of competition and monopoly are *conceivably* measurable, but measurements are practically impossible. Measurements of propensities, preferences and anticipations are surely not feasible on a sufficiently large scale to be helpful in the solution of our problems. But even the most essential magnitudes—prices, costs, sales, profits—cannot be measured with any degree of accuracy.[26] Some of this will become apparent in other parts of this volume, especially in the chapters dealing with operational concepts.

Measurement is sometimes believed to be independent of theory. Some others regard measurement as a prerequisite of theory. This reverses the true roles of the two. Measurement *presupposes theory*, although the latter may be primitive, should be tentative, and frequently is implicit rather than explicit.[27] Of course, measurement may result in the revision, qualification, or disqualification of a theory, but this does not modify the fact that, quite apart from the obvious theoretical foundation of all *indirect* measurements, even "the simplest direct measurements depend upon theoretic assumptions." [28]

---

this applies also to the social sciences: "perfectly good measurement in atomic physics (as well as in biology and in the social sciences) may 'kill' or annihilate a system. . . ." *op. cit.*, p. 377.

[26] On the inherent difficulties in obtaining price and cost data see Fritz Machlup, *The Economics of Sellers' Competition: Model Analysis of Sellers' Conduct* (Baltimore: Johns Hopkins Press, 1952), Chapter 1.

[27] For an illuminating discussion of this issue see Tjalling C. Koopmans, "Measurement Without Theory," *Review of Economics and Statistics*, Vol. XXIX (1947), pp. 161–172.

[28] Morris R. Cohen, *op. cit.*, p. 97.

Fictitious Accuracy

Concepts must be adapted to the purposes for which they are constructed. Revisions of theories may compel re-adaptations of the concepts to which they relate. Moreover, different questions asked about seemingly the same set of phenomena may require slightly different concepts. For example, prices paid by consumers (that is, "delivered prices") may be relevant for one problem while another may refer to prices received by producers (that is, mill-net prices, net of transportation and distribution cost). Clearly, if we need statistical data about prices of certain products, it will make a difference whether they are to be used in one context or another, and theory must be applied in making the choice.

The relativity of the relevance of concepts, and hence of statistical data, is often overlooked; especially when statistics are regularly published, the temptation is great to mistake the data for accurately measured facts. The following example may serve as a warning against such a mistake. Some years ago the Department of Commerce revised several basic concepts and methods of estimation for its statistics of the United States national income (in current dollars, not "real income"). Evidently it had been felt that the concepts previously employed were not relevant to the sort of problems for which national income figures were most frequently demanded and that the changed concepts were more relevant. As a result of the revision, the "national income" of 1945, which had been reported at 161 billion dollars, was raised to 182.8 billion, that is, by 21.8 percent. And while the 1946 "national income" had been above that of 1945 on the basis of the old method, it was below the 1945 income on the basis of the new method.

Even apart from differences in basic definitions and classifications, the discrepancies in the results of repeated or simultaneous measurements of the same so-called economic facts are embarrassingly large.[29] Thus, two different methods of measuring the size of the labor force—both methods used by the U.S. Bureau of the Census for April 1950—resulted in a discrepancy of 3½ mil-

[29] For a veritable chamber of horrors in this class of "statistical findings" see Oskar Morgenstern, *On the Accuracy of Economic Observation* (Princeton: Princeton University Press, 1950), pp. 50–64.

lion people.[30] In the absence of similar control measurements in most of the areas of statistical investigation we do not know the extent to which gross inaccuracies exist in the data available for empirical research and naively regarded as "the facts."

[30] Clarence D. Long, "Discussion: Statistical Standards and the Census," *The American Statistician,* Vol. 6 (1952), p. 11.

ON VERIFICATION AND OPERATIONALISM

INTRODUCTION TO PART THREE

Chapter 5, "The Problem of Verification in Economics," reproduces an article first published in the *Southern Economic Journal*, [22, 1955]. An Italian translation of it appeared in *L'Industria* in 1958 and, a year later, in a monograph on *La verifica delle leggi economiche* [with Terence W. Hutchison and Emile Grunberg] (Milano: Editrice L'Industria, 1959). Two Spanish translations were published, one in the *Revista de Economía Politica*, Vol. 9 in 1958, the other in a collective volume edited by J. Hortala Arau, *Lecturas sobre teoría económica*, Vol. I (Barcelona: Departmento de Teoría Económica, 1969). The article was reprinted in English in *Selected Economic Writings of Fritz Machlup* (New York: New York University Press, 1976).

This chapter discusses the meanings of verification, confirmation, falsification, and disconfirmation of special and general hypotheses; the methodological positions of builders of aprioristic systems, at the one extreme, and of ultra-empiricists, at the other; and the difference between demands for direct tests of fundamental assumptions, or postulates, and for merely indirect tests through checking the correspondence of deduced consequences with observed sequences of events. A novel feature of the exposition is a graphic "model of the use of an analytical apparatus." It shows a "machine of pure theory," which processes an "assumed change" (of an independent variable, considered as the input) into a "deduced change" (of a dependent variable, considered as the output), where input and output may have empirical counterparts in the world of observables, while the machine itself is a mental construction designed for heuristic purposes. It can be tested only by its performance, that is, its yielding conclusions more consistently corresponding with observed changes than alternative machines can do.

Chapter 6, "Operational Concepts and Mental Constructs in Model and Theory Formation," was written in honor of Gustavo del Vecchio and published first in the *Giornale degli Economisti*, Vol. 19, New Series, in 1960. It was reprinted in *Studi di Economia, Finanza e Statistica in Onore di Gustavo del Vecchio* (Padova: Cedam, 1963). It was also included in *Selected Economic Writings of Fritz Machlup* (New York: New York University Press, 1976).

The essay is divided into three sections: I. The Concepts of Physics —dealing chiefly with the demand for operational definitions according to the methodological tenets of Percy Bridgman; II. Empirical Laws and Pure Theory—presenting a list of synonyms and antonyms used by nine different philosophers; III. Construct and Model—showing first the relationships among constructs, models, and theories, then attempting a definition of *construct*, and finally examining the possible reference of mental constructs to observable phenomena.

Chapter 7, "Operationalism and Pure Theory in Economics," was written for a collected volume, edited by Sherman Roy Krupp, *The Structure of Economic Science* (Englewood Cliffs, N.J.: Prentice-Hall, 1966). An Italian translation appeared in *L'Industria* in 1967.

This essay is designed to supplement the preceding one chiefly by providing more illustrations. It offers, for example, a specific theoretical economic argument concerning the effects of a surtax on imports; the argument proceeds in eleven separate steps; then the nature of the concepts employed at each step is examined in order to show which of them have or may conceivably have operational counterparts and which cannot possibly have any such referents; but the main point is that all concepts at every step in the theoretical arguments are pure constructs and are to be nothing but pure constructs if the logical coherence of the argument is to be secured. Operational concepts are needed, first, to help us in the choice of the theoretical apparatus most suitable to deal with particular problems; and second, to help us test the efficiency of the theoretical system chosen.

No textual changes were made in any of the three articles. Perhaps I should have made a few deletions in order to avoid repetition. On the other hand, where the problems discussed are complex, repetition may work as reinforcement and thus serve as an aid to comprehension.

Chapter 5

THE PROBLEM OF VERIFICATION
IN ECONOMICS

I

It will be well for us first to clear the ground lest we get lost in the rubble of past discussions. To clear the ground is, above all, to come to a decision as to what we mean by verification and what it can and cannot do for our research and analysis.

The Meaning of Verification

A good book of synonyms will have the verb "verify" associated with the more pretentious verbs "prove," "demonstrate," "establish," "ascertain," "confirm," and with the more modest verbs "check" and "test." The verbs in the former group would usually be followed by a "that"—"we shall prove that . . ."—the verbs in the latter group by a "whether"—"we shall check whether. . . ." Besides this difference between "verify that" and "verify whether," there is the difference between verification as a process and verification as an affirmative result of that process. By using *"test"* for the former and *"confirmation"* for the latter we may avoid confusion. Where the distinction is not necessary, "verification" is an appropriate weasel-word, meaning both test and confirmation.

Verification in research and analysis may refer to many things including the correctness of mathematical and logical arguments, the applicability of formulas and equations, the trustworthiness of reports, the authenticity of documents, the genuineness of artifacts or relics, the adequacy of reproductions, translations and paraphrases, the accuracy of historical and statistical accounts, the corroboration of reported events, the completeness in the enumeration of circumstances in a concrete situation, the reliability and exactness of observations, the reproducibility of experiments, the explanatory or predictive value of generalizations. For each of these pursuits, the term verification is used in various disciplines. But we intend to confine ourselves to the last one mentioned: the verification of the explanatory or predictive value of hypothetical generalizations.

Although definitions are sometimes a nuisance rather than an aid, I shall try my hand at one, and say that verification in the sense most relevant to us—the

* A paper presented at the Annual Conference of the Southern Economic Association in Biloxi, Mississippi, on November 19, 1954. The author is indebted to several of his colleagues, but chiefly to Dr. Edith Penrose, for criticism and suggestions leading to improvements of style and exposition.

1

testing of generalizations—is *a procedure designed to find out whether a set of data of observation about a class of phenomena is obtainable and can be reconciled with a particular set of hypothetical generalizations about this class of phenomena.*

Truth and Reality

I have carefully avoided the words "truth" and "reality," although the Latin *veritas* forms the root of the term defined. I eschewed references to truth and reality in order to stay out of strictly epistemological and ontological controversies. Not that such discussions would be uninteresting or unimportant; he who never studies metaphysical questions, and even prides himself on his unconcern with metaphysics, often does not know how much in fact he talks about it. To stay away from metaphysics one has to know a good bit about it.

The function of words chosen—testing, checking, confirming—is precisely to enable us to leave the concepts of truth and reality in the background. If I should slip occasionally and say that a proposition is "true" or a phenomenon is "real," this should be taken merely as an unguarded way of speaking; for I mean to say only that there seems to be considerable "support" or "evidence" for the proposition in view of a marked *correspondence* or consistency between that proposition and statements about particular observations.

Special and General Hypotheses

My definition of verification related only to hypothetical generalizations. But the status of *special hypotheses about single events or unique situations* (and their causes, effects, and interrelations) also calls for examination, for it is with these that economic history and most of applied economics are concerned. Such special hypotheses—to establish the "facts"—are of course also subject to verification, but the rules and techniques are somewhat different from those of the verification of general hypotheses.

In a murder case we ask "who done it?" and the answer requires the weighing of several alternative special hypotheses. Such special hypotheses may be mental constructions of unobserved occurrences which could have taken place in conjunction with occurrences observed or conclusively inferred. It is an accepted rule that a special hypothesis will be rejected if it is contradicted by a single inconsistency between a firmly established observation and any of the things that follow logically from the combination of the special hypothesis and the factual assumptions of the argument.

But this weighing and testing of special hypotheses in the light of the known circumstances of the case always involves numerous *general* hypotheses. For example, the generalization that "if a man is at one place he cannot at the same time be at another place" may be of utmost importance in verifying a suspicion that Mr. X was the murderer. And whenever observations have to be interpreted and special hypotheses applied to reach a conclusion about what are the "concrete facts," the argument will presuppose the acceptance of numerous general theories or hypotheses linking two or more (observed or inferred) "facts" as possible (or probable) causes and effects. This is the reason why it has to be said over and over again that most of the facts of history are based on previously formed general hypotheses or theories. Although this has been an important theme in the discussion of the relation between theory and history, and one of the central issues in the *Methodenstreit* in economics, it is not an issue in our discussion today. At the moment we are concerned with the verification of general hypotheses and theories, not of propositions concerning individual events or conditions at a particular time and place. But this much ought to be said here: to establish or verify "historical facts," we must rely on the acceptance of numerous general hypotheses (theories); and to verify general hypotheses we must rely on the acceptance of numerous data representing "facts" observed or inferred at various times and places. We always must take something for granted, no matter how averse we are to "preconceptions."

Theories, Hypotheses, Hunches, Assumptions, Postulates

No fixed lines can be drawn between theories, hypotheses, and mere hunches, the differences being at best those of degree. There are degrees of vagueness in formulation, degrees of confidence or strength of belief in what is posed or stated, degrees of acceptance among experts, and degrees of comprehensiveness or range of applicability.[1]

A hunch is usually vague, sometimes novel, original, often incompletely formulated; perhaps more tentative than a hypothesis, although the difference may lie just in the modesty of the analyst. A hypothesis may likewise be very tentative; indeed, some hypotheses are introduced only for didactic purposes, as provisional steps in an argument, in full knowledge of their inapplicability to any concrete situation and perhaps in preparation for a preferred hypothesis. Distinctions between hypotheses and theories have been suggested in terms of the strength of belief in their applicability or of the comprehensiveness (range) of their applicability.[2] But so often are the words theory and hypothesis used interchangeably that there is not much point in laboring any distinguishing criteria.

Perhaps it should be stressed that every hypothesis may have the status of an "assumption" in a logical argument. An assumption of a rather general nature which is posited as a "principle" for an argument or for a whole system

---

[1] The belief that a "hunch" is something fundamentally different from a "theory" may be responsible for certain antitheoretical positions of some historians and statisticians. Those who claimed the priority and supremacy of fact-finding over "theoretical speculation" might have accepted the contention that you cannot find facts without having some hunch. But this is practically all that the theorists meant when they claimed that theory must precede fact-finding, whether historical or statistical, and that history without theory, and measurement without theory are *impossible*. There are kinds of fact-finding which presuppose full-fledged theories; some simpler kinds may start with vague hunches.

[2] "A hypothesis is an assumption . . . tentatively suggested as an explanation of a phenomenon." Morris R. Cohen and Ernest Nagel, *An Introduction to Logic and Scientific Method* (New York: Harcourt, Brace, 1938), p. 205.—"A hypothesis . . . is . . . a theory which has, at present at least, a limited range of application. It is promoted to the status of a theory if and when its range is deemed sufficiently large to justify this more commendatory appelation." Henry Margenau, "Methodology of Modern Physics," *Philosophy of Science*, Vol. II (January 1935), p. 67.

of thought, but is neither self-evident nor proved, is often called a "postulate." Just as there may be a connotation of tentativeness in the word "hypothesis," there may be a connotation of arbitrariness in the word "postulate."[3] But since no fundamental assumption in an empirical discipline is definitive, and since all are more or less arbitrary, it is useless to insist on subtle distinctions which are (for good reasons) disregarded by most participants in the discussion.[4]

Confirmation versus Non-Disconfirmation

How is a hypothesis verified? The hypothesis is *tested* by a two-step procedure: first deducing from it and the factual assumptions with which it is combined all the conclusions that can be inferred, and second, confronting these conclusions with data obtained from observation of the phenomena concerned. The hypothesis is *confirmed* if reasonable correspondence is found between the deduced and the observed, or more correctly, if no irreconcilable contradiction is found between the deduced and the observed. Absence of contradictory evidence, a finding of non-contradiction, is really a negation of a negation: indeed, one calls a hypothesis "confirmed" when it is merely *not dis*confirmed.

Thus, the procedure of verification may yield findings compelling the rejection of the tested hypothesis, but never findings that can "prove" its correctness, adequacy or applicability.[5] As in a continuing sports championship conducted by elimination rules, where the winner stays in the game as long as he is not defeated but can always be challenged for another contest, no empirical hypothesis is safe forever; it can always be challenged for another test and may be knocked out at any time. The test results, at best, in a "confirmation till next time."

Some logicians, following Popper, use "falsification" for a finding of irreconcilable contradiction; and since a hypothesis can be definitely refuted or "falsified," but not definitely confirmed or "verified," some logicians have urged that we speak only of "falsifiable," not of verifiable propositions. Because the word "falsification" has a double meaning, I prefer to speak of refutation or disconfirmation. But the dictum is surely right: testing an empirical hypothesis results either in its disconfirmation or its non-disconfirmation, never in its definitive confirmation.

[3] Cf. Wayne A. Leeman, "The Status of Facts in Economic Thought," *The Journal of Philosophy*, Vol. XLVII (June 1951), p. 408.—Leeman suggests that economists prefer the term "assumption" because it "escapes . . . the undesirable connotations" of the terms "hypothesis" and "postulate."

[4] "So far as our present argument is concerned, the things (propositions) that we take for granted may be called indiscriminately either hypotheses or axioms or postulates or assumptions or even principles, and the things (propositions) that we think we have established by admissible procedure are called theorems." Joseph A. Schumpeter, *History of Economic Analysis* (New York: Oxford University Press, 1954), p. 15.

[5] There are no rules of verification "that can be relied on in the last resort. Take the most important rules of experimental verification: reproducibility of results; agreement between determinations made by different and independent methods; fulfillment of predictions. These are powerful criteria, but I could give you examples in which they were all fulfilled and yet the statement which they seemed to confirm later turned out to be false. The most striking agreement with experiment may occasionally be revealed later to be based on mere coincidence. . . ." Michael Polanyi, *Science, Faith and Society* (London: Cumberlege, 1946), p. 13.

Even if a definitive confirmation is never possible, the number of tests which a hypothesis has survived in good shape will have a bearing on the confidence people have in its "correctness." A hypothesis confirmed and re-confirmed any number of times will have a more loyal following than one only rarely exposed to the test of experience. But the strength of belief in a hypothesis depends, even more than on any direct empirical tests that it may have survived, on the place it holds within a hierarchical system of inter-related hypotheses. But this is another matter, to be discussed a little later.

Nothing that I have said thus far would, I believe, be objected to by any modern logician, philosopher of science, or scientist. While all points mentioned were once controversial, the combat has moved on to other issues, and only a few stragglers and latecomers on the battlefield of methodology mistake the rubble left from long ago for the marks of present fighting. So we shall move on to issues on which controversy continues.

II

Which kinds of propositions can be verified, and which cannot? May unverified and unverifiable propositions be legitimately retained in a scientific system? Or should all scientific propositions be verified or at least verifiable? These are among the controversial issues—though my own views are so decided that I cannot see how intelligent people can still quarrel about them, and I have come to believe that all good men think as I do, and only a few misguided creatures think otherwise. But I shall restrain my convictions for a while.

Critizing extreme positions is a safe pastime because one may be sure of the support of a majority. But it is not for this reason but for the sake of a clear exposition that I begin with the presentation of the positions which *extreme apriorism*, on the one side, and *ultra-empiricism*, on the other side, take concerning the problem of verification in economics.

Pure, Exact, and Aprioristic Economics

Writers on the one side of this issue contend that economic science is a system of *a priori* truths, a product of pure reason,[6] an exact science reaching laws as universal as those of mathematics,[7] a purely axiomatic discipline,[8] a system of pure deductions from a series of postulates,[9] not open to any verification or refutation on the ground of experience.[10]

---

[6] "The ultimate yardstick of an economic theorem's correctness or incorrectness is solely reason unaided by experience." Ludwig von Mises, *Human Action: A Treatise on Economics* (New Haven: Yale University Press, 1949), p. 858.

[7] "There is a science of economics, a true and even exact science, which reaches laws as universal as those of mathematics and mechanics." Frank H. Knight, "The Limitations of Scientific Method in Economics," in R. G. Tugwell, ed., *The Trend of Economics* (New York: Crofts, 1930), p. 256.

[8] "Economic theory is an axiomatic discipline. . . ." Max Weber, *On the Methodology of the Social Sciences* (Glencoe, Ill.: Free Press, 1949), p. 43.

[9] "Economic analysis . . . consists of deductions from a series of postulates. . . ." Lionel Robbins, *An Essay on the Nature and Significance of Economic Science* (London: Macmillan, 2nd ed., 1935), p. 99.

[10] "What assigns economics its peculiar and unique position in the orbit of pure knowl-

We must not attribute to all writers whose statements were here quoted or paraphrased the same epistemological views. While for Mises, for example, even the fundamental postulates are *a priori* truths, necessities of thinking,[11] for Robbins they are "assumptions involving in some way simple and indisputable facts of experience."[12] But most of the experience in point is not capable of being recorded from external (objective) observation; instead, it is immediate, inner experience. Hence, if verification is recognized only where the test involves objective sense-experience, the chief assumptions of economics, even if "empirical," are not independently verifiable propositions.

This methodological position, either asserting an *a priori* character of all propositions of economic theory or at least denying the independent objective verifiability of the fundamental assumptions, had been vigorously stated in the last century by Senior[13] and Cairnes,[14] but in essential respects it goes back to John Stuart Mill.

Mill, the great master and expositor of inductive logic, had this to say on the method of investigation in political economy:

> Since . . . it is vain to hope that truth can be arrived at, either in Political Economy or in any other department of the social science, while we look at the facts in the concrete, clothed in all the complexity with which nature has surrounded them, and endeavor to elicit a general law by a process of induction from a comparison of details; there remains no other method than the *a priori* one, or that of 'abstract speculation.'[15]
>
> By the method *a priori* we mean . . . reasoning from an assumed hypothesis; which is not a practice confined to mathematics, but is of the essence of all science which admits of general reasoning at all. To verify the hypothesis itself *a posteriori*, that is, to examine whether the facts of any actual case are in accordance with it, is no part of the business of science at all but of the *application* of science.[16]

This does not mean that Mill rejects attempts to verify the results of economic analysis; on the contrary,

> We cannot . . . too carefully endeavor to verify our theory, by comparing, in the particular cases to which we have access, the results which it would have led us to predict, with the most trustworthy accounts we can obtain of those which have been actually realized.[17]

edge and of the practical utilization of knowledge is the fact that its particular theorems are not open to any verification or falsification on the ground of experience." Ludwig von Mises, *op. cit.*, p. 858.

   [11] Ludwig von Mises, *op. cit.*, p. 33.

   [12] Lionel Robbins, *op. cit.*, p. 78, also pp. 99–100.

   [13] Nassau William Senior, *Political Economy* (London: Griffin, 3rd ed., 1854), pp. 5, 26–29.

   [14] John E. Cairnes, *The Character and Logical Method of Political Economy* (London: Macmillan, 1875), especially pp. 74–85, 99–100.

   [15] John Stuart Mill, "On the Definition of Political Economy; and on the Method of Investigation Proper to It" in *Essays on Some Unsettled Questions of Political Economy* (London, 1844, reprinted London School of Economics, 1948), pp. 148–49.

   [16] *Ibid.*, p. 143.

   [17] *Ibid.*, p. 154.

The point to emphasize is that Mill does not propose to put the *assumptions* of economic theory to empirical tests, but only the *predicted results that are deduced from them*. And this, I submit, is what all the proponents of pure, exact, or aprioristic economic theory had in mind, however provocative their contentions sounded.[18] Their objection was to verifying the basic assumptions in isolation.

Ultra-Empirical Economics

Opposed to these tenets are the ultra-empiricists. "Empiricist" is a word of praise to some, a word of abuse to others. This is due to the fact that there are many degrees of empiricism. Some economists regard themselves as "empiricists" merely because they oppose radical apriorism and stress the dependence of theory on experience (in the widest sense of the word); others, because they demand that the results deduced with the aid of theory be compared with observational data whenever possible; others, because they are themselves chiefly concerned with the interpretation of data, with the testing of hypotheses and with the estimates of factual relationships; others, because they are themselves engaged in the collection of data or perhaps even in "field" work designed to produce "raw" data; others, because they refuse to recognize the legitimacy of employing at any level of analysis propositions not independently verifiable. It is the last group which I call the ultra-empiricists.[19] Then there are the ultra-ultra-empiricists who go even further and insist on independent verification of all assumptions by objective data obtained through sense observation.

The ultra-empiricist position is most sharply reflected in the many attacks on the "assumptions" of economic theory. These assumptions are decried as unverified, unverifiable, imaginary, unrealistic. And the hypothetico-deductive system built upon the unrealistic or unverifiable assumptions is condemned either as deceptive or as devoid of empirical content,[20] without predictive or

---

[18] "Aprioristic reasoning is purely conceptual and deductive. It cannot produce anything else but tautologies and analytic judgments." While this sounds like an "empiricist's" criticism of the aprioristic position, it is in fact a statement by Mises. (*Op. cit.*, p. 38.) Mises emphasizes that "the end of science is to know reality," and that "in introducing assumptions into its reasoning, it satisfies itself that the treatment of the assumptions concerned can render useful services for the comprehension of reality." (*Ibid.*, pp. 65–66.) And he stresses that the choice of assumptions is directed by experience.

[19] It is in this last meaning that empiricisms has usually been discussed and criticized in philosophy. In the words of William James, radical empiricism "must neither admit into its constructions any element that is not directly experienced, nor exclude from them any element that is directly experienced. For such a philosophy, *the relations that connect experiences must themselves be experienced relations, and any kind of relation experienced must be accounted as 'real' as anything else in the system.*" William James, *Essays in Radical Empiricism* (New York: Longmans, Green, 1912), pp. 42–43.

[20] "That 'propositions of pure theory' is a name for . . . propositions not conceivably falsifiable empirically and which do not exclude . . . any conceivable occurrence, and which are therefore devoid of empirical content. . . ." T. W. Hutchison, *The Significance and Basic Postulates of Economic Theory* (London: Macmillan, 1938), p. 162.

explanatory significance,[21] without application to problems or data of the real world.[22] Why deceptive? Because from wrong assumptions only wrong conclusions follow. Why without empirical significance? Because, in the words of the logician Wittgenstein, "from a tautology only tautologies follow."[23]

If the ultra-empiricists reject the basic assumptions of economic theory because they are not independently verified, and reject any theoretical system that is built on unverified or unverifiable assumptions, what is the alternative they offer? A program that begins with facts rather than assumptions.[24] What facts? Those obtained "by statistical investigations, questionnaires to consumers and entrepreneurs, the examination of family budgets and the like."[25] It is in research of this sort that the ultra-empiricists see "the only possible scientific method open" to the economist.[26]

This, again, is the essence of the ultra-empiricist position on verification: the ultra-empiricist is so distrustful of deductive systems of thought that he is not satisfied with the indirect verification of hypotheses, that is, with tests showing that the results deduced (from these hypotheses and certain factual assumptions) are in approximate correspondence with reliable observational data; instead, he insists on the independent verification of all the assumptions, hypothetical as well as factual, perhaps even of each intermediate step in the analysis. To him "testable" means "directly testable by objective data obtained by sense observation," and propositions which are in this sense "non-testable" are detestable to him.

The Testability of Fundamental Assumptions

The error in the antitheoretical empiricist position lies in the failure to see the difference between *fundamental* (heuristic) hypotheses, which are not inde-

[21] ". . . that propositions of pure theory, by themselves, have no prognostic value or 'causal significance.'" T. W. Hutchison, *op. cit.*, p. 162.—The clause "by themselves" makes Hutchison's statement unassailable, because nothing at all has causal significance by itself; only in conjunction with other things can anything have causal significance. But if Hutchison's statement means anything, it means an attack against the use of empirically unverifiable propositions in economic theory, regardless of their conjunction with other propositions. Indeed, he states that "a proposition which can never *conceivably* be shown to be true or false . . . can *never* be of any use to a scientist" (*ibid.*, pp. 152–53).

[22] With regard to the "fundamental assumption" of economic theory concerning "subjectively rational" and "maximizing" behavior, Hutchison states that "the empirical content of the assumption and all the conclusions will be the same—that is, nothing." *Ibid.*, p. 116.

[23] Ludwig Wittgenstein, *Tractatus Logico-Philosophicus* (London: Routledge & Kegan Paul, 1951), p. 167.

[24] ". . . if one wants to get beyond a certain high level of abstraction one has to begin more or less from the beginning with extensive empirical investigation." T. W. Hutchison, *op. cit.*, p. 166.

[25] *Ibid.*, p. 120. This does not answer the question: "what facts?" Precisely what data should be obtained and statistically investigated? What questions asked of consumers and entrepreneurs?

[26] *Ibid.*, p. 120. I could have quoted from dozens of critics of economic theory, from adherents of the historical, institutional, quantitative schools, and these quotations might be even more aggressive. I have selected Hutchison because he is the critic best informed about logic and scientific method.

pendently testable, and *specific* (factual) assumptions, which are supposed to correspond to observed facts or conditions; or the differences between hypotheses on different levels of generality and, hence, of different degrees of testability.

The fundamental hypotheses are also called by several other names, some of which convey a better idea of their methodological status: "heuristic principles" (because they serve as useful guides in the analysis), "basic postulates" (because they are not to be challenged for the time being), "useful fictions" (because they need not conform to "facts" but only be useful in "as if" reasoning), "procedural rules" (because they are resolutions about the analytical procedure to be followed), "definitional assumptions" (because they are treated like purely analytical conventions).

A fundamental hypothesis serves to bring together under a common principle of explanation vast numbers of very diverse observations, masses of data of apparently very different sort, phenomena that would otherwise seem to have nothing in common. Problems like the explanation of the movements in wages in 13th and 14th century Europe, of the prices of spices in 16th century Venice, of the effects of the capital flows to Argentina in the 19th century, of the consequences of German reparation payments and of the devaluation of the dollar in the 1930's; problems like the prediction of effects of the new American quota on Swiss watches, of the new tax laws, of the increase in minimum wage rates, and so forth,—problems of such dissimilarity can all be tackled by the use of the same fundamental hypotheses. If these hypotheses are successful in this task and give more satisfactory results than other modes of treatment could, then we accept them and stick by them as long as there is nothing better—which may be forever.

That there is no way of subjecting fundamental assumptions to independent verification should be no cause of disturbance. It does not disturb the workers in the discipline which most social scientists so greatly respect and envy for its opportunities of verification: physical science. The whole system of physical mechanics rests on such fundamental assumptions: Newton's three laws of motion are postulates or procedural rules for which no experimental verification is possible or required; and, as Einstein put it, "No one of the assumptions can be isolated for separate testing." For, he went on to say, "physical concepts are free creations of the human mind, and are not, however it may seem, uniquely determined by the external world."[27]

Much has been written about the meaning of "explanation." Some have said that the mere *description* of regularities in the co-existence and co-variation of observed phenomena is all we can do and will be accepted as an *explanation* when we are sufficiently used to the regularities described.[28] There is something to this view; but mere resignation to the fact that "it always has been so" will not for long pass as explanation for searching minds. The feeling of relief and satisfied curiosity—often expressed in the joyous exclamation "ah haahh!"— comes to most analysts only when the observed regularities can be deduced from

[27] Albert Einstein and Leopold Infeld, *The Evolution of Physics* (New York: Simon and Schuster, 1938), p. 33.

[28] Cf. P. W. Bridgman, *The Logic of Modern Physics* (New York: Macmillan, 1927), p. 43.

general principles which are also the starting point—foundation or apex, as you like—of many other chains of causal derivation. This is why Margenau, another physicist, said that an explanation involves a "progression into the constructional domain. We explain by going 'beyond phenomena.' "[29] But this clearly implies that the explanatory general assumptions cannot be empirically verifiable in isolation.

Logicians and philosophers of science have long tried to make this perfectly clear. Although appeals to authority are ordinarily resorted to only where an expositor has failed to convince his audience, I cannot resist the temptation to quote two authorities on my subject. Here is how the American philosopher Josiah Royce put it:

> One often meets with the remark that a scientific hypothesis must be such as to be more or less completely capable of verification or of refutation by experience. The remark is sound. But equally sound it is to say that a hypothesis which, just as it is made, is, without further deductive reasoning, capable of receiving direct refutation or verification, *is not nearly as valuable to any science as is a hypothesis whose verifications, so far as they occur at all, are only possible indirectly, and through the mediation of a considerable deductive theory,* whereby the consequences of the hypothesis are first worked out, and then submitted to test.[30]

And here is the same idea in the words of the British philosopher of science, Richard B. Braithwaite:

> For science, as it advances, does not rest content with establishing simple generalizations from observable facts. It tries to explain these lowest-level generalization by deducing them from more general hypotheses at a higher level. . . . As the hierarchy of hypotheses of increasing generality rises, the concepts with which the hypotheses are concerned cease to be properties of things which are directly observable, and instead become 'theoretical' concepts—atoms, electrons, fields of force, genes, unconscious mental processes—which are connected to the observable facts by complicated logical relationships.[31]

And he states that "the empirical testing of the deductive system is effected by testing the lowest-level hypotheses in the system."[32]

Assumptions in Economics, Pure and Applied

Examples of *fundamental assumptions* or "high-level generalizations" in economic theory are that people act rationally, try to make the most of their opportunities, and are able to arrange their preferences in a consistent order; that entrepreneurs prefer more profit to less profit with equal risk.[33] These are

---

[29] Henry Margenau, *The Nature of Physical Reality* (New York: McGraw-Hill, 1950), p. 169.

[30] Josiah Royce, "The Principles of Logic," in *Logic, Encyclopaedia of the Philosophical Sciences*, Vol. I (London: Macmillan, 1913), pp. 88–89.

[31] Richard Bevan Braithwaite, *Scientific Explanation: A Study of the Function of Theory, Probability and Law in Science* (Cambridge: University Press, 1953), p. ix.

[32] *Ibid.*, p. 13.

[33] For most problems of an enterprise economy no exact specifications about "profit"

assumptions which, though empirically meaningful, require no independent empirical tests but may be significant steps in arguments reaching conclusions which are empirically testable.

Examples of *specific assumptions* are that the expenditures for table salt are a small portion of most households' annual budgets; that the member banks are holding very large excess reserves with the Federal Reserve Banks; that there is a quota for the importation of sugar which is fully utilized. Examples of *deduced "low-level hypotheses"* are that a reduction in the price of table salt will not result in a proportionate increase in salt consumption; that a reduction in the discount rates of the Federal Reserve Banks will at such times not result in an increase in the member banks' lending activities; that a reduction in sugar prices abroad will not result in a reduction of domestic sugar prices. All these and similar specific assumptions and low-level hypotheses are empirically testable.

Perhaps a few additional comments should be made concerning the fundamental assumptions, particularly the postulate of rational action, the "economic principle" of aiming at the attainment of a maximum of given ends. Any independent test of this assumption by reference to objective *sense*-experience is obviously impossible. Those who accept findings of introspection as sufficient evidence may contend that the fundamental assumption can be, and constantly is, verified. Those who accept findings of interrogation (that is, replies to questions put to large numbers of introspectors) as "objective" evidence may contend that the assumption of "maximizing behavior" is independently testable. But such a test would be gratuitous, if not misleading. For the fundamental assumption may be understood as an idealization with constructs so far removed from operational concepts that contradiction by testimony is ruled out; or even as a complete fiction with only one claim: that reasoning *as if* it were realized is helpful in the interpretation of observations.[34]

Economists who are still suspicious of non-verifiable assumptions, and worry about the legitimacy of using them, may be reassured by this admission: The fact that fundamental assumptions are not directly testable and cannot be refuted by empirical investigation does not mean that they are beyond the pale of the so-called "principle of permanent control," that is, beyond possible challenge, modification or rejection. These assumptions may well be rejected, but only together with the theoretical system of which they are a part, and only when a more satisfactory system is put in its place; in Conant's words, "a theory is only overthrown by a better theory, never merely by contradictory facts."[35]

(whose? for what period? how uncertain? etc.) will be needed. There are some special problems for which "specific assumptions" concerning profit are needed. Needless to say, the assumption about entrepreneurs will be irrelevant for problems of centrally directed economies.

[34] Or, again in a different formulation: the fundamental assumption is a resolution to proceed in the interpretation of all data of observation as if they were the result of the postulated type of behavior.

[35] James B. Conant, *On Understanding Science* (New Haven: Yale University Press, 1947), p. 36.

III

What I have said and quoted about assumptions and hypotheses on various "levels" of abstraction may itself be too abstract, too remote from our ordinary terms of discourse, to be meaningful to many of us. Perhaps it will be helpful to try a graphical presentation of a simple model of an analytical system combining assumptions of various types.

A Model of an Analytical Apparatus

The design for the model was suggested by the usual metaphors about an analytical "apparatus," "machine," or "engine of pure theory." Something goes into a machine and something comes out. In this case the input is an assumption concerning some "change" occurring and causing other things to happen, and the output is the "Deduced Change," the conclusion of the (mental) operation. The machine with all its parts furnishes the connection between the "assumed cause," the input, and the "deduced effect," the outcome. The main point of this model is that *the machine is a construction of our mind, while the assumed and deduced changes should correspond to observed phenomena, to data of observation, if the machine is to serve as an instrument of explanation or prediction.* In explanations the analytical machine helps select an adequate "cause" for an observed change; in predictions it helps find a probable "effect" of an observed change.[36]

The machine consists of many parts, all of which represent assumptions or hypotheses of different degrees of generality. The so-called *fundamental assumptions* are a fixed part of the machine; they make the machine what it is; they cannot be changed without changing the character of the entire machine. All other parts are exchangeable, like coils, relays, spools, wires, tapes, cylinders, records, or mats, something that can be selected and put in, and again taken out to be replaced by a different piece of the set. These exchangeable parts represent *assumptions about the conditions* under which the Assumed Change must operate. Some of the parts are exchanged all the time, some less frequently, some only seldom. Parts of type A, the Assumed Conditions as to "type of case," are most frequently exchanged. Parts of type B, the Assumed Conditions as to "type of setting," will stay in the machine for a longer time and there need be less variety in the set from which they are selected. Parts of type C, the Assumed Conditions as to "type of economy," are least exchangeable, and there will be only a small assortment of alternative pieces to choose from.

Now we shall leave the engineering analogies aside and discuss the status of all these assumptions regarding the operational and observational possibilities and the requirements of verification.

Verified Changes under Unverified Conditions

Both the Assumed Change and the Deduced Change should be empirically verifiable through correspondence with data of observation. At least one of the two has to be verifiable if the analysis is to be applied to concrete cases. Hence

---

[36] On the problem of prediction versus explanation see the chapter on "Economic Fact and Theory" in my book *The Political Economy of Monopoly* (Baltimore: Johns Hopkins Press, 1952), pp. 455 ff.

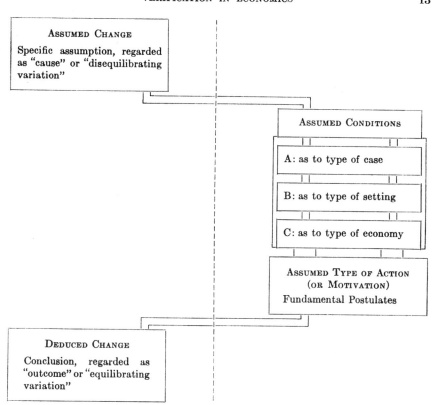

FIG. 1. A MODEL OF THE USE OF AN ANALYTICAL APPARATUS

On the right side is the "machine of pure theory," a mental *construction* for heuristic purposes; on the left side are assumptions of independent and dependent variables whose *correspondence* with data of observation may be tested.

the concepts employed to describe the changes should, if possible, be operational. This raises no difficulty in the case of most kinds of *Assumed Change* in whose effects we are interested, for example: changes in tax rates, customs duties, foreign-exchange rates, wage rates, price supports, price ceilings, discount rates, open-market policies, credit lines, government expenditures, agricultural crops—matters covered in reports and records. There are difficulties concerning some other kinds of Assumed Change, such as improvements in technology, greater optimism, changed tastes for particular goods—things for which recorded data are often unavailable. As regards the *Deduced Change* the requirement that it be operational will usually be met, because we are interested chiefly in effects upon prices, output, income, employment, etc.,—magnitudes reported in statistical series of some sort. To be sure, the figures may be unreliable and the statistical concepts may not be exact counterparts to the analytical concepts, but we cannot be too fussy and must be satisfied with what we can get.

In principle we want both Assumed Change and Deduced Change to be capable of being compared with recorded data so that the correspondence between the theory and the data can be checked. The analysis would be neither wrong nor invalid, but it would not be very useful if it were never possible to identify the concrete phenomena, events, and situations, to which it is supposed to apply. Once we have confidence in the whole theoretical system, we are willing to apply it to concrete cases even where only one of the two "changes," either the "cause" or the "effect," is identifiable in practice, rather than both. For example, we are prepared to base policy decisions on explanations or predictions where one of the phenomena cannot be isolated in observation from the complex of simultaneous variations. For purposes of verification of the entire theory, however, we shall have to identify both the phenomena represented by the Assumed Change and the Deduced Change—although such verification may be practical only on rare occasions.

We need not be particularly strict concerning the verification of the *Assumed Conditions*. Regarding them, a casual, perhaps even impressionistic empiricism will do, at least for most types of problems. The Assumed Conditions refer to personal characteristics, technological or organizational circumstances, market forms, enduring institutions—things of rather varied nature. Few of the Conditions are observable, except through communication of interpretations involving a good deal of theorizing by the parties concerned. Often the Conditions are not even specified in detail, but somehow taken for granted by analysts working in a familiar milieu. All of the Conditions are hypothetical parameters, assumed to prevail at least for the duration of the process comprising all the actions, interactions and repercussions through which the Assumed Change is supposed to cause the Deduced Change.

Assumed Conditions of Type A, that is, as to *"type of case,"* refer to conditions which may vary from case to case and influence the outcome significantly, but are sufficiently common to justify the construction of "types" for theoretical analysis. Here is a list of examples: type of goods involved (durable, non-durable, perishable; inferior, non-inferior; taking up substantial or negligible parts of buyer's budget; substitutable, complementary; etc.); cost conditions (marginal cost decreasing, constant, increasing; joint costs, etc.); elasticity of supply or demand (positive, negative, relatively large, unity, less than unity); market position (perfect, imperfect polypoly; collusive, uncoordinated oligopoly; perfect, imperfect monopoly); entry (perfect, imperfect pliopoly); expectations (elastic, inelastic; bullish, bearish; certain, uncertain); consumption propensity (greater, smaller than unity); elasticity of liquidity preference (infinite, less than infinite, zero).

Assumed Conditions of Type B, that is, as to "type of setting," refer to conditions which may change over brief periods of time—say, with a change of government or of the political situation, or during the business cycle—and are apt to influence the outcome in definite directions. A list of examples will indicate what is meant by conditions prevailing under the current "setting": general business outlook (boom spirit, depression pessimism); bank credit availability (banks loaned up, large excess reserves); central bank policy (ready to monetize government securities, determined to maintain easy money policy, willing to let interest rates rise); fiscal policy (expenditures fixed, adjusted to tax revenues, geared to unemployment figures; tax rates fixed, adjusted to maintain revenue, etc.); farm program (support prices fixed, flexible within limits, etc.); antitrust policy (vigorous prosecution of cartelization, etc.); foreign aid program; stabilization fund rules; trade union policies.

Assumed Conditions of Type C, that is, as to *"type of economy,"* refer to conditions which may vary from country to country and over larger periods of time, but may be assumed to be "settled" for a sufficiently large number of cases to justify taking these conditions as constant. Examples include legal and social institutions; private property; freedom of contract; corporation law; patent system; transportation system; enforcement of contracts; ethics of law violations; social customs and usages; monetary system (gold standard, check system, cash holding habits).

Assumed Conditions are exchangeable because the effects of an Assumed Change may have to be analysed under a variety of conditions: for example, with different degrees or forms of competition, different credit policies, different tax structures, different trade union policies, etc. But it may also be expedient, depending on the problem at hand, to regard a variation of an Assumed Condition as an Assumed Change, and *vice versa.* For example, the problem may concern the effects of a wage rate increase under various market conditions or, instead, the effects of a change in market position under conditions of automatic wage escalation; the effects of a change in monetary policy with different tax structure, or the effects of a change in the tax structure under different monetary policies.

After listing the many examples of the various types of Assumed Conditions it will probably be agreed that a rigid verification requirement would be out of place. Usually the judgment of the analyst will suffice even if he cannot support it with more than the most circumstantial evidence or mere "impressions." Suppose he deals with a simple cost-price-output problem in a large industry, how will the analyst determine what "type of case" it is with regard to "market position?" Lacking the relevant information, he may first try to work with a model of perfect polypoly[37]—although he knows well that this cannot fit the real situation—and will note whether his deduced results will be far off the mark. He may find the results reasonably close to the observed data and may leave it at that. For to work with a more "realistic" assumption may call for so many additional assumptions for which no relevant information is available that it is preferable and unobjectionable to continue with a hypothesis contrary to fact. When a simpler hypothesis, though obviously unrealistic, gives consistently

[37] Under perfect polypoly the individual seller assumes that his own supply will not affect any other seller or the market as a whole and, thus, that he could easily sell more at the same price and terms. This condition was also called "pure competition," "perfect competition," or "perfect market" (although it has little to do with any effort of "competing" or with any property of the "market"). See Fritz Machlup, *The Economics of Sellers' Competition* (Baltimore: Johns Hopkins Press, 1952), pp. 85–91, and pp. 116 ff.

satisfactory results, one need not bother with more complicated, more realistic hypotheses.

Ideal Type of Action, Unverified but Understood

While solid empirical verification is indicated for the Assumed Change, and casual empirical judgments are indicated for the Assumed Conditions, the *Assumed Type of Action* forms the fundamental postulates of economic analysis and thus is not subject to a requirement of independent verification.

Various names have been suggested for the fundamental postulates of economic theory: "economic principle," "maximization principle," "assumption of rationality," "law of motivation," and others. And their logical nature has been characterized in various ways: they are regarded as "self-evident propositions," "axioms," "*a priori* truths," "truisms," "tautologies," "definitions," "rigid laws," "rules of procedure," "resolutions," "working hypotheses," "useful fictions," "ideal types," "heuristic mental constructs," "indisputable facts of experience," "facts of immediate experience," "data of introspective observation," "private empirical data," "typical behavior patterns," and so forth.

Some of these characterizations are equivalent to or consistent with each other, but some are not. How can a proposition be both *a priori* and empirical, both a definition and a fact of experience? While this cannot be, the distinctions in this particular instance are so fine that conflicts of interpretation seem unavoidable. Logicians have long debated the possibility of propositions being synthetic and yet *a priori*, and physicists are still not quite agreed whether the "laws" of mechanics are analytical definitions or empirical facts. The late philosopher Felix Kaufmann introduced as a middle category the so-called "rules of procedure," which are neither synthetic in the sense that they are falsifiable by contravening observations nor *a priori* in the sense that they are independent of experience;[38] they are and remain accepted as long as they have heuristic value, but will be rejected in favor of other rules (assumptions) which seem to serve their explanatory functions more successfully.

If this debate has been going on in the natural sciences, how could it be avoided in the social sciences? If issues about "self-evident," "inescapable," or "indisputable" insights arose concerning the physical world, how much more pertinent are such issues in the explanation of human action, where man is both observer and subject of observation! This, indeed, is the essential difference between the natural and the social sciences: that in the latter the facts, the data of "observation," are themselves results of interpretations of human actions by human actors.[39] And this imposes on the social sciences a requirement which does not

[38] Felix Kaufmann, *Methodology of the Social Sciences* (New York: Oxford University Press, 1944), pp. 77 ff, especially pp. 87–88.

[39] ". . . the object, the 'facts' of the social sciences are also opinions—not opinions of the student of the social phenomena, of course, but opinions of those whose actions produce his object. . . . They [the facts] differ from the facts of the physical sciences in being . . . beliefs which are as such our data . . . and which, moreover, we cannot directly observe in the minds of the people but recognize from what they do and say merely because we have

exist in the natural sciences: that all types of action that are used in the abstract models constructed for purposes of analysis be "understandable" to most of us in the sense that we could conceive of sensible men acting (sometimes at least) in the way postulated by the ideal type in question. This is the crux of Max Weber's methodology of the social sciences, and was recently given a refined and most convincing formulation by Alfred Schuetz.[40]

Schuetz promulgates three postulates guiding model construction in the social sciences: the postulates of "logical consistency," of "subjective interpretation," and of "adequacy." The second and third of these postulates are particularly relevant here:

> In order to explain human actions the scientist has to ask what model of an individual mind can be constructed and what typical contents must be attributed to it in order to explain the observed facts as the result of the activity of such a mind in an understandable relation. The compliance with this postulate warrants the possibility of referring all kinds of human action or their result to the subjective meaning such action or result of an action had for the actor.
>
> Each term in a scientific model of human action must be constructed in such a way that a human act performed within the life world by an individual actor in the way indicated by the typical construct would be understandable for the actor himself as well as for his fellowmen in terms of common-sense interpretation of everyday life. Compliance with this postulate warrants the consistency of the constructs of the social scientist with the constructs of common-sense experience of the social reality.[41]

Thus, the fundamental assumptions of economic theory are not subject to a requirement of independent empirical verification, but instead to a requirement of understandability in the sense in which man can understand the actions of fellowmen.[42]

IV

We are ready to summarize our conclusions concerning verification of the assumptions of economic theory. Then we shall briefly comment on the verification of particular economic theories applied to predict future events, and on the verification of strictly empirical hypotheses.

Verifying the Assumptions

First to summarize: We need not worry about independent verifications of the fundamental assumptions, the Assumed Type of Action; we need not be

---

ourselves a mind similar to theirs." F. A. v. Hayek, "Scientism and the Study of Society," *Economica, New Series*, Vol. V (August 1942), p. 279. Reprinted F. A. v. Hayek, *The Counter-Revolution of Science* (Glencoe, Ill.: Free Press, 1952).

[40] Alfred Schuetz, "Common-Sense and Scientific Interpretation of Human Action," *Philosophy and Phenomenological Research*, Vol. XIV (September 1953), pp. 1–38. *Idem.*, "Concept and Theory Formation in the Social Sciences," *The Journal of Philosophy*, Vol. LI (April 1954), pp. 257–273.

[41] Schuetz, "Common-Sense, etc.," p. 34.

[42] Disregard of this requirement is, in my view, the only serious flaw in the otherwise excellent essay on "The Methodology of Positive Economics" by Milton Friedman, *Essays in Positive Economics* (Chicago: University of Chicago Press, 1953), pp. 3–43.

very particular about the independent verifications of the other intervening assumptions, the Assumed Conditions, because judgment based on casual empiricism will suffice for them; we should insist on strict independent verifications of the assumption selected as Assumed Change and of the conclusion derived as Deduced Change; not that the theory would be wrong otherwise, but it cannot be applied unless the phenomena to which it is supposed to apply are identifiable. *Simultaneous verifications of Assumed Change and Deduced Change count as verification—in the sense of non-disconfirmation—of the theory as a whole.*

Now it is clear why some writers insisted on the *a priori* nature of the theory and at the same time on its empirical value for the area of Applied Economics; for one may, if one wishes, regard the theory, or model, as a construction *a priori*, and the directions for its use, the instructions for its applications,[43] as an empirical appendage in need of verification. Returning to the analogy of the analytical machine, one may say that the machine and its parts are always "correct," regardless of what goes on around us, whereas the *choice* of the exchangeable parts and the *identification* of the events corresponding to the Assumed and Deduced changes may be wrong.

Testing the Predictive Values of Theories

We have examined the empiricists' charges against the theorists—charges of contemptuous neglect of the requirement of verification—and have concluded that these charges must be dismissed insofar as they refer to a failure to verify all assumptions directly and in isolation from the rest of the theory. We must yet examine another count of the charge of insufficient attention to verification: an alleged failure to test the correspondence between Deduced (predicted) and Observed outcomes. These kinds of tests are obligatory.

If verification of a theory takes the form of testing whether predictions based on that theory actually come true, one might think that this can be done in economics no less than in the physical sciences. It cannot, alas, because of the non-reproducibility of the "experiments" or observed situations and courses of events in the economy. For, while certain types of events, or "changes," recur in the economy often enough, they recur rarely under the same conditions. If some significant circumstances are different whenever a phenomenon of the same class recurs, each recurrence is virtually a "single occurrence." Economic theory applied to single events, or to situations significantly different from one another, cannot be tested as conclusively as can physical theory applied to reproducible occurrences and conditions.

Not long ago I was challenged to admit that my theories, even though applied to ever-changing circumstances, could be tested provided I were prepared to make unconditional predictions which could be compared with actual outcomes. Of course, I could only dare make unconditional predictions—without hedging about probability and confidence limits—where I was absolutely certain that my diagnosis of the situation (i.e., of *all* relevant circumstances) *and* my foreknowl-

---

[43] Cf. Milton Friedman, *op. cit.*, pp. 24–25.

edge of government and power group actions *and* the theory on which the prediction rests were all perfectly correct. Suppose that I was so foolhardy as to be sure of all this and that I did make a number of unconditional predictions. Still, unless reliable checks were possible to verify separately every part of my diagnosis and of my anticipations regarding government and power group actions, my theory could not be tested. There could be lucky "hits" where wrong diagnoses would compensate for mistakes due to bad theories; there could be unlucky "misses" where wrong diagnoses spoiled the results of good theorizing. Despite a large number of good hits the theories in question could not be regarded as confirmed, even in the modest sense of not being disconfirmed, because a joint and inseparable test of diagnosis, anticipations, and theory says nothing about the theory itself.

Where the economist's prediction is *conditional*, that is, based upon specified conditions, but where it is not possible to check the fulfillment of all the conditions stipulated, the underlying theory cannot be disconfirmed whatever the outcome observed. Nor is it possible to disconfirm a theory where the prediction is made with a stated *probability* value of less than 100 percent; for if an event is predicted with, say, 70 percent probability, any kind of outcome is consistent with the prediction.[44] Only if the same "case" were to occur hundreds of times could we verify the stated probability by the frequency of "hits" and "misses."

This does not mean complete frustration of all attempts to verify our economic theories. But it does mean that the tests of most of our theories will be more nearly of the character of *illustrations* than of verifications of the kind possible in relation with repeatable controlled experiments or with recurring fully-identified situations. And this implies that our tests cannot be convincing enough to compel acceptance, even when a majority of reasonable men in the field should be prepared to accept them as conclusive, and to approve the theories so tested as "not disconfirmed," that is, as "O. K."

Strictly Empirical Hypotheses

All this seems to circumscribe rather narrowly the scope of empirical verification, if not empirical research, in economics. But to draw such a conclusion would be rash. For there is a large body of economics apart from its theoretical or "hypothetico-deductive" system: namely, the empirical relationships obtained through correlation of observations, but not derivable, or at least not yet derived, from higher-level generalizations. Every science has such a body of strictly empirical hypotheses, no matter how fully developed or undeveloped its theoretical system may be.

I define a strictly empirical hypothesis as a proposition predicating a regular relationship between two or more sets of data of observation that cannot be

[44] This statement, it should be noted, refers to *general* theories which are part of a hypothetico-deductive system, not to strictly empirical hypotheses obtained by statistical inference. The predictions in question can never be in precise numerical terms, because no numerical magnitudes can be deduced from the assumptions of the type used in "general theory."

deduced from the general hypotheses which control the network of interrelated inferences forming the body of theory of the discipline in question. The distinction is made in almost all disciplines; it is best known as the distinction between "empirical laws" and "theoretical laws," though several other names have been used to denote the two types of scientific propositions. The philosopher Morris Cohen spoke of "concrete laws" in contrast to "abstract laws." Felix Kaufmann, though using the terms empirical and theoretical laws, characterized the former as "strict laws," the latter as "rigid laws." The physicist Henry Margenau contrasted "epistemic" or "correlational laws" with "constitutive," "exact," or "theoretical" laws. And Carl Menger, the founder of the Austrian School and protagonist in the *Methodenstreit*, distinguished "empirical laws" from "exact laws," the latter dealing with idealized connections between pure constructs, the former with "the sequences and coexistences of real phenomena."[45]

The study of the "sequences and coexistences" of the real phenomena depicted in statistical records yields correlational and other empirical findings which have to be tested and modified whenever new data on the same class of phenomena become available. While the constructs and deductions of the theoretical systems will influence the selection, collection and organization of empirical data, the particular relationships established between these data by means of correlation analysis and other statistical techniques are not deducible from high-level assumptions and can neither confirm nor disconfirm such assumptions. But these relationships, especially the numerical estimates of parameters, coefficients, or constants, are themselves subject to verification by new observations.

Verification of Empirical Hypotheses

Every one of us has lately been so much concerned with statistical demand curves, saving and consumption functions, investment functions, import elasticities and import propensities that a description of these and similar research activities is not necessary. The trouble with the verification of the empirical hypotheses derived by means of statistical and econometric analysis is that successive estimates on the basis of new data have usually been seriously divergent. Of course, such variations over time in the numerical relationships measured are not really surprising: few of us have expected these relationships to be constant or even approximately stable. Thus when new data and new computations yield revised estimates of economic parameters, there is no way of telling whether the previous hypotheses were wrong or whether things have changed.

That the numerical relationships described by these empirical hypotheses may be subject to change—to unpredictable change—alters their character in an essential respect. Hypotheses which are strictly limited as to time and space are not "general" but "special" hypotheses, or *historical propositions*. If the relationships measured or estimated in our empirical research are not universal but

---

[45] Carl Menger, *Untersuchungen über die Methode der Socialwissenschaften und der Politischen Oekonomie insbesondere* (Leipzig: Duncker & Humblot, 1883), pp. 28, 36.

historical propositions, the problem of verification is altogether different—so different that according to intentions expressed in the introduction we should not be concerned with it. For we set out to discuss verification of *generalizations*, not of events or circumstances confined to particular times and places. If all propositions of economics were of this sort, the dictum of the older historical school, that economics cannot have "general laws" or a "general theory," would be fully vindicated.

If a hypothesis about the numerical relationship between two or more variables was formulated on the basis of statistical data covering a particular period, and is later compared with the data of *another period*, such a comparison would be in the nature of a verification only if the hypothesis had been asserted or expected to be a universal one, that is, if the measured or estimated relationships had been expected to be constant. In the absence of such expectations the test of a continuing "fit" (between hypothesis and new data) is just a comparison between two historical situations, an attempt to find out whether particular relationships were stable or changing. A genuine verification of a previously formulated hypothesis about a given period calls for comparisons with additional data relating to the *same period*, to check whether the previous observations and their previous numerical description had been accurate. In brief, a historical proposition can only be verified by new data about the historical situation to which it refers. This holds also for geographic propositions and comparisons between different areas.

However, although the changeable "structures"[46] estimated by statistical and econometric researchers are nothing but historical propositions, there are probably limits to their variations. For example, we may safely generalize that the marginal propensity to consume cannot in the long run be greater than unity; or that the elasticity of demand for certain types of exports of certain types of countries will not in the long run be smaller than unity. Statements about definite limits to variations of special or historical propositions are again general hypotheses; they are not strictly empirical but universal in that they are deducible from higher-level generalizations in the theoretical system of economics. The various successive estimates of changeable structures may then be regarded as verifications of general hypotheses according to which certain parameters or coefficients must fall within definite limits. Since these limits are usually rather wide, verification will of course not be the rigorous kind of thing it is in the physical sciences with its numerical constants and narrow margins of error.

But neither this nor anything else that has been said in this article should be interpreted as intending to discourage empirical testing in economics. On the contrary, awareness of the limits of verification should prevent disappointments and present challenges to the empirical worker. May he rise to these challenges and proceed with intelligence and fervor by whatever techniques he may choose.

[46] In the sense used by Tjalling Koopmans and other econometricians.

Chapter 6

OPERATIONAL CONCEPTS AND MENTAL CONSTRUCTS IN MODEL AND THEORY FORMATION

When Einstein invented the Special Theory of Relativity he developed as a by-product a new type of concept or definition. Instead of defining certain terms by stating the essential properties or qualities of the « object » to which the terms are supposed to relate, he defined them by the physical operations which an observer performs in order to ascertain the presence of the object or to measure its magnitude. His immediate concern was to make precise the meaning of the « simultaneity » of two events occurring at different places; and he demonstrated that this required *specifying the operations used by the observer*.

The physicist Bridgman generalized this procedure and proposed « operationalism » as a universal program of scientific discourse: nothing but operational definitions should be used in physics, or in any scientific discipline. This program was quickly endorsed by representatives of several fields, including philosophers. Its appeal is easily understood because it fitted perfectly the mood prevailing in many quarters: it particularly suited the radical empiricists in their insistence on factual observations, the logical positivists in their leanings toward physicalism, the behaviorists in their antagonism to non-observables.

On the other hand, the claim that concepts used for theory formation should be operationally defined was rejected by many, and most vigorously by theoretical physicists who had come to a position best described as « constructionism » (if not fictionalism). Among them was Einstein himself, who besides having proposed the *operational concept* had also emphatically endorsed the use of *purely mental constructs* in theoretical physics. In order to get the dichotomy between operational concepts and pure constructs into proper perspective, we shall have to review some of the positions taken, chiefly by physicists, on the question of the most appropriate type of concept in theory formation.

I. THE CONCEPTS OF PHYSICS

FREELY INVENTED CONCEPTS

Einstein never tired of reiterating that the basic concepts of physics were « free inventions of the human intellect » rather than « abstractions from experience »; that their « fictitious character » should be « evident » from the fact that alternative conceptual schemes can be constructed; and that the role of experience lies partly in « suggesting » some of the conceptual elements and chiefly in testing the correspondence between « separate experiences » and the « conclusions » of — that is, the « logical deductions » from — the theoretical system (1).

Einstein gave many examples of the « freely invented ideas and concepts » of physics; he mentioned « mass, force, and an inertial system » and added that « these concepts are all free inventions »; he mentioned the « ideal conductor or insulator », the « concept of a plane wave », etc., and remarked that each of these is a « fiction which can never be realized »; and he generalized: « Physical concepts are free creations of the human mind, and are not, however it may seem, uniquely determined by the external world » (2). In reply to a skeptic who was in search of the « physically real » and questioned the use of « purely fictitious concepts », Einstein wrote that « There is only one way from the data of consciousness to ' reality ', to wit, the way of conscious or unconscious intellectual construction... We happen to put more trust in these constructions than in the interpretations which we are making with reference to our sensations » (3).

Bridgman was fully familiar with the role of « mental constructs » in physics, designed « to deal with physical situations which we cannot directly experience through our senses, but with which we have contact indirectly and by inference. Such constructs usually involve the element of invention to a greater or less degree » (4). But he was evidently

---

(1) ALBERT EINSTEIN, « On the Method of Theoretical Physics », *Essays in Science* (New York: Philosophical Library, 1934), pp. 12-21.

(2) ALBERT EINSTEIN and LEOPOLD INFIELD, *The Evolution of Physics* (New York: Simon and Schuster, 1938), pp. 310, 311, 75, 110, 33.

(3) Einstein's letter to Samuel, in Herbert L. Samuel, *Essays in Physics* (New York: Harcourt, Brace, 1952).

(4) PERCY W. BRIDGMAN, *The Logic of Modern Physics* (New York: Macmillan, 1927), p. 53.

dissatisfied with such arbitrary procedures. Commenting on Poincaré's dictum concerning the multiplicity of possible explanations of any phenomenon, he said: « This is very unsatisfactory. We want to be able to find the *real* mechanism » (5). But he was not equally opposed to all constructs. He regarded « body stress », although it is « forever beyond the reach of direct experience », as « a good construct » and was prepared « to ascribe physical reality to it because it is uniquely connected with other physical phenomena, independent of those which entered its definition ». He disliked the construct of the « electric field » because of the absence of « a single physical operation by which evidence of the existence of the field may be obtained independent of the operation which entered the definition ». He was quite partial to the construct of the « atom » because, although « no one has ever directly experienced an atom, and its existence is entirely inferential », so much independent new information pointing to the atom has been accumulated « until now we are as convinced of its physical reality as of our hands and feet » (6).

OPERATIONAL CONCEPTS AND « OPERATIONALISM »

But what Bridgman really was driving at was the exclusive use of operationally defined concepts: « the proper definition of a concept is not in terms of its properties but in terms of actual operations » (p. 6). « In general, we mean by any concept nothing more than a set of operations; *the concept is synonymous with the corresponding set of operations*. If the concept is physical, as of length, the operations are actual physical operations, namely, those by which length is measured » (p. 5). (At this point Bridgman makes what we shall see later was an unguarded aside, as he added: « if the concept is mental, as in mathematical continuity, the operations are mental operations »). There is « much freedom of choice in selecting the exact operations » (p. 9). « If we have more than one set of operations, we have more than one concept, and strictly there should be a separate name to correspond to each different set of operations » (p. 10, similarly p. 23).

Operationalism (or operationism, as it is called by psychologists who are probably in a hurry) as a program is then anchored to neo-positivistic tenets: « If a specific question has meaning, it must be possible to find operations by which an answer may be given to it ».

---

(5) BRIDGMAN, *ibid.*, p. 49.

(6) *Ibid.*, pp. 54-59.

If such « operations cannot exist », the question has no meaning (p. 28). Bridgman believes « that many of the questions asked about social and philosophical subjects will be found to be meaningless when examined from the point of view of operations. It would doubtless conduce greatly to clarity of thought if the operational mode of thinking were adopted in all fields of inquiry as well as in the physical » (p. 30).

Bridgman's position and program are subject to several criticisms. It will be useful to comment here on the following six issues:

1) The type of operations - physical, statistical, or purely mental.

2) The « synonymity » between concept and operations.

3) The operation as a criterion of meaning.

4) The multiplicity of operations, meaning, and concepts.

5) The relation between operations and « real existence ».

6) The desirability of using only operational concepts in theory formation.

Criticism is directed ostensibly against Bridgman, but really against the many writers who have embraced « operationalism » as a requirement of scientific discourse. Several of Bridgman's remarks were casual, tentative, perhaps even parenthetic; why should they be subjected to detailed criticism? The answer is that some of Bridgman's followers have endorsed his methodological platform with such intransigeance that it seems best to select his statements as the target, though with apologies for any unfairness that may be involved.

TYPE OF OPERATIONS

In order to make sense of the program of operationalism it is necessary to ascertain precisely what is meant by an « operation » or a « set of operations ». Bridgman's remark about « mental operations » defining « mental concepts » elicited the following comment from Margenau:

« Originally there seemed little doubt that *experimental* operations, processes leading to measurement, were envisaged. Later, however, Bridgman has spoken of paper-and-pencil operations and even of mental operations. This seems like a retreat, for if thought were included among the operations, nobody could possibly find fault with operationalism, nor would it be saying much » (7).

Bridgman could not possibly have meant what he said about mental operations. It would have contradicted his fundamental position and repudiated his entire methodological platform. But there is a plausible interpretation of what he wanted to say. Having asserted that concepts have no meaning unless they are defined in terms of operations, he found it necessary to concede that the concepts of pure mathematics are not meaningless. He tried to accomplish this by admitting the legitimacy of « mental operations » to give meaning to purely « mental concepts » — but undoubtedly he intended to confine his approval to the mental concepts of the pure formal disciplines, not to extend it to « mental concepts » in empirical sciences. The admission ticket was good only for concepts in logic and mathematics, not for concepts in physics or other empirical subjects (and perhaps not even for « philosophical subjects »).

What kinds of operations are then approved under the program? « Physical operations » for physical concepts, to be sure; but what for biological, psychological, economic concepts? I submit that Bridgman was thinking of all sorts of *instrumental* operations and all sorts of *statistical* operations involving recorded data derived from observation. The readings of instruments and the records of other types of observation, with the workings of the instruments and the steps of the human observers fully specified, are evidently what is meant by the operations in question.

SYNONYMITY BETWEEN CONCEPT AND OPERATIONS.

I have some difficulty with the language used in this discussion. I am accustomed to distinguish the *word* by which an idea is called and the *idea* itself; to refer to the word as the « term », and to the idea as the « concept »; and to understand a definition to be a statement expressing the equivalence of the two. If the definition thus tells what is meant by a word, one should think that *a clear statement of the concept is a definition of the term which denotes it*. I cannot understand, then, why one should speak, instead, of the « definition of the concept » (as Bridgman does) and why one should avoid (as some

---

(7) HENRY MARGENAU, *The Nature of Physical Reality: A Philosophy of Modern Physics* (New York: McGraw-Hill, 1950), p. 232.

philosophers do) speaking of an « operational concept », and insist on speaking, instead, of the « operational definition of the concept » (8).

Granting now that a definition of a term may contain as an essential element a description of the operations by which one may find or measure the denoted « object ». I fail to see how one may possibly hold for all kinds of things that the set of operations should be synonymous with the definiendum. While this equivalence makes sense for such things as « distance », « time », « velocity », « weight », « temperature », and other physical quantities, it makes no sense for most other things, physical or otherwise. It becomes particularly inappropriate when taxonomic definitions are wanted. There are guide books in botany and zoology, designed to aid the student to ascertain by appropriate observations or operations the class, order, genus, species (or whatever classificatory groupings are employed) of a particular specimen. To consider the observer's operations in such a case as « synonymous » with the concept under examination would be absurd. (The operations applied to identify a particular cactus or spider can surely never become synonymous with the plant or animal in question). The demand for an operational definition would in such instances not be different from the obvious determination to employ appropriate procedures to ascertain the presence of the essential properties of the object defined, and there can be no question of a synonymity between concept and operations.

OPERATIONS AS A CRITERION OF MEANING

It is important to distinguish between three possible roles that may be assigned to the identifying or measuring operations: 1) the operations may be regarded as synonymous with the object; 2) they may be regarded as essential directions for finding the object; and 3) they may be regarded as a test or criterion of meaning. The third, in effect, implies a threat or attempted intimidation designed to obtain conformance: « If you don't prescribe physical or statistical operations, your term and concept will be declared meaningless! ».

This command under penalty of « denial of meaning » is somewhat highhanded. It goes even further than the edicts of the pragmatists

---

(8) I am aware of the distinction, made by scholastic philosophers, between the *definitio rei* and the *definitio nominis,* but I do not see that this is relevant to the quibble in the text above. To me an « operational concept » is the same as an « operationally defined term ».

and neo-positivists, who had made analogous pronouncements with regard to *propositions,* rather than mere concepts. Reichenbach, for example, had argued that « meaning » was a predicate of whole sentences, not of single words; words could have « sense » only, while « meaning » is transferred to words by the proposition in which they are employed (9). The criterion of meaning of propositions lies in their truth-value, probability-value, or verifiability; and it was not even necessary, according to Reichenbach, to insist on the « technical possibility » of verification; « physical possibility » would be sufficient, and in some cases one might generously accept merely « logical possibility » of verification — though ordinarily this would not, in his opinion, be very sound (10). The most frequently cited verdict on this issue is Wittgenstein's: « the meaning of a proposition is the method of its verification » (11).

Now, it may be held that the direct verifiability of a proposition depends on the operationality of the concepts which comprise it. The operationality of the concepts would then be a necessary condition of the verifiability of the proposition, though it would certainly not be a sufficient condition. (Indeed, a sentence may link an operationally defined subject with an operationally defined predicate and yet be patently meaningless.) This relationship between operational concepts and verifiable propositions has probably been the basis of the occasional demands for « operational propositions » (12). Unfortunately, writers on verification have all too often overlooked the important difference between the (direct) verification of a single empirical proposition and the (indirect) verification of a theoretical system consisting of several propositions, some of which need not be directly verifiable and need not be composed of operational concepts. These not directly verifiable propositions and these non-operational concepts may be perfecty meaningful.

---

(9) HANS REICHENBACH, *Experience and Prediction* (Chicago: University of Chicago Press, 1938), pp. 19-21.

(10) REICHENBACH, *ibid.,* pp. 37-46.

(11) LUDWIG WITTGENSTEIN, *Tractatus Logico-Philosophicus* (London: Routledge and Kegan Paul, 1951), paraphrased, according to Reichenbach, p. 49, by the Vienna Circle.

(12) The economist Samuelson speaks of « the derivation of operationally meaningful theorems ». PAUL A. SAMUELSON, *The Foundations of Economic Analysis* (Cambridge, Mass.: Harvard University Press, 1947), p. 3. The demand for « operational propositions » is especially insistent in DONALD F. GORDON, *Operational Propositions in Economic Theory,* « Journal of Political Economy », Vol. LXIII (1955), pp. 150-161.

All in all, the contention that concepts must be operational in order to be meaningful is untenable and has in fact been almost universally rejected. Even those who cling to the program that most of the concepts of an empirical science « ought » to be operational no longer deny that non-operational concepts may have meaning.

MULTIPLICITY OF OPERATIONS, MEANINGS, AND CONCEPTS

The insistence on the principle « different operations—différent concepts » has been criticized, chiefly because of « the consequence... that in the case of any ordinary scientific object... the multiplicity of methods of detecting its presence would result in a corresponding family of distinct meanings for the term ». This criticism was attributed to a « failure to distinguish between verification and inference » (13). If we make this distinction and realize that our experiments do not « verify » the presence of the object but merely allow us to « infer » it, then the multiplicity of alternative operations « does not give rise operationally to an embarrassing multiplicity of meanings for one and the same term. The same object can be inferred from different sets of operations... » (14).

There is no reason to be « embarassed » when a term has different meanings; indeed, we ought to get used to it and be careful to distinguish them. But it is undeniable that sometimes it is actually one object, and not a family of objects, that is identified by different sets of operations; and in these instances the rule « different operations — different concepts » would indeed be a nuisance. (For example, a salt crystal identified by crystallographic techniques is still the same object when it is identified by chemical techiques.) The trouble, I submit, lies in the failure to distinguish metric concepts — measurable physical or statistical quantities — from concepts of sensory or imagined objects. In the case of numerically determinate quantities it is perfectly proper to insist that different metric operations yield or imply different concepts. But in all other cases different operations may point to, or identify, the same object.

The confusion has been the illegitimate extension of a principle from its proper (very narrow) area of application — measured quan-

---

(13) GEORGE BOAS and ALBERT E. BLUMBERG, *Some Remark in Defense of the Operational Theory of Meaning*, « Journal of Philosophy », Vol. 28 (1931), p. 549.

(14) *Ibid*, p. 550.

tities — to a wide area to which it does not apply. It is no surprise to find that the question of the « multiplicity of concepts » is resolved by the same clue that was previously seen to suggest the answer to the question of the « synonymity between concept and operations ».

RELATION BETWEEN OPERATIONS AND REAL EXISTENCE

In his attitude, hostile or tolerant, toward non-operational mental constructs, Bridgman, as we have seen, was guided by their more or less distant relationship to operational bases of inference. He was willing to concede that there can be « good constructs » — if they are uniquely connected with independent physical operations — and he went so far as to « ascribe physical reality » and « existence » to these constructs. Apparently there is a close connection, in the operationalist's mind, between physical operations and « real existence ».

It is rather peculiar that a physicist with a strong positivist bent should be so seriously concerned with ontological problems. One might think that a physicist, so anxious to eschew « speculation » and to trust nothing but physical observations and operations, would carefully stay away from metaphysical problems and not plunge headlong into ontology. (Or perhaps it is not so peculiar after all, since there are so many writers who first vociferously and solemnly exorcize all metaphysics as unbecoming to an earnest scientist but then keep talking about reality and real existence.)

The really strange thing in this business about the « real existence » of the objects described in mental constructs is its logical inconsistency with the pronouncements about the synonymity between concept and operations. What operationalists evidently wanted to achieve by such pronouncements was to avoid the hypostatization of an idea, to avoid the mistake of positing the independent existence of the defined thing separate from the operations by which it is defined. For Bridgman, « the union between object and means of observation or measurement is indissoluble » (15). But if the concept is nothing more than the set of operations, the concept cannot possibly at the same time be an object with an independent existence apart from the operations.

----

(15) ROBERT E. BASS, Review of Bridgman's *The Nature of Some of our Physical Concepts*, in « Philosophy and Phenomenological Research », Vol. XIV (1954). p. 416.

Exclusive Use of Operational Concepts in Theory Formation

Even if the operationalist concedes that the physicist at present must still use some constructs of a non-operational type, his hope is that, as his science is perfected, it will use only operational concepts. This is just the opposite of the position of most philosophers of science, who stress the« symbolic aspects » of science: « We are beginning to understand how very far from being a literal generalization about observable features of observable phenomena the theories of any advanced science must be taken to be. The more advanced the science, the greater the part played in its theories by unobservables... » (16).

But physicists themselves have rejected the operationalist program in no uncertain terms. Perhaps it would be considered unfair to cite Eddington (17) or Jeans (18) as witnesses for the opposition on operationalism, because their views are often characterized as ultra-rationalistic. But one does not risk a charge of bias if one produces the testimony of Born, who went out of his way to argue against rationalism and « to offer a balanced position » on the « relationship between theory and experiment » (19). Born shows that the ultra-empiricist position taken by Heisenberg was untenable: « Heisenberg felt that quantities which had no direct relation to experiment ought to be eliminated. He wished to found the new mechanics as directly as possible on experience... But if it is taken (as many have taken it) to mean the elimination of all non-observables from theory, it leads to nonsense » (20). Born proceeds to give examples of non-observable quantities which are indipensable to physical theory.

In a more direct discussion of operational definitions, he regards them as « very useful in classical physics where one has to do with quantities accessible to direct measurements... For instance, it is reasonable to introduce temperature by describing the thermometric operations... But the operational definition is rather out of place if you wish to extend » the idea to questions involving atomic nuclei and electrons, quantum theory

(16) MAX BLACK, The Definition of Scientific Method, in « Science and Civilization » (Madison: University of Wisconsin Press, 1949), p. 90.

(17) Sir ARTHUR S. EDDINGTON, The Nature of the Physical World (New York: Macmillan, 1928).

(18) Sir JAMES H. JEANS, The New Background of Science (New York: Macmillan, 1933).

(19) MAX BORN, Experiment and Theory in Physics (Cambridge University Press, 1943, Dover Publications. 1956), p. 2.

(20) Ibid., p. 18.

and wave mechanics. With regard to Schroedinger's « wave function » Born remarks: « there are in principle no means to observe it, hence no « operational » definition » (21).

It is clear, therefore, that the exclusive use of operational concepts in physical theory is impossible; and that a program which would restrict theory to such concepts is, and will remain, impractical. It would still be possible, however, to champion a program of giving preference to operational concepts whenever available and of admitting non-operational concepts only when no operational substitutes can be found.

Exclusive Use of Pure Constructs in Theory Formation

The idea that the physical theorist should build his system with a mixture of concepts, some taken over from the experimentalist — « made in the laboratory » — others freely invented — « made in the study » — is not accepted by all physicists. Even before the operationalist program was formulated, Ernst Mach (often labeled as a positivist) had stated that « All universal physical concepts and laws... are arrived at by idealization » (22). And many others, likewise, have held that even where empirical concepts are available they should be replaced by purified and idealized concepts for use in a consistent theoretical system.

While it would not be possible to find empirical (operational) counterparts to all mental constructs of physics, there is no difficulty in constructing purely abstract counterparts to all empirical concepts. This, indeed, is what theorists have done all the time, knowingly or unknowingly. This transformation of empirical concepts into pure constructs has been called the « method of successive definition » (23). Margenau likes to distinguish « epistemic definitions » (empirical, operational) and « constitutive definitions » (representing « a postulated grouping of constructs »). He holds that « without epistemic definitions science degenerates to speculation; in the absence of constitutive

---

(21) *Ibid.*, p. 39.

(22) Ernst Mach, *Erkenntnis und Irrtum* (Leipzig: J. A. Barth, 2nd ed. 1906) p. 92.

(23) « There is an abstraction of concepts from experience, the discovery of laws expressed in terms of the concepts, the definition of the original concepts to a higher order of approximation in view of the greater accuracy in the definition of conditions, the redefinition of concepts in terms of laws, the reinterpretation of original concepts in terms of the new ». V. F. Lenzen, *The Nature of Physical Theory* (New York: Wiley, 1931), pp. 274 ff.

(24) Margenau, *op. cit.*, pp. 232-243, esp. p. 240.

definitions it becomes a sterile record of observational facts » (25). But he makes it clear that only constitutive definitions « allow the establishment of systems » (26), and that « explanation involves a further progression into the constructional domain. We explain by going « beyond phenomena » (27).

The need for « constitutive definitions in terms of other constructs » is exemplified with regard to the concept of temperature: « Temperature, so long as it is defined operationally in terms of thermometer readings, is a rationally fruitless concept or indeed a set of different unconnected concepts. To unify them and to give them meaning, one must add that temperature is the mean kinetic energy of molecules. This is the constitutive definition which closes the ring and allows us to use the notion of temperature in calculations as well as in measurements » (28).

Thus, while operational concepts alone will allow the establishment of statistical correlations and the formulation of empirical laws (uniformities or regularities observed), pure constructs alone will allow the establishment of theoretical systems applicable to a vast range of phenomena in need of explanation.

II. EMPIRICAL LAWS AND PURE THEORY

That there is a difference between concepts used in empirical generalization and concepts used in abstract theory is not a recent discovery, nor an insight limited to physicists. Many biologists, economists and, of course, philosophers have long been fully aware of the difference, though there has been a question whether the difference is in kind or only in degree.

A DIFFERENCE IN DEGREE OR IN KIND?

It is quite understandable that some writers claim that the difference, however wide, is only one in degree because even the empirical concepts, « extracted from experience » and embodied in

---

(25) *Ibid.*, p. 243.
(26) *Ibid.*, p. 237.
(27) *Ibid.*, p. 169.
(28) MARGENAU, in a letter to the author, November 18, 1959.

experimental and observational data, presuppose mental processes including selection, abstraction, reconstruction, combination, reflection, ratiocination, and some idealization. In other words, « conceptualization » implies various thought processes which carry the objects of experience some distance away from whatever it is that supposedly is being observed. The mental construct, the concept used in abstract theory, is formed by means of more idealization, more invention, more construction, to remove it further from the domain of « phenomena » and « data » into the domain of pure « construction ». If there is no border passed on the way from concrete experience to abstract construction, one may refuse to see more than a difference in degree between the more « real » and the more « ideal » concepts.

If, however, the differences in the *formation* of concepts are considered together with the differences in the *use* of these concepts, the contrast becomes obviously categorical. Propositions which link empirical concepts in inductive generalizations are definitely *a posteriori,* dependent on experience and subject to direct verification by further experience. Propositions, on the other hand, which link mental constructs in hypothetico-deductive systems are in the nature of heuristic conventions, and therefore *a priori* — unless accompanied by a statement directing the application of the system to concrete data of experience (29).

That a theoretical system (a) whose concepts and propositions may have been suggested by experience, (b) whose purpose is to serve as explanation of experience, and (c) whose explanatory and predictive usefulness is testable by experience, should nevertheless be *a priori* has long been puzzling even to students of logic. Yet, « Logically... a proposition is *a priori* if it must be presupposed and cannot be proved or disproved within the system to which it is *a priori* » (30). The abstract theoretical propositions of science which are integral parts of a theoretical system have the character of postulates, for which no direct empirical proof is sought; only the system as a whole is tested by the correspondence between consequences deduced from the system and the data of experience which it is designed to explain

---

(29) Morris R. Cohen, *Reason and Nature: An Essay on the Meaning of Scientific Method* (New York: Harcourt, Brace, 1931), pp. 137-143. Milton Friedman, *The Methodology of Positive Economics,* « Essays in Positive Economics (Chicago: University of Chicago Press, 1953), pp. 24-25.

(30) Cohen, *op. cit.,* p. 138.

or predict. It is the *a priori* character of the theoretical propositions containing the mental constructs that differentiates these propositions sharply from the empirical propositions containing empirical (operational) concepts (31).

« Empirical » or « Concrete » Laws versus « Exact » or « Abstract » Laws

Using again physics as his example, the philosopher Morris Cohen contrasts « concrete laws » about « concrete things » with the « abstract or universal laws » of « developed sciences » which are « concerned with the relations between possible or ideal things or elements ». Of course, we « might not be interested in these ideal relations if they did not throw light... on the actual world »; but « there can be no doubt that the more developed a science is the more are its laws formulated in terms of such abstract or ideal elements » (32). « In thus deliberately sacrificing the concrete fullness of ordinary or ''experiential'' descriptions for the sake of abstract universality, science opens itself to the taunt that it is artificial ». But « the conceptual order which science seeks to attain » is superior in heuristic value to the « so-called perceptual order of common-sense experience »; indeed, the « most powerful organum for the apprehension and controlling of nature that man has as yet discovered is description in terms of ideal entities such as perfect levers, ideal gasses, perfectly continuous bodies, the velocity of light in an unattainable perfect vacuum, and the like » (33).

There are of course certain difficulties in applying the abstract laws and ideal concepts to uncontrolled reality since, according to Cohen, « every abstract or universal law asserts what would happen if only certain conditions prevailed and everything else remained indifferent. Prediction is possible to the extent that nature does offer us instances where the action of bodies can be accounted for by a limited number of factors, and the effects of all other influences either balance each other or are so small as to be negligible or unnoticeable. But theoretically it is true that no actual phenomenon can exclusively embody a single universal law, since in general every actual pheno-

---

(31) Margenau recognized the decisive step across the frontier from the realm of *a posteriori* to that of *a priori* when he said: « The contingency of correlation had given way to logical necessity ». *Op. cit.*, p. 28.

(32) Morris Cohen, *op. cit.*, pp. 100-101.

(33) *Ibid.*, pp. 104-105.

menon is the meeting place or intersection of many laws. Yet every true law is actually embodied in all instances of it, and it is that which enables us to analyze phenomena and arrange them in significant order. But while abstract laws are always necessary for the understanding of phenomena, their sufficiency varies in different fields » (34).

We might quote or cite other philosophers who presented the same ideas in slightly different language, but the formulation most interesting to economists is probably that by the economist Carl Menger. Speaking of the « types » and « typical relations » which are the elements of scientific discourse, Menger showed that they are of different degrees of « exactness » (35). Empirical-realistic research, working with « real types » — which can never be exact — attempts to formulate « empirical laws », stating « regularities — not necessities — in the succession and conjunction of phenomena » (36). Exact theoretical analysis, on the other hand, working with ideal types (« *strenge Typen* ») — which do not occur in reality — attempts to formulate « exact laws », stating the logically necessary relationships between the exact types.

The real types, the « basic forms of real phenomena », are of course also the result of abstraction, since several aspects of the phenomena observed are disregarded (37). But the abstraction does not proceed to a complete idealization, and the real type thus allows « more or less wide leeway for peculiarities ». For example, « real gold, real oxygen or hydrogen, real water » cannot be subject to « exact laws »; to arrive at « exact laws » one must construct « exact types », such as « absolutely pure gold, pure oxygen », etc., « no matter whether or not these ever exist as separate phenomena in reality, or indeed whether they can ever be produced as separate phenomena in their purity ». The exact types, which « exist only in our idea », are « prerequisites for the attainment of exact laws » (38).

Menger conceded that the findings of pure theory « look inadequate and unrealistic, in economics as well as in any other discipline. But this should be self-evident inasmuch as the results of exact

---

(34) *Ibid.*, pp. 105-106.

(35) CARL MENGER, *Untersuchungen über die Methode der Socialwissenschaften und der Politischen Oekonomie insbesondere* (Leipzig: Duncker & Humblot, 1883), p. 25.

(36) *Ibid.*, p. 36.

(37) *Ibid.*, p. 67.

(38) *Ibid.*, p. 41.

theories... are true only under definite pre-suppositions », usually under assumptions not satisfied in the real world (39). Yet, without the « exact laws » of pure theory we could not hope to understand the complicated relations and interdependences between phenomena of the real world.

A LIST OF SYNONYMS AND ANTONYMS

Terminology has changed over the years, in the philosophy of science not less than in most other areas of discussion and controversy. The same ideas have been expressed in very different words (and sometimes the same words have been used to express different ideas). Perhaps, to facilitate comparisons between expressions used in different fields, for different approaches, by different writers, it may be useful to present a tabulation of analogous or equivalent « phrases» relating to the dichotomy between the concrete-empirical and the abstract-theoretical. In most of the literature these words are used to modify the noun « laws »; some writers, however, have special tastes concerning the meaning of « law » and want to reserve this tag for only

Empirical Laws involving operational concepts	Theoretical Laws involving mental constructs
Empirical laws (1)	Exact laws (1)
Inductive generalizations	Deductive principles
A posteriori findings (in applied theory)	A priori postulates (in pure theory)
Material, experiential propositions	Formal, systematic propositions
Factual-observational generalizations	Hypothetico-deductive systems
Statements of regularities in data of observation (2)	Resolutions to follow analytical stipulations (2)
Generic propositions (3)	Universal propositions (3)
Concrete laws (4)	Abstract laws (4)
Empirical laws (4)	Universal laws (4)
Empirical laws (5)	Analytical laws (5)
Empirical laws (6)	Theoretical laws (6)
Synthetic universal propositions (6)	Rules of scientific procedure (6)
Strict laws (6)	Rigid laws (6)
Correlational statements (7)	Theoretical explanations (7)
Epistemic connections (7)	Constitutive connections (7)
Low-level generalizations (8)	High-level hypotheses (8)
Inductive generalizations (9)	Scientific laws (9)

Notes: Among the writers who have used these particular or very similar expressions were: (1) Carl Menger, (2) Henry Poincaré, (3) John Dewey, (4) Morris Cohen, (5) T. W. Hutchison, (6) Felix Kaufmann, (7) Henry Margenau, (8) Richard B. Braithwaite, (9) E. F. Caldin.

(39) *Ibid.*, p. 54.

the one kind or only the other kind of proposition. If they feel strongly about this usage they may substitute their favorite term for what they may regard as a misnomer.

It is not claimed that the phrases collected here on the two sides of the table are perfect synonyms or antonyms, but only that they reflect the same dichotomy in concept and theory formation (40).

III. CONSTRUCT AND MODEL

In the preceding pages the word « model » has been used sparingly. Since « model » is now being used, especially by economists, with greater frequency than any other methodological term, its place in the context of our discussion should be examined. In particular, its relation to the « construct », on the one hand, and to « theory », on the other, ought to be clarified, — though it should first be noted that there are many who have used model as a synonym of construct, and others who have used it as a synonym of theory.

« Model » as a Catch-All Word

« Model » is indeed a very handy word; it can be pressed into service as a substitute for over a dozen other words, and its convenient vagueness allows its user to avoid commitment to any strict idea. In different contexts « model » has been used in lieu of concept, mental construct, conceptual scheme, schema, ideal type, abstraction, idealization, useful fiction, fictitious construction, schematic representation, analogy, hypostatisation of analogies, postulate, assumption, system of fundamental assumptions, axiomatic system, hypothesis, theory, law, system of related variables, system of equations, and probably other things. The existence of such « catch-all » words is a boon, not only for sloppy thinkers and writers, but also for thoughtful ones when they have a good reason for postponing commitment to a definite idea. Many writers, however, do not intend to be vague but wish to convey a rather definite idea when they use the word « model », and thus it might be useful to delineate a narrower meaning that places

---

(40) The dichotomy stressed by Herbert Dingle, *Science and Human Experience* (New York: Macmillan, 1932), between « abstractions from observation » and « elaborations of hypotheses », (p. 51), is not equivalent to the dichotomies displayed in the list, but must be regarded as a subdivision of theoretical laws.

it between « construct » and « theory », related to both but not synonymous with either.

This is not to say there is anything wrong with using « model » as a synonym of either « construct » or « theory » — as it has often been used — but it should not be synonymous with both. Schumpeter used model and theory as equivalent terms when he stated: « The total or ″ system ″ of our concepts and of the relations that we establish between them is what we call a theory or a model » (41). Others have used the word model when they referred to single constructs — such as economic man, or profit maximizer. But there is need for a word connoting more than a construct and less than a complete theory; « model » can do this very well.

Form and Composition of Models

Models may come in several forms. They may be pictorial or plastic (« still models »), mechanical, hydraulic, or electro-magnetic (« mobile models »), verbal, geometric, algebraic (« symbolic models »). We are concerned here only with the last three forms. But in all forms the function of a model is to exhibit connections, relationships, interdependences. There would be no reason for making a model except to show how some things « hang together » or of what « elements » they are composed or how they « work » or are « adjusted ».

The elements of which a verbal or mathematical model is composed and whose interrelations it is designed to demonstrate are mental constructs (considered as « variables » if they are shown in functional relationships with other « magnitudes »). The logical relationship between mental constructs and mental models is quite simple: *models are made up of interrelated constructs*. But, in order to be applicable to concrete situations, should the model not be made up of operational concepts instead?

Lest a negative answer shock those who realize that « application » must mean reference to empirical data and, hence, to operational concepts, let us repeat that the question was inquiring into the kind of concept of which models are « made up », composed. The answer is that theoretical models are composed of nothing but mental constructs, some of which, however, may have operational counterparts — and

---

(41) Joseph A. Schumpeter, *A History of Economic Analysis* (New York: Oxford University Press, 1954), p. 562.

this is all that is needed to secure applicability of a model. In many theoretical models some of the indispensable concepts cannot be operational, and some of those that can are too inexact for use in a logically consistent system (42).

Perhaps an illustration from model construction in economics will clarify this statement. Think of the model of a competitive industry, designed to demonstrate the effects of changes in cost or in demand upon price and output. The operational concepts that we have of industry, firm, cost, demand, price, and output would obviously not do for this purpose. For example, the Census Bureau's concepts of « industry », the legal or organizational concepts of « firm », the accounting concepts of « cost », these operational concepts cannot be substituted for the idealized concepts of the model; for « demand » there is no operational concept at all; and no practically available operations can unambiguously identify one « price » and one « output » of a product in all its varieties of qualities, shapes, calipers, colors, finishes, lot sizes, delivery terms, credit terms, etc. « Price » and « output » in the theoretical model are mental constructs, and the consequences deduced from the model are « exact » in the sense that they abstract from all the complications surrounding the price and output observations of actual business. Of the « exact » (imagined) deduced consequences the « inexact » (observed) changes of magnitudes actually measured (by necessarily inaccurate statistical operations) are only very unsatisfactory *counterparts,* and the correspondence between the two cannot be anything but rough.

We shall presently furnish additional illustrations of the discrepancies between the abstract constructs employed in economic models

---

(42) This position, taken by many philosophers of science, is forcefully presented by F.S.C. Northrop. He distinguishes two main classes of concept: « concepts by intuition », which include « concepts by inspection », and « concepts by postulation », which include « concepts by imagination », « concepts by intellection », and « logical concepts by intuition ». He states that « An operation in the denotatively given sense of the term is a concept by intuition »; and concludes that « in a properly constructed, deductively formulated scientific theory every concept in the theory, as deductively formulated, must be a concept by postulation. Utter confusion and nonsense enter into scientific discourse when concepts by intuition are put in the same proposition with concepts by postulation... When concepts belonging to two different worlds of discourse are treated as if they belonged to the same world of discourse, nonsense is the result ». Filmer S. C. NORTHROP, *The Logic of the Sciences and the Humanities* (New York: Macmillan, 1947), p. 128-29.

and the operational counterparts available to empirical researchers. But first we should proceed with our discussion of the relationship between construct, model, and theory.

The Model and the Theory

We have regarded a model as a system of interrelated constructs; and we have indicated that a theory may be more than a model. A theory may be regarded as a model plus a specification of the empirical observations to which it applies (43). The same distinction is sometimes expressed by the terms « pure » and « applied » theory (which, however, are also used with other meanings). « Model » may stand for « pure theory », working only with mental constructs; when the kinds of empirical data are specified to which the model is supposed to apply we may speak of applied theory.

This does not mean that a theory will *replace* the pure constructs of the model or models that compose it with empirical (operational) concepts. But it does mean that for *some* of the constructs empirical counterparts will have to be suggested, namely, for those variables whose changes are interpreted as the supposed « causes » and the deduced « effects » of the events simulated by the model (44). Thus, to repeat, applicable or applied theory consists of two parts: (1) a pure model and (2) a specification of the empirical facts (described, ordinarily, in term of real types or operational concepts) whose changes it will explain or predict.

This, unfortunately, is still too simple a statement since the explanatory and predictive tasks of applied theory cannot as a rule be attempted with just one model. It will usually take a combination of models (plus specifications of empirical applications) if problems arising in complex situations and complex developments are to be analyzed. Thus, applied theory ordinarily requires several models — and some of them may even be models built in different disciplines, say political science or sociology, since the models of economics alone may

---

(43) MILTON FRIEDMAN, *The Methodology of Positive Economics*, « Essays on Positive Economics » (Chicago: University of Chicago Press, 1953), pp. 24-25.

(44) For a detailed exposition of these ideas see FRITZ MACHLUP, « The Problem of Verification in Economics », *Southern Economic Journal*, Vol. XXII (1955), pp. 12-14. An Italian translation was published under the title *Il problema della verifica in economia*, « Industria » (1958, n. 3), and in the book *La verifica delle leggi economiche* by F. MACHLUP, T. W. HUTCHISON, and E. GRUNBERG, Milano 1959.

leave the analyst helpless and would need to be supplemented by relevant models borrowed from other fields of inquiry. Thus, whereas a model is a combination of constructs, applied theory may be a combination of models. This deserves to be given explicit recognition.

A few words should be added with respect to econometric models. Econometric models are applied to empirical data of the past — in order to obtain the so-called structure of the model by means of statistical estimates of the numerical values of the variables and parameters — and then tried out in predicting some empirical data of the future. The fact that the numerical values of variables and parameters are derived from statistical operations may make some of us think that the terms in the equations are not pure constructs, but operational concepts after all. This would be a mistake, as one may judge from the fact that the econometrician often examines several alternative operations for obtaining his estimates and selects what appears to him to be the closest approximations to the variables included in the model. In other words, he knows that he cannot get exactly what he wants; the constructs of the model which have *any* operational counterparts usually have *several* such counterparts, each deficient in some way, deviating from the exact (ideal) construct for which it can be only a poor analogue. It should therefore be clear that the econometric model, before numerical values have been estimated, consists of pure constructs, notwithstanding the fact that the builder of the model tries hard to design it only with constructs for which he can hope to find statistically operational counterparts. Moreover, since he immediately proceeds to apply his model to data of observation, his model is always in the nature of a theory: it specifies the empirical (operational) concepts the magnitudes of which, he hopes, it can « explain ».

MORE ILLUSTRATIONS OF OPERATIONAL COUNTERPARTS

It may be desirable to add some examples illustrating more sharply the difference between pure constructs and operational concepts in economics. Let us first elaborate on the model of the « competitive market », to which we have previously referred. Like any quantitative model, it contains two kinds of constructs: *variables* and functional *relations* between variables. The simplest market model contains only two variables — price and quantity — and two functional relations between them — supply and demand. The « simplicity » is achieved by the implicit or explicit assumptions of *ceteris paribus* and *mutatis mutandis*; that is to say, all things not included in the model but possibly suspected of having some influence upon quantities supplied or demanded are assumed either to remain unchanged or to change as they must change in logical connection with the variables officially recognized in the model. (For example, the amount of money or income buyers have left over after they make a purchase cannot be assumed to remain unchanged if the demand function is not of unit elasticity). The reference to « other things » possibly of influence implies an admission that these things are in effect part of the model, though playing silent roles, so to speak, and not listed among the cast. It would be preferable, from several points of view, to enumerate all possibly relevant variables and stipulate the silent roles they have to play in the model — such as to remain unchanged. (Stipulations regarding money incomes, real incomes, cash balances, liquidity reserves, for example, would be useful in many market models).

Every beginning student of economics is (or should be) repeatedly warned of the hypothetical nature of the functional relations between the variables. There are no « observable » supply or demand functions — unless one means merely the chalk symbols which the teacher produces on the blackboard for students to observe. All the values of the functions are imagined; the supply function assigns hypothetical quantities offered in the market to hypothetical prices paid, and the demand function assigns hypothetical quantities demanded to these prices, but since the prices and quantities are hypothetical only, they cannot be observed by anybody. (It may be said for the benefit of readers who are comforted by the thought of « conceivable operationality » that with much fantasy one may design a grand « experiment », with heroic controls of all relevant factors, to ascertain all values of the functions. But one must add, in all honesty, that the « operations » required to establish the functions as empirical observations are not practically possible). The so-called statistical supply and demand curves have not really been « observed »; they are the result of highly imaginative computations with data recorded at different times under different conditions and manipulated on the basis of unverifiable assumptions which range from « plausible » to « contrary to fact ».

But not only the *relations* between variables in the model are constructions of our minds; the *variables* themselves are pure constructs even where several quite acceptable operational counterparts for them can be found. Think of an exceptional firm which produces only one homogeneous product, say fiberboard, only of first quality, but in different calipers; the firm measures its output by weight. The buyers of the board use it for purposes for which only square measure is significant. Perhaps a wholesaler buys it by the ton and sells it by the square foot. The recorded quantity of fiberboard sold and bought may at the same time increase in terms of tons and decrease in terms of square feet. Two different quantities would then result from our statistical inquiries. If one now thinks of the possible combinations between different sizes, different shapes, different qualities, and different products made by the same firms, one must realize that the « quantity produced » or « quantity sold » within a given period can be measured by a variety of operations, so that one must choose among a variety of operational concepts of output, none of which may be precisely the thing that fits the pure construct used in the model.

Matters are much more complicated regarding the other variable, price. What are the usual operations by which we obtain price data for an economic or econometric research problem? We may compile daily quotations from newspapers or weekly or monthly quotations from trade journals; we may send questionnaires to some or all producers, or to some or all users; we may use, or may choose to neglect (with drastic results sometimes), changes in freight costs to adjust the data for f.o.b. mill prices and delivered prices (or for changes in the « interpenetrations » of distant markets by distant producers, which may alter prices paid and net prices received in opposite directions); we may manipulate the data in order to account for some changes in the composition of output while we may choose to neglect other changes in composition where we cannot think of a « good » way of adusting the raw data; we may be able to learn of secret discounts, and may take them into account; but, on the other hand, we may not find out about such practices. The diligent researcher may end up with dozens of different series of prices for the same commodity; and he will realize that they all contain so many « impurities » that none can be said to be a very good analogue of the pure construct.

Not that our operational difficulties relate only to manufactured commodities or to personal services, where the assumption of homogeneity is so far from being fulfilled. Take a relatively homogeneous commodity, foreign exchange in the form of bank balances payable on demand by telegraphic order. The researcher looking for data — for the daily rates (bid and ask) in the important financial centers — will find his task encumbered by difficult choices. He may first turn to one of the most reliable newspapers, *The New York Times,* and copy the daily reports of the foreign-exchange markets. If he then compares his data (say, for 1947 to 1957) with the analogous data from the *Zürcher Zeitung* or the *Journal de Genève,* he will discover discrepancies. Before he gets too desperate, somebody may explain to him that the American paper has felt some (moral) inhibitions about reporting rates illegal under the laws of friendly nations, and confined itself to reports of transactions legal and authorized by the authorities in all countries involved — which under exchange restrictions may be only a small part of the actual transactions. In order to obtain complete information about the rates involved in illegal exchange transactions the researcher will have to turn to *Pick's Currency Reports,* published in New York by an expert who receives reliable reports from dealers all over the world. Now, which of these rates were *the* foreign-exchange rates to be explained, if not predicted, by our theory? The choice between these differing operational concepts of foreign-exchange rates may depend on the type of problem to be answered. But certainly one cannot say that there is an unambiguous operational concept of the price of foreign exchange that corresponds to the pure construct used in our abstract model of the exchange market.

One more illustration, also from international finance. When the trade balance of the United States turned from strongly positive to strongly negative in the years 1957 to 1959, while the balance of long-term capital movements and financial aid had not appreciably changed, accepted theory suggested that prices in the United States must have increased relative to prices in other industrial nations. Price statistics, however, did not verify this suggestion. But what did these operational price concepts really measure? Did they permit comparisons of prices of comparable qualities of comparable products with comparable delivery terms? Reconstruction and growth of European industry probably brought with it drastic improvements in the quality of engineering goods and in the terms of delivery. Assume that in the early 1950's a certain machine or machine tool was offered at similar prices in England and in America, but that delivery terms were 24 months in England and only 6 months in America; assume that in the late 1950's prices in both countries were 10 per cent higher, but English manufacturerers were now able to make prompt delivery. This would easily explain a switch of demand from American to English products, although relative prices, as recorded, were unchanged. In other words, the operation by which the statisticians establish prices and price changes fails to catch significant changes in the things for which prices are paid; and a quantification of these changes does not seem practicable, so that we cannot hope to devise more refined operations that would yield operational concepts more nearly corresponding to the pure constructs used in the model.

These illustrations may have driven home a methodological point often overlooked by positivistically inclined economists who complain about the paucity of verifications of theory. The point is that the difficulty of verification lies less in the « excessive » purity of the abstract constructs and models than in the gross impurities in the operational concepts at our disposal. Empirical tests employing inadequate operational concepts are, quite properly, not accorded much weight and, hence, the theories so tested survive any number of apparently contradictory « experience ».

DEFINITION OF « CONSTRUCT »

Not many writers have attempted to define « construct », and those who have seem to have had limited purposes in mind and thus have come up with narrow definitions. I shall try my hand at a definition which may suit the purposes of the formal sciences as well as the empirical sciences, the natural sciences as well as the social sciences. I submit this definition as a basis for discussion in the hope that it will call forth suggestions for improving it.

A mental construct is a concept designed for purposes of analytical reasoning that cannot be adequately defined or circumscribed in terms of observables or in terms of operations with recorded data derived from observation. It is the result of a mental construction, either (1) without reference to empirical data, as in the case of the constructs of pure mathematics, or (2) with some indirect reference to facts of experience but derived through idealization, heroic abstraction, or invention, as in the case of the constructs of empirical sciences. The constructs of empirical sciences may be divided into (a) constructs used as explanatory links between observable phenomena where the question of the existence of a direct « counterpart » in the real world remains problematic, as in the case of a nuclear « particle » so called; (b) constructs used for purposes of hypothetical reasoning where the existence of a « counterpart » in the real world is regarded as highly improbable, if not impossible, as in the case of imaginary « perfection » such as the physical concepts of the perfect gas, the perfectly rigid lever, perfect blackness, or the economic concepts of the economic man, perfect foresight, perfect competition; and (c) constructs which, though they have direct « counterparts » in the real world, must for purposes of hypothetical reasoning be kept free from the uncertain attributes, deviations, or associations that commonly attach to empirical concepts and would blur or vitiate the analytical (implicative) connections with other constructs of a theoretical system. Constructs in the social sciences are often in the nature of « ideal types », formed with a strong admixture of inner experience and « understanding » of the subjective meanings.

THE EMPIRICAL REFERENCE OF IDEAL TYPES AND OTHER CONSTRUCTS

Before we discuss the special kind of empirical reference which is inherent in the ideal types employed in the social sciences — a reference to inner experience — we should comment on the general kind of empirical reference that is involved in the formation of virtually *all* mental constructs. This seems advisable because some writers have made much of an apparent difference between concepts « arbitrarily constructed » and concepts « derived from experience ». The distinction is misleading since experience will necessarily affect the construction of any sort of concept, and there will be a dose of the arbitrary in the formation of any concept, however realistic (45).

The role of experience in the formation of a mental construct will be indicated, in turn, for a construct in physics and for a construct in economics. Take the « neutrino » as a relatively novel construct of physics. It got its start when experimental data failed to fit the consequences deduced from the accepted theoretical system (including the postulated law of the conservation of energy). The inclusion of a new

---

(45) "Inner experience" and "subjective meanings" are anathema to many scientists, especially to many American psychologists who have embraced "operationism" with great fervor. For example: « Since science is empirical and excluded private data, all of its concepts must be çapable of operational definition ». Edwin G. BORING, *The Use of Operational Definitions in Science*, in the « Symposium on Operationism » published by the « Psychological Review », Vol. 52 (September 1945), p. 244. The editor of that Review added to the terminological confusion by speaking of « construct-terms » which could or could not be operationally defined (*loc. cit.*, p. 241). Another participant in the symposium attempted to set this straight: « A construct is something constructed. The initial data of science are not constructed. They are given ». CARROLL C. PRATT, « Operationism in Psychology », *loc. cit.*, p. 262. The term "construct" was coined in order to contrast this kind of concept with empirical concepts; to use it for any sort of concept would make it a useless term.

construct in the system seemed to be the best device for making the system yield deduced consequences that fitted the data. The new construct — the neutrino — was called a « particle » by analogy with experiences of other things. It was designed to give (in conjunction with all other variables and relations constructed for the system) results that corresponded to the experimental data; yet, it was not an object of observation or any other kind of direct experience. In other words, the reference to observed phenomena is only indirect.

Now think of the « money illusion » as a relatively novel construct of economics. It probably got its start when observations of (increased) consumer price and of (unchanged) amounts of labor available seemed to contradict deductions from a model which included labor supply as an increasing function of real-wage rates. The inclusion of a new construct seemed to be the best device for removing from the model the effect which the reduction of real-wage rates (implied in increased consumer prices) would have upon the quantity of labor supplied, and thus for allowing the deduced consequences of an increase in effective demand to fit better the actual supposed (or hoped for) observations. The new construct — the money illusion —, since it had to offset the effects of another construct, namely, « perfect rationality », was called an « illusion » by analogy with a type of inner experience shared by many (who, though normally quite sensible, sometimes fail to wake up to certain realities). With the help of the new construct the consequences deduced from the enlarged system promised to correspond to what was thought to be the record of observation; but the construct is without direct reference to observables and no one could reasonably claim to have any direct experience of illusions suffered by other minds. The reference to observed phenomena is entirely indirect.

In many respects the empirical reference of the constructs is the *same* for natural and social sciences: (1) Inadequate correspondence between deduction (from an accepted model) and empirical observations sets off a search for new constructs. (2) The inclusion of the new constructs into the model is designed to achieve closer correspondence between deductions and observations. (3) The invention and design of the new constructs is affected by analogical reasoning based on various kinds of experience, though not necessarily related to the problem at hand. (4) The modified model is tested by the correspondence between the modified deductions and observations. A significant *difference* exists, however, in point (3), for it is a very special type of experience that affects invention and design of a new construct in the social sciences: each construct must pass the test of empathic understanding or imagined introspection; that is to say, it must satisfy the postulates of « subjective interpretation » and of « consistency with the constructs of commonsense experience » (46).

This does not mean that these ideal types are « realistic ». They are not, because the selection of the supposedly relevant trait, motive, attitude, or mode of thinking that is idealized in the construct implies the exclusion of many other traits, motives, attitudes, or modes of thinking which we all, in everyday life, know we have and which we suppose others likewise have; and this unnatural isolation of one element from all the rest makes the construct definitely unrealistic. Yet human experience is undoubtedly behind the creation of the construct, and the construct, however nonhuman in its artificial limitation dictated by the purpose of the model, must be so designed that an act performed « in the way indicated by the typical construct would be understandable » (47) by people possessing experiences of the kind involved. (Perhaps it needs to be added that an act can be « understandable » to me even if I myself were not disposed to act the same way in the same circumstances).

Experience, Realism, Relevance, and Truth

That the constructs (ideal types) of the social sciences are derived from experience and consistent with the constructs of common-sense experience does not make them « *empirical* ». Nor does it make them, or the models for which they are used, « *realistic* »; nor does it make them, or the models, « *relevant* »; nor does it make the theories for which they are used « *true* ». A few words about the widespread confusion between experience, realism, relevance, and truth may be an appropriate conclusion of this essay.

The origin or derivation of a concept has nothing to do with its logical nature. It may be « derived » from or « inspired » by experience, and yet be a « pure construct » (« ideal type »). It is empirical only to the extent that it embodies the result of observation (including experimentation), usually in the form of records of instrument readings and/or testimonies and other communications. That the records in the

---

(46) Alfred Schuetz, « Common-Sense and Scientific Interpretation of Human Action », *Philosophy and Phenomenological Research*, Vol. XIV (1953), p. 34.

(47) Schuetz, *loc. cit.*, p. 34.

social sciences always go back to some person's interpretations of subjective meanings — such as « costs », « prices », depreciation », « profits », « purchase », « loan », « gift », « theft », « marriage », « illegitimate child » — is characteristic for the science of society (48). (This subjective interpretation is inherent in the abstract constructs as well as in the empirical concepts of the social sciences). The more manipulations (computations, corrections, adjustments) are made with the raw data contained in the record, the more refining decisions are made on the basis of preconceived theory and intelligent judgment, the further removed from the direct findings of observation and the less empirical will be the resulting figures.

The confusion between realism and relevance can best be cleared up by emphasizing the fact that they are usually opposites. To draw a picture in all « realistic » detail means to include all that hits the eye, however irrelevant it may be for a particular purpose; to draw a model with only the « relevant » features means to leave out the realistic appearances. If Johnny wants to know how a steam locomotive *looks,* we shall show him a photograph on which he will see all that is on the surface of the thing. If he wants to know how a steam locomotive *works,* we shall show him a model that includes very little of the realistic picture, but instead a few things not visible there: a schematic drawing of a cylinder, a piston, a valve, etc. An explanatory model should not be realistic; it should exhibit what are considered the relevant variables and relations.

Formal logic has taught us that a proposition is either « true » or « false ». A scientific theory, perhaps, may be true or false, but the scientist will reserve his judgment. He may be firmly convinced that his theory is « true », but he will be mindful of the fact that thousands of theories, once held to be true, have had to be rejected or modified or reformulated; hence all he will say is that his theory is the best he has got, and that it has « not yet » been disconfirmed.

Of course, this business of disconfirming has something to do with experience and with relevance. For it is by means of empirical tests,

---

(48) The « facts » of the social sciences cannot be « observed » with the five senses. If Mr. A is observed carrying an object from Mr. B's store, the observers cannot know whether he has bought it, borrowed it, stolen it, or was given it as a present. Perhaps A and B do not agree, one regarding the transaction as a gift, the other as a theft. The subjective meanings of the actors and the interpretations by record keepers and record analysts are essential.

through comparisons of the deduced consequences of the theory with empirical data recognized as their adequate counterparts, that the theory may eventually be rejected — in favor of a better one. And this will happen if the model embodied in the theory does not contain the relevant, or not all the relevant, variables for the problem at hand. Thus there is after all a connection between experience, relevance, and truth — but it certainly does not mean that the relevant concepts in a good theory must be « empirical ».

Chapter 7

OPERATIONALISM AND PURE THEORY IN ECONOMICS

SOMETHING LIKE A "CULTURAL LAG" CAN BE found if one compares different fields of learning. Certain methodological ideas have arrived in some fields many years later than in others—sometimes after they had been discarded by the others. Certain "teachings" about scientific method and about the "proper" formation of concepts and theories have reached a particular discipline long after other disciplines had recognized them as errors.

Cases in point are the rejection of "causality" and all causal theories; the championing of "description" in opposition to "explanation"; the taboo against "nonobservables" and against mere "constructions of the mind"; the contemptuous characterization as "pseudo problems" of all questions to which only nonverifiable answers can be given; the insistence that only "operationally defined" concepts be used in scientific theories; the demand that every assumption employed in a theory be tested independently; the assertion that theories are "empty" (of empirical content) if they include postulational propositions; the contention that theories must not be wider in scope than the empirical evidence available for their support. It might be possible to date the birth of each of these positions and to supply a time schedule of their arrivals in various disciplines.

The time schedule of "departures" of these ideas from the various disciplines would be difficult to ascertain, for there are cultural lags also among different representatives of the same discipline. Although most physicists, for example, have outgrown virtually all the positions enumerated, others—including some well-recognized authorities in special areas —may not have been keeping up with developments in the philosophy of science and may repeat the methodological precepts they were taught when they were students decades earlier. This holds for biologists, psychologists, sociologists, economists.[1]

It would be an interesting undertaking to show how little the methodological propositions stated by a writer are related to his own research and analysis. Many do the things they pronounce impossible or illegitimate, and many fail to do what they declare to be essential requirements of scientific method. These differences between the actual formation of substantive scientific theories and the statements of "theories of theory formation" should not surprise us. Most of us know how to walk, but do not know what our brains, nerves, muscles, etc., have to do in order to make us walk. Some great athletes have quite outlandish theories about the superiority of their techniques, but these ideas, however silly, do not affect their performance. Hence, a great physicist or a great economist may, without any consequences for his scientific work, embrace and proclaim the most naïve and outdated methodological principles. Students of methodology should beware of the temptation to rely on authority in accepting the methodological pronouncements of a great figure in his field.

The present essay attempts neither a survey of methodological thought in economics nor a review of the debate on a particular methodological issue. Its aim is much more modest: to offer a clear, but critical, presentation of the principles of "operationalism" (or "operationism") in economic concept and theory formation.[2]

---

[1] Perhaps some examples may be in order. The rejection of causality and the championing of mere description (rather than explanation) became fashionable in the last quarter of the nineteenth century. Many years later, Schumpeter was one of the first economists who embraced the excommunication of causality (1906), but later he was one of the most vigorous to plead for its reinstatement. The anathema against explanation and the exhortation for "description only" are still maintained by Samuelson (1964). I know of no philosopher of science who still clings to such views.

[2] For a more elaborate analysis of operationalism in physics and economics, see my article on "Operational Concepts and Mental Constructs in Model and Theory Formation," *Giornale degli Economisti*, 19 (September-October, 1960), 553-582. Reprinted in Universitá Commerciale Luigi Bocconi, Milano, ed., *Studi di Economia, Finanza e Statistica in Onore di Gustavo del Vecchio* (Padova: Cedam, 1963), pp. 467-496.

THE TENETS OF OPERATIONALISM

Operationalism insists that "the proper definition of a concept is . . . in terms of actual operations"; claims that pure constructs, designed "to deal with . . . situations which we cannot directly experience through our senses," should (although sometimes indispensable) be replaced as soon as possible by operationally defined concepts; denies that a "question has meaning" if one cannot "find operations by which an answer may be given to it"; and demands that "the operational mode of thinking [be] adopted in all fields of inquiry." [3]

This program concerns both the formation of *concepts* and the formation of *theories*. It is possible to accept a modified "operational" position for theory formation without accepting the program for concept formation. However, since this modified position removes the idea of operationalism far from what it originally meant—and employs the word "operational" merely as an equivalent for "verifiable"—we shall understand the principles of operationalism as they were originally proclaimed.

Whose operations were referred to? Clearly, the scientist's, observer's, experimentalist's, surveyor's, technician's, interrogator's, statistician's operations were meant. *What kind* of operations? "Physical operations" were required for physical concepts; this, evidently, meant chiefly experimental operations. In other empirical disciplines the operations would include setting up instruments, taking certain measurements, making controlled observations of all sorts, going through certain routines in recording, compiling, computing, and so forth.

Two contentions in the early operationalist position cannot meaningfully be maintained: (1) that the operations defining a concept are "identical with the concept"; and (2) that "mental operations" are still within the compass of the requirements of operationalism.

The asserted identity between the concept and the set of operations that defines it can conceivably be maintained for certain metric concepts (distance, time, velocity, weight) but not for other things. Concepts of (sensory or imagined) objects or events can be defined through sets of operations, but these operations are not identical with the concepts. The operations by which scientists identify a chemical substance, a gas, an animal, a disease, an earthquake, a revolution, an inflation, a strike, etc., are surely not "identical" with the things defined.

The admissibility of "mental operations" was probably only a momentary lapse, induced by the need to reconcile the exaggerated statement

---

[3] All quoted phrases are from Percy W. Bridgman, *The Logic of Modern Physics* (New York: Macmillan, 1927), pp. 6, 53, 28, 30.

about the prescribed operations being "a criterion of meaning" with the recognition that the formal disciplines—mathematics and logic—cannot be condemned as "meaningless." If "operations" are a prerequisite of meaning and if mathematical propositions evidently have "meaning," mental operations must be approved. However, if this approval is extended to empirical sciences, the entire platform of operationalism is compromised. For the formation of concepts in empirical sciences, definitions can admit only operations with data of experience, with records of observations, with "protocol statements."

The question is only whether the operations that define concepts must be *actually* performed (or performable) or whether merely *conceivable*, but not practically possible, operations are also acceptable. Conceivable operations with not yet invented instruments or not yet discovered techniques are perhaps acceptable if there is an honest expectation that these operations may soon be practically possible. On the other hand, conceivable operations of a more "imaginative" character, based on developments which nobody can reasonably expect to become reality, ought to be disqualified as criteria for allegedly "operational" definitions (for example, operations with a mind-reading device that records the hypothetical thoughts and choices of millions of people in thousands of hypothetical situations). If such fictitious operations were admitted, the difference between operational concepts and pure constructs would disappear and the demand for "operational definitions" would become senseless. This demand, in essence, is for concepts of things *observed*, for empirical data from the sensory domain, in contradistinction to concepts of things *imagined* or *postulated* in the domain of mental construction.

For the operationally defined concepts of economics the relevant operations are largely based on reports and on records compiled from reports, such as balance sheets, profit-and-loss statements, bank statements, market quotations, price lists, customhouse statements, income-tax returns, census returns, and so forth. Most of the data, both the raw data from the original reports and the manipulated data from the compilations, are numerical; but also nonnumerical "events," reported in newspapers, trade journals, and other publications, may be among the data entering into and emerging from the operations described or prescribed in the definitions.

It is one of the commandments of operationalism that the propositions which form a "theory" should be composed solely of operational concepts. Unfortunately, "theories" made of such material are only what some philosophers have called "low-level generalizations" or "statements of empirical uniformities and regularities." The "general theories," the "high-level generalizations" of a "theoretical system," from which any number of propositions about all sorts of relationships can be deduced, are made of different stuff. The differences between these two types of theory will be examined presently, but first we have to make sure that we understand the nature of the building material of theoretical systems, namely, "pure constructs" and how they differ from operational concepts (as "operationally defined terms" may be called).

PURE CONSTRUCTS AND OPERATIONAL CONCEPTS

What is given to us and what is constructed by us are obviously different things. Concepts based on operations with data from the *protocol* domain,[4] on records concerning sensory observations and experiences, on knowledge about concrete objects, magnitudes, and events, may be regarded as *empirical* and as containing all the impurities and the inexactness inevitable in the reporting, recording, and computing by erring, perhaps lying, and certainly not infallible humans. Concepts based on imagination, invention, and postulation, on pure reason in the domain of mental *construction,* on idealization, hypothesization, and heuristic fictions, on nominalistic conventions adopted because of their analytical convenience and logico-deductive fertility, may be regarded as *theoretical* and endowed with the purity and fictional exactness afforded by uninhibited, abstract speculation.

I am deliberately overstating the contrast between the two types of concepts when I stress the extreme polarities empirical–theoretical, concrete–abstract, given–constructed, reality–fiction, observation–idealization, impure–pure, and so forth. One could immediately show that the empirical concepts contain plenty of theorizing, abstraction, purification, and so forth and that the theoretical concepts are not all that free, uninhibited, and speculative (or they could not serve in theories applicable to explain observations of the real world). The *operations* with the data of observation are usually designed to produce empirical concepts that somehow fit the constructs of a theoretical framework, and the *construction* of purely fictitious ideal types is usually designed to aid in the formation of theories of explanatory and predictive usefulness. The requirements of *theoretical* usefulness of operational concepts and *empirical* usefulness of pure constructs are powerful constraints in the formation of the two types of concepts.

These constraints both in the choice of operations with the "givens" and in the choice of design for the "construction" should not be understood to reduce a difference in kind to a difference in degree. Despite all

---

[4] The term "protocol" was introduced by the early neopositivists of the Vienna Circle, evidently because in German this word stands for the "record" (of a testimony) or the "minutes" (of a conference). The idea is that the data given to the scientist are in the form of a record ("protocol"). Bridgman's "operations" refer to the original observations that are recorded, to the manner of recording, and to what is done with the data recorded. Hence, operationalism is by its very nature associated with the "protocol domain."

psychological and practical similarities, the logical difference remains. Its chief implication is that the various constructs ("constructed concepts") in a comprehensive theoretical system are *logically interrelated*, whereas various empirical concepts ("operational concepts") are at best linked by *inductive generalization* or statistical correlation. Conclusions deduced from a set of hypothetical propositions containing only pure constructs follow by *logical necessity*—though they may not be applicable to the concrete situations in need of explanatory or predictive judgments. Conclusions based on inductive generalizations about observed objects, magnitudes, or events possess some more or less definite *probability value* —though they may not be helpful in conveying any genuine understanding of the causal connections involved.

Illustrations may be needed to clarify matters, and I shall choose some from economics. The term "price" in the proposition "an increase in supply will lower the price" has a different meaning from the term "price" in the proposition "the price of steel in 1933 was 15 per cent lower than in 1932." In the first proposition, "price" is a pure construct; in the second, an operational concept. What are the operations employed in ascertaining the steel price in a particular period? A large variety of operations could be used: One could procure the price lists of all steel producers and compute some sort of average, weighted or unweighted; one could ascertain their sales proceeds—gross or net of discounts, commissions, transport costs—and divide them by the total tonnage shipped; one could secure reports from steel buyers and arrange, weight, or otherwise manipulate their figures in various ways; one could rely on reports from the largest middlemen; one could propose as many as fifty different sets of operations, all sensible and reasonable, but yielding different findings. Depending on the changes in the composition of steel shipments, the average per ton may have fallen while list prices were raised (but more of cheaper types, shapes, or qualities were shipped). The average of "delivered prices" may have increased while the average of f.o.b. prices declined (transportation costs being higher, perhaps because of steel being shipped over greater distances). The average of prices may be different depending upon whether new orders received, or production, or actual shipments are taken into account.

None of these operational concepts of "steel price" corresponds completely to the simple construct "price," because the latter abstracts from the score of complications presented by "reality," particularly from differences in qualities, shapes, alloys, etc.; from differences among producers; from differences between prices quoted and prices agreed; from differences between prices paid by the buyer and prices received by the seller (net of commissions, sales taxes, transportation costs); and so forth. Many statements about the pure construct "price" would not hold for some of the operational concepts. It is perfectly possible, for example, that an "increase in supply" of steel—provided an operational counterpart could be found for this construct [5]—will under certain conditions be associated with an increase, not a reduction, in the price of steel. This could happen either because of a particular choice of operations—computing, for example, average proceeds per ton, although the increase in supply had caused also a change in the composition of physical sales in favor of more expensive qualities—or because other things changed at the same time. *Ceteris paribus* is always a construction rather than an operational concept.

Many more illustrations could be chosen from micro-economic analysis. Among the most revealing are the concepts of "cost" and "profit," but the reader may be left to his own devices in comparing the wide variety of operational concepts and the smaller selection of pure constructs designated by these terms. The fact that the underlying data available for the statistical operations by disinterested observers come from reports derived from accounting operations that leave much leeway for subjective judgment by interested parties is only one of the difficulties in choosing appropriate operational concepts of cost and profit; much more significant is the fact that virtually all practically possible operations refer to historical (*ex post*) data, whereas most of the pure constructs that are relevant for the theoretical system refer to expected (*ex ante*) values.

Macro-economic terms present the same problems. Against the fictitious purity, simplicity, and exactness of the pure constructs of national income, consumption, *ex ante* saving, investment, imports, trade balance, and all the rest, the impurities, complications, and inaccuracies of their operational counterparts are appalling. Anyone who has done empirical work with national-income statistics or foreign-trade statistics is aware of thousands and thousands of arbitrary decisions that the statisticians had to make in executing the operations dictated or suggested by one of the large variety of definitions accepted for the terms in question. One cannot expect with any confidence that any of the theories connecting the pure constructs of the relevant aggregative magnitudes will be borne out by an examination of their operational counterparts. If imports, for example, are measured by the declared values of merchandise crossing the border of the nation and passing the customhouse during a stated period, this cannot be but a very imperfect surrogate of the imports supposedly purchased in consequence of certain changes in relative prices or total income, according to some general theoretical propositions.

Of course, passages or cross-connections between the domain of construction (the pure theories with their pure constructs) and the

---

[5] See Footnote 7, page 63, for an explanation of this doubt. The point is that an observable increase in the "quantity supplied" (perhaps in response to an increase in demand) may be associated with an unchanged or even reduced "supply."

domain of recorded data are needed; these connections are possible wherever an operational concept comes particularly close to a pure construct.[6] At these points "rules of correspondence" will direct the theorist to the data, and the empirical researcher to the pure theory. But from what has just been said about operational concepts and pure constructs, it should be clear why only the latter qualify as building material for general propositions within theoretical systems.

EMPIRICAL THEORIES AND PURE THEORY

Although most writers use the terms "empirical" and "theoretical" as opposites, and thus contrast "empirical correlations" with "theoretical relationships," there are some who speak of "empirical theories." The term "theory" in this phrase means nothing but "inductive generalization," that is, a statement of an expectation or probability that the same co-existence, sequence, or numerical relation that has been observed among certain objects, events, or magnitudes in the past will also be found in future constellations of the same classes of observations. If such inductive generalizations are termed "theories" by some writers, one has to understand it as an extension of the dictionary meanings of theory. There are others, who use the designation "empirical laws" for this sort of proposition. If my reading of contemporary philosophers of science is correct, they prefer to speak of these generalizations as "correlational statements," "observed links among protocol data," or "statements of empirical uniformities." The term "theory" is more frequently reserved for those general constructions which, by permitting logical inferences from premises to conclusions (and from causes to consequences), help us understand (interpret, explain) some observed "facts" from the protocol domain.

Empirical (correlational) statements are necessarily composed of operational concepts. This does not mean that no theoretical elements are contained in these concepts. There is no such thing as "mere description." The pre-scientific reports are already permeated with some theorizing on the part of the reporters as well as of those whose instructions or directives they follow. In addition, the subsequent operations with these protocol data are influenced by theorizing of a higher order, especially if the arrangement of the data is designed for "scientific" purposes. But still, despite the treatment which the raw data must undergo, despite selections, abstractions, adjustments, corrections, and other manipulations, they still belong to the protocol domain. For, since the treatment of the recorded data must be equal and uniform in accordance with technical rules stipulated for particular classes of data, the "facts" are still "stubborn," at least in their relative dimensions. The admixture

[6] On "The Need for Operational Concepts," see page 65.

of theory, however, may be substantial; indeed, the operations for the production and processing (or perhaps "fabrication") of the empirical data are designed and redesigned to make the resulting operational concepts as closely corresponding to some theoretical construct as possible.

Theoretical systems are composed entirely of pure constructs. This assertion, plausible though it is, contradicts the pronouncements of a large number of scientists and philosophers. They accept a constructed, nonempirical concept only where some notion is indispensable but no suitable operational concept can be found. They want as many terms as possible, within a theoretical system, to be operationally defined. Only where operational concepts are unavailable would they provisionally admit pure constructs; and they see progress in science when theoretical concepts are replaced by empirical concepts.

The opposite position, argued in the present essay, also has numerous supporters. They see progress in science when empirical concepts are replaced by theoretical concepts, for only by redefinitions, transforming all terms into pure constructs, can a logico-deductive system be developed. Fortunately, such redefinitions require only some superior constructive minds; it is always possible to replace an empirical concept by a theoretical construct. (On the other hand, attempts to discover practicable operations to obtain an operational counterpart for a pure construct may be frustrated by the nature of things. The search for operational proxies for some theoretical constructs may be quite hopeless.) The replacement of empirical by theoretical concepts, or of operational by pure concepts, is, to state it once more, needed for the following reasons: The roughness, or degree of exactness, of empirical concepts depends upon the technical possibilities provided by the state of the arts. The impurities and inaccuracies inherent in most or all practicable operations with sensory observations and recorded data destroy the logical links between different concepts. But without logical interrelations the propositions containing these concepts do not afford logically necessary conclusions. In the possibility of deducing such conclusions lie the sole purpose and value of any theoretical system.

ILLUSTRATION: A THEORETICAL ARGUMENT AND THE CONCEPTS USED

The entire discussion of empirical generalizations and theoretical systems—especially with all the jargon used about "operations with data from the protocol domain" and the "purity and exactness of concepts in the domain of construction"—may be lost on readers who are not given an opportunity to see "what's what" in an illustration. Hence, we shall offer an example of a theoretical economic argument, followed by an examination of the nature of the concepts employed.

In 1964 the new Labor government of the United Kingdom imposed a 15 per cent tax on imports. Economists were probably asked to analyze the probable and possible effects of this measure. The following argument might have been formulated by an analyst using his knowledge of economic theory.

0. Effective on a certain day, a tax of 15 per cent ad valorem is levied on all imports.
1. Assuming that both the foreign supply of imports and the domestic demand for imports have elasticities greater than zero and smaller than infinity, the prices of imports including the tax will rise by less than 15 per cent; that is, foreign suppliers will obtain reduced net prices. The physical volume of imports will decrease.
2. The amount of foreign exchange demanded for payments for imports will decrease, both because of the reduced quantities of goods imported and the reduced foreign prices of some of these goods.
3. Depending upon whether the elasticity of the domestic demand for imports is greater or smaller than unity, the total amount of domestic money spent for the reduced quantity of imports will be decreased or increased, but a portion of this expenditure (less than 15 per cent since the tax is on import values, not retail prices) will go to the Treasury.
4. With consumer expenditures for imported goods decreased or increased, expenditures for domestic products may increase or decrease; however, only if the elasticity of the demand for imported goods were less than unity (which one may doubt) would consumer expenditures for domestic products decrease. In addition, if the Treasury were to spend some or all of its revenue from the import tax, this would further increase total effective demand for domestic products.
5. Increased demand for domestic products will sooner or later result in (a) higher prices, (b) increased profits for domestic producers, (c) increased demand for, and prices of, productive factors, especially labor, (d) increased costs and supply prices, not only of import substitutes and domestic goods, but also of export goods.
6. The increased prices of domestic products will lead to an increase in the (domestic) demand for imports and to a reduction in the quantity of exports demanded (abroad).
7. With regard to some particular imports, special situations—in terms of elasticities of competitive foreign and domestic supply and demand or in terms of monopolistic market positions—may require special analysis.
8. With regard to some particular countries, the possibility of retaliatory measures and their effects may require special analysis.
9. With regard to the labor market, the possibility of escalated trade-

union pressures because of increased costs of living may require special analysis.

10. With regard to the domestic credit market and official monetary policy, the possibility of an increased demand for funds and of an expansion of bank credit may require special analysis.

11. With regard to international capital movements, the possibility of increased or reduced outflows of foreign long-term and short-term funds, in the light of expectations induced by the tax measure, may require special analysis.

Although this argument is far from complete, it more than suffices for our purpose—for an examination of the nature of concepts employed.

(1) "Foreign supply of imports" and "domestic demand for imports" mean hypothetical quantities as functions of hypothetical prices. No operational concept can be devised to ascertain these functions. Even as pure constructs the imagined functions can be unambiguously visualized only for one import good, or for a bundle of import goods of uniform composition. For many import goods, each with a separate set of supply and demand functions, the problem of "aggregation," even in imagination, would present difficulties. The theorist, however, accepts the single-commodity function as a satisfactory analogy for the many-commodities case. But even if there were "in reality" only one import commodity, the supply and demand functions would still not be operational. A so-called "statistical demand function" is a *tour-de-force* and its results cannot be accepted as a usable operational proxy for a construct, let alone as a part of a theoretical argument.[7] The other concepts, in this first point of the argument, are "domestic prices of imports," "net prices obtained by foreign suppliers," and "physical volume of imports."

---

[7] "Every beginning student of economics is (or should be) repeatedly warned of the hypothetical nature of the functional relations between the variables. There are no 'observable' supply or demand functions—unless one means merely the chalk symbols which the teacher produces on the blackboard for students to observe. All the values of the functions are imagined; the supply function assigns hypothetical quantities offered in the market to hypothetical prices paid, and the demand function assigns hypothetical quantities demanded to these prices, but since the prices and quantities are hypothetical only, they cannot be observed by anybody. (It may be said for the benefit of readers who are comforted by the thought of 'conceivable operationality' that with much fantasy one may design a grand 'experiment,' with heroic controls of all relevant factors, to ascertain all values of the functions. But one must add, in all honesty, that the 'operations' required to establish the functions as empirical observations are not practically possible.) The so-called statistical supply and demand curves have not really been 'observed'; they are the result of highly imaginative computations with data recorded at different times under different conditions and manipulated on the basis of unverifiable assumptions which range from 'plausible' to 'contrary to fact.' " *Giornale degli Economisti*, Vol. XIX, p. 574.

They all have operational *counterparts,* but they are pure constructs as used in the argument.

(2) The "amount of foreign exchange demanded for payments for imports" is another pure construct. An operational counterpart is available in countries with strict foreign-exchange controls, where each application for foreign exchange must specify the purpose for which the foreign payment is made. Even there the operational counterpart will be quite inexact for several reasons, one of which is that payments made in one period may be for goods ordered much earlier.[8] In any case, an operational concept corresponding to this pure construct is "practically possible," but in countries with convertible currencies nobody will bother actually to perform or direct the relevant operations.

(3) For the construct "expenditures for imported goods" operational counterparts could be obtained if necessary. The cost would be inordinately high if complete enumeration were wanted, but estimates could be made without a large bureaucratic apparatus. For purposes of the present theoretical argument, the theoretical construct is all that is needed.

(4) The same comment applies to the construct "expenditures for domestic products." For "Treasury expenditures" the operational counterpart is actually available, though it would be difficult to ascertain whether increased expenditures were in fact induced by the increased revenues, or would have been made in any case. Actual expenditures, public and private, may serve also as a proxy for "effective demand," though this term stands again for a pure construct in the argument.

(5) For some of the concepts used here as theoretical constructs one could obtain more or less approximate operational counterparts. Exceptions are (a) "increased profits" because *ex post* reported figures would not correspond to the *ex ante* ideas of those who decide on higher production volumes; (b) "increased demand for productive factors" because one can at best ascertain purchases, employment, prices, and wage rates but not "demand"; and (c) "supply prices" because one can ascertain only prices actually paid or received but not the hypothetical prices for hypothetically supplied quantities.

(6) The "demand for imports" has already been disqualified as a candidate for operational ambitions. The "quantity of exports demanded" stands a better chance.

(7)–(11). Only two more concepts which would present serious dif-

---

[8] Another reason is that under exchange restrictions many invoices will be a little "padded" so that the payor can get a little more foreign currency than he needs to pay for the particular import.

ficulties if they had to be operationally defined will be mentioned: "monopolistic market positions" and "trade-union pressures" (since demands for higher wages are made almost constantly, how can "pressures" be quantified?).

What this exercise has shown is that for *some* of the concepts used in the theoretical argument operational counterparts are available; for *others* they could be obtained if it were really necessary; for a *third group* they could not be obtained even with the greatest expense and ingenuity; but that in the theoretical argument itself *all* concepts were pure constructs, not operationally but nominalistically defined.

THE NEED FOR OPERATIONAL CONCEPTS

If operational concepts are not wanted, not even admitted for membership in a purely theoretical argument, does this mean that there is no use for them at all? No, they are wanted, indeed urgently needed, for two purposes: (1) when one has to decide what kind of theoretical apparatus will be suitable for answering particular questions, and (2) when one wishes to verify or test the theoretical apparatus.[9] (Regarding these two purposes, the significance of the "rules of correspondence" should be recalled.)

The theoretical economic argument, used above as an illustration, was intended to answer the question "What consequences could be expected from the imposition of a tax on imports?" This presupposes that we possess an empirical concept of "tax on imports" and can define it by unambiguous operations. We do have such a concept at our disposal, and we can define it explicitly. The operations may consist in looking for a law enacted by the legislature, for decrees making the law effective, and for records of tax offices about the law being executed. An even simpler set of operations would be to look for reports by importers paying the tax. There is no difficulty at all concerning an operational definition of "tax on imports."

For purposes of verification it does not suffice to have an operationally defined concept as the clear counterpart of the starting step that sets the theoretical apparatus in motion. We also need operational counterparts for some of the conclusions furnished by that apparatus, that is, for the consequences deduced from the propositions in the logical argument. Fortunately, some of the "consequences" inferred in our illustration have operational brothers or cousins. This is true at least for the prices and quantities involved. Several other "consequences" have no operational relatives and are, therefore, not testable. But no one expects a theoretical

[9] See the author's article, "The Problem of Verification in Economics," *Southern Economical Journal*, 22 (1955), 1-21.

system to be tested at every use. Occasional tests under favorable conditions suffice to establish confidence in the system, which will then be used in many instances where the results cannot be verified through satisfactory "correspondence" between all deduced consequences and observed facts.

The theoretical models designed for showing the effects of changes in tax rates, tariffs, wage rates, interest rates, and similar variables have been tested often enough to satisfy us concerning their general usefulness. To be sure, there have been numerous disappointments; but, when these occurred, acceptable reasons could usually be found. The most frequent reason for disappointment, that is, for a lack of correspondence between deduced consequences and observed facts, has been some unexpected change in conditions, some simultaneous event that had not been assumed to occur and, therefore, was not taken into account in the theoretical argument. In order to maintain our confidence, the "auxiliary hypotheses" employed to excuse failures and to reconcile expected with actual observations ought to be testable. This presupposes that the crucial constructs used in these hypotheses possess operational counterparts. Only then can one prove that the alleged disturbance has not only been "assumed" but that something of this sort has actually occurred according to available evidence.[10]

OPERATIONAL THEORIES, SO-CALLED

It is not easy to know what the economists who used the phrase "operational theory" really meant by this designation. They have not furnished any illustrations or examples for their designation. Technical jargon is usually not enough to make things clear. Thus, if I fail to understand them and misinterpret their intentions, they will have to forgive me.

What the economists could have meant when they called for "operational theory" is approximately what has been advanced in the preceding section, namely, that a theory ought to have sufficient links with the protocol domain, with data of observation. Links are "sufficient" if they allow us to choose intelligently the theoretical arguments that apply to particular "concrete" situations and, in addition, if they allow us to subject the theoretical system to occasional verification against empirical evidence.

The only good reason for calling such theories "operational" is because their links with empirical data require the availability of *operational counterparts* to some of the crucial theoretical constructs. Although the

---

[10] It has been said that a good economist is one who will be able to explain next year why his predictions of last year have not come true this year.

phrase has been used here almost constantly, it is well to repeat that by "operational counterpart" of a theoretical construct we mean an "operationally defined" term that can be accepted as a satisfactory empirical referent or proxy for the construct.

There is, however, the alternative meaning of "operational theory" as propositions containing exclusively operationally defined terms. This would be what has been called "empirical theory" or inductive generalizations. It usually correlates a small number of narrowly defined concepts, that is, *classes of data,* and since there is little or anything that can be deduced from it except that the same relations among these classes of data will probably recur in the future, it applies only to a very narrow choice of "cases." For example, an empirical generalization in the field of "taxes on imports" would presuppose that we have had many previous experiences with and observations of import taxes together with other things, such as prices and quantities of imports and amounts of foreign exchange sold by monetary authorities. We could, of course, never have anything like a "general price theory." And we would not be allowed to apply an empirical theory of the effects of sales or excise taxes to a case of import taxes, apart from the fact that such a theory would not include the variables relevant to the case of import taxes (such as imports, foreign exchange, etc.).

Thus, without a sufficient number of past observations in connection with import taxes we could not present, under the principles of empiricism and operationalism, an argument about the effects to be expected from the imposition of such a tax. These principles prohibit us from going beyond the specific empirical evidence, that is, beyond the established correlations among recorded data of a narrowly defined type. As soon as we go beyond these data and their correlations, we are in the domain of construction and have risen above inductive generalizations. Empiricists and operationalists may deplore it, but this is the only way of developing a general theoretical system fertile with useful inferences.

ON IDEAL TYPES AND
THE INTERPRETATION
OF REALITY

INTRODUCTION TO PART FOUR

Part Four is composed of four essays: one newly written for this volume, another published in German in 1960 and translated into English for inclusion in this volume, the third published first in French in 1967 and then in English in 1970, and the fourth first published in English in 1972. The earlier publications were to honor either some anniversary or the memory of a respected scholar; the German essay was written in memory of the German economist Walter Eucken; the French version of the third essay was published in a festschrift for Jacques Rueff, the French economist; the English version of the same essay was included in a volume in memory of Alfred Schutz, the Austrian–American philosopher and sociologist; and the fourth was one of the *Essays in Honour of Lord Robbins.* All four essays deal with the ideal type, a construct designed for the interpretation of social reality.

Chapter 8, "The Ideal Type: A Bad Name for a Good Construct," is intended as an appetizer to the next three courses. I composed it in order to allay my misgivings concerning the heavy doses of doctrinal history administered to the reader of Chapter 9. A brief exposition of the basic ideas that underlie the ideal type should help the reader endure the hardships he might confront if he accompanied me on the strenuous tour through the intellectual history offered in

Chapter 9. I hope that my effort will succeed, and will encourage the reader to go on.

Chapter 9 is entitled "Ideal Types, Reality, and Construction." The German original was published in *Ordo* Vol. 12 (1960); the entire issue of that annual publication was devoted to honoring the memory of Walter Eucken, who had died in 1950. This is the reason why I treated Eucken's views on the ideal type in great detail and gave him so much more space than I did to Carl Menger, Max Weber, Werner Sombart, and most other participants in this discussion. However, with all my respect for Eucken, I was quite critical of his methodological position and did not pull my punches; I was sure he would not have wanted me to do so. The translation from the German gave me much trouble, as I explain in a prefatory note to the chapter.

Chapter 10 bears the title "Homo Oeconomicus and His Class Mates." It was first published in French, under the title "L'homo oeconomicus et ses collègues" in Jacques Rueff, *Les Fondements Philosophiques des Systèmes Economiques* (Paris: Payot, 1967), which contained selected writings by Rueff himself as well as essays contributed in his honor. Since my essay was largely based on the social phenomenology of Alfred Schutz, the editor of a collective book published in memory of this great philosopher asked me to contribute the English version of my essay to the memorial volume, Maurice Natanson, ed., *Phenomenology and Social Reality: Essays in Memory of Alfred Schutz* (The Hague: Nijhoff, 1970). It is this version reproduced here as Chapter 10, with the omission of a three-page subsection, "The Ideal Type According to Alfred Schutz," which at the editor's request had been taken from the 1960 essay in *Ordo* and inserted into the English version of the "Homo Oeconomicus." We surely do not need to have exactly the same statement appear in Chapters 9 and 10.

At the end of Chapter 10, I tried to show that the ideal type "economic man" was in some respects quite different from his class mates, that is, from other members of the class "ideal type." Economic Man had been terribly misunderstood and misrepresented in the literature, especially by antitheoretical economists and antieconomists. Lionel Robbins had referred to the much denounced man as "The Universal Bogey." I chose this designation for the title of my contribution to the Robbins festschrift, Maurice Peston and Bernard Corry, eds.,

Essays in Honour of Lord Robbins (London: Weidenfeld & Nicolson, 1972). My essay was reproduced without change (except for the correction of a misprint in the very last sentence) in the *Selected Economic Writings of Fritz Machlup* (New York: New York University Press, 1976). It is now Chapter 11 in the present volume.

When I was invited to contribute to the festschrift for Robbins, I had been at work on a project in intellectual history for which I had tentatively chosen the title "The Life and Work of Homunculus Oeconomicus." I found it expedient as well as suitable to use my accumulated notes and working papers for this essay in honor of Robbins; my contribution to the festschrift would thus be a well researched and well thought-out study in areas in which Robbins himself had always excelled: doctrinal history and logical analysis. The essay presents the views of 14 authors, and of course my own, on the good and bad deeds of Economic Man, born *in vitro*, in the economist's mental test tube.

Chapter 8

THE IDEAL TYPE:
A BAD NAME FOR A GOOD CONSTRUCT

To answer the question "how concepts are formed"—either in the minds of ordinary people in their everyday business of thinking, talking, and acting or in the minds of scientists describing or explaining natural or cultural phenomena—has been a major task of philosophers. Some were chiefly interested in the genesis of concepts, in the mental processes that result in concepts (or notions); others wanted to know what kinds of processes were especially efficient or particularly reliable in the formation of "good" concepts. By this, supposedly, they meant the concepts most useful in the acquisition of *true knowledge*—a goal that has led to millions of printed pages of discourses on what is knowledge and what is truth.

PSYCHOLOGY AND LOGIC OF
CONCEPT FORMATION

In any case, inquiries into concept formation have long been regarded as studies of the genetics of concepts or of the technology of concept formation; but inasmuch as the genesis or the techniques in question refer to processes in the mind, and the concepts themselves are mental, the inquiries fell into the domain of psychology.

This epistemological allocation, however, was not acceptable to logicians. They showed that the psychology of concept formation was one thing, but the logic of formed concepts, and especially interrelated concepts, was another.

The demand that logical problems be separated from psychological problems has proved fruitful. A concept, once formed and formulated, has, so to speak, a life of its own, independent both of the actual thinking processes that went on in the minds of the concept formers and of those that will go on in the minds of the concept users. The independent existence of the concept—independent of its creator as well as of its user—is then left for the logicians to take care of. Perhaps one may say, in the language of Sir Karl Popper, that the concept has become an inhabitant of "World Three," the world of objective knowledge, quite apart from "World Two," the psychological world of subjective experiences. According to this view, thought processes are in World Two, but the contents of thought are in World Three. Whether or not this extreme epistemological position is accepted, the dominant view today is that "psychologism in logic . . . is largely a thing of the past; the attempt to reduce the norms of logic to laws of thought is now merely a historical curiosity." [1]

CONSTRUCTS BASED ON SUBJECTIVE MEANINGS

These remarks seem to prejudge the central issue addressed in this essay and the other three essays collected in this part, "On Ideal Types and the Interpretation of Reality." For, if the ideal type is a concept constructed with a view to the essential role of the subjective meaning meant by a person acting in the social world, are we not plainly and flagrantly back in psychologism, without a passport or visa to the objective world of logic? "Alas, you are," would be the answer of some methodologists, who reject the ideal type as a legitimate construct for theory formation in the social sciences. I shall argue, however, that constructs "typifying" subjective meanings can

[1] Gerard Radnitzky, "Popperian Philosophy of Science as an Antidote against Relativism," in *Essays in Memory of Imre Lakatos*, edited by Robert S. Cohen, *et al.*, (Dordrecht, Netherlands: D. Reidel Publishing Co., 1976), p. 505.

be objective in character; and I shall attempt to defend the claim that ideal types can be members in good standing of the class of scientific constructs. This defense, I am aware, will not be easy, because many champions of the use of ideal types in descriptions and explanations of social phenomena and human affairs have engaged in most explicit psychologizing. Thus I shall have to fight against both sides: against the psychologizing exponents of ideal-typical reasoning and against the logical antagonists of ideal-typical reasoning.[2]

In this engagement on two fronts, I have two strikes against me even before I begin: the ideal type is a misnomer. In the ordinary senses of these words, *the ideal type is neither ideal nor a type.* The type is not "ideal" in the usual, evaluative sense of this adjective. Indeed, the adjective in this instance is not supposed to refer to an ideal but, instead, to an idea—which is a less common use of the adjective. And the noun thus modified is not supposed to refer to a "type" in the sense of a characteristic image or representation of a group or class or as a symbol for a kind (of something) frequently encountered in reality. Instead, it is supposed to be a mental construct of imagined (and often imaginary) aspects of imagined (and often imaginary) persons, of their actions and reactions, and of processes, events, or material things presumed to result from these actions and reactions. Hence, the word "type" is even more misleading than the word "ideal." Why not scrap the expression and thereby get rid of a bevy of pseudo-problems? Perhaps we should. However, poor terminology cannot be the only reason why that ill-starred notion has been suspect and controversial for three-quarters of a century. The misnaming of the concept may have contributed to the misunderstandings, but the methodological difficulties would have existed even if the most felicitous name had been found for the poor creature. To change its name would not resolve the specific

[2] The dichotomy of psychology versus logic, although I have called it fruitful, is also misleading in that it seems to overlook the problems of the cultural influences upon individual minds. Too many psychologists, and even more nonpsychologists, have thought of psychology as the study of mental processes in disregard of inter-subjective experiences, experiences of "other minds," shared experiences, and the learning of concepts formed or suggested by others. One may, of course, favor a meaning of psychology wide enough to encompass all phenomena of the social world that influence the thought processes of the individual.

problems of the methodology of the social sciences. If the issues remain with us, we may just as well put up with the ill-chosen name; name-changing this late in the game may make it harder for studious readers to learn from the literary exchanges of the past.

TWO SETS OF DISTINCTIONS

Having intimated that there are specific problems regarding the methodology of the social sciences, I feel obliged to say wherein they lie and what this essay and the other essays on the ideal type will do to explicate them. The logic of conceptualization requires two sets of distinctions, of which the first holds for all empirical sciences, while the second relates to a difference between natural and social sciences. The first distinction was discussed in Chapters 6 and 7 and will again be given some space in Chapter 9. It relates to the separation of the empirical and theoretical domains for which concepts are designed. The two domains cultivate different concepts: *Operational* (empirical, epistemic) concepts, defined by observational, experimental, or statistical operations, are needed for empirical propositions [correlational laws]. *Exact* (abstract, pure) constructs, formed by idealization, invention, and construction, are needed for nomologic-theoretical propositions [theoretical laws].

The second difference is based on methodological characteristics separating the sciences of human culture and society from the sciences of nature, inorganic and organic. The question arises whether this second difference is to be more effectively advertised by using separate names for the concepts employed. In the methodological writings of German philosophers and social scientists, historians as well as theorists, such a special term has been used for almost 80 years: the "ideal type."

Exact constructs in the physical sciences, that is, nonempirical, idealized concepts such as pure water, pure alcohol, perfect gas, perfect vacuum, zero friction, perfect conductor, etc., etc., can be defined without any reference to any person, living or dead, real or imaginary. In contradistinction, idealized constructs (ideal types) employed in everyday social life by ordinary people, but also in narratives by social historians, in *belles lettres* produced by writers of

FRITZ MACHLUP

any sort, in empirical generalizations by sociologists, and in theoretical arguments by economists—in brief, concepts relating to the social world—cannot be formed or used without explicit or implicit reference to meanings meant by persons real, imagined, or imaginary. I shall presently try to elucidate the meaning of meant meanings, but before I do I should like to repeat that, in my opinion, this difference, that is, the need for an inherent relation to acting, thinking, or feeling persons, is sufficiently important to warrant the explicit distinction between the idealized constructs in natural sciences and the idealized constructs in social history and social sciences: The difference justifies the use of a separate designation for constructs related to man, culture, and society. "Ideal type" has been this designation.

My attempt at elucidation will be helped by illustrations. We can divide them into those of personal ideal types, material ideal types (including course-of-action types) and ideal types of personal feelings. We shall quickly discover, however, that the material ideal types are usually closely related to personal ideal types, inasmuch as the material objects in question are either the results of human actions and can be defined only in terms of the intentions or other subjective meanings entertained by acting persons. The same holds true for course-of-action types that include no material objects. Similarly, the ideal types of the third kind, those of personal feelings, again relate closely to personal ideal types, since it would be unthinkable that feelings exist without a person having them.

PERSONAL IDEAL TYPES

I begin with a string of (anonymous) personal types: friend, enemy, stranger, homecomer, messenger, liar, boss, servant, wife, husband, bachelor, lover, thief, judge, buyer, borrower, investor. Let us pick out one of this list to take a closer look at, say, the *thief*. The ideal type of the thief is inseparably connected with the intention of a person to take possession of another person's property against the will of the latter. If you observed someone carrying a physical object out of a house or shop, you could not possibly know whether the person had purchased the object or borrowed it or was taking it to have it repaired on orders from the owner or was taking back what he had previously lent. Alternatively, the thought of a thief may be in the mind of the person from whom the object was taken, who regarded it as his property. There may even be an honest difference of opinion about whose property the object really is and/or whether the object was being removed from the premises as the result of a loan, a gift, or a theft. In any case, the definition of a thief implies interpretations on the part of the person taking an object, on the part of the person from whom the object is being taken, or on the part of bystanders, observers, policemen, witnesses, juries, or judges.

In other words, there is no thief unless somebody thinks so. That thought may be in the mind of him who steals (or has stolen); or in the mind of the one from whom something is (or was) stolen; or in the mind of a third person, for example, the judge. The observable fact, that somebody is carrying a physical object from a house or shop, does not establish the physically nonobservable fact of "theft." It takes somebody's knowledge of who has the property right to that physical object, or who has authorized its removal; neither the right nor the authorization is physically observable—unless one means by "physical" the sound waves generated by the owner of the object as he makes an oral claim, or the ink lines he produces on a piece of paper as he puts such a claim in writing. However, such a verbal (spoken or written) statement is again nothing but an expression of a thought concerning a nonphysical, nonobservable situation.

I need not discuss other examples of personal ideal types in the same detail, but I invite the reader to think of the ideal type of a *liar* and of its necessary connection with the person's knowledge and intentions. The ideal type of a liar involves subjective interpretations of the truth-value or probability-value of what he knows and, in addition, an interpretation of his intentions. Just think of a person who intends to tell a lie but actually tells the truth, because what he believes to be true is in fact untrue, and what he actually tells, though he intends it to be a lie, is actually true.

Think of statements about *husbands* and *wives;* these ideal types are connected with interpretations of law or custom, and on interpretations of the legality of a wedding certificate. Assume that the officer of the state or church who conducted the wedding was not duly authorized to perform such an act, but that the couple was unaware of this lack of legitimate authority. You would have the couple "live in sin" if you accepted the interpretation and bureaucratic definition by third persons who discovered the illegality of the marriage. Someone may think that there can be hard evidence for the statement that two cohabitants are legally married, and that this kind of evidence is of the same order of reliability as that of an assayer confirming the fineness of gold or that of a chemical analyst reporting on the relative purity of water. All three are equally objective affidavits about expert findings after honest searches and tests. However, the assayer's and the chemist's evidence relate to tests involving operational concepts of gold and water, not the "exact" constructs. The operational concept of a husband may involve no more than an examination of a wedding certificate and a corroborating search of the official marriage register. The difference between the constructs of natural and cultural phenomena lies not in the domain of empirical observation but rather in the domain of theoretical construction. The ideal type "husband," which is employed in propositions concerning a husband's typical conduct, involves a consciousness, a subjective meaning, entertained by the husband regarding his being married to a particular wife; or, alternatively, this ideal type may serve in propositions concerning a wife's typical conduct, in which case it involves a subjective meaning in her mind regarding her being married to a particular man.[3] The physically observable ink symbols in the marriage register maintained by the state or church have hardly anything to do with the thinking or acting of the people concerned.

For the personal ideal types employed in economic theory, the references to motivation and intention are rather obvious. They are most conspicuous in the exceptional instances of economic results of nonintended actions, when, for example, the economist speaks of "unintended saving" or "unintended investment," as a saver or an investor finds out only afterwards [ex post] what he has done. The case of a collector of paintings is a good example of unobservable thought processes: You may have to ask him whether he bought a picture for the enjoyment he would get out of looking at it or whether he bought it only or chiefly as an investment. In many economic problems, the role of expectations is paramount; and the importance of uncertainty is pervasive in economic analysis. Gen-

[3] Any association between our ideal husband—or rather ideal-typical husband—and Oscar Wilde's *Ideal Husband* is merely coincidental.

eral economic theory, as well as special fields within economics, deal with mind-related, intention-related, and value-related constructs. Designations such as welfare economics, management science, game theory, etc., point clearly to the fact that the subject matter of these fields of inquiry is essentially concerned with meant meanings on the part of idealized actors and decision-makers.

MATERIAL IDEAL TYPES

Illustrations of material ideal types may also help our understanding of what is involved, particularly since the two adjectives—material and ideal—seem to contradict each other. The point is that many material [physical] objects cannot be defined except with reference to ideas in somebody's mind. What is a table? An object of wood, metal, stone, cement, plastic, of a certain minimum or maximum height or size? It may be all of these things, but the essential point is that there is somebody who thinks of the possibility of placing something on it, say, a book, a paper, a cup, or a plate. There is no table unless there is somebody who thinks about placing something on it. The table is defined by the use people may intend to make or expect others to make of it.

Similarly, there is no chair unless somebody thinks of sitting on it. There is no hat without someone thinking of putting it on his or her head. There are no trousers unless someone considers putting his legs into them. There is no hurdle unless someone thinks of jumping over it, or of his or her incapacity to jump over it. There is no path unless someone thinks that he or she or others may walk on it.

For all these, and for thousands of similar things, the characteristic of the object defined is the thought in the mind of a subject—though the thought, the mind, and the subject may all be unspecified or even imagined.

IDEAL TYPES OF FEELINGS

It is hardly necessary to demonstrate that because feelings or sentiments cannot be defined in physical terms they are essentially subjective and hence subject only to introspective observation—

apart from physical (physiognomic) symptoms observable by outside observers. It is just for this reason that extreme empiricists and old-fashioned behaviorists deny that feelings can be admitted into scientific discourse. That symptoms are not the real thing should be obvious. As Herbert Feigl has said so perceptively: "It has become increasingly clear that the early ('radical') behavioristic identification of the meaning of subjective terms with behavioral terms (designating symptoms) will not do. Embarrassment is not identical with blushing; pain is not identical with cringing or writhing.[4]

Of course, if we see someone blush (or cringe), we do not know for sure that he is embarrassed (or in pain), but as a rule we accept symptoms of, or statements about, emotions as pointing to actual emotions felt by the person in question; and we can do it because we have experienced such emotions. "We make a step from introspection to empathy."[5]

We need not be concerned with the restrictive definitions of *science* and *scientific* which opinionated ultra-empiricists have wished to impose upon the scientific enterprise. The fact that I feel love or hate or pain, and the fact that many other people tell us that they feel love or hate or pain, is adequate ground for assuming that people are sufficiently similar to allow scientific inquiries into human feelings. Even if their full understanding presupposes personal subjective experience of such feelings, they are intersubjectively established, can be objectively discussed, and can be related to other ideal types, especially to ideal types of actions and reactions.

Many ideal types of feelings, emotions, sentiments are employed in sociological research. But only a very few of them are employed in economics, because economic theorists try to single out a minimum of such constructs as fundamental postulates for their hypothetico-deductive system. Sometimes they have thought that the isolation of *one* motive—the greatest possible gratification of self-interest—would be sufficient. This may do for some kinds of problem, but ordinarily it is helpful at least to subdivide the principle of utility maximization. John Stuart Mill distinguished three objectives of

---

[4] Herbert Feigl, "Philosophical Tangents of Science," in *Current Issues in the Philosophy of Science*, edited by Herbert Feigl and Grover Maxwell (New York: Holt, Rinehart and Winston, 1961), p. 984.

[5] Helmut R. Wagner, from an unpublished letter to me.

economic decision-making, which had to be integrated in some fashion: maximum income combined with maximum leisure and minimum waiting. These three goals can be expressed as preferences for higher income, less toil, and earlier consumption ["time preference"], or as a propensity to consume more with less work and also sooner; they can also be roughly translated into the qualities of appetite, laziness, and impatience. But this may not be enough, as it is clear that other motivations may be important in some problems. For example, the desire for prestige, recognition, and popularity; the aversion to risk-taking and to serious uncertainty; the fear of penalties for violations of laws, ordinances, customs, and traditions. Most important, especially for the theory of public policy, the widespread human trait of envy, often equivalent to a feeling for equity and justice.

With more feelings and desires mixed into one system of human action, its generality is ever more diminished. For purposes of greater determinacy, the theorist will set aside some of the motives or goals and let his train of deductive reasoning take a straighter route towards a single destination—maximum satisfaction, maximum income, even maximum profit—without taking dangerous curves to get around impediments of all sorts. The results will then be determinate, though rather general. It is better, however, to be approximately right than absolutely lost in the labyrinth of an excessively complex "realistic" ideal-typical world.

WHAT'S IN A NAME?

I am satisfied that the constructs employed in the theoretical analysis of the social world deserve a separate name. But, as I have said before, *ideal type* is a bad name. Neither the adjective nor the noun conveys the intended meaning (except to those who have been indoctrinated and have learned to disregard the ordinary senses of the words); moreover, the phrase does not in any way point to what is regarded as the distinguishing feature of the construct.

Can we perhaps coin a better phrase to replace the misnomer? Howard Becker, Talcott Parsons, and others have struggled with the problem of finding a good English rendition of the German *sinnhaft* and *sinnadäquat,* which Max Weber had used to point to the subjective foundation of ideal types in the social sciences. Becker came up with the expression "constructed type;" [6] Parsons with the phrase "adequate on the level of meaning; [7] others spoke of "meant meaning" and "subjectively intended meaning." [8] If *meaning* is used without a modifying adjective, one invites confusion of the dictionary meaning of a term or phrase with the subjective intentions and thoughts of an acting (ideal) person in his social world. To guard against such confusion one had better speak of meant meanings or "subjective interpretations." Even better, a reference to the actor's *mind,* rather than his meaning, may express the fundamental idea. But how can this be explicitly incorporated into the name of what is now tacitly implied in the designation *ideal type?*

The words *ideal type* could be replaced by the simple term *construct.* The reference to an actor's mind could be made in the form of a participle linking mind with construct, as in "mind-based construct," "mind-presuming construct," or "mind-related construct." None of these phrases, however, is either euphonious or self-explanatory. I doubt that the bad name now in use should be given up before a really good name is found.

Shakespeare, in *Romeo and Juliet,* spoke of loved and unloved names:

> What's in a name? That which we call a rose
> By any other name would smell as sweet.

Applying his dictum to our case, I would have to say

> What's in a name? That which we call ideal type
> By any other name would be as hard to grasp.

---

[6] Howard Becker, *Through Values to Social Interpretation: Essays on Social Contexts, Actions, Types, and Prospects* (Durham, N.C.: Duke University Press, 1950), p. 160 and *passim.*

[7] Talcott Parsons, ed., *Max Weber: The Theory of Social and Economic Organization* (Glencoe, Ill.: The Free Press, 1947), pp. 109–10.

[8] Howard Becker, *Systematic Sociology on the Basis of the Beziehungslehre and Gebildelehre of Leopold von Wiese* (New York: Wiley, 1932), pp. 56–61, 409, and 709.

Chapter 9

IDEAL TYPES, REALITY, AND CONSTRUCTION

Notes on the Translation from the German: *I acknowledge with gratitude valuable assistance in the difficult task of translating the original German text into readable (?) English. A first draft was made by Mrs. Martha Coorssen De Rooy, then of Bethlehem, Pennsylvania, and a first revision by Miss Susan Ray of New York. Their problem was that an attempt at literal translation would yield a succession of words but no intelligible sentences. Only a free translation could secure intelligibility, but then the translator could not be sure whether he was conveying the meaning intended by the author. When I set out to revise the second draft of the translation, I felt at liberty to offer a freer rendition of my own text, but I had the same trouble with translating the quotations from the works of some 20 German authors, most of them writing in a highly idiosyncratic language expressing the most complex, almost inexpressible thoughts. I have done my best to find a compromise between "faithful" and "intelligible" translation. Most of the authors, if they were alive, would, I am sure, appreciate my difficulties and forgive any distortions of their statements.*

I found no English equivalent for the simple preposition bei, *as in*

"Der Idealtypus bei Weber." I decided to avoid this difficulty in six of the original German subheadings by composing altogether new subheadings, which may serve as better guideposts through the essay.

A MENTAL CONSTRUCTION: VON THÜNEN

> Imagine a very large town, at the center of a fertile plain which is crossed by no navigable river or canal. The plain itself consists of completely homogeneous land of which every part is equally suitable for cultivation. At a great distance from the town, the plain ends abruptly in an uncultivated wilderness, by which this State is completely separated from the rest of the world.[1]

Thus Thünen began his work, *The Isolated State*, which appeared in its first edition in 1826. He had no name for his method of thinking through or analyzing complicated problems with the aid of mental constructions. He was, however, aware of the fact that "assumptions deviating from reality" are needed if "some of the many simultaneously operating forces are to be exhibited and comprehended." He considered this "form of representation" as "the most important contribution" in his entire work.[2]

A hundred years later, Thünen might have spoken about a heuristic fiction or an ideal type or a model. The names change, but the ideas remain much the same. But before we embark upon discussions of the history of ideas, we must look more closely at the assumptions that underlie Thünen's construction.

The assumption of an "uncultivated wilderness" has a clear purpose: It puts definite limits on the available space and isolates it from the rest of the world. There may have been times when completely isolated states or areas existed in reality, but we are not concerned here with describing such exceptional situations. The assumption of the state's hermetic isolation would be just as interesting if there had never been any isolated economic regions. It serves the *mental* isolation of the posed *problem*, and it can do so in the present case

---

[1] Johann Heinrich von Thünen, *Der isolirte Staat* (Hamburg: Perthes, 1826). English translation *Von Thünen's Isolated State*, edited by Peter Hall (Oxford: Pergamon, 1966).

[2] *Isolirte Staat*, Preface to 2d ed. (1842), pp. vi ff.

FRITZ MACHLUP

by excluding foreign trade and its effects. Instead of the wilderness, Thünen could equally well have used an iron curtain (Model Stalin and Co.) or a cordon of flames (Model Wotan and Loge). "Experiences" with or observations of wildernesses, iron curtains, and cordons of flames may be psychologically interesting for the form in which the model builder happens to have developed his ideas, but they are completely irrelevant for the model itself and for its usefulness.

Reality, or experience with reality, is equally irrelevant for the assumption of the absence of "navigable rivers and canals." To be sure, areas without navigation exist in reality, but this is quite immaterial for the problem in question. It is completely unimportant whether one has ever known ("experienced") such a region or whether one chooses to "abstract" from all the shipping that actually takes place in any observed economic region. The assumption has but one purpose: to simplify the formal solution of the problem of the economic determination of location. It is for the same purpose that the model prescribes a "plain" rather than a region with hills and valleys.

Finally, the assumption of the "completely homogeneous land" is likewise only a heuristic fiction. Again, it makes no difference whether or not there ever existed a large area with soil of absolutely equal quality or whether we merely "abstract" from the differences in quality actually observed or instead "construct" a pure Utopia. If "in reality" all soil were equal, then, but only then, would the mental image be "realistic" in this respect. But this is completely immaterial. If the element of "distance" is to be mentally isolated, we have to eliminate other influences upon choice of location and production, and it is for just this purpose that we assume homogeneity of the soil.

Thünen added still more assumptions before he could begin his analysis, and a few additional ones were obviously made tacitly. The assumptions of the profit motive and of unrestricted competition were especially important, for without them the actions of the inhabitants of his isolated state would not have been uniquely determinate. But here we need not go into further detail; for we are only concerned with the method of "thinking things through" with the aid of counterfactual assumptions. As Max Weber once said, "In order to grasp the real causal relationships, we construct unreal ones."[3]

Walter Eucken designated Thünen's mental image as an ideal type. He was anxious to point out that Thünen derived that type "in examining the concrete economy" and succeeded with its help in "emphasizing *one* aspect of the concrete economy." For Eucken, the derivation from concrete cases, from "actual reality," was an essential characteristic of the ideal type. Indeed, Eucken criticized Max Weber for not having seen this clearly: He regretted that Weber's "views about the formation of types are still prevalent today."[4] To this methodological controversy we shall return later.

DESCRIPTIVE AND NORMATIVE TYPES: PLATO, ARISTOTLE, MODERN SCIENCE

Weber never maintained that he (as Schelting believed) was the discoverer of the ideal type; and Eucken was correct in saying that one is not bound to abide by Weber's teachings about the nature of the ideal type. In any case, the concept of the ideal type was not new, and the term was not coined by Weber. I assume that a survey of the historical development of the idea is in order.[5]

Without any strain, we can trace the notion of "types" back to Greek philosophy. Plato employed the type as "a schematic representation, expressing the essence of a thing,"[6] though most inter-

---

[3] Max Weber, *Gesammelte Aufsätze zur Wissenschaftslehre* (Tübingen: J. C. B. Mohr [Paul Siebeck], 1922), p. 287.

[4] Walter Eucken, *Die Grundlagen der Nationalökonomie* (Berlin-Göttingen-Heidelberg: Springer Verlag, 6th ed., 1950), p. 269. (*The Foundations of Economics,* translated by Terence W. Hutchison [London and Edinburg: Hodge, 1950]).

[5] The literature includes numerous works about the history of the idea and about the epistemology of the use of types, and particularly the ideal type. I only want to name the following: Bernhard Pfister, *Die Entwicklung zum Idealtypus* (Tübingen: J. C. B. Mohr [Paul Siebeck], 1928); Eugen Seiterich, *Die logische Struktur des Typusbegriffes bei William Stern, Eduard Spranger und Max Weber* (Freiburg im Breisgau: Herder & Co., 1930); Heinz Haller, *Typus und Gesetz in der Nationalökonomie* (Stuttgart: W. Kohlhammer, 1950). For a treatment on the grounds of formal logic, see Carl G. Hempel and Paul Oppenheim, *Der Typusbegriff in Lichte der neuen Logik* (Leiden: A. W. Sijthoff, 1936).

[6] Quoted from André Lalande, *Vocabulaire technique et critique de la philosophie,* 5th ed. (Paris: Presses Universitaires de France, 1947), p. 1133.

preters of Plato regard his conception of the type as a normative one. "Aristotelian types . . . are closer to 'real types,'" maintained Walter Eucken, who characterized as "real types" many of the concepts that Weber and others had designated as ideal types.[7] Views on this point may differ, however, since there is also a strong normative element in the Aristotelian types.[8]

Concepts of "types" have been used in all fields of knowledge, though more often at some times than at others. Wilhelm Wundt speaks about an "emergence" of the types-concept in modern sciences—in fact, surely, a reemergence. "One of the most significant phenomena in the more recent development of the sciences," wrote Wundt, "is the fact that the same notion [of the 'type'] appears almost simultaneously in the most diverse branches: zoology, botany, crystallography, chemistry, linguistics."[9]

EXACT IMAGINATION, SELECTIVE EXAGGERATION, LOGICAL ISOLATION: GOETHE, COMTE, MILL, COURNOT

It is especially noteworthy that, in his essays on natural sciences, Goethe emphatically recommended ideal-type thinking and the use of "exact imagination" [*Phantasie*]. He spoke of "idea" and "archetype" [*Urbild*]. "No organic being completely corresponds to its underlying idea; we see the higher idea behind each being."[10] Karl Viëtor, the Goethe scholar, commented as follows: "*Goethe's* morphological research and *Schiller's* aesthetic speculation are the be-

---

[7] Eucken, *Grundlagen*, p. 268.

[8] Aristotle, *Nichomachean Ethics*, Book 10. Another view regarding the Platonic and Aristotelian types may be quoted here: "The concept of type can be seen in the sense that it characterizes the perfect essence of a class, no matter whether one prefers to imagine it, in the Platonic way, as the transcendental idea which appears only incompletely in the individual entities, or, in the Aristotelian way, as an effective, molding force that shapes the individual specimens of the class. It is the concept of the ideal type, which has occupied all scientific thinking without interruption since the days of Hellenistic philosophy, through the scholasticism of the Middle Ages, up to the present day. This ideal type, however, has a basically teleological meaning. . . . It is not a statement of what is, but rather of what ought to be." Georg Jellinek, *Allgemeine Staatslehre*, 2d. ed. (Berlin: O. Häring, 1905), p. 33.

[9] Wilhelm Wundt, *Logik*, 4th ed., vol. 2 (Stuttgart: F. Enke, 1920), p. 55.

[10] Flodoart von Biedermann, ed., *Goethe's Gespräche*, vol. 4 (Leipzig: Biedermann, 1910), p. 267.

ginning of the typological method of observation, which later played such a large role . . . , above all in Germany, in inquiries into the history of ideas. The method consists in emphasizing the fundamentals, so that an idealized schema emerges, an ideal type, which does not occur in reality." [11] And Viëtor quotes Goethe's *Morphology* (1817–1823), where Goethe states that the "schematic image" should serve as a thread "by which we can help ourselves through the labyrinth of living forms [*Gestalten*]." [12]

The expression *type idéal* appears several times in the work of Auguste Comte, not only in the chapter on biology [13] but also in the chapter on sociology. Comte emphasized the element of exaggeration inherent in the ideal type, for example, in his reference to "ce juste degré d'exagération qu'exige nécessairement l'indication d'un type quelquonque, audessous dequel la réalité ne sera jamais que trop maintenue." [14] Thus Comte also belongs in this line of ideological descent, even if within his positivistic system such an "ideal type" has still another shade of meaning.

John Stuart Mill did not, as far as I know, use the term *ideal type*, yet the concept is inherent in his method. His definition of political economy as "such of the phenomena of the social state as take place in consequence of the pursuit of wealth" shows a typically ideal-typical constitution of this branch of inquiry. "It makes abstraction of every other human passion or motive." He selects only three (partially conflicting) motives as the guiding ones: the (ideal-typical) economic decision maker prefers to be richer rather than

[11] Karl Viëtor, *Goethe: Dichtung, Wissenschaft, Weltbild* (Bern: A. Francke, 1949), p. 384.

[12] Goethe, *Works*, vol. 2.6, p. 279. Quoted in Viëtor, *Goethe*, p. 384.

[13] Comte speaks first of the tendency "à transformer artificiellement l'espèce en un seul individu, immense et éternel" and then immediately of the fact that "on peut considérer avec justesse cette subordination volontaire et systématique de la vie végétale à la vie animale comme le type idéal vers lequel tend sans cesse l'humanité civilisée, quoiqu'il ne doive jamais être entièrment réalisé. Il suit de là que pour la nouvelle science fondamentale . . . une telle notion devient convenable comme tendant à présenter sous une forme plus energique l'ensemble des caractères distinctifs de la vie humaine proprement dite, et à indiquer d'un seul aspect le but général de notre espèce." Auguste Comte, *Cours de la Philosophie Positive*, vol. 3 (Paris: Bachelier, 1838), Leçon 40, pp. 298–99.

[14] Ibid., vol. 4 (1839), Leçon 50, p. 553.

poorer, to work less rather than more, to consume earlier rather than later. But Mill adds an important comment: "Not that any political economist was ever so absurd as to suppose that mankind are really thus constituted, but because this is the mode in which science must necessarily proceed." [15]

Many writers who used the expression *type* differentiated between *type* and *genus* [*Gattung*], depending on the kind of abstraction employed in forming the concept. According to Cournot, for example, the genus is a "logical" and the type a "rational" abstraction, whereby the former is said to be "artificial" and the latter "natural." Furthermore, Cournot uses the expressions *type* and *model* as synonyms and employs *type* primarily in cosmological and biological (morphological) discussions.[16] A few German logicians of this period pointed to differences in the formation of concepts by means of "abstraction" and "construction," and to differences in the kind of abstraction—especially between "isolating" and "generalizing" abstraction; but they did not use (or did not yet use) the expressions *type* and *formation of types* in this connection. Hermann Lotze [17] and Wilhelm Wundt [18] should be mentioned as leading innovators in the questions concerning differences in the kinds of abstraction.

This brings us chronologically to Carl Menger and his analysis of different conceptions of types. It calls for a more detailed discussion.

[15] John Stuart Mill, "On the Definition of Political Economy; and on the Method of Investigation Proper to It," printed in part in *A System of Logic*, vol. 2 (London: John W. Parker, 1843), pp. 570–72, and in its entirety in *Essays on Some Unsettled Questions of Political Economy* (London: John W. Parker, 1844). I have modernized somewhat the formulation of the three ideal-typical motives emphasized by Mill. In view of Mill's explicit comment, it is unbelievable that so many of the critics of classical economics have misled their readers by asserting that the classical writers had accepted "economic self-love" (egoism) not just as heuristic hypothesis but as factual assumption. Was it prejudice, incomprehension, or just carelessness that explains the critics' misrepresentation?

[16] Antoine Augustin Cournot, *Traité de l'enchaînement des ideés fondamentales dans les sciences et dans l'histoire* (Paris: L. Hachette & cie., 1861), vol. 1, book 1, Chapter 5, pp. 74 ff; Book 2, Chapter 11, pp. 290 ff; Book 3, Chapter 3, pp. 347 ff.

[17] Herman Lotze, *Logik* (Leipzig: Hirzel, 1874), pp. 40 ff., 169 ff., idem, *Grundzüge der Logik und Encyklopädie der Philosophie*, 3rd ed. (Leipzig, 1891), pp. 64 ff., 68 ff.

[18] Wilhelm Wundt, *Logik*, vol. 2, *Methodenlehre* (Stuttgart: F. Enke, 1883), p. 11.

REAL TYPES AND STRICT TYPES: CARL MENGER

Carl Menger introduces the notion of types in the first pages of his work on the methodology of the social sciences.[19] He explains that, according to general experience, "certain phenomena repeat themselves, sometimes with greater, sometimes with lesser sameness; they recur even as circumstances change. We call these phenomenal forms *types*. [The same] is true of the relationships between concrete phenomena. [We can] observe certain, sometimes more, sometimes less regularly recurring relations between the same phenomena (for example, regularities in their succession, their development, their coexistence,—relations that we call *typical*." Menger cites money, prices, and the rate of interest as examples of typical phenomena. Besides *typical phenomena* there are *typical relations* among phenomena. Thus

> The regular decrease in the price of a commodity consequent upon an increase in supply, the increase in the prices of commodities consequent upon an increase in the quantity of money, the decline in the rate of interest consequent upon substantial accumulation of capital, and so forth, present themselves to us as typical relations among the economic phenomena [pp. 4–5].

> Without knowledge of typical relations we would lack not only . . . deeper comprehension of the real world, but would also be incapable of any cognition of things beyond direct observation, i.e., incapable of predicting and controlling events of the future. . . . What is said here holds for all areas of the world of phenomena, and hence also of the human economy [p. 5]. We understand phenomena through theories, in that we preceive, and take notice of, phenomena in every concrete case only as exemplifications of a general regularity [p. 33].

Such regularities can be established in two ways: (1) through a "realistic-empirical" approach, which derives from the phenomena of "empirical reality" so-called "*real types*" and gives an account of the "actual regularities in the succession and the coexistence of real phenomena" in the form of "*empirical laws*" [p. 36]; and (2) through an "exact" theoretical approach, which seeks to go to the bottom of

[19] Carl Menger, *Untersuchungen über die Methode der Socialwissenschaften und der politischen Ökonomie insbesondere* (Leipzig: Duncker & Humblot, 1883).

the simplest elements of things real, constructs *"strict types"* from them, and formulates strict typical relations among them in the form of "exact laws" [p. 41]. All this, in Menger's view, holds no less for the natural sciences than for the social sciences.

> Natural phenomena too, in their "empirical reality," offer us neither strict types nor strict typical relations. Real gold, real oxygen and hydrogen, real water—not to mention the more complicated phenomena of the inorganic, let alone the organic world—are in their full empirical reality neither of a strictly typical nature, nor can exact laws concerning them be observed in empirical research [pp. 36–37].

Yet, in the natural sciences, "exact laws"—Menger explains why he does not want to call them "natural laws" or "laws of nature"—are formulated, which, however, relate only to "strictly typical phenomena"—such as "perfectly pure oxygen, perfectly pure alcohol, perfectly pure gold—which may never have existed except "in our idea" [p. 41].

Menger did not use the expression "ideal type"; however, his "strict type," which occurs only in our "idea"—and contrasts with the "real type" obtained from "observation" of "empirical reality," [p. 55] —is probably close enough to the ideal type. The strict, purely idealized type contains the "simplest elements" of reality, which "just because they are the simplest have to be thought of as being strictly typical" [p. 41].

> Exact science, therefore, does not investigate the regularities in the succession, etc., of *real* phenomena; rather, it investigates how, from . . . the simplest, in part clearly unempirical elements of the real world, in their (likewise unempirical) isolation from all other influences, more complicated phenomena develop. It does this irrespective of whether those simplest elements or, respectively, their relevant complications, can actually be observed in the real (from human art unaffected) world, indeed, whether those elements can ever be produced in their perfect purity [pp. 41–42].

The "realistic-empirical" approach to economics shares the same objective with the "exact" approach, namely, to obtain *general* knowledge, *universal* propositions. Hence, it should not be confused with the "historical science of the economy," whose task is to obtain "knowledge of concrete phenomena in their *individual* nature and their *individual* conjunctions [p. 12]. We understand a concrete phenomenon in a specifically *historical* way (through its history) when we investigate its individual process of emergence or development, i.e., by realizing the concrete circumstances under which it came into being, and specifically, how it has become as it is, in its particular uniqueness" [p. 14].

Menger, we may repeat, developed his concepts of types for the "theoretical comprehension" of both natural and social phenomena [p. 16]. It also bears repetition that he distinguished between two kinds of types and typical relations. The "real types" are something observed in empirical reality; *observed regularities* in their conjunction or succession are called *empirical laws*. The "strict, purely idealized types" are something constructed from elements of the real world that are isolated by a thought process; and the *logically necessary relations* between them are called *exact laws*. They are of service in causal explanations of reality; of human, social, cultural as well as of physical, biological, natural phenomena.

ISOLATING ABSTRACTION AND MEANT MEANINGS: WUNDT, DILTHEY

The year 1883 was especially fertile in the area of methodology: Besides Carl Menger's challenging book, the great works of Wilhelm Dilthey [20] and Wilhelm Wundt,[21] and a major paper by Wilhelm Windelband [22] appeared in that year.

Wundt's views were rather close to those of Menger. This is not so strange, since both Menger and Wundt accepted the intellectual heritage of John Stuart Mill. In his earlier writings, Wundt spoke less about types, except when he was referring to natural history, where the concept of type was generally distinguished from that of species.[23]

[20] Wilhelm Dilthey, *Einleitung in die Geisteswissenschaft* (Leipzig: Duncker & Humblot, 1883).

[21] Wilhelm Wundt, *Logik*, vol. 2, *Methodenlehre* (Stuttgart: F. Enke, 1883).

[22] Wilhelm Windelband, "Kritische oder genetische Methode?" Paper delivered in 1883. Reprinted in *Präludien* (Freiburg im Breisgau: Mohr, 1884), pp. 247–79.

[23] Wundt, *Methodenlehre*, p. 459. In later, considerably expanded editions of his work, Wundt had much to say about types in the social sciences. This, however, was after Weber's articles had appeared.

FRITZ MACHLUP

What were for Menger the "realistic-empirical" and the "exact" approaches to scientific knowledge were for Wundt the "concrete" and the "abstract" [p. 593]. He made the same distinction for the natural sciences, in which it had often been found necessary "to distinguish, besides the causal or genuine natural laws, *empirical laws,* which presented only a functional relation between two facts [or events]. In the very same sense, the statistical regularities [in social science] now have the right to be called empirical laws" [p. 577]. Wundt left no doubt, however, that "insofar as the statistical regularities are at all open to a causal interpretation, such an interpretation can never be obtained from [the data] themselves." Indeed, we usually have derived the *abstract laws* beforehand "from the general characteristics of human nature; and mass observation provides only a numerical confirmation" [pp. 578–79]. In the "abstract theory of economics," for example, one has singled out in "isolating abstraction" one of the generally influential "motives of human action"—"self-interest"— and deduced from it consequences "by presupposing an ideal state in which each individual at every moment" recognizes not only his interest but also the correct means of pursuing it, has moreover the will to act accordingly, and is not hindered in doing so [p. 588].

Discussing the task of history, Wundt emphasizes something that Menger had not seen, or at least did not pursue, namely, the function of the understanding of subjective meaning. Wundt wrote: "The task of historical interpretation . . . cannot be put on the same footing as the explanation of natural phenomena; instead, it restricts itself to the demonstration of a psychologically understandable connection among the individual historical facts established through criticism. If such a connection is demonstrated, then we have thereby obtained an understanding of the events" in question [p. 539].

It was Dilthey who made the understanding of subjective meaning and the "types of human nature" not only the foundation of history, but also the foundation of the social sciences, indeed of all moral sciences [*Geisteswissenschaften*].

> A type of human nature always stands between the historian and his sources, from which he wants to bring individuals and events to life; in the same sense, that type stands between the political

thinker and the reality of society, for which he [the political thinker] wants to draft the rules of its further development. Science aims merely to give this subjective type adequacy and fertility [p. 32].

On the strength of principles of this kind, Dilthey raised the demand for unlimited autonomy of the moral sciences and their methodology. He undertook "to build a new foundation for the moral sciences by a special theory of knowledge, to justify and support their autonomous formation, as well as to eliminate forever the subordination of their principles and their methods under those of the natural sciences [p. 109].

In an evaluation of the attempts of the empirical and the historical schools at grasping social reality as a whole, Dilthey comes to the following conclusion: "The structure [*Zusammenhang*] of society that is inferred from this empirical interpretation, is not inferior to that which the speculative schools have posed, a construction designed from abstract elements" [p. 124]. Dilthey was obviously not satisfied with that. Did he want *more* reality or *nothing but* reality?[24]

GENERALIZING, INDIVIDUALIZING, UNDERSTANDING: WINDELBAND, RICKERT, SIMMEL

Windelband's contribution to methodology was undoubtedly of great importance, and it is an injustice that he is often mentioned nowadays merely as a connecting link between other writers. *Before* Windelband, the historian Droysen had clarified the difference between law-formulating and narrative sciences, mentioned that we "understand that which *is* only when we comprehend it as that which has *become*," and maintained that historical science must de-

[24] Dilthey wrote: "This *whole, complete, unadulterated experience* has never until now been used as the base for philosophizing" [p. 123; emphasis supplied]. If Dilthey intended this to mean that it cannot be done, I would agree. But this, evidently, he did not mean. He seems to want to get away from abstraction and construction and to grasp "the whole" in one thrust. The purpose Dilthey gives for this attempt is noteworthy: "For such is the powerful soul of present-day science: an insatiable desire for reality . . ., if possible, to comprehend the whole of the world and to attain the means for intervening in the course of human society" [p. 123].

velop its own concepts "because its method is essentially that of understanding." [25] *After* Windelband, the philosopher Rickert demonstrated the difference between generalizing and individualizing sciences with such clarity that one seldom finds it still necessary to refer to Windelband's writings.[26]

Heinrich Rickert [27] is so important for this discussion primarily because he showed so very clearly "that the formation of scientific concepts is in all circumstances equivalent to isolating abstraction" [p. 64], that it is never the "task of cognition [to furnish] a picture of reality" [p. 214], and that it is within the "principle of individualizing concept-formation [to require frequently] a value-related concept-formation" [p. 275]. Probably best known, however, of Rickert's contributions to the theory of knowledge in general is his rejection of a distinction between natural and cultural sciences on the basis of their *subject matter or contents* [pp. 166–67], and his claim that the real difference lies in the *tasks and methods*: The (historical) cultural sciences must individualize, whereas the natural sciences must generalize [p. 278]. In accordance with this point of view, he needed a new definition of *nature*, characterized by the method of cognition: "Empirical reality . . . becomes nature when we observe it with regard to the general; it becomes history when we observe it with regard to the particular and individual" [p. 224]. On these definitions, economics (economic theory) becomes a "natural science"; however, for most of Rickert's followers, including Max Weber, this conclusion was unacceptable.

Many of Rickert's propositions about the relationship between concrete reality and the comprehension of reality are among the most frequently quoted statements in German methodological literature. For example: that "*every* empirical science must select from reality that which seems essential and, hence, must depart from reality in its immediacy" [p. 224]. Also, "if the concepts of natural

[25] Johann Gustav Droysen, "Erhebung der Geschichte zum Rang einer Wissenschaft," Review of the book by Thomas Buckle, *Historische Zeitschrift* (1862); reprinted in Droysen, *Historik* (Munich and Berlin: R. Oldenbourg, 1937), pp. 56–57.

[26] Wilhelm Windelband, "Geschichte und Naturwissenschaft," Rektoratsrede [Presidential Address], 1894, printed in *Präludien* (Freiburg im Breisgau: Mohr, 1884), vol. 2. See also his main work, *Einleitung in die Philosophie* (Tübingen: J.C.B. Mohr [Paul Siebeck], 1914; 3d ed., 1923).

[27] Heinrich Rickert, *Die Grenzen der naturwissenschaftlichen Begriffsbildung* (Tübingen: Mohr, 1902; 2d. ed., 1913).

science [generalizing science] still included the observable, real-looking [*anschauliche*] and individual forms [*Gestaltung*] of reality, they would not be of any help for an orientation in the real world" [p. 199]. To the development of the concept of the subjective-meaning-based ideal type, Rickert contributed through his observations about the formation of "value-related" and "relative-historical concepts." Even if Max Weber took exception to many of Rickert's propositions, there can be no question about Rickert's strong influence upon Weber.[28]

It remains to add a reference to Georg Simmel.[29] His contribution to the development of Weber's ideal type consisted primarily in his finding that "value-relatedness," which Rickert had seen only in "relative-historical concepts" (and, therefore, deemed useful only for gaining insights into the particular and unique), was significant for general theory as well. Moreover, Simmel, as Max Weber said, "deserves credit for . . . having clearly distinguished . . . the objective 'understanding' of the meaning of an expression from the subjective 'interpretation' of the *motive* of a (speaking or acting) person. In the first case we 'understand' what is spoken, but in the latter we 'understand' the person speaking (or acting)."[30]

With that we have come to Max Weber.

IDEAL TYPES CONSTRUCTED WITH
UNDERSTANDING OF MEANT MEANINGS: WEBER

The term "ideal type" was not used by the direct predecessors of Max Weber, at least not before Weber introduced it. According to Marianne Weber's statement and Bernhard Pfister's confirmation,[31]

[28] "Contemporary logic and epistemology, above all Heinrich Rickert's theory of knowledge, in which the separation of practical valuation and theoretical 'value-relatedness' was particularly important, afforded the mental tools" needed for Weber's methodological thought. Marianne Weber, *Max Weber: Ein Lebensbild* (Tübingen: J.C.B. Mohr [Paul Siebeck], 1926), p. 324.

[29] Georg Simmel, *Probleme der Geschichtsphilosophie* (Leipzig: Duncker & Humblot, 1892; 2d ed., 1905; 3d ed., 1923). The relevant questions are raised for the first time in the second edition in remarks about Rickert's work.

[30] Max Weber, *Gesammelte Aufsätze zur Wissenschaftslehre* (Tübingen: J.C.B. Mohr, 1922), p. 93.

[31] Marianne Weber, *Max Weber*, p. 327. Bernhard Pfister, *Die Entwicklung zum Idealtypus* (Tübingen: J.C.B. Mohr [Paul Siebeck], 1928), pp. 138–39.

Weber took over the expression "ideal type" from Georg Jellinek, who, however, had used it as a normative concept.[32] Weber's ideal type is to serve "understanding," not to evaluate social actions or establish norms.

For Max Weber, as for others before him, scientific explanation is causal attribution, which is obtained in the natural sciences through comprehending external relationships and in the cultural sciences through the *understanding* of subjective-meaning relationships.[33] Natural phenomena are comprehended, social conduct is understood. The understanding interpretation of human action and its results or "products" calls for concepts "adequate to the subjective meanings of the actor [*sinnadäquat*], obtained through the mental isolation and magnification of certain elements of reality, [but] nowhere to be found empirically in the real world." [34] These concepts are Weber's ideal types.

Thus, ideal types according to Weber are not simply idealized types but rather types constructed only for the explanation of social and cultural phenomena, with the proviso that these types are connected with meanings meant by persons, particularly in the context of action. They serve not only the generalizing, but the historical cultural sciences as well. Sociology, the generalizing treatment of the social world, "is a science which attempts the interpretive understanding of social action." [35] Understanding in this context means understanding of subjective meanings meant by acting persons.

[32] According to Jellinek the "ideal type [is] not that which is, but that which ought to be. With this it becomes also a standard of value of what is given." Jellinek adds: "Two classes of such ideal types are to be distinguished. The type is either a free construction of our speculation . . ., or existing states [countries] or some of their institutions are transformed into an ideal type." With the ideal type Jellinek contrasts the "empirical type," which is found "by the inductive method, that is, by means of careful comparison." He distinguishes also between "development types" and "existence types." Georg Jellinek, *Allgemeine Staatslehre*, 2d ed., pp. 33, 35, 38. (The first edition of the work appeared in 1900.)

[33] Max Weber, "Roscher und Knies und die logischen Probleme der historischen Nationalökonomie," *Schmollers Jahrbücher für Gesetzgebung, Verwaltung und Volkswirtschaft*, vols. 27, 29, and 30 (1903, 1905, and 1906). Reprinted in *Gesammelte Aufsätze zur Wissenschaftslehre* (Tübingen: J.C.B. Mohr, 1922), pp. 93 ff. I know of no English translation of this essay.

[34] Ibid., p. 190.

[35] Max Weber, *Wirtschaft und Gesellschaft* (vol. 3 of the *Grundriss der Sozialökonomik*) (Tübingen: J.C.B. Mohr [Paul Siebeck], 1922), p. 1. An English translation of Part 1 by Alexander M. Henderson and Talcott Parsons was published under

"Meaning" (in the sense of the definition of interpretive [*verstehende*] sociology) is either (1) the actual meaning meant (*a*) by an acting person in an historically given case or (*b*) meaning meant by a number of acting persons in an average and approximate way in a given number of cases or (2) the hypothetical subjectively meant meaning in a conceptually constructed *pure type* of a hypothetical acting person or persons in a given type of action [p. 17]. In all these cases, "understanding" denotes an interpretive grasp of the meaning or meaning-relationships (*a*) of what is really meant in individual cases (as in a historical approach) or (*b*) of what is meant in an average or approximate way (as in sociological investigations of mass-phenomena), or . . . (*c*) of what is scientifically constructed in the *pure* type (ideal type) of a frequently occurring phenomenon. Such ideal-typical constructions are exemplified by the concepts and "laws" formulated in pure economic theory. They state what course human conduct of a particular kind *would* take *if* it were *strictly* rational (in a subjective sense built into the type), unaffected by error and emotion and, furthermore, *if it* were completely and uniquely oriented toward only one objective, namely, economizing. In reality, action rarely [if ever] corresponds to the idealized conduct hypothesized in the ideal type . . . and even then it does so at best approximately [p. 4].

Sociology seeks to formulate type-concepts and *general* uniformities of empirical courses of actions. This is in contrast to history, which attempts causal analysis and explanation of *individual* actions, structures, and personalities possessing cultural significance. . . . Among the various bases on which its concepts are formulated and its generalizations worked out, is an attempt to justify its important claim to be able to make a contribution to the causal explanation of some historically and culturally important phenomenon. As in the case of every generalizing science, the abstract character of the concepts of sociology is responsible for the fact that, compared with actual historical reality, they are relatively lacking in fullness of concrete content. To compensate for this disadvantage, sociological analysis can offer a greater precision of concepts. This precision is obtained by striving for the highest possible degree of adequacy on the level of [subjectively intended] meaning. . . . This aim can be realized in a particularly high de-

---

the title *Max Weber: The Theory of Social and Economic Organization* (Glencoe, Ill.: The Free Press, 1947). My page references are to the German text. Weber's definition of interpretive sociology in the 1922 work is much clearer than the exposition in Weber's earlier methodological articles, though it is still difficult to comprehend and almost impossible to translate into reliable English. For a possibly helpful commentary I refer the reader to my introduction to this part.

FRITZ MACHLUP

gree in the case of concepts and generalizations which formulate *rational* processes [rational from the actor's point of view]. But sociological investigation attempts to include in its scope various irrational phenomena, as well as prophetic, mystic, and affectual modes of action, formulated in terms of theoretical concepts which are adequate on the level of [subjectively intended] meaning. In *all* cases, rational or irrational, sociological analysis both abstracts from reality and at the same time helps us to understand it, in that it shows with what degree of approximation a concrete historical phenomenon can be subsumed under one or more of these concepts. . . . For this purpose sociology formulates pure ideal types of the corresponding forms of action which in each case involve the highest possible degree of logical integration by virtue of their complete adequacy on the level of [subjectively intended] meaning. But precisely because this is true, it is probably seldom, if ever, that a real phenomenon can be found which corresponds exactly to one of these ideally constructed pure types. The case is similar to a physical reaction which has been calculated on the assumption of an absolute vacuum [pp. 9–10; Henderson and Parsons, p. 109–110].

Weber's ideal type was at the same time narrower and wider than the pure constructs or ideal types of earlier methodologists had been. He had narrowed it down from a construct designed to explain phenomena *of every kind*, natural as well as social, to one that was to serve only the explanation of social phenomena. On the other hand, it should serve in generalizing as well as historical inquiries. His ideal type, moreover, was subject to the requirement of "understanding meant meanings." Some of these modifications were not fully understood by those who considered themselves heirs to Weber's methodology and proceeded to reinterpret, adapt, and apply it. In the process, most of them managed to reduce its applicability.

INCONSISTENT ASSIGNMENTS FOR THE IDEAL TYPE: OPPENHEIMER, SCHELTING, MISES, SOMBART

For Weber, the ideal type, as he understood it, can have fundamentally different forms, contents, subjects, and functions; it can refer to individual historical events and to abstract-theoretical generic concepts as well; "every individual ideal type consists of conceptual elements that . . . have, in turn, been formed as ideal types"; ideal types can be constructed of various kinds of "developments"; and, besides ideal types of behavior, interrelations, processes, and institutions, there are also ideal types of ideas and ideal types of ideals.[36] This manifold diversity may seem confusing, but it need not be, inasmuch as everything that has to do with human feeling, thinking, and acting, whether it be treated in a theoretical-abstract or a historical-concrete manner, can be understood in terms of ideal types. There are those, however, who do not agree with this statement.

Hans Oppenheimer wants only ideal types that have "historical meaning" and he regrets that Weber made a "logically impossible jump" when he wanted to pattern the meaning "of social behavior in general," the concepts of pure sociology, into ideal types.[37]

Alexander von Schelting raises just the opposite objection. He objects to Weber's designating as ideal types the concepts of "empirical-historical cultural science," which present "complexes of purely ideational, non-causally interconnected elements of meaning," but do not serve the understanding of causal relationships. Schelting would bestow the term "ideal type" only upon the "concepts of real-causal relationships," upon the forms of greatest purity of meaning, such as the universal concepts and rules of pure sociology and economic theory.[38]

Ludwig von Mises finds that sociology, inclusive of economic theory, aims not at understanding, but at comprehending.[39] He holds that "the laws of sociology [are] not ideal types and are not average types," and sociological concepts are not constructions that are obtainable, as Weber said, "through one-sided magnification of one or a few aspects." Mises maintained, finally, "that the form of thinking in ideal types is not appropriate for the theoretical, law-stating science of sociology but, instead, only for social history" [p. 169]. The

[36] Max Weber, *Gesammelte Aufsätze zur Wissenschaftslehre*, pp. 201–5.

[37] Hans Oppenheimer, *Die logik der soziologischen Begriffsbildung, mit besonderer Berücksichtigung von Max Weber* (Tübingen: J. C. B. Mohr, 1925), p. 70.

[38] Alexander von Schelting, *Max Webers Wissenschaftslehre* (Tübingen: J.C.B. Mohr, 1934), pp. 332–33 and 354–60.

[39] Ludwig von Mises, *Grundprobleme der Nationalökonomie* (Jena: Gustav Fischer, 1933), pp. 124 ff.

ideal type thus serves history but accomplishes nothing for economics. The laws of economics are purely aprioristic necessities of logical thought, deduced from the "fundamental categories of (rational) action" [p. 13].

Werner Sombart accepts these economic laws as "genuine laws about meaning [and] a priori truths, [as] rational schemata [models] in which or by which it is shown how the course of economic events would run if certain conditions were fulfilled and everybody acted perfectly rationally." However, he characterizes them as "fictional laws" and maintains that they have "nothing to do with reality and with inquiries into the real world." Sombart, moreover, refuses to speak in this context of "ideal types," because what is involved here are "certainly not 'types,' but rather 'ideal' constructions of an entirely different nature." [40] He deplores that so many "try to use the type-concept only with reference to the human soul and perhaps the human body," and that the separation of the type "from the concept of genus is not sharp enough" [pp. 241–42]. Sombart demands that one keep apart, and not confuse, concepts of individuals, of types, and of genera. All three can be found not only in the knowledge of nature, but also in that of culture, though "the proper area of application for the type concept is in the cultural sciences." All three kinds exist as ideal concepts and as real concepts. "Ideal concepts [are those] by which the essence of the subject can be expressed in complete purity; . . . real concepts . . .are those that comprehend the subjects in their accidental (empirical, historical) form." In contradiction to Weber, Sombart believes that a "concept of the individual . . . can never be a 'type' " [pp. 245–46].

THE DISCUSSION CONTINUED:
WEIPPERT, SPRANGER, SPIETHOFF

Georg Weippert agrees with Sombart in that the "rational schemas" of pure economics are not of ideal-typical character, and that Weber did not comprehend the difference between "meaning-adequacy [and] utmost rationality," and therefore failed "to separate

[40] Werner Sombart, *Die drei Nationalökonomien* (Munich and Leipzig: Duncker & Humblot, 1930), pp. 258–60.

cleanly the 'ideal types' from the 'rational schemas.' " [41] On the other hand, Weippert defends Weber against the attacks by Oppenheimer and Schelting and criticizes their misleading endeavor to limit the ideal type either to only "pure-meaning" types [*sinnreine Typen*] of social action or only to "meaning-related" types [*sinnhafte Typen*] of specifically historical phenomena. According to Weippert, the ideal type is an instrument for the understanding of meant meanings not only for sociology, but also for history [pp. 282–84]. However, "no ideal type is fiction [and,] in contrast to the ideal type, the 'model' is . . . in principle independent of reality [and] all insights gained from models . . . always have under given assumptions . . . a priori validity as pure results of logical thought" [pp. 292, 294]. Yet, after all his troubles with the "clean" distinction between the "rational schemas" with their derived "fictional laws" and the genuine ideal types with derived "laws of essence," Weippert still comes to the conclusion that "under a purely formal, logical aspect . . . there is really no difference between the ideal type and the rational schema" [pp. 307–8].

Eduard Spranger believes that one needs "a psychology of forms of experiences" and a "theory of structure" before one can study "systematic history of ideas." [42] We can leave aside what he says about the relationship between type and structure and about the "direction and stratification of value-dispositions," which determined the structure [p. 21]. All that is important here is that Spranger assigns a large role to the "average type," besides the "ideal type." The difference between the two lies in the modes of procedure: "If one obtains the type by induction from the repeated experience of similar cases, an average type emerges. If one obtains the type through a priori construction from a law that one imagines as being realized in its purity, an ideal type results." [43] The inductive procedure is "like making a set of superimposed photographs of all historical phenomena" [p. 282].

[41] Georg Weippert, "Die idealtypische Sinn- und Wesenserfassung und die Denkgebilde der formalen Theorie," *Zeitschrift für die gesamte Staatswissenschaft,* vol. 100 (1940), pp. 294–97.

[42] Eduard Spranger, *Der gegenwärtige Stand der Geisteswissenschaften und die Schule* (Leipzig-Berlin, 1922).

[43] Eduard Spranger, *Psychologie des Jugendalters* (Leipzig: Quelle & Meyer, 1925), p. 20.

Arthur Spiethoff contrasts (as did Carl Menger) a "real type" with the "ideal type." His "real type represents the regularities of a recurring historical subject purified of its historical uniquenesses." [44] The real type serves "intuitive theory" [*anschauliche Theorie*], perhaps better: "graphically descriptive" theory, which strives for "a picture of reality." In contrast to it, the ideal type serves "pure theory" and is "a mental model" [p. 637]. The ideal type is obtained either through "remodeling" [*Zurechtmachung*] or through "construction," and Spiethoff believes that Weber's "types" are "remolded ideal types," and not "free, purely mental constructions . . . independent of experience" [p. 657].

> The quality of high fidelity to reality inherent in intuitive [graphically descriptive] theory . . . is obtained through the observation of reality and is genuine reality. . . . [But] the pictures of reality are not photographs, but paintings. . . . The phenomena are selected on the basis of a very special viewing of the whole. . . . Since it is a painting rather than a photograph, it represents a mental image, and particularly an image that is inevitably and necessarily determined as much by the person of the researcher as a painting is determined by that of the artist. However, since it also comprises disturbing [deviating] phenomena and not only homogeneous ones, and since it includes not only some but all essential factors that determine the phenomenon as a whole, it is not an ideal type, but a real type [pp. 637–40].

The choice of the seven participants presented here in the discussion of the ideal type and the selection of their statements for reproduction or paraphrase were, of course, quite arbitrary. Completeness would surely have been impossible, and an expansion in the number of participants in the discussion or of their statements would not be necessary for my purposes. These purposes were to show that each of the seven wanted to narrow down the ideal type from the wide scope designed by Weber, that their views about the proper procedure in the formation of types differ in many respects, that their interpretations of what Weber had really meant are anything but mutually consistent (let alone unanimous), and that the result-

[44] Arthur Spiethoff, "Anschauliche und reine volkswirtschaftliche Theorie und ihr Verhältnis zueinander," in Edgar Salin, *Synopsis: Festgabe für Alfred Weber* (Heidelberg: Schneider, 1948), p. 614.

ing confusion is great. I have made for myself a list of different positions regarding the supposedly proper nature and uses of the ideal type, and then let the seven authors cast their votes in an imaginary poll about the "truth" of each position statement.[45] The results showed continuing switches in the line-up of the opposition. Similar switches between approving and opposing groups may happen in almost all scientific discussions; but on the issues here in question, the crisscrossing is especially flagrant and signifies serious confusion in the intellectual situation. In order to save space, I refrain from reproducing my tabulation, but recommend that the reader repeat the mental experiment.

I wish to present the views of two other authors, and in much greater detail—Alfred Schutz and Walter Eucken: Schutz because, in my opinion, he understood Weber best, was his best interpreter, and went on to develop what was best in Weber's methodology; Eucken because he spoke out most vehemently against the confusion between real and ideal types, and thereby challenged me to inquire into what the real type really is and what it is for.

PERSONAL AND MATERIAL IDEAL TYPES OF VARYING DEGREES OF ANONYMITY: SCHUTZ

A fundamental point in Schutz's work [46] is that the formation of any ideal type depends on the problem which it should help clarify or solve [pp. 210–20].This sounds ridiculously simple and trite, but it has to be said because there has been so much argument about the logical nature of the ideal type and whether it should be constructed this way or in some other way—questions that can be answered only with reference to the particular problem that concerns us at the particular moment.

Schutz distinguishes between personal ideal types and material

[45] If I were to say that, on the basis of my knowledge of their published work, I formed ideal types of each of the seven authors, whom I then caused to give ideal-typical replies to my questions in accordance with the ideal-typical views built into their personal ideal types, I might get the approval of some writers, but at least Sombart and Schelting would object to my way of speaking.

[46] Alfred Schutz, *Der sinnhafte Aufbau der sozialen Welt* (Vienna: Springer Verlag, 1932). In English, *The Phenomenology of the Social World*, translated by George Walsh and Frederick Lehnert (Evanston, Ill.: Northwestern University Press, 1967); hereafter cited as W. and L.

(or course-of-action) types, but he recognizes an "inner relation" between the two. The personal ideal type constructed on the basis of the theory of subjective understanding

> is such only by virtue of its capacity to make the course of action that can bring about the result observed understandable to us [as a necessary consequence]; for this purpose, the personal type must be endowed with all those ideal-typical experiences and motivations as will lead to the ideal-typical course of action; in other words, a model of consciousness is constructed to fit, i.e., to be "adequate" to a certain course of action, and for this ideal-typical consciousness the subjective, motivational meaning-relationship that determines the ideal-typical actions must be congruent to the objective context of meanings [p. 215; sentence omitted by W. and L., p. 190].

The private world of the man in the street, who thinks about the actions of the persons around him and who acts in anticipation of their reactions, is "constituted" of the ideal types he has constructed on the basis of his experiences. Any scientific analysis of the social world has to begin, therefore, with the problems of the acting individual, but must soon proceed to ideal-typical concepts of reduced concreteness, of lesser specific content; it requires ideal types of greater "anonymity, [because] the concreteness of the ideal type is inversely proportional to the level of generality of the past experiences out of which it is constructed" [p. 222; W. and L. p. 195].

Personal ideal types can be "characterological, habitual, [or types that are] to a high degree anonymous and void of content [concreteness]" [p. 222–29]. In addition, there is the class of "so-called social collectives"—such as state, economy, nation, working class—which contains "completely heterogeneous kinds of ideal types of quite different degrees of anonymity" [p. 226; W. and L., p. 198]. Schutz shows

> that the concepts of social action and social relationship undergo many modifications, depending on whether the object of the "other-orientation" is of directly experienced social reality, the world of mere contemporaries, the world of predecessors, or the world of successors [p. 251; W. and L., p. 219]. Of course, only the world of contemporaries and the world of predecessors, but not the world of persons confronted face-to-face, are appropriate subjects of the social sciences; it follows that sociology, even when it deals with

the actions of a single individual, must do so in terms of ideal types [p. 259; W. and L., p. 227].

Schutz "makes a sharp distinction between the construction of the ideal type and the application of this type as an interpretive schema to real concrete actions" [p. 260; W. and L., p. 228]. He considers it to be "the basic postulate of social science that the motives ascribed to the ideal type must be both causally adequate and adequate on the level of meant meanings" [p. 262; W. and L., p. 229]. The double requirement that (1) the constructed types be acceptable as efficient causes of the effects that are to be explained, and (2) at the same time plausible in the sense of reflecting the meant meanings in the minds of acting individuals, has important implications: It implies that each of the ideal types

> must be formulated as a *pure* construct (that is, without any admixture of type-transcending behavior; and, furthermore, that it must be compatible with our experience of the world in general and therefore with our experience of other people in general and of the particular person whose acts we are seeking to understand by means of the construct. Another demand of the postulate is that the construct be based only on repeatable behavior [p. 270; W. and L. p. 236].

As to the application of ready-made, already existing rather than newly constructed ideal types to concrete courses of action, "the postulate of adequacy states that the type must be *sufficient to explain the action without contradicting previous experience* [p. 270; W. and L., p. 236]. There must, of course, be an "objective probability [chance]" that the ideal-typical motives to which the action is attributed, were also in fact effective.

> But there is no limitation whatsoever regarding the ways of constructing ideal types or regarding the techniques or principles of their formation. Both "empirical" [47] and "eidetic" [48] ideal types can be formed; though taken as invariant, the ideal type may be obtained by whatever method of generalization, abstraction, formali-

[47] " 'Empirical' is used here in the sense of the sum and substance of experiences of the outside world."

[48] "That is to say, ideal types derived from speculative insights into the essence of things [*in Wesensschau erfasst*]."

zation, idealization, or imagination, provided only that the principle of meaning-adequacy is observed [p. 219; W. and L. p. 244].

In other words, the type must be understandable and acceptable as corresponding to possibly intended meanings of acting individuals.

According to Schutz's conception, pure economic theory is "a perfect example of an objective meaning-complex about subjective meaning-complexes, in other words, of an objective meaning-configuration stipulating the typical and invariant subjective experiences of anyone who acts within an economic framework" [p. 280; W. and L. p. 245].

Schutz never speaks of real types (just as Max Weber avoided this term).[49] Any ordinary person in his everyday communication with his fellow men and contemporaries, the historian in his interpretation of past events, and the theorist in his formulation of general laws of the social world—all use ideal types; none is concerned with real types in the sense used by some of Weber's followers. Could it be that Weber and Schutz overlooked something that could be designated by this term? Let us turn to the work of Walter Eucken, who had much to say about the real type.

CONTRASTING REAL AND IDEAL TYPES OF VARYING DEGREES OF REALISM: EUCKEN

Walter Eucken succeeded, as hardly anyone before or after him, in endowing his treatise on the foundations of economics [50] with in-

[49] Weber did use a counterpart to his ideal type, which he called *Richtigkeitstypus*. A literal translation would be "correctness type" or "accuracy type." Weber used it chiefly to contrast subjectively rational action (*zweckrationales Handeln*) with objectively rational action (*richtigkeitsrationales Handeln*). Max Weber, "Über einige Kategorien der verstehenden Soziologie," *Logos*, Vol. 4 (1913); reprinted in *Gesammelte Aufsätze zur Wissenschaftslehre* (Tübingen: J.C.B. Mohr [Paul Siebeck], 3rd ed., 1968), p. 433. In addition, Weber recognized a *Durchschnittstypus* (average type). Max Weber, "Soziologische Grundbegriffe," *Grundriss der Sozialökonomik*, 3rd Abt.: *Wirtschaft und Gesellschaft* (1921), Part I, Ch. 1; reprinted in *Gesammelte Aufsätze zur Wissenschaftslehre*, 3rd ed., pp. 560–61 [2nd ed., pp. 521–22]. Neither of these two types, however, was assigned the explanatory role that Weber gave to the ideal type. Only the ideal type, with its inherent reference to subjective rationality, could explain human action.

[50] Walter Eucken, *Grundlagen der Nationalökonomie* (Berlin-Göttingen-Heidelberg: Springer Verlag, 1st ed., 1939; 6th ed., 1950). Page references are to the

sights of the most diverse sorts; seldom does one find such a firm and yet so smooth an integration of theoretical, historical, and methodological discourse. Eucken knew how to support his statements of economic theory quite casually with epistemological interpretations, and to elucidate them with light-flashes of economic-historical narratives. But it is only with one detail of his exposition that we have to be concerned here: his comments about the real type and its differentiation from the ideal type.

Eucken deplores that

> both kinds of types are continually confounded, and thus two logically entirely different mental tools are designated by the same name. . . . Nowadays both the real types and the genuine ideal types are called ideal types [pp. 41–42]. [The two kinds of type] are to serve different purposes, are obtained by different procedures, and have different logical character [p. 235]. [For the two types] the relation to the historically given past and present is different, both with regard to man acting as an economic unit and with regard to economic institutions. Likewise, the relation to rationality is different in the two types [p. 236].

The failure to see the difference that Eucken believes he sees goes back to Max Weber:

> What Weber says about the formation of ideal types is not only incomplete, but also contains serious defects. He recognized neither the fundamental difference between real types and ideal types, nor their logical character, nor the dissimilarity of the methods of abstraction that lead to the formation of these types. As a result, *the* type that he [Weber] names ideal type, is a concept with indefinite content. Weber, though he criticized the widespread incorrect use of real types, at the same time accepted Bücher's economic stages and interpreted them as ideal types. . . . Likewise, he designated the medieval "town economy" as an ideal type; the same name he gave to the "Robinson Crusoe economy," which is a genuine ideal type, formed in an entirely different way. Hence Weber contributed to the common confusion between ideal types and real types. . . . As his views about the formation of types still prevail in our days, and since clarification of this im-

---

sixth edition. An English translation by Terence W. Hutchison appeared under the title *The Foundations of Economics* (London and Edinburgh: Hodge, 1950).

FRITZ MACHLUP

portant complex of problems is impossible without an argument with Max Weber, a criticism of his writings is unavoidable. It is not a matter of developing a new concept of ideal type *against* Weber, but rather of rendering exact and complete what Weber had seen only vaguely and partially [pp. 268–69].

Just where does Eucken think this fundamental difference lies? If he believes that "the dividing line must be drawn clearly" [p. 236], where does he want to draw it? Let Eucken speak for himself:

> Regarding the difference between "real type and ideal type": Bücher's self-sufficient "domestic economy" is a real type. This type, the closed "domestic economy" is supposed to describe economic reality in antiquity and in the early Middle Ages. Thünen's "isolated state," on the other hand—a state in which a large city lies in the middle of a fertile plain of absolutely homogeneous soil, entirely separated from the rest of the world by a surrounding uncultivated wilderness and in which perfect competition rules everywhere—is an ideal type for use as a mental model. With his isolated state, Thünen does not describe any actual reality, nor does he want to do so. But he obtained this type through investigating the concrete economy; he selected and isolated *one* side of the concrete economy; and the theoretical propositions gained by working with this ideal type serve, in their application, the discovery of concrete relationships. In the same way I have found forms of economic order—economic systems, forms of centrally-managed economy, market forms, monetary systems, in short, an entire morphological system—and I found them in concrete reality. Yes, there they really *are*. Science has to discover them there. But these forms of economic order do not exist there in purity, but "blended together" in manifold ways. . . . By separating them in order to emphasize individual points or, in other words, by mentally extracting and isolating them from the blending in which they exist in the real economy, and thus by obtaining them in their pure form, we come into possession of types that do not individually portray economic reality; instead, they are "ideal" in a logical sense [p. 269].

That the "isolated state" is an ideal type is clear. But why, I must ask, is the self-sufficient "domestic economy" for Eucken a real type? Simply because Bücher thought that it "described" something factual, a reality of the past? Or because it was depicted in too great detail? To be sure, there are useful and useless ideal types, and many ideal types are of no use because they contain details that are irrelevant for the relationships under investigation; but why should this make them "real types"?

Let us listen further:

> The single aspects of the individual phenomenon . . . are lifted out and "ideal types" are thereby obtained. This kind of abstraction is in sharp contrast to the "generalizing" abstraction, which is designed to focus on that which is common to many factual states of affairs, and which is the working technique of the constructors of economic stages and economic styles; this is quite different from the "selectively emphasizing" (or "isolating") abstraction operating on individual factual states of affairs [p. 70]. We reduce the concrete state of affairs . . . to pure forms through pointedly selective emphasis [p. 71].

Yet, I must ask, is the difference between "generalizing" abstraction and "isolating" abstraction really sufficient to separate the concepts obtained? After all, we receive most of the concepts with which we work, in ordinary everyday life as well as in scientific research, from others, often from generations of predecessors. If we accept from one of our teachers the concept of "communism" and the concept of "centrally administered economy," how do we know what kind of observations and what kind of mental operations he (or *his* teacher) have used in order to form these concepts? Of course, Eucken is right in holding that the type "market economy" is far more helpful in theoretical analysis than is the type "capitalism." But this is a matter of applicability and of the directions for use, not of the production method that was employed in obtaining the type.

In order to clarify the difference in the method of production of types, Eucken resorts to an analogy. With regard to the historical school and its method, to its "building of cross-sections through history and its constructions of separate theories for every single cross-section," he says:

> The builders of cross-sections created their types through "generalizing abstraction," by *stepping back* from reality, by *neglecting* details—and thereby they came to results that did not correspond to the real economy and are of no use as foundations of theoretical work. I have proceeded in the opposite fashion from the very beginning. I have sought, as resolutely as possible, to dig into the individual factual circumstances, into the concrete individual households and industrial establishments; and thus I have *magnified*

vision of the individual phenomenon to the highest degree. To use a metaphor: as one seeks to seize the silhouette of a town visible from a distance, so economic stages or economic styles are formed, which are supposed to represent the essential or normal of the economy of a certain era. I do something entirely different: I go— to continue the metaphor—into the town and then into the individual houses and inspect them from cellar to roof. The single economic structures are thoroughly examined. On the strength of isolating, "pointedly emphasizing abstraction," I have there encountered the ideal-typical economic systems with their many forms of centrally managed economy, market forms, and currency systems. I have thus found the forms of economic order in historical reality. I have uncovered them in the process of examining the factual states of affairs of the present and the past [pp. 162–63].

What has been my intention to do with this morphological system? The single forms of which it is composed yield no images of concrete reality, although they were obtained from exact observation of reality. They are neither photographs nor paintings and do not want to be either. Nor are they thought to be part of a definite historical milieu. I have shown, however, that on their basis —because they present simple and clear constellations of circumstances—one can find theoretical propositions, that is, general assertions, about necessary interrelationships of conditions [p. 163].

What was said here about the applicability of the ideal-typical forms of economic system could hardly be more poetically formulated. But the story of the "discovery" of these forms through "house searches" and "exact observation of reality," the idea that these forms of economic order were actually "found" or detected, is, in my opinion, unacceptable. Forms of economic order are *schemas of interpretation* with which we can explain some or many things in reality (namely, observed phenomena), but they [the schemas] can neither be found nor observed, neither from a distance nor at close range. Eucken, however, does not like this to be so. He struggles against the idea that one can make progress in perception and cognition by means of more thorough reflection, by thought experiments, heuristic fictions, mental constructions, or free invention. He always wants to reassure himself and his reader that everything he says, and everything that can be said correctly, has been directly "obtained from concrete reality."

Here are a few examples of this attitude:

An exact and at the same time systematic elaboration of the constitutive elements of form must not be the result of the positing of axioms or of speculative reflections. Otherwise a break between historical experience and theoretical inquiry would occur at this point. Building models arbitrarily would be a serious mistake, though this mistake has been made often enough. The new stage of analysis is not to be achieved by moving away from the real economic world. On the contrary . . . we must . . . penetrate even deeper than before into the individual historical economic structures if we want to solve the problems now before·us [p. 78].

The diversity of factual circumstances compellingly requires the building of these forms [of economic order]. The "pointedly emphasizing" analysis of the *factual* circumstances has therefore to decide about the kind and shape of the patterns of supply and demand, *not the deduction from a priori posited conditions.* The diversity [of the real world] cannot be conquered in any other way but through investigation of the concrete facts: It [the investigation] must advance to the point of contact with the real essence of the matter—with the economic plan and its conditions. Only from there can the types be worked out successfully. There are as many typical forms as are found in reality, but not so many as can be mentally constructed. Despite my intensive investigation of reality I have not been able to find more forms than I have here presented [p. 106].

One more comment about the "fundamental forms" to which the "analysis that has penetrated to the real economy with the aid of 'pointedly isolating abstraction' " supposedly has led:

They are not types designed to copy [or portray] the economy, they are not real types such as the economic styles or economic stages. They are pure forms, genuine ideal types, every one of which reproduces only *one* aspect of the factual circumstances that are found to exist. However, this does not mean Utopias, as Max Weber mistakenly called them. Utopias are presented as contrasts to concrete reality, placed in juxtaposition to it. *Genuine ideal types are obtained from concrete reality* [p. 123].

Let us set this controversial point aside for the time being and return to the question of whether or not we have at last learned where the line between ideal type and real type is to be drawn. Unfortunately, we have not. Perhaps it will help if we survey the examples of real types which Eucken presented in his book: "town economy"; "capitalism" [p. 41]; "independent economy" [*Eigenwirtschaft*]; [self-sufficient] "household economy"; "regional economy" [*Landschaftswirtschaft*] [p. 46]; "communist economy [p. 127]; "medieval man"; "capitalist man" [p. 221]; "stages, styles, or real-typical economic systems" [pp. 251–52]; [early] "household economy" [*Oikenwirtschaft*] [p. 254]. This brief catalogue undoubtedly contains a few types that are poorly suited for theoretical analysis, and others that are rather useless for historical interpretation, although they were originally intended for it. Yet every single one of these concepts *may* be an ideal type, and a few can be nothing but ideal types, because no observed characteristics can be specified for them at all.

Eucken also gives us examples of real types that he formed himself: "From the point of view of their behavior with regard to conjunctural fluctuations, *three types* of economic order can be distinguished. They are all real types" [p. 195]. The three types are economic orders in which certain structural elements "dominate." Eucken designates them as real types, evidently because these structural elements are embodied in the type, but not in complete purity and exclusivity. Yet the fact that Eucken can *think* about how an economic system in which these or those forms are "predominant," or how it would react to certain changes in conditions, shows, I submit, that he is here talking about *ideal types* of mixed economies. Theorizing with *complicated* ideal types is, of course, possible only if one has previously constructed *simple* types and developed the relations that are ideal-typically associated with them. One can then combine several simple types with one another and can form all possible composite models, which, however, do not lose thereby their character as ideal types.

In an exemplification of "pointedly emphasizing abstractions" for the forming of ideal types, Eucken points out that pure forms are obtained from "*one* household, *one* industry, *one* farm, *one* feudal manor. ... Generalizing abstraction, on the other hand, is carried out with surveys covering *many* concrete cases from which common traits are noted and formed as generic concepts. From surveying a large number of ancient estates the generic concept and real type 'Oikos Husbandry' [*Oikenwirtschaft*] has emerged; and from surveying a large number of medieval towns the real type 'town economy' has been formed" [p. 254]. Reading Eucken's statement, I cannot help saying that the question how many single houses, industrial establishments, estates, and towns are visited and observed before one selects to isolate or accentuate one or more features for the purpose of type formation is quite irrelevant. The fact that one often selects for special emphasis one single feature or element for the formation of an ideal type does not mean that one has to refrain from examining a larger number of particular individual persons, objects, institutions, towns, or other things. The number of elements or characteristics that one considers essential and therefore wants to emphasize in the formation of a concept has nothing to do with the number of concrete (personal or material) individuals that one decides to examine.

Two further remarks about real types should be quoted here, for they can possibly provide a clue to what Eucken really meant. In a negative characterization of pure ideal types of economic systems he says that they "do not—in contrast to styles or stages or real-typical economic systems—claim to *portray* in a comprehensive fashion economic realities in certain cross-sections" [p. 235]. In a comment on economic stages and styles—which he calls real types while others call them ideal types—Eucken writes:

> *During* their construction one believes that such "ideal images" or "ideal types" could be constructed with some casual magnanimity, neglecting many historically conjoined facts, just because it is only a question of ideal representation. *After* their construction, however, one hears declarations to the effect that, through them, the concrete economy has been "captured" or "portrayed" or "copied." *At first* the contention was that the type "town economy" represented an ideal type, and that facts that did not agree with the picture were insignificant. *Later* the claim is made that the type "town economy" be recognized as the image of the economy of a particular era, say, that of the Middle Ages since the twelfth century. Thus an open invitation is tendered to subjectivity and arbitrariness in the creation of a historical picture [p. 253].

Eucken points here to the bold assertion made by builders of types that they "portray" or "copy" the real world. Eucken has good reason to be angry about such silly assertions; but one cannot label a concept as "real type" simply because someone falsely maintains that it "portrays" actual reality. There is no such thing as a picture of economic reality, since reality consists only of interrelations of meanings without anything visible and portrayable. The visible and observable artifacts of economic activity are such things as price lists, invoices, order forms, payroll sheets, ledgers, business reports, financial statements, etc. We shall have more to say about this later. If someone maintains that his types "portray" a "town economy," a "money system," or "capitalism," he is talking nonsense and should not be taken seriously.

Now, if this criterion too, which Eucken proposed for identifying generic concepts as "real types," is eliminated, then no reason is left for characterizing them as real types. It may well be that certain types were constructed with an excessive number of elements—too large for theoretical analysis—and that, moreover, the elements were poorly chosen and proved to be irrelevant when the types were put to use in causal reasoning. If so, these types are simply *useless ideal types*—and Eucken is right, of course, in criticizing and rejecting them.

THE REAL TYPE: MENGER ONCE AGAIN

In this dilemma we cannot ask Max Weber for advice, for he did not speak of the real type. We have to go back to Carl Menger, in whose methodological investigation the two kinds of types played an important role and were clearly set apart. Unfortunately, the wording of his definitions was not clear enough to avoid misunderstandings. His examples, however, are suitable for the task of shedding light on our questions.

First of all, we have to remember that Menger's real and ideal types were supposed to be useful for explanatory purposes in the natural as well as in the social sciences. I propose to discuss Menger's distinction with reference to three areas of application: chemistry, physics, and economics.

1. The *chemical* ideal types "pure oxygen," "pure hydrogen," "pure water," and "pure gold" are juxtaposed by the real types oxygen, hydrogen, water, and gold in impure forms with agreed tolerances for various impurities. The ideal types expressed in

formulas are used for the derivation of abstract ("exact") laws. The real types, on the other hand, are used for the practical determination of the chemical materials, partly for experimental use in laboratories with a view to comparable, and measurable, empirical results, partly for quality controls in industry production.

2. The *physical* ideal types "perfect vacuum," and "perfectly frictionless movement," have no counterparts that are formed in real types; the ideal types "perfect lever," "ideal gas," etc., do have such counterparts in the form of the real types "lever," "gas," etc., which are accepted as definitions of what one may in the laboratory or workshop reasonably regard as lever, gas, etc. Again, the ideal types are useful in the derivation of relationships in the form of law statements, whereas the real types serve, for example, for the specification of the rules and procedures to be observed in the laboratory in the performance of experiments and in the evaluation of the results.

3. The *economic* ideal types *"homo oeconomicus,"* "isolated state," and "equilibrium" have no counterparts in the form of real types. The ideal types "pure deposit bank," "pure entrepreneurial profit," and "free-market price" are juxtaposed by corresponding real types such as deposit bank, profit, and price. Abstract models are formed with the aid of ideal types for the derivation of abstract-law statements, whereas the real types often serve in describing the concrete situations in which the theories may be tested, or in determining the concrete phenomena which the statistician needs for his enumerations, estimations, measurements, and calculations.

THREE TYPICAL EXAMPLES OF REAL TYPES IN ECONOMICS

Let us reflect for a moment on the three examples of real types in economics just mentioned. Why do we need a real type "deposit bank?" It is needed for several purposes. For instance, the statistician should be enabled to determine the number of deposit banks in a country, to report on their deposit liabilities, their assets, etc. He needs guidelines to determine which of the existing financial institutions, perhaps registered by the state, are to be considered banks and which banks considered deposit banks. The same real type is needed for those in charge of economic policy, who are called upon to take advantage of the teachings offered by theoreticians for application in certain economic situations. Finally, the real type is needed for the economic historian who is to report on the state of banking in a particular period and has to determine whether the institutions named in the archives and described in the available records can reasonably be designated as deposit banks.

Why do we need a real type "profit?" As a matter of fact, we need several real types of profit, one for tax purposes, another for purposes of dividend policies of business corporations, a third for deliberations regarding investment plans, a fourth for the statistics concerned with the national economic accounts, etc. The real type profit describes the operations to be executed by those who have to calculate the amount which, for specified purposes, is to be regarded as profit. It should be clear to economists that these real types have only weak family resemblances to the ideal type of "pure entrepreneurial profit," since they usually include also other kinds of income—particularly, interest and rents of all sorts.

There is a large variety of real types called "price"; the number of these real types is so large not only because different techniques of inquiry lead to different reports, or because for different purposes different kinds of information are sought, but also because there are several different sources of the information recorded. In collecting statistics of retail prices, the numbers written on the price tags and labels on goods in shops, stores, or shop windows may be noted and reported; for some types of commodities, one relies on printed price lists or catalogues, for others on the invoices filed in the business offices or recorded in entries in business ledgers; for wholesale prices, especially for goods traded on commodity exchanges, one may find information in the business sections of daily newspapers or in specialized trade journals. For these and many other sources, the empirical researcher obtains his material for the determination of actual prices; the definition of the real type "price" provides the description of the steps the researcher takes to get his "observations." Of course, he knows full well that often these "real prices" are not really "real"— think, for example, of secret discounts or rebates—but he will in general have to restrict himself to what is written or printed in black on white. All this holds, no matter whether the purpose of the exercise is a historical narrative or a series of empirical data employed for causal explanations of other events, or a set of so-called observations designed for use in the testing of theoretical propositions.

THE RELATION BETWEEN REAL TYPES AND IDEAL TYPES

All of these real types are useful, or even necessary, in observing phenomena of the real world, whereby "real" is best equated with "in black on white." [51] Thus it is understandable that the real type is held to be the adequate concept of realistic-empirical research. *As soon as one passes from observation, classification, comparison and calculation (correlation, regression, etc.) to reflection and theorizing about causal relationships among phenomena, one consciously or unconsciously replaces the real types with ideal types.* For example, as soon as one asks whether certain prices have risen during a period of time as the result of an increase in demand or because of a decrease in supply, one no longer thinks of price tags, price lists, price files, or price reports, etc. but, instead, of ideal-typical decisions on the part of ideal-typical buyers and sellers in an ideal-typical market. In short, *the real type is a category of observation, classification, description, and measurement, while the ideal type is a category of reflection and argumentation.*

This does not mean, however, that the empirical researcher can do without ideal types. He certainly cannot succeed in his work without reflection, otherwise he cannot know whether the real types—which are the material at his disposal—have any relevance for his task. First, as a historian or statistician he must ask himself whether the reports, the data available to him, are accurate or whether he should perhaps adjust, correct, or altogether reject them. He is not capable of such

[51] Although I have obtained my interpretation of the meaning of the word *Realtypus* from Carl Menger's explanations, I must not hold Menger responsible for it. I am certain that my proposition will meet resistance, but I hope that it will not be rejected without reflection. Perhaps one may prefer to waive all definitions of *real type* and drop the expression completely. I would accept such a decision without any regret, inasmuch as better terms are available for the notion in question.

FRITZ MACHLUP

judgments unless his intellectual equipment includes the ideal types appropriate for tackling the problems he confronts. Second, he must ask himself whether the so-called facts of the real world that he puts before himself or before others as the things to be explained really are facts and not just "hot air," emanating from misunderstandings, errors, distortions, false reports, misprints, and so forth. For this judgment, he needs ideal types, not only for explaining possible connections among concrete events and conditions, but also for confirming the reports of such facts. Third, he must ask himself whether the material with which he wants to test some of the theories on which he has relied is suitable for verification or falsification. To make such a judgment, he requires an examination of the comparability and correspondence of the factual material (the data) arranged according to available real types with the ideal types that are included, in the form of (independent or dependent) variables or parameters, in his models of actions, interactions, and processes.

Every real type has one or more ideal types as theoretical counterpart. *Many an* ideal type has one or more real types as empirical counterpart. However, many an ideal type has *no* empirical counterpart. Such an ideal type—without any "relatives" in the empirical domain—may nevertheless be a necessary link in the thought process that is required for a meaningful explanation of the relationships among certain phenomena of the social world.

THE REAL IN THE REAL TYPE
AND THE IDEAL IN THE IDEAL TYPE

Names are often poorly chosen, and logicians and epistemologists have often been unfortunate in their lack of linguistic imagination: They have not had the knack of choosing the most expressive words. With regard to the two types in question, we must say that if the adjectival halves of the terms are to have any good meaning, let us ask ourselves what actually is the real in the real type (as we understand it), and the ideal in the ideal type.

The real in the real type is, in my opinion, the set of phenomena visible, audible, or tangible to the observer, or the records, descriptions, estimates or measurements of any factual events or phenomena made by the (concerned or unconcerned) observers. It is not necessary that these objects of observation be themselves experiences of tangible things. They may also relate to inner experiences, insofar as these were retained and recorded by the one who experiencd them (or by others who witnessed the reports) in an audible or visible form. The real in this connection rarely, if ever, means "complete empirical reality," because there are no observations without abstraction. But with all omissions, witting or unwitting, what is observed is still a directly observable phenomenon, a written (graphic) record, or some otherwise visible testimony of something experienced.

The scientifically most frequent and most important form of real type is a series of numbers presented to the analyst assigned to furnish adequate explanations or employed by the analyst for the testing (verification, falsification) of his explanations or predictions.

The ideal in the ideal type lies in its belonging to the domain of ideas, of thought, its transcendence from the sensually perceptible. The thought of something real is and remains a thought or idea even if it has for its content something that is perceptible. In the narrower sense of the word, the *ideal* in the ideal type is the thought of meaning-relationships among remembered or imagined persons, thoughts of their actions and reactions and of the results of their actions and reactions.

OPERATIONAL CONCEPTS AND PURE CONSTRUCTS

The pair of concepts, real type and ideal type, is almost unknown in Anglo-American literature. In their place, another pair of terms is customarily used: the *operational concept* and the mental *construct*.[52] (English logicians coined the word *construct* in order to distinguish *constructum* from *constructio*, the former being the result of an act of construction.)

---

[52] I introduced *Konstrukt* as a new word in German in the original German text of this essay and in a short monograph. See Fritz Machlup, *Der Wettstreit zwischen Mikro- und Makrotheorien in der Nationalökonomie* (Tübingen: J.C.B. Mohr [Paul Siebeck], 1960), p. 32.

An operational concept is defined by the description of the operations which the researcher undertakes in the determination or measurement of an observed situation or event.[53] A *construct* is a concept formed for purposes of theoretical analysis which cannot be defined in terms of objects of observation and of operations with such objects.[54] Operational concepts and constructs are needed in all fields of empirical knowledge. Now the question arises, whether one may equate *operational concept* with *real type*, and *construct* with *ideal type*, or whether it is better to use a specific terminology for the social sciences. Only a short time ago, I wrote sceptically about the question of whether one should give different names to this pair of concepts in the social and natural sciences: "Granted that there is the additional postulate (or precept) of 'understandability' [*Verstehbarkeit*] in the social sciences, could one not bear this in mind even without being reminded of it by the use of special terms?"[55] However, after having referred once again to the large amount of German literature on the ideal type and having partially reread it, I do not dare to recommend that expressions so carefully analyzed and tenderly cultivated be entirely dropped. The German social scientist who continues to speak of real and ideal types separates himself from his colleagues in other countries and remains partially incomprehensible to them in this respect. This, however, is not necessarily so much of a loss in comparison with the discontinuance of a grand tradition. Yet, the German sociologist should at least know which expressions can promote mutual understanding, and from this point of view it is perhaps important to say that the real type, as I understand it, is an *operational concept,* and the ideal type is a pure *construct,* useful in the social sciences to remind us of the importance of understanding subjective and intersubjective meanings of social action and social phenomena.

[53] Percy W. Bridgman, *The Logic of Modern Physics* (New York: Macmillan, 1927).

[54] I have elsewhere attempted to define *construct* and to distinguish its main forms. See Fritz Machlup, "Operational Concepts and Mental Constructs in Model and Theory Formation," *Giornali degli Economisti*, Vol. 19 (New Series, 1960), pp. 553–82. Reproduced as Chapter 6 of the present volume.

[55] Fritz Machlup, *Der Wettstreit*, p. 43.

THE POSITIVISTIC PREJUDICE
AGAINST CONSTRUCTION

My suggestion may give offense to those who harbor a strong prejudice: *Construction* is often suspect, for it is thought to be the work of inventive and mysterious fancy, willful toying with empty thoughts, metaphysical speculation, perhaps even the conjuring tricks of a swindler. Is it not imperative for the scientist to take his concepts from empirical reality if they are to be of use in explaining empirical reality?

I have in this essay reproduced a good many statements to this effect, and we have seen that many of them are strongly supported by an authority as recognized as that of Walter Eucken. In the intellectual situation of our days, one may easily risk one's scientific reputation by questioning the empirical source of scientific concepts. I cannot help, nevertheless, being so bold as to challenge and contradict the empiricist position and, in particular, Walter Eucken's. Fortunately, my stand has the support of the authority of Max Weber, who did not hesitate to designate his ideal types as outright constructions, indeed as Utopias. I may add that some of the sociologists and philosophers who have translated Weber's works into English have rendered ideal type as "constructed type" and have defined it as a construct.[56]

The fear of being guilty of the scientific misdemeanor of "construction," which so much distresses the worshippers of unadulterated reality, has caused them to distinguish between "reconstruction" and "free construction," between "construction on the solid ground of reality" and "free-floating construction," between "reductive

[56] H. Stuart Hughes, a great admirer of Weber's, wrote about "the creation of useful fictions, as Max Weber was later to elaborate them, as models for critical understanding. . . . Only with Max Weber do we reach a theory of fictions that has had enough internal consistency to maintain itself as a permanent contribution to social thought." Finally he compares Weber's methodology with Vaihinger's philosophy of "As-if": "Vaihinger's notion of a fiction in science was approximately the same as what Weber was to call an 'ideal type' ". Although pragmatism and fictionalism have much in common, they are nevertheless fundamentally different: "Pragmatism equated usefulness with truth; fictionalism, on the other hand, maintained that the two questions were separate—that an idea might be palpably false but nonetheless have 'great practical importance.' " Henry Stuart Hughes, *Consciousness and Society* (New York: Knopf, 1958), pp. 65, 107, 110, 111–12.

model" and "constructive model," and finally between "purified ideal type" and "constructed ideal type." All these, in my opinion, are distinctions without differences. They have about as much scientific value as pious averments of faith.

An ideal type is a pattern of interpretation, a means of cognition, a mental tool. How a tool is fabricated is important for the toolmaker, but not for those who use it. And how the tools already at hand were manufactured and where they came from is entirely immaterial as long as they are useful. An ideal type is to help us solve problems. If it does that, the question of its origin or derivation is unimportant. Whether an idea for the solution of a problem was born in detailed empirical work, in massive statistical calculations, or in pure contemplation, or whether it has emerged from the search of archives, from the scrutiny of ancient documents, from the surveying or polling of thousands of respondents, or has been generated in pure speculation, makes not a whit of difference for finding out whether the idea is good or bad, useful or useless, for the explanation of possible, probable, or necessary relationships. Even if someone who has never before been engaged in such inquiries were suddenly to have a good idea come into his head, an idea that may prove helpful in solving a problem of explanation—even if it had come to him in a dream—we should accept this idea with gratitude. We must rise above prejudice against ideas of questionable origin when these ideas prove superior to others of more respectable origin. "Good extraction" or "lineage" is no guarantee for performance.

In competition with German products, manufacturers in other countries once believed that a label "Made in Germany" would arouse the nationalistic prejudice and mistrust of wide circles of consumers overseas and would lead to the rejection of these imports. The good quality of the wares, however, soon overcame the prejudice and transformed the mistrust into trust. Similarly, there are those who would exploit the mistrust of mental products of "questionable" origin. Prejudiced adherents of empiricist epistemology have resorted to a policy of requiring, so to speak, psychological certificates of origin for mental products; they think that products imported directly from the realm of "observed reality" will find more approval than imports from the realm of "speculation." Perhaps in these intellectual exchanges too, the mistrust—the positivistic preju-

dice—will soon disappear and mental constructions that prove efficient will be accepted, with or without certificates of origin.

POSTCRIPT

For the sake of brevity, I have formulated many of my propositions
much more apodictically than may seem appropriate. For that I ask
forgiveness. Moreover, I am aware that much more should be said
about the problems of appropriate concept formation; that it would
be important, for example, to examine them more thoroughly in the
light of the insights of logical, methodological and epistemological
research of the last half-century. I am thinking especially of Karl
Jaspers, Ernst Cassirer, and Karl Popper, but also of several others.
Perhaps I can attempt this some time in the future in another context. My main purpose in this essay has been to pose questions that
made it possible for me to argue with Walter Eucken. Those who
have known him well will testify that he would not have taken my
criticism amiss.

ANOTHER POSTCRIPT AFTER
EIGHTEEN YEARS

One of the most significant methodological developments in the
years since the first publication of this essay has been the steady increase in the professional appreciation of the work of Alfred Schutz,
especially his posthumously published writings.[57] His "social phenomenology," if I may use this expression, has solved some of the
problems dealt with in my essay and has finally buried others. In the
light of Schutzian thought, I would now be inclined to forget all the

[57] No less than 22 titles in English or German by Schutz have appeared since his
death in 1959. This includes some double counting, since some articles were reproduced in his volumes of collected works, but it also understates his posthumous
publications in that numerous translations into languages other than English and
German have been published. The literature on Schutz's work has grown by leaps and
bounds. Eight books have appeared between 1965 and 1977 which have Schutz's
name in the title. The number of articles dealing comprehensively with Schutz's
writings has grown to 179; of these, 75 have Schutz's name in the title.

FRITZ MACHLUP

talk about the "real type"; the empirical concepts used in the collection of empirical data do not need the fancy designation proposed by extreme empiricists in the social sciences. On the other hand, the elaboration and reformulation of the "ideal type" remains a task worthy of the efforts of students of the methodology of the social sciences.

Chapter 10

HOMO OECONOMICUS AND HIS CLASS MATES

PREFATORY NOTE

A French rendition of this essay, under the title "L'Homo oeconomicus et ses collègues," was included in *Les Fondements philosophiques des systèmes économiques,* a volume published in 1967 in honor of Jacques Rueff, member of the Académie Française. Since the ideas presented in my essay have been significantly influenced by the work of Alfred Schutz, since my intellectual debt to him is gratefully acknowledged in text and footnotes, and since my strong emphasis on some Schutzian theses can be regarded as homage and obeisance to my old friend and mentor, the inclusion of the English version of my essay in this volume in memory of Alfred Schutz is entirely appropriate.

I have been working on a short biography of *homo oeconomicus* and have found it fascinating. The history of this idea is largely a history of misunderstandings and misinterpretations reflecting the course of the debate of the methodology of the social sciences. Reserving most of this ideological history for a longer publication, I propose to offer here my observations on some of the controversial issues involved.

Two problems should be clarified right at the outset: One is the question of the legitimacy and expediency of selecting specific traits or objectives of men through the mental construction of an abstract, partial man (*homo partialis*), in the face of the strong opposition of many writers who reject such a willful dissection of whole man (*homo totus*). The other problem relates to the difference, too often overlooked, between the construction of personal types for the understanding of particular men – historical personages, men in the news, acquaintances, friends – and the construction of personal types designed to aid in the analysis of things, events, and observed changes which are interpreted as the results of actions or reactions by persons who may be unknown and unidentified.

THE DISSECTION OF HOMO TOTUS

Writers without analytic tastes or talents have strongly protested against breaking up "whole man" into ideal types each endowed with only one quality (or a small selection of qualities) or exhibiting the pursuit of only one motive or objective. This anti-analytic position, the resistance to the analytical dissection of *homo totus* into many separate constructs isolating particular human traits or functions, is difficult to understand, let alone defend. After all, no real man could possibly have all the qualities or pursue all the objectives singled out in separate conceptual constructions needed for the understanding of human action. For example, *homo cholericus* and *homo phlegmaticus* are mutually exclusive types, who could not *both* be "embodied" in one real person. To be sure, we may need dozens of ideal types to interpret the conduct of any one person of our acquaintance or to understand different aspects of his behavior in particular situations; but never can *all* possible types become relevant in connection with any real man.

Analysis of human action with the aid of constructs isolating, idealizing, and exaggerating some human trait or function is needed both for historical and for theoretical investigation. That is to say, the "breaking up" of "whole man" is needed for understanding the actions of *historical* persons, known to us either personally or indirectly through reports, as well as for explaining and predicting the probable consequences of actions of *anonymous* persons known to us merely in their general roles in society. Such social roles may be those of consumers, producers, buyers, sellers, employers, workers, lenders, borrowers, landlords, tenants, bankers, depositors, and so forth, all social roles involved in generalizations in economics; or of voters, candidates, rioters, soldiers, officers, worshippers, priests, judges, thieves, actors, spectators, and in hundreds of other roles involved in generalizations in political science and sociology.

THIS ONE VERSUS ANY ONE

Having mentioned a variety of social roles, I should make it clear that every real person acts at various times in many different roles and that the interpretation of his actions presupposes the availability, in the minds of the interpreters, of a large collection of ideal types. Thus, our friend, Mr. *This*

One, may be a consumer, buyer, seller, worker, borrower, tenant, depositor, voter, worshipper, spectator (to choose from our list) and also a husband, father, trade unionist, tax payer, glee-club member, bowler, poker player (to mention a few additional roles he plays in society). To understand Mr. *This One's* movements, gestures, and words, interpreters need to be familiar with at least as many ideal types of behavior as there are roles in which he acts, and probably many more since in each of these roles there are several possible ways of acting.

The simultaneous or consecutive use of many separate ideal types is usually required in inquiries about *particular* persons, acting alone or in groups. In inquiries about events explainable as consequences of actions of *anonymous* persons, the interpreters can often do with a very small set of ideal types. For example, for the explanation of a rise in the price of a commodity in a competitive market it will, as a rule, be quite irrelevant that the buyers are also voters, husbands, poker players, and what not, and whether they are choleric or phlegmatic, selfish or altruistic, pious or irreligious. In such inquiries the bloodless type of a Mr. *Any One*, representing a mere buying robot equipped with a stipulated "behavior equation" or "objective function," will be the most serviceable analytic instrument.

FOUR CONTROVERSIAL ISSUES

Homo oeconomicus should be understood as an anonymous type, constructed for the interpretation of effects of human action. Economists, but also sociologists, philosophers, historians, and other writers, have debated a large variety of issues concerning the nature and the standing of *homo oeconomicus.* Among other things, they have argued whether Economic Man could serve as a realistic description of human decision-making or only as a heuristic fiction; whether the authors who had used Economic Man in their theoretical inquiries had actually believed him to be realistic or only fictitious; whether Economic Man was employed in explanations of decisions of businessmen only or also of consumers; and whether Economic Man should or should not be regarded as an ideal type (in Max Weber's sense). These four controversial questions, particularly the fourth one, will be selected for discussion in the present essay.

The points of view about the "realism" of Economic Man range from assertions of reasonable *lifelikeness* to characterizations as pure and useless *fiction.* No writer, to my knowledge, has ever claimed that all men were always actuated by egoistic motives or by a desire to maximize money gains. All that supporters of Economic Man as a "realistic type" of man engaged in economic activities claimed was that enough people often enough followed the lure of pecuniary advantage to make the outcome of market activities roughly correspond to the conclusions deduced from the assumption of profit-maximizing behavior.[1] Others claimed much less; and a few asserted that it would make no difference if the hypothesis of maximizing behavior were entirely unrealistic, provided only that the use of this theoretical postulate led us to deductions useful in predicting correctly the consequences of changes in observable data.

On the other hand, those who repudiated *homo oeconomicus* as a useful aid in economic theory denied not only the realism of the assumption of "maximizing behavior" but also its methodological standing as a heuristic fiction. They contended that abstraction from the large bulk of reality, and isolation of a small fragment of it, was an arbitrary and illegitimate procedure and they rejected the methodological tenet that unrealistic, fictitious constructions could be of any use in the explanation of real phenomena.

This controversy, as an issue in methodology, cannot be settled either by empirical tests or by formal logical demonstration. The second controversy, however, as a question about the history of economic thought, is easy to decide. One merely has to take the trouble to reread what the authors who befriended *homo oeconomicus* actually wrote about him.

The critics of "classical" economists derided them for their alleged failure to recognize that *homo oeconomicus* was a fiction (or caricature) and for their alleged naiveté in mistaking him for a true picture of reality. This charge was repeated over and over in the writings of the historical schools. But these critics had evidently neglected to check the sources, or they would have found very clear statements of the real position of the theorists whom they attacked. John Stuart Mill, for example, said most explicitly that "Political Economy presupposes an arbitrary definition of man, as a being who invariably does that by which he may obtain the greatest amount of necessaries, conveniences and luxuries, with the smallest quantity of labour and physical self-denial . . ." He stressed that "Political Economy . . . reasons from *assumed* premises – from premises which might be totally without foundation in fact, and which are not pretended to be universally in accordance with it . . ." And, in justifying the isolation of economic motives, he

---

[1] "The propositions of the theory of variations do not involve the assumption that men are actuated *only* by considerations of money gains and losses. They involve only the assumption that money plays *some* part in the valuation of the given alternatives." Lionel Robbins. *An Essay on the Nature and Significance of Economic Science* (London: Macmillan, 2nd ed. 1935), p. 98.

exclaimed: "Not that any political economist was ever so absurd as to suppose mankind are really thus constituted . . ."[2]

It is almost comical how the anti-theorists reveled in delight when, having demonstrated the fictional and fictitious nature of Economic Man, they believed they had refuted the classical school and demolished economic theory. One especially quixotic knight errant must have been terribly pleased with himself when he characterized "pure theory" as a big "circus of commodities with value-and-price acrobats on the mathematical trapeze and the *homo oeconomicus* as clown."[3] Evidently he did not realize that his supposedly devastating analogy would be quite acceptable to many a theorist. Not a circus but a puppet stage was the simile used for pure economic theory by Alfred Schutz, one of the most profound writers on the methodology of the social sciences.[4] Max Weber, likewise, fully accepted the critics' contention that the "rational constructions" of "pure economics" were "pure fictions."[5]

Sombart summarized the argument nicely when he spoke of "the legendary *homo oeconomicus*, the spook and bogie against whom generations of economists of the historical schools have waged their embittered windmill

---

[2] The last sentence is part of Mill's statement on the method of political economy as the science concerning itself only with "such of the phenomena of the social state as take place in consequence of the pursuit of wealth. It makes entire abstraction of every other human passion or motive; except those which may be regarded as perpetually antagonizing principles to the desire of wealth, namely, aversion to labour and desire of the present enjoyment of costly indulgences . . . The science then proceeds to investigate the laws which govern these several operations, under the supposition that man is a being who is determined . . . to prefer a greater portion of wealth to a smaller, in all cases, without any other exception than that constituted by the two counter-motives already specified. Not that any political economist was ever so absurd as to suppose that mankind are really thus constituted, but because this is the mode in which science must necessarily proceed. . . . In order to judge how he [man in society] will act under the variety of desires and aversions which are concurrently operating upon him, we must know how he would act under the exclusive influence of each one in particular . . ." John Stuart Mill, *A System of Logic*, Vol. II (London: Parker, 1843), pp. 570–572; "On the Definition of Political Economy; and on the Method of Investigation Proper to It," *Essays on Some Unsettled Questions of Political Economy* (London: Parker, 1844), pp. 137–139, and 144.

[3] Friedrich von Gottl-Ottlilienfeld, *Wirtschaft als Leben*, (Jena: Gustav Fischer, 1925).

[4] ". . . the [social] scientist replaces the human beings he observes as actors on the social stage by puppets created by himself and manipulated by himself." Alfred Schutz, "The Problem of Rationality in the Social World," *Economica*, New Series, Vol. X (May 1943), reprinted in *Collected Papers*, Vol. II (The Hague: Martinus Nijhoff, 1964), p. 81.

[5] *Max Weber on the Methodology of the Social Sciences* ed. Shils and Finch (Glencoe, Ill.: Free Press, 1949), p. 44. Translated from *Gesammelte Aufsätze zur Wissenschaftslehre* (Tübingen: J. C. B. Mohr, 2nd ed., 1951), pp. 190 ff.

battles, but who in the bright light of reason turns out to be a very harmless creature, namely, the fictitious subject deciding on the fictitious actions in our explanatory rational models [*Schemata*]."[6]

The third controversial issue is on the question whether *homo oeconomicus* is a businessman or a consumer or both. It is true that the writers of the classical school were more concerned with production, costs, and profits than with consumption and utility. But it is probably a misunderstanding to hold that "the classical scheme is not at all applicable to consumption or the consumer."[7] The hypothesis of utility maximization in the theory of the household is methodologically on a par with the hypothesis of profit maximization in the theory of the firm. Most expositors of economic theory have therefore decided to treat all "maximizing behavior" as the fundamental assumption implied in the "economic principle."

The fourth issue — whether *homo oeconomicus* is or is not an ideal type in the sense of Max Weber — has led to an extensive literary feud, especially among German writers (for whom methodological problems, however subtle, often assume an importance beyond the comprehension of the more pragmatic Anglo-Saxon economists). The literature on this subject, though impressive, is almost unknown outside the circle of Max Weber-exegetes. I think a taste of this debate on the "ideal type" will be worthwhile.

Merely in order to document the differences of opinion on this point, we may cite a recent history of theory in which Economic Man is, without the shadow of a doubt, treated as an ideal type,[8] and an epistemological discourse in which this characterization is emphatically rejected.[9] In general,

[6] Werner Sombart, *Die drei Nationalökonomien* (München und Leipzig: Duncker & Humblot, 1929), p. 259. The English translation is mine.

[7] Ludwig von Mises, *Epistemological Problems of Economics* (Princeton, N.J.: Van Nostrand, 1960), p. 179.

[8] "In spite of many disagreements, Menger, Jevons, and Walras claimed that only the economic man evaluates goods and services according to marginal utility. This fictitious man, an heritage of early classicism, had no clear-cut profile. As an ideal type he was sometimes identified as a materialist utilitarian, and then again as a bookkeeper who balances thoroughly cost and utility." Emil Kauder, *A History of Marginal Utility Theory* (Princeton, N.J.: Princeton University Press, 1965), p. 116. Still more recent is the brief assertion that " 'Economic man' is an 'ideal type.' " Jerome Rothenberg, "Values and Value Theory in Economics," in Sherman Roy Krupp, ed., *The Structure of Economic Science* (Englewood Cliffs, N.J.: Prentice-Hall, 1966), p. 228.

[9] "Yet neither is the *homo oeconomicus* an ideal type in Max Weber's sense." Ludwig von Mises, *op. cit.*, p. 180. "It was a fundamental mistake of the Historical School ... and of Institutionalism ... to interpret economics as the characterization of the behavior of an ideal type, the *homo oeconomicus*. According to this doctrine traditional or orthodox economics does not deal with the behavior of man as he really is and acts, but with a fictitious or hypothetical image ... Such a being does not have and never did have a counterpart in reality, it is a phantom of a spurious armchair philosophy ...

FRITZ MACHLUP

the contradiction could be due to disagreements on the meaning of "Economic Man" or on the meaning of "ideal type". Both these disagreements exist, but it is chiefly the second that explains why writers either affirm or deny that *homo oeconomicus* is an ideal type.[10]

THE IDEAL TYPE OF THE "IDEAL TYPE"

While it was obvious to all that any concept classified as "ideal type" was a mental tool, helpful in thinking and talking about certain phenomena, writers have differed on whose tool it was and for what purposes. Some claimed it as an exclusive property of historians for use in their interpretations of individual historical personalities, actions, events, institutions, and ideas. Others claimed the ideal type for exclusive use in sociology, others again for use in both history and sociology. Several writers assigned it to all social sciences, but solely for purposes of reasoning and generalizing, that is, for general theory, not for historical description. Others, however, regarded the ideal type as the appropriate concept for both historical and theoretical investigations of any phenomena, processes, personalities, and artifacts of the cultural world, hence for the social sciences, history, and the humanities. Finally, there were some who included the theoretical natural sciences among the users of ideal types.

Even if this really were the meaning of classical economics, the homo oeconomicus would certainly not be an ideal type. The ideal type is not an embodiment of one side or aspect of man's various aims and desires. It is always the representation of complex phenomena of reality; either of men, of institutions, or of ideologies." Ludwig von Mises, *Human Action: A Treatise on Economics* (New Haven: Yale University Press, 1949), p. 62.

[10] A survey of some of the literature on Max Weber's "ideal type" yields a conspicuous division on this question. Among those who affirm that Economic Man is an ideal type are Schelting, Spranger, Eucken, Spiethoff, and Schutz; among those who deny it are Hans Oppenheimer, Mises, Sombart, and Weippert. See Alexander von Schelting, *Max Webers Wissenschaftslehre* (Tübingen: J. C. B. Mohr, 1934); Eduard Spranger, *Der gegenwärtige Stand der Geisteswissenschaften und die Schule* (Leipzig-Berlin: B. G. Teubner, 1925); Walter Eucken, *Grundlagen der Nationalökonomie* (Berlin-Göttingen-Heidelberg: Springer-Verlag, 1st ed. 1939, 6th ed. 1950); Arthur Spiethoff, "Anschauliche und reine volkswirtschaftliche Theorie und ihr Verhältnis Zueinander," *Synopsis: Festgabe für Alfred Weber*, ed. Edgar Salin (Heidelberg: Verl. Schneider, 1948); Alfred Schutz, *Der sinnhafte Aufbau der sozialen Welt* (Wien: Springer, 1932); idem, *Collected Papers* (The Hague: Nijhoff, Vol. I, 1963, Vol. II, 1964); Hans Oppenheimer, *Die Logik der soziologischen Begriffsbildung, mit besonderer Berücksichtigung von Max Weber* (Tübingen: J. C. B. Mohr, 1925); Ludwig von Mises, *Grundprobleme der Nationalökonomie* (Jena: Fischer, 1933); Werner Sombart, *Die drei Nationalökonomien* (München und Leipzig: Duncker & Humblot, 1929); Georg Weippert, "Die idealtypische Sinn- und Wesenserfassung und die Denkgebilde der formalen Theorie," *Zeitschrift für die gesamte Staatswissenschaft*, Vol. 100 (1940).

But this is not all. Some wanted to reserve the designation "ideal type" for class concepts – though it would probably be a null class if one were to look for empirical counterparts of "ideal" types designed for theoretical investigations – whereas others extended the designation to refer to the mental image of any particular person or individual member of a class. (Thus, not only the class "economist" but also "Jacques Rueff" would be an ideal type; not only "city" but also "Paris"; not only "battle" but also the "Battle of the Marne"; not only "depression" but also the "Great Depression".)

Most of those engaged in the debate on the ideal type attempted to restrict the use of this appellation in one way or another. Since they pretended to interpret what Max Weber "really meant" (or "ought to have meant") it is noteworthy that Weber himself wanted none of the restrictions proposed by his interpreters, with one exception: he did consider the ideal type as a concept particularly appropriate for human action and effects of human action. (This is because the ideal types involve "meant meanings" attributed to the actors in question, which is not relevant for concepts pertaining to things in inanimate nature.) The other restrictions, however, were not intended by Weber, and he said so without reserve.

How was it then possible for the Weber interpreters to arrive at so many divergent interpretations of his ideas about the ideal type? There are probably several explanations, apart from the infelicitous choice of words – of whose most common meanings the reader has to be disabused before he can begin to grasp what Weber meant. (Only after the normative connotation of "ideal" and the empiric-taxonomic connotation of "type" have been exorcized can the intended meanings of "mental construction" emerge.) Foremost among the possible explanations are, it seems to me, Weber's writing style and people's reading habits. Weber developed his concepts only slowly and therefore could not at the outset present a comprehensive exposition showing their full scope. Thus he would at one place discuss the ideal type employed in historical research, at another place the ideal type in sociological theory, elsewhere again the ideal type in pure economics. Most readers approach a work with rather firm preconceptions and, though ready to accept gladly what fits in with their own position, are not receptive to ideas drastically deviating from their own; they either fail to notice them or they consciously reject them.[11]

---

[11] Perhaps there is no excuse for the denial that Economic Man is an ideal type in Max Weber's sense, since Weber himself had affirmed it explicitly. For example: "Economic theory is an axiomatic discipline ... Pure economic theory ... utilizes ideal-type concepts exclusively. Economic theory makes certain assumptions which scarcely ever correspond completely with reality but which approximate it in various degrees and

Thus, if a reader approaches Weber's writings convinced that the concepts of history must be differently constituted from the concepts of theory, he may accept a newly proposed phrase for one notion but not for another He may have been so impressed with the undeniable differences in concept formation in different areas of discourse, that he is willing to embrace a new designation for one kind of concept, in order to contrast it with others, but quite unprepared to adopt new language that brackets ideas which he is anxious to keep apart. Thus Weber was singularly unsuccessful in persuading his readers of the basic similarities in the formation of concepts in the domain of human action. These similarities were of great importance to Weber. He failed to get the common characteristics of these concepts across, largely because he violated the expository rule that one should not be silent about differences when one wishes to stress similarities, or about similarities when one wishes to stress differences.

If "Protestantism" is an ideal type, how could I agree that my "Aunt Molly" is also an ideal type? If "slavery" is an ideal type, how can I understand that "architecture" is also one? If "socialism" is an ideal type, how come that "Saint Augustine," "Egyptian hieroglyphs," "Spanish literature," "Robinson Crusoe," "Napoleon Bonaparte," "constitutional monarchy," "oligopoly," "witch hunting," "Arthur Miller," "tragedy," "International Monetary Fund," "deposit banking," and "*homo oeconomicus*" are all ideal types too? The point is that *all* these persons, activities, institutions, constellations, artifacts, ideas, etc., can be understood only in terms of "meant meanings" by (particular or anonymous) actors of whom we have formed some mental image, however unrealistic or selective.

The differences among these ideal types are, of course, important too. But only later, Alfred Schutz provided us with a more discriminating terminology. Thus, for example, he pointed out the differences between various kinds of "personal ideal types," not only according to their place in time but also according to their place in our thought systems (e.g., "characterological ideal types" and "functional ideal types"). And, most significantly, he taught us that the ideal type is not only the fundamental concept of the social scientist and the historian but also, or even primarily, the basic concept of the ordinary man thinking about his everyday experiences with and relations to his partners and contemporaries. "The construction of the

---

asks: how would men act under these assumed conditions if their actions were entirely rational? It assumes the dominance of pure economic interests and precludes the operation of political or other non-economic considerations." Max Weber, *On Methodology of the Social Sciences*, pp. 43–44.

categories and models of the social sciences is founded on the pre-scientific common-sense experience of social reality." [12]

PRE-SCIENTIFIC COMMON-SENSE AND SCIENTIFIC THINKING

The key to the understanding of the ideal type is the realization that not only scholars – historians, economists, social theorists – think about their subjects with the aid of ideal types, but that *everybody does so in his everyday life.*

Even the small child has probably formed his ideal type of his mother, whom he expects to comfort him with her gentle voice, stroking hands, and warm breasts. The schoolboy has formed ideal types of his teacher, his classmates, the doctor, the minister, and his favorite television personalities. The adult has formed ideal types of many people whom he meets repeatedly face-to-face as well as of others whom he does not know personally but with whose reactions he reckons in several connections. For example, he may expect a policeman to blow a whistle and give him a summons if he fails to stop his car at a red traffic light, or a postman to collect a letter which he deposits in a mailbox. The ideal type I have formed of my wife has something to do with my punctuality in coming home for supper, for it includes her getting worried if I am late.

There is no essential difference in the construction of ideal types as commonsense concepts of ordinary people and as scientific concepts of the historian or social scientist, except of course that the concepts designed for scholarly investigation have to satisfy certain requirements of consistency and relevance, requirements which are usually not checked by the ordinary man in everyday life. Perhaps, though, a middle category should be distinguished between that of the ordinary man in his own social relations and the scholarly observer engaged in serious professional investigations, namely, the category of the non-scholarly observer of the social scene. The bystander, onlooker, spectator, the listener and viewer of broadcasts, the audience in theaters and cinemas, the reader of books, stories and news – all these can understand what they see, hear, or read only to the extent that they have formed the ideal types relevant to the scenes observed or described.

The lines separating acting man, lay observer, and scientific observer look rather definite. *Acting man* is engaged in practical activities and relies

---

[12] Alfred Schutz, *Collected Papers*, Vol. II (The Hague: Martinus Nijhoff, 1964), p. 21. Schutz's earlier book, *Der sinnhafte Aufbau der sozialen Welt* (Vienna: Julius Springer, 1932) was translated into English and published under the title *The Phenomenology of the Social World* (Evanston, Ill.: Northwestern University Press, 1967).

on his collection of ideal types in the interpretation of the actions, and in predicting the reactions, of his "partners". The *lay observer* is an outsider, merely a curious audience, relying on his collection of ideal types in the interpretation of the actions of the people observed or described. The *scientific observer* is also an observer, making use of ideal types and models in his collection, but his interest in the matter investigated stems from his desire to add to the body of scientific knowledge. Upon closer inspection, however, the lines of separation among the three kinds of interpreters of the social stage become less definite. The lay observer, for example, may identify himself so intensively with one or more of the actors observed that his involvement in the scene may be such that he thinks and feels as if he were himself participating in a real-life situation affecting his own welfare. A man acting in his personal affairs may have scientific training enabling him to apply the techniques of his science, say, economics or psychology, to advantage in interpreting and predicting the actions and reactions of his "partners". By and large, however, we may take the distinctions to be valid and significant.

SELECTING THE RELEVANT TYPE

We spoke of the collection of ideal types at the disposal of actors and observers for use in their interpretations, but we have not indicated how they select the type relevant in the specific situation. Ordinarily, the necessary skill is acquired by experience. Know-how cannot easily be taught in any other way; and with regard to some ideal types, a stock of "inner experience" is necessary for a full understanding of the movements, gestures, or words of other people. Explicit directions or rules would more often mislead than help.

Assume, for example, that some primitive soul, having been exposed to a disquisition to the effect that the *homo oeconomicus* has to do primarily with money matters, propounded the rule that all situations involving money and its expenditure or nonexpenditure are most appropriately interpreted with the aid of the ideal type of Economic Man. Anyone who followed this rule would be sadly frustrated in his attempts to understand what goes on. Any number of situations involving money require a variety of characters – logical, psychological, and functional types – for their interpretation and could never be elucidated by the application of the ideal type of the *homo oeconomicus*, no matter whether he be regarded as a profit maximizer or a maximizer of utility.

To illustrate the principle that the money theme is not decisive in the selection of the appropriate ideal type, I shall present a sequence of vignettes, each in form of a scene with two persons on the stage, which can be understood only with the aid of special personal ideal types. After each "scene" I shall designate the ideal type in evidence.

Scene 1

"How dare you," Robert shouted in a husky voice, staring at the ten-dollar bill which George had put on the table before him. His face was flushed with anger, his eyes protruding, the veins at his temples formed thick blue cables. He took the bill, tore it into small pieces and threw them into George's face.
[The relevant ideal type is *homo cholericus.*]

Scene 2

"Boss, we've got to close down the mill at Hungerville. Our new plant in the city can easily take care of all our orders at a cost 36 per cent below that of the Hungerville mill."

"How many people would lose their jobs at Hungerville?"

"Six hundred and fifty, boss."

"I cannot do it. Most of these people have been with us for years. Who will take care of them if we don't?"

"They can go on relief. Every week that we keep the mill open means a net loss of 50,000 dollars. Are you running a business or a charity?"

"Call it what you will, the mill stays open as long as I have the money, or as long as I can borrow or steal it. I am not going to lay off any of my workers."
[The relevant type is *homo caritativus.*]

Scene 3

"Another shot of gin," he ordered in a bellowing voice.

Jim, the saloon keeper, reached for the bottle and said casually: "It's all right with me, Dick, but your wife won't like it if you spend half your week's pay on getting drunk again."

"This'll be the last one," promised Dick.

"The last till the next," teased Jim.

"What business is it of yours? I can do what I please with my own money." He emptied his glass in one gulp. "Okay, give me another. No one's going to tell me what I can't do."

"Dick, I'm glad to sell you all you can pay for. Here's your drink. But you told me you wanted the kids to get enough to eat. And your wife said you promised to reform and bring the money home for the rent and the grocery bill."

"The hell with her, and the hell with the kids. Give me another shot. I need my gin and, by gosh, I'm going to have it."

[The relevant ideal type is *homo alcoholicus.*]

Scene 4

John looked at her, took her hands, and then spoke in a low voice. "Listen, darling, I'm letting you have the money. But you should know: This money would not only have paid the note that falls due tomorrow but also for the half-interest I hoped to buy in the firm. Without this money I'll lose my option to become a partner and, what's more, by not paying the note I'll lose my honest name. But I don't care what happens. There's only one thing I care for: you. I love you. I adore you."

He tooks her into his arms and pressed her against his body. He drew her face toward his and let his lips touch hers.

[The relevant ideal type is *homo amorosus.*]

Scene 5

"This machine will pay for itself within eight months; it's the best investment you've ever made, Mr. Halo."

"You're absolutely right, Mr. Newtime," the industrialist replied solemnly, "but as long as I can't pay for it in ready cash on delivery, Halo and Son is not going to order the machine."

"But, Mr. Halo, we'll be delighted to take your note payable in six months, or, indeed, to let you have it on open terms of credit."

"Sir, Halo and Son, will not borrow. The First National has been trying to talk us into taking a million-dollar loan at 3½ per cent. No, we shall remain true to the traditions of our firm as they have been observed by my father, my grandfather, and my great-grandfather, Mr. Polonius Halo. We are neither borrowers nor lenders, and this, sir, is final."

[The relevant ideal type is *homo traditionalis.*]

Scene 6

"That's bunk!" He puffed several times on his cigar, dropping some of its overload of ashes on his bulging vest. "That's sheer bunk! You don't win an election with good intentions and such stuff. I've been running this machine for twenty-six years and I know it must be greased. After all, we nominated you not just because you're a reputable businessman, but a successful one with all the dough it takes to grease the party machine."

"Sorry, much as I want to win the election, and much as I recognize your experience as party boss, I don't want to buy votes."

"Well, well, we can put it differently. You're not buying votes, you're selling yourself. As a businessman, you know that you can't sell anything without paying for advertising. Political patronage is fine, it costs you nothing and gets you support. But it ain't enough. We need money. And one more thing: you'll have to create a few jobs in your business for some trusted party workers."

"What'll my stockholders say to that?"

"Nothing if they don't know it. Moreover, they'll like it fine having a state senator managing their investments. This will be businesslike government and statesmanlike business."

[The relevant ideal type is *homo politicus*.]

Scene 7

"We've just learnt, J.C., that the Chicago order went to Gregg's. Those blasted chiselers must have made all sorts of concessions. I'd been promised the order and was sure we had it."

"Damn it, that order would have been just right for our Wisconsin mill. What are our chances on the big Cleveland deal?"

"You never know, J.C. The Gregg people are after it, too, and they tell me Cone Brothers are at least 2 points below our price. If we don't want to lose this order, we'll have to come down too."

"Nothin' doing. If we shade our price, the whole industry will be demoralized. Gregg's, Cone's, Gannef's and all the rest will just fall all over themselves and no one will know what the right price really is."

"Are we going to sit back, J.C., and watch one dirty chiseler after another steal the nicest orders from us?"

"No use getting mad. You have to let them get away with it once in a while, as long as they keep their senses most of the time. If we start cutting prices, the bottom drops out of the market, and we'll have to fight over every single order, even the smallest. Let's stick to our list prices and avoid chaos."

[The relevant ideal type is *homo oligopolisticus*.]

THE ROLE OF HOMO OECONOMICUS

I could easily have produced a scene depicting *homo oeconomicus* at work. I refrained from doing so, because it might have confused the reader about the proper role of this ideal type, a role quite different from that of those exhibited in the vignettes presented.

The point is that the personal types relevant in the seven scenes were suitable for interpreting observations of men's actions, whereas the ideal type of *homo oeconomicus* is designed for interpreting observed *consequences* of men's actions. The difference is significant. In the scenes presented we listened to what some people said and we watched their movements and gestures. (Only in Scene 1 was the "watching" important; in the other scenes we chiefly "listened" to the dialogue.) The purpose of the *homo oeconomicus* is not to help us understand observations of people – that is, we neither watch anyone's movements and gestures nor listen to their conversations – but rather to understand observations of records, such as reports on prices, outputs, employment, and profits, which are evidently *results* of people's actions. Almost never can we observe the actions themselves. (Exceptions are our self-observations – introspection – as we change our minds concerning things to buy, assets to hold, etc.).

We observe, for example, price data and attribute changes in some prices to changes in certain cost items or to changes in tariffs, excise taxes, or total incomes; or we attribute changes in price indices to changes in interest rates or the quantity of money. But these causal attributions presuppose our assuming the intervention of people making decisions in reaction to changes in their opportunities to buy, sell, work, hire, lend, borrow, produce, etc. The "scenes" of people making these decisions are not observed but only imagined. The ideal type relevant for these imagined scenes is *homo oeconomicus*.

Chapter 11

THE UNIVERSAL BOGEY: ECONOMIC MAN

The 'bogey' to whom this essay will be devoted is Economic Man. It was Lionel Robbins who suggested that *homo oeconomicus* would probably not have become 'such a universal bogey' if those who wrote so contemptuously about him had known him better.[1] He has been quite unpopular even among some good economic theorists, who contended that they could do better without him. Others who appreciated his services, were nevertheless intimidated by the irate accusations persistently reiterated by his detractors; so they decided to avoid his name. He was admitted into most respectable company under such aliases as 'behaviour equation' or 'objective function', names by which his enemies would not recognise him.[2]

Antitheoretical economists and anti-economists in general have raged and roared with fury about that wicked and despicable Economic Man. To deal with their accusations may appear 'foolish and exasperating ... to any competent economist' but, nevertheless, Robbins thought it was 'worth some further examination.'[3] I have found it entertaining to read the angry charges against the innocent creature and I propose, before engaging in still further examinations of the nature and significance of Economic Man, to share with the reader some of the juiciest denunciations.

1.   Robbins, Lionel, *An Essay on the Nature and Significance of Economic Science,* 1935, p. 97.
2.   I do not know who was the first to use the name objective function, but he certainly had no feeling for language or he would have sensed the possibility of misunderstandings. Objective as an adjective is the antonym of subjective; as a noun it is a synonym for goal or aim; what is it if it precedes and modifies a noun? French translators have had hard times; they were prone to mistranslate objective function as *fonction objective* instead of *fonction d'objectif.* Coiners of new terms and phrases ought to feel morally obliged to test them for non-ambiguity and intelligibility.
3.   Robbins, *An Essay on The Nature and Significance of Economic Science,* 1935, p. 94.

99

A SAMPLE OF DENUNCIATIONS

What irked the critics most was that the Man's 'desire of wealth' had frequently (and unwisely) been described as a desire to acquire or possess *material* goods satisfying *physical* wants, and sometimes as a desire for *pecuniary* gains; and the goal of getting the most out of what he has had been identified with *selfishness*. Thus we read in the work of John Barton, an early and almost forgotten critic of the Ricardians, that 'a reasoner who is incapable of measuring and appreciating the higher influences, confining his views to this one sordid and narrow motive, must infallibly arrive at conclusions as false as they are grovelling.'[4]

The members of the earlier Historical School in Germany were still quite civil in their rejection of Economic Man. Opposed chiefly to the use of abstraction and the emphasis on egoism, they wanted to have 'abstract' man replaced by 'real' man, and self-interest exorcised by strong appeals to ethical values. The British branch of the Historical School, led by Leslie, was not very original. Leslie mainly commended the 'realism' of the Germans in repudiating abstract and unhistorical concepts and in deprecating the 'Love of Money'.[5] He thought he was disposing of Economic Man by reminding us that money bought not only material things but also intangibles that satisfied the finest cultural aspirations – such as cleanliness and knowledge.

The American Henry C. Carey showed some originality in the venom he directed at the Classical School and especially at Mill. He quotes Mill first on economic motives – to acquire wealth, to avert labour, and to enjoy consumption – and then on population – pressing wages down to the subsistence level – and proceeds to make the following observation regarding these two assumptions:

> That having been done, we have the political-economical man, on one hand influenced solely by the thirst for wealth and on the other so entirely

---

4. Barton, John, *A Statement of the Consequences Likely to Ensue from Our Growing Excess of Population if not Remedied by Colonization,* 1830, p. 47. (Reprinted in John Barton, *Economic Writings,* Regina, Sask.: Lynn Publishing Co., 1962, p. 293.)

5. Leslie, Thomas Edward Cliffe, 'The Love of Money', in *Essays in Political Economy,* 1888, pp. 1-8. (This essay was first published in 1862.)

100

under the control of the sexual passion as to be at all times ready to indulge it, however greatly such indulgence may tend to prevent the growth of wealth.[6]

Fascinated by Carey's angry exclamations, I cannot resist quoting him more extensively. He expects the reader of the classical writings to wonder:

He [the reader] might perhaps ask himself, has man no other qualities than those here attributed to him? Is he, like the beasts of the field, solely given to the search for food and shelter for his body? ... Has he no feelings of affections to be influenced by the care of wife and children? ... That he did possess these qualities he would find admitted, but the economist would assure him that his science was that of material wealth alone, to the entire exclusion of the wealth of affection and of intellect ... and thus would he ... discover that the subject of political economy was not really a man, but an imaginary being moved to action by the blindest passion...[7]

Again:

The British School of Economists recognizes, not the real man of society, but the artificial man of their own system. Their Theory, occupied with the lowest instincts of humanity, treats its noblest interests as mere inter-polations of the System.[8]

And again:

Such is the error of modern political economy, its effects exhibiting them-selves in the fact that it presents for our consideration a mere brute animal to find a name for which it desecrates the word 'man' ...[9]

To set him apart from this brute, Carey spells 'real MAN' with capital letters.

A disciple of Carey's, Robert Ellis Thompson, angry about the free-

6.   Carey, Henry C., *Principles of Social Science,* Vol I. 1858, p. 29. In a later book, *The Unity of Law,* 1872, p. 59, he repeats this statement almost literally, except for the insertion, after 'politico-economical man', of the words 'or monster'.

7.   Carey, *Principles,* p. 30; also *Unity,* p.61.

8.   Carey, *Principles;* p.xiii, in the table of contents describing § 5 of Ch. I.

9.   Carey, *Unity,* p. 61.

101

traders' interest in the 'consumer' (as distinct from 'producer') and their opposition to protective tariffs, managed to combine his antagonisms against the 'consumer', against the 'economic man', and against all abstract reasoning in one statement:

> Who this consumer is, that is neither a producer as well, nor directly dependent upon the prosperity of other people who are producers, is hard to say. ... But most likely he is an innocent *ens logicum,* manufactured by the same process of abstraction by which the economists devised their economical man – 'a covetous machine inspired to action only by avarice and the desire of progress'. That is, they cut away or stole away (abstracted) the better half of the real being, and persisted in treating the remaining human fragment (if we can call it human) as a living reality.[10]

One more sample of this group of writers may be offered, John Ruskin – in my opinion, one of the most overrated writers of nineteenth-century England. He too protested vigorously against the classical economists 'considering the human being merely as a covetous machine' – although he prided himself on never having read any book on political economy except Smith's *Wealth of Nations.* This is what he had to say about the economic principle operating in exchange and commerce:

> So far as I know, there is not in history record of anything so disgraceful to the human intellect as the modern idea that the commercial text, 'Buy in the cheapest market and sell in the dearest,' represents, or under any circumstances could represent, an available principle of national economy.[12]

THE GROUNDS OF THE OPPOSITION

Some of the strictures and denunciations included in this sample can probably be best explained as the result of misunderstandings – due to ignorance or incompetence. But not all opposition to Economic Man is of this sort. The ranks of the opposition are not filled entirely with

10. Thompson, Robert Ellis, *Social Sciences and National Economy,* 1875, p. 269.

11. Ruskin, John, *Unto This Last,* 1901, p. 2. The four essays collected in this book were first published in 1861. The phrase 'covetous machine' was widely quoted, for example, also by Thompson, in 1875, in the passage reproduced above.

12. Ruskin, *Unto This Last,* p. 59.

102

anti-analysts, anti-theorists, anti-classicists, anti-liberals, and anti-economists. Some eminent economic theorists, skilled in analysis and respectful of classical economics, have also condemned the use of the concept of Economic Man. What are the grounds of their opposition?

Several such grounds should be distinguished, since different critics have different quarrels with Economic Man's nature, character, and function. One issue relates to the breaking up of Whole Man into parts and the construction of a Partial or Fragmented Man, who has only a few specific traits or objectives; there are those who object vigorously to all analytical dissection of man (as if it were physical vivisection). Other controversial questions are whether the construction of an abstract Partial Man is sound either in the sense that all disregarded traits or objectives can reasonably be dispensed with without vitiating the conclusions deduced with the help of the construct, or in the sense that the traits or objectives which are singled out for emphasis are sufficiently realistic to yield useful conclusions. Several objectors deny both propositions, some only one. There is a group of economists who are greatly worried that we may obtain only 'hypothetical' rather than incontrovertible, categorical, or 'positive' conclusions. Some object to the use of heuristic fictions and counterfactual assumptions; they hold that no worthwhile inferences can come from untrue hypotheses. The largest number of critics merely take exception to poor formulations of the behaviour equation called Economic Man.

In order to avoid the impression that the parties to this controversy can be nicely tagged and boxed, we had better go back for a bit of doctrinal history; we shall confine it, however, to a few of the main protagonists: John Stuart Mill, Nassau Senior, Walter Bagehot, John E. Cairnes and Philip H. Wicksteed.

THE HYPOTHETICAL NATURE OF SCIENTIFIC DISCOURSE

Re-reading John Stuart Mill after reading the comments and observations of his critics, one cannot help finding a strong suspicion confirmed: that many authors, even highly respected ones, read with insufficient care or poor retention. Far too many of the methodological issues raised about Mill's procedure, and about his (unnamed) Economic Man, had been anticipated and largely resolved by Mill.

103

Mill insisted on the hypothetical nature of all science — reasoning from assumed premises — and on the especially hypothetical nature of economics (Political Economy) — presupposing 'an arbitrary definition of man'.[13] He stressed the 'uncertainty inherent in the nature of these complex phenomena [in the moral sciences in general] ... arising from the impossibility of being quite sure that all the circumstances of the particular case are known to us sufficiently in detail'.[14]

'Man..., the subject matter of all moral sciences' has to be dealt with 'under several distinct hypotheses'. The major division, in Mill's exposition, is between 'ethics' and 'social economy', and a branch of the latter was 'political economy'. 'The science of social economy embraces every part of man's nature, in so far as influencing the conduct and condition of man in society ...'. 'Political economy', in contradistinction, 'does not treat of the whole of man's nature as modified by the social state, nor of the whole conduct of man in society. It is concerned with him solely as a being who desires to possess wealth, and who is capable of judging of the comparative efficacy of means for obtaining that end.'[15] The fundamental assumption is that man will 'prefer a greater portion of wealth to a smaller...'[16] This is, I submit, a common-sense way of formulating the postulate of maximising.

Mill makes it perfectly clear that this basic hypothesis may be contrary to fact. 'Political Economy' he states, 'reasons from *assumed* premises — from premises which might be totally without foundation in fact, and which are not pretended to be universally in accordance with it...'[17] Several times Mill points to the fictitious character of the fundamental hypothesis of economic science, in particular to the 'entire abstraction of every other human passion or motive', except 'desire of wealth', 'aversion to labour', and 'desire of the present enjoyment of costly indulgences'.[18] He cautiously warns the reader against mistaking

13.   Mill, John Stuart, 'On the Definition of Political Economy; and the Method of Investigation Proper to It' *Essays on Some Unsettled Questions of Political Economy*, p. 144.

14.   Mill, *Political Economy*, p. 150.

15.   Mill, *Political Economy*, pp.134-137. [The same sentences appear in Mill's *System of Logic.*]

16.   Mill, *Political Economy*, pp.138-139.

17.   Mill, *Essays*, p. 137.

18.   Mill, *Essays*, pp. 137-138.

104

a heuristic counterfactual hypothesis for a statement of fact:

> Not that any political economist was ever so absurd as to suppose that mankind are really thus constituted ... [But] the manner in which it [Political Economy] necessarily proceeds is that of treating the main and acknowledged end as if it were the sole end; which, of all hypotheses equally simple, is the nearest to the truth... This approximation is then to be corrected by making proper allowance for the effects of any impulses of a different description, which can be shown to interfere with the result in any particular case.[19]

POSITIVE TRUTH AND MERE SUPPOSITION

Not all classical or post-classical writers were agreed on the hypothetical or postulational character of Economic Man, or of the Economic Principle. Several of them, before Mill as well as afterwards, wanted the basic assumption recognised as a factual premise, stating an unquestioned, positive truth. The most out-spoken critic of merely hypothetical economics was Senior.

Long before Mill, Senior had formulated the 'First Proposition' of Political Economy: 'That every person is desirous to obtain, with as little sacrifice as possible, as much as possible of the articles of wealth'.[20] In later reformulations he omitted the reference to 'articles' and was careful to point out that wealth included such intangibles as 'power', 'distinction', 'leisure', 'benefits for acquaintances and friends', and even contributions of 'advantage to the public'.[21] However, Senior was dissatisfied with Mill's reliance on a hypothesis which, in Mill's words, was not 'universally in accordance with fact' or was even 'totally without foundation in fact'. From mere suppositions only conclusions of uncertain truth or applicability could be inferred. Senior wanted economic science to state positive truths, not just hypotheses. 'It appears to me', he wrote in 1852, 'that if we substitute for Mr. Mill's hypothesis, that wealth and costly enjoyment are the *only* objects of human desire, the statement that they are universal and constant objects of desire, that they are desired by all men and at all times, we shall have laid an equally firm foundation for our subsequent

19.   Mill, *Essays,* pp. 139-140.
20.   Senior, Nassau W., *Introductory Lecture on Political Economy,* 1827, p.30. Quoted from Bowley, Marian, *Nassau Senior and Classical Economics,* 1937, p.46.
21.   Senior, *An Outline of the Science of Political Economy,* 1836, 6th ed. 1872, p. 27.

reasonings, and have put a truth in the place of an arbitrary assumption'.[22]

USEFUL FICTIONS

Senior's ambition for economic science — to yield absolutely true, not merely hypothetical propositions — was criticised by Walter Bagehot, who also criticised earlier classical economists for confusing useful fictions with established facts. For example, Bagehot claimed that Ricardo 'thought that he was considering actual human nature in its actual circumstances, when he was really considering a fictitious nature in fictitious circumstances'.[23]

According to Bagehot, 'English political economists are not speaking of real men, but of imaginary ones; not of men as we see them, but of men as it is convenient to us to suppose they are'.[24] The convenience lies in the simplicity of disregarding elements of lesser relevance. For this reason, 'Political Economy deals not with the entire real man as we know him in fact, but with a simpler, imaginary man..., because it is found convenient to isolate the effects of this force from all others'.[25]

Bagehot thus sided completely with Mill and against Senior, who wanted positive 'truths' in place of mere 'hypotheses'.

PREMISES AND CONCLUSIONS

John E. Cairnes defended Senior on some points and criticised him on others. He took his side on the question of fact or fiction in the assumption regarding the economic motive. The fundamental assumption of economics is, for Cairnes, not a mere supposition, let alone a counterfactual hypothesis, but a proposition which rests on well established facts of experience: 'The economist starts with a knowledge of ultimate causes.'[26] For their discovery or confirmation 'no elaborate process of induction is needed', for we have 'direct knowledge of these

22.   Senior, Nassau W., *Four Introductory Lectures on Political Economy*, 1852, p. 62. Quoted from Bowley, *Nassau Senior*, p.61.
23.   Bagehot, Walter, *Economic Studies*, 1880, p. 157.
24.   Bagehot, *Economic Studies*, p. 5.
25.   Bagehot, *Economic Studies*, p. 74.
26.   Cairnes, John E., *The Character and Logical Method of Political Economy*, 1st ed. 1858, 2nd ed. 1875, p. 87.

106

causes in our consciousness of what passes in our own minds...' After all, 'every one who embarks on any industrial pursuit is conscious of the motives which actuate him in doing so'.[27]

However — and here Cairnes dissents from Senior's position — that the economist can start with 'facts' rather than a 'hypothesis' does not guarantee that his conclusions are anything but hypothetical. For, in Cairnes' view,

> an economist, arguing from the unquestionable facts of man's nature — the desire of wealth and the aversion to labour — and arguing with strict logical accuracy, may yet, if he omit to notice other principles also affecting the question, be landed in conclusions which have no resemblance to existing realities. But he can never be certain that he does not omit some essential circumstance, and, indeed, it is scarcely possible to include all: it is evident, therefore, that... his conclusions will correspond with facts *only in the absence of disturbing causes,* which is, in other words, to say that they represent not positive but hypothetic truth.[28]

Thus Cairnes accepts one half of Senior's and one half of Mill's position: 'the premises are not arbitrary figments of the mind', but the conclusions are hypothetical and 'may or may not correspond to the realities'.[29] He attributed Senior's dilemma, regarding the question whether economics was a positive or a hypothetical science, to 'an ambiguity of language'. If the two adjectives are used 'with reference to the character of [the] premises' of a science, they may point to a genuine difference: the 'positive' premises of the physical sciences, dictated by 'the existing facts of nature', can be contrasted with the 'hypothetical' premises of the science of mathematics, which are 'arbitrary conceptions framed by the mind'.[30] If, however, the two adjectives are used 'with reference to the conclusions of a science', the advanced physical and other empirical sciences may be regarded as both positive and hypothetical: positive in the sense that there is a probability that the conclusions deduced from the premises 'represent positive realities', and hypothetical in the sense that these conclusions can be true only 'on the hypothesis that the premises include all the

27. Cairnes, *Character and Logical Method*, p. 88.
28. Cairnes, *Character and Logical Method*, pp. 63-64. (Emphasis in the original.)
29. Cairnes, *Character and Logical Method*, p. 62.
30. Cairnes, *Character and Logical Method*, pp. 60-61.

107

causes affecting the result', of which we 'can never be sure'.[31]

Cairnes' view, in a nutshell, is that 'it is surely possible that the premises should be true and yet incomplete — true so far as the facts which they assert go, and yet not including all the conditions which affect the actual course of events'.[32]

EGOISM, TUISM, AND SIMPLIFIED PSYCHOLOGY

Cairnes' disquisitions were lost on Philip Wicksteed, who embraced Senior's position on several issues. Like Senior, Wicksteed (quite rightly) insisted on keeping maximising behaviour apart from egoism and from the desire to possess material goods; like Senior, Wicksteed rejected mere suppositions as the basis of economic deductions; and like Senior, Wicksteed was not satisfied with a merely 'hypothetical science'.

Wicksteed was well advised in restating the irrelevance of material possessions and of self-interest, simply because so many exponents of economic theory continued to advertise these false criteria of economic conduct. But the issues had been fully discussed and understood by many. If wealth was defined as material goods, this was partly a device to eschew problems of statistical estimation, which were especially difficult with regard to intangible values. This, at least, was Malthus' explanation, back in 1812. The issue as to whether the scope of egoism had to be narrowed to the fulfilment of bodily desires or could be extended to include 'higher' impulses had already been discussed by Hobbes,[33] back in 1651. Why then, in the opinion of so many eminent writers, the desire to attain with given means a maximum of ends (objectives, satisfaction, utility) had to be identified with egoism or self-interest is nowadays difficult to understand. Senior was one of the few who recognised that the economic motive could accommodate altruism along with any other preferences of the acting individuals. Yet we find reversions at much later, more enlightened times. Edgeworth, for example, in 1912 stuck to the old, unreconstructed view according to which 'the first principle of pure economics' was 'the prevalence of self-interest'.[34]

31.   Cairnes, *Character and Logical Method,* p. 61.
32.   Cairnes, *Character and Logical Method,* p. 68.
33.   Hobbes, Thomas, *Leviathan,* 1651.

108

Wicksteed offered the most patient exposition of the egoism-altruism issue. He has no difficulty demonstrating that it is quite irrelevant whether a decision-maker acts on the basis of a preference system that includes only his personal interests or also those of his family, his friends, his clients, his compatriots, or any *alteri.*[35] In any case the principle of 'true economy', that is, of 'making the best of existing conditions',[36] yields the same results, regardless of whether the 'maximum advantage'[37] is desired only for the decision-maker himself or for other beneficiaries.

Wicksteed makes one exception to the possible inclusion of other persons' interests among the aims of a decision-maker: the interests of a trading partner must not actuate his behaviour. If I bargain with you, I, *ego*, may think of my own interests or of the interests of others, *alteri,* but I must not think of you, *tu,* and of your interests. Hence, egoism and altruism are both all right, but 'tuism' must be ruled out. 'It is only when tuism to some degree actuates my conduct that it ceases to be wholly economic'.[38] Thus, 'The specific characteristic of an economic relation is not its "egoism", but its "non-tuism" '.[39]

Wicksteed, although he could accommodate altruism along with egoism, thought that he had to exclude tuism, probably because otherwise the terms of an exchange between two transactors would be indeterminate. He evidently overlooked that an isolated exchange, outside a competitive market, would be indeterminate in any case, with or without tuism. On the other hand, if the market is competitive, a trader may wish to give his trading partner a 'break', and thus include the partner's interests in his own considerations, without any harm to the determinateness of the market price; the 'rebate' in the case of the 'tuistic' trader would be an understandable deviation.

Wicksteed rejected the construction of Economic Man, less because of the awkward traits of materialism and egoism with which some

34. Edgeworth, Francis Y., 'Contributions to the Theory of Railway Rates, III', *Economic Journal,* Vol. XXII, 1912, p. 199. Reprinted in *Papers Relating to Political Economy,* Royal Economic Society, 1925, Vol. I, p. 173.
35. Wicksteed, Philip H., *The Common Sense of Political Economy* 1910, pp. 170-183.
36. Wicksteed, *Political Economy,* p. 94.
37. Wicksteed, *Political Economy,* p. 70.
38. Wicksteed, *Political Economy,* p. 181.
39. Wicksteed, *Political Economy,* p. 180.

model-makers had endowed him than because of the other two limit-ations: the 'artificial simplification' through isolation of selected mo-tives and abstraction from all others, and the restriction to 'hypo-thetical' conclusions which is involved in the reliance on unrealistic assumptions. In his arguments against these limitations Wicksteed en-gages in a great deal of verbal hair-splitting, particularly when he tries to do away with an 'economic motive' and replaces it by an 'economic relation'.

Wicksteed's stance in his opposition to an abstract construct of man resembles that of the anti-analytic, anti-vivisectionist holists: he rejects 'the hypothetically simplified psychology of the Economic Man' and the convention of 'imagining man to be actuated by only a few simple motives; and he proposes that we 'take him as we find him... under the stress of all his complicated impulses and desires'.[40] Many of Wicksteed's observations are perfectly sound, for example, when he states that

> a man may be just as strenuous in the pursuit of knowledge or of fame, or in his obedience to an artistic impulse, as in the pursuit of wealth... The demands of vanity may be as imperious as those of hunger, so that all the motives and passions that actuate the human breast may either stimulate or restrain the desire to possess wealth. How, then, can we isolate that desire as a 'motive'?[41]

And in a similar vein:

> There is no occasion to define the economic motive, or the psychology of the economic man, for economics study a type of relation, not a type of motive, and the psychological law that dominates economics dominates life. We may either ignore all motives or admit all to our consideration, as occasion demands, but there is no rhyme or reason in selecting certain motives that shall and certain others that shall not be recognised by the economist.[42]

We shall later justify how we can reasonably regard these obser-vations as sound and yet irrelevant. The apparent contradiction has to do with the distinction between (spontaneous) action and (induced) reaction, and with the differences in complexity in explaining the two types of decision-making. Wicksteed was one of many who failed to

40.   Wicksteed, *Political Economy*, p. 4.
41.   Wicksteed, *Political Economy*, p. 164.
42.   Wicksteed, Philip H., 'The Scope and Method of Political Economy in the Light of the "Marginal" Theory of Value and Distribution', *Economic Journal*, Vol. XXIV, March 1914, p. 9.

110

recognise these differences. His opposition to the basic simplifying assumption was based on a methodological tenet:

> We have now to ask further, are these psychological data, whether facts or principles, to include all the psychological considerations that actually bear upon the production, distribution, etc. of wealth, or are we artificially to simplify our psychology and deal only with the motives supposed to actuate the hypothetical 'economic man'? In the latter case political economy will be a hypothetical science. In the former it will aim at positivity.[43]

Here we meet again the objection Senior had raised against Mill's 'hypothetical science'. The ambition for something 'more positive', which would assure *true* deductions from *true* assumptions rather than merely valid deductions from fundamental postulates, moved Wicksteed, as it had moved Senior, to oppose the construction of a simplified model in favor of a supposedly complete one. This ambition reached its extreme in Ludwig von Mises' praxeology, the all-embracing theory of human action, in which economic action, rational action, and action of any kind become one and the same.[44]

THE OBJECTIVES OF ECONOMIC MAN

From the sample of quotations offered here it should be clear that the exact content of the 'fundamental hypothesis' embodied in the construction of *homo oeconomicus* has changed from one economic treatise to another. Many critics have suffered from a tendency to interpret the descriptions of Economic Man too narrowly and too literally. The differences in the scope of Economic Man's aspirations can perhaps be visualised in the following schema: Economic Man is assumed to seek (A) more wealth with given sacrifices of other advantages, (B) the largest gains in exchange and trade, (C) greatest pleasure with given pain, (D) highest returns from given resources, (E) highest pecuniary and nonpecuniary benefits from business, or (F) maximum utility from given means.

In some of the constructions proposed, Economic Man was only a

43. Wicksteed, Philip H. 'Political Economy and Psychology', *Palgrave's Dictionary of Political Economy*, 1926, Vol. III, p. 142.
44. von Mises, Ludwig, *Nationalökonomie: Theorie des Handelns und Wirtschaftens*, 1940, also English edition, *Human Action: A Treatise on Economics*, 1949.

111

consumer, only a trader, only a producer, only an investor, only a businessman. Some writers insisted that the construct could never fit some of these roles, whereas others were convinced that it fitted them all, indeed, a few were even prepared to extend it to other roles, such as the politician, the government, or society as a collective decision-maker.

Within each of the constructs several further variations can be found. The wealth which the first Economic Man sought to maximise was thought of as a stock by some, as a flow by others; as consisting of material consumer goods, of material assets of any sort, of tangibles and also intangible goods and services, or of money or general purchasing power. The failure to distinguish between a stock and a flow of 'wealth' has trapped a good many, friends and foes of Economic Man. Smith said 'wealth' but explained that he meant 'the necessaries and conveniences of life', hence, a stream of income. Mill said 'necessaries, conveniences, and luxuries', but at the same time spoke of the desire to 'possess' wealth. No wonder that critics with literal minds found these descriptions wanting and thought the whole conception useless.

The idea of confining wealth to material goods was supposed to serve statistical convenience, to ease quantitative estimation. But, surely, where no statistical operations were intended or needed, it was supererogatory to subject the construct to an operational constraint. The distinction between physical wants 'of a low order' (Jevons) and gratification of higher values was entirely uncalled for. The substitution of money or general purchasing power for goods and services of any sort was all right, but of course not with the disparaging connotation of a miser's 'love of money', avarice and cupidity. The difference between selfish and nonegoistic desire of wealth is understandable in the light of the discussions of utilitarian philosophy, but proved irrelevant to the maximisation postulate. In the same context, emphasis on the 'calculus of pleasure and pain' and the conception of Economic Man as a 'pleasure machine' (Edgeworth) were instances of misplaced hedonism and made it harder for the student of economics to arrive at an understanding of 'utility maximisation'.

The Economic Man in business was also having serious problems of a schizophrenic nature: was he a pure maximiser of money profits or did he have also other objectives, was he subject to various pulls and pressures of conflicting obligations, responsibilities, loyalties, and preferences? The problems of the multi-goal firm in business have been

112

much discussed in the last thirty years and perhaps we should only remind the reader that most of these problems are serious only as far as spontaneous business action is concerned, but quite innocuous with regard to reactions and responses to changes in the conditions confronting the firm.[45]

THE LOGICAL NATURE OF ECONOMIC MAN

Homo oeconomicus is the metaphoric or figurative expression for a proposition used as a premise in the hypothetico-deductive system of economic theory. This settles, however, only the question of the logical *status,* not of the logical *nature* of the proposition, especially regarding its derivation, evidence or truth value.

Alas, this question has remained as controversial as it ever was. We have sampled some of the methodological positions defended in the older literature and have seen that Mill, Senior, Cairnes, Bagehot and Wicksteed had rather different views on the subject. We have not quoted any of the pronouncements of Mises, Knight, Robbins, Samuelson or Friedman — to name only a few of the major living disputants on economic methodology — chiefly because their views are more widely known, and known to contradict one another. The fundamental assumptions of economic theory — the 'economic principle', 'the postulate of rationality', the 'assumption of maximisation', or whatever they have been called — have been characterised in so many different ways that an enumeration must suffice:

> ... they are regarded as "self-evident propositions", "axioms", "*a priori* truths", "truisms", "tautologies", "definitions", "rigid laws", "rules of procedure", "resolutions", "working hypotheses", "useful fictions", "ideal types", "heuristic mental constructs", "indisputable facts of experience", "facts of immediate experience", "data of introspective observation", "private empirical data", "typical behaviour patterns", and so forth.[46]

Going from *a priori* statements and axioms, via rules of procedure, useful fictions and ideal types all the way to empirical data, the spectrum of logical possibilities seems to be complete. Since there is no

45.   Machlup, Fritz, 'Theories of the Firm: Marginalist, Behavioral, Managerial', *American Economic Review*, Vol. LVII, March 1967, pp. 1-33; and 'Corporate Management, National Interest, and Behavioral Theory', *Journal of Political Economy*, Vol. 75, October 1967, pp. 772-774.

113

way to settle conflicts of methodological taste, we shall refrain from attempting arbitration.

One suggestion, however, may be permissible and, indeed, may stand a good chance of being acceptable to the representatives of the most divergent views. It is probably agreed that *homo oeconomicus* is not supposed to be a real man, but rather a man-made man, an artificial device for use in economic theorizing. Thus, he is not a *homo* but a *homunculus*. It is *homunculus oeconomicus* we have been talking about all along.

THE FUNCTION OF ECONOMIC MAN

Economic Man, I repeat, is a figurative expression for a proposition which serves as a premise in the theoretical system of economics. To ask for the function of the construct Economic Man is, in effect, to question the need for that premise. To put it bluntly: is the behaviour equation expressed by that construct really necessary — necessary, that is, for the theoretical system in which it is employed?

I shall try to answer this question in the form of an argument that focuses on the most important tasks of economic theory, namely, the explanation of changes in output and changes in price (exchange value). Illustrations will help illuminate the argument.

Changes in output. The output of any product never, or hardly ever, increases unless some producers allocate additional productive services to the particular activities or improve the techniques of production. The output of any product never, or hardly ever, decreases unless some producers reduce the quantities of productive services allocated to the particular activities. Hence, changes in output can be satisfactorily explained only by stating (a) the conditions under which producers are likely to take any of these actions, and (b) the general motive or objective that is likely to induce them to respond in the specified way to the stated changes in conditions.

Changes in price. Prices of anything sold, bought, or exchanged never rise unless some suppliers ask for higher prices and buyers are

46. Machlup, Fritz 'The Problem of Verification in Economics', *Southern Economic Journal,* Vol. XXII, July 1955, p. 16.

willing to pay them, or some buyers bid higher prices and suppliers are willing to accept them. Prices of anything sold, bought, or exchanged never fall unless some suppliers offer to sell for reduced prices and buyers are willing to pay less, or some buyers bid lower prices and suppliers are willing to accept less. Hence, changes in prices can be satisfactorily explained only by stating (a) the conditions under which suppliers and buyers are likely to take such decisions, and (b) the general motive or objective that is likely to induce them to respond in the specified way to the particular changes in conditions.

A universal principle. There are obviously many different changes in conditions that could have the results mentioned and, likewise, one could think of a variety of motives or objectives that would induce the stated responses. No theoretical system, however, can be built if *all* premises vary from case to case; at least *one* premise must be found that can serve to deduce applicable conclusions in a very large number of cases. If no such universal premise could be found, but all assumptions had to be chosen from a large variety of possibilities, it would be impossible ever to predict the outcome of any change in conditions with any degree of confidence. A fundamental postulate acceptable as universal premise of at least approximate universal relevance is needed, and it stands to reason that an assumption of a pervasive and invariant objective or behaviour equation can serve in this capacity. Three examples shall be given in order to clarify the meaning of uniformity or universality in the basic hypothesis.

First example: more research.. We do not doubt that many a person may, as Wicksteed reminded us, 'be just as strenuous in the pursuit of knowledge' as in the desire for more wealth. Would it then be wise if we tried to explain the large increase in the number of persons devoting their time to research and development, say, for space ships and moon shots, as a result of their thirst for knowledge? Or are we not better advised to point to the improved job opportunities and pay levels offered these persons in the research and development activities financed by government and industry — conditions of which they were glad to take advantage?

Second example: more music. Undoubtedly many persons 'may be just as strenuous in the obedience to an artistic impulse' as in the desire for more wealth. Should this lead us to attribute the increase in the

115

number of professional musicians solely to heightened obedience to their artistic impulses? Or had we not better look for the cause in such pecuniary factors as the offer of more positions in more symphony orchestras thanks to larger appropriations of funds to musical organisations, out of increased tax revenues due to higher national incomes?

Third example: vanity and sloth.　　No one in his right mind has any doubt that 'vanity' and 'love of ease' are strong motives of human action. But are there many changes in quantities produced or in prices paid and received that would be most credibly explained by changes in the love of ease or by changes in the degree of vanity? To be sure, an increase in incomes or earnings opportunities may affect prices and production in ways that could be explained by reference to given degrees of desires of leisure or prestige, but the substantive change is then on the pecuniary side, not in the system of subjective valuations.

Action and reaction.　　The preceding three examples should have illuminated the clue for solving the issue: the economist's chief task is not to explain or predict human action of every sort, or even all human action related to business, finance, or production, but instead only certain kinds of people's reactions (responses) to specified changes in the conditions facing them. For this task a *homunculus oeconomicus,* that is, a postulated (constructed, ideal) universal type of human reactor to stated stimuli, is an indispensable device for a necessary purpose.

Example of an exception:　　We must not be dogmatic and exclude exceptions to the rule. For we cannot always find the explanations in economic reactions or adjustments to changes in opportunities that present themselves in changes of prices or incomes. Consider the following case: All during the 1950s and later, there was a substantial flow of Austrian maids and waitresses to England, where they could earn much better wages than at home. In the 1960s, however, there began a movement of English girls to Austria, where their wages were lower. Needless to say, wage differentials can explain why Austrian girls go to England, but not why English girls go to Austria to work in hotels and pensions. What hypotheses could be adduced? We may have two plausible explanations: one, the English girls' newly discovered love for learning – learning to speak German, to ski, to have fun –; the other, newly obtained information about these existing opportunities. The

116

first explanation posits a change in *preferences,* perhaps a fashion, the second a change in the availability of *information,* perhaps furnished by employment agents or by travel agents. These hypotheses are, of course, not inconsistent with the economic principle (utility maximisation), but if the bulk of all cases were of this kind, the usefulness of our theoretical system would be much reduced. For most of our explanatory and predictive assignments we need to assume given preferences and given information.

No quantitative predictions. The conclusions deduceable from the theoretical system with its objective function as fundamental assumption will, by and large, be only qualitative, that is, they will indicate only the direction of change to be expected from certain changes in conditions. No exact quantitative predictions can be derived from the system, although it may be possible to give plausible limits for the deduced changes. For example, the imposition of an excise tax on the product of an oligopolistic industry will be most unlikely to result in a price reduction, but similarly unlikely to result in a price increase by several times the amount of the tax. The increase will most probably be greater than zero and not much greater than the tax. If this appears 'plausible', it is so only from the conjunction of the maximisation assumption with several assumptions concerning cost and demand conditions, possibly also managerial ambitions, political considerations, and institutional constraints. There are other instances in which quantitative estimates may be possible, for example, in macroeconomic problems, but there the estimates are usually derived from correlational regularities (empirical laws), which themselves are not deduceable from any general hypotheses and for which no claims of universality can be made. On the other hand, these empirical laws will not have any great standing — apart from their place in economic history — if they are not at least understandable by reference to individual reactions consistent with the economic principle.

Conclusion. I move the following resolution: The fundamental assumption — whether it be regarded as a conventional postulate, a useful fiction, or a well-known fact of experience — of maximising behaviour, that is, of utility-maximising reactions of households and firms, is recognised as a useful and probably indispensable part of the theoretical system of economics. This assumption has frequently been hypostatized into the symbolic figure or 'personal ideal type', the Economic Man.

117

ON COMPARISONS
BETWEEN NATURAL
AND SOCIAL SCIENCES

INTRODUCTION TO PART FIVE

The social sciences are often called the soft sciences—in contrast with the natural, the hard sciences. Unfortunately, what makes the social sciences soft makes them also hard in a different sense: hard to master, hard to advance, and hard to apply.

Three essays on the peculiarities of the social sciences and on comparing them with the natural sciences form the content of Part Five. Chapters 12 and 13 were written as contributions to festschrifts, one for Ernest Nagel, the philosopher, whose methodology was steeped in logical positivism; the other was for Ludwig Mises, the economist, whose methodology derives from an extreme apriorism. I have great respect for both these thinkers. Chapter 14 was written as my presidential address to the Southern Economic Association in 1960.

Chapter 12, "If Matter Could Talk," was published in Sidney Morgenbesser, Patrick Suppes, and Morton White, eds., *Philosophy, Science, and Method: Essays in Honor of Ernest Nagel* (New York: St. Martin's Press, 1969). It was republished in *Selected Economic Writings of Fritz Machlup* (New York: New York University Press, 1976).

As the essay's title suggests, its major theme is that the objects studied by the natural sciences do not tell the scientist whether and why they "do" what they are observed to do or to have done, whereas the objects studied by the social sciences tell their stories, true or false. I do not assert that the helpful or misleading "tales told by men" constitute the most important difference between the methodological problems of natural and social sciences, but I find the emphasis on this point to be a distinct aid in comprehending most of the other issues in comparative methodology. My comments on Nagel's treatment of the social sciences are designed to shed light on the difficulties which logical empiricism has in dealing with the problematic issues of inquiry into social action.

The essay "The Inferiority Complex of the Social Sciences," Chapter 13 of the present collection, was originally published in Mary Sennholz, ed., *On Freedom and Free Enterprise: Essays in Honor of Ludwig von Mises* (Princeton, N.J.: D. Van Nostrand Co., 1956). It is reproduced here without change.

The paper presents an argument against scientism, that is, against the demand that the social scientist apply exclusively the methods found useful in the natural sciences, however ill-adapted they may be for his purposes. The scientistic appeal invokes restrictive definitions of scientific method and of science as including only those disciplines that employ "the" scientific method. Economists persuaded or intimidated by such bigotry develop an inferiority complex, which drives them to employ techniques of analysis and presentation that are, at best, unnecessarily difficult and awkward but, at worst, downright misleading and counterproductive.

In a way, the next essay, Chapter 14, asking the question "Are the Social Sciences Really Inferior?" is a natural sequel to the previous chapter. If many social scientists suffer from an inferiority complex, this may be either because they falsely believe their work to be inferior or because it really is. This essay was first published in the *Southern Economic Journal*, Vol. 27 (1961). It was reprinted several times: in Maurice Natanson, ed., *Philosophy of the Social Sciences* (New York: Random House, 1963); in Gloria B. Levitas, ed., *Culture and Consciousness: Perspectives in the Social Sciences* (New York: Braziller, 1967); and in Leonard I. Krimmerman, ed., *The Nature and Scope of Social Science* (New York: Appleton-Century-Crofts, 1969). The essay was also published in Italian in two different translations: in the journal *L'Industria* [1961], and in Ellen B. Hill, ed., *Alcuni aspetti delle scienze sociali oggi* (Centro Sociale, Vol. 11, 1964).

Inferior in what respect? This must be answered before any sense can be made of the previous question, especially since, if *A* is inferior to B in quality Q, A is necessarily superior to B in the contradictory quality. Thus I examine how the social sciences compare with the natural sciences on specific matters ranging from invariability of observations, through verifiability of findings and constancy of numerical relationships, to standards of admission and requirements. After the score card is made, the question arises "So what?" What pragmatic conclusions should be drawn from a finding that the social sciences are in fact inferior on this or that score? For example, that they are more complex, yield few, if any, numerical constants, lead to less safe predictions of observable events, or produce deductive results that are difficult to test empirically. What consequences should be drawn from such conclusions? Common sense suggests that we take due notice and go on with our work.

Chapter 12

IF MATTER COULD TALK

The differences between the natural and the social sciences have been both exaggerated and minimized. To some, especially Anglo-American writers, the differences have seemed so categorical that they decided to appropriate the designation "science" for the natural sciences and to deny it to the study of social phenomena. Others, especially German writers, insisted on the scientific character of the study of cultural phenomena but still held that natural and "cultural" sciences were so fundamentally different that they required "contrary" methodological approaches.

These extreme positions had to be countered; it was important to show that in most respects, especially regarding the logic of inquiry, cognition, generalization, verification, and application, there were no fundamental differences between natural and social sciences. Philosophers of science who applied themselves to this task have, however, in their zeal to correct the errors of the exaggerators of contrast, sometimes gone too far in minimizing genuine differences. To recognize these differences may do a great deal for the comprehension of both the unity and the departmentalization of science.

This essay is intended to present an issue which has an important bearing on the difference between the natural and the social sciences. Following my inclination to dramatize ideas when I want the reader to share my appraisal of their importance, I shall introduce the issue by means of a short story or parable.

A PARABLE

They had debated the proposal to telephone the physical laboratories at Harvard, Princeton, and Chicago and notify their counterparts in these institutions of their exciting observations; but then they felt unsure and decided to call a psychiatrist.

"Doctor, please come to the physics laboratory, Columbia University. A group of seven men—three professors and four assistants—apparently are suffering from strange hallucinations, although none of us has taken alcohol, LSD, or any other drugs. We all hear voices. They seem to come from inside our machines and apparatuses, in clear English. If we are not crazy, we are going crazy. Please come immediately."

When the psychiatrist arrived, he found the physicists engrossed in conversation, not with one another but each with some persons hidden in all sorts of containers, cabinets, and machines.

"Are you making fun of us? Is this a hoax, or what?" Professor R. spoke into an apparatus of stainless steel, cylindrical in shape.

"Nothing of the sort," a voice answered from the inside of the apparatus. "We simply have decided to end our silence and cooperate with you in your research work by telling you all we know."

The professor greeted the psychiatrist and introduced him to his colleagues and assistants. At this point he was called to the telephone. He returned after several minutes.

"The same thing happened in Princeton. Professor W. was on the phone. Apparently it started there at the same time as here. At the Forrestal Laboratory the people panicked after the stellarator started talking. . . ."

He was interrupted by a newcomer. "Someone from the *New York Times* called. He wants you to comment on a dispatch from Moscow. There are two strange headlines in *Tass*. One says: 'New Elementary Particles Are Russian'; the other says: 'Genes Pass Resolution Siding with Lysenko'."

Before Professor R. was able to answer, Dr. M., an instructor, entered. He was excited and, without waiting for his chief's nod or question, he began to report on his lab section. He had been talking to a group of undergraduates, demonstrating various cases of Brownian motion. As he spoke about the random walk of molecules and about molecular collisions at various pressures, someone shouted, "Stop that nonsense!" When he looked around to see which student had made this impertinent remark, the voice continued. It was obviously coming from the protective chamber with the suspended mirror, whose movements were being tracked by the fluctuations of a reflected light beam. This is what he heard: "It is time that you cease and desist from misleading your students. What you teach about us molecules is simply not true. This is no random walk and we are not pushing one another all over the place. We know where we are going and why. If you will listen, we shall be glad to tell you." He had not waited for more, but had rushed here to report and get Professor R. to witness the event and to hear what the molecules were about to tell.

"Oh," said Professor R., "you mean they are going to tell us what they *think* they are doing. By all means, let them go ahead."

A SKETCH OF THE HISTORY OF THE THEME

I shall resist the temptation to spin this yarn further. To do so might be fun—but each of us can do it in his spare time and make a short story long. The parable has served to pose the issue, that is, to ask what problems would arise in the natural sciences if inanimate matter began to talk. It is a fantastic idea, to be sure, but an idea worth exploring. Before I proceed, however, I shall acknowledge how it came to me.

The theme—that animals, trees, and inanimate objects could be endowed with the gift of human speech—is, of course, as old as literature. Legends, fables, and fairy tales are the best-known sources; in Homer's *Iliad* we encounter a talking horse, that of Achilles; Aesop's fables and the tales by the Grimm brothers and by Hans Christian Andersen are full of talking and chatting foxes and wolves, trees and flowers, storks and ducks, the sun and the wind, and teakettles, mirrors, and street lamps. In addition, there are the stories of Orpheus, who moved rocks and rivers by his songs; and there have been many anthropomorphic parts in epic and lyric poetry, in tragedy and in comedy.

As a youngster I delighted in reading books by Carl Ewald; among them was one with beautiful *Tales Told by Mother Nature* about talking animals and objects.[1] There was one in which earth and a comet had a discussion, joined in by the moon; another featured a chat between a spider and a mouse. A conversation between the sea and various plants and birds occurred in one tale, and another had a talk, with interesting implications of

1. Carl Ewald, *Mutter Natur Erzählt* (Stuttgart: Franckh, 1910); *idem, The Spider and Other Stories* (New York: Scribners, 1907); *idem, The Old Post and Other Nature Stories* (London: Dent, 1922).

conscious cooperation, between a soldier-crab and a sea-anemone. There was also a most informative debate among five germs: tuberculosis, cholera, and diptheria complaining about man's warfare against them, mold bragging about its great power, and yeast defending man as its best friend.

Much later I became acquainted with the writings of E. B. White and I fell in love with *Charlotte's Web*. But the most philosophical stories of this genre are in the poems by Christian Morgenstern. The manifesto of the "West Coasts," protesting the semantic willfulness of man and declaring their semantic independence,- belongs in the notebook of every language philosopher. But none of the human talk of these nonhuman beings and things included, to my knowledge, any allusions to the problem of scientific procedure.

In methodological and epistemological discussions of the social sciences, references to a cognate, though inverted, theme can be found: Several writers have mentioned that the natural sciences lacked two sources of information—inner experience and verbal communication—which were of essence in the social sciences. We are familiar with statements by social scientists reflecting about their advantage—in some measure compensating for several disadvantages—in having access to data of inner experience unavailable to natural sciences. Thus Friedrich von Wieser wrote: "We can observe nature from the outside only, but ourselves also from within. And since we can do it, why should we not make use of it?"[3]

The emphasis here was on the scientific observer's ignorance of how it feels to be a molecule, an electron, or a gene, contrasted with his knowledge of how it feels to be a human being, suffering pain, enjoying pleasures, and making decisions. There was little emphasis, as far as I know, on the scientific observer's inability to interrogate, and receive communications from, inanimate objects, in contrast with his ability to interrogate, and listen to verbal reports from, large samples of the members of human society.

Some philosophers of science, to be sure, have likened the controlled experiments in the physical, chemical, or biological laboratories to "inter-

2. Christian Morgenstern, "Die Westküsten," in *Galgenlieder* (Berlin: Bruno Cassirer, 1926), pp. 42–43.
3. Friedrich von Wieser, "Das Wesen und der Hauptinhalt der theoretischen Nationalökonomie: Kritische Glossen," *Jahrbuch für Gesetzgebung, Verwaltung und Volkswirtschaft im Deutschen Reich*, 35. Jahrgang (1911). p. 402.

rogations" and "cross-examinations." But, notwithstanding the cleverness of such metaphors, the observation of physical (chemical, biological) changes in response to controlled variations in conditions is essentially different from verbal replies to verbal questions. To watch the change in the speed with which molecules move as temperature is increased is not the same thing as to ask them why they are moving faster, and then to listen to the introspective explanations they might offer in reply—if they were able to talk.

Whether the fact that the natural scientist does not have to bother with verbal communications from observed objects was ever emphasized, or even mentioned, by early writers on the philosophy of science—this I must leave to the historian of ideas. I do know, however, where I encountered the idea. It came to me through Alfred Schütz,[4] who in turn gave credit to Hans Kelsen.[5]

In his theory of law, Kelsen discussed the problem of contradiction between self-interpretation and the analyst's interpretation of the written constitution of a state. What should we make of the contentions, stated in such a document, that the particular state was a federation, a democracy, a republic, if we find these contentions contradicted by our "objective" interpretation of many of its substantive provisions? Should we disbelieve and discard the self-characterization? The same problem appears frequently in connection with statutory law. Several statutes in the United States, for example, tell in their preambles that they are enacted to preserve competition and reduce monopoly, while their actual effect—intended or unwitting—is to reduce competition and increase monopoly.

It was this type of contradiction that prompted Kelsen to make a general observation about the "considerable difference between the subjects of cognition in juridical science, and indeed in all social sciences, and the subjects of cognition in the natural sciences. A rock does not say: I am an animal."[6]

---

4. Alfred Schütz, *Der sinnhafte Aufbau der sozialen Welt* (Vienna: Springer, 1st ed. 1932, 2nd ed. 1960), pp. 281–282.
5. Hans Kelsen, *Allgemeine Staatslehre* (Berlin: Springer, 1925), p. 129.
6. Kelsen, *loc. cit.* Fascinated by this story of the rock, I made the rock expand its tale: "I came here because I did not like it up there near the glaciers, where I used to live; here I like it fine, especially this nice view of the valley." Fritz Machlup, "Are the Social Sciences Really Inferior?" *Southern Economic Journal,* Vol. XXVII (January 1961), pp. 176–177; reprinted in Maurice Natanson, ed., *Philosophy of the Social Sciences* (New York: Random House, 1963), p. 166.

THE ISSUE CLEARLY POSED

The implication is clear: If a rock said of itself that it was an animal, the geologist could not be content with a statement on its chemical composition, physical form and structure, and geological origin; he would also have to explain why the rock was telling something that contradicted the geologist's finding. He would have to explain why the rock was wrong, did not know what it was talking about, or was trying to confuse those who listened to it.

It is one of the characteristics of the natural sciences that their subjects of investigation do not talk about themselves. Moreover, the

facts and events [studied by natural scientists] are neither preselected nor preinterpreted; they do not reveal intrinsic relevance structures. . . . The facts, data, and events with which the natural scientist has to deal are just facts, data, and events within his observational field, but this field does not "mean" anything to the molecules, atoms, and electrons therein.

But the facts, events, and data before the social scientist are of an entirely different structure. His observational field, the social world, . . . has a particular meaning and relevance structure for the human beings living, thinking and acting therein. They have preselected and preinterpreted this world by a series of common-sense constructs of the reality of daily life, and it is these thought objects which determine their behavior, define the goal of their action, the means available for attaining them. . . . The thought objects constructed by the social scientists refer to and are founded upon the thought objects constructed by the common-sense thought of man living his everyday life among his fellow men. Thus, the constructs used by the social scientist are, so to speak, constructs of the second degree, namely constructs of the constructs made by the actors on the social scene whose behavior the [social] scientist observes and tries to explain in accordance with the procedural rules of his science.[7]

7. Alfred Schutz, "Common-sense and Scientific Interpretation of Human Action," *Philosophy and Phenomenological Research*, Vol. XIV (September 1953), p. 3; reprinted in Alfred Schutz, *Collected Papers*, Vol. I (The Hague: Martinus Nijhoff, 1962), pp. 5–6.

NO DIFFERENCE IN LOGIC

The inherent "meaning structure" of human action prompts Schütz, as it did Max Weber, to proclaim the postulate of subjective interpretation.[8] This postulate requires the social scientist to ask what model of an individual mind can be constructed and what typical content must be attributed to it in order to explain the observed facts as the results of the activity of such a mind in an understandable relation.[9] This does not mean that only *one* model of an individual mind would fit the observed facts. Several different models of various degrees of specificity or generality may be adequate for the explanation of the same set of observations, so that the social scientist has the same problem that the natural scientist has of choosing among alternative hypotheses. Thus, Schütz's "postulate" leaves more freedom to the social scientist than the term may suggest.

Ernest Nagel, however, remains skeptical concerning this postulate. He concedes that many social scientists seek "to explain such [i.e., social] phenomena by imputing various 'subjective' states to human agents participating in social processes"; but he questions "whether such imputations involve the use of logical canons which are different from those employed in connection with the imputation of 'objective' traits to things in other areas of inquiry."[10]

Precisely what is meant here by "different logical canons"? If Nagel means no more than that the effort "to 'understand' social phenomena in terms of 'meaningful' categories"[11] "does not annul the need for objective evidence, assessed in accordance with logical principles that are common to all controlled inquiries,"[12] he is not in any disagreement with either Weber or Schütz. Schütz, too, calls for "methodological devices for attaining ob-

---

8. The idea of subjective interpretation—*Verstehen*—was first advanced by Wilhelm Dilthey. He, however, confined it to interpretations of history and literature. Wilhelm Windelband and Heinrich Rickert extended the postulate to the social sciences, or rather "cultural" sciences, which they, however, regarded as strictly historical in character. (For citations, see footnote 30, below.) It is Max Weber to whom we owe the further extension of the principle to generalizing (and predictive) social sciences. Whether for Weber subjective interpretation was a requirement or merely an important aid in the analysis of social phenomena is still controversial.

9. Schutz, *Collected Papers*, Vol. I, p. 43.

10. Ernest Nagel, *The Structure of Science* (New York: Harcourt Brace, 1961), p. 481.

11. *Ibid.*

12. *Ibid.*, p. 485.

jective and verifiable knowledge of a subjective meaning structure"[13] and insists "that the principal differences between the social and the natural sciences do not have to be looked for in a different logic governing each branch of knowledge."[14]

THE NATURE OF THE DIFFERENCE

Nagel believes that the differences which the Weber school stresses between the explanation of social phenomena and that of natural phenomena lie chiefly in the "personal experience," "sympathetic imagination," and "empathic identification" that are possible for the social scientist and may aid him in his efforts "to *invent* suitable hypotheses."[15] But Nagel denies that these differences are essential as far as the *validity* of explanatory hypotheses is concerned. He explicates his position by the following illustration:

> . . . we can *know* that a man fleeing from a pursuing crowd that is animated by hatred toward him is in a state of fear, without our having experienced such violent fears and hatred or without imaginatively recreating such emotions in ourselves—just as we can *know* that the temperature of a piece of wire is rising because the velocities of its constituent molecules are increasing, without having to imagine what it is like to be a rapidly moving molecule. In both instances "internal states" that are not directly observable are imputed to the objects mentioned in explanation of their behaviors. Accordingly, if we can rightly claim to *know* that the individuals do possess the states imputed to them and that possession of such states tends to produce the specified forms of behavior, we can do so only on the basis of evidence obtained by observations of "objective" occurrences—in one case, by observation of overt human behavior (including men's verbal responses), in the other case, by observation of purely physical changes. To be sure, there are important differences between the specific characters of the states imputed in the two cases; in the case of the human actors the states are psychological or "subjective," and the social scientist making the imputation may indeed have first-hand personal experience

13. Schutz, *op. cit.*, p. 36.
14. Alfred Schütz, "Concept and Theory Formation in the Social Sciences," in *Collected Papers*, Vol. I, p. 65.
15. Nagel, *op. cit.*, p. 484.

of them, but in the case of the wire and other inanimate objects they are not.[16]

I should like to raise some questions about four points in Nagel's formulation:

(1) Our knowledge of the state of "fear" of the fleeing man and of the "hatred" animating his pursuers does, of course, not presuppose that we can "identify" with the people observed. It does, however, presuppose that we know what fear and hatred "really" are. We could not know what fear is if we had never felt it or at least, as some would say, if we had not been told about it by persons who had.[17] The same is true for hatred. The meaning of these words could never be grasped except on the basis of direct personal experience or perhaps (but perhaps not) on the basis of verbal communications from some who have had such experience.[18]

(2) When Nagel extends the concepts of "observation of 'objective' occurrences" and of "overt human behavior" to include "men's verbal responses," he loses the clue to the problem. That fearing and hating men can tell us about their fears and hates, whereas molecules cannot tell us about their slower or faster movements, is a difference, not only "important," as Nagel concedes, but essential enough to justify the postulate of subjective interpretation à la Weber and Schütz. For the men talking to us may deny any fears and hates that we impute to them, or claim that they are animated by feelings which we fail to impute to them in our objective interpretation of their actions. Molecules, on the other hand, never con-

---

16. *Ibid.*

17. I cannot resist recalling the operatic dialogue between young Siegfried, in Richard Wagner's music drama, and old Mime: Siegfried asking what fear is and how one could learn how to fear, and Mime first trying to teach him fear by describing his own feelings of anxiety and then, when this proves unsuccessful, promising that Siegfried would soon learn it by personal experience when he encounters Fafner, the dragon.

18. We may know what fear and hatred felt like when we felt them and how we think we acted at those times; we may also know how other people acted when they reported fearing and hating and how they described their feelings. We then try to find a correspondence or similarity—an overlap among the relevant features common to these sets of private and public observations.

tradict our hypotheses by verbal depositions—except in our parable or similar pieces of fiction.[19]

(3) Nagel's illustration contrasts a concrete observation of a particular human situation, that is, a single instance of a (poorly bounded) class of social phenomena, with a well-bounded class of physical phenomena reproduced thousands of times in thousands of laboratories. We shall come back to this lack of parallelism when we discuss the difference between the constructs used in universal laws and those used in reports on particular events.

(4) The "important differences" that Nagel recognizes are those between physical and psychological states, with the possibility of "firsthand personal experience" of psychological states on the part of the social scientist. This emphasis is at the expense of even more important differences, especially that the subjects of inquiry in the social sciences can give us their opinions about our explanations of social phenomena; that their opinions may sometimes be helpful, sometimes misleading; that they may be contradictory, some saying one thing, some another; and that large portions of several social sciences have as their subject matter verbally stated theories of social "actors," or, at least, their interpretations of the actions and intentions of their "partners."

It is in reaction to this fourth point, to Nagel's emphasis on "firsthand personal experience" (and "empathic identification"), that Schütz exclaims that subjective understanding or *Verstehen* "has nothing to do with introspection."[20] What Schütz wants to say here, I suppose, is that "subjective

19. I realize that we can build instruments which tell us by means of signals in English about the physical state of matter. For example, the gauge in my automobile tells me whether the water in the radiator is "cold" or "hot." If the gauge is out of order, the "report" may be wrong. Yet, we would never say that the water was "lying" about its temperature. It is not the water that tells us about its feeling cold or hot; the gauge gives us signals by means of a mechanism which man has invented, built, and installed.

In this example, as Karl Deutsch called to my attention, there is a gap between the report by the gauge and the response by the driver. Gaps of this sort can sometimes be bridged. In the human body, signals are often coupled to a response without the intervention of consciousness, as for example by various feedback mechanisms, studied by neurophysiologists. Analogous mechanisms are designed by man: self-steering apparatuses. The difference between *automatic* and *conscious* responses in the case of human behavior is, I believe, relevant to the scientific procedures in different behavioral sciences. The "strictly behavioral" scientist studies unconscious reactions of the body; in contradistinction, the "social" scientist studies conscious reactions of man to signals received from his environment, including actions of other persons.

20. Schutz, *op. cit.,* p. 56.

understanding" goes far beyond introspection and does not always require it. It merely requires the construction of at least one model of the actor or of the type of actor, that is, an imaginative construction of perceptions, memories, and preferences that is adequate for explaining (and for predicting) the observed behavior or the observed consequences of presumed behavior.

TALES TOLD BY MOLECULES

Let us go back to the end of our parable, where the molecules, after denying the story told by the physicist, offered to tell all they knew about themselves. The lesson of the parable was not that the physicist had never been a molecule and thus had no introspective knowledge about molecules but that the tales told by the molecules would become data and problems for the physicist to deal with. The self-interpretations of the molecules and their interpretations of the actions and reactions of their fellow molecules would become integral parts of the scientists' observational field.

Whether the tales told by inanimate matter would help or hinder the scientists' work is difficult to say. New discoveries will sometimes complicate, mess up, or even destroy the nicest and most widely accepted scientific models of natural phenomena, and thus increase the "mystery" of nature for the time being. Yet, in the long run such discoveries may prove to have been significant steps in the search for "truth." On the other hand, the newly discovered facts may turn out to be errors of observation, and the scientists' efforts to accommodate them in their theoretical system may have been sheer waste. In the same sense, any verbal reports mysteriously made by inanimate matter—on the witness stand, on the psychoanalyst's couch, on questionnaires, or in informal interviews—would certainly mess up the scientists' systems of ordered knowledge; in the long run, the value of such reports may prove to be positive or negative. Undoubtedly, most scientists would prefer not to be bothered by any confessions, true or false, of their now conveniently silent subjects of observation.

The most irritating disturbances would come from contradictory communications. They would raise, among other problems, the question of who, if anyone, is right, or "more credible." Assume, for example, that some molecules explained their movements as part of a well-designed plan of action, others as emotional reactions to irritations from their fellow molecules, while a few molecules admitted that they had been pushed around in random collisions with others. The scientist would probably regard the few respondents who had the "correct" story as particularly honest and intelligent molecules. But he would still be confronted with the problem of explaining why the others were liars or, at least, confused and unreliable witnesses.[21]

TALES TOLD BY MEN

In all social sciences, theorists, empirical researchers, and practitioners are greatly hampered by (deliberately or unwittingly) false reports from men telling about their own actions. However, the question for the social scientist is not whether the reports received from human actors are helpful or unhelpful; in many instances such verbal reports are the only data at their disposal and may be the very subject matter of their investigations. (This is the case, for example, in economic inquiries about prices, which *are* reports from buyers or sellers.)

Even where the communications (from those who take actions which, or the consequences of which, the social scientist studies) are *not* the sole data for inquiry, but where the communications are data supplementary to a record about physically observable phenomena, even then the social scientist must not disregard them. He must account for them, whether they are a help or a nuisance.

Strangely enough, the discussion of these problems has often taken it for granted that the social scientists, especially those accepting the Weber position on subjective understanding, regard introspective or communicated

21. The first step of a scientist confronted with contradictory and dubious confessions (by hitherto silent matter) would be to ascertain how relevant the different motivations reported are for the actual movements observed. He may find that several different confessions would account for the same movements (under the same conditions). In this case he might have no *prima facie* reason for preferring one "subjective explanation" to another. The differences could become more significant as his range of experimental findings expands and yields critical data allowing or requiring him to exclude one or more of the previously eligible explanations. In any case, however, he would have to search for explanations of the contradictory "subjective" explanations. The record of the contradictory reports presents problems which call for investigation.

insights as always helpful in their work. Thus, Nagel, questioning the superiority of "interpretative explanations" in the social sciences, asks, "Do we really understand more fully and with greater warranted certainty why an insult tends to produce anger than why a rainbow is produced when the sun's rays strike raindrops at a certain angle?"[22]

The answer probably depends on who "we" are. If we are physicists, the answer is "no"; if we are persons untrained in physics, the answer is "yes." But if we are interested in the philosophy of science, the comparison is moot. The point is that the very notions of "insult" and "anger" have no meaning outside the consciousness of those who have been insulted and angered or who have been told by some who have. At the same time, those who tell us about insults suffered and anger felt may be trying to mislead us—and perhaps themselves.

The problems of misleading tales from men engaged in all sorts of activities is well-known to social scientists. Economists have often complained about the misinformation received from persons who do the very things which economic theory tries to explain but who contest the theorists' explanations. We may recall the perpetual disagreements between practitioners and theorists of banking. David Ricardo, 150 years ago, spoke about the directors of the Bank of England who did not understand what they were doing or what they were talking about; and about dealers in foreign exchange who reported rates which could not possibly be correct. Generations of economists have written about generations of commercial bankers who failed to grasp the implications of their actions and often misinterpreted their own intentions.[23] Writers on the theory of the business

----

22. Nagel, *op. cit.*, p. 483.
23. That commercial banks "create" credit and money is now known to practically all sophomores studying elementary economics and is fully recognized by the official authorities reporting statistics on the supply of money. Yet, the majority of commercial bankers have stubbornly denied it in interviews, public speeches, and print. The economist can explain the failure of the bankers to form a correct image of their actions and of the consequences of their actions: The banker receives deposits from customers, which adds to his reserves; he grants loans to customers, who then draw on the bank, which will reduce his reserves; thus he cannot lend more than he has received. What the banker does not realize and cannot observe is that many of the deposits he receives are from persons who had received payments from those who had obtained loans from other banks and even from himself. Thus, the banker does not know what he really does or brings about because he cannot observe it. He may, of course, learn it from economists. But his uninstructed opinion —and frequently also his opinion unshaken by attempted instruction—contradicts the economists' theories.

firm have repeatedly been criticized by businessmen who disliked the fundamental hypotheses of the theorists and offered contradictory explanations of business conduct.[24]

SILENT NATURE VERSUS TALKING MAN: ONLY ONE OF THE DIFFERENCES

How fortunate, in contrast, are the physicists, say, those in particle theory: They do not have to put up with denials or contradictions of their propositions by verbal communications from electrons and positrons. Imagine how a physicist would react to positrons protesting that they have unjustly been called "antiparticles," or to photons denying that they were "carriers" of the electromagnetic field.

Think of the long faces of biologists if the *Tass* headline, featured in my parable, became true and genes really passed a resolution siding with Lysenko! Or if cells divided in an opinion poll about the differences between viruses and microbes. And how disturbing to microbiologists it would be if a society of cells endorsed the selection of a scientist for the Nobel Prize and cited with approval his use of an anthropomorphic analogy: ". . . a cell consists of molecules which must work in harmony. Each molecule must know what the others are doing."[25] Some microbiologists might then take heart when they learned that a minority of the cells had dissented, protesting against anthropomorphism as inappropriate in the explanation of their interactions.

To be sure, these events—the message received from particles, genes, cells, etc.—need not at all change any predicted outcomes of actual movements observed by the scientist. The trouble caused by the messages might consist only in the extension of the scientist's task: He would have to explain

24. This refers to the assumption that the firm attempts to maximize profits. At the bottom of the controversy, in which so-called business economists and professors of management science often take the side of the businessman contradicting the economic theorist, lies the confusion between the "firm" as an organization—a group of persons with a variety of objectives, somehow coordinated—and the "firm" as a pure construct in the analytical role of an intervening variable in the theory of prices, inputs, and outputs.

25. Andre Lwoff, "Interaction among Virus, Cell, and Organism" (Lecture delivered in Stockholm upon receiving the Nobel Prize in Physiology), *Science*, Vol. 152 (27 May 1966), p. 1216.

the processes behind the misleading messages. On the other hand, some of the messages might give clues useful in the modification of existing theories.

Perhaps I am giving too much play to the contrast between silent nature and talking man. Claims for recognition of several other issues in the discussion of differences between natural and social sciences have been made. Without deciding the relevance and relative importance of the various issues, and fully recognizing that some of them are closely related and partly overlapping, I propose to offer a list designed to point up some notable distinctions. The list will include the question of introspection, although Schütz preferred to have it put aside. All the issues refer to the relationship of the investigator to his subject matter, that is, in the social sciences, to man, human action, or the effects of human action.

The investigator in the social sciences

(1) can feel and think like the men whose actions he investigates;

(2) can talk with other men, learn about their experiences, thoughts, or feelings, and ascertain that these are similar to his own;

(3) can listen to verbal communications, or read written communications, among persons whose actions he investigates, or among persons of the same type;

(4) can receive verbal communications, solicited or unsolicited, directly from the persons, or type of persons, whose actions he investigates;

(5) can make mental constructs and models of human thinking and acting, and can construct theoretical systems involving relationship among ideal-typical actions, counteractions, and interactions;

(6) can interpret, with the use of his abstract models and theories, particular (concrete) observations of human conduct;

(7) can interpret, with the use of his abstract models and theories, particular (concrete) data as results of certain types of action;

(8) cannot build useful constructs and theories in disregard[26] of constructs and theories formed and communicated by men of the type he observes;

(9) cannot obtain useful data (i.e., the "givens" he is supposed to ex-

26. While he may not completely disregard constructs and theories communicated by the subjects, he may contradict them for adequate reasons.

plain) except through verbal (and often also numerical) reports from men engaged in the activities he investigates.

Following Schütz, I regard point 8 as the most significant. But it is obviously connected with several other points, especially with point 4. Since point 4 is most easily comprehended, even by laymen and scientists with an aphilosophical or antiphilosophical orientation, I have chosen this point as the one to emphasize and dramatize.

OBSERVATION AND EXPLANATION IN ECONOMICS

My emphasis on the importance, for the invention and acceptance of theoretical models in the social sciences, of communicated interpretation of human actions by the actors themselves may give a false impression. For, alas, these "prescientific" or naïve interpretations may be very poor clues to a satisfactory theory of the network of actions, reactions, and interactions which the social scientist has to explain. This warning, however, should not support the opposite position, namely, that complete absence of verbal communications from the participants in social actions would facilitate the construction of a good theory. Indeed, certain institutions and processes could never be satisfactorily explained by observers of overt behavior exclusive of men's verbal responses.

Assume an anthropologist arrives from a populated planet (I do not know whether Mars still qualifies for this designation)—a scholar with a great gift for observation but without any knowledge of human institutions, practices, or languages. He sets himself the task of explaining the working and the function of the stock market. He might observe the traders, jobbers, messengers, brokers, and customers, their movements, their gestures, and their shouts for any length of time, but he would not even come close to a superficial description of the actual process, not to speak of the function of the institution.

Now endow him with the ability to speak and to understand the language, and permit him to interview every one of the people engaged in the activities of the stock market. He would end up with information, but he would not understand enough of what goes on to know the economic functions of the stock market, particularly its role in the utilization of investible funds and in the formation of capital. Since probably 999 out of 1000 persons working on the stock market do not really know what it does and how it does it, the most diligent observer-plus-interviewer would remain largely ignorant. Alas, economics cannot be learned either by watching or by interviewing the people engaged in economic activities. It takes a good deal of theorizing before one can grasp the complex interrelations in an economic system. And this theorizing consists mainly in constructing ideal types of motivated conduct of idealized decision-makers and combining them in abstract models of interactions.

From time to time attempts have been made, in economic literature, to do without the fundamental hypothesis of economic theory, that is, without the assumption that households and firms pursue a definite objective, such as maximization of satisfaction and profits. For example, it has been proposed "to start with complete uncertainty and nonmotivation" and rely on "the principles of biological evolution and natural selection" to explain and predict the course of economic events.[27] The principle of conscious "adaptation" by firms seeking more profits was to be replaced by a principle of "adoption" of successful firms by the environment. The survival of the "viable" firms and the elimination of the nonviable ones were supposed to be the result of "competition."

This proposal depends on the assumption of competition; but competition in markets depends on the desire of human decision-makers to make profits. Competition among hungry animals for scarce food can be understood without reference to any "thoughts" expressed by the animals. Competition among well-nourished men cannot. Of course, competition among athletes in a sport contest, competition among scholars in intellectual endeavors, and competition among businessmen in trade and industry are different matters, each presupposing different motivations. The point is that the existence of the profit motive must be presupposed to explain competition in business. If firms in particular lines of activity make good profits, the emergence of newcomers trying to get a share in the market can be expected only if one assumes that there are men who prefer more money to less and, therefore, decide to enter the industry that seems to offer

27. Armen A. Alchian, "Uncertainty, Evolution, and Economic Theory," *Journal of Political Economy,* Vol. LVII (June 1950), pp. 221 and 211.

relatively large profits.[28]

One of the most important phenomena of the social world, inaction or "negative action" ("intentional refraining from action"), necessarily escapes sensory observations,[29] other than the nonactor's verbal statement of his "reasons," that is to say, a statement of his (perhaps wrong or misleading and certainly introspective) theory about his way of thinking. Where inaction is a mass phenomenon, the construction of an ideal type of man who would "understandably" not react to a particular change in conditions is required.

UNIVERSAL AND PARTICULAR, THEORY AND HISTORY

One of the worst stumbling blocks in the methodological analysis of the social sciences was the insistence of many (chiefly German) philosophers of science on a categorical difference between natural and cultural sciences. The cultural sciences, they argued, were not "generalizing," like the natural sciences, but were, instead, "individualizing" in the sense that their only concern and interest were individual events at particular times and places.[30] For these writers, the social sciences were essentially "history." Confronted with the general theoretical system of economics, a foremost representative of this school of thought stuck to his principles and without hesitation separated economics from the other social sciences by designating it as a natural science.[31] The cultural sciences were "by definition" concerned only with historical events.

However widespread this notion was at one time, nowadays it is at best a chapter in the history of ideas. Philosophers of science, irrespective of their differences on many issues, are now fully agreed that almost all disciplines

28. Edith Penrose, "Biological Analogies in the Theory of the Firm," *American Economic Review*, Vol. XLII (Dec. 1952), pp. 804–819 (esp. pp. 809–816); *idem*, "Rejoinder," Vol. XLIII (Sept. 1953), pp. 603–609.

29. Schutz, *Collected Papers*, Vol. I, p. 54.

30. Among the major representatives of the categorical differentiation between generalizing and individualizing sciences were Wilhelm Dilthey, *Einleitung in die Geisteswissenschaften* (Leipzig: Duncker & Humblot, 1883); Wilhelm Windelband, *Präludien* (Tübingen and Leipzig: Mohr, 1903); and Heinrich Rickert, *Die Grenzen der naturwissenschaftlichen Begriffsbildung* (Tübingen Mohr, 1902, 2nd ed. 1913). See footnote 8, above.

31. Rickert, *op. cit.*, p. 224.

have a core of *general* propositions, with applicability to *concrete* situations or *particular* cases. This is true of the natural and the social sciences alike. Of course, application does not mean that the propositions of the discipline will be sufficient to explain a concrete situation, change, or event (or to predict actual outcomes or to prescribe for desired outcomes). As a rule, propositions of several disciplines will have to be brought to bear on explanations (predictions, prescriptions) in particular cases. No discipline is self-sufficient when it comes to applications. Incidentally, there is much division of labor among those professing a discipline, some of them specializing in formulating, reformulating, and disseminating general propositions —theorists; others on applying them to particular cases—applied scientists and engineers (including social engineers).

Perhaps a few words should be said about one discipline which is exclusively concerned with applications of general propositions from other disciplines to particular situations and events: I refer to history. The historian is an applied sociologist, political scientist, psychologist, social psychologist, economist, anthropologist, archaeologist, military scientist, philologist, linguist, physiologist, biologist, chemist, geologist, physicist, statistician, and what not. Since he deals chiefly with human history, he is predominantly an applied social scientist and will, where propositions of natural sciences are relevant to historical research, either rely on generally known propositions (for example, that certain chemical substances are deadly poisons) or turn to specialists for advice. The historians who explain Caesar's decision to cross the Rubicon and the historians who explain Roosevelt's decision to devalue the dollar apply different mixtures of social sciences, although psychology is a strong ingredient in both.

I have said that almost all disciplines—though not history—have a core of general propositions with (usually indirect) applicability to concrete situations or particular cases, and that this is true for natural and social sciences alike. Yet, strangely enough, when we search modern treatises on the philosophy of science for illustrations in all sorts of contexts, we find a consistent inconsistency: The natural sciences are, practically without exception, illustrated by general laws or by propositions about empirical regularities, whereas the social sciences are illustrated by particular instances, singular observations, and historical events. Whatever may have been responsible for this discrimination in analysis and exposition, it cannot help being misleading. Indeed, it has, I believe, led the philosophers themselves into erroneous positions concerning the very issues we have been treating in the present essay.

To show what I have in mind I shall present and briefly examine three propositions, all in the form of questions about price increases:

(1) Why did the United States Steel Corporation raise the prices of certain steel products in April 1962 by 3½ percent?

(2) Why did prices, as measured by the cost-of-living index, rise in the United States by 7 percent from 1956 to 1958?

(3) Why will prices increase if, with a given labor force, given facilities of production, and given technological knowledge, total bank credit is expanded and aggregate spending by government and business increases?

Only the third question is a problem of economic theory. The first is chiefly a problem of business history. To answer it, many things besides economic theory have to be known; indeed, economics may be relatively irrelevant in explaining why corporate management took the particular decision. Psychology, sociology, politics, management science, industrial relations, accounting, and several other disciplines may be involved; a professional economist may, of course, know enough of all these fields to answer the question without calling in a team of experts from ten other departments. (The reader may want to be reminded that the particular price decision precipitated a row between the President of the United States and the President of the United States Steel Corporation.)

The second question is one of historical statistics. Since it involves mass conduct, that is, decisions and actions of millions of anonymous people selling and buying thousands of different things, we expect that propositions of economic theory are of paramount but not of exclusive relevance. The full explanation calls for knowledge in a variety of fields: political science, law and diplomacy, military science, logistics, technology, engineering, trade-union politics, and other arts and sciences. (The reader may have to be told that military actions in Egypt, the closing of the Suez Canal, the rerouting of oil shipments, and several other things played significant roles, besides fiscal, monetary, and labor policies.)

The third question is pure economics, and nothing but economics, because it does not refer to any particular event in time and space. It is answered by reference to general propositions in the form of "universal laws" or fundamental hypotheses. These hypotheses involve constructs of idealized human action based on (assumed) objectives to maximize profits and satisfactions. The hypothetical price increases are explained as the results of certain types of hypothetical actions which, in turn, are understood in terms of "meanings" on the part of hypothetical human actors—of homunculi made to order to suit the economist's purposes.[32]

NAGEL ON PROPOSITIONS OF SOCIAL SCIENCES

I am not sure whether Nagel sees the concepts and theories of the social sciences in this or in a very different light. For he does not choose for his illustrations general propositions of social sciences, but rather singular events involving particular persons at a specified time and place. He states this most clearly when he discusses MacIver's example of the man fleeing from a pursuing crowd and finds that it involves "an assumption, singular in form, characterizing *specified* individuals as being in certain psychological states at *indicated* times. . . ."[33]

At one point Nagel discusses a point of economic history: Southern cotton planters were "unacquainted with the laws of modern soil chemistry, and mistakenly believed that the use of animal manure would preserve indefinitely the fertility of the cotton plantation." He holds that the "social scientist's familiarity with those laws" will help him explain the gradual deterioration of the soil and the consequent need for virgin land to maintain the output of cotton.[34] I submit that it is not the "social scientist" who needs this knowledge of soil chemistry; it is the historian who, in explaining the events and changes he has selected for investigation, has to know all sorts of things, including some general laws of physics, chemistry, agronomy, and so forth. If the historian happens to have competence (or a university degree) in economics or any other social science, this does not make

32. Most economists are satisfied that *some* people—in sufficient number to be significant—really act in ways similar to the programmed decision-making by the homunculi. But there are also economists who do not care about even that much correspondence between real and imagined men, as long as the conclusions that can be derived from conjunctions between the constructed types and certain sets of specified conditions broadly correspond to the observed records of events that have actually occurred after conditions of the specified sort have actually existed.

33. Nagel, *op. cit.*, p. 482. The emphasis is mine.

34. *Ibid.*, p. 476.

physics, chemistry, or agronomy a part of social science. The exhaustion of the soil used in cotton production may be a *result* of human action (deficient fertilization), partly explained with the aid of economic theory, and in turn also a *cause* of human action (cultivation of additional land), again in part explained in terms of economics. However, this does not make the exhaustion of the soil the province of economics. Technology is not a social science, even if it plays a great role in many classes of phenomena with which social scientists have to deal. My main point is that concrete events in history, particular cases in the real world, are rarely, if ever, explained with the aid of a single discipline but require application of several fields of knowledge.

In his critical discussion of "meaningful" or "interpretative" explanation in the social sciences, Nagel tries to show that the imputation of motives or sentiments to human agents is quite unreliable.

> We may identify ourselves in imagination with a trader in wheat, and con-jecture what course of conduct we would adopt were we confronted with some problem requiring decisive action in a fluctuating market for that commodity. But conjecture is not fact. The sentiments or envisoned plans we may impute to the trader either may not coincide with those he actually possesses, or even if they should so coincide may eventuate in conduct on his part quite different from the course of action we had imagined would be the "reasonable" one to adopt under the assumed circumstances.[35]

We may note that in this illustration Nagel again refers to our imagined identification with a *particular* trader in wheat, even asks about "the sentiments and envisioned plans" which he *actually* possesses, and raises questions about his *actual* conduct. Since I may assume that Nagel is not alluding to the psychoanalysis of a wheat dealer of his acquaintance, but rather to the methodology of economic analysis, I take the liberty of offering an interpretation of the "actual" role which "interpretative" explanation has in economics, and I propose to do this with an illustration involving traders in wheat.

The economist is concerned with questions of the following kind: How will the price of wheat be affected by a report of a drought; by a reduction in the import quota for wheat; by a reduction in the rate of interest; by an increase in freight rates; by an announcement that the ice cover on the

---

35. *Ibid.*, p. 483.

Great Lakes will delay the opening of shipping for several weeks? These questions can be answered with the aid of general propositions of economic theory. The answers do not presuppose that the economist knows any wheat dealer personally, let alone his psychological make-up. They do presuppose, however, that the economist has constructed an ideal type of dealer conduct. Its main feature is that dealers would rather make more money than less. This imputation of the profit motive to anonymous characters—"intervening variables" between, say, a newspaper report and a quotation of a higher price on the wheat exchange—is necessary for a full understanding of the causal connections.

HUNCHES

I cannot pretend to know why Nagel, like most other philosophers of science, confines himself, in illustrations from social sciences, to propositions about concrete events and particular persons. I have a hunch, however, that the explanation is related to the main issue of this essay: that human actors can talk about themselves, their actions, and the events they experience. If they could not, Nagel would not be able to question his wheat dealer in order to ascertain whether he "actually possesses" the sentiments and plans that an economist may have imputed to the dealer or, more likely, to a hypothetical dealer of a heuristic model.

Perhaps, if molecules could talk, and told about their individual sentiments and plans, the philosopher of science would be tempted to switch his attention from general to particular propositions about molecular motions. (Physicists, though, might soon learn to discount the tales told by molecules.) If genes could talk, philosophers of science would perhaps emphasize the divergences between the geneticists' readings of the hereditary code and the genes' own translations into English (even if biologists decided to disregard the confessions of the genes).

One may venture the thought that the development of the computer has opened an area in which the contrast between silent matter and talking man may vanish and the procedures of natural and social scientists converge. Assume for a moment that scientists can observe both the input and the output of a modern computer but have no access either to the information storage or to the program tape. Could they explain the behavior of the computer? This is similar to the task of explaining human behavior without knowing either the memory (information storage) or the skills and preferences (program tape) of the actors.[36]

For a primitive explanation of the computer's behavior, purely empirical methods (linking frequencies of various kinds of input and output) might suffice, though one might not have much confidence in the findings. For a more thorough and more powerful explanation, we would want to construct models of the (unknown) memory stored in the computer and of the (unknown) program tape directing its actions. If some philistines should now rebel against my assumptions and insist that we not reconstruct (imagine) but inspect (observe) the memory and the program in the computer, they would merely reestablish the contrast between natural and social sciences: After all, there is no way for the social scientist to "inspect" human memories and programs. He can introspect, he can receive and interpret verbal communications about introspections by others, and, most importantly, he can construct models of individual minds deemed adequate for the explanation and prediction of human "output."

36. I am indebted to Karl Deutsch for a stimulating discussion of these points.

Chapter 13

THE INFERIORITY COMPLEX OF THE SOCIAL SCIENCES

I⊤ IS said and repeated over and over again that the social sciences are so very young, relatively speaking. Why is it that social scientists insist on this as a statement of fact and why do they consider it worth-while repeating?

The habit of not-so-very-young women of understating their age and emphasizing their youthfulness probably rests on the observation that, as a rule, younger women are regarded as more eligible, desirable and attractive, partly because from some point on beauty is a decreasing function of age, partly because inexperience and innocence are associated with youth and are highly valued by many men. This, however, is not a helpful analogy for us. Innocence, inexperience, beauty—these are surely not the attributes which social scientists wish to claim for their subjects as means of attracting more followers and admirers.

Another analogy may come closer to an explanation. Very young children are forgiven when they misbehave and do silly things. Perhaps social scientists wish to claim this privilege of childhood in order to secure the indulgence of the adult world; as if they were saying: "Pardon us for being so dumb, but we are still so very young." By implication they seem to promise: "Wait till we grow up, wait just a few hundred years, then you will see how smart we shall be." In any case, apparently, while they are children they should be accorded the privilege of being silly; after all, children do not know what they are doing.

161

The closest analogy, in my opinion, is the well-known apology of many people in games and in sports, trying to account for their awkwardness and clumsiness. If they admit that they are old practitioners of the game or sport, their poor performance may be attributed to lack of intelligence or talent; but for "novices" they are not doing so badly. Thus, "Excuse me, I am just a beginner," is an often-heard apology from participants in sports and games who have a feeling of inferiority. This is what is probably behind the social scientists' pronouncements emphasizing how young the social sciences really are: "Please do not think we are stupid; we are merely beginners."

Only those who feel that their accomplishments are unsatisfactory and inferior to those of others have a reason to point to the fact that they are relatively new at their business and thus should not be expected to be any better than they are. Whether or not they actually are poor performers is not of the essence: an inferiority complex may or may not be justified by some "objective" standards. It is the *feeling* of inferiority which makes the sufferers over-apologetic, excessively aggressive, or looking for other sorts of compensations.

The trouble with the protestations by social scientists is that their story about their "young" science is not true. We have only to open our text-books on the history of social theory, political science, or economics to find that we have no right to engage in that baby talk about being mere children, or in those novices' excuses of being mere beginners. Our subjects are as old as any; the scholars and writers in classical Greece had as much interest in problems of society as in problems of the physical world, and their achievements in the former are not less than those in the latter.

But the social science "youngsters" or "beginners" will quickly protest against my reference to our ancient predecessors and will proclaim: "What they did must not be called 'science'! Only recently has social thought become social *science.*" Such pronouncements force me to return to the analogy of the "beginner" in sports. When I once heard the familiar "I am just a beginner" from a ski bunny whom I had seen snow-plowing many years before, I was impolite enough to remind her of it. But undaunted she said: "Oh, that does not count! That was not the right technique; you cannot call it skiing!"

This is precisely the line these perennial beginners, the social scientists, are trying to sell: "Oh, what all these people, long ago, were doing was not the right scientific method, you cannot call it

Social Science!" I do not buy this line about the "right method" and want to warn against it. The old students of society used whatever method they believed was right and expedient, and they thought— 2500 years ago, 2000, 1000, 200 years ago—that they had succeeded in acquiring more knowledge, and more accurate knowledge, about human action than the man-in-the-street had. That should make them social scientists in no less "good standing" than anybody who uses the most fashionable methods of our day.[1]

That the old scholars engaging in the study of society did not call themselves "social scientists" is surely irrelevant. Until recently their subjects were part of "moral philosophy," just as physics was part of "natural philosophy." The fact that Newton and his contemporaries considered his work as natural philosophy does not prevent us from calling him a physicist (although he also wrote much on philosophy and theology and believed that his contributions to these subjects were of major importance). It is not by what *name* it was called, nor by what *method* was used, nor by what *success* was had from the point of view of posterity that we should judge whether a certain body of knowledge at some time past was "science." Knowledge is "scientific" if it is impartial, systematic, and more complete or more accurate than "popular" knowledge at the time. The fact that in the course of the last hundred years several writers have proposed rather narrow definitions of "science"— restricted in terms of particular subject matters or particular methods—and were allowed to get away with these restrictive definitions, has caused anguish to many social scientists. If the restriction had always been in terms of *subject matter* and had excluded social phenomena once and for all, less serious harm would have followed [2] —because the study of society could do nothing to "qualify" for the title of "science." But many of the restrictions were in terms of particular *methods* and this created an ambition on the part of social scientists to earn the right to the honorific title by adopting as

---

[1] "We cannot refuse the name *science* to logic or to the non-quantitative branches of mathematics . . . etc. Nor is there good reason for refusing the adjective *scientific* to such works as Aristotle's *Politics* or Spinoza's *Ethics* and applying it to statistical 'investigations' or 'researches' that do not advance the understanding of anything." Morris R. Cohen, *Reason and Nature: An Essay on the Meaning of Scientific Method* (Glencoe, Ill.: Free Press, 1953), p. 89.

[2] Of course, there are so many connections between physical nature and social phenomena, that a division of disciplines as "sciences" as far as they relate to "nature" and "non-scientific studies" as far as they relate to "human action" would be rather silly. Just think of physical and cultural anthropology, of physical and human geography, of physiological and social psychology.

far as possible, and even farther, the methods that were elected as the definitional characteristics of "Science."

It is in terms of some of these restrictive definitions that the social sciences are deemed to be so very young. Those who insist that a science must be a system of deductions inferred from a small number of axioms or postulates will date the birth of economic science with the publication of Ricardo's *Principles* and will reject the scientific character of political science, sociology and most other social disciplines. Those who insist that a science must be exclusively based on a series of inductions from a large number of exact observations and precise measurements of objectively discerned phenomena, will date the science of sociology as a rather recent creation and will reject the scientific character of economics, political science and most other disciplines commonly counted among the social sciences. These are only two of a large number of definitional restrictions. When in a recent textbook on the methodology of social science the author states that "If we are honest we have to admit that the *first century* of social science has left us somewhere short of victory,"[3] we can infer that he proclaims Auguste Comte as the progenitor of social science and accepts his method of "positivism" as the essential criterion of "science."

Perhaps it ought to be said that there exists no method-oriented definition of science under which all parts and sections of physics, chemistry, biology, geology and other generally recognized natural sciences could qualify as "sciences." Definitions of science which stress the theoretical *system*, the network of logically interrelated hypotheses using mental constructions of ideal exactness, undoubtedly exclude large parts of chemistry and biology. Definitions stressing repeatable experiments and verified predictions clearly exclude the parts of biology, geology and cosmology which deal with the evolution of life, of the earth and of the universe. And even within physics—the discipline which is the science *par excellence* because most definitions of science were formulated with physics in mind as *the* model—the authorities are by no means agreed as to whether the deductive system or the inductive technique constitutes its scientific nature.[4]

It would be interesting to catalogue the definitions of science

[3] John Madge, *The Tools of Social Science* (New York: Longmans, Green & Co., 1953), p. 290. (*Italics supplied.*)

[4] For an exposition of the former view see Henry Margenau, *The Nature of Physical Reality: A Philosophy of Modern Physics* (New York: McGraw-Hill, 1950). For an expression of the latter view see P. W. Bridgman, *The Logic of Modern Physics* (New York: Macmillan, 1927).

proposed or adopted by writers in different fields or in specialized branches of larger disciplines. They all formulate the specific characteristics in such a way that their own kind of work would still qualify as "scientific," while they have little concern, if not undisguised scorn, for fellow workers in their own discipline, in cognate fields, or in fields with which they are entirely unfamiliar. Many a scholar thus excluded from the honorary fraternity of "true scientists" suffers from severe frustrations and develops an inferiority complex, or aggravates the one he had to begin with. In defense against the humiliating "rejection" he either tries to change the definition of science [5] by enlarging the extension of "scientific method" just enough to have his own particular working techniques covered or he adopts working techniques which, however unsuitable to the subject matter or problems under investigation, are safely approved, or can somehow be represented, as "scientific."

A mere enumeration of the subjects now customarily regarded as social sciences will suffice to make it clear that a demand that they follow the same methods (let alone, the same method) is entirely impractical, if not fantastic. The list includes Sociology, Cultural Anthropology, Social Psychology, Human Geography, Demography and Population Theory, Ethnography and Ethnology, Political Science, Economics, History, International Studies. This list is incomplete and overcomplete, depending on whether particular fields are granted "autonomy." [6] Moreover, it can easily be shown that many

[5] An analysis of the attitude of German social scientists may well show that their inferiority complexes are relatively smaller than those of their Anglo-American colleagues. For they do not suffer from frustrations resulting from restrictive definitions of science. The German *Wissenschaft* cannot meaningfully be restricted to exclude any kind of scholarly inquiry, be it in the social sciences, the humanities, philosophy, or jurisprudence. When a lawyer writes an article for a law review he writes a scientific paper (Wissenschaftliche Arbeit); and the historians of literature, the philologists, the philosophers, the mathematicians, the sociologists, they all are scientists (Wissenschaftler) no less and no more than the physicists and biologists. Feeling secure in their title and status as scientists, they do not have to "assert themselves" as scientists and do not have to show off with working techniques unsuited to their work but "acceptable" under some restictive definition of science. This is not to say that German scholars or German social scientists are free from inferiority complexes—yet one source at least is removed.

[6] Sociology, for example, may be given a larger scope so that it may comprise some of the other subjects enumerated; or its scope may be narrowed so that other subjects, such as criminology, become independent. International Studies, which merely emphasize the international aspects of political science, economics, geography, and history, have recently been granted autonomy in many university curricula. History, customarily listed among the social sciences, is sometimes regarded instead as a "method" of social science and sometimes as an "application" of social sciences; again, there are those who insist on excluding it entirely from the social sciences, grouping it with "humanistic studies" (or cultural sciences).

of the supposedly separate fields are largely interdependent. Finally, most of the subjects call for several approaches, descriptive, historical, statistical, and theoretical, which have to be skillfully integrated in the application to concrete problems. An insistence on the use of "the" scientific method for all would be nonsensical.

What is really meant by "the" scientific method? In its narrowest sense, scientific method is supposed to mean *experimental* method, or the demand that every proposition be "verified" by repeated laboratory experiments with strict controls of all conditions. In a wider sense, scientific method is supposed to mean *statistical* method, or the demand that every proposition be "verified" by numerous sets of statistical data relating to sufficiently comparable situations. If no wider extension of the definition is conceded and if no proposition is deemed "scientifically" acceptable unless it is confirmed by such scientific method—alas, only a *minute* fraction of all propositions about human action in society would be acceptable, and only the most *insignificant* propositions at that. Needless to say, all sorts of additional concessions are proposed in order to accommodate other kinds of scientific inquiry. But there is no epistemologically defensible borderline short of the widest meaning of scientific method, defined in the *Encyclopaedia Britannica* "any mode of investigation by which impartial and systematic knowledge is acquired." Such largess would give away any pretensions by which one scholar may assert superiority over another on grounds of the purity and sanctity of his method; it would remove any need for feelings of guilt or inferiority on the part of scholars who ably and diligently add to our store of knowledge by inquiries which are neither experimental, nor statistical, nor quantitative, nor of predictive usefulness. But this largess in the meaning of scientific method is not widely accepted and we must continue to labor under the restrictive definitions and to bear the consequences of the inferiority complex of the social sciences.

These consequences or manifestations of the inferiority complex of the social sciences are chiefly in the form of scientistic [7] compensations. Some of them are old and may yield to treatment; for some more recently observed forms no cures have as yet been developed. Some, though satisfactorily described have not even been given

[7] This expression, introduced though not coined by F. A. Hayek, is almost self-explanatory: It expresses the desire of an investigator of social phenomena to apply in his studies methods found useful in the natural sciences however ill-adapted for his own purposes. See F. A. Hayek, *The Counter-Revolution of Science: Studies on the Abuse of Reason* (Glencoe, Ill.: Free Press, 1952), p. 15. The present paper owes much to Hayek's essay.

technical names, and I shall have to propose nomenclature. Although there are probably several more, we shall deal here only with the following: (1) Historicism, (2) Institutionalism, (3) Holism, (4) Behaviorism, (5) Operationism, (6) Metromania, (7) Predictionism, (8) Prescriptionism, (9) Mathematosis, and (10) Experimentomania. Needless to say, most of the afflicted will not recognize their attitudes as aberrations in any sense, but will insist that they, and they alone, have the right insights and all others are "unscientific."

Before I attempt to formulate the briefest possible statements of the symptoms and manifestations of these conditions, it may be well, in order to avoid even temporary misunderstandings, to anticipate here in the form of examples some explanations that will later be given in greater detail. A historian need not be a historicist—indeed, few historians are—and, moreover, even a fanatic historicist may be an excellent historian. Scholars engaged in social statistics, quantitative economics, econometrics, mathematical economics, or mathematical analysis in the other social sciences—however exclusively their interests may be in quantitative and numerical research and analysis—may be far removed from the attitudes characterized as metromania and mathematosis; and even some who are afflicted may produce useful results. Thus, their work is not in question here. What I find unhealthy in the ten listed attitudes or beliefs is, above all, the attempt to urge certain methods on others in the name of "science" and to disparage the research of others, not perhaps because their arguments or findings are fallacious, self-contradictory, or contradicted by evidence, but because they fail to employ the method claimed to be the only "scientific" one.

Historicism insists on the accumulation of historical facts as the only legitimate beginning and as the sole basis of social research; on the prohibition of the use of theory in the interpretation of past events, though sometimes admitting that theories might eventually be distilled from large masses of historical data; but the validity (not merely applicability) of any such theories will be strictly limited as to time and place. What laboratory experiments are to the natural sciences historical research is to the social sciences: just as the experimental method is required in the study of nature, the "historical method" is required in the study of society and makes it "scientific." Pure theory is useless speculation, sheer metaphysics; history is the scientific method of the social sciences.

Institutionalism, sharing with historicism the view that social theory cannot be general theory and is neither "perpetual" nor "cosmopolitan," holds that human attitudes, objectives, and organizations —all called "institutions"—are subject to human control and, hence, must not be taken as fundamental assumptions in the analysis of human action; instead, social sciences must concentrate on factual descriptions of the institutions and their evolution; thus they will be based on facts rather than on speculation and preconceptions.

Holism (derived from "the whole" rather than "the holy") takes several forms; one insisting on the notion that the whole is prior (logically and historically) to its parts and that, therefore, the study of society must start with the "social wholes" or collectives—the nation, the community, the market, etc.,—rather than with the individual and some of his motivations and actions; another insisting that different aspects of human action should not be separated in analysis, but that social conduct and organization should be studied realistically and "as a whole." To start with the individual and to isolate particular aspects of his actions is held to be unrealistic speculation, whereas the observation of the undissected whole will permit scientific social research.

Behaviorism insists on confining social sciences (as well as psychology *per se*) to the establishment of regularities in the physical behavior of man under strictly controlled conditions. All interpretation of human action on the basis of introspective insights or in terms of mental constructions, postulating the existence of motivations or preferences, is rejected as speculative; in order to be scientifically sound research must be restricted to objectively discernible facts, observable and describable in physical terms.

Operationism (or operationalism) insists on the exclusive use of so-called operational concepts in scientific discourse; that is, all concepts must be defined in terms of operations, chiefly physical operations of the scientific observers. Mental constructs without operational counterparts—idealized concepts—are either rejected outright or only temporarily admitted on the expectation that they will soon be replaced by operational concepts. "Conceivably operational" concepts are sometimes, in exceptional cases and only grudgingly, condoned for want of "practically operational" concepts. As a concession it was (somewhat inconsistently) proposed to admit "mental operations" besides physical operations, but this was not widely accepted since it would open the door to metaphysical speculation.[8]

---

[8] Operationalism has been urged upon both natural and social sciences. In the social sciences, behaviorists are perhaps the truest observers of operationalism.

Metromania, stemming from a fixation on the dogma that "science is measurement," [9] takes the form of attempts to measure everything however faintly connected with the subject under investigation and to imagine the resulting figures to be relevant, and of urgent claims that any proposition not amenable to quantitative verification be rejected as "unscientific." The questions of the stability of computed numerical relations and of their historical relativity are usually ignored and ever new statistical figures for different or longer time intervals are produced in order to devise "corrected" parameters or coefficients "explaining" the measured magnitudes of social reality.

Predictionism, impressed by the success of natural scientists in predicting the outcome of controlled laboratory experiments, sees the sole purpose and justification of scientific inquiry in the formulation of propositions instrumental in successful predictions of events in the real world, including the social world in which only few relevant factors can be controlled or even reliably ascertained, let alone measured. Generalizations of merely explanatory, not predictive, usefulness are rejected as speculative.

Prescriptionism insists, in emulation of the great practical achievements of the physical sciences, on practical usefulness of the findings of research in the social sciences; it demands their use in devising improved social institutions and, especially, in economic organization that satisfies the needs of mankind substantially better than the present one; embracing the dogma *"savoir pour prévoir pour pourvoir,"* [10] it denounces pure theory as apology of the *status quo* and, in the name of "science," calls for action to carry out the prescriptions. These are usually for social control of economic life either on the basis of "scientific socialism" or by governmental planning and interventions.[11]

Mathematosis is the urge, incited by admiration of the paramount use of mathematics in the physical sciences, to employ higher mathematics in expressing propositions that could equally well be expressed in ordinary language. Purely "literary" arguments are

Another expression of operationalism in the social sciences is the demand that social scientists employ only statistically measurable concepts.

[9] Lord Kelvin.

[10] Auguste Comte. The teachings of certain brands of pragmatism are also invoked by prescriptionists.

[11] What distinguishes prescriptionism from controlism, interventionism, socialism and other programs of economic policy is its appeal to "science." It urges these practical applications of scientific findings as the *raison d'être* of science, as a requirement of the true scientific spirit.

scorned, and ideas or problems not reducible to mathematical formulation are suspected of being "metaphysical" or "pseudo-problems."

Experimentomania combines the firm conviction that practical experiments alone are "scientific" with the illusion that social research will eventually be "solidly" founded on practical experiments under strictest controls; all present research techniques are regarded as preparations for eventual experimental research, and research problems are invented that are immediately amenable to laboratory techniques even if they are of little relevance to any hypotheses significant in the systems thus far employed in the various social sciences.

All these attitudes, beliefs, and ambitions use the flag of "true science" as a means for gaining support and allegiance and for combatting the non-believers. Their own method is the best—not perhaps because it has proved particularly fruitful and has yielded results not obtained by other methods—but because it is the only "truly scientific" one. All other methods ought to be rejected—not perhaps because they have not been instrumental in producing or confirming knowledge or insights—but because they are "not scientific."

There is at least one other notion that the described attitudes, beliefs, ambitions have in common. The social scientists who display them are apparently ashamed of the one thing that really distinguishes social sciences from natural sciences, namely, the fact that *the student of human action is himself an acting human being* and therefore has at his command a source of knowledge unavailable to the student of the phenomena of nature. The student of atoms, electrons, magnetic fields, enzymes, genes, etc., is himself none of these things and has no immediate experience of them, whereas the student of human thinking and acting is a thinking and acting human being and knows a good deal about the subject of his inquiries before he starts inquiring. The close and unbreakable link between pre-scientific everyday knowledge and scientific knowledge about the subject matter of social sciences is both an aid and a burden. It is an aid in that it furnishes the social scientist with an initial stock of experiences, working hypotheses, and interpretations of fundamental importance. It is a burden in that it saddles him with the obligation to work with constructs that are understandable to him and his fellow men in terms of their everyday experiences; that is to say, he is under the obligation to make his scientific constructs correspond in all relevant respects to the constructs that are used in everyday life in the common-sense interpretation of our fellow men's actions.[12]

Social scientists laboring under the inferiority complex they have developed under the frustrating notion that the methods of the natural sciences are the only truly scientific ones refuse both to recognize the "obligation" and to take advantage of the "aid" just mentioned. They mistake the prescription of scientific "objectivity" for a proscription of "subjectivism"—confusing "subjective" in the sense of not impartial with "subjective" in the sense of cognizant of inner experiences.

But we must also guard against a possible misunderstanding: that we do not respect the positive and constructive values in the described attitudes, convictions, and ambitions; such values should be recognized. Thus we must be sure not to confuse historians with *historicists*, nor to discount the value of good historical work merely because its author happened to cling to historicist views aggressively critical of all theoretical analysis. We must not underestimate the importance of descriptive work on the institutional features of our social organization, even if its author is a firm believer in *institutionalist* methodology and should be deadly opposed to all general theory. We should admit that the *holists'* fervor for integrated studies, though often destructive in their rejection of isolating abstraction, may at times result in the discovery of data and the development of promising hypotheses. We must acknowledge that *behaviorists* have done good work and have come out with significant findings, even if their campaign against introspection and speculative reasoning about intervening variables probably has obstructed progress in the social sciences more than a little. Although it is true that the attempts of the *operationalists* to ban pure constructs has had obscurantist effects, we must grant that they have been successful in developing a number of statistically operational concepts as useful counterparts for pure constructs and thus have contributed much to our stock of factual information. We must not take all specialists in social statistics, quantitative economics, or econometrics for *metromaniacs;* moreover, while some metromaniac may have wasted money on piling up mountains of stultifying statistics, and may have misdirected some of our best talents, his enthusiasm for empirical work has probably been productive also of useful quantitative studies, for which he deserves credit regardless of the damage done by his preaching about his exclusive scientific method.

[12] See Alfred Schuetz, "Common-Sense and Scientific Interpretation of Human Action," *Philosophy and Phenomenological Research*, vol. XIV, September 1953, p. 34.

The *predictionists* are of course perfectly right in encouraging the formulation of generalizations useful for prediction and testable by the success of predictions based on them, and we must thank them for such encouragement, despite the gratuitous and harmful disparagement of purely explanatory hypotheses. The *prescriptionists* have frequently turned the attention of the social analyst to practical problems of immediate urgency when the latter was preoccupied with spinning hypotheses of remote applicability; for this they must be given credit even if most of the time their zeal has badly messed up theoretical analysis as well as practical policy-making. We should be careful not to regard every mathematical analyst as a *mathematotic;* and even the latter should be thanked for having contributed to substantial improvements in the mathematical training of social scientists, useful for a better selection of talents and also for greater elegance of exposition. Perhaps there is also something good to say about the achievements of the social science *experimentomaniacs,* though I have not yet been able to find anything.

In brief, good historical and institutional studies, interesting holistic hypotheses and behavioristic research, the development of operational concepts, improved quantitative-empirical research, encouragement of attempts to predict and to test, attention to the practical problems of the day, and better training in mathematics —all these are highly desirable things in the social sciences. What is harmful is the attitude of snubbing, disparaging, excommunicating, or prohibiting the working habits of others and of preaching a methodology that implies that they are inferior in scientific workmanship.[13]

Good "scientific method" must not proscribe any technique of inquiry deemed useful by an honest and experienced scholar. The aggressiveness and restrictiveness of the various methodological beliefs which social scientists have developed—in subconscious attempts to compensate for their feelings of inferiority vis-a-vis the alleged "true scientist"—are deplorable. Attempts to establish a monopoly for one method, to use moral suasion and public defamation to exclude others, produce harmful restraints of research and analysis, seriously retarding their progress.

[13] Lest someone think that I myself have engaged in such activities, he had better re-read the last sentence with greater care. For I have not said anything against the *working* habits of others and have not questioned anybody's scientific workmanship. I have dealt with their claims of exclusive possession of the one and only scientific method.

Chapter 14

ARE THE SOCIAL SCIENCES
REALLY INFERIOR?[1]

IF WE ASK whether the "social sciences" are "really inferior," let us first make sure that we understand each part of the question.

"*Inferior*" to what? Of course to the natural sciences. "Inferior" in what respect? It will be our main task to examine all the "respects," all the scores on which such inferiority has been alleged. I shall enumerate them presently.

The adverb "*really*" which qualifies the adjective "inferior" refers to allegations made by some scientists, scholars, and laymen. But it refers also to the "inferiority complex" which I have noted among many social scientists. A few years ago I wrote an essay entitled "The Inferiority Complex of the Social Sciences."[2] In that essay I said that "an inferiority complex may or may not be justified by some 'objective' standards," and I went on to discuss the consequences which "the *feeling* of inferiority"—conscious or subconscious—has for the behavior of the social scientists who are suffering from it. I did not then discuss whether the complex has

[1] Reprinted from *The Southern Economic Journal* (Vol. XXVII, No. 3, January 1961, pp. 173–184), with the permission of that journal and the approval of the author.
[2] Published in *On Freedom and Free Enterprise: Essays in Honor of Ludwig von Mises*, ed. Mary Sennholz, pp. 161–172.

an objective basis, that is, whether the social sciences are "really" inferior. This is our question to-day.

The subject noun would call for a long disquisition. What is meant by "*social sciences*," what is included, what is not included? Are they the same as what others have referred to as the "moral sciences," the "Geisteswissenschaften," the "cultural sciences," the "behavioral sciences"? Is Geography, or the part of it that is called "Human Geography," a social science? Is History a social science —or perhaps even *the* social science *par excellence*, as some philosophers have contended? We shall not spend time on this business of defining and classifying. A few remarks may later be necessary in connection with some points of methodology, but by and large we shall not bother here with a definition of "social sciences" and with drawing boundary lines around them.

The Grounds of Comparison

The social sciences and the natural sciences are compared and contrasted on many scores, and the discussions are often quite unsystematic. If we try to review them systematically, we shall encounter a good deal of overlap and unavoidable duplication. None the less, it will help if we enumerate in advance some of the grounds of comparison most often mentioned, grounds on which the social sciences are judged to come out "second best":

1. Invariability of observations
2. Objectivity of observations and explanations
3. Verifiability of hypotheses
4. Exactness of findings
5. Measurability of phenomena
6. Constancy of numerical relationships
7. Predictability of future events
8. Distance from every-day experience
9. Standards of admission and requirements

We shall examine all these comparisons.

Invariability of Observations

The idea is that you cannot have much of a science unless things recur, unless phenomena repeat themselves. In nature we find many factors and conditions "invariant." Do we in society? Are not conditions in society changing all the time, and so fast that most events are unique, each quite different from anything that has happened before? Or can one rely on the saying that "history repeats itself" with sufficient invariance to permit generalizations about social events?

There is a great deal of truth, and important truth, in this comparison. Some philosophers were so impressed with the invariance of nature and the variability of social phenomena that they used this difference as the criterion in the definitions of natural and cultural sciences. Following Windelband's distinction between generalizing ("nomothetic") and individualizing ("idiographic") propositions, the German philosopher Heinrich Rickert distinguished between the generalizing sciences of nature and the individualizing sciences of cultural phenomena; and by individualizing sciences he meant historical sciences.[3] In order to be right, he redefined both "nature" and "history" by stating that reality is "nature" if we deal with it in terms of the *general* but becomes "history" if we deal with it in terms of the *unique*. To him, geology was largely history, and economics, most similar to physics, was a natural science. This implies a rejection of the contention that all fields which are normally called social sciences suffer from a lack of invariance; indeed, economics is here considered so much a matter of immutable laws of nature that it is handed over to the natural sciences.

This is not satisfactory, nor does it dispose of the main issue that natural phenomena provide *more* invariance than social phenomena. The main difference lies probably in the number of factors that must be taken into account in explanations and predictions of natural and social events. Only a small number of reproducible facts will normally be involved in a physical explanation or prediction. A much larger number of facts, some of them probably unique historical events, will be found relevant in an explanation or prediction of economic or other social events. This is true, and methodological devices will not do away with the difference. But it is, of course, only a difference in degree.

The physicist Robert Oppenheimer once raised the question whether, if the universe is a *unique* phenomenon, we may assume

[3] H. Rickert, *Die Grenzen der naturwissenschaftlichen Begriffsbildung.*

that *universal* or *general* propositions can be formulated about it. Economists of the Historical School insisted on treating each "stage" or phase of economic society as a completely unique one, not permitting the formulation of universal propositions. Yet, in the physical world, phenomena are not quite so homogeneous as many have liked to think; and in the social world, phenomena are not quite so heterogeneous as many have been afraid they are. (If they were, we could not even have generalized concepts of social events and words naming them.) In any case, where reality seems to show a bewildering number of variations, we construct an ideal world of abstract models in which we create enough homogeneity to permit us to apply reason and deduce the implied consequences of assumed constellations. This artificial homogenization of types of phenomena is carried out in natural and social sciences alike.

There is thus no difference in invariance in the sequences of events in nature and in society as long as we theorize about them —because in the abstract models homogeneity is assumed. There is only a difference of degree in the variability of phenomena of nature and society if we talk about the real world—as long as heterogeneity is not reduced by means of deliberate "controls." There is a third world, between the abstract world of theory and the real unmanipulated world, namely, the artificial world of the experimental laboratory. In this world there is less variability than in the real world and more than in the model world. But this third world does not exist in most of the social sciences (nor in all natural sciences). We shall see later that the mistake is often made of comparing the artificial laboratory world of manipulated nature with the real world of unmanipulated society.

We conclude on this point of comparative invariance, that there is indeed a difference between natural and social sciences, and that the difference—apart from the possibility of laboratory experiments—lies chiefly in the number of relevant factors, and hence of possible combinations, to be taken into account for explaining or predicting events occurring in the real world.

Objectivity of Observations and Explanations

The idea behind a comparison between the "objectivity" of observations and explorations in the natural and social sciences may be conveyed by an imaginary quotation: "Science must be objective and not affected by value judgments; but the social sciences are inherently concerned with values and, hence, they lack the disinterested objectivity of science." True? Frightfully muddled. The trouble is that the problem of "subjective value," which is at the very root of the social sciences, is quite delicate and has in fact confused many, including some fine scholars.

To remove confusion one must separate the different meanings of "value" and the different ways in which they relate to the social sciences, particularly economics. I have distinguished eleven different kinds of value-reference in economics, but have enough sense to spare you this exhibition of my pedagogic dissecting zeal. But we cannot dispense entirely with the problem and overlook the danger of confusion. Thus, I offer you a bargain and shall reduce my distinctions from eleven to four. I am asking you to keep apart the following four meanings in which value judgment may come into our present discussion: (a) The analyst's judgment may be biased for one reason or another, perhaps because his views of the social "Good" or his personal pecuniary interests in the practical use of his findings interfere with the proper scientific detachment. (b) Some normative issues may be connected with the problem under investigation, perhaps ethical judgments which may color some of the investigator's incidental pronouncements—obiter dicta—without however causing a bias in his reported findings of his research. (c) The interest in solving the problems under investigation is surely affected by values since, after all, the investigator selects his problems because he believes that their solution would be of value. (d) The investigator in the social sciences has to explain his observations as results of human actions which can be interpreted only with reference to motives and purposes of the actors, that is, to values entertained by them.

With regard to the first of these possibilities, some authorities have held that the social sciences may more easily succumb to temptation and may show obvious biases. The philosopher Morris Cohen, for example, spoke of "the subjective difficulty of maintaining scientific detachment in the study of human affairs. Few human beings can calmly and with equal fairness consider both sides of a question such as socialism, free love, or birth-control."[4]

---

[4] M. Cohen, *Reason and Nature*, p. 348.

This is quite true, but one should not forget similar difficulties in the natural sciences. Remember the difficulties which, in deference to religious values, biologists had in discussions of evolution and, going further back, the troubles of astronomers in discussions of the heliocentric theory and of geologists in discussions of the age of the earth. Let us also recall that only 25 years ago, German mathematicians and physicists rejected "Jewish" theorems and theories, including physical relativity, under the pressure of nationalistic values, and only ten years ago Russian biologists stuck to a mutation theory which was evidently affected by political values. I do not know whether one cannot detect in our own period here in the United States an association between political views and scientific answers to the question of the genetic dangers from fallout and from other nuclear testing.

Apart from political bias, there have been cases of real cheating in science. Think of physical anthropology and its faked Piltdown Man. That the possibility of deception is not entirely beyond the pale of experimental scientists can be gathered from a splendid piece of fiction, a recent novel, *The Affair*, by C. P. Snow, the well-known Cambridge don.

Having said all this about the possibility of bias existing in the presentation of evidence and findings in the natural sciences, we should hasten to admit that not a few economists, especially when concerned with current problems and the interpretation of recent history, are given to "lying with statistics." It is hardly a coincidence if labor economists choose one base year and business economists choose another base year when they compare wage increases and price increases; or if for their computations of growth rates expert witnesses for different political parties choose different statistical series and different base years. This does not indicate that the social sciences are in this respect "superior" or "inferior" to the natural sciences. Think of physicists, chemists, medical scientists, psychiatrists, etc., appearing as expert witnesses in court litigation to testify in support of their clients' cases. In these instances the scientists are in the role of analyzing concrete individual events, of interpreting recent history. If there is a difference at all between the natural and social sciences in this respect, it may be that economists these days have more opportunities to present biased findings than their colleagues in the physical sciences. But even this may not be so. I may underestimate the opportunities of scientists and engineers to submit expert testimonies with paid-for bias.

The second way in which value judgments may affect the investigator does not involve any bias in his findings or his reports on his findings. But ethical judgments may be so closely connected with his problems that he may feel impelled to make evaluative pronouncements on the normative issues in question. For example, scientists may have strong views about vivisection, sterilization, abortion, hydrogen bombs, biological warfare, etc., and may express these views in connection with their scientific work. Likewise, social scientists may have strong views about the right to privacy, free enterprise, free markets, equality of income, old-age pensions, socialized medicine, segregation, education, etc., and they may express these views in connection with the results of their research. Let us repeat that this need not imply that their findings are biased. There is no difference on this score between the natural and the social sciences. The research and its results may be closely connected with values of all sorts, and value judgments may be expressed, and yet the objectivity of the research and of the reports on the findings need not be impaired.

The third way value judgments affect research is in the selection of the project, in the choice of the subject for investigation. This is unavoidable and the only question is what kinds of value and whose values are paramount. If research is financed by foundations or by the government, the values may be those which the chief investigator believes are held by the agencies or committees that pass on the allocation of funds. If the research is not aided by outside funds, the project may be chosen on the basis of what the investigator believes to be "social values," that is, he chooses a project that may yield solutions to problems supposed to be important for society. Society wants to know how to cure cancer, how to prevent hay fever, how to eliminate mosquitoes, how to get rid of crab grass and weeds, how to restrain juvenile delinquency, how to reduce illegitimacy and other accidents, how to increase employment, to raise real wages, to aid farmers, to avoid price inflation, and so on, and so forth. These examples suggest that the value component in the project selection is the same in the natural and in the social sciences. There are instances, thank God, in which the investigator selects his project out of sheer intellectual curiosity and does not give "two hoots" about the social importance of his findings. Still, to satisfy curiosity is a value too, and indeed a very potent one. We must not fail to mention the case of the graduate student who lacks imagination as well as intellectual curiosity and undertakes a project just because it is the only one he can think of, though neither he nor anybody else finds it interesting, let alone important. We may accept this case as the exception to the rule. Such exceptions probably are equally rare in the natural and the social sciences.

Now we come to the one real difference, the fourth of our value-references. Social phenomena are defined as results of human action, and all human action is defined as motivated action. Hence, social phenomena are explained only if they are attributed to definite types of action which are "understood" in terms of the values motivating those who decide and act. This concern with values—not values which the investigator entertains but values he understands to be effective in guiding the actions which bring about the events he studies—is the crucial difference between the social sciences and the natural sciences. To explain the motion of molecules, the fusion or fission of atoms, the paths of celestial bodies, the growth or mutation of organic matter, etc., the scientist will not ask why the molecules want to move about, why atoms decide to merge or to split, why Venus has chosen her particular orbit, why certain cells are anxious to divide. The social scientist, however, is not doing his job unless he explains changes in the circulation of money by going back to the decisions of the spenders and hoarders, explains company mergers by the goals that may have persuaded managements and boards of corporate bodies to take such actions, explains the location of industries by calculations of such things as transportation costs and wage differentials, and economic growth by propensities to save, to invest, to innovate, to procreate or prevent procreation, and so on. My social-science examples were all from economics, but I might just as well have taken examples from sociology, cultural anthropology, political science, etc., to show that explanation in the social sciences regularly requires the interpretation of phenomena in terms of idealized motivations of the idealized persons whose idealized actions bring forth the phenomena under investigation.

An example may further elucidate the difference between the explanatory principles in non-human nature and human society. A rock does not say to us: "I am a beast,"[5] nor does it say: "I came here because I did not like it up there near the glaciers, where I used to live; here I like it fine, especially this nice view of the valley." We do not inquire into value judgments of rocks. But we must not fail to take account of valuations of humans; social phenomena must be explained as the results of motivated human actions.

The greatest authorities on the methodology of the social sciences have referred to this fundamental postulate as the requirement of "subjective interpretation," and all such interpretation of "subjective meanings" implies references to values motivating actions. This has of course nothing to do with value judgments impairing the "scientific objectivity" of the investigators or affecting them in any way that would make their findings suspect. Whether the postulate of subjective interpretation which *differentiates* the social sciences from the natural sciences should be held to make them either "inferior" or "superior" is a matter of taste.

Verifiability of Hypotheses

It is said that verification is not easy to come by in the social sciences, while it is the chief business of the investigator in the natural sciences. This is true, though many do not fully understand what is involved and, consequently, are apt to exaggerate the difference.

One should distinguish between what a British philosopher has recently called "high-level hypotheses" and "low-level generalizations."[6] The former are postulated and can never be *directly* verified; a single high-level hypothesis cannot even be *indirectly*

---

[5] H. Kelsen, *Allgemeine Staatslehre*, p. 129. Quoted with illuminating comments in A. Schutz, *Der sinnhafte Aufbau der sozialen Welt.*

[6] R. B. Braithwaite, *Scientific Explanation: A Study of the Function of Theory, Probability and Law in Science.*

verified, because from one hypothesis standing alone nothing follows. Only a *whole system* of hypotheses can be tested by deducing from some set of general postulates and some set of specific assumptions the logical consequences, and comparing these with records of observations regarded as the approximate empirical counterparts of the specific assumptions and specific consequences.[7] This holds for both the natural and the social sciences. (There is no need for *direct* tests of the fundamental postulates in physics—such as the laws of conservation of energy, of angular momentum, of motion—or of the fundamental postulates in economics—such as the laws of maximizing utility and profits.)

While entire theoretical systems and the low-level generalizations derived from them are tested in the natural sciences, there exist at any one time many unverified hypotheses. This holds especially with regard to theories of creation and evolution in such fields as biology, geology, and cosmogony; for example (if my reading is correct), of the theory of the expanding universe, the dust-cloud hypothesis of the formation of stars and planets, of the low-temperature or high-temperature theories of the formation of the earth, of the various (conflicting) theories of granitization, etc. In other words, where the natural sciences deal with non-reproducible occurrences and with sequences for which controlled experiments cannot be devised, they have to work with hypotheses which remain untested for a long time, perhaps forever.

In the social sciences, low-level generalizations about recurring events are being tested all the time. Unfortunately, often several conflicting hypotheses are consistent with the observed facts and there are no crucial experiments to eliminate some of the hypotheses. But every one of us could name dozens of propositions that have been disconfirmed, and this means that the verification process has done what it is supposed to do. The impossibility of controlled experiments and the relatively large number of relevant variables are the chief obstacles to more efficient verification in the social sciences. This is not an inefficiency on the part of our investigators, but it lies in the nature of things.

[7] F. Machlup, "The Problem of Verification in Economics," *Southern Economic Journal*, XXII, 1955, 1–21.

Exactness of Findings

Those who claim that the social sciences are "less exact" than the natural sciences often have a very incomplete knowledge of either of them, and a rather hazy idea of the meaning of "exactness." Some mean by exactness measurability. This we shall discuss under a separate heading. Others mean accuracy and success in predicting future events, which is something different. Others mean reducibility to mathematical language. The meaning of exactness best founded in intellectual history is the possibility of constructing a theoretical system of idealized models containing abstract constructs of variables and of relations between variables, from which most or all propositions concerning particular connections can be deduced. Such systems do not exist in several of the natural sciences—for example, in several areas of biology—while they do exist in at least one of the social sciences: economics.

We cannot foretell the development of any discipline. We cannot say now whether there will soon or ever be a "unified theory" of political science, or whether the piecemeal generalizations which sociology has yielded thus far can be integrated into one comprehensive theoretical system. In any case, the quality of "exactness," if this is what is meant by it, cannot be attributed to all the natural sciences nor denied to all the social sciences.

Measurability of Phenomena

If the availability of numerical data were in and of itself an advantage in scientific investigation, economics would be on the top of all sciences. Economics is the only field in which the raw data of experience are already in numerical form. In other fields the analyst must first quantify and measure before he can obtain data in numerical form. The physicist must weigh and count and must invent and build instruments from which numbers can be read, numbers standing for certain relations pertaining to essentially non-numerical observations. Information which first appears only in some such form as "relatively" large, heavy, hot, fast, is later transformed into numerical data by means of measuring devices such as rods, scales, thermometers, speedometers. The economist can begin with numbers. What he observes are prices and sums of moneys. He can start out with numerical data given to him without the use of measuring devices.

The compilation of masses of data calls for resources which only large organizations, frequently only the government, can muster. This, in my opinion, is unfortunate because it implies that the availability of numerical data is associated with the extent of government intervention in economic affairs, and there is therefore an inverse relation between economic information and individual freedom.

Numbers, moreover, are not all that is needed. To be useful, the numbers must fit the concepts used in theoretical propositions or in comprehensive theoretical systems. This is rarely the case with regard to the raw data of economics, and thus the economic analyst still has the problem of obtaining comparable figures by transforming his raw data into adjusted and corrected ones, acceptable as the operational counterparts of the abstract constructs in his theoretical models. His success in this respect has been commendable, but very far short of what is needed; it cannot compare with the success of the physicist in developing measurement techniques yielding numerical data that can serve as operational counterparts of constructs in the models of theoretical physics.

Physics, however, does not stand for all natural sciences, nor economics for all social sciences. There are several fields, in both natural and social sciences, where quantification of relevant factors has not been achieved and may never be achieved. If Lord Kelvin's phrase, "Science is Measurement," were taken seriously, science might miss some of the most important problems. There is no way of judging whether nonquantifiable factors are more prevalent in nature or in society. The common reference to the "hard" facts of nature and the "soft" facts with which the student of society has to deal seems to imply a judgment about measurability. "Hard" things can be firmly gripped and measured, "soft" things cannot. There may be something to this. The facts of nature are perceived with our "senses," the facts of society are interpreted in terms of the "sense" they make in a motivational analysis. However, this contrast is not quite to the point, because the "sensory" experience of the natural scientist refers to the *data*, while the "sense" interpretation by the social scientist of the ideal-typical inner experience of the members of society refers to basic *postulates* and intervening variables.

The conclusion, that we cannot be sure about the prevalence of non-quantifiable factors in natural and social sciences, still holds.

Constancy of Numerical Relationships

On this score there can be no doubt that some of the natural sciences have got something which none of the social sciences has got: "constants," unchanging numbers expressing unchanging relationships between measurable quantities.

The discipline with the largest number of constants is, of course, physics. Examples are the velocity of light ($c = 2.99776 \times 10^{10}$ cm/sec), Planck's constant for the smallest increment of spin or angular momentum ($h = 6.624 \times 10^{-27}$ erg sec), the gravitation constant ($G = 6.6 \times 10^{-8}$ dyne cm^2 gram^{-2}), the Coulomb constant ($e = 4.8025 \times 10^{-10}$ units), proton mass ($M = 1.672 \times 10^{-24}$ gram), the ratio of proton mass to electron mass ($M/m = 1836.13$), the fine-structure constant ($\alpha^{-1} = 137.0371$). Some of these constants are postulated (conventional), others (the last two) are empirical, but this makes no difference for our purposes. Max Planck contended, the postulated "universal constants" were not just "invented for reasons of practical convenience, but have forced themselves upon us irresistibly because of the agreement between the results of all relevant measurements."[8]

I know of no numerical constant in any of the social sciences. In economics we have been computing certain ratios which, however, are found to vary relatively widely with time and place. The annual income-velocity of circulation of money, the marginal propensities to consume, to save, to import, the elasticities of demand for various goods, the saving ratios, capital-output ratios, growth rates—none of these has remained constant over time or is the same for different countries. They all have varied, some by several hundred per cent of the lowest value. Of course, one has found "limits" of these variations, but what does this mean in comparison with the virtually immutable physical constants? When it was noticed that the ratio between labor income and na-

[8] M. Planck, *Scientific Autobiography and Other Papers*, p. 173.

tional income in some countries has varied by "only" ten per cent over some twenty years, some economists were so perplexed that they spoke of the "constancy" of the relative shares. (They hardly realized that the 10 per cent variation in that ratio was the same as about a 25 per cent variation in the ratio between labor income and non-labor income.) That the income velocity of circulation of money has rarely risen above 3 or fallen below 1 is surely interesting, but this is anything but a "constant." That the marginal propensity to consume cannot in the long run be above 1 is rather obvious, but in the short run it may vary between .7 and 1.2 or even more. That saving ratios (to national income) have rarely been above 15 per cent in any country regardless of the economic system (communistic or capitalistic, regulated or essentially free) is a very important fact; but saving ratios have been known to be next to zero, or even negative, and the variations from time to time and country to country are very large indeed.

Sociologists and actuaries have reported some "relatively stable" ratios—accident rates, birth rates, crime rates, etc.—but the "stability" is only relative to the extreme variability of other numerical ratios. Indeed, most of these ratios are subject to "human engineering," to governmental policies designed to change them, and hence they are not even thought of as constants.

The verdict is confirmed: while there are important numerical constants in the natural sciences, there are none in the social sciences.

Predictability of Future Events

Before we try to compare the success which natural and social sciences have had in correctly predicting future events, a few important distinctions should be made. We must distinguish hypothetical or conditional predictions from unconditional predictions or forecasts. And among the former we must distinguish those where all the stated conditions can be controlled, those where all the stated conditions can be either controlled or unambiguously ascertained before the event, and finally those where some of the stated conditions can neither be controlled nor ascertained early enough (if at all). A conditional prediction of the third kind is such an "iffy" statement that it may be of no use unless one can know with confidence that it would be highly improbable for these problematic conditions (uncontrollable and not ascertainable before the event) to interfere with the prediction. A different kind of distinction concerns the numerical definiteness of the prediction: one may predict that a certain magnitude (a) will change, (b) will increase, (c) will increase by at least so-and-so much, (d) will increase within definite limits, or (e) will increase by a definite amount. Similarly, the prediction may be more or less definite with respect to the time within which it is supposed to come true. A prediction without any time specification is worthless.

Some people are inclined to believe that the natural sciences can beat the social sciences on any count, in unconditional predictions as well as in conditional predictions fully specified as to definite conditions, exact degree and time of fulfilment. But what they have in mind are the laboratory experiments of the natural sciences, in which predictions have proved so eminently successful; and then they look at the poor record social scientists have had in predicting future events in the social world which they observe but cannot control. This comparison is unfair and unreasonable. The artificial laboratory world in which the experimenter tries to control all conditions as best as he can is different from the real world of nature. If a comparison is made, it must be between predictions of events in the real natural world and in the real social world.

Even for the real world, we should distinguish between predictions of events which we try to bring about by design and predictions of events in which we have no part at all. The teams of physicists and engineers who have been designing and developing machines and apparatuses are not very successful in predicting their performance when the design is still new. The record of predictions of the paths of moon shots and space missiles has been rather spotty. The so-called "bugs" that have to be worked out in any new contraption are nothing but predictions gone wrong. After a while predictions become more reliable. The same is true, however, with predictions concerning the performance of organized social institutions. For example, if I take an envelope, put a certain address on it and a certain postage stamp, and deposit it in a certain box on the street, I can predict that after three or four days it will be delivered at a certain house thousands of miles away. This prediction and any number of similar predictions will prove correct with a remarkably high frequency. And you don't have to be a social scientist to make such successful predictions about an organized social machinery, just as you don't have to be a natural scientist to predict the result of your pushing the electric-light switch or of similar manipulations of a well-tried mechanical or electrical apparatus.

There are more misses and fewer hits with regard to predictions of completely unmanipulated and unorganized reality. Meteorologists have a hard time forecasting the weather for the next 24 hours or two or three days. There are too many variables involved and it is too difficult to obtain complete information about some of them. Economists are only slightly better in forecasting employment and income, exports and tax revenues for the next six months or for a year or two. Economists, moreover, have better excuses for their failures because of unpredictable "interferences" by governmental agencies or power groups which may even be influenced by the forecasts of the economists and may operate to defeat their predictions. On the other hand, some of the predictions may be self-fulfilling in that people, learning of the predictions, act in ways which bring about the predicted events. One might say that economists ought to be able to include the "psychological" effects of their communications among the variables of their models and take full account of these influences. There are, however, too many variables, personal and political, involved to make it possible to allow for all effects which anticipations, and anticipations of anticipations, may have upon the end results. To give an example of a simple self-defeating prediction from another social science: traffic experts regularly forecast the number of automobile accidents and fatalities that are going to occur over holiday weekends, and at the same time they hope that their forecasts will influence drivers to be more careful and thus to turn the forecasts into exaggerated fears.

We must not be too sanguine about the success of social scientists in making either unconditional forecasts or conditional predictions. Let us admit that we are not good in the business of prophecy and let us be modest in our claims about our ability to predict. After all, it is not our stupidity which hampers us, but chiefly our lack of information, and when one has to make do with bad guesses in lieu of information the success cannot be great. But there is a significant difference between the natural sciences and the social sciences in this respect: Experts in the natural sciences usually do not try to do what they know they cannot do; and nobody expects them to do it. They would never undertake to predict the number of fatalities in a train wreck that might happen under certain conditions during the next year. They do not even predict next year's explosions and epidemics, floods and mountain slides, earthquakes and water pollution. Social scientists, for some strange reason, are expected to foretell the future and they feel badly if they fail.

Distance from Every-day Experience

Science is, almost by definition, what the layman cannot understand. Science is knowledge accessible only to superior minds with great effort. What everybody can know cannot be science.

A layman could not undertake to read and grasp a professional article in physics or chemistry or biophysics. He would hardly be able to pronounce many of the words and he might not have the faintest idea of what the article was all about. Needless to say, it would be out of the question for a layman to pose as an expert in a natural science. On the other hand, a layman might read articles in descriptive economics, sociology, anthropology, social psychology. Although in all these fields technical jargon is used which he could not really understand, he might *think* that he knows the sense of the words and grasps the meanings of the sentences; he might even be inclined to poke fun at some of the stuff. He believes he is—from his own experience and from his reading of newspapers and popular magazines—familiar with the subject matter of the social sciences. In consequence, he has little respect for the analyses which the social scientists present.

The fact that social scientists use less Latin and Greek words and less mathematics than their colleagues in the natural science departments and, instead, use everyday words in special, and often quite technical, meanings may have something to do with the attitude of the layman. The sentences of the sociologist, for example, make little sense if the borrowed words are understood in their non-technical, every-day meaning. But if the layman is told of the special meanings that have been bestowed upon his words, he gets angry or condescendingly amused.

But we must not exaggerate this business of language and professional jargon because the problem really lies deeper. The natural sciences talk about nuclei, isotopes, galaxies, benzoids, drosophilas, chromosomes, dodecahedrons, Pleistocene fossils, and the layman marvels that anyone really cares. The social sciences, however,—and the layman usually finds this out—talk about—him. While he never identifies himself with a positron, a pneumococcus, a coenzyme, or a digital computer, he does identify himself with many of the ideal types presented by the social scientist, and he finds that the likeness is poor and the analysis "consequently" wrong.

The fact that the social sciences deal with man in his relations with fellow man brings them so close to man's own everyday experience that he cannot see the analysis of this experience as something above and beyond him. Hence he is suspicious of the analysts and disappointed in what he supposes to be a portrait of him.

Standards of Admission and Requirements

High-school physics is taken chiefly by the students with the highest I.Q.'s. At college the students majoring in physics, and again at graduate school the students of physics, are reported to have on the average higher I.Q.'s than those in other fields. This gives physics and physicists a special prestige in schools and universities, and this prestige carries over to all natural sciences and puts them somehow above the social sciences. This is rather odd, since the average quality of students in different departments depends chiefly on departmental policies, which may vary from institution to institution. The preeminence of physics is rather general because of the requirement of calculus. In those universities in which the economics department requires calculus, the students of economics rank as high as the students of physics in intelligence, achievement, and prestige.

The lumping of all natural sciences for comparisons of student quality and admission standards is particularly unreasonable in view of the fact that at many colleges some of the natural science departments, such as biology and geology, attract a rather poor average quality of student. (This is not so in biology at universities with many applicants for a pre-medical curriculum.) The lumping of all social sciences in this respect is equally wrong, since the differences in admission standards and graduation requirements among departments, say between economics, history, and sociology, may be very great. Many sociology departments have been notorious for their role as refuge for mentally underprivileged undergraduates. Given the propensity to overgeneralize, it is no wonder then that the social sciences are being regarded as the poor relations of the natural sciences and as disciplines for which students who cannot qualify for *the* sciences are still good enough.

Since I am addressing economists, and since economics departments, at least at some of the better colleges and universities, are maintaining standards as high as physics and mathematics departments, it would be unfair to level exhortations at my present audience. But perhaps we should try to convince our colleagues in all social science departments of the disservice they are doing to their fields and to the social sciences at large by admitting and keeping inferior students as majors. Even if some of us think that one can study social sciences without knowing higher mathematics, we should insist on making calculus and mathematical statistics absolute requirements—as a device for keeping away the weakest students.

Despite my protest against improper generalizations, I must admit that averages may be indicative of something or other, and that the average I.Q. of the students in the natural science departments is higher than that of the students in the social science department.[9] No field can be better than the men who work in it. On this score, therefore, the natural sciences would be superior to the social sciences.

The Score Card

We may now summarize the tallies on the nine scores.

    1. With respect to the invariability or recurrence of obser-

[9] The average I.Q. of students receiving bachelor's degrees was, according to a 1954 study, 121 in the biological sciences, and 122 in economics, 127 in the physical sciences, and 119 in business. See D. Wolfle, *America's Resources of Specialized Talent: The Report of the Commission on Human Resources and Advanced Training*, pp. 319–322.

vations, we found that the greater number of variables—of relevant factors—in the social sciences makes for more variation, for less recurrence of exactly the same sequences of events.

2. With respect to the objectivity of observations and explanations, we distinguished several ways in which references to values and value judgments enter scientific activity. Whereas the social sciences have a requirement of "subjective interpretation of value-motivated actions" which does not exist in the natural sciences, this does not affect the proper "scientific objectivity" of the social scientist.

3. With respect to the verifiability of hypotheses, we found that the impossibility of controlled experiments combined with the larger number of relevant variables does make verification in the social sciences more difficult than in most of the natural sciences.

4. With respect to the exactness of the findings, we decided to mean by it the existence of a theoretical system from which most propositions concerning particular connections can be deduced. Exactness in this sense exists in physics and in economics, but much less so in other natural and other social sciences.

5. With respect to the measurability of phenomena, we saw an important difference between the availability of an ample supply of numerical data and the availability of such numerical data as can be used as good counterparts of the constructs in theoretical models. On this score, physics is clearly ahead of all other disciplines. It is doubtful that this can be said about the natural sciences in general relative to the social sciences in general.

6. With respect to the constancy of numerical relationships, we entertained no doubt concerning the existence of constants, postulated or empirical, in physics and in other natural sciences, whereas no numerical constants can be found in the study of society.

7. With respect to the predictability of future events, we ruled out comparisons between the laboratory world of some of the natural sciences and the unmanipulated real world studied by the social sciences. Comparing only the comparable, the real worlds—and excepting the special case of astronomy—we found no essential differences in the predictability of natural and social phenomena.

8. With respect to the distance of scientific from every-day

experience, we saw that in linguistic expression as well as in their main concerns the social sciences are so much closer to pre-scientific language and thought that they do not command the respect that is accorded to the natural sciences.

9. With respect to the standards of admission and requirements, we found that they are on the average lower in the social than in the natural sciences.

The last of these scores relates to the current practice of colleges and universities, not to the character of the disciplines. The point before the last, though connected with the character of the social sciences, relates only to the popular appreciation of these disciplines; it does not aid in answering the question whether the social sciences are "really" inferior. Thus the last two scores will not be considered relevant to our question. This leaves seven scores to consider. On four of the seven no real differences could be established. But on the other three scores, on "Invariance," "Verifiability," and "Numerical Constants," we found the social sciences to be inferior to the natural sciences.

The Implications of Inferiority

What does it mean if one thing is called "inferior" to another with regard to a particular "quality"? If this "quality" is something that is highly valued in any object, and if the absence of this "quality" is seriously missed regardless of other qualities present, then, but only then, does the noted "inferiority" have any evaluative implications. In order to show that "inferiority" sometimes means very little, I shall present here several statements about differences in particular qualities.

> "Champagne is inferior to rubbing alcohol in alcoholic content."
> "Beef steak is inferior to strawberry jello in sweetness."
> "A violin is inferior to a violoncello in physical weight."
> "Chamber music is inferior to band music in loudness."
> "Hamlet is inferior to Joe Palooka in appeal to children."
> "Sandpaper is inferior to velvet in smoothness."
> "Psychiatry is inferior to surgery in ability to effect quick cures."
> "Biology is inferior to physics in internal consistency."

It all depends on what you want. Each member in a pair of things is inferior to the other in some respect. In some instances it may be precisely this inferiority that makes the thing desirable. (Sandpaper is wanted *because* of its inferior smoothness.) In other instances the inferiority in a particular respect may be a matter of indifference. (The violin's inferiority in physical weight neither adds to nor detracts from its relative value.) Again in other instances the particular inferiority may be regrettable, but nothing can be done about it and the thing in question may be wanted none the less. (We need psychiatry, however much we regret that in general it cannot effect quick cures; and we need biology, no matter how little internal consistency has been attained in its theoretical systems.)

We have stated that the social sciences are inferior to the natural sciences in some respects, for example, in verifiability. This is regrettable. If propositions cannot be readily tested, this calls for more judgment, more patience, more ingenuity. But does it mean much else?

The Crucial Question: "So What?"

What is the pragmatic meaning of the statement in question? If I learn, for example, that drug E is inferior to drug P as a cure for hay fever, this means that, if I want such a cure, I shall not buy drug E. If I am told Mr. A is inferior to Mr. B as an automobile mechanic, I shall avoid using Mr. A when my car needs repair. If I find textbook K inferior to textbook S in accuracy, organization, as well as exposition, I shall not adopt textbook K. In every one of these examples, the statement that one thing is inferior to another makes pragmatic sense. The point is that all these pairs are *alternatives* between which a choice is to be made.

Are the natural sciences and the social sciences alternatives between which we have to choose? If they were, a claim that the social sciences are "inferior" could have the following meanings:

1. We should not study the social sciences.

2. We should not spend money on teaching and research in the social sciences.

3. We should not permit gifted persons to study social sciences and should steer them toward superior pursuits.

4. We should not respect scholars who so imprudently chose to be social scientists.

If one realizes that none of these things could possibly be meant, that every one of these meanings would be preposterous, and that the social sciences and the natural sciences can by no means be regarded as alternatives but, instead, that both are needed and neither can be dispensed with, he can give the inferiority statement perhaps one other meaning:

5. We should do something to improve the social sciences and remedy their defects.

This last interpretation would make sense if the differences which are presented as grounds for the supposed inferiority were "defects" that can be remedied. But they are not. That there are more variety and change in social phenomena; that, because of the large number of relevant variables and the impossibility of controlled experiments, hypotheses in the social sciences cannot be easily verified; and that no numerical constants can be detected in the social world—these are not defects to be remedied but fundamental properties to be grasped, accepted, and taken into account. Because of these properties research and analysis in the social sciences hold greater complexities and difficulties. If you wish, you may take this to be a greater challenge, rather than a deterrent. To be sure, difficulty and complexity alone are not sufficient reasons for studying certain problems. But the problems presented by the social world are certainly not unimportant. If they are also difficult to tackle, they ought to attract ample resources and the best minds. Today they are getting neither. The social sciences are "really inferior" regarding the place they are accorded by society and the priorities with which financial and human resources are allocated. This inferiority is curable.

SOME ASPECTS AND APPLICATIONS OF ECONOMIC METHODOLOGY

INTRODUCTION TO PART SIX

The three chapters brought together in this part have less in common than the chapters joined under single headings in previous parts. On the other hand, they share one feature: They are all more closely related to economics than to other social sciences.

Chapter 15, "Why Economists Disagree," was first published in the *Proceedings of the American Philosophical Society*, Vol. 109 (February 1965).

Economists may disagree for four reasons: differences in word meanings (semantics), differences in reasoning (logic), differences in factual assumptions (diagnosis of actual conditions, future public policies, and people's probable reactions), and differences in value judgments (ethical, normative preferences). The first two differences are easily resolved, the other two, however, cannot be resolved so long as some facts are unknown, and perhaps unknowable, and so long as people differ in the relative weights they give to social "priorities." Economists' views are publicized most often on questions of public policy, and rarely on questions of pure theory. Public policy, however, is necessarily based on diagnoses of factual situations and on value judgments. This explains the widespread impression that disagreements are more frequent among economists than among students of other sciences.

Chapter 16, "Theories of the Firm: Marginalist, Behavioral, Managerial," was first given as my presidential address to the American Economic Association in December 1966. It was published in the *American Economic Review*, Vol. 57 (March 1967) and republished in several anthologies: Douglas Needham, ed., *Readings in the Economics of Industrial Organization* (New York: Holt, Rinehart, and Winston, 1970); Michael Schiff and Arie Y. Lewin, eds., *Behavioral Aspects of Accounting* (Englewood Cliffs, N.J.: Prentice-Hall, 1974); only partially in Edwin Mansfield, ed., *Microeconomics: Selected Readings* (New York: W. W. Norton, 1971); in full in *Selected Economic Writings of Fritz Machlup* (New York: New York University Press, 1976). It also appeared in a Spanish translation in *De Economía*, Vol. 23 (1970). Since the essay is available in so many places, why reproduce it again? The answer is that a collection of my methodological writings would not be complete without this piece.

My address "revisited" after 20 years the widely noted Lester–Machlup controversy on "Marginal Analysis and Empirical Research," which had taken place in the pages of the *American Economic Review* in 1946 and 1947. (My 1946 article was republished in no fewer than 10 anthologies.) Lester had asserted that the findings of his empirical research on wage rates, sales, and employment had refuted the marginal-productivity theory of the individual firm's (or the industry's) demand for labor. In response, I had contended that each and every one of the empirical findings was fully consistent with the theory, if correctly understood, and no alternative (let alone better) theory had been offered to replace it. The revisit to the battlefield satisfied me that during the interval of 20 years alternative theories of the firm had indeed appeared on the scene: behavioral theories and managerial theories. They were addressed, however, to different applications, namely, to explanations of the conduct of individual firms that are not under pressure of effective competition and hence have substantial freedom of action. In contradistinction, the general theory of marginalist reactions of firms to events or changes applies essentially to industries with effective competition—and hence with profits insufficient to pursue objectives other than survival through maximization of net income.

In arguing my case, I review the pertinent literature and methodological insights relevant to the issues at hand. Among these are whether behavioral theory can acquire "generality beyond the specific firms studied"; whether the assumption of pursuit of objectives other than profit maximization, say, a specified set of managerial goals, can be merged within one combined formula of maximizing or optimizing behavior; whether a theory of a hypothetical (ideal–typical) firm with a single decision-maker can be replaced effectively (that is, with adequate predictive capability) by a theory of a firm in which decisions are made by several multiminded committees; whether a behavioral theory of the firm will ever be able to explain the effects of external events on prices and production as efficiently as traditional theory has done on the basis of simple marginal analysis; whether the existence of uncertainty and risk aversion makes marginal analysis unworkable, and whether alternative theories can cope with it satisfactorily; whether the extension of marginalism to total utility (comprising all possible satisfactions besides money profits) can be of real help in applied theory; whether the subjective interpretation of sales functions and cost functions involves "empty tautologies"; whether "imperfect information" available to management would lead to determinate decision-making or to unpredictable "satisficing" behavior; whether a marriage between marginalism and managerialism can last or is doomed to end in divorce. This preview, though it may look forbidding, is far from complete.

Regarding the contested marginal-productivity theory of demand for factors of production, I still find it robust and capable of resisting the onslaught of rival theories, at least in the foreseeable future. However, I am less concerned about the survival of any particular theory than I am interested in the methodological principles that regulate the validity of the tests and of the attempts at refutation.

Chapter 17, "On Positive and Normative Economics," is the major part of an essay written in 1967 for a symposium at the New School for Social Research in honor of Adolf Lowe. It was published in Robert L. Heilbroner, ed., *Economic Means and Social Ends: Essays in Political Economics* (Englewood Cliffs, N.J.: Prentice-Hall, 1969). The essay, though printed in one piece, consisted of "An Analysis of the Ideas" (which went from p. 99 to p. 124) and "Some Thoughts on Lowe's Instrumentalism" (pp. 124–129), which is included in this volume in Part Seven as Chapter 24.

The analysis of the ideas on positive and normative economics begins with a rounding-up of different meanings of positive and of normative, but soon comes to the conclusion that a trichotomy would account for differences in the logical character of economic propositions better than a dichotomy: They may be positive, normative (evaluative), or instrumental. What cause and effect are in a positive statement, means and ends are in an instrumental one; the normative statement is about the comparative evaluation of the end. I then proceed to a logical analysis of normative statements and present twelve different ways in which economists are concerned with values. A special section is devoted to a discussion of the nature of welfare economics.

Chapter 15

WHY ECONOMISTS DISAGREE

In asking why economists disagree, one evidently takes it as a fact that they do; and, moreover, that they disagree more, in frequency or amplitude, than the learned men professing other disciplines. Evidence of the existence of disagreements among economists is plentiful and notorious. Whether their disagreements are more frequent and more serious than those in other fields is a question to which we shall return later. Certainly their disagreements appear to be greater, and this is enough to justify an inquiry into the causes.

Economists develop general statements on relationships between certain events, magnitudes, and changes of magnitudes, and on the basis of these general statements they offer explanations, predictions, and prescriptions. As long as their discourse is quite abstract, confined to purely deductive inferences from definitions, postulates, and their implications, no one else cares much about whether economists agree or disagree with one another. When they begin, however, to apply their theoretical systems to concrete situations and arrive at conspicuously different explanations, glaringly different predictions, and shockingly different prescriptions, the audience cannot help wondering whether economists really know enough to be taken seriously.

In a comprehensive treatment of my topic I would start with examples of divergent explanations—say, of the Great Depression—then proceed to examples of divergent predictions—say, of post-war economic activity in the United States—and finally come to examples of divergent prescriptions. Such a program would be too big to fit into a twenty-minute nutshell. I shall, therefore, select only one illustration: disagreements on prescriptions for the international monetary system. This choice is indicated because we have recently finished a careful analysis of these disagreements.

DISAGREEMENT ON INTERNATIONAL
MONETARY PRESCRIPTIONS

Central bankers had become disgusted with the economists' squabbles and had decided not to listen to the economists' advice. Understanding this attitude, we proposed an inquiry into the sources of disagreement on international monetary prescriptions. An international study group of 32 economists from eleven countries was brought together for a series of conferences and worked hard on the assigned problems. The group included representatives of several feuding schools of thought. Indeed, quite deliberately, it included extremists on matters of international monetary reform, advocates of the most irreconcilable plans. For only a direct confrontation of the divergent views could afford a full and fair analysis of the sources of disagreement.

The findings of the study were written up and a report was published in August of this year.[1] It will furnish most of the illustrations for my paper today.

THE CHOICE OF POLICIES

To simplify matters I have prepared an exhibit showing some of the differences in the prescriptions of the money doctors concerning

[1] *International Monetary Arrangements: The Problem of Choice.* A Report on the Deliberations of an International Group of 32 Economists (Princeton: International Finance Section, Princeton University, 1964.)

the price of gold, the foreign-exchange rates, the foreign reserves held by the national monetary authorities, and the targets of domestic monetary policy.

Conflicting Prescriptions by the Money Doctors

The Price of Gold
1. Leave it unchanged
2. Raise it sharply (double it)
3. Raise it gradually (2 to 4% a year)
4. Reduce it gradually (2 to 4% a year)
5. Reduce it from time to time
6. Leave it to the free market, with governments buying or selling as they like
7. Leave it to the free market, with governments selling their stocks only gradually, avoiding a drastic fall of the price

Foreign-Exchange Rates
1. Keep them fixed forever
2. Keep them fixed as long as possible, then adjust to new fixed level
3. Keep them pegged, readjust peg from time to time
4. Let them float freely within fixed limits, which are secured by official sales and purchases
5. Let them float without limit but with official sales and purchases at the discretion of the monetary authorities
6. Let them float freely without any official sales and purchases

Foreign Reserves of National Monetary Authorities (Central Banks)
1. Gold, U.S. $, U.K. £
2. Gold, U.S. $, U.K. £, French fr., German DM, Dutch fl., etc.
3. Gold, U.S. $, U.K. £, composite currency unit
4. Gold, composite currency unit
5. Gold only
6. Gold, IMF unit
7. Gold, U.S. $, U.K. £, IMF unit
8. IMF unit only
9. Nothing

Targets of Domestic Monetary Policy
1. Secure balance of foreign payments at fixed exchange rates
2. Secure stability of domestic price level
3. Secure full employment of labor
4. Secure desired growth rate of gross national product

The list could easily be expanded by adding both to the classes of policy and to the alternative recommendations in each class. But as it stands it will suffice to convince anybody of the fact that the choice of prescriptions is wide and bewildering.

FOUR CAUSES OF DISAGREEMENT

In general we can distinguish four possible causes of disagreement among experts advising on policy: differences as to the meaning of words, differences in logic, differences in factual assumptions, and differences in value judgments.

The first two—semantic and logical differences—can be easily resolved. Differences as to facts can be resolved in principle, if the needed empirical evidence is available; but all too often it is not. Normative differences cannot usually be resolved. But even where facts cannot be ascertained and value judgments cannot be reconciled, the mere identification of the differences can serve an important purpose.

Let us discuss all of these in turn.

Different Word Meanings

Terminologies differ and there are no universally accepted definitions of terms. A good deal of economic disagreement is only apparent and disappears as soon as an understanding of word meanings is reached.

Here is a list of words, all used in the discussion of international problems, that mean different things to different economists: money, supply of money, demand for money, velocity of circulation, hoarding, dishoarding, currency, credit, banks, gold standard, devaluation, inflation, deflation, flexible exchange rates, stable price level, full employment, economic growth, balance of payments, financing, surplus, deficit, equilibrium, adjustment, liquidity—and I could go on and on. Yet the situation is not like that in the Tower of Babel, since any group of economists can, if they wish, make an *ad hoc* agreement on the glossary for use in a particular discussion. If, however, one compares published statements by economists not in a semantic cartel, one may get an impression of substantive agreement where the authors actually disagree, or an impression of disagreement where they actually agree with one another.

To illustrate the possibility of semantic confusion in the context of the policy recommendations previously enumerated, let us look at two pertinent terms. "Devaluation" may be understood to refer to (1) an increase in the official price of gold, not necessarily associated with increased prices of foreign currencies; (2) an increase in the official prices of all or some foreign currencies, not necessarily associated with an increase in the price of gold; or (3) increases in both. Arguments for or against "devaluation" will evidently depend on just what is meant. I have avoided this term in my exhibit of conflicting prescriptions.

Similarly, arguments for or against "flexible exchange rates" may depend on what "flexible" is supposed to mean. It may refer to any of the things recommended as points (2), (3), (4), (5), and (6) of our list concerning foreign-exchange rates, and even more variants are possible. Intelligent discussion presupposes agreement on terminology.

Different Logical Reasoning

We have no real differences in logic—the rules of formal logic are the same for all of us—but there may be logical fallacies behind some of the disagreements. This may happen when two or more of the factual assumptions on which an argument is supposed to rest are inconsistent with one another—but the inconsistency becomes manifest only after some of the hidden implications of the assumptions are laid bare in an analytic process that calls for even more skill in theorizing than many trained economists can muster.

Here is an example: Some economists contended that a country would develop a deficit in its trade balance if money incomes in foreign countries were increasing at a slower rate than labor productivity, and that the conditions of supply and demand might be such that a devaluation of the currency of the deficit country would not cure the deficit. It was later demonstrated that the conditions under which the deficit would develop and the conditions under which it could not be cured by devaluation are mutually inconsistent.[2]

It goes without saying that disagreements due to such logical flaws will not persist among competent economists. As soon as the inconsistencies are demonstrated, the argument in question is withdrawn.

Different Factual Assumptions

The most prolific source of disagreement lies in differences of factual assumptions. It is not customary for experts to state all the assumptions that underlie their conclusions; it would be much too cumbersome. But when they have reached very different conclusions, then we are forced to go back and find out what implicit assumptions they have made. Such assumptions may refer to single events, sequences and conjunctions of events, lasting institutions and temporary constellations of circumstances, economic reactions (mass behavior) and decisions (policies), political reactions and decisions, interrelations between economic and political behavior, etc. Any of these assumptions may be made with respect to the past, the present, or the future.

Assumptions about the past usually relate to matters on which no historical evidence is available. For example, the composition of private short-term capital movements and of "errors and omissions" in the balance of payments of the United States during recent years is unknown and can only be assumed. These assumptions may be pertinent to the solution of the problems with which we are concerned.

Assumptions about the present may be similar in nature: they are part of a "diagnosis" based on guesses or estimates not testable at the time, if ever. For example, the amount of the present stocks of gold held by the Soviet Union and of the hoards of gold owned by private investors and speculators are unknown. Lacking this information, we must resort to making assumptions.

Assumptions about the future may be (1) extrapolations and

[2] Harry G. Johnson, "Increasing Productivity, Income-Price Trends, and the Trade Balance," *Economic Journal* 64 (Sept., 1954): pp. 462–485.

projections of past reactions ("behavior functions"), (2) predictions of events or conditions regarded as probable for a variety of stated or statable reasons, or (3) sheer forecasts based on "insights" of several unspecified kinds. For example, ratios of imports to national income ("propensities to import") are projected into the future; attitudes of central-bank managers which have been typical in the past are supposed to remain unchanged; political group pressures are anticipated to develop under certain conditions and to result in particular decisions by national authorities. The "probabilities" that such assumptions will actually be borne out by the future course of events are debatable. Some of the underlying propositions may become testable in the future, but at present they can, at best, be judged as "sound," "likely," or "realistic" on the basis of verified information which throws some indirect light on them. To bring tacit or implied assumptions of this sort into the open can be essential in an evaluation of differences of opinion.

With respect to economic policy recommendations, it is of particular significance to state clearly all assumptions about political attitudes, because diverse judgments about what is politically "unacceptable," "impossible," or "impractical" may be responsible for wide disagreement among economists. Authorities or legislators charged with making the decisions have a right to know what an economist thinks, not about their likes and dislikes, but about the effects a particular measure, policy, or institution would be likely to have if it were adopted. Hence, the economist should frankly state what he would recommend if the constraint of "political feasibility" were removed, that is, if he could assume the absence of political resistances he thought were preventing the acceptance of certain proposals.

For an illustration of these abstract propositions we may remain close to our previous examples and select from our exhibit the prescription of flexible exchange rates (in one of the forms which minimize official interventions in the market). Several economists testified that they proposed other systems chiefly because they assumed that the political resistance to flexible exchange rates was too strong to be overcome. Another group of experts oppose flexible rates and favor fixed rates chiefly because of particular assumptions they make about the attitudes of future managers of central banks; they assume, particularly, that central-bank managers trying to avoid inflationary credit policies (urged upon them by political pressure groups) will succeed more easily when they can point to dwindling foreign reserves under fixed exchange rates than they could by pointing to a declining exchange rate of their currency under a system of flexible rates. (Advocates of flexible rates regard this assumption as an unrealistic speculation about political prejudices prevailing in the future.) Another assumption relevant to the advocacy or rejection of flexible rates relates to the comparative probability that governments resorting to restrictions in the foreign-exchange markets would do so more readily in order to avoid losses of reserves in the case of fixed rates or to avoid depreciation in the case of flexible rates. Again, another assumption relates to the economic effects of possible apprehensions which importers and exporters may have concerning foreign-exchange restrictions, on the one hand, and exchange depreciation, on the other.

Now it should be clear that all these are matters on which we lack knowledge. Nothing else can be done than to make assumptions about what one thinks would be most likely to happen. And nobody can reasonably complain if different experts have different judgments regarding these probabilities.

One more example. The success of a certain monetary arrangement may depend on whether wage rates can be kept from being pushed up faster than productivity increases. Those who assume that no excessive wage-push will occur may prescribe one monetary arrangement, whereas those who fear that the wage-push cannot be avoided may properly prescribe something else. There will be several variants of recommendations according to several possible views about what will happen, may happen, could happen, or might happen. Who can reasonably demand that economists ought to "know" such future developments?

There are some kinds of "behavior functions" about which we may eventually learn more than we know at present and on the stability of which one may possibly be less pessimistic than I seem to be. Particularly one sect among the economists, the econometricians, have great faith in the stability of numerical relationships in economic life, and they promise us that we shall soon know more about future behavior than we do now. But even they recognize that certain inde-

FRITZ MACHLUP

pendent variables, or exogenous magnitudes, will always have to be assumed.

Economists need not feel ashamed about their ignorance of an unknowable future. They can do no better than make assumptions, and it would be an inexcusable deception of the public if in the face of extreme uncertainty they conspired to make the same assumptions. Without such collusion, however, it is most unlikely that they will make the same assumptions; consequently, they will arrive at different conclusions and different recommendations.

Different Value Judgments

Even identical choices of all relevant assumptions of fact would not secure agreement on policy recommendations if the advisers held different preferences in the pursuit of objectives.[3] Indeed, with different aims and purposes, but the same factual assumptions, recommendations cannot possibly be concordant, except in freakish instances of semantic confusion or logical fallacy.

The hierarchy of values ruling our opinions may be quite different from person to person; and even where a broad, general ranking happens to be the same, the comparative weights are likely to differ. The things different people have in mind when they talk about total welfare, and which they group under such headings as total income, employment opportunities, stability, growth, income equality, freedom, etc., cannot all be "maximized" at the same time. As a rule, more of one will mean less of something else; and how much we should be prepared to sacrifice on other scores for the sake of a gain on a particular score is a matter on which people will always differ.

Although we have been told *de gustibus non disputandum*, a discussion on differences in value judgment may be useful. For it happens too often that a partisan of a cause takes a strong position without realizing that only some of his values are "ultimate" (or "terminal") while most are only "instrumental" (or "derived"). An instrumental value implies a combination of an ultimate value judg-

[3] By "adviser" I mean anybody offering advice, paid or unpaid, upon request or unsolicited, in the government or in the opposition, as an interested party or as a disinterested expert.

ment and of factual assumptions about the causal connections between the "instrument" and the presumed effects to which ultimate value is attached. These implied assumptions of fact, however, may be invalid or partially invalid; or the assumptions may be correct in linking the "instrument" with the desired effects, but incomplete in that they disregard some side-effects that would be undesirable even in the advocate's own system of values.

The objectives of a stable price level, full employment, and a faster growth rate are usually lumped together as an economic holy trinity. That they conflict with one another in many circumstances is well known, but that they are also on different levels of intermediacy to ultimate values is commonly overlooked. Fast growth, defined as a sustained rate of increase of income or consumption per head, implies that our children will be much better off than we are and that young people will enjoy increasing incomes as they grow older. This is an ultimate value, or quite close to one. A stable price level, on the other hand, is "good" only in that we may regard it as instrumental to something else. We may assume, for example, that instability in the price level leads to unwanted redistributions of real income. Hence, stability of the price level promotes "equity" in income distribution, which may be an ultimate value for us. (Alas, the actual effects of changing prices upon distribution may be quite uncertain.) Or we may assume that price inflation reduces efficiency in the use of productive resources, which implies smaller outputs of goods and services that might *ceteris paribus* be obtainable at stable prices. Hence, stability of the price level may promote a larger output, which is an ultimate value. (Alas, the assumption that the *cetera* would be *paria* may be questioned.) Or, as a third possibility, we may assume that rising price levels will reduce the rate of saving and the rate of investment, which in turn may reduce the rate of growth. Hence, stability of the price level is valued because it is assumed to promote growth, the ultimate value in this chain of derivation. (Alas, the assumption of this causal connection is sometimes attacked as irrelevant compared with the presumed direct effects upon growth of the expansionary policies which only "incidentally" inflate the price level.)

It happens that my own judgment of the relevant probabilities makes me inclined to accept the value of price stability. But I recognize that it is not a value *per se* and certainly not an absolute value.

FRITZ MACHLUP

If it is instrumental in attaining certain recognized benefits, its realization will usually involve some cost in the form of sacrifices of alternative benefits. This cost is left out of account by single-minded champions of price stability; on the other hand, the cost is probably overestimated by some advocates of the monetary policies which presumably promote full employment and faster growth.

If we understand that many objectives of economic policy are only instrumental values, we come to understand that judgments of fact and judgments of value may be hopelessly tangled. One who favors a certain policy may do so either because of the high value he puts on its expected main effects or because of the low probability he assigns to the occurrence of certain undesired side-effects. For example, those who sing the praises of price stability, and consequently preach austerity and continence in monetary and fiscal policy, usually believe that, as a matter of fact, the employment of labor will not be greatly affected by aggregate spending. Conversely, those who wave the flag of full employment, and consequently cry out for greater courage or indulgence in monetary and fiscal expansion, usually believe that, as a matter of fact, full employment secured by freer spending need not drive up prices. Is it that value judgments affect judgments of fact? Should we perhaps call in one or more psychoanalysts to disentangle the normative and the positive elements in the economists' disagreements?

Some of the values that influence economic policy recommendations are partly instrumental and partly ultimate. For example, the imposition of foreign-exchange restrictions of the discretionary and discriminatory kind (that is, where a government official can grant or reject a request for an allocation of foreign exchange) is opposed by many economists; but some object to such restrictions largely because of probable economic side-effects of the governmental controls—for example reduced efficiency in production—which they regret, while others are chiefly motivated by a distaste for the directly implied reduction of freedom. Both value judgments should first be broken down to bring out what factual assumptions are involved and to what extent ultimate values—national income, personal liberties—are impinged upon.

A similar mixture of values complicates attitudes with regard to "national sovereignty." Certain monetary institutions or arrangements, for example, are being opposed because they are likely to reduce the economic independence, autonomy, or sovereignty of the nation. The judgment in question may be one regarding intermediate values—when it is feared that harmful or unnecessarily costly measures or actions would be imposed upon the nation from abroad; or one regarding an ultimate value—when foreign pressures are resented *per se,* not because of their consequences. In the former case, the ultimate value may be a higher national income, jeopardized by the imposed actions; in the latter case, the ultimate value is the feeling of pride of self-determination. For instance, a nation may be quite willing to take certain actions under anonymous pressures, under the force of circumstances, but resist or reject the same actions if they are recommended by a foreign government or an international body. (In other words, the nation may resent "being told," though it would be prepared to make the same choice of policy by its own free will.) In the first case, the judgment is not about the value of national free will but about other values foregone by the actions recommended or demanded from the outside. A dissection of value judgments of this sort will be required if the sources of disagreement on certain plans for reform of the international monetary system are to be laid bare.

COMPARISONS WITH NATURAL SCIENTISTS

Our exploration of the sources of disagreement on economic policy recommendations has yielded some of the insights required to answer the question raised at the outset: whether disagreements among economists are wider and more numerous than disagreements among practitioners in other fields. Let us make some comparisons with natural scientists, particularly physicists and biologists.

The fact that we have analyzed disagreements on policies is of great importance. For, if there is an impression that natural scientists are broadly in agreement about the greater part of the body of knowledge that constitutes their discipline, this impression is gained from observing them in concerns far removed from policy recommendations. Most physicists or biologists do not feel called upon publicly to offer opinions on public policy involving their fields of study. Those, however, who are engaged in policy development, either in their capacity as government advisers, or as private citizens speaking out on public affairs, disagree with one another not one bit less than do economists.

Are examples needed to support this point? We need only recall a few more or less recent controversies—about work on the hydrogen bomb, about testing nuclear devices in the air, in water, and underground, about the Mohole project, about the appropriations for research in high-energy physics, about the manned orbital laboratory and the unmanned Mars exploration within the space program—to realize that disagreements among the policy-advising scientists have been ample and fought about with vigor, heat, and often with bitterness. We also find similar entanglement of judgments of value with assumptions of fact. Think only of the question of fallout and its genetic consequences. Or of the question of shelters and the possibilities of reducing nuclear casualties. On issues of this sort one could observe the same phenomenon that we have seen in the economists' controversies: a correlation between normative and positive judgments. Ethical and political inclinations apparently affected the protagonists' views on pure questions of fact, for example, on the effects of radiation through fallout upon mutation of genes.

We have not here discussed why economists disagree on matters of prediction and even explanation, and hence we are less equipped for comparisons with scientists' disagreements on these scores. It is essential, however, to distinguish propositions about sequences of events under specified conditions, assumed as given or actually controlled, from propositions about sequences of events where conditions can be neither controlled nor known with certainty. Impressions of general agreement among scientists refer to the artificial world of the controlled experiment or to a very stable world in which the essential factors are known to remain unchanged (for most practical purposes). When scientists step out of these worlds into a world in which they cannot control all important variables, cannot know their magnitudes, or cannot expect these magnitudes to remain unchanged for sufficiently long periods, disagreements came up thick and fast.

To predict in a world that they do not control, the natural scientists have to make assumptions about unknown or uncertain variables, and their various judgments of relevant facts may differ as widely as the judgments of social scientists differ. The differences and unreliabilities of their predictions are most notorious with regard to such matters as tomorrow's rainstorm, next winter's snow conditions, next autumn's crops, next decade's death rate, or with regard to the exact time it will take for Venice to be sunk or for New York to be drowned under a heightened sea level, or whether we shall find living organisms on Mars, or whether nuclear power will be competitive with conventionally generated energy.

To explain past events in the real-life world, where things happen that have not been expected, is to assume numerous antecedent occurrences and conjoined conditions for which no, or only circumstantial, evidence is available. Thus, the scientists' explanations of particular earthquakes, landslides, floods, conflagrations, explosions, collisions, shipwrecks, and many other past catastrophes may forever remain controversial. In countless litigations expert witnesses testify on opposite sides, supporting their conclusions by different assumptions of fact, not testable with the information available. Similarly, the scientists' explanations of the evolution of the universe, the genesis of stars and planets, the biography of the earth, the origin of life, the evolution of man—all these are based on uncertain knowledge and tentative hypotheses, highly controversial and changing over the years.

The point I am trying to make is this: the exact-construct-world and the controlled-laboratory-world of the scientist are different from the real-life-world.[4] As long as scientists deal with the former two worlds, that is, in their theoretical analysis and experimental research, differences of opinion may be infrequent and not conspicuous enough to arouse public notice. As soon as they have to deal with the real-life-world, that is, as forecasters, experts, consultants, strategists, and advisers on public policy, differences of opinion will be wide and frequent. It happens that these are regarded as the nonscientific roles of the scientists, who are best known and respected for their strictly scientific achievements.

Economists also have an exact-construct-world, created for purely theoretical analysis; but no outsider cares what they do with it or

[4] Fritz Machlup, "Are the Social Sciences Really Inferior?" *Southern Economic Journal* 27 (January, 1961): pp. 173–184.

FRITZ MACHLUP

appreciates the broad agreement of the analysts about the theoretical system that constitutes their discipline. The economists' work becomes known only where it deals with the real-life-world, in which most things are unknown and almost everything is uncertain. In explaining, predicting, and prescribing for this uncertain world, economists will unavoidably disagree. Some purists among the economists have contended that they, *qua economists*, cannot give advice or make policy recommendations; that those who recommend or prescribe do so in their capacity as citizens or politicians. Such restrictive definitions of economics may be good for their ego but will not help their public image. For, regrettably, it is only in their roles as practical experts, forecasters, consultants, and policy advisers that economists are known to the public. They have thus acquired the reputation of professional wranglers, incapable of ever agreeing with one another.

Chapter 16

THEORIES OF THE FIRM:
MARGINALIST, BEHAVIORAL, MANAGERIAL

Last year, when it was my task to plan the program for the annual meeting of our association, a friend suggested that, with twenty years having passed since the outbreak of the "marginalism controversy," it was appropriate to review what has since happened to the embattled theory of the firm. The topic did not fit the general theme I had chosen for the 1965 meeting, but I reasoned that 1966 would give me a good opportunity to undertake the review myself.

The Battlefield Revisited

So let us recall that literary feud and the warriors, and let us revisit the battlefield. The major battlefield was the *American Economic Review*, with six articles and communications between March 1946 and March 1947 [16] [43] [21] [17] [22] [44]. There had been earlier gunfire elsewhere, chiefly in the *Oxford Economic Papers* in 1939 [14]. But, since the shooting then was not returned and it takes at least two opponents to join battle, it must be agreed that the real hostilities were the exchanges in the *AER*.

The fight was spirited, even fierce. Thousands of students of economics, voluntary or involuntary readers, have been either shocked or entertained by the violence of some of the blows exchanged and may have thought that the opponents must have become mortal enemies forever. These readers would have been wrong. Even before we came out for the last round of the fight, we exchanged friendly letters. (December 1946) assuring each other that we would bear no grudges.

We have remained the best of friends; for several years now Richard Lester and I have been colleagues in the same department; and, as a token of our friendship, he has generously accepted my invitation to share this platform with me today as chairman of the session. Thus the veterans of both sides of the War of 1946 are now joined in revisiting

---

* Presidential address delivered, in a shorter version, at the Seventy-ninth Annual Meeting of the American Economic Association, San Francisco, December 28, 1966.

the battlefield. This, incidentally, does not mean that either of us has succeeded in converting the other to the "true faith."

What was the outcome of the controversy? Who won? We could not possibly say if we have not first agreed on precisely what the shooting was about. I have heard it said that Machlup won the battle but Lester won the war. What this means, however, cannot be known unless we know what the issues and objectives of the war had been. Was it merely to make economics safe for or from marginalism? Were there not several other issues being fought over?

Some of the Major Issues

There were no doubt a good many contentions of all sorts—major, minor, essential, incidental, interpretative, factual, methodological, substantive, and all the rest. To present a complete catalogue of the issues involved would be too ambitious a task for this occasion, but a partial listing might be helpful.

The chief issue, of course, was whether marginal analysis was invalid and ought to be discarded, especially as far as the theory of prices, cost, wages, and employment in manufacturing industry is concerned. This issue, however, implied the question of the correct interpretation of marginal analysis, including the tenets of the marginal-productivity principle. In this connection, differences in the models of the firm customarily used in different kinds of analysis became relevant. Involved here was the question of whether the postulate of maximizing money profits led to conclusions very different from those derivable from assumptions of conduct guided by a variety of largely nonpecuniary considerations.

Underlying all these questions were some issues of general scientific methodology: the legitimacy and usefulness of abstract theorizing on the basis of unrealistic assumptions, or perhaps on the basis of assumptions regarded as "reasonable" though not "universally true." These issues, in particular, were whether an assumption of profit maximization as the effective objective of the firm in the theoretical model may be accepted as a tenable hypothesis only if it can be verified that all or a majority of those who actually run business firms in the real world agree that this is their only or major objective, that they are capable of obtaining all the information and of performing all the calculations needed for the realization of that objective, and are really carrying out the actions found to be optimal in this fashion; or, alternatively, whether all these tests may be dispensed with and the assumption of profit maximization nevertheless accepted as a fruitful postulate from which conclusions can be derived which correspond with what can be observed in the records of prices and quantities.

FRITZ MACHLUP

Concerning the empirical testing of theoretical conclusions, there were issues of the validity of surveys through mailed questionnaires and of the proper interpretation of responses to various types of questions about managerial judgment. In the background of the whole controversy, but undoubtedly of pervasive significance, was the comparative acceptability of empirical findings to the effect that the elasticity of demand for labor was virtually zero and of the conventional theoretical inference that the elasticity was normally above zero.

Realizing how manifold were the issues of the controversy, one can appreciate that no clear decision can be made about its outcome. Some of the issues had been raised decades or centuries before 1946 and were not decided in this confrontation one way or the other. Attacks on the assumption of maximizing behavior and on the lack of realism in price theory have occurred with great regularity ever since "economic man" and similar postulates were introduced. The running battles between the classical and the historical schools were largely on these points. The *Methodenstreit* of 1883-84 dealt essentially with the same issues. And in the United States, institutionalism may be seen as a movement animated by the same spirit of protest against abstract theory.

However, the particular form of explicit marginalism (under the name of "theory of the firm") which became the target of the attacks of 1939 and 1946 had only come into being in the 1930's—if one suppresses the memory of the great master of 1838 [9]. Ironically, some interpreter of recent history of economic thought—I have forgotten who it was—regarded the 1933-34 versions of the theory of the firm [8] [32] [41] as the theorists' concession to institutionalism, as attempts to supplement the neoclassical model of the firm under atomistic competition with some "more realistic" models allowing for a greater variety of conditions. It was this theory of the profit-maximizing firm in all sorts of market positions, in monopolistic and oligopolistic competition as well as in pure and perfect competition, that was attacked by the researchers in Oxford; and it was the marginal-productivity principle in the explanation of the demand for labor on the part of the individual firm that was the prime target of the attack of 1946.

If the chief aim of the attack was to force the abandonment or subversion of marginalism, and if the chief aim of the defense was to turn back the subversive forces and secure the reign of marginalism once and for all, then, to be sure, the war of 1946 ended in a draw. Look at the textbooks and you will find that marginalism has continued to dominate the teaching of microeconomics, perhaps though with occasional reservations and references to current attempts at greater realism. But look at the journals and monographs and you find that research on alternative approaches to the theory of the firm is regularly reported with the implication that a superior theory may eventually replace marginalism. This replacement, however, according to the proponents of the best-known alternatives to marginalism, is expected chiefly with regard to industries where firms are few and competition is ineffective. The marginalist solution of price determination under conditions of heavy competition is not seriously contested.

In pointing this out, I am not trying to claim that marginal analysis is invincible and forever irreplaceable. If I follow the philosophy of science which, instead of pronouncing theories "false" or "true," distinguishes only between those "rejected" and those "still open to criticism" [30, pp. 246-48], the only victory that can be claimed for the cause of marginalism is that it is still open to criticism. I must go beyond this and concede that some anti-marginalist suggestions have led in recent years to a number of revisions in the marginal analysis of the firm which amount to the incorporation of other goals besides money profits into expanded marginalist objective functions.

The Alternative Approaches

In their arguments against the profit-maximization model the various alternative approaches to the theory of the firm are very much alike; only their positive programs can distinguish them.

The program of behaviorism is to reject preconceptions and assumptions and to rely only on observation of overt behavior. Thus, behaviorism rejects the assumption of marginal analysis that economic action is directed by the objective to maximize the attainment of ends with given means, and that business action can be deduced from a postulate that firms attempt to maximize money profits. Instead, we are directed to *observe* how businessmen really act and by what processes they reach decisions.

Perhaps it is not entirely fair to suggest here an association between "behaviorism" and the working program of the proponents of a "behavioral theory of the firm" [10]. In any case, behavioral research proposes to observe and study the "real processes," in the sense of a "well-defined sequence of behaviors" by which decisions are reached in "actual business organizations." The hope—faithfully inductive—is to develop a theory "with generality beyond the specific firms studied" [10, p. 2]. Such a theory will be based on "four major sub-theories" regarding "organizational *goals*, organizational *expectations*, organizational *choice*, and organizational *control*" [10, p. 21]. It is assumed that five organizational goals—a production goal, an inventory goal, a sales goal, a market-share goal, and the profit goal—become the subject of bargaining among the various members of the "coalition" which make up the business organization but that the goals are continually adapted and are being pressed with varying force [10, pp. 40-43]. The behavior theory of the firm, with regard to the determination of prices and outputs, will run in terms of a "quasi resolution of conflict" within the organization, of an "adaptively rational, multiple-objective process" with responses to "short-run feedback on performance" and with continuing "organizational learning" [10, pp. 269-70].

This behavioral approach has been characterized as striving for "realism in process," in contrast to approaches aiming at more "realism in motivation" [48, p. 11]. Such realism in motivation is felt to be needed chiefly because of the separation of ownership and control in the modern corporation, whose managements have great power and wide discretion.

In principle, I could expect three different views to be taken regarding the relative independence of corporation management: (1) Whereas owners would run their business chiefly with a view to a maximum of money profits, managers run it with several supplementary and partly competing goals in mind. (2) Whereas owners, especially wealthy ones, would often allow nonprofit considerations to enter their decision-making, managers have a sense of dedication and identification with the business that makes them the more single-minded seekers of profits. (3) Even if managers are inclined to indulge in seeking other goals as long as profits look satisfactory, they are as professionals, trained in the art and science of management, able to make better profits than the owners could ever hope to make running their own show.

What consequences can be drawn from this? One attitude would be to stick with the assumption of profit maximization because it is the simplest and is applicable with much less detailed information to the largest field.[1] Another attitude would be to insist on starkest realism with a complete catalogue of goals and indices of their effectiveness in each firm. A third attitude would be to select two or three of the most

---

[1] "To use marginalism in the theory of the firm it is not necessary to assert that firms attempt to maximize money profits only nor to deny that a goodly portion of all business behavior may be nonrational, thoughtless, blindly repetitive, deliberately traditional, or motivated by extra-economic objectives. It merely presupposes that the 'rational-economic' portion of business conduct is by and large sufficiently important to affect what is going on in the world to an extent large enough to warrant analysis; and that the substitution of money profits for a composite of pecuniary and nonpecuniary rewards simplifies the analysis so much that the gain in expediency far exceeds the loss in applicability" [23 pp. 30-31]. A similar view is expressed by Scitovsky: "Empirical studies of businessmen's behavior suggest the need for modifying or qualifying the assumption of profit maximization here and there, rather than scrapping it altogether. Accordingly, . . . we shall retain the assumption that the firm aims at maximizing its profit. But we shall regard this assumption as a working hypothesis rather than as a universal rule" [37, p. 111].

important managerial objectives of a type that can be reduced to quantitative analysis and to combine them in a single manageable "objective function." This third approach merges marginalism with managerialism in that it integrates money profits with other managerial goals within one formula of "maximizing behavior."

The question is whether managerial marginalism is prescribed for general application or only for so-called noncompetitive cases. Its most prominent proponents prefer to use the old formula, based on profit maximization, in situations where competition is effective and managerial discretion therefore narrowly circumscribed. In the next sections we shall discuss matters that at first blush may seem unrelated to this issue but on reflection can shed indirect light on it.

The Analogy of the Theoretical Automobile Driver

One of the best remembered points in my exposition was the use of an analogy designed to warn against mistaking theoretical variables and their links for realistic descriptions of observable processes. This was the analogy of the "theory of overtaking" automobiles on the highways [21, pp. 534-35].

Analogies are often misleading, but in this particular case it served its main purpose: to show that the theoretical variables need not be estimated and the theoretical equations need not be solved through actual calculation by the actors in the real world whose idealized types are supposed to perform these difficult operations in the models constructed for the explanation of recorded observations.[2] The critics of marginal analysis believed they had refuted it if they could show that the exact numerical calculations of marginal magnitudes—cost, revenue, productivity—were difficult or impossible to perform by real decision-makers.

Yet, my analogy was only partially successful. An implication which should have been obvious has been widely overlooked: that the type of action assumed to be taken by the theoretical actor in the model under specified conditions need not be expected and cannot be predicted actually to be taken by any particular real actor. The empiricist's inclination is to verify the theoretically deduced action by testing individual behavior, although the theory serves only to explain and predict effects of mass behavior.

We may illustrate this again by means of the same analogy, the theory of overtaking. Assume a change of driving conditions occurs, say, that the roads have become wet and slippery and fog has reduced visi-

---

[2] The theoretical automobile driver had to estimate, among other things, the speeds of three vehicles and the distances between them, and to perform calculations involving potential acceleration and a few other things, before he could decide to overtake the truck ahead of him. An actual driver simply "sizes up" the situation and goes ahead.

bility. Theory enables us to predict that traffic will be slower and accidents more frequent, but it does not enable us to predict that any particular driver will drive more slowly or have an accident. The model of the reactions of the individual driver was not designed to explain the actual driving of any particular operator but only to explain the observable consequences of the observed change of conditions by deducing from the model the theoretical reactions of a hypothetical driver.

Our analogy can also show us the limitations of the model: the prediction will hold only if there is a large number of automobiles on the road. If only a very few cars are around, there may be no accident and there need not be a reduction in their speed. Conceivably, the operators may all be good and self-confident drivers. Marginal analysis of hypothetical driver reaction will suffice for explaining and predicting the consequences of a change in driving conditions if the number of automobiles on the highways is large. If the number is small, behavioral research will be needed, though it may or may not be worth the cost.

Still another use can be made of our analogy: to show the vast differences in the scope of questions to which answers can or cannot be expected with the aid of a given theory, for example, from the theory of overtaking as sketched in my article. Compare the following four questions: (1) How fast will traffic move? (2) How fast will the automobile driven by Mr. X move? (3) How will the speed of traffic be affected by fog? (4) How will the speed of Mr. X's driving be affected by fog?

The theory sketched by me offers no answer to the first question, because each of the variables specified may have very different values for different cars and drivers; it has no answer to the second question, and only a suggestion, a rebuttable presumption, for answering the fourth question, because the theory is not really concerned with particular persons or their actions and reactions. The theory is equipped only to answer the third question, regarding the effects of a change in driving conditions on automobile traffic in general, and even this answer will be qualitative only, without good clues to numerical results. It may be interesting to get answers to all four questions, but since Question 3 can be answered with a fraction of the information that would be needed to answer the other questions, it would be foolish to burden the models designed for Question 3 with irrelevant matters, or to reject such models because they cannot do what they are not designed to do.[3]

<hr>

[3] A behavioral theory of automobile driving would probably study the process by which the decision to pass a truck is arrived at in a sequence of bickering among the members of the family: Mama and Sis trying to argue against taking an unnecessary risk, Sonny egging on his Dad to speed up and pass the truck "crawling" ahead of them. Moreover, the theory would not be satisfied with "explaining" the decision to overtake but it would

Confusion of Purposes

The same sort of confusion about the scope of problems and models for their solution has been fostered in recent writings on the theory of the firm: models have been condemned or rejected because they could not be used for purposes for which they had not been designed, and significant differences in the questions to be answered have been obscured or underemphasized.

Let us again pose four typical questions and see which of them we might expect to answer with the aid of "price theory." (1) What will be the prices of cotton textiles? (2) What prices will the X Corporation charge? (3) How will the prices of cotton textiles be affected by an increase in wage rates? (4) How will the X Corporation change its prices when wage rates are increased?

Conventional price theory is not equipped to answer any but the third question; it may perhaps also suggest a rebuttable answer to the fourth question. But Questions 1 and 2 are out of reach. We could not obtain all the information that would be required for their answers and there is, therefore, no use burdening the models with variables remaining silent and inactive throughout the show.

We ought to guard against an easy misunderstanding of our denial that conventional price theory can predict actual prices of specified goods. Prediction of future prices of a particular commodity may in fact be quite manageable if we know its present price. It should be obvious, however, that this is Question 3, not Question 1. Or, one may be able to predict prices on the basis of good information on production cost. But this presupposes that we know the demand for the commodity and assume it will remain unchanged; which again comes down essentially to evaluations of changes of some variables with others held constant, that is, to Question 3.

If the number of firms producing cotton textiles is large and the X Corporation does not supply a very large part of the aggregate output of the industry, price theory may suggest an answer to Question 4, although this is not the purpose of the theory and there may be a considerable chance for the suggested answer to be wrong. The point is that a model of a theoretical firm in an industry consisting of a large number of firms can do with a much smaller number of assumptions, provided the model is used to predict, not the actual reactions of any one particular firm, but only the effects of the hypothetical reactions of numerous anonymous "reactors" (symbolic firms). If it were to be applied to predictions of reactions of a particular firm, the model would have to

---

also wish to determine the speed of driving, the frequency and length of stops at roadside stands, and all the rest.

FRITZ MACHLUP

be much more richly endowed with variables and functions for which information could be obtained only at considerable effort and with results that may or may not be worth the cost of the required research.

My charge that there is widespread confusion regarding the purposes of the "theory of the firm" as used in traditional price theory refers to this: The model of the firm in that theory is not, as so many writers believe, designed to serve to explain and predict the behavior of real firms; instead, it is designed to explain and predict changes in observed prices (quoted, paid, received) as effects of particular changes in conditions (wage rates, interest rates, import duties, excise taxes, technology, etc.). In this causal connection the firm is only a theoretical link, a mental construct helping to explain how one gets from the cause to the effect.[4] This is altogether different from explaining the behavior of a firm. As the philosopher of science warns, we ought not to confuse the *explanans* with the *explanandum*.

Misplaced Concreteness

To confuse the firm as a theoretical construct with the firm as an empirical concept, that is, to confuse a heuristic fiction with a real organization like General Motors or Atlantic & Pacific, is to commit the "fallacy of misplaced concreteness." This fallacy consists in using theoretic symbols as though they had a direct, observable, concrete meaning.

In some fields, investigators are protected from committing the fallacy, at least with regard to some of their problems, by the fact that a search for any empirical counterpart to the theoretical construct seems hopeless. Thus, some physicists working on particle theory were able

---

[4] The same statement can be made about the household. The "household" in price theory is not an object of study; it serves only as a theoretical link between changes in prices and changes in labor services supplied and in consumer goods demanded. The hypothetical reactions of an imaginary decision-maker on the basis of assumed, internally consistent preference functions serve as the simplest and heuristically satisfactory explanation of empirical relationships between changes in prices and changes in quantities. In other words, the household in price theory is not an object of study.

Behavioral studies of real households are something entirely different. A realistic, behavioral theory of the household might conceivably distinguish the large, children-dominated household from a simpler, father-dominated one. The decisions in the children-dominated household, where mother frequently and father occasionally try to exercise some influence, are probably not consistent, since different preference systems are made explicit at various times, with varying decibels and gestures deployed to make them prevail over the preferences of other members of the family.

One can imagine studies on the behavior of particular households selected at random or in structured samples. If the researcher learns that a spoiled brat in a family wants to eat nothing but beef and throws a tantrum every time his mother tries to feed him other kinds of meat, a reduction in the price of chicken will probably not substantially increase the consumption of chicken in this family. Thus, the weight of the child's taste in the decision process of the family can explain a low elasticity of its demand for chicken. But none of this has much bearing on general price theory.

to answer the question "Does the Neutrino Really Exist?" [11, pp. 139-41] laconically with "Who cares?" and to explain that any belief in the "real existence" of atoms, electrons, neutrinos, and all the rest, would hold up the progress of our knowledge. Some biologists working in genetics warned, after empirical genes were discovered, that these "operational genes" should not be confused with the "hypothetical genes," which had been useful constructs in explanatory models before the discovery of any empirical referents [42, p. 814]. Economists, however, know for sure that firms exist as empirical entities and, hence, they have a hard time keeping the theoretical firm and the empirical firm apart.

For certain economic problems the existence of the firm is of the essence. For example, if we study the size distribution of firms or the growth of the firm, the organization and some of its properties and processes are the very objects of the investigation. In such studies we insist on a high degree of correspondence between the model (the thought-object) and the observed object. For other problems, however, as for problems of competitive-price theory, any likeness between the theoretical construct of the firm and the empirical firm is purely coincidental.

Economists trained in scientific methodology understand this clearly. I might quote a dozen or more writers, but will confine myself to one quotation, which states that "in economic analysis, the business firm is a postulate in a web of logical connections" [15, p. 196]. Let me add the statement of another writer, who however was plaintiff rather than advocate when he wrote that "It is a fascinating paradox that the received theory of the firm, by and large, assumes that the firm does not exist" [45, p. 249].

Here is what I wrote on one of the several occasions when I have discussed this problem:

> . . . the firm in the model world of economic micro-theory ought not to call forth any irrelevant associations with firms in the real world. We know, of course, that there are firms in reality and that they have boards of directors and senior and junior executives, who do, with reference to hundreds of different products, a great many things—which are entirely irrelevant for the microtheoretical model. The fictitious firm of the model is a "uni-brain," an individual decision-unit that has nothing to do but adjust the output and the prices of one or two imaginary products to very simple imagined changes in data [26, p. 133].

I went on, of course, to say that this purely fictitious single-minded firm, helpful as it is in competitive-price theory, will not do so much for us in the theory of monopoly and oligopoly. To explain and predict price reactions under monopoly and oligopoly we need more than the

FRITZ MACHLUP

construct of a profit-maximizing reactor.[5] I shall come back to this after discussing the demands for "more realistic" assumptions where they are plainly irrelevant and therefore out of place.

Realistic Models of the Firm under Competition

Many of the proponents and protagonists of a more realistic theory of the firm are quite aware of the fact that the managerial extension and enrichment of the concept of the firm was not needed except where firms in the industry were large and few, and not under the pressure of competition. There are many very quotable statements to this effect.[6]

Too many students, however, want a realistic model of the firm for all purposes. They forget the maxim of Occam's Razor that unnecessary terms in a theory be kept out (or shaved off). These students seem to miss in a simplified model the realistic trimmings of the observable world; they distrust such a model because it is obviously

[5] You may wonder whether I have changed my mind on these matters. Incidentally, I hold that it is important for scholars and scientists to have an open mind, and the only evidence showing that they do are instances in which they have actually changed their minds. On this particular issue, however, I cannot oblige. Whether I am right or wrong, I have been consistent regarding these points. Let me quote from an article I wrote 28 years ago: "The problem of oligopoly is by definition the problem of the effects of the actions of few, giving a greater importance to the behavior of each member of the group. . . . The theory of the oligopoly price involves an interpretation of the significant motives behind the actions of a small number of people. . . . Even the most superficial theory will have to include many more ideal types of behavior in order to handle the problem of *few* sellers than it takes to handle the problem of a *mass* of competitive sellers" [20, p. 235].

On the other hand, I must plead guilty to a charge of the same error of misplaced concreteness against which I have just warned. It occurred in a sentence in which I spoke of various magnitudes (subjectively) "perceived or fancied by the men whose decisions or actions are to be explained (the business men) . . ." [21, p. 521]. If this sentence referred only to oligopolistic or monopolistic behavior, it would not be so bad, for, as I said above, the theoretical constructs of decision-makers in this case have a closer correspondence to real businessmen than the constructs in the theory of competitive prices. But the sentence was supposed to apply to the constructs of the firm in any position whatever. Hence it was a misleading sentence in that (1) it gave the impression that the decision-makers in question were *real* men (real businessmen, whom you could interview) and (2) it said that the actions of these men were to be explained, whereas the purpose of the theory was not to explain observed actions but only observable *results* of imagined (postulated) reactions to observable events.

I apologize for this error. Not that I do not approve of a busy shuttle-traffic between the domain of theoretical construction and the domain of empirical observation, but we must never fail to specify the side of the frontier on which we happen to be. The theoretical terms may have empirical referents (counterparts), but to believe, or allow an impression of belief, that the two are identical is a methodological fallacy.

[6] "When the conditions of competition are relaxed . . . the opportunity set of the firm is expanded. In this case, the behavior of the firm as a distinct operating unit is of separate interest. Both for purposes of interpreting particular behavior within the firm as well as for predicting responses of the industry aggregate, it may be necessary to identify the factors that influence the firm's choices within this expanded opportunity set and embed these in a formal model" [48, pp. 2-3].

"descriptively false." In view of this sentimental hankering for realism, it may be helpful to survey some of the inclusions which various writers have proposed in order to meet the demands for greater realism in the "theory of the firm," and to examine their relevance to the theory of competitive price. The following considerations are supposed to supplement, qualify, restrict, or replace the objective of maximizing money profits.

(1) Entrepreneurs and managers cannot be expected to have an inelastic demand for leisure; indeed, one must assume that this demand is income-elastic so that higher profit expectations will cause them to sacrifice some income for the sake of more leisure [36, p. 356]. (2) Managers are anxious to avoid resentment on the part of their colleagues and subordinates and will, therefore, not enforce their orders with the sternness required for maximization of profits; similarly, minor functionaries do not want to disturb the routines of their superiors and, hence, they often abstain from suggesting improvements which would maximize profits [31, p. 452]. (3) Managers are more interested in their own salaries, bonuses, and other emoluments, than in the profits of the firm or the income of its owners [27, pp. 226-27]. (4) The realization of certain asset preferences (for example, liquidity as against inventories and fixed assets) may be in conflict with profit maximization [5, p. 99]. (5) The flow and biased screening of information through the various levels of management may cause systematic misinformation resulting in earnings far below the maximum obtainable [27, p. 229]. (6) The objective of maintaining control in the hands of the present control group may require a sacrifice of profit opportunities [31, p. 455]. (7) The preference for security may be so strong that even relatively conservative ways of making higher profits are eschewed [12, pp. 270-71]. (8) The striving for status, power, and prestige may be such that it results in conduct not consistent with a maximum of profit [1, p. 145] [28, p. 207] [13, p. xii] [27, p. 227]. (9) The wish to serve society, be a benefactor, or soothe one's social conscience, may militate against actions or policies that would maximize profits [7, pp. 16-17] [13, pp. 339-40]. (10) The instinct of workmanship [46, p. 187], a desire to show professional excellence [1, p. 146], a pervasive interest in feats of engineering, may lead to performance in conflict with highest possible profits. (11) Compromises among the different goals of executives with different interests—production, sales, personnel relations, finance, research and development, public relations, etc.—are sure to "compromise" the objective of maximum profits [10, p. 29]. (12) A variety of influences may be exerted on management decisions, perhaps pulling in different directions and possibly away from maximum profits, as for example influences from labor organizations, suppliers of materials,

customers, bankers, government agencies [13, p. 340] [12, p. 270] [28, pp. 195-205].

I shall not prolong this catalogue even if it is far from complete. Let us admit that each of the possible deviations from maximum profit may be "real" in some circumstances. But how effective and significant are they? If the industry is effectively competitive—and it does not have to be "purely" competitive or "perfectly" competitive—is there much of a chance that the direction in which firms react, through their decisions regarding prices, inputs and output, to a change in conditions would be turned around by any of the "forces" listed? Before we say apodictically no, we should examine a few of the reservations.

Security and Managerial Coordination

Let us single out two items which have been given especially wide play: the "objective of security" and the question of "managerial co-ordination."

The demand for the recognition of a separate "security motive" conflicting with the profit motive deserves a good discussion. But when I prepared for it, I reread what I had written on this subject and found that I could not improve on it. Will you do me the favor of reading it [23, pp. 51-53 and 424-28] and, if you like it, make your students read it?

That there are no business profits without risks and that there is not much point in treating the two quite separately; that it would be silly to call a decision one of profit-maximizing if it increased risk and uncertainty so much as to reduce the chance of survival; that the notion of long-run profits comprises all considerations of risks of loss; that, in terms of my automobile-driving analogies, only a fool would assume that maximization of speed means driving 120 miles an hour regardless of curves and bumps; these are some of the things that have to be said in this connection. But the most essential point to be made is that in the economics of *adjustment to change* the issues of security, survival, and maximum profit are merged. How primitive again to confuse new ventures and daring moves with mere responses to stimuli, obvious reactions to change. If a change in conditions calls for a certain reaction in the name of maximum profits, the very same reaction is called for also in the name of security of survival.

The other matter is of a more "behavioral" nature: the coordination of different goals and judgments on the part of different members of the management and the deviations from profit maximization that may be involved in the process. Frankly, I cannot quite see what great difference organizational matters are supposed to make in the firm's price reactions to changes in conditions. Assume, for example, the import duties on foreign products competing with the products of domestic industry are raised, with a resulting increase in the demand for the products of the firm. Why should the clashes and compromises of divergent opinions reverse the direction of the change that would be "dictated" by the simple rule of profit maximization? Perhaps one vice president wants to raise prices without increasing output, while another wants to increase output without (at least at the moment) raising prices. No matter what their compromise will be, it is likely to conform with what the simple rule suggests. But if not, so what? Remember we are talking about industries with more than a few firms and with free entry.[7]

Other Qualifications to Competitive Price Theory

Substitution between income and leisure looks like the strongest reason for a qualification in cases in which the change in conditions is such that not only the locus of maximum profits is shifted but also the amount of profit obtainable is changed. Take again the example of a tariff increase shutting out foreign competition. The firms in the industry will find that given outputs will now fetch higher prices and that increased outputs can be sold at prices higher than those prevailing before tariffs were raised. And profits will be higher in any case, so that managers—even owner-managers—will be inclined to relax their efforts. Yet would anybody seriously argue that the substitution of leisure (coffee breaks, cocktail parties, golf) for potential profits would be such that total output would be reduced instead of increased? It is not a likely story, and where the industry consists of several or many firms, the small probability vanishes quickly. What remains of the argument is that total output would increase, in reaction to the tariff increase, somewhat less than it would if the managers were eager beavers and did not relax in their efforts when profits increased. Thus, the elasticity of supply of the products in question is a little smaller. But since we do not know how much it would be anyhow, the unknown substraction from an unknown number should not cause the economic theorist any serious anxieties. (And if the politicians who push for the tariff increase decide to push less hard if we tell them that their friends in the industry will enjoy some of the added protection in the form of more leisure and recreation, we would not really mind.)

Even if formal accuracy demanded that we accept the maximization of the decision-maker's total utility as the basic assumption, simplicity and fruitfulness speak for sticking with the postulate of maximization of money profits for situations in which competition is effective. The question is not whether the firms of the real world will *really* max-

---

[7] A great champion of more realistic theories of the firm summed up his reflections on their implications for general economics with this statement: "We shall not be far wrong in concluding . . . that the impact of more realistic theories of the firm on static price analysis is likely to be small" [6, p. 42].

imize money profits, or whether they even *strive* to maximize their money profits, but rather whether the *assumption* that this is the objective of the theoretical firms in the artificial world of our construction will lead to conclusions—"inferred outcomes"—very different from those derived from admittedly more realistic assumptions.

The second qualification in my list—regarding bosses, colleagues and subordinates—is quite irrelevant, except perhaps for questions of welfare economics, where it matters whether firms "really" do all they can to maximize efficiency. For theories concerned with *changes* in prices, inputs, and outputs in response to *changes* to conditions (of production, resource availability, and product demand) the strictness with which efficiency is watched in the firm does not matter. The effects of the tariff increase in our illustration, or the effects of changes in wage rates, interest rates, tax rates, and so forth, are if there is effective competition, essentially independent of the relations among the various levels in the managerial hierarchy of the firm.

It would take too much time here to go through our entire list of reservations. Anybody who makes the effort will find that some of the "realistic assumptions" proposed for inclusion in the theory can affect (by an unknown amount) the magnitude but not the direction of any change that is likely to result from a specified change in conditions; and that other assumptions will not even do that much. In short, they are all irrelevant for purposes of competitive price theory.

Oligopoly, Monopoly, and Managerial Discretion

I repeat: In the theory of competitive price the "real existence" of firms is irrelevant; imaginary (postulated) agents pursuing a simple (postulated) goal react to assumed changes in conditions and thereby produce (or allow us to infer) changes in prices, inputs, and outputs [24, pp. 13-14]. The correspondence between these inferences (deduced changes) and actual observations (observed changes in prices, inputs, and outputs, following observed changes in conditions) is close for two reasons: (1) The number of firms in the real world is so large that it suffices if some of them react as posited by the theory; and (2) the profits of firms are only about "normal," that is, excess profits are about zero, because of competitive pressures from newcomers (pliopolistic pressures [23, pp. 211-23]), so that profits below the maximum obtainable would in fact be net losses in an economic sense.

These two reasons do not hold in the theories of oligopoly and monopoly price.[8] For these theories the real existence of firms (that is, an

---

[8] The idea that profit maximization is the appropriate hypothesis for the theory of competitive price but not necessarily for the theory of monopoly or oligopoly price has been expressed repeatedly over the last century.

Pareto, for example, said that "pure economics" cannot tell us anything about the con-

empirical counterpart to the theoretical construct) is required, because the explanation of changes in prices, inputs, and outputs is at the same time an explanation of decisions of some particular firms, in the sense of organizations of men acting in particular, sometimes unpredictable, ways. Various attempts have been made to develop patterns of oligopolistic and monopolistic conduct and to correlate these patterns with types of organization or with types of personalities exercising ultimate decision-making power. The success has thus far been small; even if the decision-making (say, pricing) in a particular firm was sometimes satisfactorily modeled (for example, in a simulated computer program), the model has usually not been transferable to other cases, to predict decisions in other firms. I do not recall, moreover, that the behavior patterns in these cases were shown to be inconsistent with the postulate of profit maximization.

Under these circumstances, retreat to simpler, less realistic models of firms in oligopoly and monopoly positions is indicated. The first approach is to apply the polypolistic model, in full awareness that the actual facts are entirely different. In many instances the use of the polypolistic model for situations which in our judgment would merit to be labeled as oligopolistic will still yield satisfactory explanations and predictions. Where this is not so, the analyst will resort to the use of models of oligopolistic or monopolistic firms, postulating the simplest possible pattern of action and reaction, dispensing with all peculiar attitudes and "special" strategies. Only where these simple models of oligopolistic and monopolistic firms yield quite unsatisfactory predictions will the analyst need to go further, to more special types of behavior, provided he finds it worth while. It depends on the research interests and on the problems under examination how much effort one wishes to invest in behavioral research where the findings hold little promise of yielding generalizations of wide applicability.

There are, however, some simple models of oligopolistic behavior

tinuing shifts of position of competing oligopolists, and we have to turn to "the observation of facts," which would show us the variety of possibilities [29, pp. 601-2].

Schumpeter, in 1928, had this to say about the dichotomy: "We have much less reason to expect that monopolists will . . . charge an equilibrium price than we have in the case of perfect competition; for competing producers *must* charge it as a rule under penalty of economic death, whilst monopolists, although having a *motive* to charge the monopolistic equilibrium price, are not forced to do so, but may be prevented from doing so by other motives" [33, p. 371].

Finally, Scitovsky in 1951 stated that "not only does the monopolist's secure market position enable him to relax his efforts of maximizing profit, but his very position may prevent his aiming at maximum profit. He may regard his immunity from competition as precarious or be afraid of unfavorable publicity and public censure; and for either reason, he may judge it wiser to refrain from making full use of his monopoly position. We conclude, therefore, that although in some cases the monopolist will aim at maximizing his profit . . . in other cases—which may well be the important ones—he will refrain from maximizing profit" [37, p. 377].

FRITZ MACHLUP

which seem to be of sufficiently wide applicability. A model that equips the oligopolistic decision-maker not under heavy competitive pressure with an objective of gross-revenue ("sales") maximization, subject to the constraint of satisfactory net-revenue ("profit") [2, p. 49], succeeds in explaining the lack of response to some cost-increasing events observed in several instances. There are other simple models explaining the same phenomenon, and one may think of good reasons for finding one model or another more satisfactory. If the sales-maximization hypothesis can explain a greater variety of observed responses or nonresponses than other hypotheses can, and if it seems to correspond better with self-interpretations offered by interviewed businessmen, it merits acceptance, at least for the time being.

An alternative to the maximization of sales is the maximization of the growth rate of sales [3, p. 1086]. This hypothesis is especially interesting because it involves an endogenous relation with profits: while some of the growth of gross revenue may encroach on profits, it does so with an automatic limit in that profits are needed to finance the investment required for the growth of sales.

Another extension of the objective function proposed on the basis of behavioral research combines two managerial preferences for specific expenses of the firm with the usual profit motive. The two additional motives are expenditures for staff personnel and expenditures for managerial emoluments; both figure prominently in the utility functions of executives of companies which, sheltered from competitive pressures, make enough profits to allow management to indulge in these personal desires [48, pp. 38-60].

All these "managerial-discretion models" are simple and sufficiently general to allow relatively wide application. We shall have more to say about them later.

Effective Competition and Managerial Discretion

In mapping out the area of applicability for theories of managerial discretion, we have spoken of "oligopoly," "monopoly," and of "firms not under heavy competitive pressure." These are rather vague guideposts, but unfortunately the literature has not been very helpful in ascertaining precisely what it is that allows or restricts the exercise of wide managerial discretion.

Some writers stress the size of the firm, suggesting that it is only in the *large* firm that management can exercise discretion. Others stress the condition of *diffused ownership* as the one that affords management the opportunity of pursuing objectives other than maximization of profits. Those who stress oligopoly as the domain for which objective functions richer than profit maximization are needed are usually not quite specific as to their criterion of an oligopoly position: it may be *fewness of firms* active in the same industry, or the subjective state of awareness of the *interdependence of price making* often characterized as "conjectural variation," or simply the *absence of aggressive competition for increasing shares in the market.* Others again stress *closed entry,* or absence of newcomers' competition, as the essential condition for a profit level sufficiently comfortable to allow managers to indulge in the satisfaction of objectives other than maximization of profits.

To combine all these conditions would probably be far too restrictive; it would confine the application of managerial-discretion models to large firms with diffused ownership, few competitors, full awareness of interdependence in pricing, absence of agressive efforts by existing competitors to increase their market shares, and little danger of new competitors entering the field. The size of the firm may actually not be relevant, and diffused ownership may not be a necessary condition for some deviations from profit maximization to occur, say, in the interest of larger sales or larger expenditures for staff. Fewness of competitors may be more significant, chiefly because the danger of newcomers' competition is likely to be small where the number of firms has been few and continues to be few; partly also because the few competitors may have learnt that aggressive price competition does not pay. The essential conditions, it seems to me, are these two: that no newcomers are likely to invade the field of the existing firms, and that none of the existing firms tries to expand its sales at such a fast rate that it could succeed only by encroaching on the business of its competitors.

Competition from newcomers, from aggressive expansionists, or from importers is sometimes called "heavy," "vigorous," or "effective." The simplest meaning of these adjectival modifiers is this: a firm is exposed to heavy, vigorous, or effective competition if it is kept under continuing pressure to do something about its sales and its profits position. Under this "competitive pressure" the firm is constantly compelled to react to actual or potential losses in sales and/or reductions in profits, so much so that the firm will not be able to pursue any objectives other than the maximization of profits—for the simple reason that anything less than the highest obtainable profits would be below the rate of return regarded as normal at the time.

I am aware of a defect in this definition: its criterion is lodged in the effect rather than in an independently ascertainable condition. Perhaps, though, "effective" is quite properly defined in this fashion, namely, by whether certain effects are realized: competition is effective if it continually depresses profits to the level regarded as the minimum tolerable. What makes it effective is not part of the definition, but has to be explained by the conditions of entry, aggressive attitudes on the part of existing firms, or imports from abroad.

If my reasoning is accepted, several formulations proposed in the literature will have to be amended. Managerial discretion will be a function, not of the independence of the management from the control of the owners, but chiefly of the independence of the management from urgent worries about the sufficiency of earnings. If one insists, one may still say that all managers are primiarly interested in their own incomes. But, since it is clear that their long-term incomes are jeopardized if profits go below the acceptable rate of return, maximization of managerial incomes and maximization of profits come to to the same thing if competition is effective.[9]

There can be no doubt about the fact that competition is not effective in many industries and that many, very many, firms are not exposed to vigorous competition. It follows that managerial discretion can have its way in a large enough number of firms to secure wide applicability of well-designed managerial-discretion models—or to invite the use of managerial total-utility models.

I was fully aware, when I wrote my 1946 article, that there were many qualifications and exceptions to the principle of profit maximization.[10] But I considered it hopeless for predictive purposes to work with total-utility maximization and I did not see the possibility of combining a few selected managerial goals with the profit motive.

Marginalism Extended: Total Utility

In order to show how hopeless it is to construct a comprehensive total-utility model and obtain from it definite predictions of the effects of changes in conditions upon the dispositions of the managers, one merely has to visualize the large variety of possible "satisfactions" and the still larger variety of things that may contribute to their attain-

---

[9] For competition to be effective it is not necessary that competition is either pure or perfect or that all or any of the markets in which the firm buys or sells are perfect.

[10] Several of my statements, if I presented them without source reference, might well be mistaken for quotations from critics of marginalism, including behavioralists and managerialists. Here are samples [21]: ". . . a business man is motivated by considerations other than the maximization of money profits"; "it is preferable to separate the non-pecuniary factors of business conduct from those which are regular items in the formation of money profits" (p. 526); "one may presume that producing larger production volumes [or] paying higher wage rates . . . than would be compatible with a maximum of money profits may involve for the business man a gain in social prestige or a certain measure of inner satisfaction"; "it is not impossible that considerations of this sort substantially weaken the forces believed to be at work on the basis of a strictly pecuniary marginal calculus"; for patriotic reasons during the war "many firms produced far beyond the point of highest money profits"; "the conflict of interests between the hired managers and the owners of the business" may call for "important qualifications" (p. 527); "the interest of the former in inordinately large outlays or investments may be capable of descriptions in terms of a pecuniary calculus, but it is not maximization of the firm's profits which serves here as the standard of conduct" (pp. 527-28); "maximization of salaries and bonuses of professional managers may constitute a standard of business conduct different from that implied in the customary marginal analysis of the firm"; and "the extent to which the two standards would result in sharply different action under otherwise similar conditions is another open question in need of investigation" (p. 528).

ment. The satisfactions consist not only in receiving money incomes, immediate or deferred, and various incomes in kind, but also in distributing incomes to others and in gaining prestige, power, self-esteem, as well as in enjoying a good conscience and other pleasurable feelings.

What makes things really complicated is that the creation of these satisfactions is related to very different flows of funds into and out of the firm: some to gross revenue (sales volume), others to net revenue; some to profits distributed, others to profits retained; some to investment outlays, others to company expenses. The managers' immediate money incomes and some of the emoluments received in kind are partly at the expense of profits, partly at the expense of corporate income taxes (and every change in tax rates changes the trade-off ratios.) The same is true of several other company expenses which add to the prestige, power, and self-esteem of the managers. Special mention may be made of the provision of stock options for managers, which are either at the expense of the owners' equity (through watering down their stock) or at the expense of potential capital gains on treasury stock earmarked for such stock options, but which, on the other hand, may be a powerful force aligning the managers' personal interests with the goal of maximizing the net profits of the firm.

The point of it all is that the total utility of managers can be increased by decisions which increase expenses at the expense of profits. (Of course, this is confined to situations where profits are high enough to stand encroachments by avoidable expenses—to situations, that is, where the firm is not hard-pressed by competition.) The question is how various changes in conditions will affect managerial decisions on inputs, outputs, and prices if the objectives of management include the gratification of preferences for certain expenses of the firm that compete with the maximization of profits.[11]

---

[11] Instead of cataloguing the various contributions to the "utility" of the management and their relationships to the sources and uses of the firm's funds, one may wish to classify the expenses of the firm with reference to "discretionary" decisions of the management influenced by the decision-makers' preferences. Here is a tentative classification of this sort:

1. Expenses required for the production of (a) current output of unchanged size, (b) additional current output, with marginal cost not exceeding marginal revenue (hence, contributing to higher profits), and (c) additional current output, with marginal cost exceeding marginal revenue (hence, reducing profits).

2. Expenses not required for the production of current output, but increasing the productive capacity or efficiency of the firm for future production.

3. Expenses for managerial personnel in the form of (a) salaries and bonuses, and (b) services rendered to them for their convenience and pleasure.

4. Expenses not required for either current or future production, but (a) expected of a profitable firm as a social service, and only slightly promoting the public image of management, (b) widely recognized as contributing to the social or national benefit and as indicative of the public spirit of the management, (c) contributing chiefly to the gratification of personal desires of supervisory and managerial personnel, and (d) largely

For purposes of illustration let us reproduce in a literary form the utility function of a management (perhaps of its "peak coordinator" [28, pp. 190-91]) in full control and confident that stockholders will not make any fuss as long as the firm makes a "normal" profit and pays out a fair share of it in dividends. Total utility, which the manager by his decisions will try to maximize, will be a function of a large number of variables, by virtue of the contributions they make to his pride, prestige, self-esteem, conscience, comfort, feeling of accomplishment, material consumption, and anticipations of future benefits and pleasures. Among the variables may be total profits of the firm, growth rate of profits, rate of profits to investment, total sales, growth rate of sales, increase in market share, dividends paid out, retained earnings, increase in market value of stock, price-earnings ratio of stock, investment outlay, salary and bonus received, stock options received (capital gains), expense accounts (consumption at company expense), services received (automobile, chauffeur, lovely secretary, theatre tickets, conferences at resorts), size of staff, expenses for public relations and advertising, expenses for research and development, technological and other innovations, leadership in wage increases and good industrial relations, expenses for public or private education and health, other contributions to public interest and patriotic causes, free time for leisure and recreation, and indications of influence over government, industry, and society. This list of variables is, of course, only representative, not exhaustive.[12]

Now what can one do with a utility function of this sort? Will it be of much use in telling us what the firm will do with its freedom of action if it has to respond to a change in conditions?

The answer will depend partly on a simple condition, namely, whether the acceptable trade-off ratios between all the factors contributing to total utility remain unchanged, or approximately the same, if any one of them, say, total profit, increases. If this were the case, we could shout hurrah or sigh a sigh of relief (depending on our temperament). For, if the marginal rates of substitution among all the various "utilifactors" are constant, the distribution of funds among them will remain unchanged with changes in conditions that increase or decrease the total of funds available. Only if the cost of any of the factors

wasteful, that is, contributing nothing, and economizing nothing but managerial effort or capability.

This list may be suggestive of the actions that may have to be taken when, after years of ease and growth, the firm finds its profits declining or disappearing.

[12] Perhaps there ought to be a place on the list for some gratifications that are more stable, less subject to quantitative variation, such as the pleasure of being known for honesty and fairness, on the one hand, and for sharpness and shrewdness, on the other, or at least the pleasure of being convinced of having and exercising these qualities. And last, though not least, there is the general feeling of gratification from "running" a large, well-known profitable, widely respected firm with growing assets and employment.

changed, say, the cost of staff personnel and, hence, the cost of prestige and other benefits that accrue from having a sizable staff, would the marginal rates of substitution be adapted to the new cost relation. In such a case we might also perhaps be able to tell the kind of response of the decision-makers.

Alas, the condition that the marginal rates of substitution are independent of the total funds available is not likely to be satisfied; in addition, certain types of change in conditions have the bad habit of affecting at the same time funds available and relative costs of utilifactors. For example, an increase in the corporate income tax will change the trade-off ratio between expensable outlays and profits in favor of avoidable expenses.

Marginalism Extended: Choice of Maximanda

If we were interested only in a formal solution, and perhaps in a proof of "existence" of an equilibrium position, we might be satisfied with the maximization of total utility by those who effectively run the firm. If, however, we want to predict the direction of the changes which a given change in conditions is likely to bring about, then mere formalism will not be enough. For predictive purposes we need *more* to go by with the help of *fewer* variables. Maximization of money profits is certainly the simplest "objective function," but it works only in the case of firms exposed to vigorous competition. The management of a firm that makes more than enough money need not go all out to maximize profits; it can afford to do a few other things that it likes, such as serving what by its own lights it regards as the national interest or indulging in other luxuries.

Would this imply "giving up" the principle of marginalism in the theory of the profitable firm? This is chiefly a semantic question. I have been inclined to use a more extended definition. In 1946, I called marginalism "the logical process of finding a maximum" [21, p. 519]. I did not say that it had to be maximization of money profits— though I struggled hard to justify the use of profit maximization in all cases. In the meantime several writers have shown that profit maximization may not be a completely unambiguous objective, even where it is used in splendid isolation from all competing goals, in that it may refuse to yield unambiguous conclusions regarding the effects of certain changes, such as the effects of changes in profit taxes. In addition, it has been shown that several workable "objective functions" can be developed that give plausible results with a few relatively simple terms added. Any of these functions that can be maximized, with or without specific constraints, would still be a part of marginal analysis.

The choice of the *maximandum* is of course a pragmatic matter: we should prefer one that yields sufficiently good approximations to what we consider reasonable on the basis of empirical research, with wide applicability and fruitfulness and with great simplicity. The compromise among these goals that we accept is, admittedly, a somewhat "subjective" standard of selection, but perfectly in line with the standard accepted in all scientific fields. Concessions to any one of these desiderata must be at the expense of the others.

Let us list some of the alternative *maximanda* that have been suggested and are available for our choice: Total quasi-rents over a short period of time (But how short? This is good only for a freshman course); total quasi-rents during the service-life of existing fixed assets (But is a replaceable part of a machine a fixed asset? This works only for a one-hoss shay); present value of all profits (after taxes) expected in the future, discounted at a "normal" or "competitive" rate; internal rate of return to equity; equity of controlling stockholders; present values of retained earnings; growth rate of equity; growth rate of total assets; growth rate of gross revenue (sales); gross revenue (sales), if net revenues (profits) are satisfactory (over what period of time?); salaries, bonuses, and other accruals (including services in kind) to management, over their entire lives; all accruals to management plus expenditure for staff personnel, compatible with minimum profits; all accruals to management, consistent with satisfactory profits and gradually rising prices of corporate stock; and, of course, the present values of the various combinations of flows mentioned.

Surely a much longer list could be prepared, but there is no use to this. The point should be clear: profit maximization proper may mean a variety of things—several entries apply to money profits—and in addition there are a few other *maximanda* of possible relevance. Incidentally, if profits or accruals to stockholders are not explicitly included in some of the entries, let no one believe that they are really out of the picture. No management could try to maximize its own accruals in the long run if it completely disregarded the interests of the stockholders. Hence, all *maximanda* are subject to the constraint of some minimum benefits to the owners of the business in the form of dividends, capital gains, or both.[13]

Subjective Information and the Charge of Tautology

I have a few remaining tasks, and one of them is to lay a ghost, one that has long played tricks on economists and led them astray. He has

[13] The four "managerial" variables included in the list—sales, growth of sales, expenses for staff, and emoluments to the management—may well be the most important deviations from profit maximization, although I may easily be persuaded of the existence of other "extravagances" of management. Among the managements of our large corporations there are so many civic-minded men, bursting with social responsibility and cocksure of their ability to know what is in the national interest, that I incline to the thought that rather serious deviations from the profit motive occur in the area of virtuous striving for the so-called

done this in their discussions of the subject of information, its availability, its uncertainty, and its subjectivity. I mean, of course, information available to the "firm," and this raises the question whether we mean the firm as a purely theoretical construct or the firm as an organization of real people or anything else.

The firm as a theoretical construct has exactly the kind of information the theorist chooses to endow it with in order to design a good, useful theory. The firm as an organization of real people has the information system that it actually happens to have and which, in some instances, the management scientists (operations researchers) have succeeded in developing. For purposes of competitive price and allocation theory, it does not make much difference whether the information which we assume the firm to have concerning the conditions of supply, production, and demand under which it works is correct or incorrect, as long as we may safely assume that any *change* in these conditions is registered correctly. If we want to inquire into the effects of a change in wage rates or tax rates or something of this sort, we must of course take it for granted that the decision-makers who supposedly react to the change have taken notice of it. But whether their "previous" store of information—from which they started when the change occurred—was accurate or not will only in exceptional instances make a qualitative difference to the reactions.

This important difference between information about conditions and information about changes in conditions has eluded several writers, who shouted "tautology" when they confronted my statements about the subjectivity of information. They reasoned like this: If firms act on the basis of information which is entirely subjective, then *anything* they do may be said to follow from whatever they believe they know: hence, the assumption of subjectivism defeats any explanatory purposes. This is a sad confusion. In teaching elementary economics we ought to be able to make our students grasp the difference between the shape and position of a curve, on the one hand, and the shift of a curve, on the other. The direction of the effects which we derive from the shift is usually, though not always, independent of the shape and position of the original curve. We need not fuss about the curve reflecting "accurate information" if we only want to see what happens when the curve shifts in a certain direction.

common good. I hope I am not excessively naive if I believe that the excess profits secured through restrictions on competition are to no small extent used for what the discretionary managers believe to be worthy causes. But I see no way of formulating any hypotheses that would enable us to predict either just what the firms' outlays in the public interest will be or how they will affect total output in the long run. I suppose that Boulding's witty question, "do we maximize profit subject to the constraints of morality or do we maximize virtue subject to the constraints of satisfactory profits? [7, p. 17] was not intended to suggest an answer with empirically fertile conclusions.

Since ghosts are hardy creatures, the laying of this one will probably not constitute a once-and-for-all execution. We shall probably see him again thumbing his nose at us in the next textbook or in the next issue of one of our journals.

Imperfect Information and the Question of "Satisficing" Behavior

The same confusion sometimes encumbers the discussions about the alleged "imperfection" of knowledge available to firms for their rational decision-making [39, pp. xxiv-xxvi, 40-41, 81-83, 241-42] and the screens and blockages in "the flow of information through the hierarchies of the organization" [27, pp. 228-29]. But what can be "imperfect" about the information on, say, a tax increase? Why should it take special theories of bureaucracy to explain how the news of a wage increase "flows" through various hierarchical levels up or down or across? Yet this, and this alone, is the information that is essentially involved in the theory of prices and allocation, since it is the *adjustment to such changes* in conditions for which the postulate of maximizing behavior is employed.

One can understand, of course, how the confusion arose. The proponents of managerial analysis have the creditable ambition to reorganize firms in such a way that their managements can really, as a matter of actual fact, maximize the results of their performance, not only in adjusting to changes in conditions, but also in making the most rational arrangements on the basis of the *complete environment* in which they operate.[14] Incidentally, not only "normative micro-economics," as management science has been called [40, p. 279], has this ambition; many propositions of welfare economics are also based on such presuppositions.

As a matter of fact, the interesting distinction made between "satisficing" and "maximizing" or "optimizing" behavior [39, pp. xxiv-xxvi] [40, pp. 262-65] had its origin in precisely the same issue; management, realizing the complexity of the calculations and the imperfection of the data that would have to be employed in any determination of "optimal" decisions, cannot help being satisfied with something less: its behavior will be only "satisficing." What behavior? The mere adjustment to a simple change or the coordinated, integrated whole of its activities? Evidently, only the latter is the overly ambi-

[14] "Economic man deals with the 'real world' in all its complexity," says Herbert Simon [39, p. xxv]. The *homo oeconomicus* I have encountered in the literature was not such a perfectionist. Incidentally, even Simon's "economic man," two years before the ambitious one just quoted, did not have "absolutely complete," but only "impressively clear and voluminous" knowledge of the "relevant aspects of his environment" [38, p. 99]. My point is that we ought to distinguish perfect or imperfect knowledge of (a) the entire environment, (b) the relevant aspects of the entire environment, (c) the relevant changes in environmental conditions.

tious aim. The theory of prices and allocation, viewed as a theory of adjustment to change, does not call for impossible performances.[15] I ask you to remember what I spelled out, twenty years ago, about the difference between exact estimates and calculations, on the one hand, and "sizing up" in nonnumerical terms, on the other [21, pp. 524-25, 534-35]. And I ask you to realize how many more good predictions can be made on the basis of the assumption that firms try to maximize their profits than on the basis of the assumption that they want no more than satisfactory profits. Take one illustration: if an easy-money policy is introduced, we expect that some firms will increase their borrowings, some firms will increase their purchases, some firms will sell at higher prices, and some firms will increase their output. But if everybody was satisfied before the change, we cannot infer any of these things. On the other hand, if we assume that firms prefer a larger profit to a smaller one, all the mentioned consequences follow from the simple model.

The Twenty-one Concepts of the Firm

Several times in this paper I have spoken of the fallacy of misplaced concreteness, committed by mistaking a thought-object for an object of sense perception, that is, for anything in the real, empirical world. My warnings might have given rise to another confusion, namely, that there are only two concepts of the firm. There are many more, and I do not wish to suppress altogether my strong taxonomic propensities. I shall offer a list of ten different contexts calling for even more different concepts, some theoretical, some more empirical.

One of my favorite philosophers, who was a past-master of the art of making fine distinctions, enumerated 13 concepts of "pragmatism" [18], 66 concepts of "nature" [19, pp. 447-56], and "a great number" of concepts of "God."[16] I am sure there are at least 21 concepts of the firm employed in the literature of business and economics,

---

[15] Suppose the government imposes a 15 per cent surcharge on all import duties. The theory of the profit-maximizing firm will without hesitation tell us that imports will decline. What will the theory of the satisficing firm tell us? "Models of satisficing behavior are richer than models of maximizing behavior, because they treat not only of equilibrium but of the method of reaching it as well. Psychological studies of the formation and change of aspiration levels support propositions of the following kinds. (a) When performance falls short of the level of aspiration, search behavior (particularly search for new alternatives of action) is induced. (b) At the same time, the level of aspiration begins to adjust itself downward until goals reach levels that are practically attainable. (c) If the two mechanisms just listed operate too slowly to adapt aspirations to performance, emotional behavior—apathy or aggression, for example—will replace rational adaptive behavior" [40, p. 263]. I admit that this is an unfair use of the theory of satisficing, but I wanted to show that everything has its place and no theory can be suitable to all problems. I suspect, however, that Simon's theory of satisficing behavior will yield neither quantitative nor qualitative predictions.

[16] Lovejoy Denied Approval by Senate Group," *The Baltimore Sun,* April 1, 1951.

but I shall exercise great forbearance and confine myself to a selection. Everyone may join in the game and fill in what I leave out. I shall first state the context, then delimit the concept, and finally add a few words of explanation.

1. In the theory of competitive prices and allocation, the firm is *an imaginary reactor to environmental changes.* By "imaginary" I mean to stress that this a pure construct for which there need not exist an empirical counterpart. By "reactor" I mean to deny that this robot or puppet can ever have a will of his own: he is the theorist's creature, programmed to respond in the predetermined way.

2. In the theory of innovation and growth, the firm is *an imaginary or a typical reactor or initiator.* Depending on which theory one has in mind, we see that several combinations are possible. In the theory of "entrepreneurial innovation" by men of very special qualities [34, pp. 78-94] the entrepreneur is neither imaginary nor a mere reactor; he is a typical initiator. By "typical" I do not refer to the ideal type of German sociology [47, p. 44] [35, pp. 20-63, 81] [25, pp. 21-57], but rather to the common-sense kind of person that many of us have met in person or, at least, have heard about. On the other hand, there are also theories of "induced invention"—assuming latent inventiveness (though an invention can never be a mere reaction)—and theories of "induced growth," employing the construct of the imaginary reactor.

3. In welfare economics, the firm is *an imaginary or a typical reactor or initiator with accurate knowledge of his opportunities.* Depending on the proposition in question, all combinations are again possible, but in any case a new requirement is introduced: accurate knowledge of the environmental conditions on the part of all reactors and initiators. For, in contrast to the theory of price and allocation, the welfare theorist wants to ascertain, not only in which direction price, input, and output will move in response to a change, but also whether this move will increase or reduce welfare. For such an exercise it is no longer irrelevant whether the subjective information of the firms is correct or false.

4. In the theory of oligopoly and monopoly, the firm is *a typical reactor and initiator in a small (or zero) interacting group.* I have explained earlier why a theory of oligopoly with nothing but imaginary reactors may not be widely applicable.

5. In the theory of organization (or bureaucracy), the firm is *a typical cooperative system with authoritative coordination.* I have accepted this formulation from one of the authorities [28, p. 187] and thus may disclaim responsibility for it.

6. In management science (or the art of business management), the firm is *a functional information system and decision-making system*

for typical business operations. The normative nature of management science should be stressed. Several management scientists include operations research among the agenda of management science. I take this to mean that the principal techniques of operations research of such matters as inventory problems, replacement problems, search problems, queueing problems, and routing problems have to be mastered by the management scientist. He should, however, make a distinction between the science and its application: the science deals with typical systems, but is applied to particular cases.

7. In operations research and consultation, the firm is *an actual or potential client for advice on optimal performance.* In this context the reference is not to the techniques and principles of operations research but rather to the particular projects planned or undertaken.

8. In accounting theory, the firm is *a collection of assets and liabilities.* It should be clear how different this concept is from most of the others.

9. In legal theory and practice, the firm is *a juridical person with property, claims, and obligations.* This may be a very deficient formulation; I defer to the experts, who will surely correct it.

10. In statistical description (such as the Census of Manufactures) the firm is *a business organization under a single management or a self-employed person with one or more employees or with an established place of business.* I have adopted here the definition used by the U.S. Census.

This exercise should have succeeded in showing how ludicrous the efforts of some writers are to attempt *one* definition of *the* firm as used in economic analysis, or to make statements supposedly true of "the" firm, or of "its" behavior, or what not. Scholars ought to be aware of equivocations and should not be snared by them.

A Sense of Proportion

I hope there will be no argument about which concept of the firm is the most important or the most useful. Since they serve different purposes, such an argument would be pointless. It would degenerate into childish claims about one area of study being more useful than another.

I also hope the specialist who uses one concept of the firm will desist from trying to persuade others to accept his own tried and trusted concept for entirely different purposes. The concept of the firm in organization theory, for example, need not at all be suitable for accounting theory or legal theory; and I know it is not suitable for either competitive price theory or for oligopoly theory.

Most of the controversies about the "firm" have been due to misunderstandings about what the other specialist was doing. Many people cannot understand that others may be talking about altogether different things when they use the same words.

I am not happy about the practice of calling any study just because it deals with or employs a concept of the firm "economics" or "microeconomics." But we cannot issue licenses for the use of such terms and, hence, must put up with their rather free use. My own prejudices balk at designating organization theory as economics—but other people's prejudices are probably different from mine, and we gain little or nothing from arguing about the correct scope of our field.

Now what conclusions from all our reviewing may we draw on the conflicts between marginal analysis, behavioral theory, and managerial theory of the firm? Fortunately, not much time is being wasted on descriptive studies of a narrowly behaviorist kind, in the sense of recording observed behavior without any prior theoretical design. Most proponents of behavioral studies of the firm are too competent theorists for that. As far as the proponents of managerial theories are concerned, they have never claimed to be anything but marginalists, and the behavior goals they have selected as worthy for incorporation into behavior equations, along with the goal of making profits, were given a differentiable form so that they could become part of marginal analysis.[17] Thus, instead of a heated contest between marginalism and managerialism in the theory of the firm, a marriage between the two has come about.

Not all marriages, these days, are permanent; divorces are frequent. Whether this marriage will last or end in divorce will depend chiefly on what offspring it will produce. If the match of the profit hypothesis with the various managerial hypotheses proves fertile of sufficiently interesting deductions, the prospects of a lasting marriage are good.

It is not easy to judge the future sterility or fertility of this marriage between marginalism and managerialism, because most of us are inclined to underrate the kinds of problem on which we have never

---

[17] While under profit maximization $MR-MC=0$, sales maximization requires that $MR=0$; hence, for some of the output sold marginal revenue is less than marginal cost, which cuts into profits. A minimum-profit constraint sets a limit to this.

In the case of maximization of the growth rate of sales the limit on nonremunerative selling is built into the objective itself because a growth of productive assets is required to support the growth of sales, and the acquisition of these assets presupposes a sufficiency of profits, either for internal financing or as a basis for outside finance [3, pp. 1086-87]. If at any time sales were pushed too hard at the expense of profits, there would arise a shortage of funds for acquiring the productive assets needed for producing more output. Thus no separate minimum-profit constraint has to be imposed, since it is inherent in the objective of maximization of the growth of sales. It should be understood, however, that the growth rate of assets under this objective is still less than it could be under straight profit maximization. (This shows why we should never speak of the "growth of the firm" without specifying by what criterion we measure it.)

worked: we have a bias in favor of our own research experience. Most of the researchers on behavioral versions of the theory of the firm look for their problems to the records of selected large corporations. They take it for granted that their theory must be designed to explain and predict the behavior of these firms. This, however, is less so in the case of economists engaged in the analysis of relative prices, inputs, and outputs. They look for their problems to the records of entire industries or industrial sectors. To be sure, some industries are dominated by large corporations, yet the accent of the analysis is not on the behavior of these firms but at best on some of the results of that behavior. Where the focus is not on the behavior of the firm, a theory that requires information on particular firms to be "plugged in" seems to them less serviceable than a more general theory, at least as long as only qualitative, not numerical, results are sought. Hence, even if the "partial-equilibrium analyst" knows full well that the actual situation is not a really competitive one, he probably will still make a first try using the competitive model with good old-fashioned profit maximization. And if the results appear too odd, appropriate qualifications may still be able to take care of them more simply than if he had started with a cumbersome managerial model. (In saying this, I am showing my bias.)

It is revealing to ask what kind of theory we would apply, at least in a first approximation, if we were called upon to predict the results of various kinds of public-policy measures. For questions regarding short-run effects of changes in the corporation income tax (or an excess-profits tax) I believe a strong case can be made in favor of a model of the firm with some managerial variables. If the problem is whether an increase in cigarette taxes is likely to be fully shifted onto the consumer or what portion of it may be absorbed by the producers, I may feel safer with a model that includes managerial objectives. If, however, the problem is what qualitative effects an increase in the import duty on a material used in several industries will have on its imports and on the prices and outputs of the various products of the industries in question, I would be inclined to work with the simple hypothesis of profit maximization. I would find it far too cumbersome in this case to go down to the level of the "real" firms; I could probably not obtain the necessary data and, even if I did, I might not be able to rely on the composite results obtained from a firm-by-firm analysis. The old theory of the firm, where all firms are pure fictions, may give me—in this case—most of the answers, in a rough and ready way, not with any numerical precision, but with sufficient reliability regarding the directions of change.

I conclude that the choice of the theory has to depend on the problem we have to solve.[18] Three conditions seem to be decisive in assigning the type of approach to the type of problem. The simple marginal formula based on profit maximization is suitable where (1) *large groups* of firms are involved and nothing has to be predicted about particular firms, (2) the effects of a *specified change* in conditions upon prices, inputs, and outputs are to be explained or predicted rather than the values of these magnitudes before or after the change, and nothing has to be said about the "total situation" or general developments, and (3) only *qualitative answers,* that is, answers about directions of change, are sought rather than precise numerical results. Managerial marginalism is more suitable to problems concerning particular firms and calling for numerical answers. And, I am sure, there are also some problems to which behavioral theory may be the most helpful approach. My impression is that it will be entirely concerned with particular firms and perhaps designed to give answers of a normative, that is, advisory nature.

It looks as if I had prepared the ground for a love feast: I have made polite bows in all directions and have tuned up for a hymn in praise of peaceful coexistence of allegedly antagonistic positions. But I cannot help raising a question which may tear open some of the wounds of the battle of 1946. The question is whether the effects of an effective increase in minimum wages upon the employment of labor of low productivity can, at our present state of knowledge, be fruitfully analyzed with any other model than that of simple marginalism based on unadulterated profit maximization.

If I answer in the negative, does this mean that we are back at the old quarrel and have not learned anything? It does not mean this. Deficiencies in marginal analysis have been shown and recognized; and a great deal of good empirical as well as theoretical work has been accomplished. But the deficiencies dealt with were not just those which the critics twenty years ago attacked. That attack questioned the applicability of marginal analysis to the employment effects of wage increases in industries with many firms presumably under heavy competition [16, pp. 64, 75-77]. In such circumstances the managerial theories of the firm, according to their proponents, do not apply. On this narrow issue, therefore, the old-type marginalist cannot retreat.

[18] As a matter of fact, it will also depend on the research techniques which the appointed analyst has learned to master; we can eliminate this bias by assuming an ideal analyst equally adept in all techniques.

REFERENCES

1. C. I. BARNARD, *Functions of the Executive.* Cambridge, Mass. 1938.
2. W. J. BAUMOL, *Business Behavior, Value and Growth.* New York 1959.

3. ———, "On the Theory of the Expansion of the Firm," *Am. Econ. Rev.*, Dec. 1962, *52*, 1078-87.

4. ———, *Economic Theory and Operations Analysis*, 2nd ed. Englewood Cliffs, N.J. 1965.

5. K. E. BOULDING, *A Reconstruction of Economics*. New York 1950.

6. ———, "Implications for General Economics of More Realistic Theories of the Firm," *Am. Econ. Rev.*, Proc., May 1952, *42*, 35-44.

7. ———, "Present Position of the Theory of the Firm," in K. E. Boulding and W. A. Spivey, *Linear Programming and the Theory of the Firm*, New York 1960, pp. 1-17.

8. E. H. CHAMBERLIN, *The Theory of Monopolistic Competition; A Reorientation of the Theory of Value*. Cambridge, Mass. 1933.

9. A. A. COURNOT, *Recherches sur les principes mathématiques de la théorie des richesses*, Paris 1838. English transl. by N. T. Bacon under the title *Researches into the Mathematical Principles of the Theory of Wealth*, New York 1897, reprinted 1927.

10. R. M. CYERT AND J. G. MARCH, *Behavioral Theory of the Firm*. Englewood Cliffs, N.J. 1963.

11. S. M. DANCOFF, "Does the Neutrino Really Exist?" *Bull. Atomic Scientists*, June 1952, *8*, 139-41.

12. R. A. GORDON, "Short-Period Price Determination in Theory and Practice," *Am. Econ. Rev.*, June 1948, *38*, 265-88.

13. ———, *Business Leadership in the Large Corporation*, 2nd ed. with a new preface, Berkeley 1961.

14. R. L. HALL AND C. J. HITCH, "Price Theory and Business Behaviour," *Oxford Econ. Papers*, May 1939, *2*, 12-45. Reprinted in T. Wilson, ed., *Oxford Studies in the Price Mechanism*, Oxford 1951, pp. 107-38.

15. S. R. KRUPP, "Theoretical Explanation and the Nature of the Firm," *Western Econ. Jour.*, Summer 1963, *1*, 191-204.

16. R. A. LESTER, "Shortcomings of Marginal Analysis for Wage-Employment Problems," *Am. Econ. Rev.*, March 1946, *36*, 63-82.

17. ———, "Marginalism, Minimum Wages, and Labor Markets," *Am. Econ. Rev.*, March 1947, *37*, 135-48.

18. A. O. LOVEJOY, "The Thirteen Pragmatisms," *Jour. Philosophy*, Jan. 2, 1908, *8*, 5-12, 29-39. Reprinted in *The Thirteen Pragmatisms and Other Essays*, Baltimore 1963.

19. A. O. LOVEJOY AND G. BOAS, *Primitivism and Related Ideas in Antiquity*. Baltimore 1935.

20. F. MACHLUP, "Evaluation of the Practical Significance of the Theory of Monopolistic Competition," *Am. Econ. Rev.*, June 1939, *29*, 277-36.

21. ———, "Marginal Analysis and Empirical Research," *Am. Econ. Rev.*, Sept. 1946, *36*, 519-54.

22. ———, "Rejoinder to an Antimarginalist," *Am. Econ. Rev.*, March 1947, *37*, 148-54.

23. ———, *The Economics of Sellers' Competition*. Baltimore 1952.

24. ———, "The Problem of Verification in Economics," *So. Econ. Jour.*, July 1955, *22*, 1-21.

25. ——, "Idealtypus, Wirklichkeit, und Konstruktion," *Ordo,* 1960-1961, 21-57.
26. ——, *Essays on Economic Semantics.* Englewood Cliffs, N.J. 1963.
27. R. J. MONSEN AND A. DOWNS, "A Theory of Large Managerial Firms," *Jour. Pol. Econ.,* June 1965, *73,* 221-36.
28. A. G. PAPANDREOU, "Some Basic Problems in the Theory of the Firm," in B. F. Haley, ed., *A Survey of Contemporary Economics,* Vol. II, Homewood, Ill. 1952, pp. 183-219.
29. V. PARETO, *Manuel d'économie politique,* 2nd ed. Paris 1927.
30. K. R. POPPER, *Conjectures and refutations.* New York and London 1962.
31. M. REDER, "A Reconsideration of the Marginal Productivity Theory," *Jour. Pol. Econ.,* Oct. 1947, *55,* 450-58.
32. J. ROBINSON, *The Economics of Imperfect Competition.* London 1933.
33. J. A. SCHUMPETER, "The Instability of Capitalism," *Econ. Jour.,* Sept. 1928, *38,* 361-86.
34. ——, *The Theory of Economic Development.* Cambridge, Mass. 1934.
35. A. SCHUTZ, *Collected Papers,* Vol. II. The Hague 1964.
36. T. SCITOVSKY, "A Note on Profit Maximisation and its Implications," *Rev. Econ. Stud.,* Winter 1943, *11,* 57-60. Reprinted in AEA, *Readings in Price Theory,* Homewood, Ill. 1952, pp. 352-58.
37. ——, *Welfare and Competition.* Chicago 1951.
38. H. A. SIMON, "A Behavioral Model of Rational Choice," *Quart. Jour. Econ.,* Feb. 1955, *69,* 99-118.
39. ——, *Administrative Behavior,* 2nd ed. New York 1957.
40. ——, "Theories of Decision-Making in Economics and Behavioral Science," *Am. Econ. Rev.,* June 1959, *49,* 253-83.
41. H. VON STACKELBERG, *Marktform und Gleichgewicht.* Vienna 1934.
42. L. J. STADLER, "The Gene," *Science,* Nov. 19, 1954, *120,* 811-19.
43. G. J. STIGLER, "The Economics of Minimum Wage Legislation," *Am. Econ. Rev.,* June 1946, *36,* 358-65.
44. ——, "Professor Lester and the Marginalists," *Am. Econ. Rev.,* March 1947, *37,* 154-57.
45. H. B. THORELLI, "The Political Economy of the Firm: Basis for a New Theory of Competition?" *Schweiz Zeitschr. Volkswirtschaft und Stat.,* 1965, *101,* 248-62.
46. T. VEBLEN, *The Instinct of Workmanship and the State of the Industrial Arts.* New York 1914.
47. M. WEBER, *On the Methodology of the Social Sciences,* transl. and ed. by E. A. Shils and H. A. Finch, Glencoe, Ill. 1949.
48. O. E. WILLIAMSON, *Economics of Discretionary Behavior: Managerial Objectives in a Theory of the Firm.* Englewood Cliffs, N.J. 1964.

Chapter 17

POSITIVE AND NORMATIVE ECONOMICS

Although there are some economists who "can't be bothered" by such exercises in "philosophy" or "mere semantics," the distinction between positive and normative plays a considerable role in present-day economic discussion. And this has been true for more than 150 years. While for some the distinction refers to a boundary between two branches of a science, for others "normative science" is a contradiction in terms, the discourse of norms or values being by definition nonscientific. The question is, of course, semantic and philosophic, but this does not make it trivial or useless. An elucidation seems worth our while.

Such an elucidation should be both historical and analytical. In the interests of conserving space, I shall confine myself here, however, to a discussion of the analytic questions.[1] The reader

---

[1] When we distinguish analytical from historical semantics, we do not suggest that the former can be independent of the latter. Words have meanings because people have used them to express certain ideas, and the meanings in which words have been used are historical data—though they are derived by way of interpretation, not observation.

If meanings have changed over time and between different groups, historical semantics will present these changes. The task of analytical semantics is largely one of rearrangements: the historical evidence and the chronology are removed and the different meanings are ordered and grouped in a systematic fashion designed to exhibit significant contrasts and relationships,

who would care to pursue the matter on a historical level may, if he is patient, wait for the publication of the history of ideas I am preparing on the issues behind the concepts "positive" and "normative."

When we embark on a methodological analysis of the ideas of "positive" and other kinds of economics, we cannot dispense with semantics. Questions of semantics and methodology are difficult to disentangle.

This is easy to comprehend. If some authors, for example, expound the intricacies of welfare economics, old or new, and conclude that certain propositions are normative in character, whereas other authors have characterized the same propositions as positive, either the difference may be semantic or it may be a matter of methodological interpretation. Obviously, it makes a difference whether "normative" in this context is to mean prescriptive, advisory, persuasive, evaluative, ethical, emotive, instrumental, or political; and whether "positive" means expository, descriptive, explanatory, predictive, nonhypothetical, nonevaluative, nonmetaphysical, nonspeculative, operational, testable, verifiable, nonpartisan, or consistent with agreed premises. But even if authors agree on the meaning of the adjectives, they may still come to different judgments on the character of the propositions in question, for they may not agree on all that is involved.

We shall begin with a brief summary of findings from the historical survey.

THE MEANINGS OF "POSITIVE"

The adjective "positive" has been used, in the literatures of economics, of the social sciences in general, and of the philosophy of science, chiefly to modify the following nouns: economics, inquiry, science, theory, problems, propositions, premises, and conclusions. The meaning of the adjective, however, has varied considerably over time and among different authors. The following list presents a quick review of some of the meanings of "positive" as a modifier of relevant nouns, the nouns being shown in parentheses:

Incontrovertible, unconditional, not merely hypothetical	(conclusions)
Empirical, not arbitrary	(premises of empirical sciences)

---

and thus to aid in the understanding of the concepts in the contexts in which they are used.

Perhaps all this can be said more simply by prohibiting the analytical semanticist from acting like Humpty-Dumpty, whose program was, "When I use a word, it means just what I choose it to mean—neither more nor less." The semanticist may analyze, but not dictate.

Probably true	(conclusions, corresponding to "positive reality")
Free from metaphysical speculation	(stage of scientific development)
Unconcerned with ultimate efficient causes	(science)
Based on facts of immediate perception	(science)
Disregarding psychic and spiritual facts	(science)
Confirmable or at least conceivably testable	(propositions)
Not merely critical or negative	(theory)
Nonpolitical, nonethical	(problems)
Neither normative nor prescriptive	(inquiry)
Not concerned with ideals or precepts	(inquiry)

This list can be reduced to a few pairs of opposites:

> Positive (constructive) versus negative (critical)
> Positive (certain) versus uncertain
> Positive (observable) versus nonobservable
> Positive (confirmable) versus nontestable
> Positive (descriptive) versus prescriptive
> Positive (factual) versus normative

In addition, there are two terms that have been used sometimes as equivalents of positive and in other instances to denote the opposite of positive. One of these terms is *"speculative,"* which for practically all philosophical positivists stands for nonobservable, if not metaphysical, and hence nonpositive. For at least two authors, however (Sidgwick and Keynes), the word meant the opposite of normative–prescriptive and, hence, the equivalent of positive–theoretical. (Thus, they would not approve the pair of opposites used by philosophical positivists: positive versus speculative.)

The other term is *"natural."* In legal philosophy, it modifies "law" to mean norms dictated by reason, social necessity, or divine order, and imposing justice and ethical precepts. In contrast to this "natural law" (of metaphysical origin), "positive law" is formally laid down, artificially instituted, not derived from general principles of justice but formulated in accepted codes, anchored in statute or formal precedent. In scientific discourse, however, "natural law" has meant law of nature, empirically tested and therefore a part of positive science, in contrast to arbitrary construction, mere fiction, product of imagination—hence, metaphysical. (This would contradict the pair of opposites in the language of legal philosophers: positive versus natural.)

THE MEANINGS OF "NORMATIVE"

The semantic record of the adjective "normative" is less voluminous and less bewildering. This is clearly reflected in the dictionaries: *The Oxford Dictionary,* which lists thirteen meanings for "positive," gives only a single meaning for "normative": "Establishing norms or standards." But this overlooks some significant differences in the use of the word by different economists, social scientists, and philosophers.

The most important differences in the meanings of "normative" relate to the degree in which the statements in question are (1) explicit with regard to the norms (objectives, values) to which they refer; (2) focused on the problem of valuation, especially on the problem of comparing particular norms (objectives) with conflicting ones; and (3) concerned with the means and techniques of attaining certain stated norms (ends) which stand high in the value systems of some but not necessarily of the person making the statements.

There are writers who would use the word "normative" to denote all statements that are advisory or hortatory in effect or intent, regardless of whether the underlying values are concealed or clearly stated, the problem of conflicting values is raised, or the objective to be attained is assumed as given and independent of the adviser's personal system of values. Others, however, prefer to remove the tag "normative" from statements that merely describe the means and techniques by which given ends can be attained. And some would remove the tag as soon as the underlying values are made explicit and unambiguous.

"POSITIVE" VERSUS "NORMATIVE"

Disregarding for the moment all other meanings of "positive," and concentrating on "positive" as the antonym of "normative," we may think of two sets of ideas associated with this pair of opposites:

Positive	Normative
Description	Prescription
Explanation	Recommendation
Theory	Practice
Theory	Policy
Thought	Action
Laws (statements of uniformities)	Rules (statements of norms)
Science	Art
Factual judgments	Value judgments

Statements in the indicative	Statements in the imperative
mood	mood
Testable propositions about facts	Nontestable expressions of feelings

We shall not discuss all these pairs of opposites, some of which reflect misunderstandings, serious or trivial. We should not fail, however, to comment on the grounds on which "practice" and "art" were placed in the normative column.

Let us not forget that the writer most responsible for the wide adoption of the terms "positive economics" and "normative economics" really proposed a triple distinction, not a dichotomy. John Neville Keynes distinguished positive, normative, and practical economics, which are concerned, respectively, with uniformities, standards, and precepts. I find it expedient to follow this tripartite division, at least for some distance.

THE TRICHOTOMY AND THE CHOICE OF TERMS

According to Keynes, positive economics tells you "what is," normative economics tells you "what ought to be," and practical economics tells you "what you can do to attain what you want." [2]

The term "practical" in this context is ambiguous; it disregards two significant differences: the one between action and advice, and the other between general advice for typical situations and specific advice for concrete (unique) situations. If what is meant is advice of a more general nature ("precept"), a more self-explanatory term had better be sought. The frequently used term "prescriptive" is not of great help either. It may prescribe standards, and thus become synonymous with "normative," or it may prescribe actions, and thus be equivalent to "practical." In this case, it leaves open whether one prescribes according to one's own standards (values), those of one's client, or some other stipulated standards. In the first of these possibilities, "prescriptive" would be both normative and practical at the same time. Let us use the term favored by Adolph Lowe, "instrumental," to denote the task of describing and prescribing actions by means of which specified objectives can be obtained.

The term "normative" as one of the triad will be examined later in greater detail, but let us agree at this point that the norms to which it refers are not rules or precepts telling you what to do or not to do to

---

[2] The first two phrases between quotation marks are Keynes', the third is mine, designed to fit what Keynes intended to express.

achieve given ends, but instead ethical (or aesthetic) standards telling you what we consider good or bad, right or wrong. The term "evaluative," referring to systems of ethical (or aesthetic) values, would probably be more expressive of the idea. In any case, in the following discussion "normative" means "evaluative."

GRAMMATICAL FORMS

Positive, normative, and instrumental statements will now be characterized by simple relationships between events A and B, alternatively seen as causes and effects and as means and ends.

> Positive: If A, then B;
> that is, B is the effect of the cause A.
> Normative: B is good;
> that is, you ought to get (strive for) B.
> Instrumental: If you want B, A will get it for you;
> that is, A will be the means for the end B.

Much has been made of the fact that normative sentences can (and ought to be) expressed in the imperative mood, whereas positive sentences would always be in the indicative mood. In the scheme above, both the positive and the instrumental propositions are stated in the conditional form, the positive one taking the cause (A) as the condition of achieving the effect (B), the instrumental one taking the end (B) as the condition for resorting to the means (A). The normative sentence can be translated in a variety of ways: it can be expressed in the indicative mood, in the imperative mood, and in conditional form.

> Indicative: B is good; indeed, B is the best.
> Imperative: Get B!!
> Conditional: (1) If you want the best, you ought to get B.
> (2) If you don't get B,
> (a) you don't know what's good for you;
> (b) you are a fool or a coward; or
> (c) you will be disliked, despised, or even punished.

It is questionable, however, whether these grammatical modifications are legitimate from a logician's point of view. Logical positivists deny the legitimacy of anything but the imperative mood. Rudolf Carnap, for example, contends that "actually a value statement is nothing else than a command in a misleading grammatical form. It may have effects upon the actions of men, and these effects may either be in accordance with our wishes or not; but it is neither true nor false. It does not assert any-

thing and can neither be proved nor disproved."[3] The contention that
the indicative mood is misleading because the value judgment "does not
assert anything" is rather pretentious. After all, if I say that I value *B*, I
do assert something about my likes and dislikes. But I know that this
does not count for logical positivists; they are not interested in my or
your tastes, maxims, or values. If I say, "Kate is the loveliest girl," they
want me to express this in the imperative mood, such as, "Kiss me, Kate!"

The translations into the form of conditional statements do not fare
much better. One should perhaps admit that forms 1 and 2a are merely
attempts to express the value judgment in a more persuasive way. Form
2b tries to reinforce the persuasion by a threat which may influence the
addressee by inducing fears of being regarded as a fool or a coward, at
least by the maker of the statement. Form 2c goes farther by threaten-
ing the addressee with sanctions if he fails to accept the value judgment
and to act accordingly. Incidentally, in this form it is not made clear
just who entertains the valuation expressed: I; we; the majority of edu-
cated people, of voters, or of all people; the government; the prince; the
dictator. But even without this specification, the statement seems to make
an assertion; the predicted sanctions for nonconformists may in fact be
imposed, and thus the statement can (at least conceivably) be tested and
confirmed or disconfirmed. Perhaps, though, the statement in form 2c has
been promoted from a value judgment to an indicative statement about
the morals and codes of a group or society and to an instrumental proposition stating something like this: "If you want to avoid social or legal
penalties, you will act to show that you too value *B*, and thus you will
resort to *A* as the appropriate means for it." In this advisory proposition,
B has become an intermediate end—namely, a means for avoiding the
sanctions imposed on those who fail to conform with the value judgment
in favor of *B*.

THE LANGUAGE OF THE COOKBOOK

Many discussions of normative science and technology refer to the
cookbook or, more generally, to the book of recipes, as an analogy for
prescriptive or normative statements. As a matter of fact, recipes in cook-
books (or technological handbooks) are commonly written in the imperative mood, and their authors thus seem to obey the logician's normative statement on the proper grammatical form of normative statements.

Some of the most frequently used imperatives in the cookbook are

---

[3] Rudolf Carnap, *Philosophy and Logical Syntax* (London: Kegan Paul, Trench,
and Trubner, 1935), p. 24. Partially reproduced in Morton White, *The Age of
Analysis* (3rd printing) (New York: Mentor Books, 1957), p. 217.

Have! Cut! Slice! Chop! Wash! Soak! Drain! Shake! Melt! Cook! Boil! Bake! Fry! Add!—all, of course, followed by quantities of victuals to which the prescribed operations are to be applied.

However, each of the sets of imperatives is under a heading, such as "Crab Cakes," "Cheese Omelet," or "Crêpes Suzette." From the logician's point of view, the heading is the premise of a hypothetical proposition, the premise stating the assumed objective. For example: "*If* you want to make a cheese omelet for *n* persons, *take* 2*n* eggs. . . ."

The imperatives of the cookbook are therefore in a grammatical form misleading for the beginning student of logic, though most helpful to the intermediate student of cooking. A logical cook could translate each recipe into a positive statement of cause and effect: "If you take 2*n* eggs . . . you will get a cheese omelet for *n* persons." But since the cookbook is organized and classified, not according to causes, but according to effects or ends, the more appropriate translation would be into instrumental statements about desired ends and required means. That is, to say as I said before, "If you want to make a cheese omelet for *n* persons, take 2*n* eggs. . . ."

This may be the point at which to digress for a discussion of whether a cookbook belongs to the science of cookery or to the art of cooking. The question is much broader, of course. Are instrumental propositions part of an "art"? Is "science" confined to positive propositions?

ART AND SCIENCE

Those who speak of cooking as an art do not mean to say that it is an art to read a cookbook and carry out its instructions, or to prepare without instruction the simple dishes commonly eaten by most of us. They refer, instead, only to the work of those rare cooks who prepare very special meals, using unusual imagination and a fine sense of taste, form, and color. The "art" in this activity lies precisely in their deviation from common practice and from common precepts.

This meaning of art, as a performance superior to that of most practitioners, is contrary to another meaning of art, as a body of precepts for practice; this is one of the dictionary definitions and has been widely used as an antonym of science. Art in this sense is, like science, systematic knowledge, but arranged in a different way, suitable for more immediate practical application. As John Stuart Mill has explained, science is a body of knowledge classified according to causes, and art is a body of knowledge classified according to effects, the causes of which are often the subject of several different sciences.

Bentham's aphorism, that science is knowledge while art is practice, places us right between the two meanings of art just contrasted. Clearly, not all knowledge is science and not all practice is art. Perhaps one may say that highly qualified knowledge (rather than common, everyday knowledge) is science,[4] while highly qualified practice (rather than common, everyday practice) is art. But since virtually all practice, and certainly all qualified practice, presupposes knowledge, it is quite possible, as some writers have proposed, to use "art" and "applied science" as synonymous terms.

Those who define art as practical knowledge have usually failed to differentiate various degrees of practicality and various degrees of practice. There are important differences between, say, a handbook of technology, technological advice in a concrete situation, actual instruction given for immediate activation, and the final, perhaps manual, execution of the instruction. Yet all four phases of practical knowledge, practical application of knowledge, and practice have indiscriminately been called art.[5] (Let us recall Menger's complaint about this confusion.)

An important idea in designating certain kinds of practical activity as art is, I submit, the recognition that these activities presuppose a combination of human qualities that cannot be obtained solely from books or lectures. These activities are "art" in that they call for judgment, intuition, inventiveness, and imagination; they call for skill in making the correct diagnoses and prognoses required for successful prescriptions and good performance. Here lies a real distinction from science, scientific knowledge, and even technology and general practical precepts.

To what extent can it be said that art is normative or contains significant normative elements? Let us recall our resolution to use "normative" as an equivalent of "evaluative"—that is, as referring to standards for judging things as good or bad, right or wrong—and not as rules helpful in the attainment of stated ends. In this sense, art is normative to the extent that the activity in question calls for judgments of value, ethical or aesthetic; it is neutral or nonnormative where no value judgments are involved. In other words, art cannot reasonably be put under the normative heading except after an examination of the value-content of the judgments employed.

That the fine arts and the performing arts presuppose commitment to aesthetic standards goes without saying. The medical arts and the engineering arts, however, may go a long way without giving up their basic

---

[4] See the discussion of the meanings of science by Joseph A. Schumpeter, *History of Economic Analysis* (New York: Oxford University Press, Inc., 1954), pp. 6–11. One of Schumpeter's definitions differentiates scientific knowledge from that of the layman and mere practitioner.

[5] The German word for art is *Kunst*, but the German language offers the compound nouns *Kunstlehre* (for art as a body of precepts, technology), *Kunstregel* (for art as a precept or rule for practical application), and *Kunstfertigkeit* (for art as technical skill).

value-neutrality. The art of making recommendations on economic policy, requiring diagnostic and prognostic skills as well as interdisciplinary intelligence, may likewise proceed on the basis of agreed ethical standards without any violation of the adviser's value-neutrality. The economic adviser practices an art, not because his recommendations serve certain ends desired by people committed to certain values, but rather because his recommendations presuppose so much more than economic science: politics, sociology, psychology, pedagogy, and diplomacy, as well as diagnostic judgment, prognostic flair, intuition, and inventiveness.

One other concept of art may be mentioned here, the one used in grouping the various academic disciplines taught by the nonvocational faculties of our universities. The "arts," in academic parlance, were originally the disciplines of the trivium (grammar, logic, and rhetoric) and the quadrivium (arithmetic, geometry, music, and astronomy). In a series of reorganizations, the universities have reassigned various disciplines among the faculties of arts and sciences. In some institutions the "reading departments" are considered as professing the arts subjects, the "laboratory departments" as professing the sciences. The adjective "normative" is not relevant to such a division of subjects. Sometimes the fields classified as the humanities are regarded as inseparable from commitments to unscientific value systems. This, too, is quite superficial, if not downright wrong. Studies in linguistics or paleography are not any less value-neutral than studies in acoustics or paleontology.

NORMS, VALUES, RULES, PRECEPTS, ADVICE, PERSUASION, AND COMMAND

Be it tedious repetition or proper reinforcement, it may be helpful to sort out, once again, the set of nouns that are related and yet differentiated in meaning: norms, values, rules, precepts, advice, persuasion, and command. (We could add many more, such as instruction, directives, recommendations, and guideposts.)

The idea common to all these nouns is that somebody's actions are to be directed: someone is told what to do or what not to do. Certain differences in connotation are not generally recognized in common parlance, and not always even in learned language analysis. Of course, the differences between advice, persuasion, and command are patent, but the difference between precepts and advice or the differences between norms, rules, and precepts are not.

Perhaps we can agree on the difference between the general or typical and the specific or concrete. Advice, persuasion, and command may refer to both, to typical as well as concrete situations (concrete as to time, space, and persons involved). Norms, values, rules, and precepts are always general, and their application in concrete cases is left to intelligent interpretation. Norms and values refer to systems of valuation which the acting individual or individuals may recognize as valid (cogent or imposed by sanctions) but may not necessarily accept as their own. (After all, persons frequently act in violation of legal, ethical, or religious norms, and in breach of social etiquette.) Precepts, on the other hand, are general advice, directing voluntary action in the interest of or toward ends desired by the decision-makers. Rules may be norms or precepts; the word has not acquired a special sense linking it to only one or the other. Norms, then, are rules of conduct, self-imposed or imposed by coercion or pressures of various sorts, which relate chiefly, though not exclusively, to social objectives, whereas precepts are rules of suitable conduct for the achievement of ends chosen by the decision-makers themselves.

These semantic explications will have justified our previous terminological decision to reserve the adjective "normative" for references to norms or value judgments, and to use the adjective "instrumental" for references to precepts that direct actions designed to attain explicitly stated objectives. In order to safeguard against misunderstandings, we should add that precepts may be used for individual or group action, and for the attainment of individual or group objectives. Thus, there are precepts for householders, telling them what to look out for in shopping, budgeting, borrowing, and so forth; and there are precepts for legislators, telling them what look out for in drafting legislation to reduce unemployment, to alleviate poverty, to accelerate growth, and to achieve other national goals. A book of precepts is instrumental and not normative in that it tells what to do *if* certain things are wanted but does not say that these things are beneficial or worth their cost.

THE LOGICAL STATUS OF NORMATIVE STATEMENTS

From the survey of the philosophical literature, it has become apparent that normative statements, or expressions of value judgments, do not enjoy an unequivocal status in logic. They are, depending on which logician pronounces the verdict, empirical propositions, analytical propositions, or no propositions at all. The differences in the verdicts are not entirely due to the differences between logical schools, but are also due in part to semantic differences, since the meaning of "normative statement" is far from unambiguous.

There are several possible ways to show that a (supposedly) normative statement is an empirical proposition. "The policies of the United States between 1963 and 1967 indicate that the avoidance of large unemployment was regarded as more important than the removal of the deficit in foreign payments." This is a statement about the system of values held or goals desired by the government (the Legislature as well as Administrations); depending on the acceptance of certain definitional and theoretical relationships, the assertion can be tested and therefore represents an empirical proposition. However, it may be denied that an assertion about values held or shared by certain persons or groups is a normative statement. That "full employment is more important than balance in foreign payments," would be a genuine value judgment. But that "full employment is held to be more important than balance in foreign payments," or is "more important to the government" or "to the majority of the people," is not a genuine value judgment.

"If a reduction in the payments deficit is desirable, but not at the price of an increase in unemployment, then the Congress ought not to increase the income tax." This looks really normative; it even employs the characteristic "ought." Yet, the statement merely asserts that a tax increase will reduce both employment and the payments deficit. It also draws a correct inference from an assumption about relative values. It does not try to persuade anyone to accept this valuation. The opposite assumption might be made, with the opposite inference, and the statement would make the same assertion: "If a reduction in the payments deficit is desirable, even at the price of increased unemployment, then an increase in the income tax is not ruled out." (In this case, the "ought" cannot legitimately be used, because it would presuppose, not only a comparison between the values of reducing the deficit and increasing unemployment, but also a comparative evaluation of all other possible side effects of the tax increase. The assumption in the "if"-clause has not gone that far.) The point is that the (indirectly) asserted relationship between tax increase and payments deficit makes the proposition empirical.

"The American people will resent an increase in unemployment and will not regard it as a fair price to pay for a reduction in the deficit." If we can agree on operational definitions for the feelings predicted in this statement (take, for example, certain replies in an opinion poll), the assertion is conceivably testable and the proposition can be characterized as an empirical one. Thus, it may be denied that a value judgment was expressed. A statement about people's reactions, even if these reactions express their evaluations, is not regarded as normative by most logicians, and surely not by radical empiricists. Indeed, when they speak of the "science of ethics," what they have in mind is an empirical study of observed or observable behavior in reaction to particular events.

That value judgments can be regarded as analytical propositions means that they can be derived by logical inference from stated assumptions—for example, from a convention or resolution about a definite system of values. Given this convention with all its "axiological rules," to use Felix

Kaufmann's phrase, one can deduce whether 3 per cent unemployment with a payments deficit of two billion dollars is better or worse than 4 per cent unemployment with a deficit of only one billion dollars, all other things being equal. The value judgment is true "in terms of given axiological rules" if it was correctly deduced from the axiological system. The trouble with this position, in my opinion, is that there are an infinite number of such value systems, and we have no criteria for choosing among them in selecting the most appropriate "convention."

According to logical positivists, value judgments are no propositions at all. The sentences in which these judgments are expressed "say nothing." A sentence stating that "a reduction of the payments deficit from two billion dollars to one billion dollars is worth an increase in unemployment from 3 to 4 per cent" asserts nothing that can be true or false and, hence, is "meaningless," according to logical positivists. I submit that this formulation of the verdict against normative statements is unduly harsh. The condemned sentence makes perfectly good sense to me, and probably to many others, even if I readily admit that what it expresses cannot be proved or disproved. In order to show the difference between "meaningless" and "nontestable," I propose that we compare the sense of the indicted and condemned statement with that of the following: "A reduction of the deficit is greenish pink and much more erudite and farther east than an increase in unemployment." Even this sentence may make sense if there is a secret code to decipher those words that destroy the sense if they are given their ordinary meanings.

The assertion that a sentence expressing a nontestable judgment is meaningless cannot be tested either, and would therefore be meaningless itself by the standard it proposes. Speaking in a more reasonable language, I find the finding of "meaninglessness" against value judgments presumptuous and overdone. It suffices to say that pure value judgments cannot be tested by empirical procedures and therefore cannot be admitted into the body of positive science.

"POSITIVE" VERSUS "NONOBSERVABLE"

By giving the floor to logical positivists in the discussion of the logical status of "normative," we have unwittingly changed the meaning of "positive": From being the opposite of "normative" it has moved—because the normative is nonobservable and nontestable—to being the opposite of "nonobservable."

The logical positivist or radical empiricist will not recognize that there is a change of meaning involved: Normative equals metaphysical equals nonobservable equals nontestable equals meaningless. For me, these are quite different qualities and, hence, their opposites are different too. I have many witnesses testifying in support of my position. Let me recall a statement of Schumpeter's complaining about these qualifications; [6] the pronouncements of John Neville Keynes, originator of the expression "positive economics"; the comments of Milton Friedman in his essay on the subject; and the remarks of Tjalling Koopmans in his methodological discourses; to mention only a few. For none of these authors is positive economics confined to propositions that are based solely on observable premises and that assert nothing but observable relationships. Some if not all of them would insist on "conceivable testability" as a criterion of eligibility for positive economics; however, the tests may be indirect, through rough correspondence of deduced consequences with observed outcomes, rather than direct, through empirical confirmation of all assumptions, including the fundamental hypotheses.

Rather than expatiate on this issue, I may refer to several earlier statements of mine in which I have attempted to show that propositions in positive economics may—nay, must—be conceived in terms of purely mental constructs, some of which do not even have operational counterparts.[7] Thus, the "positive" in positive economics is definitely not the equivalent of "observable."

"POSITIVE" VERSUS "NONTESTABLE"

I may repeat that many, perhaps most, economists nowadays insist on conceivable testability of the propositions of positive economics, although some are satisfied with indirect tests, applied to the conclusions, and do not require direct tests of the premises.[8]

However, the insistence on empirical testing (as against merely logical demonstration) is not implied in the designation "positive" economics. The designation is given only to separate this body of knowledge from

---

[6] "The word 'positive' as used in this connection has nothing whatever to do with philosophical positivism. This is the first of many warnings . . . against the dangers of confusion that arises from the use, for entirely different things, of the same word by writers who themselves sometimes confuse the things" [J. A. Schumpeter, *History of Economic Analysis*, ed. E. B. Schumpeter (New York: Oxford University Press, Inc., 1954), p. 8n].

[7] Fritz Machlup, "Operational Concepts and Mental Constructs in Model and Theory Formation," *Giornale degli Economisti*, XIX (*Nuova Serie*) (1960), 553–582; "Operationalism and Pure Theory in Economics," in *The Structure of Economic Science*, ed. Sherman Roy Krupp (Englewood Cliffs, N. J.: Prentice-Hall, Inc., 1966), pp. 53–67; and "Idealtypus, Wirklichkeit und Konstruktion," *Ordo*, XII (1961), 21–57.

[8] In addition to the articles cited in the preceding footnote, see Fritz Machlup, "The Problem of Verification in Economics," *The Southern Economic Journal*, XXII (1955), 1–21; and "Rejoinder to a Reluctant Ultra-Empiricist," *The Southern Economic Journal*, XXII (1956), 483–493.

normative and perhaps also from practical or instrumental economics. In other words, the "positive" in positive economics is not meant to be synonymous with "testable."

THE ECONOMIST'S CONCERN WITH VALUES

It now seems well established that the "positive" in positive economics means nonnormative, nonevaluative. Moreover, the meaning of "normative," though perhaps not sufficiently cleanly defined, seems fairly well circumscribed. There is little danger, therefore, that a knowledgeable economist will confuse "value references," many of which he cannot avoid in his studies and reports, with "value judgments" incompatible with his value-neutrality and scientific objectivity. Noneconomists, however, including philosophers discussing the problem of "values" in scientific activity, may easily fall into error. Indeed, we could cite a good many confused dicta of philosophers of science reflecting on the supposed difficulties of purging the social sciences of nonscientific evaluations.

It may, therefore, be in order to examine the many kinds of values and value references with which the economist may have to concern himself. We must find out which ones, if any, are likely to lead him into making normative statements or expressing value judgments inadmissible in positive economics.

My list—may I be forgiven for my irrepressible propensity to produce lists?—has twelve items, referring to valuations by the economist, by those who produce the events he analyzes, by those for whom he makes his analyses, or by those whom he wishes to influence. More specifically, the values of possible concern to the economist are those of individuals as micro-economic decision-makers and micro-political decision-makers (items 1 and 2); of social groups or society as a whole (items 3 and 4); of the government (item 5); of the clients to whom the economist reports (item 6); of the symbolic clients whose "welfare function" he assumes as given (item 7); of his own values in his capacity as analyst (items 8–10); and of his own values in his capacity as adviser and persuader (items 11 and 12). Here is the list:

1. Values (estimates of utility, tastes, preferences) which the individuals, in the economist's models, are assumed to have and by which they are assumed to be guided as micro-economic decision-makers (household and business managers) in reaction to changes in their opportunities.
2. Values which individuals, acting alone or in groups, may reveal as micro-political decision-makers in voting for advocates of certain programs and for changes of constitutional provisions, in writing to

newspapers and legislators, in lobbying, haranguing, demonstrating, or revolting.

3. Values which social groups or society as a whole, represented by writers, speakers, and preachers, leaders in schools, clubs, associations, parties, or communities, or any influential or vocal group, may express and by which the values of individuals as micro-economic decision-makers are shaped or influenced.

4. Values which society, as either anonymous group or political institution, expresses in the form of legal norms, ethical codes, or moral suasion and which operate as constraints on, or even prohibitions or suspensions of, individual preference systems and micro-economic decisions.

5. Values which guide the government (legislators and administrators) in its decisions affecting micro-economic decision-makers by changing through coercive measures or incentives the opportunities open to them.

6. Values of the economist's clients (business firms, trade or labor organizations, government agencies) which he takes as the basis for his analysis, leading to his recommendations of optimal policies to attain their objectives.

7. Values of the economist's symbolic client—the local community, nation, or world community—which he assumes to be given in the form of a "social welfare" function as a basis for his unsolicited policy recommendations designed to serve the public interest thus defined.

8. Values of the economist as analyst which influence him in the choice of his research projects, of the problems to be analyzed, and of the hypotheses to be entertained and examined.

9. Values of the economist as analyst which influence him in the choice of his research techniques and analytical procedures, in the weights he attaches to various types of evidence, in the elegance of his logical demonstrations, and in his eagerness to subject his findings to suitable empirical tests.

10. Values of the economist as analyst which influence him in the choice of his terminology and in the acceptance of available statistical data for purposes of measurement of magnitudes taken as operational counterparts of his theoretical constructs (such as national product at market prices, with the given distribution of income).

11. Values of the economist as adviser or persuader which influence him in substituting his own value judgments, chiefly those of the supposed interest of society, for those of his actual or symbolic clients, but without deliberate falsification of his data or conscious bias in his findings.

12. Values of the economist as adviser or persuader which influence him to use inappropriate or fabricated data, employ improper methods of calculation, and give false evidence, either in an attempt to secure material advantages for his clients and himself or, alternatively, in the hope of persuading people or governments to take political action in the supposed interest of society.

While the verdict is absolutely clear regarding the last item, we must ask which of the other values or value-concerns might contaminate the economist's product and violate his value-neutrality.

THE ECONOMIST'S SCIENTIFIC OBJECTIVITY

We need not feel nervous regarding the first five items. These values, either assumed or revealed through actual conduct, are part of the subject matter with which economists deal: they are data needed for the analysis of various kinds of problems.

Item 1, the values of household and business managers, which influence their decisions to buy, sell, hire, lend, borrow, and so forth, are "given" to the analyst, who employs models of decision-making and of supply and demand to explain changes in prices and quantities of goods and services. When the economist speaks of subjective-value theory, it is not his theory which is subjective. He deals objectively with the subjective values of the economic decision-makers whose actions or reactions produce observable changes which the economist has to explain. Whether the subjective values, the preferences of the acting decision-units, are (behaviorally) revealed or merely (postulationally) assumed is a question which may concern the radical empiricist (logical positivist), not because of any suspicion of a transgression into the normative domain, but only because of the nonempirical nature of merely assumed values.

Item 2 enters only rarely into economic analysis. It may become relevant in analyses of policy measures or of events likely to incite political reactions. The analysis of problems in which political reactions play a significant role can be perfectly objective, absolutely neutral with regard to the values behind the observed or predicted reactions.

Item 3 is important chiefly in problems with strong infusions of sociological elements, such as the effects of advertising, patriotic or educational campaigns, or changes in fashion or other habits (alcohol, smoking, drugs), to mention only a few social (moral) influences on people's preferences. Valuations that change valuations are subjects of study, and have in fact been studied, without inviting deviations from value-neutrality.

Item 4 hardly needs explanation. To give only one example, the effects of legal or ethical prohibitions upon decisions regarding production, employment, supply, and demand can be analyzed without any normative (evaluative) undertones or overtones.

Item 5 is quite similar. The "official" valuations which, for example, cause the U. S. Government to impose a tax on the purchase of foreign securities but exempt securities issued by less developed countries or by Canada and Japan are data which the analyst can accept and take into account without being deflected from his scientific objectivity.

Item 6 brings us closer to the danger zone, for we are now looking at an economist working on policy recommendations for government, special-interest organizations, business firms, or other clients. Of course, such recommendations cannot help being value-directed. Yet, if the values are not too complex and can be stated in the form of specific objectives, like the tasks assigned to an engineer, chemist, or physician, then the economist's analysis is not basically different from straight causal reasoning. Instead of inquiring for the effects of some action or measure, he has to inquire what actions or measures would cause the effect desired by the client. This procedure, which, following Adolph Lowe, we have called instrumental analysis, does not involve the analyst's value judgments and is not normative in character.

Item 7 is quite problematic, for in this case the "client"—a symbolic client—does not specify his objectives or value-function. The economist arrogates to himself the role of judge of what constitutes the public interest. To be sure, he has many clues that tell him that the community likes a larger income, more employment, faster growth, more equality of income and wealth, better schools, cleaner air and water, better roads, bigger parks, better fishing, and more freedom. If he had only one objective to worry about, he could do his instrumental analysis and maintain his innocent value-neutrality. But with a multitude of social objectives and no specification of an indifference map that would give him the community's marginal rates of substitution between competing goals, "objective" instrumental analysis is impossible. We conclude that this kind of economic analysis—welfare economics—is normative. But let us take this as a rebuttable conclusion, to be reconsidered in the next section.

Item 8 presents no problems to us, though only because the problems involved were authoritatively treated and definitely resolved by Max Weber sixty years ago. Since not every writer has studied and understood Weber's arguments, there have been occasional recurrences of suspicion. Myrdal, for example, thought he could reopen the case and renew the charges that the values which influence a scholar to become interested in a certain topic and particular problem, and to formulate his first hypotheses, would inevitably produce a bias in his analysis. These charges cannot be sustained unless the entire notion of scientific objectivity in any area of inquiry is to be discarded. For the same situation exists in all sciences, the physical and biological included. There is necessarily a valuation behind the choice of topic and problem, and a preconception behind the choice of preliminary hypotheses. But this does not imply anything concerning a lack of scientific objectivity in the analysis itself, in any of the sciences—physical, biological, or social.[9]

Item 9 is analogous to item 8. No scientist can help being influenced by his valuations of alternative methods of research and analysis. In many instances strong preferences for particular techniques, usually developed in the investigator's earlier training, may have a role even in his choice of problems to be researched. No doubt these values on the part of the analyst exist and may effectively influence the choice of his rules of procedure. To admit this, however, is not to admit any insincerity in his endeavor to reach correct solutions. To be sure, some of the favored techniques may hinder or prevent him from getting "true" findings, but this does not imply violation of his value-neutrality with respect to the results of his inquiries.[10]

Item 10 presents more difficult problems, chiefly because an economist's value judgments regarding choice of terminology and acceptance of available statistical data sometimes prevail over the analyst's zeal to obtain and report unbiased findings. The use of value-loaded language is perhaps less treacherous than the use of value-blended statistics, because any design to persuade with emotive or prejudicious words is more easily detected than an attempt to lie with statistics. However, the situation is not quite as serious as it may appear from these comments. The persuasive or emotive effects of value-loaded words may wear off with time or may be removed by proper cautions. And the use of value-blended statistical data may be disclosed or exposed by critical notes. (I am not referring here, incidentally, to fabricated data or to deliberately improper uses of data, both of which belong to item 12. The statistics referred to here as value-blended cannot be cleansed of their value contents. For example, any assemblage of goods, such as the national product, can be measured only in terms of prices or values; whether one uses current market prices, officially fixed prices, prices of some base period, hypothetical prices that would result with a different distribution of income, labor-cost prices, or another standard, some prices have to be used, and the decision may be influenced by value judgments concerning the "right" system.) [11] We

---

[9] Professor Ludwig von Mises used to tell his students about the value judgment that induced chemists and biologists to do research on insecticides. The researchers' interest in these problems stemmed from an obvious bias: they were not impartial in siding with man and against the bugs. But this did not vitiate the scientific character of their endeavor. In the social sciences, research on means to preserve peace is guided by a preference for peace and a clear bias against war. Does this vitiate the research—apart from possible wishful thinking by some of the researchers?

[10] For a good discussion of items 8 and 9, see T. W. Hutchison, *"Positive" Economics and Policy Objectives* (London: George Allen & Unwin, 1964), Chap. 2.

[11] See Fritz Machlup, *The Political Economy of Monopoly* (Baltimore, Md.: The Johns Hopkins Press, 1952), pp. 459–461.

may conclude that transgressions into normative territory are possible on these counts, but that the implied threats to scientific objectivity are not serious enough to make even the purist fret and squirm.

Item 11 is closely related to item 7 in that the economic adviser (or pleader) often is not given sufficiently full specifications of the objectives to be attained and has to fill in with his own value judgments where the specifications leave blanks. The resulting bias may be, and usually is, unconscious, since most people innocently believe that they know what is wanted, either by their clients or by the community. The normative character of this sort of advice will be examined more closely in the next section.

Item 12 presents the most obvious instance of valuations leading to conscious bias and even deliberate fraud. To speak here only of a lack of scientific objectivity is unduly charitable. But let no one think that economists, or social scientists in general, have a monopoly on cheating. Hoaxes, fraud, biased testimonies, and cases of false evidence occur in all fields: in the physical and biological sciences, the engineering sciences, and even the humanities. I have supplied examples elsewhere.[12]

ADJUDICATING CHARGES OF BIAS

The point-by-point treatment of types of valuation calls for a brief summary, preceded by a restatement of the essential issue.

The issue is not whether value judgments *may* intrude into the economist's analyses and reports, or if they *may* impart a bias to his work, destroying his scientific objectivity. There is no question that this may happen and does happen. The real question is whether this is in the nature of all economic analysis or, perhaps, of certain kinds of economic analysis, and if it is therefore *unavoidable* in either all or some kinds of economic analysis.

The values or value-concerns enumerated in items 1–5 are quite irrelevant to the issue. While concern with valuations of this sort distinguishes the social sciences from the natural sciences, none of these value-concerns has any bearing on the issue of value-neutrality and bias.

The values described in item 6, the stated objectives assigned to the economist as an "engineer" in instrumental analysis, present no danger to his scientific objectivity in his work. He is given the task of solving certain problems and of reporting to his clients how they can get what they want.

---

12 Fritz Machlup, "Are the Social Sciences Really Inferior?" *The Southern Economic Journal*, XXVII (1961), 175–176. Reprinted in *Philosophy of the Social Sciences: A Reader*, ea. Maurice Natanson (New York: Random House, Inc., 1963), pp. 163–164.

Whether he himself approves of their objectives or dislikes them may affect his work, but need not. Ethical conflicts may arise if he has qualms about the social desirability of his clients' or employers' objectives. I can even imagine some zealot supplying wrong answers in an attempt to thwart their "evil" designs. In such cases, however, it is the substitution of his own value judgments for those of his clients or employers that changes the character of his work, transforming it from instrumental into normative.

Almost the same problem arises in cases of incomplete specification of the objectives sought by the advisees—cases under item 11. The economic adviser, not having been given exact and complete instructions about the advisees' valuations of side effects, alternative means, and conflicting goals, has to use his own judgment. In this case, his value judgments are not substituted for those of his clients, but supplement them in more or less essential ways. Where he can do it in an explicit and unambiguous manner, he merely writes the missing part of the specifications of his assignment. If so, no harm is done to the scientific objectivity of his work. Often, however, the value system that supplements the simple set of objectives furnished by the clients or advisees is too complex to be unambiguously specified. In this case, the economist's analysis and report cannot help being colored by his hidden valuations and, thus, are no longer scientifically objective.

The suspicions and charges relating to items 8 and 9—concerning the choice of problem and preliminary hypotheses—were dismissed. Adjudicated long ago, they can worry only those who have not done their homework and have skipped the required reading.

Regarding item 10—value-loaded terms and value-blended figures—we merely advise caution on the part of both producers and consumers of economic reports. Where our language provides only value-loaded words and our statistics furnish only value-blended measurements, reports may have persuasive effects, intentional or unintentional. To deny the scientific objectivity of economics on these grounds would be a vast exaggeration.

This leaves the value problem of item 7 as the most sensitive of all. It is the problem of the normative nature of welfare economics, which we have resolved to consider once more.

THE NORMATIVE CHARACTER OF WELFARE ECONOMICS

Where the objectives are fully and unambiguously specified, the analysis of the best ways to attain the objectives is instrumental, not normative. But where there is any deficiency or ambiguity in the specification, the analyst cannot provide answers without (consciously or unconsciously) filling the gaps *ad hoc* according to value judgments he himself entertains at the moment. This is an undertaking that is hardly compatible with scientific objectivity. The findings of what is "better" or "best" for society under the circumstances become a function of the analyst's predilections.

We have to find out just what it means to have a full specification of social objectives. But before we try to answer this question, it will be helpful to show how a specified map of social preferences would be used in an analysis that determines the social optimum or, more modestly, an improvement of the given state of affairs.

If there were only two social goals, a two-dimensional map with indifference curves would show the acceptable trade-offs between them. The trade-off rates, or marginal rates of acceptable substitution,[13] would of course be very different for different combinations of goal achievement. Assume, for example, that the two goals are "present consumption" and "rate of increase of growth of national product." The acceptable trade-off rates (represented by the slope of the indifference curve) in a range of low consumption and fast growth would be quite different from the acceptable trade-off rates in a range of high consumption and slow growth. Although this should be obvious to the trained economist, it does not tally with his frequent references to a "given hierarchy" of social goals.

The social indifference curves have to be brought together with social possibility curves for the same two goals. The slopes of these curves tell how much of each goal would have to be given up in order to get a little more of the other. In other words, they show the rates of required sacrifice. Again, these rates will be quite different for different combinations of goal achievement. They can be regarded as marginal rates of potential substitution.

The social possibility curves are opportunity or transformation functions, showing the *required* trade-offs between alternative goal achievements—that is, the *cost* of more of one in terms of less of the other. The social indifference curves are preference or welfare functions, showing the *acceptable* trade-offs between alternative goal achievements—that is, the *utility* of more of one in terms of less of the other. The optimum solution would be that combination at which required and acceptable trade-off rates are equal.

To ascertain the required trade-off rates is one of the most important tasks of the economist. To pretend knowledge of the acceptable trade-off rates between social goals is the heroic assumption of welfare economics. Even for only two social goals, the assumption of knowing the acceptable trade-off rates for all possible combinations of goal achievement would

---

13 "Acceptable marginal rates of substitution" may be the preferred expression. I said "marginal rates of acceptable substitution" in order to indicate that all points on such a curve are equally acceptable, and that movement along such a curve represents an "acceptable substitution."

be rather extravagant. To assume knowledge of all acceptable trade-off rates among a multitude of social goals for all possible combinations is well-nigh fantastic.

Even if we think only of the most commonplace menu of social goals offered to the voter in political platforms, we must be overwhelmed by the enormity of the task of imagining, let alone ascertaining, the trade-offs acceptable to just one representative citizen. For there are not only the full arrays of rates of employment, consumption, private investment, public expenditures, growth of GNP, foreign aid, income equality, and so forth—to mention only quantifiable goals—but there are also questions of the composition of these aggregate magnitudes. The same rate of employment may be the composite of several different distributions among regions, occupations, age groups, and racial and ethnic groups; the same rate of consumption may be the composite of different distributions among consumer groups (social groups, income groups) and among consumption items (food, housing, automobiles, entertainment, alcohol, tobacco); the same rate of investment may mean very different outlays in different sectors (agriculture, mining, manufacturing, public utilities, transportation); the same rate of public expenditures may comprise substantial variations in the appropriations for different purposes (defense, research, education, health, highways); and analogous illustrations could be given for each of the quantifiable goals.

If we think of the nonquantifiable objectives our agony increases, for there are innumerable combinations among all sorts of psychic income. Most important are the legal and institutional arrangements to increase or reduce various kinds of economic, political, intellectual, and religious freedoms, many of which conflict with one another as well as with other objectives, such as employment, production, investment, equality, etc. There are also activities to increase national prestige, with acceptable trade-offs against the achievement of other objectives.

The usual reflections on welfare economics have concentrated on measurable increases or decreases in total output or income, and on associated changes in the distribution of income. By making ingenious assumptions concerning side payments through which gainers would compensate losers, the relevance of income distribution for the evaluation of particular measures or changes was eliminated, and total income was made the sole determinant of economic welfare.

With a single social objective and a single constraint—increase in aggregate income with no reduction in any individual incomes—the problem of assessing alternative public policies became manageable. But as soon as one recognizes the existence of several partly conflicting objectives, the possibility of a unique solution, even the determination of the direction of change, disappears—unless the value system of one man can be repre-

sented as that of the community. That man can only be the economist himself, and the social optimum is then clearly a personal opinion which cannot
be proved right or wrong. In addition, this Grand Arbiter of Social Welfare
would probably be incapable of specifying his preference functions fully
and in advance; many of his findings would be *ad hoc*, for particular occasions, improvised and not predictable.[14]

An illustration may help to make this clear. The Congress of the United
States has been working on a new copyright law extending the term of
protection to the lifetime of the author plus fifty years. Although it has
not occurred to any legislator to ask for an economic appraisal of the
effects of this provision, let us assume that an economist is commissioned
to advise. He may be able to say something about the probable movement along the possibility function. He may predict that the increase
in incentives for publishers and authors will lead to the publication of
additional books (including five novels per year, eight mystery stories,
six books on sex, and seven new textbooks, two of which will be on elementary economics with poor chapters on welfare economics); that the
prices of books, especially those published long ago but still selling in
considerable quantities, will go up by 10 per cent; that private consumer
spending on books will be only slightly affected, as consumers will buy
fewer books with a somewhat larger outlay of money, but that the budgets
of public libraries and libraries of educational institutions will have to be
increased; that the appropriations to education departments of states and
public-school districts will have to be raised because of the higher prices
of most textbooks; that these expenditures will be met partly by raising
taxes and partly at the expense of other educational outlays, including
teachers' salaries; that expenditures for lawyers' fees and court costs will
go up because of the increase in litigation of copyright cases; and that the
chief redistributive effects will be from book readers, researchers, teachers,
and taxpayers to the grandchildren of the authors of the (very few) successful books. Now all this is on the possibility or transformation side of
the prediction. What about the evaluation of the changes involved?

The welfare economist will have to decide how much "society" will
delight in the publication of the additional titles (including those on sex
and economics); how much "society" will resent paying higher taxes; how
much it will appreciate the decrease in teachers' salaries and increase in
lawyers' incomes; and, especially, how much it will relish the thought that

---

14 This can also be said of particular decisions on problems of individual households and firms, but with different implications. It means only that their reactions
cannot always be correctly predicted and, unless odd decisions cancel out, predictions of reactions of aggregate supply and demand may be less than accurate. The
problem is quite different with regard to a single Grand Arbiter of Social Welfare.

some fortunate heirs of authors will receive royalties on the literary products of their late grandfathers or great-aunts.

The use of value-loaded language in the exposition of this piece of
applied welfare economics may have revealed the value judgments of
the present writer. Whether these judgments agree with those of the
majority of the people or of the legislators in Congress is not known, but is
quite unlikely. The best that I can say in support of my value judgment is
that I presume that most other people would agree with me if, but only if,
they thought about the problem hard enough.

The point of my illustration, however, was not that my valuations may
be peculiar prejudices not shared by others; what I intended to show was
that my value system could not possibly have been specific on the merits
or demerits of potential gifts to unknown grandchildren of authors of books
that still enjoy sales long after their publication. This spot on my social-
welfare function was completely blank until the problem arose and I had
to fill in the relevant valuations for the occasion. I could, of course, assert·
that my appraisal of the legislative action represents a logical inference
from my value system and that I can *now* give the necessary specification
for others to check my logic. I still doubt that this will meet the objections
that the whole procedure is "unscientific."

One more difficulty should be considered: the welfare economist's valuations of future benefits derived from present sacrifices, and of present
benefits obtained at the cost of future sacrifices. Some welfare economists
are very generous toward future generations and are prepared to give away
much of the income of their own contemporaries. Others are quite stingy
and resent making sacrifices for the yet unborn great-grandchildren of
their friends and fellow taxpayers. ("Why should I do so much for posterity? What has posterity done for me?") Any social indifference map
presupposes given sets of rates of time preference (generosity or stinginess *vis-à-vis* future generations), and thus is the result of entirely subjective inclinations.

It may seem that a way out of this and all similar difficulties would be
not to specify just one social-value system, but to give the client or advisee
(that is, the representatives of society) a large set of alternative systems
from which to choose. This is not really practicable, however, simply because there are an infinite number of possible preference systems. It is
not feasible to propose a sufficiently large number of alternative value
systems to do justice to the existing variety of tastes and preferences. It is
not feasible to tell those in the seats of government that they have a choice
among millions of different value systems and that, corresponding to each,
there may be a different answer to their specific questions. The welfare
economist, if he is very conscientious, will at best specify a small sample

of alternative welfare functions and, in limiting the open choices in this way, will again have engaged in normative economics.

STAYING PURE VERSUS COMING CLEAN

Having concluded that welfare economics is normative in character, the purists among us may cry, "Unclean! Unclean!" whenever they see a piece of welfare analysis. This would be unfortunate. Even if welfare economics is impure, it is a necessary part of our work.

The recent fashion for "cost-benefit analysis" represents a healthy recognition of the danger of choosing blindly and of the advantages of making choices on the basis of a rational consideration of alternatives. It is true that the considerations include estimates of benefits that rest on more or less arbitrary valuations, but this does not imply that we would be better off if we avoided all "unscientific" estimates and made our decisions without considering what the effects might be and how we would like them.

Honesty demands that we be frank about the evaluative nature of our appraisals and recommendations. But this does not mean that we must write long methodological introductions to each and every policy memorandum. If we did, we would only increase the percentage of memoranda reaching their final destination—the files—without being read by those to whom they were addressed. This would be too bad. A great deal needs to be done to improve the quality of economic policy advice. We can meet the demands of honesty by discussing and justifying the value assumptions made in the analysis and, even better, by showing how the findings would be affected if we varied the value assumptions. As a rule, we probably will indicate which value position we regard as the most "reasonable." Most of us will do this in a rather unmistakable way, since we are usually convinced that our own ethical values are more ethical than others.

Part Seven

ON VARIOUS
METHODOLOGICAL
POSITIONS

INTRODUCTION TO PART SEVEN

The nine chapters, mostly short, in this last part of the volume deal with methodological writings of several social scientists: three sociologists and seven economists. Some of my discussions were written as book reviews, others as replies or rejoinders to papers they had published. Only one of my pieces was a longer appraisal of the cumulative methodological contributions of an author over a period of 44 years.

This appraisal is republished here as Chapter 18, "Schumpeter's Economic Methodology." It was originally published in the *Review of Economics and Statistics*, Vol. 33 (May 1951), a year after Schumpeter's death, and then collected as one of 20 evaluative essays in a volume edited by Seymour E. Harris, *Schumpeter, Social Scientist* (Cambridge, Mass.: Harvard University Press, 1951).

My essay stresses Schumpeter's lifelong effort to combine historical, statistical, and theoretical analysis. But it also shows significant changes in Schumpeter's position, for example, from an early rejection of the search for "causality" to a statement that "the question of causation is the Fundamental Question"; or from an early lack of interest in "motives of human conduct" to the almost loving formation of an ideal type of the "dynamic entrepreneur" who fills the "leadership function" in the economic system. The two of Schumpeter's most significant contributions to the methodology of the social sciences were, in my opinion, first the realization that the numerical data that make economics the most naturally quantitative of all sciences (more so than physics) would nevertheless neither form the basis of induction nor permit their use for verification or refutation of economic theories; and, second, the emphasis upon (and perhaps also the coinage of the phrase) "methodological individualism," a procedural rule that is quite independent of political individualism but implies a rejection of methodological collectivism.

Chapter 19, "Gunnar Myrdal on Concealed Value Judgments," is the republication of my review of the English translation of his book *The Political Element in the Development of Economic Theory.* My review was published in the *American Economic Review,* Vol. 45 (December 1955).

Myrdal's book is a sharp attack on classical utilitarianism and economic liberalism. The former, he charges, was "little more than a more elaborate formulation of the natural law doctrines," and the latter is "unrealistic in its premises and fallacious in its deductions." Strangely enough, he is much harder on the British ideologies (leading up to welfare economics) than on the Austrians. He rejects as metaphysical the idea that one can judge social policy from a "purely economic point of view." While I found Myrdal's strictures against concealed value judgments largely justified, though often exaggerated, I was unable to understand, let alone accept, his remedial prescriptions. He wants economics to engage, to the exclusion of its traditionally analytical and empirical research, in surveys and analyses of the people's attitudes; our problem is that of "the social psychology of the character of groups." This notion was advanced in the German edition of Myrdal's book, published in 1930. The Myrdal of 1954 no longer pushed these proposals, but in his battle against nonexplicit value judgments he had become even more extreme. He had come to hold that economists were biased not only in their policy recommendations or policy analyses, in their welfare economics, in their interventionist or anti-interventionist preconceptions, and in their national-income measurements, but also in all their empirical observations, theoretical concept formations, and primarily in their choice of problems and data to be analyzed.

"Paul Samuelson on Theory and Realism," Chapter 20 of this volume, was originally published as a note in the *American Economic Review* Vol. 54 (September 1964). I wrote it in reply to Samuelson's paper "Problems of Methodology: Discussion," in which he had criticized "theories which employ unrealistic assumptions" and had concluded with the dictum that "if the abstract models contain empirical falsities, we must jettison the models, not gloss over their inadequacies."

Samuelson, dismissing as nonsense the view that the assumptions may be "wider" than the theory and the theory wider than the consequences, proclaims that the consequences inferred from a theory must in turn imply the theory. This restriction constitutes, I hold, the most extreme empiricism ever propounded. It is generally agreed that a theory must be wider than any of the consequences deduced; indeed, it is the very function of theory to permit inferences regarding future events. Samuelson, the brilliant economic theorist, fortunately has never accepted the constraints which Samuelson, the stern methodologist, wishes to impose. In my paper, I present one of Samuelson's famous theorems—on the international equalization of the prices of equal productive factors—which he deduces from a large set of abstract, unrealistic assumptions, some of which are patently counterfactual. And he explains observed facts of life by divergences of real conditions from the ideal ones that form the basis of his theorem. Good for him and good for economic theory!

Chapter 21 discusses three books by sociologists. Under the title "Three Writers on Social Theory: Madge, Rose, and Zetterberg" it republishes my review from the *American Economic Review*, Vol. 45 (June 1955), of John Madge, *The Tools of Social Science;* Arnold M. Rose, *Theory and Method in the Social Sciences;* and Hans L. Zetterberg, *On Theory and Verification in Sociology.*

My review deplores Madge's "scientistic preconceptions, his ultraempiricism, positivism, and behaviorism," but rejoices in the fact that Rose's book answered and corrected virtually all of Madge's misunderstandings and misjudgments. Rose's distinction between "a pile of discrete bits of knowledge" and "an integrated body of propositions" is given honorable display. Zetterberg's position is shown to be similarly enlightened, especially when he asks that "miniature theories" be integrated, and holds that "we explain something by demonstrating that it follows the laws of other phenomena."

Chapter 22 is on "John Neville Keynes' Scope and Method." It was originally published in the *Southern Economic Journal* Vol. 23 (January 1957) as a review of the reprinting (by Kelley and Millman) of the fourth edition of John Neville Keynes' renowned book, *The Scope and Method of Political Economy*, which had first appeared in 1890, at the end of the *Methodenstreit* between Menger and Schmoller: Keynes set out to represent both sides without prejudice.

Political economy, according to Keynes, deals with uniformities, ideals, and precepts: It does the first as a science, the second as ethics, the third as an art (though in this art it has to join forces with "political and social science" as well as social philosophy). The first two are positive and normative economics. As to the former, Keynes emphatically states that mere description cannot constitute a science: "Economics is of necessity a science of cause and effect." The role of observation and experiment in science are discussed in connection with Mill's canons of induction. The impossibility of obtaining exact numerical data does not preclude mathematical methods in economics. "One of the most important functions of mathematical analysis is to discover determinate relations between quantities whose numerical values are unassignable." J. N. Keynes' methodological views are so sound and are set forth so lucidly that I have nothing but praise for his good sense. As I say in my review, "teachers in all fields of economics will render a service to their students if they urge them to read this fine little book."

"Terence W. Hutchison's Reluctant Ultra-Empiricism" is the title of Chapter 23, which reprints without change my "Rejoinder to a Reluctant Ultra-Empiricist" from the *Southern Economic Journal*, Vol. 22 (April 1956). This rejoinder was prompted by a reply Hutchison had written to my paper on "The Problem of Verification in Economics" (reprinted as Chapter 5 of this volume). All three pieces— article, reply, and rejoinder—were included in the Italian book by

Machlup, Hutchison, and Grunberg, *La verifica delle leggi economiche* (Milano: Editrice L'Industria, 1959), and in the Spanish journal *Revista de Economía Política*, Vol. 9 (1958).

Hutchison protested my characterization of his position as ultra-empiricism, which I had defined as a demand for direct empirical testing of propositions used as fundamental assumptions in a theoretical system. There was a misunderstanding of the meaning of indirect testing. Hutchison meant by it that a proposition that was not *itself* empirically testable directly was still acceptable if it was reducible by *direct* deduction to other empirically testable propositions. To me *conjunction of logically independent propositions and derivation of their joint consequences* is the essence of indirect testing. The difference between the two positions can be seen most clearly in connection with my "analytical apparatus" or "machine of pure theory." Hutchison would want to subject the fundamental postulates which are parts of my machine to empirical tests. I would test only the inputs (assumed changes) that are fed into the machine, and the outputs (deduced changes) that come out of the machine; and I would say that the machine has proved itself—has passed the test together with the whole caboodle—if the correspondence of the assumed and deduced changes of variables *outside* the machine with their observed proxies is satisfactory. Another strategic difference in our basic understanding is that Hutchison admits only two categories of propositions: those that can be proved false by empirical tests and those that are meaningless. I recognize a third category, namely, variously called resolutions or rules of procedure (complex-analytic propositions, constitutive nonepistemic propositions, research programs, and so on). They are neither falsifiable nor meaningless; they may be applicable and efficient, or inefficient and inapplicable, but they cannot be proved false.

With Chapter 24, "Adolf Lowe's Instrumental Analysis," we come back to where we left off in Chapter 17. The last six pages of my contribution to the Lowe symposium, published in Robert L. Heilbroner, ed., *Economic Means and Social Ends*, were devoted to a review of Lowe's methodological views and are here reprinted without change apart from an expansion of the first paragraph.

For Lowe, instrumentalism is not what it means to other writers on philosophy or economics. Given an initial state of affairs ("macro-state") and another state to which we wish to move ("macro-goal"), given, further, certain "laws of nature" (physical laws), "engineering rules," and empirical generalizations "concerning sociopsychological relations," Lowe's questions are (1) What path is suitable to that movement? (2) What patterns of micro-behavior are appropriate to keep the system on that path? (3) What micro-motivations are capable of generating suitable behavior? (4) What political control can be designed to stimulate suitable motivations? Lowe holds that the analysis that answers these questions is based neither on positive nor on normative economics. My objections are twofold: If there are several goals and several paths toward their attainment, *normative* economics is indispensable for rational choices; and if judgments are needed regarding "suitable" paths, "appropriate" micro-behavior, "capable" micro-motivations, and adequate (or efficient) political controls, *positive* economics is indispensable. Nor can I help venting my misgivings about all the goal-choosing and control-imposing tasks that Lowe assigns to the authorities, though he makes some soothing provisos for the sake of political freedom. Since Lowe expresses the hope that the instrumental analysts will avoid crossing over the "critical boundary" into normative economics, I may say that I am far less afraid of the analysts' value judgments than I am of the bureaucrats' power to manipulate and coerce people.

Chapter 25, "Friedrich Hayek on Scientific and Scientistic Attitudes," reproduces a few pages from my article "Friedrich von Hayek's Contribution to Economics," first published in the *Swedish Journal of Economics,* Vol. 76 [December 1974, pp. 498–531,] and reprinted in Fritz Machlup, ed., *Essays on Hayek* (New York: New York University Press, 1976, pp. 45–50). The selected pages are designed to review Hayek's work on the philosophy of science.

With his strictures against "scientism," a term he had taken from French writings, Hayek intended no slight of scientific method or of the methods appropriate to natural sciences. He merely criticized the "slavish imitation of the method and language" of the natural sciences in the study of society. He explains that "the scientistic as distinguished from the scientific view is . . . a very prejudiced approach which, before it has considered its subject, claims to know what is the most appropriate way of investigating it." My review touches upon several other of Hayek's insights into methodological problems. It quotes some of his statements on "degrees of explanation" and "degrees of abstraction." It calls attention to Hayek's warnings against economists who are only economists and may through their narrow concentration on their specialty become a positive danger to society. The review concludes with references to Hayek's essay, "The Primacy of the Abstract," in which he talks about the existence of subconscious rules that guide perception; this has often been recognized by eminent psychologists and philosophers, but unfortunately is disregarded by the believers in the primacy of the concrete.

Chapter 26, the last in this volume, has the title "Spiro Latsis on Situational Determinism." It reproduces my article, "Situational Determinism in Economics," published in the *British Journal for the Philosophy of Science*, Vol. 25 (1974) and written in reply to an article Latsis had published in 1972 under the same title.

By situational determinism, Latsis meant a theoretical system that allowed for only a "single exit," determined by the specific situation. In a model of a firm run by a single mind, conducting its business with the aim of maximizing profit but under the pressure of effective competition (so that the highest possible profits will be just enough to cover the lowest possible costs), any particular change in the *situation* will have a *determinate* effect. Hence the expression in the titles of Latsis' article and my reply. Latsis contrasted this kind of economic determinism with "economic behavioralism," which substitutes for the single goal of profit maximization pursued by a single decision-maker a collection of different goals pursued by a collection of different managers, without however postulating or specifying either the managers' attitudes or their goals but, instead, trying to obtain these unknowns by empirical research. This is indeed a research program different from simple marginal analysis. It may yield insights into the ways a particular firm is managed at a particular time by a particular team of executives. Whether it can yield generalizations that apply to other firms at other times, run by other types of managers, is an open question. Latsis had examined the "two rival research programs" from the point of view of the "Methodology of Scientific Research Programmes" (MSRP), advanced by the logician Imre Lakatos, and he had many interesting things to say on both marginal and behavioral analyses of the firm. The chief points in my reply are that the two research programs are not really rivals, since they deal with different problems; and that behavioralism will be successful only if it succeeds in furnishing determinate solutions, and thereby becomes behavioral determinism.

Perhaps I may take this opportunity to bring to the reader's notice a book, *Method and Appraisal in Economics,* edited by Spiro Latsis (Cambridge: Cambridge University Press, 1976). It has just reached my desk as I am writing this part's introduction. It contains a very informative and interesting discussion of "alternative methodologies of economics" and of "the Methodology of Scientific Research Programmes" developed by Imre Lakatos. Latsis distinguishes three major methodologies of economic and social inquiries: apriorism, falsificationism, and conventionalism. He labels me a conventionalist —in the sense of one who accepts as meaningful and useful basic propositions that make no assertions but are conventions (resolutions, postulates) with regard to analytic procedure. I accept this label.

Chapter 18

JOSEPH SCHUMPETER'S ECONOMIC METHODOLOGY

The very first article which Schumpeter published—in 1906—was a plea for the use of the *mathematical* method in economic theory.[1] Two months before his death—in November 1949—he delivered a paper pleading for the use of the *historical* method in business-cycle analysis.[2]

Can the fact that the 23-year-old Schumpeter stood up for mathematical economics and the 67-year-old Schumpeter for economic history be taken as indicative of a trend in his development? Such a trend would be typical of great minds in our field. Yet those who know Schumpeter's work well will know that his was not an evolution from the youthful keenness of a mathematical turn of mind to the mature perspective of a historical one. For they know that Schumpeter never lost the one and never lacked the other. They have seen how consistently throughout his 44 years of writing he worked for a "combination of historical, statistical, and theoretical analysis" and

[1] "Über die mathematische Methode der theoretischen Ökonomie," *Zeitschhrift für Volkswirtschaft, Sozialpolitik und Verwaltung*, 15 Band (1906), pp. 30–49.

[2] "The Historical Approach to the Analysis of Business Cycles," Universities-National Bureau Conference on Business Cycle Research, November 25–27, 1949.

"their mutual peaceful penetration." [3] They have seen how Schumpeter from the very beginning insisted that there was "no contradiction between the historical and the abstract approaches, and that the only difference was in their interest for different problems." [4] They have seen how he would accompany a strong plea for econometric research and mathematical economics by the reassurance that "nothing is farther from our minds than any acrimonious belief in the exclusive excellence of mathematical methods." [5] Indeed, they have seen how he could acclaim "Léon Walras as the greatest of all economists" [6] and Walras and v. Wieser as "the two authors to whom [he] felt closest affinity," [7] and then turn around and pay most reverent homage to Gustav v. Schmoller, the militant leader of the historical school. [8]

Schumpeter spoke sometimes of the sterility of methodological debates, and once he wrote: "Not the first, but the last chapter of a system should deal with its methodology." [9] Yet his very first article as well as his first book were on the methodology of economics; and indeed almost everything he ever wrote contained general methodological discussions or comments. What may have driven him constantly back to the theme which apparently he wished to avoid and which he regarded as neither very "meaningful nor fruitful"? [10]

I submit that, with his superior understanding of general epistemology and scientific method and his extensive learning and reading in many fields of knowledge, he could not stand the methodological nonsense that was continually advertised by the various "authorities" in the field. When others reiterated their bigoted patter,

[3] *Business Cycles: A Theoretical, Historical, and Statistical Analysis of the Capitalist Process* (New York, 1939), p. v.

[4] *Das Wesen und Hauptinhalt der theoretischen Nationalökonomie* (Leipzig, 1908), p. 7.

[5] "The Common Sense of Econometrics," *Econometrica*, 1 (1933), p. 5.

[6] *Ibid.*, p. 9.

[7] *Das Wesen*, p. ix.

[8] "Gustav v. Schmoller und die Probleme von heute," *Schmollers Jahrbuch für Gesetzgebung, Verwaltung und Volkswirtschaft im Deutschen Reich*, 50 Jahrg. (1926), pp. 337–88.

[9] *Das Wesen*, p. xv. Cf. Dr. Schneider's essay in this issue.—Ed.

[10] "Gustav v. Schmoller," p. 337. Elsewhere Schumpeter has said: "The armor of methodological commentaries I renounce completely." (*The Theory of Economic Development*, Cambridge, Mass., 1934, p. 4.)

Schumpeter could not help coming back with his own message, which urged methodological tolerance and was intolerant only of illiteracy and intolerance itself.

METHODOLOGICAL TOLERANCE

At the time Schumpeter began to write, hoping to contribute "to the epistemology of our science," [11] most Continental economists' blood was still boiling from the excitement of the *Methodenstreit*, and his own teachers had not forgiven their foes. Schumpeter attempted reconciliation between the warring schools by emphasizing that no method can be universally good or bad, and that we should abstain from claiming "general validity" or superiority for any method.[12]

"Each method has its areas of application," he said, and by way of example he added that one could not use the historical method for developing the theory of prices, or the abstract method for "the problem of the organization of the economy." [13] He explained the existing antagonism between theorists and historians by the fact that "description and theory call for different methods, and appeal to persons of very different talents and natural turns of mind." [14] But, "unless one chooses to characterize all reflection as essentially antidescriptive theory, and all observation as essentially antitheoretical description,

[11] *Das Wesen*, pp. 117–18; also p. xii.

[12] "The method which we have found useful need not on this account have general validity. Surely we shall *try* to continue applying it, but the attempt may turn out good or bad; and in the latter case our method would no more be generally bad than it would be generally good in the first case." *Ibid.*, p. xiv.

[13] *Ibid.*, p. 7.

[14] *Ibid.*, p. 42. Schumpeter lamented, however, that so many believed they saw methodological contrasts where none existed. For example, he denied that the methods of Ricardo and Malthus were different. He denied especially that Malthus' work was more historical and less theoretical in nature than Ricardo's, although many who wrote about them were convinced of it and even Ricardo and Malthus themselves thought so. Said Schumpeter: "It is quite common for scholars in a controversy, when they make no headway with concrete arguments, to blame each other for using faulty methods. Ricardo lost his patience with his clumsier opponent, and the latter called anything he could not grasp 'too abstract'. That is all." "Epochen der Dogmen- und Methodengeschichte," *Grundriss der Sozialökonomik* 1. Abteilung (Tübingen, 1914), p. 60.

one will have to admit . . . that both 'methods' often converge and become indistinguishable." [15]

The social sciences, said Schumpeter, suffer from two deep-seated and pernicious ills: "first, from that almost childish narrow-mindedness which regards its own method of work as the only possible one, wishes to make it the universal one, and considers that one's foremost task is to annihilate all others in holy anger; second, from that complete lack of even elementary knowledge of all branches of learning outside one's own." [16] Schumpeter made this diagnosis of the state of the social sciences in a spirit of disgust over certain "positivist" criticisms of economic theory and he asked impatiently: "When at last will the day come when all will realize . . . that the ocean of facts has innumerable different aspects which call for innumerable different modes of approach?" [17]

ECONOMIC SCIENCE

The rejection of absolutism in economic methodology, and the equal respect for modes of approach which had been presented as mutually exclusive—a conciliatoriness which could be misjudged as weak eclecticism—rested in Schumpeter's case on very strong convictions in matters of scientific procedure. Speaking for the founders of the Econometric Society he stated: ". . . we have no common credo beyond holding: first, that economics is a science, and secondly, that this science has one very important quantitative aspect." [18]

From the very beginning Schumpeter had held that, methodologically, economics was more closely akin to the natural sciences than to other social sciences.[19] Later he went beyond this position when he stated: "There is . . . one sense in which economics is the

---

[15] "Gustav v. Schmoller," p. 375.

[16] "Die 'positive' Methode in der Nationalökonomie," *Deutsche Literaturzeitung,* xxxv Jahrgang (1914), p. 2101.

[17] *Ibid.,* p. 2108.

[18] "The Common Sense," p. 5.

[19] "Über die mathematische Methode," p. 36; *Das Wesen,* p. 533.

most quantitative, not only of 'social' or 'moral' sciences, but of *all* sciences, physics not excluded. For mass, velocity, current, and the like *can* undoubtedly be measured, but in order to do so we must always invent a distinct process of measurement. This must be done before we can deal with these phenomena *numerically*. Some of the most fundamental economic facts, on the contrary, already present themselves to our observation as quantities made numerical by life itself. They carry meaning only by virtue of their numerical character. There would be [physical] movement even if we were unable to turn it into measurable quantity, but there cannot be prices independent of the numerical expression of every one of them, and of definite numerical relations among all of them." [20]

Schumpeter's emphasis on the character of economics as a quantitative science, as an equilibrium system whose elements are "quantities of goods," led him to regard it as unnecessary and, hence, as methodologically mistaken for economics to deal with "economic conduct" and with the "motives of human conduct." [21] He conceded that a relationship between the value functions which the economist must assume and certain psychological or physiological facts may well exist, but this relationship "is only of philosophical interest. For the economic *results* it is irrelevant and it can never be the task of the economist to go into these matters." [22]

His conclusion, a strict denial of any "methodological or material connection" between economics and psychology,[23] has long remained a contested issue. But Schumpeter himself was by no means obstinate or narrow in the matter. In his own analytical work he soon found it fruitful to discuss types of human motivation and conduct. This was particularly true when he came to elaborate his model of economic development, for which he needed the conduct model of the "dynamic entrepreneur," of the man filling the "leadership function" in the economic system.[24]

[20] "The Common Sense," pp. 5–6. (Italics in the original.)
[21] *Das Wesen*, pp. 28, 30, 154, 542, 568.
[22] *Ibid.*, p. 542. (Italics in the original.)
[23] *Ibid.*, p. 544.
[24] In the first edition of the *Theorie der wirtschaftlichen Entwicklung* (Leipzig, 1912) he distinguished a "hedonic-static" and a "dynamic-energetic" type of economic conduct (p. 128) and proceeded to offer a "psychological explanation" (p. 134).

FUNCTIONAL VERSUS CAUSAL
RELATIONSHIPS

In his earlier writings Schumpeter tried to discard "causality" as a conception relevant for economic theory. He wanted "to avoid the concepts 'cause' and 'effect' and to replace them by the more perfect concept of the function." [25] His reason for this preference was that the latter, "carefully developed by mathematics, has a content which is clear and unambiguous while the concept of causation has not." [26]

On this point Schumpeter changed his mind. The "epistemological indictment" of the concept of causation, he later held, need not extend to its common-sense meaning. And "our mind will never be at rest until all our measurements and descriptions of mechanisms and propositions about relations are linked to the causes indicated in such a way that they may be understood to follow from them or, to put the same thing in our language, until we have assembled in one model causes, mechanisms, and effects, and can show how it works. And in this sense, whatever we may object, the question of causation is the Fundamental Question, although it is neither the only one nor the first to be asked." [27]

But, be it functional or be it causal relationships that to him were fundamental, Schumpeter never changed his views regarding the proper way to establish them. Even if general, economic, and industrial *history* are "really the most important contributors to the understanding" of our problems,[28] and even if *statistical* research appears to be required by the quantitative and numerical nature of economic science, it is economic *theory* which in its "schemas" or "models" and in its "theorems" defines and describes (or constructs) the relevant relationships. The "raw facts are, as such, a meaningless jumble" [29] and "it is absurd to think that we can derive [even] the contour

[25] *Das Wesen*, p. xvi.

[26] *Ibid.*, p. 47.

[27] *Business Cycles*, p. 34. As early as 1911 Schumpeter had abandoned his dislike of the concept of causation; for example, when he stated: "When we succeed in finding a definite causal relation between two phenomena, our problem is solved if the one which plays the 'causal' rôle is noneconomic." *The Theory of Economic Development*, pp. 4–5.

[28] *Business Cycles*, p. 13.

[29] *Ibid.*, p. 30.

lines of our phenomena from our statistical material only." [30] No "statistical method, however refined" [31] will help us toward this goal. "We must put our trust in bold and unsafe mental experiments or else give up all hope." [32]

ASSUMPTIONS, MODELS, FACTS, AND VERIFICATIONS

The model or schema (as it was invariably called in Schumpeter's earlier work) rests entirely on assumptions and "is, thus, a creation of our discretion, just as any other exact science. . . . To be sure, neither our 'assumptions' nor our 'laws' lie in the real world of phenomena. . . . But this does not preclude them from *fitting* the facts. How can this be? Simply because in constructing our schema we proceeded, no doubt arbitrarily, but reasonably in that *we designed the schema with the facts in mind.*" [33]

This is the "decisive point" in Schumpeter's epistemological position: "On the one hand, our theory is in essence *arbitrary*, and on this are based its system, its rigor, and its exactness; on the other hand, it *fits* the phenomena and is *conditioned* by them, and this alone gives it content and significance." [34]

That our hypotheses, "although just as arbitrary as our definitions" are conditioned by "facts," distinguishes them, in Schumpeter's view, from "aprioristic speculations." [35] He concedes that "some of our refinements upon common sense are logically anterior to the facts we wish to study and must be introduced first, because our factual discussions would be impossible without them." [36] But this must not be confused with the aprioristic position in economic theory. Schum-

---

[30] *Ibid.,* p. 13.

[31] *Ibid.,* p. 30.

[32] *Ibid.,* p. 13.

[33] *Das Wesen,* p. 527. (Italics in the original.) Schumpeter refers in this connection to the analogy of the tailor who uses his discretion in cutting the cloth and making the coat, which nonetheless is expected to fit.

[34] *Ibid.,* p. 533. (Italics are mine.) It is noteworthy how closely these formulations—published in 1908—correspond to the most recent statements with respect to the methodology of physics.

[35] *Ibid.,* p. 46. Remarks such as "aprioristic, unscientific speculations, little better than scholasticism," can be found in many of Schumpeter's writings. See, e.g., *Vergangenheit und Zukunft der Sozialwissenschaften* (Leipzig, 1915), p. 74.

[36] *Business Cycles,* p. 31.

peter insists that the "basic assumptions" of pure theory rest on "observation of facts," only that most of them "are so simple and are so strikingly confirmed by everyday experience as well as historical experience that it would be a shame to waste paper printing any special compilations of facts to confirm them." [37]

If facts—the simple facts of our immediate everyday experience as well as "statistical and historical facts"—"induce the theoretical work and determine its pattern," can they also fill "the function that theorists usually assign to them—the function of verification?" [38] No, said Schumpeter, and he explained his answer with reference to statistical facts: "But no statistical finding can ever either prove or disprove a proposition which we have reason to believe by virtue of simpler and more fundamental facts. It cannot prove such a proposition, because one and the same behavior of a time series can analytically be accounted for in an indefinite number of ways. It cannot disprove the proposition, because a very real relation may be so overlaid by other influences acting on the statistical material under study as to become entirely lost in the numerical picture, without thereby losing its importance for our understanding of the case. It follows that the claim usually made for statistical induction and verification must be qualified. Material exposed to so many disturbances as ours is, does not fulfill the logical requirements of the process of induction." [39]

QUANTITATIVE AND NUMERICAL ECONOMICS

The position that statistical research serves more to ask than to answer questions of the economic theorist is sometimes regarded as antagonistic to empirical research. This was surely not so in Schumpeter's case. Indeed, by correcting the inflated claims of statisticians of the purely inductive school, he did more to bring about the coalition of statistical and theoretical analysts than could have been done in any other way. And in taking a most active part, or lead, in the promotion of econometrics, he worked for that mutual penetration

[37] "Die 'positive' Methode," p. 2104.
[38] *Business Cycles*, p. 32.
[39] *Ibid.*, p. 33.

FRITZ MACHLUP

of quantitative economic theory and statistical observation which had been his program during his entire career.

In his 1906 article, in which he championed the use of the "mathematical method" in economics, he was careful to distinguish between quantitative and numerical relations. He contended that the establishment of quantitative relations need not wait for numerical data and, indeed, must precede them.[40] But that the numerical data would eventually have to be supplied through statistical research was clear to him. In his 1908 book, he coined the expression "*rechnendes Verfahren*" for this necessary cooperation between economic theory and statistics. And he said: "I expect much from it; even the most modest result, no matter how much it will be ridiculed and criticized —as it surely will be, since nothing is easier than to criticize first attempts—will be a colossal step forward on the road of the development of our discipline." [41]

This econometric program he presented more than twenty years before the foundation of the Econometric Society.

ECONOMIC DYNAMICS

We have pointed out how tolerant Schumpeter was with regard to methodological rivalries; he was similarly tolerant in terminological questions. He had originally adopted the terms "Statics" and

[40] "The most important thing is, first, to find the existence of functional relations and, second, to know as many properties of these functions as possible. One can, then, establish algebraic expressions even if their numerical magnitudes cannot be found." "Über die mathematische Methode," p. 37. Quite apart from any numerical magnitudes, the mathematical method, according to Schumpeter, is "just *the* appropriate instrument" of exposition because the use of "systems of simultaneous equations for the representation of economic interrelationships affords a comprehension [*Überblick*] of them that cannot otherwise be attained with the same clarity." "Epochen," p. 110.

[41] *Das Wesen*, p. 607. An interesting suggestion for statistical research designed to yield numerical values for quantitative relationships was made by Schumpeter in 1914, when he called for "more exact data on the propensity to save [*Intensität des Spartriebs*] in different social strata." ("Die 'positive' Methode," p. 2105.) Similar remarks, made in 1915, on the significance of statistical research for our "knowledge about the shape of the demand curve" and even for the evaluation of the benefits and costs of particular measures of economic policy can be found in *Vergangenheit und Zukunft*, p. 125.

"Dynamics" as suitable for his purposes. His 1908 and 1911 books made ample use of the terms; indeed, he stated that his "exposition rests on the fundamental distinction between 'Statics' and 'Dynamics'." [42] By 1926, in the second edition of his *Theory of Economic Development*, he found that the terms had been used by others with "innumerable meanings" and, in order to avoid confusion, he used "theory of the circular flow" for what in 1911 he had called Statics, and "theory of development" for what he had called Dynamics.[43] By 1939, when he published his book on *Business Cycles*, he used the terms Statics and Dynamics, "in deference to Professor Frisch," to distinguish theorems which include "values of variables which belong to different points of time" from others where all variables refer to the same point of time.[44]

After this digression on Schumpeter's willingness to give up his private meanings of the terms when he found that in the public domain, or rather at the hands of respected colleagues, they had acquired different but precise meanings, we may turn to a discussion of the ideas for which he had originally used them.

"Statics and Dynamics are completely different fields, dealing not only with different problems, but also with different methods and different material." [45] Statics is the equilibrium system operating with given basic assumptions, mechanisms, and data, to show the effects of small and continuous changes of these data.[46] Large and discontinuous changes call for the method of "Dynamics." But Schumpeter emphasized that neither "smallness" or "continuity" need be taken literally, and that it would be against his principles to give "an absolute, inflexible rule" determining an "exact boundary line" between Statics and Dynamics. There are, on the one hand, many safe applications for static theory; on the other, there are problems for which it would be clearly inappropriate and dynamic theory is prescribed. "In-between, however, there is a range which is methodologically and epistemologically most interesting; the

[42] *Das Wesen*, p. xix. He stated, however, that the terms were not felicitous (p. 182) and subject to gross misuse (pp. 614–15).

[43] *The Theory of Economic Development*, pp. 60–64. The English edition was translated from the second German edition, which was published in 1926.

[44] *Business Cycles*, p. 48.

[45] *Das Wesen*, p. 182.

[46] *Ibid.*, pp. 183, 458–59, 464–65.

range, namely, where it is advisable to use our [static] method—although its presuppositions are strictly not fulfilled—because it in fact leads to usable results; but also . . . where . . . we may prefer . . . [Dynamics] because we do not get enough out of [Statics]. To proceed correctly here calls for tact and judgment, or almost 'instinct', and it is here that we are confronted with perhaps the most fascinating questions of epistemology." [47]

Some of the problems which J. B. Clark had regarded as essentially dynamic, such as increase in population or capital, are for Schumpeter mere changes of data, disturbances of the static equilibrium; and "these changes are small per annum and therefore do not stand in the way of the applicability of the 'static' method." [48] Changes in technique and productive organization, however, are truly dynamic problems, because they represent discontinuous "revolutionary change." Dynamics (or "theory of development") is needed to deal with "such changes in economic life as are not forced upon it from without but arise by its own initiative, from within." Development in this sense is "a distinct phenomenon, entirely foreign to what may be observed in the circular flow or in the tendency toward equilibrium. It is spontaneous and discontinuous change in the channels of the flow. . . ." [49]

The really revolutionary change which Schumpeter proposed for the structure of economic theory was to banish some of the most important economic concepts, such as profit, entrepreneurship, and interest, from the realm of Statics and to deport them to Dynamics. This methodological revolution has not been fully successful even with those who thought in terms of Schumpeter's original terminology. Most of them have continued to find some useful work which these concepts can do in Statics, from which they were to be locked out.

METHODOLOGICAL INDIVIDUALISM

A Schumpeterian innovation which was fully successful in the sense that it has been explicitly accepted by some and implicitly by

[47] *Ibid.*, p. 185.
[48] *The Theory of Economic Development*, pp. 60, 63.
[49] *Ibid.*, pp. 63, 64.

practically all modern economists is the distinction between political and methodological individualism.[50]

The distinction is essential because political and methodological individualism are often mistakenly considered to be the same, but in fact "have nothing in common. The former starts from general premises, such as that freedom contributes more than anything else to the progress of mankind and to the common welfare, and proceeds to a series of practical assertions; the latter does nothing of the sort, asserts nothing and has no particular premises. It means merely that in the description of certain economic processes one had better begin with the actions of individuals." [51] Some people may, of course, endorse both political and methodological individualism; but it is equally possible that a socialist finds methodological individualism preferable for use in his analysis, or that a political individualist chooses to employ "social categories" [collectives] in his. The significance of the conceptual separation is, to Schumpeter, that economic theory may employ a sound individualistic or "atomistic" method without burdening itself with a political program such as *laissez faire*.[52]

Schumpeter rejects methodological collectivism—which he calls the "*soziale Betrachtungsweise*" or the "use of social categories"—simply because it "has no appreciable advantages, and thus is superfluous," in economic analysis. He does not deny strong social influences upon the conduct of the individual, the close ties between the members of the social group, or the importance which social entities may have for sociological analysis. But he is concerned with pure economic analysis, and for it methodological individualism—although not preferable on any *a priori* grounds—has proved most useful.

Again, "that social influences determine the conduct of the individual, and that the individual is a microscopically small factor, is all admitted but entirely irrelevant for our purposes. What matters

[50] I assume Schumpeter was the first to make the distinction, or at least that he coined the words necessary to express it, because he said that he was "proposing the name 'methodological individualism'." (*Das Wesen*, p. 94.)

[51] *Ibid.*, p. 90.

[52] *Ibid.*, p. 91. See also *Business Cycles*, p. vi.

FRITZ MACHLUP

for us is not how these things really are but how me must schematize or stylize them in order to serve best our purposes. . . ." [53]

PURE SCIENCE VERSUS PRACTICAL AIMS

"Our purposes" which are to be served by the methods in question are the development of a satisfactory economic theory—not the development of economic policies. Schumpeter was most emphatic on this point. He bitterly decried attempts to use "pure theory" in the solution of questions of practical politics.[54]

Even in his book on *Business Cycles,* a subject on which few writers refrain from making or discussing policy recommendations, Schumpeter wrote in the preface: "I recommend no policy and propose no plan. . . . But I do not admit that this convicts me of indifference to the social duty of science. . . . What our time needs most and lacks most is the understanding of the process which people are passionately resolved to control. To supply this understanding is to implement that resolve and to rationalize it. This is the only service the scientific worker is, as such, qualified to render." [55]

One frequently hears the old dictum that correct prediction is the best or only test of whether a science has achieved its purposes. What this saying naïvely overlooks is the difference between prediction in physical or mental experiments, or under circumstances where events can by and large be controlled, and prediction in the real world of uncontrolled phenomena. Economic forecasting has come in for a good deal of not quite undeserved disparagement. One can hardly picture the task of the economic forecaster better than Schumpeter has done in this sentence: "It is unreasonable to expect the economist to forecast correctly what will actually happen as it would be to expect a doctor to prognosticate when his patient will be the victim of a railroad accident and how this will affect his state of health." [56]

[53] *Das Wesen,* pp. 93–94. In lieu of "schematize and stylize" Schumpeter in later years would have used "model."
[54] *Ibid.,* p. 575.
[55] *Business Cycles,* p. vi.
[56] *Ibid.,* p. 13.

Schumpeter was convinced that the advance of knowledge in our field was retarded because "economic problems have most of the time been approached in a practical spirit, either indifferent or hostile to the claims of scientific habits of thought. No science thrives, however, in the atmosphere of direct practical aim, and even practical results are but the by-products of disinterested work at the problem for the problem's sake. We should still be without most of the conveniences of modern life if physicists had been as eager for immediate 'application' as most economists are and always have been. . . . Nobody who craves for quick and short answers to burning questions of the day will care to entangle himself in difficulties which only patient labor can clear in the course of many years." [57]

[57] "The Common Sense," p. 6.

Chapter 19

GUNNAR MYRDAL ON CONCEALED VALUE JUDGMENTS

This is a review of Gunnar Myrdal's book The Political Element in the Development of Economic Theory, *translated from the German by Paul Streeter (Cambridge, Mass.: Harvard University Press, 1954), 248 pages.*

This book was published in Swedish in 1930 and in German in 1932. Originally "planned as a frontal attack on the dogmas of the older generation" of Swedish economists (Cassel, Heckscher, etc.)— economic liberals strongly opposed to government intervention in economic activities—the book turned out to be a "history of ideas" concerned with the evaluative, normative and political elements in economic theory (pp. vi-x). The chief aim was to expose the fallacy of deriving political applications from any theoretical system that failed to make explicit the value judgments on which it was based. No "political conclusions" can follow "from mere premises of facts" and/or from objective (neutral, nonevaluative) aprioristic premises (p. 18, and in many other places).

Myrdal attempts to show that almost all economists from the early physiocrats to the present, however sincere in assuring us of the objectivity of their arguments and of the positive, nonnormative character of their systems, have in fact inserted, at some point of their analysis, some value-laden concepts, if not direct valuations.

This was rather obvious in all "natural law" theories, and the utilitarians criticized them vigorously on that account. But "it is part of the thesis of this book that . . . the direct contribution of utilitarianism amounted to little more than a more elaborate formulation of the natural law doctrines" (p. 27). Myrdal presents this thesis in a lively discussion and, in the process, traces "the general outline of the arguments of utilitarian philosophy" (p. 52). Although critical throughout, he ends this exposé with an admission of some "beneficial effect" of utilitarianism on economic thought: "One can get a certain idea of the horrors from which utilitarianism has preserved economic theory by looking at economic writings such as those of O. Spann, which sprang from German political philosophy" (p. 54). But Myrdal cannot forgive the utilitarians their basic "doctrine of harmony" and their belief in the existence of a "social optimum" in an objective sense.

In the chapters on the "classical" and "neo-classical" theories of value Myrdal undertakes to show that most explanations of price, whether based on labor, production cost, objective use value, subjective utility, real cost, or on a mere logic of choice, had normative or evaluative implications. His arguments will be fully convincing only to those of his readers who agree with him that "nearly all our terms . . . are value-laden" including " 'productivity,' 'equilibrium,' 'balance,' 'adjustment,' " and that some "directly normative concepts" which "are best eliminated altogether" include "utility," "real or subjective costs," "welfare," "social utility," "real national income," "minimum social sacrifice," "economy," and "economical" (pp. 20–21). In some of his pronouncements Myrdal goes far beyond the thesis he set out to prove; for example, when he declares that "the subjective theory of value . . . neither conveys knowledge of facts, nor does it solve practical problems. It is an abstract, barren construction of great complexity for the uninitiated. It is one of those systems so common in the social sciences which yield only pseudo-knowledge. An abstract theory of price formation without a theory of value does not even pretend to describe empirical facts: it is primarily concerned with formulating questions" (p. 96).

This sounds remarkably like the antitheoretical strictures in the writings of the institutionalists. But Myrdal is not one of their friends. For "they criticize nearly everything in the classical heritage—except the basic normative approach. Without being quite clear about it themselves they are as much dominated by the general welfare concept as the classical writers" (p. 4). Lest some reader wonders just

FRITZ MACHLUP

what Myrdal wants economists to do if they are neither to be all-empirical nor abstract nor normative, we repeat that he wants them to make explicit the value judgments which must be hidden somewhere beneath their arguments and conclusions.

In his critique of economic liberalism, Myrdal first disassociates himself from the "severest critics" and allegedly "deadliest opponents of liberalism": Veblenians, theoretical socialists, labor politicians, conservative interventionists and protectionists, because they all accept some of the general presuppositions of liberal theory (pp. 104–05). Myrdal's objection to liberalism is that it "sets out to isolate an 'economic' factor in political life" and "gives a scientific appearance to an individualist, anti-interventionist prejudice" (p. 137). He criticizes the customary separation of the sphere of "production and exchange" from the sphere of "distribution" and the belief "that the desirability of liberalism could be proved" for the former. This view, that "*national income* is maximized in a free economy, even although its *distribution* could be improved by political interference," he regards as "the least vulnerable position of liberalism" (p. 129). He rejects it chiefly on the ground that an objective measurement of national income would presuppose an "objective" yardstick, instead of the market prices which are affected by an income distribution which in turn can be affected by political intervention (p. 132).

Myrdal also rejects as unwarranted and unfair the liberal contention that the burden of proof always rests on those who advocate intervention. Since "there are in the real world many deviations from free competition, it is difficult to decide whether any particular intervention would bring the fictional state of free competition nearer or remove it further. Hence, the onus of proof cannot rest on the person who advocates intervention simply because it is an intervention." To Myrdal, economic liberalism is "unrealistic in its premises and fallacious in its deductions" (p. 138).

Myrdal's discussion of liberal economic theory is of course not as general as might appear from these selected quotations. On the contrary, it includes a review of the anti-interventionist arguments of Smith, Bentham, Malthus, Ricardo, McCulloch, James and John Stuart Mill, as well as the British neoclassical economists. Myrdal is especially hard on the British ideologies leading up to "welfare economics." By contrast, "in Austria, economics has never had direct political aims in spite of the close connection of the Austrian marginal utility theory with utilitarian philosophy. The Austrians were pre-occupied with value theory and never elaborated a detailed theory of welfare economics. The same is true of the Lausanne school" (p. 128). How did the anti-interventionist writings of the Austrian von Mises escape Myrdal's attention?

The concept of an "economy" or *Volkswirtschaft* as "a collective subject of economic activity" (p. 140), regarded either as a "reality" or as a construct like that of the "communist fiction," is analyzed in a separate chapter together with ideas about "social value" (as presented in the theories of J. B. Clark and von Wieser). Another chapter is given to a survey of the theory of public finance, because "the political conclusions" in this field are "based on even more self-contradictory and on even looser premises than the conclusions in other fields" (p. 157). It is in this chapter that Myrdal gives critical attention to Swedish economists, especially Wicksell and Lindahl.

There can be no serious quarrel with Myrdal's main theses that "valuations should not be incorporated into economics by means of fallacious arguments," that "economic reasoning is often obscured by the fact that normative principles are not introduced explicitly," and that "the basic concepts are frequently charged with normative implications" (pp. 191–92). Others of Myrdal's theses leave much room for argument. For example, he contends: "The idea that one can judge social policy from a 'purely economic point of view' is thoroughly metaphysical. It assumes tacitly that there is such a thing as the interest of society as a whole, and that particular interests, though superficially antagonistic, are at heart reconcilable" (p. 195). This and similarly provocative pronouncements call for serious consideration. Unfortunately, however, Myrdal is not satisfied with presenting supporting arguments for his theses and offering pertinent illustrations from the writings of great economists. He goes on repeating himself far more than might be needed for pedagogic purposes, he extends his criticism to matters not relevant to his argument, he makes gratuitous (and misleading) remarks about "unrealistic assumptions" and "abstract theories," and he finally offers some rather absurd suggestions for an improved "technology of economics."

The improvements which Myrdal expects are to be attained chiefly through an "analysis of the field of social interests" (p. 199). Yet, "a technology of economics should not be built upon economic interests, but upon social attitudes. 'Attitude' means the emotive disposition of an individual or a group to respond in certain ways to actual or potential situations." However, "no direct conclusion can be drawn from the way people think and talk to their attitudes." Especially "a technology of economics should not accept attitudes which are based upon erroneous conceptions of the real world. Ideally, it would have to build on attitudes which the individuals with false opinions, given their general emotional dispositions, would have if they knew all the facts; or . . . all that is actually known by contemporary experts." But since this is impossible, "the technology of economics . . . should confine itself to empirically observable group attitudes, including potential attitudes which would become actual in certain carefully specified conditions." Thus, "our problem is . . . part of the psychology of character and, since we are concerned with social groups, it is a problem of the social psychology of the character of groups. The technology of economics is a branch of modern, psychologically oriented sociology." All this Myrdal advances in dead earnest although he recognizes that attitudes change all the time, and can be changed by propaganda—which "will weaken the basis of a technology of economics by making it more difficult to determine the relevant attitudes" (pp. 200–06). It is a mystery, at least to this reviewer, how such a keen critic of all harmony-of-interest doctrines manages to end up with a proposal that economics, theoretical and practical, be based on surveys and analyses of the (anything but harmonious) "attitudes" of the people.

It should be noted that Myrdal of 1954 no longer subscribes to all the ideas advanced by Myrdal of 1930. Some of them he now recognizes to have been "naive empiricism," and he retracts his anti-theoretical position to some extent by this prefatorial statement: "Facts do not organize themselves into concepts and theories just by being looked at; indeed, except within the framework of concepts and theories there are no scientific facts but only chaos" (p. vii). But in some respects he has become even more extreme: while in 1930 he still thought that some basic concepts in economic theory might be free from value connotations, he now holds that valuation enters all observation of facts and all formation of concepts from the very outset. All our "questions are an expression of our interest in the world, they are at bottom valuations. Valuations are thus necessarily involved already at the stage when we observe facts and carry on theoretical analysis, and not only at the stage when we draw political inferences from facts and valuations" (p. vii). Philosophers have often discussed this issue and have concluded that a pragmatic attitude in asking questions must not be confused with an evaluative or normative attitude in carrying out scientific research and analysis.

Myrdal wrote his book before the advent of the new welfare economics, the compensation principle and the social welfare function. The reader of the book will find many occasions to wonder what Myrdal would have said about the answers recently proposed by modern welfare economists. In order to satisfy this curiosity at least to some extent, Paul Streeten of Oxford University has furnished an appendix to the book, on "Recent Controversies." In the brief space of ten pages he succeeds in giving a most informative survey of the main issues discussed in the welfare literature of the last decades. The excellent organization, clear exposition and concise treatment of the problems can serve as a model to many economists—including Myrdal.

Streeten deserves commendation also for the translation of the book. There are only a very few terms in which he has not caught the exact meaning of the original expressions: *Rechtsstaat* should be rule of law, not "state of justice"; the *sozialpolitische Schule* is not the "socio-political school" but the social policy (social security or social justice) school; *Wahlhandlungstheorie* is not "behaviorist interpretation of choice" but pure logic of choice. The last of these is the most serious misunderstanding, for truistic and behavioristic theories of choice are true opposites, whereas the translator links them several times as parallels or complements. For example, he speaks of "a purely formal, behaviourist utility and value theory" (p. 99), substituting "behaviourist" for "subjective." But on the whole the translation is not only correct but also written in a pleasant and polished English. Few foreign authors have had the fortune of finding a translator bringing so much competence and care to that usually thankless task.

FRITZ MACHLUP

Chapter 20

PAUL SAMUELSON ON THEORY
AND REALISM

In a discussion of "Problems of Methodology" at an AEA meeting [4], Paul Samuelson embarks on a critique of theories which employ unrealistic assumptions. He concludes with this strong indictment of "unrealistic, abstract models": "If the abstract models contain empirical falsities, we must jettison the models, not gloss over their inadequacies" [4, p. 236].

Let us first indicate how Samuelson reaches this judgment. He defines a theory "as a set of axioms, postulates, or hypotheses that stipulate something about observable reality [4, p. 233]. Denoting the theory as B, the "consequences" derived from it as C, and the "assumptions" antecedent to it as A, he argues that A, B, and C must actually be identical in meaning, mutually implying one another. Thus, he holds, if the assumptions are empirically false, and the theory therefore unrealistic, the deduced consequences cannot possibly be empirically valid. In other words, an unrealistic theory cannot yield realistic consequences.

Samuelson also considers the possibility that the assumptions are *wider* than the theory, and that the theory is *wider* than the consequence, so that there is a subset $C-$ of C, while A is a subset of $A+$. In this case $A+$ may imply B, without B implying $A+$; and C may imply $C-$, without $C-$ implying C. If $C-$ happens to be empirically valid, does this "validate" the wider theory B, or the even wider set of assumptions, $A+$? Samuelson explicitly rejects this. He regards as "nonsense" the claim that the validity of $C-$ justifies holding an unrealistic theory B, let alone the completely unwarranted set of assumptions $A+$.

What Samuelson does here is to reject *all theory*. A theory, by definition, is much wider than any of the consequences deduced. If the consequences were to imply the "theory" just as the theory implies the consequences, that theory would be nothing but another form of the empirical evidence (named "consequence") and could never "explain" the observed, empirical facts.

In addition, Samuelson errs in another way. We never deduce a consequence from a theory alone. We always combine the postulated relationships (which constitute the theory) with an assumption of some change or event and then we deduce the consequence of the *conjunction* of the theoretical relationships and the assumed occurrence. Thus, we do not infer C or $C-$ from B, but rather from the conjunction of B and some occurrence O. If $C-$ can be deduced from B *cum* O; and if both O and $C-$ are found to *correspond* to data of observaton which can be regarded as the empirical counterparts (referents, proxies) of the theoretical O and $C-$; then we rule that the theory B has sustained the test. This test does not prove that B is "true," but we have no reason to "jettison" B—unless we have a better theory B'.

Let us now leave aside the argument by which Samuelson reached his decision against "unrealistic, abstract models" and theories; let us, instead, confront Samuelson's judgment with Samuelson's pattern of theorizing when he discusses, not methodology, but substantive propositions of economics. Let us choose the brilliant performance with which he demonstrated an important proposition in the theory of international trade.

In his ingenious papers on international factor-price equalization [2] [3], Samuelson shows "that free commodity trade will under certain specified conditions, *inevitably* lead to *complete* factor-price equalisation" [2, p. 181]. He admits that "it would be folly to come to any startling conclusions on the basis of so simplified a model and such abstract reasoning," but he submits— very rightly, in my opinion—that "strong simple cases often point the way to an element of truth present in a complex situation" [2, p. 181].

What are his assumptions, hypotheses, conditions? Here is the list:

1. There are but two countries, America and Europe.
2. They produce but two commodities, food and clothing.
3. Each commodity is produced with two factors of production, land and labour. The production functions of each commodity show "constant returns to scale". . . .
4. The law of diminishing marginal productivity holds. . . .
5. The commodities differ in their "labour and land intensities". . . .
6. Land and labour are assumed to be qualitatively identical inputs in the two countries and the technological production functions are assumed to be the same in the two countries.
7. All commodities move perfectly freely in international trade, without tariffs or transport costs, and with competition effectively equalizing the market price-ratio of food and clothing. No factors of production can move between the countries.
8. Something is being produced in both countries of both commodities with both factors of production. . . .

From this he concludes: "Under these conditions, real factor prices must be exactly the same in both countries (and indeed the proportion of inputs used in food production in America must equal that in Europe, and similarly for clothing production)" [2, p. 182].

In his "intuitive proof" he goes so far as to state this: "I have *established unequivocally* the following facts:

> Within any country: (a) a high ratio of wages to rents will cause a definite decrease in the proportion of labour to land in both industries; (b) to each determinate state of factor proportion in the two industries there will correspond one, and only one, commodity price ratio and a unique configuration of wages and rent; and finally, (c) that the change in factor proportions incident to an increase in wages/rents must be followed by a one-directional increase in clothing prices relative to food prices" [clothing being the more labor-using commodity, food the more land-using commodity] [2, p. 187].

It may be fair to state that Samuelson had characterized the problem as "a purely logical one" [2, p. 182]. But he sometimes uses language of empirical operations, for example, when he speaks of "observing the behaviour of a representative firm." It should be clear, however, that what he "observes" is merely the logical consequence of a set of assumptions; that the "behaviour" is purely fictitious; and that his representative firm is only an ideal type, a theoretical construct. Let me quote the sentence: ". . . if we *observe* the *behaviour* of a *representative firm* in one country it will be exactly the same in all essentials as a representative firm taken from some other country —regardless of the difference in total factor amounts and relative industrial concentration—provided only that factor-price ratios are really the same in the two markets" [2, pp. 187-88, emphasis supplied].

At the end of his discussion Samuelson evaluates some important qualifications which he finds help to "reconcile results of abstract analysis with the obvious facts of life concerning the extreme diversity of productivity and factor prices in different regions of the world" [2, p. 196]. These "qualifications" to the theorem furnish Samuelson with the "causes" of the factor-price diversities. In other words, he does not hesitate, quite rightly in my view, to explain the observed facts of life—factor-price differentials—by the divergences of real conditions from the ideal ones which form the basis of the factor-price equalization theorem.

Would the Samuelson of the *A-B-C* argument against unrealistic, abstract models approve of the Samuelson of the intuitive proof of the factor-price equalization theorem? Frankly, I do not know. Perhaps both Samuelsons make a distinction between a theorem and a theory, meaning by the former a proposition deduced from counterfactual assumptions and postulates, and by the latter a proposition stipulating something about observable reality. But the Samuelson of the *Foundations of Economic Analysis,* who preceded both other Samuelsons, did pledge allegiance to a program emphasizing "the derivation of *operationally meaningful* theorems" [1, p. 3].

Since, according to Samuelson, a theorem deduced from counterfactual hypotheses cannot yield empirically true consequences, and does not contain operationally defined terms, it is not immediately clear just what an "operationally meaningful theorem" is supposed to be. If it is supposed to be a "strong simple case" pointing the way to "an element of truth present in a complex situation" [2, p. 181], then we have no quarrel. For, I submit, this is what the bulk of economic theory does. It is based on counterfactual assumptions, contains only theoretical constructs and no operational concepts, and yields results which, we hope, point to elements of truth present in complex situations. To call such theorems "operationally meaningful" is to confer on them a designation which is slightly deceptive; but in any case it gives them the recognition which Samuelson, as critic of the Friedman position, or "the F-twist," wants to deny.

I conclude that Samuelson, one of the most brilliant theorists in present-day economics, produces his best work when he deduces from unrealistic assumptions general theoretical propositions which help us interpret some of the empirical observations of the complex situations with which economic life confronts us.

REFERENCES

1. PAUL SAMUELSON, *Foundations of Economic Analysis*. Cambridge, Mass. 1947.
2. ――――, "International Factor-Price Equalisation Once Again," *Econ. Jour.*, June 1949, *59*, 181-97.
3. ――――, "International Trade and the Equalisation of Factor Prices," *Econ. Jour.*, June 1948, *58*, 163-84.
4. ――――, "Problems of Methodology—Discussion," *Am. Econ. Rev., Proc.*, May 1963, *53*, 231-36.

Chapter 21

THREE WRITERS ON SOCIAL THEORY: MADGE, ROSE, AND ZETTERBERG

This is a review of three books on social theory published in 1953 and 1954: John Madge, The Tools of Social Science *(New York: Longmans, Green and Co., 1953, 308 pages); Arnold M. Rose,* Theory and Method in the Social Sciences *(Minneapolis: University of Minnesota Press, 1954, 351 pages); Hans L. Zetterberg,* On Theory and Verification in Sociology *(New York: The Tressler Press, 1954, 78 pages).*

"If we are honest we have to admit that the first century of social science has left us somewhere short of victory." I do not want to be less honest than Mr. Madge is (p. 290) but I should like to submit that some twenty-four hundred years of known social science have left us where we are, and that we shall always be short of victory because there is no end to the battle for knowledge, social or natural. To Madge social science is only a hundred years young because for him it all began with the establishment of the positivist science of sociology.

The "tools of social science" to which Madge devotes his text are "documents" (37 pages), "observation" (27 pages), "the interview" (110 pages) and "experiment" (36 pages). The last is "the apex of scientific method." The "mental experiment is an invaluable dress-rehearsal but it is no substitute for the real thing." There "can often be an orderly progress through search of documents, through observations, through the various forms of questioning, before we are ready for the rigour of experiment" (p. 292). Has he no place for theory at all? Madge is willing to forgive the "theoretically inclined social scientist" because "the desire to explain and to unify social facts, the search for a consistent framework, these cannot be condemned even by the extreme empiricist, because this desire has motivated much valuable empirical research" (p. 291). But "too many hypotheses are based on ideal and logically tidy considerations . . ." (p. 118). "The only safe source of knowledge about human beings is what we can see and hear, and everything else is guesswork." The techniques described by Madge "have therefore an ostensibly behaviourist foundation" (p. 34).

With all his scientistic preconceptions, his ultra-empiricism, positivism, and behaviorism, Madge is also an adherent of epistemological relativism, of the coexistence of conflicting truths in social science. To him "the only tenable view is Mannheim's perspectivist view of many truths, each shared only by those who have shared experiences and have agreed between themselves on social aims" (p. 5). And "to postulate an objective social science is to ask for something which is probably unattainable, and may even be undesirable" (p. 6).

A clue to one of the sources of Madge's superstitions can be found in the singular nouns in the title of his first chapter: "The Method of Social Science." If, instead of proclaiming the coexistence of competing truths, he came to recognize the coexistence of different methods and of several social sciences, he would be less myopic also in other matters and less liable to misguide his readers.

For every misunderstanding and misjudgment in Madge's book a pointed criticism and correction can be found in the book by Arnold M. Rose. The very first chapter (a paper which had won the 1952 prize of the American Association for the Advancement of Science for essays in social theory) contains a good statement on the nature of theory and on the testing of deduced hypotheses. But the best antidote to Madge's scientistic methodology can be found in Chapter 14 on "problem orientation versus method orientation." Rose quotes approvingly the psychologist Maslow, who protested against the "over-valuation of quantification for its own sake," against the "creation of a false and pernicious hierarchical system among the sciences," and against the "creation of a scientific orthodoxy, which in turn (a) tends to block the development of new methods, (b) tends to exclude many problems from the jurisdiction of science and (c) tends to make scientists 'safe' rather than daring" (p. 254).

Rose objects to the "primacy of method," according to which "a body of disciplines known as the 'behavioral sciences'—psychology, sociology, and social anthropology, plus a very small section of political science and economics—is distinct from a body of disciplines known as 'documentary sciences'—history, ethnology, political science, law, institutional and labor economics (the rest of economics is put in a class by itself)" (p. 249). In Chapter 15, on "Generalizations in the Social Sciences," there are, besides excellent comments on determinism versus probabilism, some admirable statements on social science as "a pile of discrete bits of knowledge" as against "an integrated body of propositions." "An adequate system of general propositions is based on an internally consistent set of assumptions and definitions, such that each proposition is capable of being logically deduced from the assumptions and definitions (in the manner of a theorem). The building up of an adequate theory—the shorthand term for the framework of assumptions and definitions as well as the propositions deducible from them—requires a constant interplay between theory and data in which the theory is regularly modified and new deductions are derived from it and once more tested by crucial facts" (p. 263).

Two chapters are explicitly addressed to economists: one on "The Potential Contribution of Sociological Theory and Research to Economics," and another on "A Deductive Ideal-Type Method." In the latter, Rose discusses the convertibility between inductive and deductive propositions and presents a good formulation of the distinction: "Inductive studies test the hypothesis that *b* follows *a* under specified conditions. Deductive studies seek to specify the conditions (assumptions) under which *b* must logically and inevitably follow *a*, and they pose for empirical research the question of the relevance of these conditions to any observable phenomena" (p. 340).

I do not know whether the Roses or the Madges are more representative of present-day sociology. But in this war of the Roses against the Magic of Scientism the third book under review sides with the former. Hans L. Zetterberg's methodological program proclaims "(1) a concern with theories (definitions and hypotheses) rather than frames of reference (only definitions) . . . (2) verificational studies rather than descriptive ones, and (3) a concern with miniature theories rather than an inclusive theory" (p. 13). These "miniature theories," however, should be integrated, not isolated. For, "we explain something by demonstrating that it follows the laws of other phenomena. To ask for an explanation in science is to ask for a theory" (p. 9). Merely "to know the labels of phenomena and to know their distribution is not to explain them" (p. 14).

Zetterberg's observations on operationalism are illuminating. For purposes of verification "only those operational definitions that have a counterpart in a nominal definition are worth while. When verifying a theory, certain measurement devices may very well be worthless [and] irrelevant" (p. 34). The evaluation of the validity of certain operational definitions for a hypothesis formulated in terms of nominal definitions is shown to be one of the most significant steps in the verification of the hypothesis. Zetterberg's book is worth while and relevant for economists.

Chapter 22

JOHN NEVILLE KEYNES' SCOPE
AND METHOD

The book by John Neville Keynes, The Scope and Method of
Political Economy, *was republished in 1955 by Kelley and Millman
(New York). This is a review.*

John Neville Keynes died in 1949 at the age of 97. Many of the
younger economists know him only as the father of John Maynard,
whom he survived by three years. Some may also know of his most
famous brainchild, his essay on *The Scope and Method of Political
Economy.* But too few are sufficiently well acquainted with this admirable book. Its reprinting as an "economic classic" should add
large numbers to that group of economists indebted to it for many
insights regarding the methodology of economics.

The first edition appeared in 1890, at the end of the decade of the
Methodenstreit between Menger and Schmoller. But little of the heat
and nothing of the fury of this controversy is in evidence in Keynes'
book. He "endeavoured to avoid the tone of a partisan, and . . .
sought, in the treatment of disputed questions, to represent both sides
without prejudice" (p. vi). In this he has succeeded remarkably well.
If he rejects in no uncertain terms the claims of the younger historical
school (pp. 314–327), he also criticizes Mill, Senior, and Cairnes,
who had insisted on the deductive and abstract nature of economic
science, for having tended "to exaggerate the characteristics of their

own method" (p. 19). By the avoidance of polemics in his eminently fair and level-headed exposition of the controversial issues, Keynes could overcome the deafness to reason to which the unconciliatory methodological analysis of Menger had provoked the opposition.

Keynes realizes that many economists dislike and discourage the study of methodology. But he regards some attention to it as necessary for all students of economics; a disregard of the "conditions of validity" of various kinds of reasoning is liable to retard the progress of knowledge (p. 4). Incidentally, I have the impression that "methodology" is no longer disliked but has become increasingly popular, especially among the uninformed who believe it means a discussion of techniques of research, or techniques of anything. (Indeed, I have encountered "the methodology of accounting" and similar expressions). Perhaps methodology would still be rejected if the users of the word knew what it meant and that their only legitimate doubts should be whether it is coextensive with "material logic" or with "philosophy of science." Methodology is the study of the logical principles by which we determine when to accept and when to reject a proposition as a valid part of a body of scientific knowledge. Needless to say, Keynes means it in this sense and he correctly mentions that economists may actually use the same method and yet disagree on methodology (p. 10).

In discussing the scope of our field, Keynes examines the three kinds of topics that commonly pass as political economy: "economic uniformities, economic ideals, and economic precepts." He regards only the first as the task of the "*science* of political economy." The other two, he proposes, might be put under the headings of "*ethics* of political economy" and "*art* of political economy," respectively, though he is sceptical about the latter because such an art would have to be based also on "political and social science" as well as on social philosophy, and thus would "be largely non-economic in character" (p. 83). The separation between positive and "ethical" economics is, according to Keynes, not only possible but imperative. In this connection he examines why positive economics has often been accused of being biased against government intervention. Keynes concludes that the accusers have confused *laisser faire* as an "assumption," or starting point of analysis, with *laisser faire* as "a maxim or rule of conduct" (pp. 67–74).

FRITZ MACHLUP

In his discussion of the differences between descriptive and constructive economics (p. 174) Keynes sides with those who hold that "mere description cannot constitute a science" and "that economics is of necessity a science of cause and effect" (p. 176). The sections on the role of observation and experiment are perhaps the most useful for students not yet well read on the subject; Keynes' illustrations of Mill's canons of induction make rewarding reading for every economist.

As one would expect from a book first published in 1890 and last revised in 1917, the comments on "statics and dynamics" are dated. Yet, in view of the frequent characterization of dynamics as the economics of change, it is refreshing to read Keynes' sound interpretation of statics as a theory of economic changes, though of "particular" rather than "fundamental" (revolutionary or evolutionary) changes (p. 147). The remarks on the "theories of economic growth and progress" will strike a sympathetic chord with some readers, but a dissonant one with others, for Keynes holds that in these problems "the part played by abstract reasoning is reduced to a minimum, and the economist's dependence upon historical generalization is at a maximum. Theories of economic growth and progress may, indeed, be said to constitute the philosophy of economic history" (p. 283).

In the theories of relative prices and incomes, on the other hand, Keynes sees little scope for empirical research; here "deduction from elementary principles . . . occupies a position of central, though not exclusive, importance" (p. 211). "This is in accordance with the ordinary logical canon, that the greater the number of causes in operation, and the more complicated the mode of their interaction, the less possible it becomes to fulfill the conditions required for valid inductive reasoning" (pp. 204–205). Moreover, even where it is "possible approximately to satisfy the conditions of valid induction, . . . the conclusion so obtained cannot be regarded as more than suggestive and provisional until deductive explanation and verification are forthcoming" (p. 213).

Keynes rejects the anti-mathematical strictures of Mill and Cairnes, and accepts Cournot's view that the "impossibility of obtaining exact numerical premises" is no reason against "the employment of mathematical methods" (p. 257). To Keynes, "political economy is essentially concerned with quantitative relations, and therefore involves mathematical notions" (p. 253). Indeed, "one of the most important functions of mathematical analysis is to discover determinate relations between quantities whose numerical values are unassignable. Functions, while remaining numerically unknown, may possess known properties; and on the assumption that certain general relations between quantities hold good, it may be possible mathematically to deduce further relations that could otherwise hardly have been determined" (p. 258).

The whole essay, written in a lucid and pleasing style, can be read in little time and "without tears." I believe that teachers in all fields of economics will render a service to their students if they urge them to read this fine little book. The publishers were well advised to include it in their series of reprints, and they deserve not only praise but a good market for it.

FRITZ MACHLUP

Chapter 23

TERENCE HUTCHISON'S RELUCTANT ULTRA-EMPIRICISM

From the tone of Professor Hutchison's reply to my article I infer that he was hurt by my characterization of his position as one of ultra-empiricism. I am sorry that I hurt or angered him; I am glad that he rejects, at least on principle, the position which I called ultra-empiricism; and I am puzzled by many of his comments which still strike me as ultra-empiricist.

I agree fully with Professor Hutchison that his opening statement—on page 9 of his book and on page 476 of his note above—is a rejection of what I call ultra-empiricism. Whereas ultra-empiricists require direct empirical testing of propositions used as fundamental assumptions in a theoretical system, Professor Hutchison in this declaration seems satisfied with the *conceivable* testability of the deduced *consequences* of these propositions. I might have quoted his statement on this point in support of my position that direct testing is not required—had he not in effect repudiated it by much of what followed it in his book. And he does it again in his note, as I shall attempt to show presently.

But do we really mean the same thing when we speak of "indirect testing"? Perhaps the crucial misunderstanding lies right here. Professor Hutchison mentions that a proposition not itself empirically testable directly must be "reducible by *direct* deduction to an empirically testable proposition or propositions." (Emphasis supplied.) This formulation suggests a requirement that the implications of any single proposition be tested independently of those of other propositions with which it is conjoined to constitute a "case." In fact, however, the *conjunction of logically independent propositions and derivation of their joint consequences* is the essence of indirect testing.

If assumption A can neither be subjected to any direct empirical test nor reduced "by direct deduction to an empirically testable proposition," its indirect verification can be accomplished by combining it with an assumption B which is directly testable; if a consequence C can be deduced from the conjunctive hypothesis A *plus* B—but not from either one alone—and if C is empirically tested, A is regarded as having passed the indirect test.

I suspect that Professor Hutchison does not accept the validity of indirect verification in this sense. Unfortunately, he makes no reference to my detailed exposition and schematic representation of the conception and operation of indirect testing. Silent on this, he professes to accept indirect testing and then proceeds to demand direct (independent) tests. I had pointed out that fundamental postulates, such as the maximization principle, are "not subject to a requirement of independent verification"; they are considered as verified, together with the whole theory of which they are a part, when the deduced consequences of their conjunction with an evident and substantive change and with assumed conditions relevant to the case are shown to correspond to observed events. Thus, if the fundamental postulate (e.g., that firms prefer more profit to less profit at equal risks[1]) is combined with assumptions about economic institutions and conditions (e.g., certain forms of competition) and with assumptions about certain substantive changes (e.g., the imposition of import quotas on certain products); and if we deduce from this conjunction of assumptions certain consequences (e.g., increases in the excess of domestic over foreign prices); and if these deduced consequences are found to be in relatively good correspondence with observed events (e.g., increases in the excess of domestic over foreign prices of bicycles) subsequent to actual changes of the kind in question (e.g., the imposition of import quotas on bicycles); then the theory is regarded as verified, and the fundamental postulate is regarded as verified with it.

Now, those who do not accept this "indirect verification" of the fundamental postulate but demand that the assumption of attempted profit maximization be

---

[1] On the problem of differences of risk and uncertainty in connection with differences in profits see my book *The Economics of Sellers' Competition* (Baltimore: Johns Hopkins Press, 1952), pp. 53–56.

empirically tested independently of the other propositions (about competition, import quotas, and bicycle prices) are the "ultra-empiricists" discussed in my article. If he understands this, I wonder whether Professor Hutchison will still deny membership in the society of ultra-empiricists or whether instead he will be eager to confirm it.

That Professor Hutchison misunderstands the essence of indirect verification is suggested by his example about the length of the unmeasured side of a triangular plot of land. If he had referred to the Pythogoras theorem as the general proposition in need of verification and to the lengths of the sides of his plot as the independently verifiable propositions, he might have come nearer to our problem, the validation of the use of universal propositions. What he really showed was (a) that he had confidence in the reliability of the Pythogoras theorem, (b) that he was sure his plot was reasonably close to a perfect right-angled triangle, and (c) that his measurements of the two short sides were reasonably accurate. The whole example has little to do with the question of the direct or indirect verification of fundamental assumptions employed in general theory.

That Professor Hutchison is not satisfied with the indirect verification of such universal propositions employed as fundamental postulates in general theory can be seen from several comments. For example, he contends (p. 478) that I have failed to state whether they are "conceivably falsifiable empirically" or rather definitions "without empirical content." (I had said they were "heuristic principles," "procedural rules," etc. See pp. 9 and 16). Then he demands (p. 478) "a specification of what a test would amount to, or of the more precise circumstances under which the generalization [of maximizing conduct] was to be regarded as 'confirmed' or 'disconfirmed.' " (I had stated repeatedly that the test consisted in checking the correspondence of observed events with the "assumed changes" and the "deduced changes" of the entire theoretical model. See especially p. 18.) It is quite obvious that Professor Hutchison, contrary to his initial declaration, wants more than indirect testing of the fundamental postulates of general theory.

Professor Hutchison asks whether my category of apriorism in economics is "so stretched to include all the middle ground up to the frontier line of 'ultra-Empiricism.' " (Since he also questions that I could name any "example of this category," he must believe that on my classification *all* economists are apriorists!) The answer is that I know very few "extreme apriorists" (e.g., Professor von Mises). The middle ground between the extreme positions is very large indeed; of the economists whom Professor Hutchison asked me to classify, it includes Zeuthen, Samuelson, Lange, and Friedman; none of them holds that no conceivable kind of experience could ever cause him to give up his theory, and none of them wants his fundamental assumptions empirically tested independently of the propositions with which they are combined when the theory is applied.

Professor Hutchison asks whether I can cite any other fundamental assumption in economics "beyond" that of "maximizing or rational action." It all depends on what one regards as fundamental. Perhaps the assumption that only limited outputs can be obtained from given resources should be called fundamental; it "underlies" all economic problems, but it does not always become a relevant step in the argument. Perhaps still other (or narrower) assumptions should be proposed for inclusion, though frankly I had not intended it.

If the question referred to the possible replacement of, rather than addition to, the assumption of maximizing conduct, my answer would be that substitutes have been proposed, but not successfully. Some writers on the equilibrium of the firm (theory of output and price) have advanced "security of survival" and similar postulates in lieu of profit maximization (for the enterprise economy), but the proposed substitutes were less simple and less comprehensive. Yet, I grant the possibility that better postulates may be proposed, and therefore I have described the "Fundamental Postulates" as "Assumed Type of Action (or Motivation)" instead of limiting them to that of "maximizing conduct."[2]

In his comments on the nature and significance of the maximization postulate Professor Hutchison conveys the impression that he recognizes as scientifically legitimate only two kinds of statements: propositions which by empirical tests can, at least conceivably, be proved to be false, and definitions without empirical content. If so, he rejects a third category of propositions used in most theoretical systems: the heuristic postulates and idealized assumptions in abstract models of interdependent constructs useful in the explanation and prediction of observable phenomena.

Such propositions are neither "true or false" nor empirically meaningless. They cannot be false because what they predicate is predicated about ideal constructs, not about things or events of reality. Yet they are not empirically "meaningless," because they are supposed to "apply" or correspond broadly to experienced events. They cannot be "falsified" by observed facts, or even be "proved inapplicable," because auxiliary assumptions can be brought in to establish correspondence with almost any kind of facts; but they can be superseded by other propositions which are in better agreement with these facts without recourse to so many auxiliary assumptions.

Logicians have long recognized this intermediate category of propositions, which are neither a priori nor a posteriori in the strict sense of these terms.[3] (One may, with Friedman, prefer to say that a theoretical system has two parts, an analytical one demonstrating valid inferences, and a synthetic one stating correct applications.[4]) I had mentioned this category of propositions in my article (p. 16), but Professor Hutchison chose to disregard my remarks on this issue.

It was necessary to bring this up again because Professor Hutchison said

[2] The assumption of maximizing conduct of the householder may, of course, be broken down into several parts—that each person has preferences, that these preferences are consistent (transitive) and can be orderly arranged, that he wishes to follow these preferences in deciding on his actions, etc.—and it is possible to call each of these a separate postulate. This, I suppose, is not questioned here.

[3] They were called "procedural rules" by Felix Kaufmann, "complex-analytic propositions" by Wm. P. Montague, "constitutive, non-epistemic" propositions by Henry Margenau.

[4] Milton Friedman, *Essays in Positive Economics* (Chicago: University of Chicago Press, 1953), pp. 24–25.

(p. 478) that if I called the fundamental assumption (of maximizing behavior) "empirically meaningful" I should mean it to be "conceivably falsifiable empirically." I do not. Resolutions to analyse certain aspects of experience with the aid of a heuristic postulate, or even of a pure fiction, are not "falsifiable" but nevertheless "empirically meaningful."[5]

At another point (pp. 478–479) Professor Hutchison realizes that I did not mean that the fundamental assumptions about human actions should or could be empirically tested, and he asks me to show "how 'empirically testable' conclusions about human actions can be deduced" from those untested or untestable fundamental assumptions. I thought I had shown it with sufficient clarity; of course, the conclusions are deduced not from the fundamental assumptions in isolation but from their conjunction with other assumptions including some whose correspondence with factual observation is established.

I can easily comply with Professor Hutchison's request by pointing to the illustration I gave above, where I showed how a relative price increase for bicycles was the empirically testable consequence deduced from the partly untested or untestable assumptions. But Professor Hutchison repeats that I had done "nothing to show that it is in any respect more difficult to confirm or 'disconfirm' assumptions, 'fundamental' or otherwise, about human actions in economic theory, than it is to confirm or 'disconfirm' the conclusions about human action." Can there be any doubt that a direct empirical test of the motivations behind businessmen's actions, such as a test whether their decisions are made in an attempt to maximize profits, would be "more difficult," to say the least, than a test that higher prices are paid for bicycles?

Perhaps it was confusing when, in addition to stating that these fundamental assumptions *need not* be independently verified empirically, I also indicated that they *cannot* be so verified. Some economists who agree that no independent verification is required would none the less hold that such verification is *possible;* and others would contend that any special tests are *unnecessary* because the assumptions are *self-evident* statements of common experience. Common experience, however, tells us merely that we (that is, I and those with whom I have talked about it) *can* follow our preferences in choosing among the alternatives open to us and that we usually do it. Common experience, moreover, tells those of us who are or were in business that we *usually* attempt to make such decisions as would promise us the highest returns, but it does not tell us that *all* businessmen do so in *all* their actions, Indeed we know, also from common experience, that there are times when many businessmen refrain from following the most profitable courses of action and instead act to meet some demands of "patriotism" or to obey the moral suasion of governmental authorities. Are there any objective tests

---

[5] Some may wonder how one may possibly interpret the "fundamental assumptions" alternatively as rules of procedure (imperative statements), definitions (resolutions), useful fictions, and "true" empirical propositions. The answer lies in the convertibility of propositions. The following formulation may suggest how it can be done: "In analysing problems of this sort *let us proceed* by assuming that things will work *as if* businessmen were always attempting to maximize their money profits (and perhaps they actually do!)".

possible by which the assumption of profit maximization could be verified independently of the uses to which the assumption is put in economic theory?

We could *conceivably* place researchers into every business office to analyse every decision that is made and check the motivations behind it. This would not be quite reliable unless our researchers were invisible, had invisible lie detectors or perhaps mind-reading apparatus. In case we are satisfied with what is *practically possible*, we could have exceptionally competent and skillful survey researchers examine in carefully devised interviews a sample of the decisions made by a sample of businessmen. The object would be to establish the relative frequency of decisions consistent with profit maximization: In what percentage of their decisions do businessmen believe that they are acting in the best (long-term) interest of their firm (that is, of its owners)? Surely, some businessmen do so some of the time; probably, most businessmen do so most of the time. But we would certainly not find that all of the businessmen do so all of the time. Hence, the assumption of consistently profit-maximizing conduct is contrary to fact.

Of course, no proposition about empirical facts can be absolutely certain; but here we are defending an assumption of which we are certain that it does not always conform to the facts. If the deviations are insignificant we can safely neglect them. But we do not know *how* significant they might be, especially because the relative strength of non-profit objectives changes with the conditions of the time, changes probably also with the kind of decisions, and changes perhaps also with several other factors. What then should be done? Just what is being done: to accept maximizing conduct as a heuristic postulate and to bear in mind that the deduced consequences may sometimes be considerably out of line with observed data. We can, to repeat, test empirically whether the outcome of people's actions is most of the time reasonably close to what one would expect *if* people always acted as they are unrealistically assumed to act. Again, the "indirect verification" or justification of the postulate lies in the fact that it gives fairly good results in many applications of the theory.

Professor Hutchison has several questions concerning the assumption of maximizing conduct; we shall call it for short the Assumption (with capital A). He asks (a) "just what content, if any, it has been meant to possess," (b) "just when, where, and how far it is applicable," (c) "what a test [of it] would amount to," (d) under what circumstances it "was to be regarded as 'confirmed' or 'disconfirmed.' " And he finds that I am "required" to indicate (e) the range of the "significance" of the Assumption, (f) "what 'work,' if any," it can do, and (g) "just why it is not a superfluous fifth wheel on the car." I shall attempt brief answers to all seven questions.

(a) I am not sure what sort of "content" it is that is in question. Does "content" refer to specific data of experience that have gone "into" the Assumption and are now an integral part of it, as in the case of a universal proposition whose subject can be defined by complete enumeration? In this sense the Assumption has no determinate "content." Or, rather, is the question whether the Assumption is to apply to empirical data of a certain class, and whether it would matter if it did or did not apply? In this sense the "content" of the assumption of profit maximization can readily be illustrated. Suppose (1) the government announces that price reductions would be in the national interest, (2) wage rates have just been raised, (3) raw-material prices have gone up, (4) no changes in technology have occurred for many years, and (5) aggregate demand has not changed. Should we expect product prices to rise or to fall? If firms did not attempt to maximize profits, they might well act in accordance with what the government publicizes to be in the national interest, and prices would be reduced. The Assumption does make a difference.

(b) The applicability—"when, where and how far"—of the Assumption, or rather of theories based on it, can be "prescribed" in broadly formulated directives, but there will always be a wide margin for the use of good judgment. The "directions for use" may be different for explanations of past events and for predictions of future events. In general, for purposes of prediction, we should *not* apply the Assumption to particular households or to particular firms, but only to large numbers of households or firms, or rather to cases where the deduced events, such as changes in prices, outputs, consumption, exports, imports, etc., are regarded as the outcome of actions and interactions of large numbers of firms and households. We should apply it only with reservations in times when strong moral suasion is exerted to make people disregard their usual preferences or interests, such as in war time when patriotic objectives are strongly pressed.

(c) Our discussion of the "kind of test" to which the Assumption should be subjected has probably been sufficient to warrant our conclusion that the test of the pudding lies in the eating and not in its ingredients. If we find no better theory to explain or predict changes in prices, outputs, etc., etc., and if our present theory does no worse than it has been doing, we may consider our Assumption as warranted.

(d) The Assumption will of course never be considered as "confirmed" for good, but only until further notice. Under what circumstances is the Assumption to be regarded as "disconfirmed"? When a theory not using this Assumption is proposed and is shown to work equally well for a wider range of problems, or with a smaller number of variables or provisos, or more reliably or more accurately for the same range of problems and with the same number of variables or qualifications—then the Assumption will have outlived its usefulness and will be sent to the limbo of "disconfirmed propositions." (And even this need not be beyond recall.)

(e) May I take the "range of the significance" to mean the same thing as the "when, where, and how far" of the applicability of the Assumption? If so, I may refer to what I said under (b). These answers, however, are strictly confined, as was my article, to positive economics, that is, to explanations and predictions of economic changes and events. Normative or evaluative economics has been outside the scope of my discussion; hence, I am not examining the significance of the Assumption for welfare economics. To give a simple example, we have been concerned with questions like "what consequences can be expected from the removal of a tariff," not with questions like "whether these consequences would be desirable" and "whether the tariff ought to be removed."

(f) The kind of "work" the Assumption does for us was indicated under (a), where its "content" was discussed.[6] Let me add two more illustrations, (A) from the theory of the household, and (B) from the theory of the firm and industry. (A) Suppose (1) the tastes for foodstuffs are given, (2) the substitutability between vinegar and lemon in salad dressings, the complementarity between salad dressings and salads, and the income elasticities of demand for both are all given with the tastes, (3) the prices of lettuce and other salads are reduced, (4) disposable incomes rise, and (5) the price of vinegar is increased. If we trust the Assumption we can predict increased consumption or increased prices of lemons (or longer queues if lemon prices are fixed, and more bootlegging if lemons are rationed). Without the Assumption we cannot say anything, for if people do not follow their preferences, act inconsistently and haphazardly, "given" scales of preference mean nothing. (B) Assume (1) the technological conditions of production are given, (2) entry into the textile industry is open, (3) the supply of productive services required for textiles is elastic, and (4) the demand for grey goods increases. On the basis of the Assumption we can explain or predict a larger output of grey goods; without the Assumption we cannot. If businessmen like smaller profits just as well as bigger profits, or even better, why should any manufacturer increase his output when demand increases? If businessmen are not tempted by opportunities to make more profit, why should anybody take up the production of grey goods? It is hard to understand how any doubt can be entertained as to "what work" the Assumption does for us.

(g) The question whether the Assumption is not really "superfluous" is, I believe, disposed of with our description of the "work" it does for us. To be sure, the same work might possibly be done by a different assumption—and we know that many versions of the fundamental "Type of Action" have been used over the years—but I doubt whether the difference can be very great. But while the Assumption might be replaced by an alternative, it cannot be eliminated without replacement; it is not a redundant part in the theory. It is perhaps possible to put an indefinite number of "behavior functions" in the place of our Assumption, with the stipulation that all consumers will consistently stick to these functions. Such a stipulation would be neither simpler nor more realistic than the Assumption; and since the required knowledge of all behavior functions would be a heavy burden for the theory of consumer behavior, this whole approach is distinctly inferior to the traditional theory. The latter has yielded a large number of generalizations as "deduced consequences" even without knowledge of the exact preference systems of consumers, merely on the basis of some very general properties of such preference systems. As for the theory of production in an enterprise economy, the Assumption appears to be indispensable. Never could a behavioristic approach provide all the millions of "entrepreneurial behavior functions" which would be needed to do the job that is now done by the simple postulate of profit maximization.

A few minor misunderstandings remain to be cleared up. The assumption

---

[6] I prefer to speak of "the work it does" rather than of "the content it has"; both are metaphors, to be sure, but the latter, I think, is quite infelicitous.

that "consumers can arrange their preferences in an order" is not, as Professor Hutchison believes (p. 479), a "variant" of the fundamental assumption, "replacing" earlier formulations in terms of "maximizing utility." Nor has it been proposed "thanks to the insistence" of Hicks and Allen, Samuelson, and Little to make the theory testable. Instead, the phrase was used by Robbins[7] and can be traced back to Čuhel[8] and the earlier Austrians; and it was proposed in order to spell out the logical prerequisites of maximizing utility.

In a footnote (p. 481) Professor Hutchison approvingly quotes I. M. D. Little concerning certain differences between physics and economics in the use of fundamental assumptions. One of the differences singled out for emphasis is supposed to be that the "concepts . . . about which people are not clear"—pure constructs, idealizations, and postulates—"do not appear in the conclusions" in physics, but do so in "welfare economics." I have not discussed welfare economics and do not intend to do so. But that the controversial, "untested" assumptions "do not appear in the conclusions" holds, as I have demonstrated, for positive economics no less than for physics.

In another footnote (p. 480) Professor Hutchison believes that he has found an ally in Professor Friedman, who held that I had come "perilously close" to a tautological formulation of the theory. But by pressing his demand for an independent empirical test of the profit maximization postulate Professor Hutchison has placed himself right in the center of the target of Friedman's attack. It was the main theme of Friedman's methodological essay that fundamental assumptions do their work even if they are contrary to fact, and that it is a mistake to attempt empirical tests for them besides those of the findings derived from the theory of which they are a part.

There is, furthermore, the charge of "tautology," which is implied in some of Professor Hutchison's strictures against my work and is made explicit in the quotation from Friedman. The judgment that a certain theory is "purely tautological" may mean rather different things: that the theory is underdetermined and can yield no specificable conclusions; that some of the important variables are unknowable or changing in undetermined ways; that the *ceteris paribus* clause is used without specifying the *cetera* or their significance for the outcome; that the deduced conclusions can never be tested against data of experience; that the theory constitutes an internally consistent and closed system; that some of the assumptions are "empirically empty." I shall comment here only on the last two meanings of the charge.

A fully developed theoretical system will always be "an internally consistent set of assumptions and definitions, such that each proposition is capable of being logically deduced from the assumptions and definitions (in the manner of a theorem)."[9] This was, and probably still is, recognized by Professor Hutchison,

[7] Lionel Robbins, *An Essay on the Nature and Significance of Economic Science* (London: Macmillan, 1932), pp. 56, 86, and elsewhere.

[8] Franz Čuhel, *Zur Lehre von den Bedürfnissen* (Wien, 1908), pp. 186–216.

[9] Arnold M. Rose, *Theory and Method in the Social Sciences* (Minneapolis: University of Minnesota, 1954), p. 263.

who once wrote that pure theory must necessarily be of a form such that "what it proves must be contained in the assumptions and cannot be obtained from any other sources." Hence, "to criticize a proposition of pure theory *as such* as tautological, or circular, or as assuming what it requires to prove, is beside the point."[10]

The assumptions that consumers act to "maximize their expected satisfaction" and entrepreneurs act to "maximize their expected profits" are sometimes considered as "empirically empty" or "tautological" because (a) we cannot know whether or not the consumers and entrepreneurs really believe that their actions are the best of the alternatives considered, (b) whatever they do can thus be interpreted as being what they consider to be "the best under the circumstances," and (c) as long as we do not know their tastes, preferences, and alternative anticipations, we cannot deduce any particular way of acting from the assumptions standing by themselves.

The point, however, is that the assumptions do not stand by themselves but are combined with other assumptions, including some about certain substantive changes which are observable by us as well as by the consumers or firms concerned. Our theory does not tell or explain what the decision makers have been doing, or have preferred to do, or have avoided to do before the changes in question occurred; it deals only with the ways in which decisions will be changed by the occurrence and its repercussions. No matter how many pounds of lemons consumers have been purchasing, they will try to purchase more; the theory tells us this from the assumptions furnished. No matter how many yards of grey goods manufacturers have been producing, they will produce more; the theory can tell us this on the basis of the assumptions supplied.[11] An assumption apparently quite "empty" or without empirical implications as long as it stands alone may become of definite empirical significance when combined in a model with other assumptions.

Finally, there is that polemical red herring dragged across the trail: veiled charges of sympathizing with controversial value judgments, "indirect" accusations based on guilt by association with others accused directly. I was first inclined to overlook it, because I thought that silence on my part would be the most eloquent response. I have been persuaded, however, that my rejoinder would be sadly incomplete without a comment on this confusion, innocent or deliberate, between positive economics and political evaluation.

Not a single passage or sentence in my article could in fairness be interpreted as dealing with political implications, value judgments, policy advice, welfare economics. Yet, in the last pages of his reply Professor Hutchison throws a heavy barrage against alleged welfare implications of my argument. Furious salvos are

---

[10] T. W. Hutchison, *The Significance and Basic Postulates of Economic Theory* (London: Macmillan, 1938), p. 36.

[11] See my reply to R. A. Gordon, who had interpreted methodological subjectivism as leaving "theory saying that businessmen do what they do because they do it." Fritz Machlup, *The Economics of Sellers' Competition* (Baltimore: Johns Hopkins Press. 2952), p. 36.

fired against the "maximum of utility for society" in connection with Walras and free competition, and against "wholesale political conclusions" in connection with Mises and liberal economic policies.

If Professor Hutchison really believes that my "doctrines on verification and verifiability" can be used (and are designed?) to "propagate sweeping political dogmas" and to defend "politico-intellectual obscurantism" he does precisely what he apparently considers objectionable in others: he confuses normative (ethical) judgments with positive propositions of economic theory. Yet, at the same time he claims to be an advocate of Professor Friedman's dictum that "It is necessary to be more specific about the content of existing economic theory and to *distinguish among its different branches*.[12] Would that Professor Hutchison practiced what he advocates.

The Johns Hopkins University   FRITZ MACHLUP

[12] Milton Friedman, *op. cit.*, p. 41. Emphasis supplied.

Chapter 24

ADOLF LOWE'S INSTRUMENTAL ANALYSIS

*In Adolf Lowe's "Toward a Science of Political Economics,"
his position paper for this symposium on* Economic Means and Social Ends, *Lowe presents the gist of his book* On Economic Knowledge. *He repeats his deep-seated objections to "traditional economics" and his plea for having it superseded by "political economics." Lowe is strongly committed to what he calls the "instru-
mental-deductive method" or, in brief, "instrumental analysis."
I have gone into the analytical semantics of the terms positive,
normative, and instrumental economics and into a methodological
analysis of the issues involved. I have thus prepared myself for an
examination of Lowe's instrumentalism.*

In order to guard against misunderstandings, it may be well to say
that Dr. Lowe's instrumentalism is neither identical with nor closely
related to John Dewey's philosophical position by the same name,
which is usually regarded as a species of pragmatism. Nor is Dr.
Lowe's instrumentalism related to that of the late Adolf Lampe,
economist of the University of Freiburg, who thought of it as advocacy of an economic system that would evolve as a compromise between liberalism, the economic system steered by free-market prices,

and socialism, the centrally directed economy. Dr. Lowe's instrumentalism is meant to be a type of analysis, differentiated from both positive and normative analyses.

The trichotomy—positive, normative, instrumental—follows the proposal of John Neville Keynes, except that Keynes used "practical," not "instrumental," to denote the third type of economics. For Keynes, moreover, the third type was firmly based on the results of positive and normative economics. Dr. Lowe, on the other hand, views instrumental analysis as independent of positive analysis, which he distrusts as inapplicable to the industrial economies of our time, and independent also of normative analysis, which he regards as meta-scientific.

THE INSTRUMENTAL INFERENCES

The scheme of things in the framework of Dr. Lowe's analytical setup, in a form in which the knowns are stated as premises and the unknowns as questions, looks like this:

1. If you are in macro-state A (the "initial" state), and
2. If you want to *move* to macro-state Z (the "macro-goal"), and
3. If L, R, and G are general laws, rules, and empirical generalizations, respectively,

then

1. What *path* is suitable to that movement?
2. What *patterns of micro-behavior* are appropriate to keep the system on that path?
3. What *micro-motivations* are capable of generating suitable behavior?
4. What political *control* can be designed to stimulate suitable motivations?

Most economists, unacquainted with Dr. Lowe's work, would see in this arrangement of premises and questions nothing that is different from their own procedures in applied economics. The second premise, stating the macro-goal, is evidently the result of normative economics, and the third premise comprises the results of positive economics—the general laws, the institutional rules and constraints, and the empirical generalizations. This, however, is not what Dr. Lowe has in mind. Although he admits that macro-goals are "the results of normative judgment," [1] he does not tell us how such judgments are justified, which would be normative economics. And the third premise, according to Dr. Lowe, does not state the results of positive economics but only those of natural sciences, engineering, and psychology. For in Dr. Lowe's framework, my notation L stands for "laws of nature," R represents "engineering rules," and G stands for empirical generalizations "concerning sociopsychological relations." [2] Thus, Dr. Lowe's instrumental analysis, as he sees it, is not based on either normative or positive economics. He holds that "only after reality has been transformed through such [Control] action" (namely, "measures of public Control suitable to bring about that conformance" of structural, behavioral, and motivational conditions which assure goal attainment) "can the instrumental inferences serve as major premises in a deductive syllogism." [3]

I submit that these contentions cannot be sustained. As soon as there are several goals and several paths toward their attainment, instrumental analysis needs normative economics, because the choices among the alternative paths and the many possible combinations of goal attainments cannot be made without complex systems of values (preferences) which cannot be assumed as objective data given to the instrumentalist. Likewise, the questions regarding the "suitable" path toward goal attainment, the "appropriate" patterns of micro-behavior, the micro-motivations "capable" of generating the required behavior patterns, and the political controls designed to stimulate the right motivations cannot be answered except on the basis of full knowledge of theoretical laws, institutional rules, and empirical generalizations about economic relations—that is, on the basis of positive economics.

[1] See *Economic Means and Social Ends*, pp. 18, 24.
[2] Adolf Lowe, *On Economic Knowledge* (New York: Harper & Row, 1965), p. 143.
[3] *Ibid.*, p. 311.

THE NEED FOR POSITIVE
AND NORMATIVE ANALYSES

Judgments about what is suitable, adequate, capable, and so forth, imply predictability, which in turn presupposes either law statements (positive theory) or firmly established correlations (significant regression coefficients). It is logically impossible to infer the suitable instruments from the "given" goals if there exists no reliable positive knowledge of the type, "If A, then B," which is the type commonly found in positive economics. (This says nothing about the way such knowledge was acquired. More often than not it may have been by way of a search for the unknown cause, A, of an observed effect, B. But this need not be "instrumental analysis.")

The inevitability of normative economics within (and not only before) instrumental analysis is a consequence of the impossibility of knowing in advance the choices that have to be made among alternative paths, alternative behavior patterns, alternative control measures. It is not just a matter of postponing decisions until we have to "cross the bridge"; it is rather complete ignorance of what bridges there may be to cross. The instrumentalist—the political economist—cannot possibly know what benefits and sacrifices may have to be compared, what compromises to be made, and therefore what values to be applied to the choices among alternative "instruments." Hence, he does not arrive at the many bridges with a ready-made evaluation kit or social-preference map for guidance in the necessary choices. The relevant preferences will have to be mapped out and justified *ad hoc* at every one of the indefinite number of questions whose existence is unknown to the chooser of the best or second-best instruments.

One may ask whether there really are quite that many alternatives to choose from for one's policy recommendations. Things would be easy if there were only one path to the desired macro-state (or even none), or perhaps only two or three, with foreseeable cost-and-benefit comparisons for which all the needed value data can be read off the prepared preference map. Such simplicity cannot be expected; I have always been able to think of countless alternatives in any problem of economic policy with which I have been concerned. For example, when the removal or reduction of the U.S. payments deficit was "given" as a very urgent macro-goal, I enumerated forty-one different types of measures capable of steering behavior along suitable paths—with an indefinite number of variations in degree of application and of possible combinations—each of them restricting to some extent the attainment of other macro-goals. And I doubt that any two of the consultants had the same comparative evaluations of the benefits that would be secured or sacrificed by the alternative courses of action. In other words, justification of values—normative economics—is part and parcel of the job of the policy adviser, the man engaged in instrumental economics.

THE CRITICAL BOUNDARY

The reader, or *this* reader at least, repeatedly frightened out of his wits by all the talk of goal-choosing and control-imposing by the authorities, is finally reassured: Dr. Lowe has us "restrict the choice of our substantive goals to such states and processes as can be brought into agreement with the strivings of the large majority of micro-units.[4] He explains this by accepting the old liberal tenet that "micro-autonomy is vindicated if it is suitable to promote political freedom, and if such freedom takes precedence over any conceivable principle according to which production and distribution can be organized."[5] However, "it is the *well-understood interest* of the micro-units that must agree with the macro-goal, rather than their crude strivings. To enlighten the individual marketer about his true interests by reducing expectational uncertainty and by suitably patterning action directives is the very function of manipulative controls."[6]

We are now definitely in normative territory. Alas, "however hard we may try to avoid choices based on value judgments pure and simple, we cannot run away from an ultimate decision as to the relative significance of the economic and the political sphere or as to the ranking of rivalling political goals."[7] Dr. Lowe justifies the inva-

4 *Ibid.*, p. 318.
5 *Ibid.*, p. 319.
6 *Ibid.*, p. 320.
7 *Ibid.*, p. 320.

sion of normative territory by granting that "liberty . . . must be adopted as a 'provisional value' if those among us who believe in absolute values are to be allowed to continue fighting for them." [8]

Dr. Lowe thinks he crossed the boundary into normative or evaluative economics only when he granted priority to political freedom over some "economic" goal or goals. This may strike us as rather strange, since he has again and again allowed some chosen macro-goal to overrule and restrain the wishes of the "micro-units." Perhaps he relies on the widely held thesis that goals anl values are subjects of value judgments only when they are compared with other goals and values or when they remain concealed, but are admitted as legitimate data in positive analysis as long as they are clearly stated and are examined only in relation to the means suitable for their attainment.

The trouble with this view is that not only the choice among alternative techniques of control but also the unquestionable "plurality of macro-goals" will always force us to engage in value judgments. The preference scales (or indifference maps) of macro-goals in the value systems of the Goal Selectors cannot be identical and cannot be fully specified. The elasticities of substitution among additional tenths of per cents of unemployment, total output, total consumption, growth, and all the rest, are too complex, and too unstable to be admissible as a "given" assumption of a supposedly scientific "instrumental analysis."

At several points Dr. Lowe tries to escape the normative task of instrumental analysis by making "the implicit assumption that the different aspirations of a goal-setter are mutually compatible and can be translated into a consistent and realizable set of targets." [9] The

[8] *Ibid.*, p. 322. I cannot help setting Dr. Lowe's view in juxtaposition to a statement made by Frank H. Knight, many years before Lowe's plea for instrumental economics: "In the field of social policy, the pernicious notion of instrumentalism . . . is actually one of the most serious of the sources of danger which threaten destruction to the values of what we have called civilization. Any such conception as social engineering or social technology has meaning only in relation to the activities of a super-dictatorship, a government which would own as well as rule society at large, and would use it for the purposes of the governors" [Frank H. Knight, "Fact and Value in Social Science," in *Science and Man*, ed. Ruth Anshen (New York: Harcourt, Brace & World, Inc., 1942); reprinted in Frank H. Knight, *Freedom and Reform* (New York: Harper & Row, Publishers, 1947), pp. 225–226].

[9] *Economic Means and Social Ends*, p. 19.

assumption of a given "hierarchy of goals," where some goals may become means for other goals but where "the precise nature of these interrelations poses a genuinely scientific problem unencumbered by any value judgment or norm," [10] serves the same purpose. But these assumptions are legitimate only as part of a logical demonstration designed to show (1) under what conditions instrumental analysis *would* be nonevaluative, and (2) that these conditions are contrary to fact. Dr. Lowe's hope that the tasks of goal-setting and policy-choosing can be separated and that those engaged in instrumental analysis need not as a rule—except where possible infringements of political freedom are involved—cross over the "critical boundary" [11] into the territory of normative analysis is, in my opinion, not justified.

However, I am neither apprehensive nor critical in any way of such crossings of the border between the Domain of the True or False and the Domain of the Good or Bad. I would do away with all pro-hibitions, customs duties, and passport requirements between the domains. Of course, I would want all imported or produced values to be declared rather than concealed. But, and this is my point in this context, I do not believe that an honest declaration at the frontier of instrumental analysis would be at all possible or helpful. The cus-toms officer may ask the traveler—the peripatetic political economist —the usual question: "Have you anything to declare? Have you any values or norms in your bag?" And the traveler may declare all the values and norms he is aware of having brought with him; however, he cannot declare those values that he will work out or develop only long after settling down, when he finds that he has to make choices for which none of the evaluations that he has ever thought about are relevant.

[10] *On Economic Knowledge,* p. 316.
[11] *Ibid.,* p. 321.

Chapter 25

FRIEDRICH HAYEK ON SCIENTIFIC AND SCIENTISTIC ATTITUDES

In an essay in which I reviewed Friedrich Hayek's contribution to economics I arranged his scholarly publications under the following headings: Money, Credit, Capital, and Cycles; Socialism, Planning, and Competitive Capitalism; Legal and Political Philosophy; History of Ideas; An Essay in Psychology; and Philosophy of Science. The last of these seems to belong in this book.

HAYEK'S PHILOSOPHY OF SCIENCE

Hayek's concern with philosophy of science in general and methodological problems of the social sciences in particular derived from his dissatisfaction with the assertions and prescriptions of social scientists regarding the "right" methods of inquiry. There were, on the one hand, those who thought that the methods of the natural sciences, especially physics, should be imitated in the social sciences; on the other hand, there were those who denied economics the status of a "science" and wanted its investigations to employ the working methods of the historians. As Hayek attempted to sort out and analyze the methodological problems of the social sciences, he found it necessary to become himself a philosopher of science.

Much of Hayek's thinking in this area is contained in his books and articles on substantive problems or on intellectual history. For example, while I chose to include his long essay on "The Counter-Revolution of Science"[1] among his work on history of ideas, one might with almost equal justification include it under the heading of philosophy of science. An even earlier publication, "Economics and Knowledge"[2] which I would rather put under the heading of Socialism, Planning, and Competitive Capitalism, contains highly significant methodological suggestions. But instead of culling Hayek's ideas on the philosophy of science from a variety of his writings, I shall concentrate here on the essays and articles that are primarily or exclusively devoted to it.

CRITIQUE OF SCIENTISM

His first major essay in this category is on "Scientism and the Study of Society"[3] a critique of the "slavish imitation of the method and language of Science" (i.e., natural sciences) in the study of society. To guard against misunderstanding, Hayek assures us that his criticisms are not aimed "against the methods of Science in their proper sphere" or "to throw the slightest doubt on their value." He adds that "the scientistic as distinguished from the scientific view is . . . a very prejudiced approach which, before it has considered its subject, claims to know what is the most appropriate way of investigating it" (p. 269). The pejorative term "scientism" had been used in French writings, as Hayek tells us with supporting documentation.

In the preface to his book of collected essays, *Studies in Philosophy, Politics, and Economics*[4] Hayek calls attention (p. viii) to

> a slight change in the tone of my discussion of the attitude which
> I then called "scientism." The reason for this is that Sir Karl Popper
> has taught me that natural scientists did not really do what most of

[1] "The Counter-Revolution of Science," Parts I–III, *Economica*, N.S. Vol. 8 (February, May, August 1941), pp. 9–36, 119–150, and 281–320.

[2] "Economics and Knowledge," *Economica*, N.S. Vol. 4 (February 1937), pp. 33–54.

[3] "Scientism and the Study of Society," Parts I–III, *Economica*, N.S. Vol. 9 (August 1942), pp. 267–291; Vol. 10 (February 1943), pp. 34–63; Vol. 11 (February 1944), pp. 27–39.

[4] *Studies in Philosophy, Politics, and Economics* (London: Routledge & Kegan Paul, Chicago: University of Chicago Press, 1967).

them not only told us that they did but also urged the representatives of other disciplines to imitate. The difference between the two groups of disciplines has thereby been greatly narrowed and I keep up the argument only because so many social scientists are still trying to imitate what they wrongly believe to be the methods of the natural sciences.

The essay on "Scientism" gives a clear account of the reasons why some of the rules of procedure claimed to be those of Science are inapplicable, or applicable only after appropriate modification, to the study of social phenomena. There is first the recognition that the "facts" of the social sciences are "opinions—not opinions of the student of social phenomena, of course, but opinions of those whose actions produce his object." Moreover, we cannot "observe" these opinions—our data—directly "in the minds of the people but [only] recognize [them] from what they do and say merely because we have ourselves a mind similar to theirs" (p. 279). Examples: sentences, crime, punishment, medicine, cosmetic, commodity, economic good, money, exchange, games, rent, scarcity, utility, price, cost, profit, etc., are all "opinions" of people. Hayek stresses the contrast "between ideas which by being held by the people become the causes of a social phenomenon and the ideas which people form about that phenomenon" (p. 285).

A thought which Hayek elaborates also in other contexts is formulated here with great clarity (p. 288):

> If social phenomena showed no order except insofar as they were consciously designed, there would indeed be no room for theoretical sciences of society and there would be, as is often argued, only problems of psychology. It is only in so far as some sort of order arises as a result of individual action but without being designed by any individual that a problem is raised which demands a theoretical explanation.

The difficulty with such "order" or "regularity" is that it "cannot be stated in physical terms, that if we define the elements in physical terms no such order is visible, and that the units which show an orderly arrangement do not (or at least need not) have any physical properties in common. . . ."

Hayek makes a "distinction between an explanation merely of the principle on which a phenomenon is produced and an explanation which enables us to predict the precise results" (p. 290) and, as an illustration of the former, he refers to "a set of equations which shows merely the form of a system of relationships but does not give the values of the constants contained in it" (p. 291).

I am tempted to quote many of Hayek's statements on behaviorism and physicalism; on attempts to explain mental processes by physical ones; on social wholes, which are not observable but are constructions of our minds to schematize supposed structures of relationships among selected actions and events; on the nature of statistical studies of social phenomena; on the claims and failures of historicism; on the complementarity between theoretical and historical work; on alleged laws of historical change and development; and on many other methodological problems with which he deals in this essay. I must not yield to this temptation, or this review will be far too long.

Hayek's distinction between scientific and scientistic attitudes has been widely accepted. More than 25 years after the publication of this lengthy essay, he was asked to write an article on "scientism" for a German encyclopedia of sociology.[5]

EXPLANATION, PREDICTION, AND SPECIALIZATION

Between 1943 and 1969 Hayek published another eleven essays in philosophy of science, seven in English, three in German, and one in French. Six of these essays were collected in his book *Studies in Philosophy, Politics and Economics*. They were on "Degrees of Explanation"[6], "The Dilemma of Specialization"[7], "Rules, Perception and Intelligibility"[8], "The Theory of Complex Phenomena"[9], "Kinds

[5] "Scientismus," in Wilhelm Bernsdorf, ed., *Wörterbuch der Soziologie*, 2nd ed. (Stuttgart: F. Enke, 1969), pp. 915–917.

[6] "Degrees of Explanation," *The British Journal for the Philosophy of Science*, Vol. 6 (November 1955), pp. 209–225.

[7] "The Dilemma of Specialization," in Leonard D. White, ed., *The State of the Social Sciences* (Chicago: University of Chicago Press, 1956), pp. 462–473.

[8] "Rules, Perception and Intelligibility," *Proceedings of the British Academy*, Vol. 48 (Oxford: Oxford University Press, 1962), pp. 321–344.

[9] "The Theory of Complex Phenomena," in Mario Bunge, ed., *The Critical Approach to Science and Philosophy: In Honor of Karl R. Popper* (Glencoe, Ill.: The Free Press, 1964), pp. 332–349.

of Rationalism" [10], and "The Results of Human Action but Not of Human Design." [11]

In the first of these essays, Hayek distinguishes positive from negative predictions, with those of disjunctive alternatives between the two. He stresses the difficulty, in as complex situations as economics presents, "that we are unable to ascertain by observation the presence and specific arrangement of the multiplicity of factors which form the starting point of our deductive reasoning" (p. 216). Falsification of a theory is not thereby excluded:

> Our tentative explanation will thus tell us what *kinds* of events to expect and which not, and it can be proved false if the phenomena observed show characteristics which the postulated mechanism could not produce.

But, in contrast with

> the supposedly normal procedures of physics . . . we do here not *invent* new hypotheses or constructs but merely *select* them from what we know already about some of the elements of the phenomena; in consequence we do not ask whether the hypotheses we used are true or whether the constructs are appropriate, but whether the factors we have singled out are in fact present in the particular phenomena we want to explain, and whether they are relevant and sufficient to explain what we observe.

In lieu of offering more quotations, attention may be called to Hayek's discussion of various issues of interest to particular groups of readers: illustrations of "explanations of the principle" (in contrast with explanations of particular observations), especially with reference to the theory of evolution by natural selection (pp. 218–220); the use of models for the explanation of "ranges of phenomena" and the problems of refuting their relevance, especially if they yield mostly "negative predictions" (pp. 220–224); the importance of "orientation" where prediction is not possible, and of "cultivation" where control is beyond our capacity (p. 225).

[10] "Kinds of Rationalism," *The Economic Studies Quarterly* [Tokyo] Vol. 15 (1965).

[11] "Résultats de l'action des hommes mais non de leurs desseins," in Emil M. Claassen, ed., *Les Fondements Philosophiques des Systèmes Economiques*. Textes de Jacques Rueff et essais rédigés en son honneur (Paris: Payot, 1967), pp. 98–106.

A few valuable insights may be presented here from Hayek's "Dilemma of Specialization." He discusses the differences in the significance to different fields of inquiry of the "concrete and particular as against the general and theoretical" (p. 463), and the consequences of "exclusive concentration on a specialty":

> The physicist who is only a physicist can still be a first-class physicist and a most valuable member of society. But nobody can be a great economist who is only an economist—and I am even tempted to add that the economist who is only an economist is likely to become a nuisance if not a positive danger.

And (p. 464)

> The degree of abstraction which the theoretical disciplines in our field requires makes them at least as theoretical, if not more so, than any in the natural sciences. This, however, is precisely the source of our difficulty. Not only is the individual concrete instance much more important to us than it is in the natural sciences, but the way from the theoretical construction to the explanation of the particular is also much longer.

Furthermore (p. 465),

> most successful research work will require a very particular combination of diverse kinds of knowledge and accomplishments, and it may take half a lifetime until we are better than amateurs in three-quarters of the knowledge demanded by the task we have set ourselves.

Unfortunately (p. 465), "not every legitimate research specialty is equally suitable as a scientific education." Hayek concludes (pp. 469–70) that in economics

> we do not know as sharp a division between the theoretician and the practitioner as there exists between the physicist and the engineer or between the physiologist and the doctor. This is not an accident or merely an earlier stage of development but a necessary consequence of the nature of our subject. It is due to the fact that the task of recognizing the presence in the real world of the conditions corresponding to the various assumptions of our theoretical schemes is often more difficult than the theory itself, an art which only those

will acquire to whom the theoretical schemes have become second nature. . . . We can, therefore, only rarely delegate the application of our knowledge but must be our own practitioners, doctors as well as physiologists.

ACTION AND PERCEPTION

Of the essay on "Rules, Perception and Intelligibility," I shall only draw attention to Hayek's important observations on "rule-guided action" and "rule-guided perception," neither of which presupposes that we can state or describe the rules that guide our actions and perceptions. I should like to make Hayek's statements of these issues required reading for any one who undertakes to talk or write about the methodology of the social sciences.

The theme of the existence of subconscious rules that guide perception is further elaborated in a brief essay on "The Primacy of the Abstract." [12] Here Hayek defends the proposition that perception of the concrete presupposes an organizing capacity of the mind; this is what he means by "primacy of the abstract." Hayek refers to the well-established fact that "most animals recognize . . . abstract features long before they can identify particulars." He goes back to the writings of many important authors, from Adam Ferguson (1767) through Immanuel Kant and Charles S. Peirce to quite recent psychologists, zoologists, and ethologists, to show that this recognition, although it contradicts a common textbook-lesson, has been of rather old vintage, forgotten or disregarded by the believers in the primacy of the concrete.

[12] "The Primacy of the Abstract," in Arthur Koestler and J. R. Smythies, eds., *Beyond Reductionism: New Perspectives in the Life Sciences* (London: Hutchinson, 1969), pp. 309–323.

Chapter 26

SPIRO LATSIS ON SITUATIONAL DETERMINISM

This article was written in response to one published under the same title by Spiro J. Latsis in this *Journal*.[1] The title puzzled me when I first saw it, but Latsis explained it in the first sentence, where he contrasted 'economic determinism' with 'economic behaviouralism' and referred to them as 'two rival research programmes in a major branch of modern microeconomic theory, in the theory of the firm'. Since I had, a few years earlier, produced a piece on

[1] Latsis [1972].

'Theories of the Firm: Marginalist, Behavioural, Managerial',[1] I realised quickly that Latsis and I were either rivals or allies in the same controversy. In the end I concluded that he was on my side more often than not. Still, on some critical questions we seem to disagree and it is, I believe, worth looking for the reasons. Not wanting to impose on the reader a reading or re-reading of our earlier pieces, I shall try to make the present article intelligible to those who are tuning in only now. A conscientious reader, however, will have to go back to Latsis's article to check my interpretation of his position.

1   Nomenclature

Economic determinism is Latsis's term for the general principles that have characterised the neoclassical programme in the theory of the firm, which attempts to explain market phenomena as the results of actions of rational agents who, in an attempt to maximise their profits, respond to the 'logic of the situation'. Situational determinism seems to be the same as marginalism inasmuch as this term refers to the logical procedure of firms equating marginal revenue and marginal cost in attempting to maximise profits.

Latsis's term, or rather a part of it, is derived from a forceful dictum by Popper: 'The analysis of the situation, the situational logic, plays a very important part in social life as well as in the social sciences. It is, in fact, the method of economic analysis.'[2] The main point regarding this simple theory of the firm is that it is based on the postulate of a single motive or objective of a single decision-maker, excluding therefore all the complications that can arise from the presence of several conflicting goals motivating several (more or less cooperating) decision-makers within a bureaucratic organisation.

The behavioural theory of the firm substitutes for the single goal of profit maximisation a collection of different goals pursued by a collection of people in executive positions in a business organisation. (Latsis proposes that 'it may be advisable to develop behaviouralist ideas first in their application to a single decision maker and later to a complex decision making structure'; he thus opposes the 'combination of behaviouralism and organisationalism'.[3] But the main tenet of behaviouralism is that the objectives of the decision-makers (and the techniques of resolving conflicts among them) should not be postulated but should first be ascertained by empirical research in actual firms, particularly by observing decision-making processes in reality. That the observations should be aided by working hypotheses and designed to develop a theory 'with generality beyond the specific firms studied'[4] justifies the term 'behavioural' as distinguished from 'behaviourist'.

Latsis mentions but does not give major billing to the third approach, the managerial theory of the firm. While the managerial theory hypothesises a few other specified goals[5] in addition to the goal of profit maximisation, it postulates

---

[1] Machlup [1967]. I shall cite an immodestly large number of my own writings in order to facilitate the work of those who want to go back and look into the development of the ideas behind this discussion.   [2] Popper [1945], *volume 2*, p. 97.
[3] Latsis [1972], footnote 3 to p. 229.   [4] Cyert and March [1963], p. 2.
[5] Baumol has proposed maximisation of sales or of the growth rate of sales as likely managerial objectives (Baumol [1959], p. 49, and [1962], p. 1086). Oliver Williamson added maximisation of expenditures for staff personnel and for managerial emoluments (Williamson [1964], pp. 38–60).

that there are rational ways to reconcile the chosen maximanda with one another, for example, by making the additional managerial goals subject to the constraint of some minimum benefits to the owners of the business. In one way or another, the accommodation of stated objectives besides that of maximum money profits in a model of the firm may justify placing managerial theories together with marginalist theories or, in Latsis's terminology, with 'situational determinism'. In any event, I shall for the present discussion accept Latsis's suggestion of only two rival research programmes in the theory of the firm.

2   *Rivals in What Sense?*

Latsis, in regarding marginalism and behaviouralism as rival theories, or rival research programmes, accepts the claims of the behaviouralists who reject the marginalist programme (or paradigm) and offer their own as a better or more promising substitute. I submit, however, that the two programmes are rivals only as long as they are supposed to serve the same purpose.

For example, if both the marginalist and the behaviouralist programmes are understood as systems designed to explain and predict the actions of particular business firms, one may regard them as rivals and may judge their comparative performance in this task. It is no doubt true that some writers in the marginalist camp have presented their theory as an instrument performing that task. However, this is not the main purpose of the marginalist theory of the firm and, if it is used for this purpose, it will be rather unreliable and will utterly fail in far too many cases.

The proper use of marginalist theory is to explain and predict the direction of changes in prices and outputs of particular products consequent upon particular events or changes in conditions. In the model that establishes a connection between these events (or changes in conditions) and the resulting changes in prices and outputs the firm is merely a link (bridge, transmission belt, transformer, automaton, or robot) between causes and effects. For this function a behavioural theory of the firm is not suitable, because it implies that the behaviour may be too varied, too idiosyncratic, too capricious (yes, too human) to be a reliable link in the chain from typical causes to typical effects. As Latsis correctly states, 'the burden of explanation shifts to the behavioural characteristics of the acting agent' (p. 229). Yet since the spectrum of such characteristics includes too many nuances and we would not know which one might apply in any concrete case, we could not hope to get much help for the stated purpose.

To be sure, the model employing this simple link-element called 'firm'— simple as long as it works merely as a robot with a one-track mind (or calculator) —can be used safely only under certain conditions ('used', that is, for purposes of explaining and predicting in particular historical situations). The most important of these conditions is that the number of real-world firms is large and that none of them has a dominant position. However, even when the model cannot be used safely (that is, with confidence that it will yield correct predictions), it will usually not work any worse than the behavioural programme with its choice of, say, 57 standard models and innumerable variants. Indeed, since the behavioural programme will rarely ever be sufficiently specified to tell us exactly which of the many possible behaviour models should be used in a particular case (particular as to industry, firm, product, place and time) we shall be at a loss trying to make the right selection. To 'misapply' the simple neoclassical model in situations in which it is not supposed to give the right answers might still give us less inaccurate results—and would surely be much less cumbersome.

Latsis understands this full well. This is what he has to say: 'In general there will be an indefinite variety of alternative decision processes for the same situational and motivational picture and each may lead to very different decisions being adopted. The actual decision may depend on more or less idiosyncratic rules or on rather stable rules related to various personality traits of the decision makers or to their social background or to other social-psychological forces' (p. 228). I am afraid, one cannot be certain that observation of the decision processes will result in any generalisations at all. This has been recognised by a student of the problem of 'simulated' behaviour, though he has not given up the hope that we shall end up with a manageable number of 'basic' models: 'In order to obtain adequate descriptions of the behaviour of individual firms, *it might conceivably be necessary to have as many models as there are firms.* . . . We doubt that this will be the case, however. Probably a relatively small number of basic models . . . will adequately describe the relevant aspects of each individual firm's actions.'[1]

The loss of generality is recognised by all behaviouralist theorists. Cyert and March, the authors of the authoritative text of the school, admit this in the following statement: 'The behaviour theory of the firm relaxes considerably the requirements of simplicity in the models, expands considerably the phenomena that can be considered explicitly, and reduces considerably the need for aggregation of phenomena into summary variables. As a result, the theory gives up some attributes of generality.'[2]

I have stated that marginalist theory will strictly apply only when competition is vigorous and therefore effective (Machlup [1967], p. 15). Latsis believes that this tells us merely 'that the perfectly competitive model is only applicable where it can be applied' (p. 212). I wonder whether this does full justice to my statement:

> The simple marginal formula based on profit maximization is suitable where (*1*) *large groups* of firms are involved and nothing has to be predicted about particular firms, (*2*) the effects of a *specified change* in conditions upon prices, inputs, and outputs are to be explained or predicted rather than the values of these magnitudes before or after the change, and nothing has to be said about the 'total situation' or general developments, and (*3*) only *qualitative answers*, that is, answers about directions of change, are sought rather than precise numerical results (1967, p. 31).

One more illustration of the use of the simple, general, marginalist theory may be helpful.

> How will the price of wheat be affected by a report of a drought; by a reduction in the import quota for wheat; by a reduction in the rate of interest; by an increase in freight rates; by an announcement that the ice cover on the Great Lakes will delay the opening of shipping for several weeks? These questions can be answered with the aid of general propositions of economic theory. The answers do not presuppose that the economist

---

[1] Cohen [1960], pp. 536–7 (my italics). [2] Cyert and March [1963], p. 281.

knows any wheat dealer personally, let alone his psychological make-up. They do presuppose, however, that the economist has constructed an ideal type of dealer conduct. Its main feature is that dealers would rather make more money than less. This imputation of the profit motive to anonymous characters—'intervening variables' between, say, a newspaper report and a quotation of a higher price on the wheat exchange—is necessary for a full understanding of the causal connections.[1]

A research programme designed to result in theories that explain and predict the actions of particular firms can never compete with the simplicity and generality of the marginalist theory which, being based on the construct of a fictitious profit-maximiser, cannot have the ambition to explain the behaviour of actual firms in the real world. The two research programmes are designed for different purposes and are therefore not real rivals.

3 *The Compromise Regarding Oligopoly*

Latsis believes that an 'appraisal of the rival research programmes is premature' (p. 233). I am quite willing to wait and give the behaviouralists more time to come up with a set of models and a set of directives and specifications telling which model to apply to which kind of firm and which kind of situation. When they do and when their models give us results superior to the 'naive' marginalist model, we shall be able to judge whether the improvement (greater accuracy, numerically determinate results) is worth the cost (need for much more information).

On one point Latsis thinks he is ready for a judgment: 'But I can say now that I see no prospect for a compromise solution whereby situational determinism retains most of the theory of the firm but concedes oligopoly to behaviouralism' (p. 233). His reasons are that each of the two approaches entails a 'pervasive methodological view', and that behaviouralism, if it has a special function in markets where sellers are few, may show also that 'even under conditions of apparently severe competition there are systematic patterns of divergence from optimising behaviour' (pp. 233–4). These are no cogent reasons. It would have to be shown that the 'divergence from optimising behaviour' in situations of effective competition is large enough to warrant the sacrifice of simplicity imposed by the behavioural programme. If a simple technique can yield good results in a large range of cases while a much more complicated and costlier technique is needed for some, should this be a compelling reason for using the costlier technique throughout? I think not. If consistency in approach is expensive or even extravagant, it is no longer a virtue.

The 'compromise solution' mentioned by Latsis preceded by several decades the proposals for a behavioural theory of the firm. One of the early proponents of the 'compromise' was Vilfredo Pareto. In his view 'pure economics' cannot yield a unique solution in the case of few sellers and 'observation' will show a variety of possibilities.[2] I cited Pareto when I discussed 'Oligopolistic Indeterminacy' in a book published in 1952, and went on to cite Alfred Schutz on the difference in analysing the effects of the behaviour of anonymous masses on the

---

[1] Machlup [1969], pp. 301–302.
[2] Pareto [1927], pp. 601–2.

one hand, and the conduct of particular individuals on the other,[1] I concluded that for an analysis of the effects of mass behaviour we can often do with far less information than we may need for an analysis of the actions of a few particular persons. (Where the outcome depends on judgments and decisions by a few individuals the selection of the appropriate model would require characterological research, or at least investigation of the 'voting records' of the individuals in question and of their influence in the hierarchy of decision-makers in the organisation.) It would be a strange methodological principle indeed that were to command us to seek the heaps of information that may be required in some cases also for problems where they are not needed.

Incidentally, to admit that the marginalist approach may fail to yield solutions in cases where the number of decision-makers is relatively small is not to concede that the behavioural approach has succeeded or is likely to succeed any better. It has not yet furnished unique solutions and accurate predictions. I have my doubts that it ever will, but I keep an open mind.

4 *Three Crucial Confusions*

In his critique of what he calls situational determinism, Latsis does not guard himself and does not warn his readers sufficiently against some of the traps in which most critics of neoclassical economics have been caught. Three confusions are rather common in the literature:

1. The confusion between action and reaction. To explain or predict anybody's actions is a far bigger job than to explain or predict his *reactions* to certain types of events or changes of conditions. Indeed, the number of possible actions is so large that the task of predicting them is almost impossible. In my earlier writings I have stressed the difference between entrepreneurial, innovative actions and typical responses to typical stimuli.[2]

2. The confusion between reactions and effects of reactions. It would be practically impossible to ascertain the reactions of millions of people to specified types of events; even to check large samples of supposed reactors would be difficult where neither the stimulus nor the response is physical. Where the stimulus is only a message, a piece of information, a becoming aware of something, and where the response is a decision (usually embodied again in some sort of message or instruction) 'direct' observation of the decision and its connection with the stimulus may be virtually impossible. To ascertain the *effects* of the decision is something quite different.[3] One can observe the effects of business decisions by consulting the records of certain changes in market prices or production volumes.

3. The confusion between the effects of reactions of particular persons and the effects of mass reactions or, more correctly, of assumed typical reactions of imaginary persons. The essential difference here is between actual people (living persons or historical personalities) and idealised, *fictitious* people invented (constructed) for the purpose of deducing from their assumed (built-in) reactions effects of the type observed in reality.[4]

[1] Machlup [1952], pp. 417, 419.   [2] Machlup [1967], pp. 7, 8, 13, 27.
[3] Machlup [1967], pp. 7, 8; [1970], pp. 123, 139.
[4] Machlup [1963], pp. 131-4, 142; [1967], pp. 6-8, 27; and [1970], p. 139.

Compounding all three pairs of contrasts into one, we confront the huge difference between (*a*) observable actions of real people and (*b*) typical effects of imagined (postulated) reactions of imagined (postulated) people to typical events or changes in conditions. Both the typical effects and the typical events to which they are attributed correspond to classes of observable changes in recorded data.

I cannot claim that Latsis himself is a victim of any of these confusions, but he does little to make his readers beware of the snares. Regarding the confusion between *action* and *reaction*, I note the almost complete absence of the words reaction and response in a discussion in which words such as actions, courses of action, decisions, decision procedures, choices, and behaviour occur several times on every page. Only once does Latsis come to grips with the problem: when he speaks of 'changes in variables in response to variations in parameters' (p. 213). Yet, this is the very essence of neoclassical microeconomics and the reader should never be allowed to confuse reactions to changes with spontaneous actions of the entrepreneurial type.

In a remark about Popper's reference to the 'logic of the situation' explaining the movements of a man crossing the street and dodging the cars,[1] Latsis exclaims: 'But entrepreneurial behaviour is usually very different from street crossing. For crossing the street we need little imagination, skill and deliberation. For entrepreneurial activity one often needs a high degree of imagination and skill; and these are processes which can hardly be reflected by crude single-exit models' (p. 224). Latsis recognises that simple models such as that of the profit-maximising firm 'have little application to actual entrepreneurial decision making' (p. 229), but he fails to tell the reader that these models were designed to explain and predict adjustments of an interdependences among market variables, not innovative, entrepreneurial activities.

The confusion between *reactions* (or actions) and the *effects* of reactions (or actions) has led many economists to aim at the wrong target. We are not primarily interested in businessmen, business decisions, business routine and business reactions; we are interested in firms only because of the effects of their actions and reactions upon production, resource use, incomes, and prices. Our main purpose is to explain and predict changes in these variables and we must look into the actions and reactions of firms only to the extent necessary for this purpose. Often this 'look' will be merely one at a mental construct (ideal type) of a firm rather than at a collection of real people in a corporate organisation. Yet, even if in specific situations the 'effects' cannot be explained without empirical research in the real people that make the particular decisions, these decisions are still only theoretical links in the chain that connects certain changes in conditions to certain changes in the variables to be explained. When Latsis offers a very interesting discussion of the 'bridge role' of certain psychological-physiological processes in the decision process of the individual and distinguishes stimulus from arousal and arousal from response (pp. 226–7) we ought to remind ourselves of the fact that even the response has only a 'bridge role' in the explanation or prediction of the variables in which we are ultimately interested: prices, incomes, allocations, and outputs.

[1] Popper [1945], *volume 2*, p. 97. My own illustration of the logic of the situation was that of an automobile overtaking a lorry on a highway. Machlup [1946], pp. 534–6; [1952], pp. 44–46, and [1967], pp. 6–7.

Latsis is fully aware of the widespread confusion between *real people* and *mental constructs* of decision-makers (which I have called 'imaginary reactors'). His awareness finds its most explicit expression in the statement that 'the neoclassical view stresses the *situation* and turns the decision making agent into a cypher' (p. 233). I cannot tell from the context whether Latsis sees this, as I do, as an advantage or rather as a defect of the neoclassical approach.

I have expressed this idea repeatedly in my writings and could select from a good many formulations. Here is one that I find especially pungent:

> the firm in the model world of economic micro-theory ought not to call forth any irrelevant associations with firms in the real world. We know, of course, that there are firms in reality and that they have boards of directors and senior and junior executives, who do, with reference to hundreds of different products, a great many things—which are entirely irrelevant for the microtheoretical model. The fictitious firm of the model is a 'uni-brain,' an individual decision-unit that has nothing to do but adjust the output and the prices of one or two imaginary products to very simple imagined changes in data.[1]

5   What Does the Firm 'Know'?

Marginalists as well as behaviouralists have fretted much about the amount of knowledge possessed by the 'firm'. Some marginalists have been overly generous, endowing the imaginary firm of their creation with 'perfect knowledge'. Some behaviouralists, on the other hand, have worried about the incompleteness, inaccuracy, and uncertainty of the information available to the real decision-makers in the business organisations of the real world; and, of course, they charged the marginalists with making ridiculously unrealistic assumptions when they hypothesised that the firm of their model was maximising its profits on the basis of 'adequate' knowledge.

Latsis seems to accept this criticism: 'Situational determinism assumes that the decision maker knows his situation better than he is assumed to know it in the conditions usually investigated in decision theory' (p. 211). And he states that 'the decision the agent will reach depends . . . also on his *decision process*, namely, the way in which he will process the incomplete information available to him' (p. 228).

Whether the imaginary firm in the marginalist model 'knows' more or less than the real people who run firms in the real world, and how perfect, complete, accurate and certain its knowledge is, depends on the purpose for which the theorist constructs his model. For some purposes—for example, for a general-equilibrium system in welfare economics in which the allocation of resources is to be optimal at least in the sense used by Pareto—the imaginary firm has to be endowed with full knowledge of its technological and organisational possibilities as well as its buying and selling opportunities in the markets. For other purposes —for example, to show the effects which changes in conditions (*i.e.* changes in any of the mentioned possibilities and opportunities) will have upon inputs, outputs, and prices in competitive industries—the knowledge required is minimal: namely, just of the *changes* in conditions, not of the conditions them-

[1] Machlup [1963], p. 133.

selves. (This is surely much less knowledge than any real person who can read the newspapers is apt to have.) No matter how incomplete, inaccurate, and uncertain the firm's knowledge is of its costs, revenues, profits, *etc.*, all that this firm has to know is the direction in which some pertinent magnitude has changed. 'What can be "imperfect"', I wrote in 1967 (p. 25) 'about the information on, say, a tax increase? Why should it take special theories of bureaucracy to explain how the news of a wage increase "flows" through various hierarchical levels up or down or across? Yet this, and this alone, is the information that is essentially involved in the theory of prices and allocation, since it is the *adjustment to such changes in conditions* for which the postulate of maximising behaviour is employed'.

Alfred Schutz likened the ideal types constructed by social scientists to puppets acting out the roles assigned to them by their constructors. The firm in competitive-price theory is one of these puppets. 'By the grace of its constructor, he [the puppet] is endowed with just that kind of knowledge he needs to perform the job for the sake of which he was brought into the scientific world.'[1] The job of the ideal type called firm may be different from problem to problem; 'we must indicate the reference scheme within which the ideal type may be utilised, that is, the problem for the sake of which the type has been constructed'.[2]

6 *How Rational is the Firm?*

The quoted formulations by Alfred Schutz come from his essay on 'The Problem of Rationality in the Social World' and might be thought of as an appropriate transition to the question how much 'rationality' one may attribute to the firm, that is, to the imaginary reactor in price theory. Most discussions of the meaning and significance of rationality in economic theory would benefit from a study of Schutz's work. Writers might learn to be more explicit about what they mean, particularly whether they refer to reasonable actions, deliberate actions (routine, use of reliable insights, anticipations of desired ends, choices among alternative means for particular ends, but also choices among alternative ends), planned actions (projects), predictable actions, 'logical' actions[3] (as contrasted with traditional and habitual ones), to mention some of the distinctions discussed by Schutz.

With regard to the theory of the firm we ought to be told whether rationality refers to consistency with the information available to the actor (or reactor) or to consistency with the objectives and the preference scheme of the actor—or perhaps even to consistency with information and insights available not to the actor but to the observer. Latsis offers an interesting discussion of pronouncements on rationality by Karl Popper and J. W. N. Watkins and develops some interesting extensions of Watkins' ideas on imperfect rationality. What Latsis has to say about the separateness of 'appraisal of the situation', 'decision to act', and 'action' (execution of the decision) deserves attention. However, it remains to be shown that the suggested analysis of the decision process, its breakdown into

---

[1] Schutz [1943]; reproduced in his [1964], p. 83.

[2] *Ibid.* Perhaps I may in this context refer to an essay of mine in which I illustrated the use of seven different characterological and habitual ideal types and contrasted them with the *homo economicus*, an ideal type 'designed for interpreting observed consequences of men's actions' (Machlup [1970], pp. 135–9).   [3] This is Pareto's term.

several constituent phases, can be of substantial help in economic theorising. I do not question its significance in psychology, on the one hand, and in organisation theory and management science, on the other. That in 'situational determinism' the 'so-called rationality principle is absorbed into the postulates characterising the *homo economicus*' is fully recognised by Latsis (p. 229). I believe that this is all to the good, but I am afraid that Latsis thinks otherwise.

7   *How Determinate is the Theory?*

This brings me to the question whether Latsis is justified in calling neoclassical microeconomics situational *determinism* in contrast to a programme of economic behaviouralism that he evidently does *not* regard as deterministic. We must ask in what sense behavioural theories of business firms can be regarded as non-deterministic.

Latsis finds that Herbert Simon committed a 'philosophical error' when he mistook 'situational determinism' for apriorism and 'psychologically observation-motivated theories for inductive ascent' (p. 229). As I see it, the fact that a model is constructed with a 'hard core' made out of fundamental hypotheses or postulates whereas other models are constructed with hypotheses derived from low-level behavioural generalisations on the basis of empirical observations should not make an essential difference in the application of the models. Any theoretical model—in contradistinction to a probabilistic model—, no matter how the built-in 'assumptions' were obtained, serves to be used in conjunction with some additional proposition—usually concerning an event or a change in conditions—so that a conclusion can be deduced from the conjunction. Both the additional proposition, which I once designated as the 'assumed change' (cause), and the conclusion, which I called the 'deduced change' (effect), are in the domain of construction but have counterparts in the domain of observation so that the correspondence can be tested.[1] In either case, the deduced change, the theoretical outcome of the whole business, is completely determined.

To put this statement in a slightly different form, any model designed to present (exhibit) a causal connection between an independent variable and a dependent variable under given conditions—conditions which may include fundamental hypotheses and a set of less fundamental assumptions on various levels of generality or specificity—must display the dependent variable as a logical consequence of all the premises in the model. Since these premises *imply* the conclusion, there can be no doubt about the *complete determinateness* of the result. Of course, whether this whole apparatus with its input and its determinate output applies to many situations of the real world, or to only a few, or to none at all, is a different matter. Determinate is only the theoretical conclusion inferred from the premises. Nobody, however, can be certain whether the apparatus, the input, and the output will fit anything in the real world and will thus *satisfactorily explain* and *approximately predict* some observable outcome of the conjunction of an observed event with actual conditions prevailing in reality. Thus, the applicability of the model with its determinate conclusion is always open to question; it is *never* certain, no matter in how many instances it has been applied with success.

In one of my earlier essays—on 'Ideal Types, Reality, and Construction'[2]—I

---

[1] Machlup [1955], p. 13.   [2] Machlup [1960–61].

tried to show that mental constructs, ideal types and theoretical models designed for causal explanation are tools which *may* be useful regardless of the origin of what has gone into their construction. The ingredients or constituent parts may be abstractions or generalisations derived from empirical research, from case studies or statistical computations, but they may also be speculative idealisations, heroic hypotheses and grandiose postulates, spun by an inventive mind. Philosophers with ultra-empiricist bias will always want to inspect the certificates of origin of the assumptions imported into a theoretical model and will call for barriers against the import of assumptions not certified as the products of an empirical workshop. Such prejudices will neither make a successful model useless nor bestow pragmatic usefulness onto a model that fails to do a good job of explaining and predicting. The worth of a conceptual scheme does not depend on the descent of its constituent concepts.[1]

8 The Wider the Choice the Harder the Choosing

The basic argument for the behavioural theory of the firm is that decisions and actions of firms in reality depend on a variety of things, including the characterological make-up of their executives and the hierarchical set-up in their organisation and coordination. In order to explain and predict the actions (including the reactions to specified events) of a particular firm, we need a wide choice of models and have to select the right model that fits the type of firm. Assuming again that 57 models will cover most, though of course not all, of the types, we can hope that one of these models will do the job. Perhaps the specifications and directions will be sufficiently precise to enable us to eliminate a major part of the collection and thus narrow the choice to eight or ten models. While each of the models can furnish a perfectly determinate theoretical result, we can never be sure which of them is the appropriate one for the case in question. This is associated with the 'loss in generality' that the behavioural theorist had to admit. The increase in specificity increases the chance of accurate results provided we pick the right model for the case before us, but it reduces the chance of our finding that model.

Even if many of the models on the shelf had been constructed after painstaking observation of the decision-making processes of certain firms, one could never be sure that they would fit the same firms at a later time. Changes in the management personnel, in the division of responsibilities, in outside influences on the decision-making people, in governmental policies (say, with regard to anti-monopoly prosecution), and many other changes, internal as well as external, may have made the model 'constructed from life' quite obsolete and, hence, entirely unreliable in subsequent applications. The model is still in excellent working order, producing fully determinate theoretical outcomes, only that the produced (deduced) solutions would now fail to explain and predict the observed actions of the 'same' firm—if its sameness is defined only in legal terms. For the analyst the firm is no longer the same.

We may now have 57 determinate theoretical solutions but may be at a loss

[1] *Ibid.* pp. 55–7. I understand that most neopositivists would agree with my denunciation of these prejudices. Unfortunately, however, some of the prejudiced writers invoke the authority of (probably misunderstood) pronouncements by neopositivist philosophers to support their rejection of 'unrealistic' assumptions.

deciding which might be the right one for a concrete case in question. The probability of a good fit is not any greater and may be smaller than if we had used a very general, deliberately unrealistic model. In saying this, I may give the impression that the general model of the profit-maximising firm is recommended here as one of the alternatives in the task of explaining and predicting actions of particular firms. It is not; this model is used properly only for the effects of reactions of imaginary firms.[1]

9   *Personal Types and Course-of-Action Types*

Many of the things suggested in the preceding pages can be said much better in the language of Alfred Schutz, or indeed in his words, except that his terminology and conceptual framework, derived from Max Weber on the one hand and Edmund Husserl on the other, have been resented and resisted in certain quarters. I am convinced that learning Schutzian language could help many in sorting out some messy notions in the methodology of the social sciences.

The social scientist, in order to grasp and interpret the 'other self', that is, people, their actions and reactions, and the effects of these actions and reactions, has to form 'a construct of a typical way of behaviour, a typical pattern of underlying motives, or typical attitudes of a personality type.[2] Such types can be

> arranged according to the degree of increasing anonymity of the relationship among contemporaries involved and therewith of the construct needed to grasp the other and his behaviour. It becomes apparent that an increase in anonymity involves a decrease in fullness of content. The more anonymous the typifying construct is the more detached is it from the uniqueness of the individual fellowman involved, the fewer aspects also of his personality and behaviour pattern enter the typification as being relevant for the purpose at hand, for the sake of which the type has been constructed. If we distinguish between (subjective) personal types and (objective) course-of-action types we may say that increasing anonymisation of the construct leads to the superseding of the former by the latter. In complete anonymisation the individuals are supposed to be interchangeable, and the course-of-action type refers to the behaviour of 'whomsoever' acting in the way defined by the construct.[3]

The social scientist, the 'scientific observer of social interaction patterns', constructs

> typical course-of-action patterns corresponding to the observed events. Thereupon he co-ordinates to these typical course-of-action patterns a personal type, namely, a model of an actor whom he imagines as being gifted with consciousness. Yet it is a consciousness restricted to containing nothing but all the elements relevant to the performance of the course-of-action patterns under observation and relevant, therewith, to the scientist's problem under scrutiny.[4]

---

[1] Still, if I were given the assignment to interpret in a concrete case the actions of a particular firm and were perplexed by having to find the correct model from among a wide choice of behaviourally specific models, I would be tempted to try first that unduly unrealistic, simplistic, anonymous general model and see what it could do for me.

[2] Schutz [1853], p. 12; [1962], p. 17.   [3] Schutz [1953], p. 13; [1962], pp. 17–18.

[4] Schutz [1953], pp. 31–32; [1962], p. 40.

Yet these models of actors are not human beings living within their biographical situation in the social world of everyday life. Strictly speaking, they do not have any biography or any history, and the situation into which they are placed is not a situation defined by them but defined by their creator, the social scientist. He has created these puppets or homunculi to manipulate them for his purpose. A merely specious consciousness is imputed to them by the scientist which is constructed in such a way that its presupposed stock of knowledge at hand (including the ascribed set of invariant motives) would make actions originating therefrom subjectively understandable, provided that these actions were performed by real actors within the social world. But the puppet and his artificial consciousness is not subjected to the ontological conditions of human beings. The homunculus was not born, he does not grow up, and he will not die. He has no hopes and no fears: he does not know anxiety as the chief motive of all his deeds. He is not free in the sense that his acting could transgress the limits his creator, the social scientist, has predetermined. He cannot, therefore, have other conflicts of interests and motives than those the social scientist has imputed to him. He cannot err, if to err is not his typical destiny. He cannot choose, except among the alternatives the social scientist has put before him as standing to his choice.[1]

The methodological principles guiding the construction of ideal types and models and their uses for, or applications to, particular problems are the same for types of different degrees of anonymity. It is a mistake to think that models containing types of greater anonymity yield fully determinate results while models with less anonymous types yield less determinate results. Any well-constructed model furnishes precisely the results the constructor wants it to furnish. Thus the most useful model has only a 'single exit', if I may use Latsis's expression. And this holds for a highly 'behavioural' model no less than for one with only fully anonymous, single-minded maximisers of profit. Indeed, if the postulate of profit maximisation in certain circumstances—*e.g.* in cases of oligopoly—fails to make the model produce completely determinate results, we regard it as unsuitable for instances of this sort and try to replace it with one that yields just the results that we want it to deliver.

10 *Behavioural Determinism*

If every good theoretical model yields just one solution—because we want to work only with models that furnish determinate solutions—but if some will do so with a simple, most general objective function while others need more specific 'psychological' and 'organisational' behaviour functions, Latsis may have to distinguish two kinds of determinism: situational determinism and behavioural determinism.

I would not choose these terms, however, because I think that the adjectives do not bring out the real difference and the noun is misleading in several respects. The problem of determinism should, in my opinion, not be brought into the discussion of model building and theory formation in the theory of the firm or in economics in general, except where probabilistic models are used. However, if

[1] Schutz [1953], p. 32; [1962], p. 41.

Latsis insists that an explanatory scheme which fully explains a specified change as an inevitable effect of a conjunction of a specified cause with specified conditions should be designated as an instance of determinism, I am willing to humour him, provided he recognises that his behavioural approach will become satisfactory only as it becomes just as 'deterministic' as the situational approach.

Neither Latsis nor the proponents of the behavioural programme have, if I understood them correctly, meant to introduce probabilistic models into the theory of the firm. They have merely proposed to distil from the findings of empirical observation of actual decision processes a bevy of behavioural types for use in empirically richer models. I conclude that the disanonymisation of the fundamental postulate of economic behaviour into a variety of particular types and subtypes of behaviour does not justify distinguishing the two research programmes by awarding to one and refusing to the other the designation 'deterministic'.

FRITZ MACHLUP
New York University

REFERENCES

BAUMOL, W. J. [1959]: *Business Behaviour, Value, and Growth*.

BAUMOL, W. J. [1962]: 'On the Theory of the Expansion of the Firm', *American Economic Review*, **52**, pp. 1078–87.

COHEN, K. [1960]: 'Simulation of the Firm', *American Economic Review*, **50**, pp. 534–40.

CYERT, R. M. and MARCH, J. G. [1963]: *Behavioural Theory of the Firm*.

LATSIS, S. J. [1972]: 'Situational Determinism in Economics', *British Journal for the Philosophy of Science*, **23**, pp. 207–45.

MACHLUP, F. [1939]: 'Evaluation of the Practical Significance of the Theory of Monopolistic Competition', *American Economic Review*, **29**, pp. 227–36.

MACHLUP, F. [1946]: 'Marginal Analysis and Empirical Research', *American Economic Review*, **36**, pp. 519–54.

MACHLUP, F. [1952]: *The Economics of Sellers' Competition*.

MACHLUP, F. [1955]: 'The Problem of Verification in Economics', *Southern Economic Journal*, **22**, pp. 1–21.

MACHLUP, F. [1960–1]: 'Idealtypus, Wirklichkeit und Konstruktion', *Ordo*, **12**, pp. 21–57.

MACHLUP, F. [1963]: *Essays in Economic Semantics*.

MACHLUP, F. [1967]: 'Theories of the Firm: Marginalist, Behavioural, Managerial', *American Economic Review*, **57**, pp. 1–33.

MACHLUP, F. [1969]: 'If Matter Could Talk', in S. Morgenbesser, P. Suppes, and M. White (*eds.*): *Philosophy, Science, and Method*, pp. 286–305.

MACHLUP, F. [1970]: 'Homo Oeconomicus and His Class Mates', in M. Natanson (*ed.*): *Phenomenology and Social Reality*, pp. 122–39.

POPPER, K. R. [1945]: *The Open Society and Its Enemies*.

SCHUTZ, A. [1943]; 'The Problem of Rationality in the Social World', *Economica*, N.S., **10**, pp. 130–49.

SCHUTZ, A. [1953]: 'Common-Sense and Scientific Interpretation of Human Action', *Philosophy and Phenomenological Research*, **14**, pp. 1–38.

SCHUTZ, A. [1962]: *Collected Papers, 1, The Problem of Social Reality*.

SCHUTZ, A. [1964]: *Collected Papers, 2, Studies in Social Theory*.

WATKINS, J. W. N. [1970]: 'Imperfect Rationality', in R. Borger and F. Cioffi (*eds.*): *Explanations in the Behavioural Sciences*, pp. 167–217.

WILLIAMSON, O. E. [1964]: *Economics of Discretionary Behaviour: Managerial Objectives in a Theory of the Firm*.

INDEX

performing and fine, 433
vs. practice, 432-434
"As if" reasoning, 497n
Assumed
change, 134, 148-152, 154, 201,
457, 495-503, 530
conditions, 77, 148-152, 154,
482-483, 487, 494, 495-503
premises, 270, 288
type of action, 153
Assumptions, see also Hypothesis,
Postulate
abstract, 455
as input for model, 79
basic to observation, 38
counterfactual, 151, 180, 287,
455, 483, 497n, 498, 501
definitional, 145
factual, 74, 140, 371-383, 384
fundamental, 4, 133, 143, 146,
147, 148-151, 288, 301, 457,
468, 495
in scientific method, 26, 39
indispensable, 15
isolated, 44
millions of, 79n
more specific, 88, 94
noneconomic, 88
nonverifiable, 143, 180, 199
not testable in isolation, 143,
145, 146, 153-155, 494
of homogeneity, 82, 90
of pure competition, 80, 81
plausible, 79
procedural, 39
realistic, 78, 79, 151
reasonable though not always true,
392
removing indeterminacy, 86-87
simplest, 103
specific, 146, 147, 149-151, 354
statistical, 48
tacit (unstated), 4, 49, 66, 69,
225, 381, 384
unproved (unverified), 27, 61, 74
unrealistic, 61, 78, 79, 82, 109,
224, 294, 392, 455, 478, 481,
528, 531
Astronomy, 19, 57, 350, 364, 434
Astrophysics, 19, 57
Atom, 23, 38, 45, 111n, 146, 161,
168, 314, 342, 352, 400
Saint Augustine, 275
Aunt Molly, 275
Austrian girls, 300
Austrian School, ix, 156, 454, 478,
501
Automobile driver, 396-397, 527n
Average type, 242
Axiological rules, 436-437
Axiom, 8, 14, 42, 51, 140n, 152, 252,
336, 481

Axiomatic system, 41, 42, 141n
Axiomatization, 43, 141-142, 274
Axioms, 8, 14, 42, 51, 140n, 152,
252, 336, 481
Ayer, Ayred Jules, 56-57n

-B-

Baconian reforms, 15
Bagehot, Walter, 287, 290, 297
Balance of payments, 124, 378,
435-436, 508-509
Balance of trade, 69, 182, 195, 379
Baltimore Sun, 416n
Bank of England, 321
Bargaining power, 102, 113-116
Barnard, Chester Irving, 402, 422
Barton, John, 284
Bass, Robert E., 167n
Baumol, William J., 407, 421, 422,
522n, 534
Becker, Howard, 220, 221
Behavior equation, 269, 283, 287,
298, 299, 381, 382, 419, 500
Behavioral
approach, 534
research, 406
sciences, 346, 487
term, 219
theory of automobile driving, 397n
theory of the firm, 373, 391-423,
460, 534
theory of the household, 399n
Behaviorism, 36, 44-45, 46, 159, 219,
317, 339, 340, 343, 394, 419,
455, 480, 486, 500, 516, 522
Benefits
compared with costs, 449, 450,
508, 509
future, 449
Benjamin, Abram Cornelius, 53n
Bentham, Jeremy, 432, 477
Bernsdorf, Wilhelm, 516n
Bias
conscious, 440, 444
economists', 454
unconscious, 122-123n, 440, 443,
444
Bicycle, 494, 495, 497
Biedermann, Flodoart von, 227n
Biographical situation, 533
Biography, 61
Biology, 38, 46, 48, 61, 79, 163,
170, 190, 228, 229, 232, 312,
322, 325, 327, 331, 336, 337n,
350, 354, 363, 365-366, 386,
400, 442, 443, 444
Bitros, George, xi
Black, Max, 168n
Bluffer, 91
Blumberg, Albert E., 166n

Boas, George, 166n, 416, 422
Bode, Karl, 90n
Body stress, 161
Books on sex, 448
Borger, Robert, 534
Boring, Edwin G., 184n
Born, Max, 168-169
Botany, 164, 227
Boulding, Kenneth E., 402, 404n, 414, 422
Bowley, Marian, 289n, 290n
Braithwaite, Richard Bevan, 4, 34, 45-47, 146, 174n, 353n
Bridgman, Percy, 3, 12, 20-21, 53n, 111n, 134, 145, 159, 160-163, 167, 191, 193n, 261n, 336n
Brownian motion, 310
Bucher, Karl, 248
Buckle, Thomas, 235n
Building code, 123-124
Bunge, Mario, 516n
Burger, Thomas, 18n
Burtt, Edwin Arthur, 53n
Business cycle, 150, 461, 470

-C-

Cactus, 164
Caesar, Julius, 327
Cairnes, John E., 142, 287, 290-292, 297, 489, 491
Caldin, Edward Francis, 174n
Capital
    formation, 325
    movements, 69, 145, 182, 199, 380
    -output ratio, 357
Capitalism, 250
Carey, Henry C., 284-285
Carnap, Rudolf, ix, 4, 12, 34, 35-38, 56, 430, 431n
Cartel, 80, 88n, 93, 108, 117, 121, 151
Cash balances, 69, 151, 181
Cassel, Gustav, 475
Cassirer, Ernst, 264
Cat
    as a thought object, 22
Causal
    analysis, 123, 240, 258, 331
    connections, 68, 225-226, 233, 384, 399, 530
    laws, 50
Causality
    emphasized, 190n, 453, 466
    Hume on, 11
    Margenau on, 40
    Popper on, 42
    rejection of, 189, 190n, 453, 466
Cause
    and effect, 112, 138, 150, 374, 399, 430, 456, 466, 469, 491,

523
    efficient, 246
    inferred from effects, 117
    relevant, 79
    ultimate, 290
Census Bureau, 177, 418
Central Bank, 64, 65, 67, 68, 147, 150, 376, 381, 382
Certainty
    Carnap on, 36-37
    of predictions, 119-120
    Reichenbach on, 29, see also A priori, Evidence, Probability, Tautology, Test, Uncertainty, Verification
Certificate of origin, 263, 531
Ceteris paribus, 179, 195, 384, 398, 501
Chamber music, 365
Chamberlin, Edward H., 89n, 393, 422
Chemistry, 217, 227, 255-256, 312, 314, 327, 329, 330, 336, 350, 361, 442, 443
Chronology, 106, 108
Cioffi, Frank, 534
Claassen, Emil-Maria, 517n
Clark, John Bates, 471, 478
Class
    of phenomena, 138, 154, 156
    vs. individual events, 75, 93, 107
Classification
    methods of, 15
    need of, 104-105
    of observed data, 258
Climate, 83
Closed shop, 83
Cognitive content, 35-36
Cohen, Kalman J., 524n, 534
Cohen, Morris, 3, 12, 19, 24-29, 54, 57n, 109-110n, 127n, 128n,, 139n, 156, 171n, 172-173, 174n, 335n, 349
Cohen, Robert S., 55n, 57n, 212n
Collective bargaining, 108, 114n
Collusion, 76, 86-99
Common sense
    prescientific, 26, 276, 324, 342, 467
    sense and illusion in, 26
    vs. developed science, 47, 47, 361
Common-sense
    concepts, 276
    experience, 27, 35, 153, 172, 186, 276
    interpretation, 153, 324, 342
    thinking, 33, 34
Communication, 150, 186, 247, 312, 313, 316, 317, 319, 320, 322-324, 332, 360
Compensation test, 122-123n, 447, 480
Competition
    aggressive, 408

Deduced
  change, 134, 148-152, 154, 397,
    457, 495-503, 530
  consequences, 133, 143-144, 177,
    194, 197, 201, 233, 252, 270,
    354, 405, 455, 481, 486, 494,
    497, 498, 500
  regularities, 145-146
Definition
  analytical, 152-496
  Croce on, 16
  epistemic vs. constitutive, 40-41,
    169
  method of successive, 169
  neglect of, 102
  of terms, 163-164
  operational, 159, 164, 169; see
    also Dictionary definitions
  real vs. nominal, 164n
Degree
  of abstraction, 73-74, 75, 77,
    110, 113, 148, 459, 518
  of acceptance, 139
  of accuracy, 128
  of anonymity, 68, 90, 244-247,
    532, 533
  of application, 509
  of certainty, 119-120
  of competition, 151
  of complexity, 105
  of comprehensiveness, 139
  of conclusiveness, 25
  of confidence, 139
  of confirmation, 37
  of conformance, 95
  of control, 120
  of divisibility, 103
  of empiricism, 143
  of exactness, 173, 197
  of explanation, 459, 516
  of falsifiability, 43
  of freedom, 86
  of generality, 67, 74, 77, 90,
    148, 315
  of intimacy, 90
  of logical integration, 239
  of mass behavior, 4
  of plausibility, 4
  of probability, 30-31, 37, 120
  of realism, 247
  of reliability, 29
  of significance, 38
  of specificity, 315
  of testability, 145
  of universality, 43
  of vagueness, 139
  of validity, 4, 69
Delivered prices, 114n, 181, 194
Delivery terms, 182-183
Demand
  effective, 185
  for exports, 157
  for foreign exchange, 69, 198, 200
  for goods, 81-82, 90, 150, 180,
    198, 357, 399n, 500
  for imports, 198
  for labor, 393
  for money, 378
  no operational concept of, 177,
    180
  statistical, 180
Demarcation
  between empirical and other sci-
    ences, 42
Demography, 337
Deposit bank, 256, 275, 321, 378
Description
  of institutions, 340
  of operations, 164
  of regularities, 145
  vs. explanation, 27, 40, 49, 189
  vs. theory, 76
Descriptive approach, 343
Destruction of output, 121
Determinism
  behavioral, 460, 533-534
  radical, 32
  situational, 459, 521-534
  vs. indeterminism, 31
  vs. probabilism, 487, 530, 533-534
Deutsch, Karl, 318n, 332n
Devaluation, 145
Development
  historical generalizations on, 491
  theory of, 470-471
Dewey, John, 174n, 505
Diagnosis of conditions, 154-155,
  371, 380, 434
Dictionary definition, 6, 9-10, 221,
  428
Digestive troubles, 91
Dilthey, Wilhelm, 232n, 233-234,
  315n, 326n
Dingle, Herbert, 175n
Disagreements
  among economists, 371-372, 375-389
Discipline, see Science
Disconfirmation, 34, 499
Documentary sciences, 487
Domain
  of construction, 197, 203, 217,
    260, 401n, 40, 146, 170, 171,
    193, 195-196
  of empirical science, 41
  of observation (perception), 217,
    260, 401n, 530
  of phenomena, 146, 170, 171
  of (protocol) data, 40, 171, 193,
    196, 197, 203
Domar, Evsey D., 8n
Downs, Anthony, 402, 415, 423
Droysen, Johann Gustav, 234, 235n
Duhem, Pierre Maurice Marie, 44
Duopoly, 89n, 94n

Dynamics
   favored, 61
   Frisch on, 470
   Schumpeter on, 469-471
Dysfunctions, 48

-E-

Easy-money policy, 416
Econometric
   analysis, 76, 156-157, 179, 181,
      339, 343, 462, 464, 468-469
   models, 76, 179
Econometric Society, 464, 469
Economic man, 176, 183, 208, 209,
      267-28 283-301, 393, 415n, see
      also Homo oeconomicus
Economic policy, 257, 371, 376-378,
      381-386, 434, 435-436, 469n,
      503, 508
Economic principle, 147, 152, 272,
      286, 289, 292, 293, 301, 394,
      see also Maximization principle
Economics
   applied, 138, 154
   as a behavioral science, 487
   as a branch of psychologically-
      oriented sociology, 479
   Braithwaite on, 46
   Carnap on, 38
   considered a natural science,
      235-236, 326, 347
   departments of, 363
   ethical, 490
   exactness in, 364
   Hempel on, 52
   institutional, 76, 94, 144n, 301,
      487
   instrumental, 430, 435, 442
   joining theory and statistics,
      468-469
   mathematical, 339, 456, 461-462,
      469, 491-492
   of science, 60
   operationalism in, 190, 197-203,
      481, 483
   positive, normative and practical,
      429, 506
   pure vs. applied, 88-89
   pure theory of, 64, 70
   purely descriptive, 77, 361
   scientific character of, 339
   scope and method of, 489-492
   theoretical vs. descriptive, 76
Economy as a whole, 74, 77, 79-81
Eddington, [Sir] Arthur S., 168
Edgeworth, Francis Ysidro, 292, 293n
Egoism, 229, 284-286, 292-294
Einstein, Albert, 44, 53n, 145,
      159-160
Elasticity

of demand, 93, 150, 157, 180, 198,
      357, 393, 399n, 500
   of import demand, 156, 191
   of substitution among goals, 510
   of supply, 150, 198, 404, 500
Electric permeability, 27
Electron, 23, 45, 146, 168, 312, 314,
      322, 342, 400
Elementology, 12-13
Embarrassment, 45, 219
Emotion
   observed or inferred, 219-220
   words loaded with, 35
Emotional
   behavior, 416n
   reaction, 320
Empirical
   applications, 41
   constants, 357
   content, 143, 144n, 189, 495, 496,
      497, 498, 501-502
   counterparts (referents, proxies)
      of theoretical constructs, 85,
      134-135, 149, 169, 175-183,
      184-187, 203, 274, 354, 364,
      401n, 406, 417, 481; see also,
      Operational counterparts
   hypothesis, 140, 155-157
   knowledge based on inner experi-
      ence, 34, 45, 185, 260, 277,
      312, 317, 357
   laws, 170, 173-174, 196, 230-232,
      233, 301
   regularities, 170, 173, 230-232,
      327
   research, 522, 531, 94, 156, 231,
      372, 413, 454, 468, 486, 487,
      491, 522, 531
   tests, 427, 438, 457, 497, 499
   theory, 41, see also Observation,
      Operations
Empiricism
   and verification, 154-157
   casual, 152, 154
   challenged, 262
   'description only' type of, 49
   epistemological, 20, 31 263
   extreme, 49, 219, 265, 455, 486
   logical, 35, 306
   naive, 479
   principles of, 203
   radical, 35, 44, 45, 143n, 154,
      159, 263, 436, 437, 441
   sensationalistic, 20
   ultra-, 133, 141, 143-144, 219,
      455, 456, 486, 493-503, 531
Employment
   aided by protection, 123-125
   effects of wage increases on, 421
   measurable, 200
   securing full, 378, 385, 436, 442
Engine of pure theory, 148

Experience
    and concept formation, 171, 187;
        see also Concept formation, Con-
        struct
    directs choice of assumptions,
        143n
    immediate, 46, 152, 185, 297
    inner, 34, 44-46, 58, 142, 152,
        184, 185, 260, 277, 312, 313,
        317, 357
    Reichenbach on, 29-31
    theoretical system tested by, 42,
        171; see also Test, Testability,
        Verification, see also Observa-
        tion, Reality
Experiment
    and operational concepts, 169
    controlled, 118n, 341, 342, 354,
        364-367, 473
    crucial, 28, 44, 354
    faulty, 42
    in economics, 109, 486
    in social sciences, 485-486
    laboratory, 256, 339, 348,
        359
    mental, 103, 109, 257, 467,
        485-486
    observation and, 491
    reproducible, 42, 137, 140n, 154,
        155, 318, 336-338
    theory and, 168
Experimentomania, 339, 342, 344
Explanation
    by deducing necessary conse-
        quences, 299, 491
    deductive-nomological, 50-52
    degrees of, 459, 516
    divergent, 376-455
    functional, 48-49
    genetic, 48-49, 50
    inductive, 52
    inductive-statistical, 52
    is causal attribution, 237
    meaning of, 145
    merely of basic principles,
        515-516
    multiplicity of, 161
    of particular events, 52-53, 517,
        518
    probabilistic, 48
    teleological, 48-49
    through construction, 170
    types of, 48-49
    vs. description, 27, 40, 49,
        189
    vs. prediction, 74, 91-92,
        116-120, 137, 148, 150, 178
    Zetterberg on, 488
Extra-economic
    factors, 92-95
    objectives, 395n

-F-

Fact
    alleged or asserted, 74, 115
    and hypothesis, 21, 25, 26
    concrete, 138, 142, 252
    defined, 110-111n
    empirical, 152
    finding of, 108, 116, 139n
    historical, 113, 339
    hypothetical, 112
    imagination is a, 23
    in natural vs. social sciences,
        111, 152n
    indisputable, 152
    inferred (deduced), 40, 74,
        110-112, 115, 138, 166
    is thought, 22
    not enough, 109
    observational, 41, 59, 88, 110,
        115, 146, 170
    of perception, 14, 21
    opinion is, 152n
    private, 34, 45-46, 111-112, 152, 184n
    psychic, 57
    public, 46
    relevance of, 25
    theory implied in, 110
    unobservable in social sciences,
        187n
    vs. fiction, 290
    vs. truth, 110, see also Data, Ex-
        perience, Observation
Fafner, 317
Fallout, 387
Falsifiability
    degree of, 42, 43
    irrelevant for fundamental hy-
        potheses, 494-497
    of a theory, 43, 140
    of economic theory, 143n
    of propositions, 152
    Popper on, 42-43, 140
    potential, 42, 495-503
    theory of, 29, 41-43, 140
    vs. verifiability, 29, 42, 140
Falsification, 42, 133, 140, 142n, 517
Falsificationism, x, 460
Farm pool, 67
Fear
    of sanctions, 431
    state of, 316, 317
Federal Reserve Banks, 147
Feeling
    for justice, 220
    genuine, 44
    ideal types of, 218-220
    knowing vs. willing vs., 13
    nontestable, 429
    of a cat, 22
    of accomplishment and satisfac-
        tion, 410, 411

of affection, 285
of being important, 96-99
of inferiority, 345
of pride, 386
of self-determination, 386
operational definitions of, 436
Feigl, Herbert, ix, 4, 12, 37n,
    43-45, 219
Ferguson, Adam, 519
Fewness
    of automobiles, 397
    of firms, 394, 401, 405-406,
        408-409, 417
    of sellers, 85-99, 525
Fiberboard, 180-181
Fiction
    heuristic, 8, 145, 152, 193,
        224-225, 251, 269, 270, 287,
        290, 297, 301, 497
    pure, 76, 147, 160, 288, 420, 497
Fictionalism, 20, 159, 262
Field of physical forces, 38, 45, 79,
    146, 161, 322, 342
Finch, Henry A., 17n, 271n
Firm
    21 concepts of, 416
    a theoretical link in a causal
        connection, 399, 405, 523, 527
    as an empirical concept, 399, 418
    elimination of nonviable, 325
    fictitious, 400, 420, 532
    in the real world, 392, 400,
        523-528
    legal or organizational concept
        of, 177, 322n, 418
    model of, 392, 439, 523-524, 528
    particular vs. large group,
        398-399, 421, 499, 523, 525, 531
    run by committees, 373
    theoretical construct of, 177,
        322n, 331, 399, 400, 527-528
    theory of, 77-85, 272, 321-322,
        372, 391-423, 500, 521-534
    with many objectives, 296, 301,
        392, 394-396, 459, 521-534
Fiscal policy, 126n, 151, 328, 385
Force
    construct of, 160
Forecasting
    by economists, 360, 381, 389, 473
    vs. predicting, 118, 119, 358
Foreign exchange
    control of, 76, 182, 200, 382, 385
    dealers, 321
    demand for, 69, 198, 200
    rates, 149, 181-182, 321, 377,
        378, 379, 381, 382
Foreign reserves, 377
Frank, Philipp, 53n
Free trade, 120, 482
Free will, 32, 33, 386
Freundlich, Erwin Finlay, 19n

Friedman, Milton, 153n, 154n, 171n,
    178n, 297, 438, 483, 495, 496,
    501, 503
Fringe benefits, 114n
Frisch, Ragnar, 470

-G-

Galileo Galilei, 15
Game theory, 90n, 218
Gene, 45, 79, 146, 310, 312, 322,
    331, 342, 387, 400
    empirical vs. hypothetical, 400
Generalization
    about social events, 347
    empirical, 51, 170, 309, 506-507,
        531
    explanatory and predictive, 137,
        344
    indispensible, 104
    inductive, 16, 43, 59, 171, 194,
        196, 203
    involves abstraction, 94n, 250,
        253, 531
    low-level vs. high-level, 45-47,
        146, 155, 353, 354
    piecemeal, 355
Generalizing propositions, 15, 94,
    229, 234-236, 237, 250, 253,
    273, 326, 347
"Gentlemen's agreement", 93
Geography, 61, 335n, 346
Geology, 61, 314, 327, 336, 347, 363
Geometry, 434
Gill, Jerry H., 58n
Goals
    conflicting, 445, 447
    for production, inventory and
        sales, 394
    incompletely specified, 444-445,
        446-450
    nonquantifiable, 447
    of a firm, 296, 301, 373, 392,
        394-396, 459, 521-534
    of individual action, 34
    organizational, 394-395
    social, 125-126, 435, 442
Gödel, Kurt, x
Goethe, Johann Wolfgang von, 227-228
Gold, 217, 231, 255
    price, 377
    real vs. pure, 173
Gordon, Donald F., 165n
Gordon, Robert A., 402, 403, 422, 502
Gottl-Ottlilienfield, Friedrich, 271n
Grammatical forms, 430, 431
Grand Arbiter of Social Welfare, 448
Grimm brothers, 311
Group attitudes
    empirical study of, 454, 479
Growth

large group vs. particular, 250,
  499
precepts for, 435
theory of, 399n, 500
Hubble, Edwin Powell, 19n
Hughes, Henry Stuart, 262n
Human action, 288, 342
  automatic vs. conscious, 318n
  defined, 112n
  explained, 65-70, 152, 153, 233,
    237
  facts and, 111
  free will and, 32-33
  ideal types of, 274, 323, 353, 497
  interpreted, 152, 277, 281, 314,
    324
  knowledge of, 335
  mass phenomena of, 66-68, 90,
    525-526
  Mises on, 295
  Nagel on, 48-50
  results of, 112, 260, 281, 323,
    330, 349, 352, 401, 515, 517,
    522
  Schutz on, 153
  understanding of, 33, 215-220,
    268-281
  undesigned, 359-360, 515, 517
  unscientific studies of, 338
  Weber on, 18
Hume, David, 11
Humpty-Dumpty, 426n
Husband, 215, 216-217, 269
Husserl, Edward, x, 33, 532
Hutchison, Terence W., 133, 143-144n,
    174n, 178n, 226n, 248n, 443n,
    456-457, 493-503
Hydrogen, 173, 214, 231, 255
Hydrogen bomb, 351, 387
Hypostatization, 167, 175, 301
Hypothesis
  about observable reality, 481
  as a gift of the gods, 26
  as a postulate, 139-140
  as an assumption, 139n
  auxiliary, 42, 202, 496
  cannot be refuted when factors
    cannot be isolated, 28
  derived from low-level behavioral
    generalizations, 530
  empirical, 140, 155-157
  equivalent of theory, 139n
  forming a deductive system, 45
  fundamental, 70, 88, 139, 144-146,
    288, 290, 295, 299, 301, 322,
    325, 329, 438
  general, 138-139, 156
  guess, 27
  heuristic, 144, 289
  in scientific method, 25-29
  low-level vs. high-level, 45-47,
    146, 155, 353

mere hunches, 139
nature of, 8
prior to facts, 25-26, 467
special, 138-139, 156
tentative, 139-140, 388
untested, 354
verifying general, 139
working, 152, 342, 395n, 522
wrong, 156
Hypothetico-deductive system, 46, 74,
    143, 155, 171, 197, 219, 297,
    336, 355, 487

-I-

Ideal
  conductor, 160
  entities, 27
  gas, 27, 172, 256
  relations, 172
Ideal type
  an abstract (ideal, mental, pure)
    construct, 18, 175, 207,
    211-221, 239, 246, 261
  a construction, not an abstrac-
    tion, 193, 242, 533
  a misnomer, 213, 220-221
  a model, 175
  a tool of theorizing, 297
  also in natural sciences, 173,
    231-232, 255-256
  an abstraction from reality, not a
    construction, 243, 250-255
  anonymous, 67, 68, 70, 89-91, 215,
    244-247, 268, 269, 328, 331,
    398-399, 525, 532, 533
  as pure fiction, 18, 88, 193, 225,
    252, 262, 297
  construction vs. application of,
    246
  contained in models of interac-
    tion, 325
  deductive method using, 487
  economic man as an, 208, 269-270,
    272-273, 298
  empirical reference of, 184-187,
    259
  Eucken on, 226, 247-255
  explaining intentional inaction,
    326
  for both history and sociology,
    242, 274
  for describing and explaining so-
    cial phenomena, 213-225
  for history, not for sociology or
    economics, 240, 274, 275
  in pure economic theory, 247, 274
  in the social (or cultural) sci-
    ences, 184-186, 212, 237-247,
    274
  intimate, 68, 89-91

involves understanding of mind,
18, 153, 184, 186, 237, 246-247
its derivation is irrelevant, 263
like a puppet, 271, 529, 533
material, 215, 218, 244-247
Menger on, 173, 230-233, 255-256
Mises on, 240-241
must be efficient cause of explanandum, 246
never operational or realistic,
61, 186, 362
not regarded as fiction, 242
of business firm, 331, 373, 525,
527
of course of action, 245, 532-533
of developments, interrelations
and institutions, 240
of dynamic entrepreneur, 454
of economic action (or reaction),
152-156, 238, 274-275, 297
of feelings, 218-220
of firm with just the knowledge
assigned to it, 529
of human action, 153
of isolated state, 226
of liar, 215-216
of motivated conduct, 325, 353
of representative firm, 483
of social collectives, 245
of specific behavior, 90, 277-280
of wheat dealer, 330-331
personal, 91, 215-218, 244-247,
267, 274, 275, 277-281, 532-533
positivists oppose, 61
postulate of adequacy of, 18, 34,
153, 234, 245-247
ready-made or newly constructed,
246
remolded vs. newly constructed,
243
Schutz on, 34-35, 153, 244-247,
532-533
used in every-day life, 245, 276
useful vs. useless, 88, 249, 255,
297
value-related, 218
vs. average type, 242
vs. real type, 173, 243, 247,
248-249, 255-256, 258-260
Weber on, 18, 153, 236-240
with normative connotation, 237
see also Construct, Model,
Idiographic propositions, 15, 347
Idiosyncratic decisions, 74, 523,
524, 531
Illegitimate child, 187
Illustration
vs. verification, 65
Imaginary
conditions, 143
perfection, 183; see also Ideal,
Perfect, Pure

person, 215-218, 290, 526, 528
vs. real firm, 399-400, 401n, 417
Imagination
exact, 227, 247
in art, 433
of sense-object, 23
pedestrian's vs. entrepreneurial,
527
sympathetic, 316
Imagined
introspection, 94, 186
objects, 166
scenes, 281
Immediately given, 37
Immobility of productive factors,
83-84, 482
Imperative vs. indicative mood,
429-430
Import
propensities, 156
quotas, 81, 118, 145, 330, 494,
495, 524
tariff, 120, 149, 202, 281, 286,
403-405, 420, 499
Imports
competition through, 408
demand for, 198, 200
measurement of, 195
surtax on, 134, 198, 201, 203,
416n
Income
distribution, 102, 122, 123n, 125,
351, 384, 440, 442, 443, 447,
477
national, 122, 122-123n, 129, 440,
443, 455, 477
of managers, 402, 409, 410, 411,
413
of the firm, 410, 411, 413
statistics, 129, 195
Indeterminacy, 74, 220
oligopolistic, 85-99
Index numbers, 113-114
Indifference curves, see social welfare function
Individualism
methodological, 454, 472
political, 454, 472
Individualizing propositions, 15,
231-232, 234-236, 326, 347
Indivisibility and competition, 103
Induction
canons of, 456, 491
considered a basis of science, 336
cult of, 24
economic data no basis for, 454
rejected by Popper, 42
too many factors in, 491
useless in economics, 468
vs. deduction, 24-25, 487
Inductive
deductive propositions convertible

into, 487
economic data no basis of, 454
explanation, 52
generalization, 8, 16, 24, 43, 8,
    16, 24, 43, 59, 171, 194, 196,
    203
inference, 11
method, 11
Inductivism, 24
Industry
    Census Bureau concept of, 177
    construct of, 74, 77-85, 177, 398
    dominated by large firms, 420
    theoretical model of, 177
    theory of, 77-85, 500
Inertia, 160
Inference
    constructs based on, 160-161
    deductive, 31, 51, 88, 196, 375
    existence based on, 161
    fact established by, 110-116
    from untrue hypotheses, 287
    inductive, 11
    probable, 16
    rules of, 52
    useful, 203
    valid, 57n, 58
Inferiority
    actual, 345-367
    complex, 306, 333-344, 345
Infield, Leopold, 145n, 160n
Inflation, 378, 384
Information
    about conditions vs. changes in
        conditions, 414, 415n, 528-529
    about opportunities, 300-301, 417
    as stimulus, 526
    assigned to the ideal-typical
        firm, 529
    firm able to obtain all, 392
    inaccurate, 528, 529
    incomplete, 83, 86, 151, 360, 361,
        373, 380, 415-416, 528, 529
    need for less, 89, 397, 526
    need for more, 407
    new, 301
    obtainable only at large cost, 399
    of management, 402
    privacy and, 356
    storage, 331-332
    subjective, 413-416, 417
    uncertain, 414-415, 528, 529
Ink symbols, 216, 217
Inner experience, 34, 44-46, 58, 142,
    152, 184, 185, 260, 277, 312,
    313, 317, 357
Insects vs. man, 443n
Instinct of workmanship, 402
Institutional economics, 76, 94,
    144n, 301, 487
Institutionalism, 339-340, 343, 393,
    476

Institutions, 150, 151, 273, 324,
    340, 341, 343, 380, 381, 494,
    507
Instrumental analysis, 429, 435, 442,
    444-450, 457, 505-511
Instrumentalism, 374, 457-458, 510n
Interaction
    among cells, 322
    among constructs, 150
    among large numbers of actors, 499
    among people, 92, 150
    models of, 325
Interconnected constructs, 156, 171,
    176, 496
Interest rate, 125n, 147, 149, 151,
    202, 230, 281, 330, 524
International
    monetary system, 376, 377-378, 386
    studies, 337
    trade, 107
Intersubjectivity, 44, 213n, 219,
    255, 261
Intervening variables, 8, 154, 322n,
    331, 343, 357, 525
Interventions, 87, 97, 106, 113,
    126n, 128, 154-155, 341, 356,
    360, 454, 475, 477, 490
Intimacy, 68, 89
Introspection, 8, 38, 44, 147, 152,
    218-219, 281, 297, 312, 313,
    318, 319, 320, 326, 332, 340,
    342
    imagined, 94, 185
Intuition
    concepts by, 177n
    role of, 8
Intuitive
    art, 433
    cogency, 44
    theory, 243
Invariability of observations,
    346-347, 365
Invention
    in art, 433
    induced, 66, 68, 417
    labor-saving, 64, 65, 67
    of constructs, 21, 40-41, 145,
        160, 169, 183, 251, 262
    of more suitable hypotheses, 316
    of new hypotheses, 517
    of physical particles, 111n
    of theoretical models, 324
Inverse-deductive method, 11
Investment, 126n, 195, 217, 257, 384,
    407, 409n, 410
Iron curtain, 225
Isolated State, 224-225, 249, 256
Isolating
    a region, 224-225
    abstraction, 229, 232-235, 250,
        252, 254, 268, 343
    effects of one force, 296

some aspects or factors involved, 110, 186, 254, 268, 270, 340

Monism
  epistemological, 31
Monopolistic
  behavior, 401, 406
  business practices, 77, 101-104
  positions, 201
  restrictions, 82-83
  wage determination, 77
Monopoly
  aided by governments, 106, 107,
    313
  exploitation of, 103
  imperfect, 96-97, 150
  labor, 108
  natural, 103
  perfect, 96, 150
  profits, 84, 96-99
  reduction of, 123
  steel, 113-116
  theory of, 82, 83, 90-91, 400,
    405-406, 417
Monsen, R. Joseph, 402, 415, 423
Montague, William Pepperell, 3, 12,
  18-20, 54, 496n
Moral
  philosophy, 335
  sciences, 233-234, 288, 346, 465
Morgenau, Henry, 162-163, 169-170,
  172, 174n, 336n, 496n
Morgenbesser, Sidney, 305
Morgenstern, Christian, 311
Morgenstern, Oskar, 90n, 129n
Mother, 276
Motive
  Carnap on, 36
  in economic conduct, 65, 95-99,
    107, 228, 288, 290, 291, 294,
    299, 330, 454, 465
  in personal ideal type, 217, 236,
    246, 353, 533
  isolating one, 219-220, 233,
    268-270, 294
  of actor, 349, 352
  other than profit, 406n, 411-412,
    498, 522-525
  patriotic, 409n, 412, 497, 499
  profit, 95, 146, 225, 325, 331,
    522-525
  Schutz on, 34
  security, 403-404
Mrs. Malaprop, 6, 7, 62
Multiple solutions, 86n
Murderer, 94n, 138
Music, 299-300, 434
Mutatis mutandis, 179-180
Myrdal, Gunnar, 454, 475-480

-N-

NSF, see National Science Foundation
Nagel, Ernest, 4, 12, 19n, 47-50, 54,

57n, 139n, 305, 306, 315-318,
  321, 329-330, 331
Napoleon Bonaparte, 275
Natanson, Maurice, 306, 313n, 444n
National
  goals, 125-126, 435, 442
  interest, 412, 413n, 440, 444,
    478, 499
  prestige, 447
  sovereignty, 385-386
National income
  maximizing, 120, 220, 383
  value judgment in measuring,
    122-123n, 440, 443, 455, 477
National Science Foundation, 7
Natural law, 427, 454, 475-476
Natural sciences
  called natural philosophy, 335
  controlled experiments in, 118n,
    341, 354, 364
  exact, 18
  vs. social sciences, 18, 32-33,
    152-153, 183, 185, 214, 231-232,
    234, 291, 305, 332, 342,
    345-367, 386-389, 444, 464,
    513-515, 518
Natural selection, 325, 517
Natural theology, 56, 57
Needham, Douglas, 372
Neopositivism, 41, 161, 165, 193n,
  531, 41, 161, 165, 193n, 531
von Neumann, John, 90n
Neurath, Otto, ix
Neurophysiology, 318n
Neutrino, 79, 127n, 184, 185, 400
New York Times, 181, 310
Newcomer, 80-81, 85, 96-97, 325, 405,
  408
Newman, Edwin, 62
Newton, [Sir] Isaac, 335
Newton's laws, 27, 145
Nobel prize, 322
Nomic universality, 49
Nomological, 18, 50, 52, 214
Nomothetic, 15, 347
Nondisconformation, 140, 154, 155,
  187
Nonobservable
  human action, 215-218
  inaction is, 326
  positive as the opposite of,
    437-438
Nonobservables
  assigned to metaphysics, 57
  Braithwaite on, 47
  Carnap on, 38
  constructs of, 138
  Hempel on, 51
  in advanced science, 168
  role of, 8
  opposition to, 159, 189
  speculation about, 427

Nonpecuniary, 98, 392, 395n
Normative
  all economic theory deemed,
    476-477
  and cognate adjectives, 426-428,
    437
  aspects of instrumental analysis,
    444
  economics, 456, 475, 505-511
  instrumental analysis need not be,
    442
  issues, 349, 351
  logical status of, 435-437
  meanings of, 374, 428
  means evaluative, 430
  methodology suspected to be, 65
  science, 425
  types, 226-227, 237, 274
  vs. prescriptive, 428
  welfare economics is, 445-450, 499
Northrup, Filmer S.C., 53n, 177n
Numerical
  analysis, 339
  calculations, 396
  confirmation, 233
  constants, 156-157, 307, 346,
    357-358, 364, 365, 367
  data, 355, 356, 454, 456, 465,
    491-492
  findings, 397
  qualitative findings rather than,
    420, 421, 524
  raw economic data are, 454, 456,
    465
  relationships, 155-157, 196, 307,
    346, 357-358, 364, 382, 465
  values not essential for func-
    tions, 491-492

-O-

Objective function, 269, 283, 295,
  299, 396, 412, 533
Objectivity
  in economics, 121, 123
  of observations and explanations,
    346, 348-353, 364
  scientific, 348-353, 364, 439-444,
    461, 475
Observables, 37, 45, 47, 51, 146,
  168, 255, 340
Observation
  and abstraction, 171, 175n, 260
  and search for new constructs, 185
  bias in economic, 455
  Braithwaite on, 45-46
  correspondence between model and,
    400, 405
  data (record) of, 47, 143, 354,
    355, 396
  domain of empirical, 146, 170,

171, 217, 260, 401n, 530
error of , 42, 319
factual, 159
guided by ideas, 28
Hempel on, 51
Hutchison on, 144
immediate, 37, 43, 46, 112
in realistic-empirical research,
  258
inaction not subject to, 326
interpretation of, 147, 277
introspective, 152, 297, 312, 317;
  see also Introspection
invariability of, 307, 346-347
Madge on, 485-486
mass, 233
object identified with method of,
  167
objective, 142, 346, 348-353, 364
of actual business, 177, 394, 531
of attitudes, 479, 531
of behavior of representative
  firm, 482-483
of decision-making process, 522,
  531, 534
of economic facts or actions, 94,
  95, 324-326, 515
of ethical views, 436
of natural phenomena, 312, 313,
  316
of new numerical data vs. readings
  of instruments, 355
of opinions, 515
of overt business behavior, 317,
  394
of regularities, 145, 155-157,
  170, 173, 230-232, 340
of sequences and coexistences,
  156, 173, 196, 230-232
of verbal responses, 317, 324
Pareto on, 88n, 525
Peirce on, 16
rarely reliable, 137, 197
silent subjects of, 319
singular, 327
suggests hypotheses, 26
supposedly exact, 251, 336
to test deduced consequences, 45,
  see also Deduced consequences
vs. experiment, 8, 491; see also
  Experiment
with too many factors, 517
yields real types, 231
Observation sentences, 30-31
Observation terms, 37, 38
Observed
  artifacts, 255
  behavior, 36, 319, 436, 482-483,
    527, 530-531
  changes, 397, 405, 494-495, 527
  consequences of assumed behavior,
    319

consequences of presumed behavior, 319

Observer, 152, 159, 163, 195, 216, 219, 259-260, 276-277, 312, 325, 529, 532

Occam's Razor, 401

Oikos husbandry, 253

Oligopolistic
behavior, 401, 406
competition, 85-99, 393-394
indeterminacy, 85-99, 525

Oligopoly, 74, 85-87, 301, 533
as ideal type, 275
defined, 97
requiring more information, 407-409
theory of, 400, 405-406, 417, 525

Ontology, 5, 19, 39, 56, 57, 59, 138, 167

Operational concepts
abstraction in, 171
as counterparts of constructs, 85, 134-135, 149, 169, 175-184, 193-203, 260-261, 343, 356, 438, 488
constructs far removed from, 147
defined, 159, 163-164, 261
equivalents of real types, 262
grossly inadequate, 183
in economics, 177-178, 440
in philosophical subjects, 163
in theory formation, 168-170
of exchange rates, 182
of feelings, 436
of price, 177
prescribed, 61, 159, 161-162, 164-165, 189
required for meaning, 20-21
used in empirical laws, 172-174, 214
useless in theoretical system, 177

Operational definition, 164, 169

Operational model, 86

Operational proposition, 165

Operational theorems, 165

Operational theory, 202, 203

Operationalism, 159-203
a criterion of meaning, 20-21, 161, 164-167
a scientistic program, 339, 340
Bridgman's, 20-21, 159-167
Einstein on, 159-160
Hempel on, 50
in economics, 190-203
in social sciences, 162
shuns pure constructs, 161-162, 167, 189, 192, 340, 343
Zetterberg on, 488

Operationism, 161, 184, 190, 339, 340; see also Operationalism

Operations
accounting, 195

actual, 161
and existence, 162
and meaning, 20-21, 161, 164-167
Bridgman on, 20-21, 159-163
description of, 164
experimental, 162, 214
instrumental, 163, 168, 191
mental, 148, 161-163
multiple, 162, 166-167
paper-and-pencil, 162
physical, 20, 159, 161, 162, 164, 167
statistical, 162, 163, 164, 177, 195, 214, 296, 343
synonymous with concept, 20, 161, 162
thermometric, 168

Operations research, 414, 418

Ophelia, 62

Oppenheim, Paul, 19n, 226n

Oppenheimer, Hans, 240, 242, 273n

Oppenheimer, Robert, 347

Optimizing, 373, 415, 525

Optimum
allocation, 121, 528
social, 446, 476, 503

Organizational
control, 394
coordination, 417, 531
expectations, 394
goals, 394-395
learning, 395
theory, 530

Organizationalism, 522

Orpheus, 311

Oscillatory movements, 87n

Ostracize, 95

Ostwald, Wilhelm, 43

Other bodies, 36, 46

Other minds, 36, 44, 152-153n, 213n, 532

Overtaking
theory of, 396-397, 527n

Owners vs. managers, 395, 402, 413

Ownership diffused, 407

Oxford English Dictionary, 9, 428

Oxygen, 173, 231, 255

-P-

Pain, 44-45, 219, 295, 296, 312

Paintings
collector of, 217
of real world, 187, 243, 251

Papandreou, Andreas George, 402, 403, 411, 417, 422

Parable, 309-311, 318, 319, 322

Pareto, Vilfredo, 88n, 406n, 423, 525, 528, 529n

Parsons, Talcott, 17n, 112n, 220, 221, 237n

Particle, 183, 185, 399
Particles
    physical, 111n, 183, 185, 322, 399
Patent
    licensing of, 77
    system, 126n, 151
Pathology of thought, 17
Patriotism, 409n, 412, 497, 499
Pearson, Karl, 11, 27
Peirce, Charles S., 16, 519
Penny-pincher, 91
Penrose, Edith, 137n, 326n
Perception
    Braithwaite on, 46
    Croce on, 16
    in common-sense experience, 172
    intelligiblity and rules of, 516,
        519
    Margenau on, 40-41
    of facts, 14, 21, 111
    preceded and conditioned by
        universalities, 28, 251, 519
    Ruggiero on, 57
    sensory, 33, 111, 142, 356
    subject to volition, 22
    thought-objects of, 23, 25
Perfect
    blackness, 183
    competition, 116, 151n, 184, 393,
        409n, 524
    conductor, 214
    continuity, 27, 172
    correlation, 111
    foresight, 184
    gas, 183, 214
    knowledge, 415, 528
    lever, 27, 172, 183, 256
    market, 151n, 409n
    monopoly, 96, 150
    pliopoly, 150
    polypoly, 91, 150, 151
    purity, 231
    rationality, 185, 529
    vacuum, 27, 172, 214, 256
Perlman, Mark, x
Personal characteristics, 90, 91, 93,
    94n, 150, 267-269, 399n, 523,
    529n
Pfister, Bernhard, 226n, 236n
Phenomenalism, 46
Phenomenology, x, 5, 17, 33, 60, 208,
    264
Philology, 327, 337n
Philosophy
    branches of, 13-14, 18
Philosophy of science
    and logic, 35, 53
    and methodology, 43, 61, 490, 513
    empiricism in, 24
    scope of, 43, 60
Photograph vs. painting, 187, 243,
    257

Photons, 127n, 322
Physical states, 318
Physicalism, 35, 36, 45, 159, 515
Physicians, 44, 92; see also Medicine
Physics, 28, 30, 32, 35, 37, 38, 39,
    46, 57, 79, 90n, 111-112, 127n,
    145, 146, 152, 159-170, 184,
    190, 214, 232, 255-256, 291,
    309-311, 312, 314, 316, 318,
    319, 321, 322, 327, 329, 330,
    331, 336, 337n, 341, 347, 350,
    354, 355, 356, 357, 359, 361,
    362-363, 364, 365, 386, 399,
    442, 443, 444, 454, 465, 474,
    501, 513, 517, 518
Physiognomy, 219
Physiology, 61, 327, 335n, 465,
    518-519, 527
Pick's Currency Reports, 182
Piltdown Man, 350
Planck, Max, 357
Planck's constant, 357
Planck's Quantum Law, 27
Plato, 226
Platonic methodology, 15
Pleasure machine, 296
Pliopoly, 150, 405
Poincaré, Henri, 21, 161, 174
Poison, 327
Poker players, 269
Polanyi, Michael, 140n
Policeman, 276
Policy
    analysis, 420
    recommendations, 383-389, 434,
        440, 442, 450, 454, 473, 508,
        511
Political
    feasibility, 381-382
    freedom, 509-511
    judgment, 4, 350, 502
    leanings, 387
    prejudices, 382
    pressures, 381-382
    reactions, 380, 441, 502
Political science, 125, 178, 268,
    327, 334, 336, 337, 352, 355,
    456, 487
Politics, 60, 67, 70, 74, 93, 127n,
    328, 404, 434, 435
Polypoly, 90, 91, 95, 96, 150, 151,
    406
Popper, [Sir] Karl, ix, 4, 12, 41-43,
    54n, 55n, 57, 58, 212, 264, 394,
    423, 514, 516n, 522, 527, 529,
    534
Position in industry, 95-99
Positive
    and cognate adjectives, 426-428
    as opposite of nonobservable,
        437-438
    as opposite of nontestable,

438-439
economics, 456, 502, 505-506, 508
meanings of, 374, 426-428
opposites of, 427
vs. hypothetical, 287-292, 295
vs. metaphysical, 57n
vs. natural law, 427
vs. normative, 55, 373-374, 385,
387, 425-450, 490, 499, 503
vs. speculative, 427
Positivism
critical of economics, 464
implying criterion of science, 336
in sociology, 485-486
logical, 12, 35, 45, 430-431, 437,
441
phenomenalistic, 37, 167
stressing sense perceptions, 27,
167
vs. rationalism, 26
Positron, 322, 362
Posterity, 449
Postulate
as a hypothesis, 139-140
concerning observable reality, 481
connotes arbitrariness, 140
deductions from, 141-142
fundamental, 27, 51, 133,
140n-142, 145, 147, 148-153,
219, 295, 299, 301, 336, 457,
460, 494, 495-503
in a theoretical system, 4, 88
not verifiable, 171
of adequacy, 18, 34, 153, 246
of logical consistency, 34, 153
of subjective interpretation, 34,
153, 186, 261, 315, 317, 342
Potato-price support, 76, 121
Pragmatism, 19n, 262n, 416, 505
Pratt, Carroll C., 184n
Praxeology, 295
Preconception
analysts', 445-446
behind choice of hypotheses, 442
indispensible, 25-27, 139, 187,
340, 442
readers', 274
regarding interventionism, 402
rejected by behaviorists, 394
scientistic, 455, 458, 486,
514-516
Predictability, 346, 358-361, 364
Prediction
behavioral approach yields no accurate, 526
by good economist, 202n
conditional, 118, 119, 358
divergent, 376
doctor's, 44, 92
impossible when too many factors
are involved, 354, 473
in natural vs. social sciences,

32, 347
no quantitative, 301, 416n
numerically specific, 359
of deduced results, 4, 143, 307;
see also Deduced consequences
of designed events, 359-360, 515
of monopolistic conduct, 91
of particular vs. mass behavior,
396-397, 398-400
of price, 398
physicist's, 92
positive vs. negative, 517
possible when few factors are involved, 28, 172, 347
Reichenbach on, 29-31
self-fulfilling, 360
tested, 140n, 143, 154-155, 307,
336, 341, 343, 355
tested more easily than explanation, 117
unconditional, 154-155, 358
vs. explanation, 74, 91-92,
116-120, 137, 148, 150, 178
vs. forecasting, 118, 119, 358,
473
Predictionism, 339, 341, 344
Preference, 296, 301, 332, 340, 383,
402, 410, 441, 448, 472, 497,
499, 500, 501, 502, 507, 508,
510, 529
Prejudice
against mental construction, 262,
263
anti-interventionist, 477
bourgeois-capitalist, 123n
empiricist, 531
nationalistic, 263, 350, 385-386
of analyst, 110
of businessmen, 94n
political, 382
positivistic, 262-264
scientistic, 455, 458, 486,
514-516
Prescriptionism, 339, 341
Prestige, 402, 409n, 410, 411, 412,
447
Pretending, 44
Price
analysis, 79
ceiling, 149
changes in, 281, 298-299, 328,
350, 499, 523
control, 87n
different meanings of, 81-82, 177,
257
discrimination, 76, 77, 105n
fixing, 8, 88n, 93, 108, 117, 121
leadership, 76, 88n, 93
mechanism, 103
operational concept of, 177,
194-195
predictions, 398

FRITZ MACHLUP

Ratiocination, 22, 171
Rationalism
  Cohen's, 24
  epistemological, 31, 516-517
  naturalistic, 20
  scientific, 20, 24, 168
  vs. positivism, 26
Rationality, 50, 88, 144n, 146, 147,
    152, 185, 238-239, 241-242, 247,
    297, 395, 415, 450, 495-496,
    522, 529-530
Rationing, 115
Ray, Susan, 223
Real type
  Aristotle's, 227
  avoided by Weber and Schutz, 247
  equivalent of operational concept,
    261
  Eucden on, 247-255
  Eucken on, 247-255
  has no place in causal theory, 258
  in economics, 256-258
  Menger on, 173, 230-232, 255-256
  never exact, 173
  obtained from observation, 231
  of recurring historical events,
    243
  Spiethoff on, 243
  vs. ideal type, 173, 243, 255-256,
    258-260
Realism
  critical, 19n
  epistemological, 19, 31
  in abstraction, 75
  in assumptions, 78
  in economic constructs and models,
    243, 247-255, 481-484
  in models of process vs. motiva-
    tion, 395
  in theory of firm, 401-403, 404n
  of economic man, 269-273
  Samuelson on Theory and, 481-484
  vs. relevance, 78, 186, 187
Realistic-empirical approach,
    230-233, 258
Reality
  a problem of ontology, 39, 59,
    138, 167
  abstraction from, 109, 224, 239,
    243, 250-255, 270
  and truth, 138
  as laboratory for experiments, 109
  comprehending, 143n
  exact observation of, 251
  explaining empirical, 262
  high fidelity to, 243
  ideal types, construction and,
    223-265
  impurities of, 173, 183
  mentally reconstructed, 243, 262
  model world vs. world of, 348,
    359, 364, 387-388, 528

  observed, 79, 92, 111, 251, 252
  physical, 21, 39, 111n, 160, 161,
    167
  pictured, 242, 243, 254, 255
  social, 34-35, 153, 207-265
  theory remote from, 20
  too complex, 109, 142
  uncontrolled, 172, 364, 387
Reder, Melvin Warren, 402, 423
Reducibility and reduction, 36, 37,
    43, 52
Reductionism, 41
Rees, Albert, 115n
Refutation
  at the core of methodology, 14
  of basic postulates, 140
  of explanatory models, 517
  of marginal-productivity theory,
    372-373
  Popper on, 42-43
  Royce on, 16, 146
Regression, 8, 258, 508
Reichenbach, Hans, 3, 12, 29-31, 53n,
    165
Relative prices, 77, 79, 125n, 182,
    491
Relativity theory, 159, 350
Relevance
  relativity of, 129
  vs. realism, 78, 186, 187
Religion, 19
Reparations payments, 145
Reproducibility, 42, 137, 140n, 154,
    155, 318, 336, 338
Reproducible
  events or facts, 347, 354, 364
  experiments, 42, 137, 140n, 154,
    155, 336, 338
Research and development, 126n, 299,
    411
Resolutions, see Conventions
Restraint of trade, 76
Ricardo, David, 290, 321, 336, 463,
    477
Rickert, Heinrich, 235-236, 315n,
    326n, 347
Risk, 93, 146, 220, 373, 403, 494
Robbins, [Lord] Lionel, 63, 64, 67,
    141n, 142, 270n, 283, 297, 501
Robinson Crusoe, 248, 275
Robinson, Joan, 393, 423
Rock, 313, 353
Romeo and Juliet, 221
Roosevelt, Franklin Delano, 327
de Rooy, Martha Coorssen, 223
Rose, Arnold M., 455, 485-487, 501
Rothenberg, Jerome, 272n
Rothschild, Kurt W., 89n, 94n, 95n,
    97n
Royce, Josiah, 3, 6, 12, 15-16, 146
Rueff, Jacques, 267, 274, 517n
Ruge, Arnold, 14n, 15n

de Ruggiero, Guido, 57n
Ruggles, Richard, 8n
Rules
    axiological, 436-437
    for action, 434
    of correspondence, 38, 39, 40-41,
        44, 140
    of game of science, 42
    of inference, 52
    of procedure, 31, 39, 55, 145,
        152, 297, 454, 457, 495, 496n,
        497n, 515
    of verification, 16, 138-140,
        144-146, 148-150, 154-157
Ruskin, John, 286

-S-

Safety regulation, 123
Salin, Edgar, 243n, 273n
Salt, 147
Sampling, 16
Samuel, Herbert L., 160n
Samuelson, Paul, 33, 165n, 190n, 297,
    455, 481-484, 495, 501
Satisficing, 373, 415-416
Saving, 125n, 126n, 156, 195, 352,
    357, 358, 384, 469n
Schelting, Alexander von, 226, 240,
    242, 244n, 273n
Schema, 76, 251, 272, 295, 466, 467,
    see also Construct, Model,
    Theory
Schiff, Michael, 372
Schiller, Friederich von, 227
Schilpp, Paul Arthur, 35n
Schlick, Moritz, ix, 35
Schmoller, Gustav von, 106n, 462,
    464, 489
Schneider, Erich, 86n, 462n
Schrödinger, Erwin, 169
Schumpeter, Elizabeth Boody, 438n
Schumpeter, Joseph A., 140n, 176n,
    190n, 406n, 417, 423, 433n,
    438n, 454, 461-474
Schutz, Alfred, x, 4, 12, 33-35, 50,
    54n, 68n, 90n, 153, 186,,
    244-247, 264, 267, 273n, 275,
    313-316, 317, 318-319, 323, 324,
    326n, 343n, 417, 423, 525, 529,
    532, 533n
Science
    a deductive system, 40, 46, 74,
        171, 197, 219, 336
    and values, 15, 17, 50, 55,
        120-121, 349-351
    dealing with uniformities, 456,
        490
    defined, 361
    ethics as, 56, 335n, 436
    formal, 57, 163

generalizing (and individualiz-
    ing), 15, 234-236, 326, 347
genesis vs. logic of, 43
history of, 43
hypothetical vs. absolutely cer-
    tain, 287-292
impartial systematic knowledge,
    338
inaccessible to laymen, 361, 433n
is exact if deductive, 40, 231
narrow definition of, 219, 309,
    334-335, 336, 337n, 338
nonobservables in advanced, 8,
    37-38, 47, 51, 138, 168, 187n
normative, 425
nothing explainable by a single,
    28, 93, 172, 327, 330, 518
of cookery, 432
requires high-level generaliza-
    tions, 45
"true", 342
vs. application, 142, 418, 433
vs. art, 428
vs. common sense, 26, 47, 276,
    324, 335, 342, 361, 476
vs. mere description, 456, 491
Scientific
    education, 518
    objectivity, 348-353, 364,
        439-444, 461, 475
    socialism, 341
    vs. scientistic attitudes, 513-519
Scientific method
    a part of logic, 9, 59
    Baconian, 15
    Cohen on, 24-29, 335n
    for economists, 144
    Nagel on, 47-49
    principles (rules) of, 42, 47, 59,
        189, 190
    Reichenbach on, 29
    restrictively defined, 306, 334,
        344, 458
    Schumpeter on, 462-464
    variety in, 11, 344
Scientism, 306, 338, 455, 458, 487,
    513-516
Scitovsky, Tibor, 123n, 395n, 402,
    406n, 423
Scope and Method of Political Econo-
    my, 489-482
Scriven, Michael, 37n
Security, 95-99, 402, 403-404, 496
Seiterich, Eugen, 226n
Selection
    for emphasis, 250, 251, 253, 254
    from conflicting value systems,
        437
    natural, 325
    of adequate cause, 148
    of adequate instruments, 508
    of appropriate model, 92, 531

FRITZ MACHLUP

8
9
0
1
2
3
4
5